Yiddish

A Linguistic Introduction

Yiddish, the language of Ashkenazic Jewry, arose some 900–1,200 years ago as a result of contact with indigenous varieties of medieval German. Over the next few centuries, it grew to cover the second-largest language area in Europe, with Yiddish-speaking colonies being created in North and South America, Palestine/Israel, Australia, and South Africa. It is estimated that just before the Nazi genocide in the Second World War, there were between 11 and 13 million Yiddish speakers worldwide.

This broad yet comprehensive introduction provides an authoritative overview of all aspects of Yiddish language and linguistics. As well as looking at key features of its syntax, phonology, and morphology, Neil G. Jacobs discusses its history, its dialectology, and the sociolinguistic issues surrounding it. Presenting linguistic data in a way that is compatible with general theoretical issues, it will be welcomed by scholars of general linguistics, Germanic linguistics, and Jewish studies alike.

NEIL G. JACOBS is Professor in the Yiddish and Ashkenazic Studies Program in the Department of Germanic Languages and Literatures, The Ohio State University. He is author of *Economy in Yiddish Vocalism: A study in the interplay of Hebrew and non-Hebrew components* (1990), and has published widely in the field of Yiddish linguistics, primarily in language history, phonology, and dialectology. He has also published in the areas of post-Yiddish ethnolects, Jewish cabaret, and Jewish geography, and edited the collection *Studies in Jewish Geography* (1998).

Yiddish

A Linguistic Introduction

Neil G. Jacobs

The Ohio State University

CAMBRIDGE UNIVERSITY PRESS
Cambridge, New York, Melbourne, Madrid, Cape Town, Singapore, São Paulo, Delhi

Cambridge University Press
The Edinburgh Building, Cambridge CB2 8RU, UK

Published in the United States of America by Cambridge University Press, New York

www.cambridge.org
Information on this title: www.cambridge.org/9780521105781

First published 2005
This digitally printed version 2009

A catalogue record for this publication is available from the British Library

Library of Congress Cataloguing in Publication data

Jacobs, Neil G.
Yiddish: a linguistic introduction / Neil G. Jacobs.
p. cm.
Includes bibliographical references and index.
ISBN 0 521 77215 X (alk. paper)
1. Yiddish language – Grammar. 2. Yiddish language – Textbooks for foreign speakers – English. I. Title.
PJ5116.J33 2004
439′.182421 – dc22 2004054626

ISBN 978-0-521-77215-0 hardback
ISBN 978-0-521-10578-1 paperback

To my teachers –
Robert P. Stockwell, Robert D. King, and Marvin I. Herzog

Contents

Acknowledgments

Several people and institutionalities have supported the creation of the present book. First and foremost, I wish to express my deepest gratitude to Joseph Salmons and Paul Glasser, who read numerous chapter drafts and offered valuable feedback at each stage of the project, spanning a four-year period. Beyond that, they made themselves available throughout this period for untold hours of "shop talk" which made the whole project a pleasure. *Joe and Paul – a fargenign.* I also owe profound thanks to Robert D. King and Molly Diesing for close reading of advanced stages of the manuscript, and for detailed feedback and suggestions. The final version has benefitted significantly from their insights. I am also indebted to Mordkhe Schaechter for numerous discussions concerning finer points of Yiddish grammar and the rise of the modern standard language. I thank the following individuals at The Ohio State University for valuable discussion during the writing of this book: Brian D. Joseph, Dieter Wanner, Anna Grotans, David Odden, Daniel Collins, Laurie Maynell, Qian Gao. I also thank the following colleagues at other universities for valuable discussion of specific points dealt with in the present book: Mark Louden, David Fertig, John te Velde, Hans den Besten. I thank an anonymous reader for valuable suggestions on the final draft. I thank the Max Niemeyer Verlag, and the editors of the *Language and Culture Atlas of Ashkenazic Jewry*, for permission to use a modified version of their map. For ongoing support of my research, including sabbatical leave during academic year 1999–2000, during which time the writing of this book was begun, I am grateful to my home department at The Ohio State University – the Department of Germanic Languages and Literatures, Bernd Fischer, Chair. I further thank the following units at Ohio State for ongoing research support: the College of Humanities; the Melton Center for Jewish Studies; the Center for Slavic and East European Studies. I have benefitted greatly from the resources of the library of the YIVO Institute for Jewish Research, in New York. I am also indebted to Joseph Galron, Judaica Librarian at Ohio State. I thank, as well, the editors at Cambridge University Press who have helped guide the manuscript toward production: Kate Brett, Andrew Winnard, Helen Barton, Alison Powell; also my copy-editor, Leigh Mueller. I gratefully acknowledge special debt to three scholars – Robert D. King, Paul

Wexler, and David Neal Miller – with whom I have spent uncountable hours over the years discussing the past, present, and future of the field of Yiddish and Ashkenazic studies. Outside the field, I have enjoyed ongoing encouragement from a team of family and friends who made a special point of asking on a regular basis about my progress on the book: Walter and Roberta Jacobs, Karen Berry, Lon Jacobs, Michael Allen, Lisa Allen, Deborah O'Connor, Michael Jory, Bridget Mulvihill-Jory, Jan Brokke, Janet Brain, Karen R. King, Dennis Percher, David A. Katz, Dave and Elaine Smith. Finally, I wish to express my deepest thanks to my wife, Joan, and daughter, Sarah, for their unfailing support, encouragement, and inspiration throughout the process of writing this book.

Notes on transcription and symbols

1. Yiddish letters – general phonetic values

Yiddish letter	Phonetic transcription	YIVO romanization
א	–	–
אַ	[a]	a
אָ	[o]	o
ב	[b]	b
בֿ	[v]	v
ג	[g]	g
ד	[d]	d
ה	[h]	h
ו	[u]	u
וו	[v]	v
וי	[oj]	oy
ז	[z]	z
ח	[x]	kh
ט	[t]	t
י	[i]; [j]	i; y
יי	[ej]	ey
ײַ	[aj]	ay
כּ	[k]	k
כ (ך word finally)	[x]	kh
ל	[l]	l
מ (ם word finally)	[m]	m
נ (ן word finally)	[n]	n
ס	[s]	s
ע	[e]	e
פּ	[p]	p
פֿ(ף word finally)	[f]	f

Yiddish letter	Phonetic transcription	YIVO romanization
צ (ץ word finally)	[c]	ts
ק	[k]	k
ר	[r]	r
ש	[š]	sh
שׂ	[s]	s
תּ	[t]	t
ת	[s]	s
Di-/trigraphs		
דזש	[dž]	dzh
זש	[ž]	zh
טש	[č]	tsh

1. Letter ו in words of Hebrew-Aramaic origin may represent the following: [u], [o], and [oj].
2. When adjacent to וו [v], ו [u] is rendered וּ, thus: וווּ [vu] 'where', פּרוּוון 'try'; syllabic י [i] adjacent to another vowel is rendered ײַ, thus: העברעיִש [hebre-iš] 'Hebrew,' אַסאָציִירן [asoci-irn] 'associate.'

Abbreviations

Yiddish dialects

AY	Alsatian Yiddish
CourlY	Courland Yiddish
CY	Central Yiddish
eCY	East Central Yiddish
eTCPY	eastern Transcarpathian Yiddish
eWY	easternmost Western Yiddish
EY	Eastern Yiddish
MWY	Middle Western Yiddish
NEY	Northeastern Yiddish
NWY	Northern Western Yiddish
PNY	Proto-Northeastern Yiddish
PSY	Proto-Southern Yiddish
PY	Proto-Yiddish
ScrY	Scribal Yiddish
SEY	Southeastern Yiddish
SL	Stam-Litvish (general Northeastern Yiddish)
StY	Standard Yiddish
SWY	Southern Western Yiddish
SY	Southern Yiddish
TCPY	Transcarpathian Yiddish
wCY	West Central Yiddish
wTCPY	western Transcarpathian Yiddish
wWY	westernmost Western Yiddish
WY	Western Yiddish
ZY	Zameter (Samogitian) Yiddish

Other linguonyms

eCG	East Central German
G	German

Gmc	Germanic
HA	Hebrew-Aramaic
Intls	Internationalisms
L	Loez
LCAAJ	*Language and Culture Atlas of Ashkenazic Jewry*
MHG	Middle High German
NHG	New High German
OHG	Old High German
Pol	Polish
Sl	Slavic
StG	Standard German
TH	Tiberian Hebrew
wCG	West Central German

Grammatical terms

ACC	accusative
ADJ	adjective
ADV	adverb
AUX	auxiliary verb
C	consonant
DAT	dative
DET	determiner
DIM	diminutive
F	feminine
G	glide
M	masculine
N	neuter gender; nucleus (in phonological discussions)
NOM	nominative
NP	noun phrase
O	onset
OBL	oblique
P	person
PL	plural
PP	prepositional phrase
PREP	preposition
R	rhyme
REFL	reflexive
S	sentence
SG	singular
V	vowel (in phonological discussions); verb (in syntactic discussions)
VP	verb phrase

Symbols

*	non-attested or reconstructed form
**	ungrammatical, non-occurring
$	Syllable boundary

1 Introduction

1.1 Aim and scope

This book provides an overview of the Yiddish language and Yiddish linguistics. It is aimed at general linguists, Germanic linguists, scholars in Yiddish and Ashkenazic studies, and scholars in general Jewish studies. It seeks to strike a balance between breadth and depth of coverage of the main issues in Yiddish linguistics: the linguistic structure, history, dialectology, and sociolinguistics. The Yiddish data are presented in a format compatible with general and theoretical linguistic discussion, accessible to linguists regardless of their individual theoretical bent. However, the task is not to engage general theoretical debate; rather, theory is used only as a tool for presentation and its place in the exposition is minimized.

There is a need for such an introduction to Yiddish linguistics. Max Weinreich's monumental *Geshikhte fun der yidisher shprakh* (1973)[1] provides a sweeping social history of Yiddish; however, it is not a grammar (historical or otherwise). The detailed grammars available (e.g., Zaretski 1926; Mark 1978) do not present the history or dialectology of the language. Birnbaum (1979a) in many respects provides both history/dialectology and a grammar;[2] however, his grammatical section is essentially a reference grammar. While individual shorter works have dealt with specific problems of Yiddish phonology, morphology, and syntax, there was – with one exception – no book-length study which attempted to look at the overall structure of Yiddish systematically, with general linguistic issues in mind. Zaretski (1926) stands alone as the one serious attempt to present a theory-oriented comprehensive Yiddish grammar, though his focus is on syntax and morphology, with only limited discussion of the phonology. Prilutski (1940) provides comprehensive discussion of Yiddish phonology and phonetics.

This book uses Yiddish as the point of departure. It is not a comparative discussion, where Yiddish is seen primarily in terms of other languages (e.g., German). This was once the case, but the field has developed and

[1] Partial translation appeared as M. Weinreich (1980).
[2] See also Weissberg (1988).

matured.[3] In the core grammar chapters (phonology, morphology, syntax) the general point of departure is modern Standard Yiddish (StY). Modern StY is largely a "common-ground" variety of Eastern Yiddish in which many of the most dialect-marked features are dropped (§7.5.1).

Several systems are employed in the present book to represent Yiddish (see "Notes on transcription and symbols"). For the most part, Yiddish data are given in romanized form. This is a regrettable necessity for reaching a broader readership. Linguistic handbooks from one hundred years ago (written for example in German, English, French) routinely included words or passages in Greek, Hebrew, Russian, etc. – often within a single book, even on the same page – without apology to the reader. However, such practice is less common today. In the present book, linguistic data are given in a modified IPA rather than in YIVO romanization. This was done in order to preserve some distinctions which are lost in YIVO romanization (e.g., /ə/ and /e/ are both rendered as <e> in the YIVO system). The use of phonetic symbols is of course necessary in discussion of phonological issues. The use of this phonetic romanization has been maintained in discussions outside the phonology for the sake of consistency in the presentation of data. The YIVO romanization, while not Yiddish orthography, does convey the regularity and systematicity of Yiddish orthography. However, the decision has been made here to use IPA-based symbols, precisely because this is a book focusing on linguistic issues, many of which are phonological. YIVO romanization is used for all bibliographic references and for Yiddish terms used in English. In some instances where an author's name has a familiar English version, this is used; e.g., *Weinreich* vs. *Vaynraykh*.

1.2 Yiddish

Yiddish arose as the indigenous language of Ashkenazic Jewry, likely some 900–1,200 years ago, via contact with indigenous varieties of medieval German in German lands. Over the next few centuries the home territory of Ashkenazic Jewry came to cover the second-largest territorial expanse (after Russian) of any language/culture area in Europe. In the late nineteenth to early twentieth centuries, a sizable Ashkenazic diaspora arose, giving rise to Yiddish-speaking colonies beyond Europe, in North and South America, Palestine/Israel, Australia, and South Africa.

In modern times, both in the European home territory and in the Ashkenazic diaspora, Yiddish served as the language of the Ashkenazic masses in everyday life, at home, in theatre, cinema, literature, politics, journalism, in

[3] See Strauch (1990), and Frakes (1993) for discussion.

schools – both secular and religious – and more.[4] Immediately prior to the Nazi German genocide of the Second World War, the number of Yiddish speakers was estimated at 11–13 million, making it the third largest Germanic language at the time (after English and German).[5] Of the 6 million Jews murdered in Germany's genocide, approximately 5 million were Yiddish speakers. Today, Yiddish speakers are to be found chiefly in centers such as New York, Israel, Melbourne, Montreal, Mexico City, Buenos Aires, and elsewhere. Birnbaum (1979a: 42) estimated the number of speakers in 1979 to be more than 5 million. Many of these may be assumed to be Holocaust survivors who have since passed away. The number of Yiddish speakers today is growing – probably in the neighborhood of some several hundred thousand to over a million – largely due to the birth rate in current Yiddish-speaking (typically, orthodox) communities. Many of these active communities have a Yiddish-language press; some have day schools in Yiddish. In Hasidic communities, traditional learning takes place in Yiddish, and Yiddish is strong as the language of home and everyday life. Yiddish-language radio programming in its heyday during the 1950s and 1960s drew large audiences in New York and other major Jewish urban centers in America. In recent decades, the field of Yiddish and Ashkenazic studies in colleges and universities has grown significantly, at both the undergraduate and graduate level. In accord with the practice common in Yiddish scholarship, the ethnographic present is used in discussion of Yiddish data, dialects, etc.

Yiddish developed a highly structured system of dialects, a modern literature, a standard language, and more – all without the support apparatus of a nation-state. Although Hebrew has served as the common sacred language of all Jewish communities throughout the world, more Jews have spoken Yiddish as their native language than have spoken Hebrew natively, and for a longer span of time. Furthermore, dating from the eighteenth century, Ashkenazim constituted the majority of the Jews in the world (the overwhelming majority beginning in the nineteenth century), and from the mid nineteenth century until the Holocaust Yiddish was the native language of the majority of the world's Jews (see chart in M. Weinreich 1980: 173).

1.3 Framing the object of investigation

To focus on a given language is to frame that language within a point of view; e.g., "German" as opposed to "Dutch," "Russian" as opposed to "Ukrainian."

[4] To varying degrees, in varying times and places, portions of Ashkenazic Jewry in modern times have adopted non-Jewish vernaculars, either as a second language, or as a primary language; see §7.

[5] Birnbaum (1979a: 40–42) arrived at a figure of approximately 12 million in 1931, and compares this with the following contemporaneous numbers: Czech – 7 million; Greek – 6 million; Rumanian – 12.5 million; Dutch – 12 million; Croat(ian)-Serbian – 10.5 million.

Classification as "language" vs. "dialect" (of that "language") depends on extralinguistic factors. However, that is part of what linguists do – they focus, somewhat arbitrarily, on a given language variety, and from there describe its history, structure, etc. In this framework sister dialects are subordinated within the superstructure of the "language," and the agenda becomes one of describing the dialects on the terms of the greater "language." At the same time, the language of focus may be seen from other perspectives – externally, e.g., Dutch in terms of German or Germanic; or typologically: SOV vs. SVO languages, agglutinating languages, etc. Furthermore, language diachrony may be viewed in terms of *stammbaum* evolution (genetic), and/or contact-induced developments. An introduction to the linguistics of a given language must balance the need for a "full picture" (of both internal and external factors) with the need to narrow the focus to the object of attention itself.

Yiddish has significant lexical and structural similarity with German; thus, Yiddish has traditionally been – and often still is – viewed by many in terms of German. However, while comparison is important, it must not be the basis for analysis. Rather, Yiddish is primarily to be described and analyzed in terms of the patterns within Yiddish itself. As a secondary task, we may compare the two systems and seek to understand and describe the nature of the complex historical and sociolinguistic relationship(s) between Yiddish and German.

Fundamental to the centering of Yiddish is the recognition of Ashkenazic Jewry as a society distinct both from other Jewries and from coterritorial non-Jewish populations. "Mapping out" the historical and perceptual geography of Ashkenaz, M. Weinreich (1980) distinguishes Ashkenaz from Germany. In the eleventh and twelfth centuries (CE), Jewish references to Ashkenaz meant the lands of Germans, i.e., non-Jews (*Encyclopaedia Judaica* 1971: III, 720); only later did the term *Ashkenaz* come to refer to Jews in or from the German lands, their culture, their Judeo-German language today called Yiddish, etc. Weinreich's ideological point is clear (Jacobs 1998): while Yiddish-speaking Jewry had an established sense of the geographic – as reflected, for example, in culture-internal division into geographic districts in the Council of the (Four) Lands (mid sixteenth century to 1764) – it had never possessed or ruled over its own nation-state in its European homeland. Use of the term *Ashkenaz* within a Yiddishist framework implies a fundamental recognition of the reality of Ashkenazic Jewish autonomy – geographic, cultural, and linguistic.

In the history of continental Ashkenaz[6] there occurred over time a shift in the center of gravity – demographic, cultural, and linguistic – from Central Europe to Eastern Europe (M. Weinreich 1980: especially 3–4). Weinreich

[6] The term *continental Ashkenaz*, to my knowledge, was coined in D. Miller (1990).

calls the early period when the center of gravity lay to the west *Ashkenaz I*, and the later period of eastern Ashkenazic predominance *Ashkenaz II*. Again, the focus is endocentric – on the changing circumstances within Ashkenaz primarily from a culture-internal perspective rather than in terms of the secondary external influences.

1.4 Development of Yiddish studies

The history of the investigation of Yiddish shows a clear path of development – dating back to the sixteenth century – from an exocentric to an endocentric enterprise (see Borokhov 1913; M. Weinreich 1923a).[7] The earliest descriptions of Yiddish are found as appendices to the Hebrew grammars (written in Latin) by Christian Semitists of the sixteenth and seventeenth centuries. Yiddish was seen as an interesting "sideline" or as a "bridge to Hebrew" (Katz 1986: 23), and thus not of primary or direct interest to the authors or their readership. Self-instructional handbooks of Yiddish (written in German) by Christian authors date from the sixteenth century and later. The handbooks contained practical information useful in business transactions, including specialized (Hebrew-origin) vocabulary used in the horse- and cattle-trade. Thus, the interest in Yiddish was a medium to facilitate the real goal – business with Jews.

The next wave of Yiddish studies consisted of pedagogical works produced by Christian missionaries and their teachers. Here, too, the interest in Yiddish was direct, but not in Yiddish *qua* Yiddish but as a means for converting Jews to Christianity. The eighteenth and nineteenth centuries saw the production of anti-Semitic works (by Germans as well as by apostates) in which Yiddish speech was described or portrayed (with varying degrees of accuracy). The nineteenth century also saw the production of criminological research on Yiddish, as a by-product of police interest in thieves' cant and other marginal speech varieties. Beginning in the late nineteenth century there arose an interest – academic, social, and political – in the investigation of Yiddish for its own sake, by Jews and non-Jews. The groundwork for the serious academic investigation of Yiddish arose earlier in the nineteenth century in the founding of the Verein für Cultur und Wissenschaft der Juden, which marked the beginning of modern Jewish studies. As Borokhov (1966[1913]: 76–77) notes, however, many of these highly assimilated Jews (in the Verein) approached Yiddish as corrupt German. Thus, it remained for the generation of the blossoming of modern Yiddish studies in the early twentieth century to establish the study of Yiddish for its own sake and on its own terms.

[7] For summary discussion of the history of Yiddish linguistics, see Katz (1986). The present outline is drawn from Jacobs and Lorenz (1998: 191–192).

1.5 Jewish languages and Jewish interlinguistics

Wexler (1981a: 99), in the abstract of his seminal paper on Jewish interlinguistics, writes: "Since the 6th century B.C., Jews have created unique variants of many coterritorial non-Jewish languages with which they came into contact; Aramaic, Greek, Arabic, Spanish, Persian, and German are just a few examples." The investigation of Jewish languages within a Jewish interlinguistic framework dates back to the nineteenth century.[8] While Wexler (pp. 104–106) classifies four types of Jewish-language genesis, the most common type is development along a diachronic chain of Jewish languages. The first shift was from Hebrew[9] to Judeo-Aramaic (= Targumic). Subsequently, a portion of the Judeo-Aramaic-speaking population shifted to Judeo-Greek; later, Judeo-Latin likely arose on a Judeo-Greek substrate, and so forth. Of course, this chain view is a simplified representation of complex sociolinguistic realities. Not all speakers took part in a given shift. For example, some Hebrew speakers remained during Judeo-Aramaic times. Furthermore, only a portion of Judeo-Romance speakers – namely, those who settled in the Rhineland in approximately the ninth–tenth centuries CE – shifted to a German-based Jewish language.

The four types of Jewish languages which Wexler distinguishes are as follows: (A) Those arising via an uninterrupted chain of Jewish languages; Yiddish provides an example of this type. (B) Those languages spoken by Jews "in the absence of any significant Jewish substratum" (Wexler 1981a: 105); these become identified as Jewish by "default" – that is, at one point the Jewish and non-Jewish variants were essentially identical, but either the non-Jews moved away, leaving this linguistic turf to the Jews (e.g., Baghdadi Judeo-Arabic), or the Jewish speakers migrated to a different region, where their speech variety was perceived of as typically Jewish, even though it was not so perceived in its original home territory. (C) Calque languages developed within Jewish culture areas for systematic translation of Biblical texts or exegesis. These are not spoken languages, but, rather, follow a specific pattern of morpheme-by-morpheme translation; this results in texts which are systematically cleansed of Semitic lexicon and morphology, but which echo the original Hebrew or Aramaic syntax or phrasing (§7.7.1). (D) This denotes instances where the Jewish speech is (virtually) identical to non-Jewish speech, except that in the former, Jews "introduce occasional Hebrew-Aramaic or Jewish elements" (p. 106). Wexler sees these as transitory situations, where a Jewish language is undergoing language death (and, at the same time, possibly signaling the first stages in the birth of a new Jewish language); examples here are the German and Dutch speech

[8] Wexler (1981a: 100); see his extensive bibliography for references.

[9] While the first Jewish shift (among the first Jews) was likely from Canaanite dialects to Hebrew, the linguistic evidence for this is beyond our reach.

of Jews undergoing shift from Yiddish, but retaining some Hebrew-Aramaic [HA] origin lexemes.

Hebrew and Targumic occupy a unique position in the chain of Jewish languages in that they are common to all subsequent type A languages. Hebrew and Targumic are also unique in that they may serve as ongoing sources of linguistic enrichment, due to their status as the languages of sacred texts, liturgy, official documents such as certificates of marriage and divorce, wills, property transactions, and the like. Yiddish contains elements from Hebrew, Aramaic, and Judeo-Greek inherited via the chain of language shift; these elements are substratal. However, new elements may be added adstratally to Yiddish, via the presence of sacred texts in Hebrew and Judeo-Aramaic, whereas Judeo-Greek does not serve as an ongoing source of new enrichment in Yiddish.

The term *Loshn-koydesh* לשון קודש 'the language of sanctity'[10] is used in Yiddish scholarship to refer to the HA component found in subsequent Jewish languages; thus conflating reference to the two distinct (though closely related) Northwest Semitic languages into a single term.[11] The terms *Loshn-koydesh* / HA further conflate those elements which are substratal, those which were at one time adstratal in a predecessor Jewish language (but substratal in subsequent Jewish languages), and those added adstratally in the Jewish language under discussion. Where linguistic evidence for the distinctions is available, distinctions may be made (§2.5). Typical in traditional Jewish diaspora societies is a situation of internal Jewish bilingualism – the ongoing symbiosis of *Loshn-koydesh* and the Jewish vernacular within a Jewish speech community (M. Weinreich 1980: 247–314). In this situation Jewish social competence requires linguistic competence not only in the Jewish vernacular, but in *Loshn-koydesh* as well. The latter entailed some knowledge of Hebrew, and, with additional education, Aramaic.

In the scenario traditionally accepted in Yiddish scholarship, Yiddish arose via the following chain of vernaculars: Spoken Hebrew – Judeo-Aramaic – Judeo-Greek – Judeo-Romance – Yiddish. In this scenario, the Slavic component entered Yiddish adstratally, and basically only in part of the Yiddish *massif.* A rough chronology of the links in the chain may be given as follows (M. Weinreich 1980: 247). Hebrew was the only spoken language of Jews until 586 BCE, which date marked the beginning of the Babylonian exile and the beginning of the shift to (Judeo-) Aramaic. Hebrew gradually declined as the

[10] Cf. Hebrew לשון הקודש which contains the definite article *ha*; its absence in Yiddish is likely due to rhythmic reasons; see §2.8; Jacobs (1991).

[11] On the case for not conflating the two, see Katz (1985: 98; 1993: 47). The grammars of the two are distinct, as are their sociolinguistic roles within traditional Ashkenazic culture. Phonologically, both the Hebrew and Aramaic elements underwent identical pre-Yiddish developments (§2.4.2). The terms *Loshn-koydesh* and *HA* are used in the present work in accordance with general practice in Yiddish linguistics, and for ease of reference and space-economy.

spoken language of Jews in the Babylonian exile, with Judeo-Aramaic becoming predominant (±500–200 BCE). For the most part, Hebrew died out as a vernacular in Palestine between *c* 200 BCE and 300 CE. However, alongside Judeo-Aramaic as the vernacular, Hebrew remained in sacral and liturgical functions, and thus served as a source of enrichment within Judeo-Aramaic, both spoken and written. The influences worked in both directions; for example, Aramaic influences are found in the Hebrew of later portions of the Bible. The symbiosis in internal Jewish bilingualism became established from this time onward as a characteristic feature of Jewish civilization. The tradition arose whereby a sacred passage was read first in Hebrew, and then in the *targum* "translation."

Internal Jewish bilingualism continued as subsequent language shifts created new Jewish languages. The *Loshn-koydesh* texts (and oral recitation or citation from these) continued as potential sources of enrichment in later Jewish languages, while Judeo-Greek and subsequent Jewish languages did not / could not fill that function. Furthermore, it can be argued that acrolectal *Loshn-koydesh* may have served to reinforce the survival and transmission of (merged) HA-origin words in the later Jewish vernaculars, giving these a boost in ways that Judeo-Greek origin words, for example, lacked. Commencing in the fourth century BCE, Judeo-Greek emerged via the shift of some speakers of Hebrew and Aramaic. This was followed by the shift of some speakers of Hebrew, Aramaic, and Greek to Judeo-Latin in the first century BCE (Wexler 1981a: 110). The exact nature of a purported Judeo-Latin is unclear. However, the important point is that the next link in the chain toward Yiddish consisted of Jewish varieties of Romance. M. Weinreich (1980) provides detailed discussion of the long history of Jewish varieties of Romance languages. He suggests that these varieties took part in daughter-dialect-specific developments (toward "Italian" and "French") while at the same time maintaining their distinctness from these. Weinreich posits a shift from two varieties of Judeo-Romance – Western (Judeo-Old French) and Southern (Judeo-Old Italian) in Loter in approximately the ninth or tenth century – to a Germanic-based language, thus creating Yiddish. Wexler (1991) supposes a different chain, whereby Yiddish arose on a Judeo-Slavic substrate, which in turn he posits arose on Judeo-Aramaic and Judeo-Greek substrates (see §2.1.6). In either scenario, Yiddish arose through language shift, as part of a continuous chain of Jewish vernacular speech. This view of Jewish linguistic continuity and adaptation is the context in which scholarship within the field of Yiddish linguistics comprehends the Yiddish language.

2 History

2.1 Approaches to the history of Yiddish

Historically, three main types of approaches have been taken concerning the origins of Yiddish. Each approach arose within the intellectual and ideological contexts of its time. Furthermore, there is a path of development among the approaches, with partial transitions evident. The first type of approach may be called essentialist, or alinguistic. This approach views Yiddish as being, for example, "corrupted Hebrew" or "corrupted German" (e.g., Wagenseil 1699). Here, the proponents were not particularly interested in linguistic developments, but rather in questions concerning the "natural" language of group X. This fits in with general pre-modern views of language. With the emergence of modern linguistic science in the nineteenth century and beyond, there arose two main opposing approaches to the origins of Yiddish. One approach saw Yiddish origins via divergence from German – that Jews once spoke "pure" German, and subsequently split off from German. The convergence approach sees Yiddish as never having been identical to German. Our present interest lies in contrasting the two linguistic approaches.

2.1.1 The age of Yiddish

Some linguistic data provide evidence for dating developments. For example, Birnbaum (1979a: 56) claims that Yiddish uniform [x] in, e.g., *bux* – *bixər* 'book-s' ([x] vs. [ç] in relevant varieties of German) suggests a pre-MHG source (thus, before *c.* 1050 CE). On the other hand, there is much other evidence for ongoing German influence upon Yiddish extending over several centuries (M. Weinreich 1928). Thus, the criteria for determining the age of a language do not consist solely in terms of a static count of linguistic features.

2.1.2 Divergence

The divergence approach arose earlier than the convergence approach. It claims that Yiddish was a variety of German, essentially identical to a non-Jewish variety or varieties, with the possible exception of lexical items specific to Judaism. Among Jewish scholars, much of this approach traces to the school of the Wissenschaft des Judentums [WdJ] 'Science of Judaism,' which arose in Germany in the early nineteenth century. While WdJ is a direct intellectual parent of modern Yiddish studies, including Yiddish linguistics, it should be seen in the context of its time and place. It arose in the wake of the *Haskole*[1] 'Jewish Enlightenment' of German Jewry. German Jewry was acculturating and assimilating to emerging German cultural and linguistic norms. While attempting to look scientifically at things Jewish (that is, with the tools of linguistics, anthropology, etc.), these were modern German Jews engaged in a modern German/European enterprise. The terms of investigation, and thus also the frames of reference, were modern European ones. The modern European political paradigm recognized and valued canonical categories such as "France," "French," "German(y)," etc. Distinct co-existing and coterritorial populations were increasingly consigned to ethnic minority status within the dominant nation-states. Dialect speech and minority languages became marginalized, accompanied by a push toward a unified standard language to serve the nation, within the framework of the nation-state. Thus, the works of *Haskole* figures and others associated with WdJ disparaged Yiddish, which was seen as a stumbling block on the way to full acculturation (see Frakes 1993: xx on M. Weinreich 1993[1923]: 229ff.). For example, Rée (1844) is of a piece with this approach. The head of a Jewish school in Hamburg, he describes the peculiarities of Jewish speech vis-à-vis normative German, and the steps taken to rid pupils of Jewish features in their speech.

The divergence approach to Yiddish origins stems from this milieu. This approach posits a logical series of developments. The speech of the *Ostjuden* (the Ashkenazim in Eastern Europe, i.e., the Eastern Yiddish [EY] speakers) is seen as a language originally German subsequently corrupted by influence from Slavic and other coterritorial non-German languages. As opposed to EY, the speech of German Jews is viewed as "purer." The "Jewish peculiarities" of Jewish German are attributed to external factors, e.g., corruption by *Ostjuden* fleeing back to Germany after the Chmielnicki pogroms of 1648–1649; the social oppression of ghettoization within Germany itself in the thirteenth century; and so forth. While the anti-Yiddish agenda of the WdJ is clear, their works do provide us today with valuable linguistic data (see M. Weinreich 1993[1923]: 231ff.).

The divergence approach is exocentric; German constitutes the frame of reference. At each stage of its development the divergence approach has continued to deal with Yiddish in terms of German. In the earliest stage of scholarship,

[1] This is the Ashkenazic pronunciation. While the *Haskole* arose in Ashkenaz, the modern Israeli Hebrew pronunciation *Haskala* is frequently encountered (and the spelling *Haskalah*).

outlined above, Yiddish simply "falls short" of German. In the following stages as well, however, German continues to be the frame of reference (though these stages constitute a transition to Yiddish linguistics as an endocentric enterprise). Thus, Şăineanu (1889) makes the case that Yiddish is not to be seen in terms of New High German [NHG], but, rather, in terms of Middle High German [MHG]. This is refined further when Landau (1895) shows that Yiddish does not stem from the MHG language of poetry, but, rather, from colloquial varieties of the MHG language. However, the interest in "locating" the German "source" dialect is still primary (see, e.g., Gerzon 1902; Eggers 1998). Even as this moves us closer to the building blocks of Yiddish, it does not tell us more precisely about the blueprint for how these blocks were put together. Sapir (1949) continues in this German-centered discourse, even as he provides linguistic description.

Frakes (1989) provides insightful discussion of Germanistic-centered approaches to Yiddish origins (e.g., Ziskind 1953), by both Jewish and non-Jewish scholars. Common to all these is a clearly exocentric approach which views Yiddish in terms of extra-Yiddish facts, situations, and paradigms. Frakes discusses at length the role of typeface used – Jewish letters or *galkhes* 'Latin letters' – in modern text editing of older texts, and how this choice often reflects the deeper ideology and basic orientation of the scholar.

2.1.3 Convergence

As Yiddish linguistics developed, it moved from an exocentric to an endocentric enterprise.[2] There occurred a shift in how Yiddish origins were viewed in relation to German. The Jewish people – specifically, its Ashkenazic branch – was the point of departure. Yiddish arose when Jews – speaking other (Jewish) languages – created something German-looking. It is the life-long scholarly contribution of Max Weinreich and Solomon Birnbaum that put Yiddish at the center of Yiddish linguistic studies. Yiddish was not to be viewed as a once-"pure" German now fallen, but, rather, as never having been German. The view of Yiddish origins traditionally accepted in modern Yiddish linguistics is the convergence approach. Even the challenges within the field to Weinreich's convergence model (e.g., Jacobs 1975; King 1979; Faber and King 1984; Katz 1987a; Wexler 1987, 1991; Manaster Ramer 1997; Manaster Ramer and Wolf 1997) represent modifications within a convergence approach.[3]

2 See Fishman (1985); Katz (1986); Frakes (1989); Sunshine (1991: 38); Jacobs and Lorenz (1998).

3 As is generally the case within academic disciplines. Interestingly, there is most often a very clear-cut divide between scholars trained in Yiddish linguistics, and those who use only the tools of German linguistics to deal with Yiddish. Yiddish linguists clearly work from a convergence approach (though aware of the German linguistic/dialectological issues). Scholars approaching Yiddish solely with the tools of German linguistics generally take a divergence approach. The

M. Weinreich's (1967) discussion of the "ghetto myth" confronts the issue straight-on. The ghetto myth – a product of post-Enlightenment assimilationist views (e.g., of the WdJ) – is the claim that Yiddish arose when German-speaking Jews were deprived of contact with "German" Germans due to the forced ghettoizations commencing in the thirteenth century. Thus, Yiddish supposedly arose as a result of pure-German-speaking Jews being deprived of contact with non-Jewish German speakers. Among the many questions which arise is why "pure German" would thrive among one group of its speakers (say, a village populated by non-Jews), but simply wither in the ghetto, where all the speakers (Jews) presumably entered as speakers of native and pure German. Weinreich demonstrates clearly that we must look to the Jewish speech community itself to understand the linguistics and sociolinguistics of Yiddish. This speech community had its own norms, conventions, evaluations, and perceptions.

The convergence approach opens up the field to serious discussion of the nature of language contact, hybridity, etc. Language origins must be seen in their social context. Yiddish never "was" German.[4] M. Weinreich (1954: 78) describes a hypothetical situation where such would have been the case: a group of non-Jewish Germans who convert to Judaism, and through the passing years incorporate more and more Jewish-specific terms into their speech. However, this was not the case with Yiddish. Rather, Jews came as distinct groups already speaking something else.[5] These substrate languages then shaped the nature of the creation of Yiddish. Weinreich called this "fusion"; linguists today would

latter thus frequently recognize EY as a language, but see WY as a type or types of German. They also frequently make errors which betray a fundamental lack of basic knowledge of Yiddish, and which betray a bias which sees Yiddish as essentially German. For example, Kloss (1952) invents a singular form *Jidde* '(Ashkenazic) Jew' based on StG *Jude* (plural *Juden*; cf. StY *jid*, plural *jidn*); see also errors in Eggers (1998), discussed in Jacobs (2001b). Kloss (1952), arguing from a Germanic rather than German linguistic perspective, sees Yiddish as always having been distinct; still, the role of perspective is evident in terms like *Nebensprache*, *Ausbausprache*, *Abstandsprache*, etc. Hutton (1999: 188–232) discusses German linguists who dealt with Yiddish before, during, and after the Nazi years. Hutton (p. 211) writes: "It is a striking fact that many of the German facilitators of Yiddish studies in the inter-war period became members of the NSDAP or evinced strong pro-Nazi sympathies." Hutton provides specific discussion of, among others, Kloss and Beranek (the latter the author of the *Westjiddischer Sprachatlas*, 1965). Many of these scholars were able to continue their academic careers in post-war Germany. For example, Beranek was appointed to a chair in Yiddish at the University of Giessen in 1961. It should be noted that some of these German-cum-Nazi scholars expressed a convergence-origins view on racial grounds – they saw Jews as racially incapable of making German fully their own true mother tongue (see Hutton 1999). Significantly, scholars trained in general contact linguistics view Yiddish in terms of convergence (e.g., Louden 2000; Thomason and Kaufman 1988). For a strongly articulated discussion of the role of ideology in Old Yiddish studies, see Frakes (1989). See also Sunshine (1991: 61ff.).

[4] M. Weinreich (1954: 79) adds "there was NO period in history before the nineteenth century in which any Jewish GROUP had spoken anything approaching 'pure German.'"

[5] In the chain of Jewish diaspora languages; see also M. Weinreich (1980: 350). Wexler (1981a: 104) writes: "A defining feature of most Jewish languages is that they have superseded previous Jewish languages which eventually became obsolete . . . Most of these languages prove to be links

use language-contact terminology like pidginization, creolization, relexification, etc. While not disputing the importance of MHG to Yiddish linguistics, the convergence approach sees German as one component in fusion-language genesis. Determining the German source dialects is important to the overall task, but it is not the "end-goal"; rather, it is merely one important factor in the overall picture. Yiddish is not a macaronic language; rather, it possesses patterns and regularities to be discovered in their own right by linguists (Frakes 1993: xviiiff.). Exocentric approaches focused on peculiarities of Yiddish vis-à-vis German. Thus, for example, Zunz (1832) and others would make specific note of the use of Hebrew words in Judeo-German (Yiddish) speech. M. Weinreich (1931), on the other hand, argues that Yiddish would not be Yiddish without the Hebrew-Aramaic [HA] component. Fusion is primary.

Three main variants of the convergence approach may be conveniently distinguished in geographical terms (which refer to the claimed birthplace of Yiddish and to the external linguistic points of reference). The following outlines the main contours of each.

2.1.4 *Loter scenario*

Max Weinreich (1980: esp. 1–45) presents the Loter scenario, according to which Jews settled approximately 1,000 years ago in communities along the Rhine, in a compact area known in Jewish sources as *Loter* (cf. German *Lothringen*). The immigrants to Loter spoke two varieties of Loez (Judeo-Romance): Western (Judeo-Old French) and Southern (Judeo-Old Italian). Here, they came into contact with varieties of German of that time and place. Temporally, this is placed at the end of the Old High German [OHG] period and the early part of the MHG period – somewhere between the ninth and twelfth centuries (pp. 423ff.).[6] However, localizing the "core" German component in Yiddish to a more specific period of German is problematic (Birnbaum 1979a: 44ff.; M. Weinreich 1980: 424ff.). Geographically, Low German is eliminated from consideration, since the German component of Yiddish underwent the Second Sound Shift (the High German sound shift; e.g., StG *zehn*, StY *cen*, vs. Dutch *tien*, English *ten*).

In the earliest period, when Ashkenaz was confined to Loter, the contact was with Rhineland – i.e., West Central German [wCG] – varieties. Later, during expansion to the east, south, and southwest (forced, in large part, by the violence of the First Crusade), the wCG-based Yiddish became coterritorial with East Central German [eCG] and Bavarian (M. Weinreich 1980: 730). Weinreich assumes for this period a remodeling based on eCG models; he sees

in a long uninterrupted chain of Jewish language shift that began some four and a half millennia ago."

[6] German continued to exert influences on Yiddish in various times and places up into the twentieth century; see M. Weinreich (1980: 424), and see below.

wCG forms as vestiges of an earlier linguistic situation. Later (from the mid thirteenth century on), migration to Eastern Europe gives rise to the introduction of a Slavic component.

The recent challenges to the Loter scenario are nevertheless only modifications of the convergence approach (see Sunshine 1991: 38). For Weinreich, Yiddish arose via fusion of elements from HA, Loez, and German. Slavic entered only later, and – with the exception of a few lexical items – only in the east. However, a number of concerns based on the linguistic data has led to the recent challenges to Weinreich's model. First, there is concern about the extremely limited presence of the Loez component. Second, there is concern over the overwhelming eCG/Bavarian nature of the German component. The two main challenges are: the Bavarian scenario, and the Judeo-Slavic scenario. Both posit more easterly origins for Yiddish, and both thus see the Loter Jews as originally distinct from the eastern group.

2.1.5 *Bavarian scenario*

This is the view that Yiddish originated on eastern German territory. It is based on the strong presence of Bavarian-like features (and, to a lesser extent, eCG features) in the German component in Yiddish. The Loter Jews are seen as a distinct group (Faber and King 1984: 407). Evidence for this comes as well from the following. Westernmost WY [wWY] does indeed contain a larger Loez component than do other varieties of Yiddish. Furthermore, the HA component often differs precisely between wWY and the rest of Yiddish (both easternmost WY [eWY] and EY); e.g., 'prayerbook' is wWY *tfilə/pfilə*, based on TH *təfilɔ:*, while eWY/EY have forms based on TH *siddu:r*. Here, wWY typically patterns with the Jewish culture areas Sepharad and Provense in its HA component, further suggestive of distinct origins for Loter and Ashkenaz. For eCG/Bavarian features, see Faber and King (1984); Faber (1987); Katz (1987a), and below. Faber and King (1984: 396) also note that while a heavy lexical influence from HA is evident universally in Yiddish, the Slavic influence is "moderate and geographically variable." That westernmost Yiddish is almost devoid of Slavicisms suggests further distinct settlement histories for Loter and Ashkenaz. Furthermore, the Slavic component in Yiddish often shows dialect variation not evident in the German component of Yiddish, possibly suggesting a more limited German (read: Bavarian) source.

2.1.6 *Judeo-Slavic scenario*

Wexler (primarily 1987, 1991) posits Yiddish origins on a Judeo-Slavic substrate (Judeo-Sorbian), which, in turn, derives from Judeo-Aramaic and Judeo-Greek predecessors. According to Wexler, Yiddish arose via relexification of Judeo-Slavic. In Wexler's scenario, Yiddish arose first in the bilingual

German-Slavic lands. Via subsequent migrations Yiddish then spread westward (as well as eastward), coming into contact in the west with the distinct Ashkenazic German which arose in Loter (Wexler 1981b). For Wexler, the higher "Slavic profile" of easternmost EY – Northeastern Yiddish [NEY] and Southeastern Yiddish [SEY] – is substratal rather than adstratal. Other varieties of Yiddish are seen as progressively more Germanized. Wexler also attempts to deal with the longstanding problem of the disappearance of the Slavic-speaking Kanaanic Jews (M. Weinreich 1980: 80ff.), who were – according to the Loter scenario – mysteriously swallowed up with little or no trace by the eastward-expanding Ashkenazim.

Among the arguments cited by Wexler (1991: 12) are: the almost complete absence of southwest German dialect features in Yiddish generally (based on Faber and King 1984); the extreme paucity of a French component in all but westernmost Yiddish (see Herzog 2000); the relative uniformity of WY as compared to the coterritorial western German dialect landscape. The latter fact, Wexler claims, suggests "a late arrival of Yiddish in the area." Wexler (1991: 88–89) dates a possible partial shift "from Judeo-Sorbian to German" to a period spanning from the ninth and tenth centuries ("earliest Jewish settlement in the Germano-Slavic lands") to the thirteenth and fourteenth centuries (marking the migration of German Jews to Poland). He suggests a date around the late thirteenth to early fourteenth century, but notes linguistic arguments for pushing this date back earlier.

Wexler's scenario is the most radical of the challenges to Weinreich's Loter scenario, and has been seen as the most controversial.[7] Yet he was the first to deal systematically with the problems of the HA and Loez components in westernmost vs. all other Yiddish. Collectively, both the Bavarian scenario and the Judeo-Slavic scenario have moved the field toward a non-Loter, eastern-origins view. The two recent approaches differ in many ways, but have much in common. Both deal directly with the clear presence of major isogloss and isopleth bundling between westernmost WY on the one hand, and all other varieties of Yiddish on the other hand. Thus, both scenarios see Loter Jewry as distinct historically, culturally, and linguistically (see also Lowenstein 1995; Herzog 2000; §3.8). Both challenges account for the problem of the very low wCG cast to Yiddish generally. Later, as Ashkenazic German and westward-diffusing Yiddish came into contact, transition dialects (of two historically distinct languages!) resulted.

2.2 The German source dialect(s)

Though formulating fundamentally different questions, both the divergence and convergence approaches are interested in determining the German source

7 See several of the "Comments to Wexler" in Wexler (1991), and Eggers (1998).

dialect(s) of Yiddish. Gerzon (1902) suggested an East Central German dialect base for Yiddish; Mieses (1924) suggested Bavarian (see Katz 1987a: 54–55 for summary). Keeping in mind Prilutski's (1917: 289) observation that no Yiddish dialect corresponds to any single German dialect, we may nevertheless look at the broader picture in an attempt to narrow down the German determinant.

Faber and King (1984: 397–398) summarize the main features in Yiddish which agree with East Central German, and those which agree with Bavarian. The features found in Yiddish which are also characteristic of East Central German listed by Faber and King are:

1. Non-affricate reflexes of Germanic *p-*, *-pp-*, and *-p*; StY *ferd* 'horse,' *epl* 'apple,' *kop* 'head'; cf. StG *Pferd, Apfel, Kopf.*
2. MHG diphthongs *ie, üe, uo* (MHG *knie, grüene, buoch*) correspond to monophthongs in East Central German and Yiddish; cf. StY *kni* 'knee,' *grin* 'green,' *bux* 'book.'
3. Retention (= non-syncope) of the vowel in unstressed prefixes *bə-* and *gə-*; cf. StY *bakumən* 'received,' *gəhat* 'had.'

The features listed by Faber and King in which Yiddish agrees with Bavarian are considerably more numerous; they are:[8]

1. Apocope – MHG *bluome, tage,* StY *blum* 'flower,' *teg* 'days.'
2. Loss of rule of final devoicing; cf. MHG *rat,* SY *rod* 'wheel.'
3. "A direct causal relationship between number 1 apocope and number 2 loss of final devoicing (see King 1980)."
4. Early and complete unrounding of front rounded vowels; MHG *über,* StY *ibər* 'over.'
5. Retention of Bavarian archaic *ec*$_{\text{NOM}}$-*enk*$_{\text{OBL}}$ 'you' "in certain dialects of Central Yiddish."[9]
6. Lack of umlaut in present indicative 2/3 P.SG of strong verbs: *du trogst* 'you carry,' *er trogt* 'he carries'; cf. StG *ich trage* 'I carry,' *du trägst, er trägt.*
7. Faber and King (1984: 398) list a seventh feature, loss of distinctive vowel length, pointing out that vowel length "is found in almost all German dialects; its absence is exceedingly rare. Both Bavarian and all dialects of Yiddish except Central Yiddish lack phonemic vowel length." This argument is overstated. The fact is that vowel length is much more present than that; it must be posited for PY, and it is found, to varying degrees, in Central Yiddish and Western Yiddish. Residual vowel length is also found in Courland Yiddish; as well, possible residual length is noted for the early twentieth century for some parts of both NEY and SEY (see U. Weinreich 1958a, 1958b).

[8] Though many of these features are widespread beyond Bavarian as well; e.g., apocope and unrounding.

[9] Actually, *ec/enk* in Yiddish was once found in areas beyond the modern Central Yiddish area, and has receded. It is also found in West Transcarpathian Yiddish (U. Weinreich 1964).

8. Diminutive formation – both Bavarian and Yiddish[10] have an *l*-based diminutive (rather than the *k*-based diminutive; see König 1978: 157). In German dialects, the *l*-diminutive is characteristic of Bavarian and Alemannic. Faber and King note that Yiddish and Bavarian both have an "intensive diminutive," i.e., a second degree of diminution (iminutive);[11] thus, StY *štot* 'city,' *štetl* 'market town,' *štetələ* 'little market town [endearing].'[12]

2.3 Hybridity and fusion

The intellectual and popular background against which Max Weinreich developed the concept of Yiddish as a fusion language (*shmeltsshprakh*) is one which saw hybridity as haphazard, sloppy, uncouth, unsystematic. Fusion, on the contrary, fit in with the structuralist principle that the individual parts of any linguistic system are to be analyzed solely in terms of their function within the whole of that system. For Weinreich, fusion is fundamental to the very origins and nature of the language (see M. Weinreich 1931, 1954: 79). This differs markedly from prior approaches to Yiddish, which saw, for example, the Hebrew-origin elements as problematic or marginal "add-ons."

On purely structural grounds it can be demonstrated that Weinreich is correct in his claim that the linguistic system of Yiddish was, from the outset, never identical to the linguistic system of any variety of German, or even of any combination of varieties of German. To take one simple example: Proto-Yiddish and the daughter dialects[13] regularly preserve a phonemic distinction /s/ vs. /z/ in word-initial position (M. Weinreich 1954: 76). The main contributors to this contrast are (in modern StY) words from HA, Loez, Slavic, and internationalisms [Intls]; thus: StY *sojnə* 'enemy,' *zojnə* 'prostitute' (< HA); *sok* 'syrup; sap' (< Sl), *zok* 'sock' (< Gmc). In the history of German, however, initial /s/ has developed (in the relevant varieties of German) in one of two ways: to /z/ /_V, and to /š/ /_C; thus: MHG *sagen* 'say,' *slâfen* 'sleep,' *stërben* 'die' > StG *sagen* [z], *schlafen*, *sterben* [š]. With one exception, it happens that the German component of Yiddish only contains items with initial *#šC* and *#zV* (StY *šlofn*, *štarbn*, *zogn*). However, as concerns the phonological system of Yiddish, this is only an accidental fact, rather than a systemic one, since the PY system contrasted /s/-/z/-/š/ word-initially, both before V and before C. (Initial /ž/ arose later via contact with Slavic.) The lexical exception with initial *sV* from the

[10] Most, though not all varieties; see Herzog 2000: 120–122; §3.5.

[11] As does Slavic, though; e.g., Polish *miasto* 'city,' *miastko*, *miasteczko*.

[12] Cf. Austrian Bavarian *stuob* 'room,' 1st DIM *stiobl*, 2nd DIM *stiobarl*. Further supporting this observation by Faber and King suggesting a Bavarian link is the fact that some varieties of CY have systematically preserved residue of the earlier /r/ in the iminutive suffix; see Jacobs (1990a: 82).

[13] With the exception of those daughter dialects which have later neutralized (some) voicing distinctions in obstruents, e.g., Alsatian Yiddish.

German component is StY conjunction *saj*, and its derivative *sajdn* 'unless' (probably from an earlier reflex corresponding to StG *es sei denn*). Similarly, comparison of Slavicisms and Intls in Yiddish and (relevant varieties of) German reveals the effects of differing system-based incorporation strategies: StY contrasts initial [s] before vowel in *socjalizm* 'socialism,' *sovetiš* 'soviet,' *salon* 'salon,' with [z] before vowel in *zavisə* 'hinge,' *zavərúxə* 'blizzard,' *zoologiš* 'zoological'; StG has [z] before vowel in *Sozialismus, Sowjet Union, Salon*, etc. Furthermore, StY initial *s* /_C and *š* /_C contrast in, e.g., *stirə* 'contradiction,' *slinə* 'saliva,' *strašən* 'threaten,' *student* 'student,' vs. *študirn* 'study,' *šlofn* 'sleep,' *štrofn* 'punish.' In StG the regular development *š* /_C yields: *Student, studieren* (both with [š]), *schlafen*, etc. In modern StG, initial *sl* is permitted, but is still somewhat marked as foreign (e.g., *Slavisch, Slowakei*), as is initial *s* /_V in, e.g., *Sushi*. On the other hand, the contrast of sibilants *s, z*, and *š* was fully productive (before vowel or consonant) already from the inception of PY; modern Yiddish (post-contact with Slavic) has a productive four-way sibilant contrast (*ž* as well).

Numerous examples of fusion and the differential structures of PY and German are found throughout the phonology, morphology, and lexicon. The syntax remains more problematic. Part of this has to do with the nature of the older documents in Yiddish, where various writing traditions (German, Hebrew-calque, as well as the heavily mixed scribal language) make it harder to know what the syntax of the vernacular was like. As concerns morphology, Yiddish from its inception contained the possibility of the *-im* noun plural suffix (something not available to German); the regularity of the *-s* plural in Yiddish (as opposed to German) may in part owe to the input from the substratal HA component (King 1990a). Similarly, the availability of periphrasis as a strategy for verb formation is distinct in Yiddish. In short, the sets of the "pieces of the puzzle" in the Yiddish system were from the start different from the potential sets in German. The inventory of available pieces – and thus, the abstractable grammatical system(s) – was uniquely Yiddish.

M. Weinreich's (1980: 30) now classic sentence demonstrates fusion at all levels of the grammar: *noxn bentšn hot der zejdə gəkojft a sejfər* 'after the blessing grandfather bought a holy book.' The component origins of the individual parts are as follows:

nox-n	benč-n	hot	der	zejdə	gəkojft	a	sejfər
G – G	L – G	G	G	Sl	G	G	HA

However, as Weinreich makes clear, the individual parts function uniquely within the system of Yiddish, to wit: while *nox* and *-n* are both from the German component, the combination is Yiddish (cf. StG *mit dem* → colloquial [miʔəm], StY *mit dem* → *mitn*;[14] see §5.9.2). The nominalized form *benčn* contains a Loez-origin root *benč-* to which is attached the German-component verbal infinitive suffix *-n* (and not a Romance-origin suffix, *-ere*; cf. Latin *benedicere* 'bless'). Slavic-origin *zejdə* combines with the German-component definite article *der*, whereas the relevant varieties of Slavic lack definite articles. Similarly, although Hebrew lacks the indefinite article, HA-component *sejfər* takes here the indefinite article *a*. Thus, *sejfər*, *zejdə*, *noxn* are Yiddish words, not Hebrew, Slavic, and German words. The nuance is perhaps self-evident, but important, and frequently missed.

Weinreich further points out the semantic difference between Yiddish *sejfər* and its Hebrew cognate. In Hebrew, the item is a general term for 'scroll' or 'book.' In Yiddish, *sejfər* 'Jewish holy book' contrasts with *bux* 'book.' Furthermore, Yiddish has regional *kniɦə* 'third stomach of a cow' solely in this meaning; in Slavic languages, the cognate word may have the meanings 'book' and 'third stomach of a ruminating animal' (e.g., in Russian). Thus, individual lexical items in Yiddish must be analyzed in terms of their function within the system of Yiddish, not externally, in terms of their stock-language function. Weinreich gives the example of Yiddish *jorcajt* 'anniversary of death,' a term specific to Jewish culture. Its constituent parts are both synchronically independent words in Yiddish – *jor* 'year,' and *cajt* 'time.' Both trace back to the German component, and both have counterparts in German (*Jahr*, *Zeit*). The meanings of *jor* and *cajt* are (*grosso modo*) the same as *Jahr* and *Zeit*, respectively. However, the compound is uniquely Yiddish; cf. StG *Jahreszeit* 'season'; here, Yiddish is forced to circumlocute: *cajt(n) fun jor* 'time(s) of the year,' since *jorcajt* is blocked.

All approaches to the history of Yiddish have noted that the Yiddish lexicon contains words from diverse source languages. However, a word is necessary about notions of specific components and semantic "domains." Some observers claimed that the Hebrew component in Yiddish is basically limited to religious life and/or High-register topics and situations, the Slavic component to nature and everyday "earthy" topics and situations, etc. This is easily refuted with examples like Yiddish *trejbərn* 'porge meat' – an activity specifically linked to Jewish religious practice – which comes from the Slavic component. Similarly, it is incorrect to say that HA-origin words are used only in H(igh)-register in Yiddish. Thus, TH *jɔ:ð* 'hand, arm,' and dual *jɔ:ðajji:m*, have yielded Yiddish *jad* 'pointer used in reading of the Torah' (thus, part of H register), and *jodajəm* 'mits, paws' (less dignified than *hant/hent* 'hand-s, arm-s'); German-origin *ejər* 'eggs' is used also for 'testicles,' but HA-origin *bejcəm* is coarser 'balls.' Thus, strictly speaking, it can be demonstrated that all components may serve all semantic domains and sociolinguistic levels throughout the language. At the

[14] Some German dialects have contracted forms with *n* (Joseph Salmons, p.c.).

same time, however, there are patterns and tendencies worth noting. For example, the Slavic component serves as the base for the expression of emotive functions, as well as for sounds in nature, for calling to animals, etc. (Stankiewicz 1985). There is furthermore a component consciousness by speakers (M. Weinreich 1980: 656–657) which may have played a role in the history and shaping of Yiddish (see §7.3).

Finally, the word order in M. Weinreich's sample Yiddish sentence should be noted. In StG (and most varieties of German), the non-finite verb typically occurs in final position, e.g., StG *Nach dem Segnen hat der Grossvater ein heiliges Buch gekauft*. In Yiddish this is not the normal word order (see §6.3.6).

The fusion approach focuses on the system of Yiddish rather than on identifying elements as "German," "Hebrew," "Slavic," etc. However, as concerns Yiddish origins, a framework is necessary for discussion of etymological sources. Weinreich distinguishes the following three terms: *stock*, *determinant*, and *component*. The term stock language refers to the external languages which are relevant to our discussion of Yiddish: German, Hebrew, Aramaic, Polish (or, less precisely, Slavic), etc. The *determinant* is that subset of a stock language which potentially could have served as a source for elements or features which surface in Yiddish. Determinant is a means of narrowing down more precisely what we mean by the term stock. The specifying of determinants is based on our knowledge of history, geography, and diachronic linguistic developments, both in the various stock languages and in Yiddish. For example, the stock language German must be narrowed down further, to High German. This (High) German component in Yiddish regularly shows effects of the Second Sound Shift (e.g., StY *cen* 'ten,' *cu* 'to'), while HA-origin items do not (e.g., *tojrə* < TH *to:rɔ:* 'Torah,' not ***cojrə*). Thus, we must assume that Yiddish arose at a time and place when the relevant varieties of German had already undergone the Second Sound Shift. As we consider and compare other features, the temporal placement of Yiddish origins is somewhat problematic in light of linguistic considerations which stretch from the late OHG period into MHG. However, comparison of MHG, Yiddish, and NHG rules out NHG as a basis for Yiddish origins.

The term *component* refers to those elements of the determinant which actually end up as part of Yiddish. Thus, the term is basically an etymological footnote concerning a given element in Yiddish. Yiddish does not consist of "scraps" of the grammars of Polish, Hebrew, German, etc. Rather, Yiddish grammar is to be analyzed in terms of its internal system. For example, Yiddish verbs like *hargənən* 'kill,' *ganvənən* 'steal,' *axlən* 'eat crudely,' *masərn* 'tattle on,' contain roots which ultimately are of Hebrew origin. In Yiddish, however, these verbs inflect according to Yiddish grammar, not Hebrew grammar.[15]

[15] In fact, these verbs are reconstructed for Proto-Yiddish from forms which are not attested in Classical Hebrew itself, and which probably arose in rabbinic Hebrew of the pre-Yiddish period (see below).

Consider the following examples of noun pluralization. StY *kačkə* 'duck' traces to the Slavic component. However, its plural is *kačkə -s*, based on regular *-s* plural for ə-final nouns in Yiddish. While the *-s* plural suffix is of debatable origin (King 1990a), it is clearly not Slavic (cf. Polish *kaczka – kaczki* 'duck-s'). We find a Gmc-origin plural strategy (umlaut + suffix) in, e.g., *sod* (< Slavic) – *sedər* 'orchard-s,' *ponəm* (< HA) – *penəmər* 'face-s.' Similarly, do we say that Yiddish plurals *tiš-n* 'table-s,' *veg-n* 'road-s,' are "German"? The StG plural forms are *Tisch-e, Weg-e*. Yiddish does not have the plural suffix *-ə*; thus, Yiddish has resorted to another available Yiddish suffix.[16] Nor must the plural allomorph be the historically "correct" one (i.e., that found in the stock language), even when that suffix is available in Yiddish; thus, StY *šabəs – šabosəm* 'Sabbath-s'; cf. TH *šabbɔ:θ – šabbɔ:θo:θ*, even though the TH plural suffix *-o:θ* survives as Yiddish *-əs* (cf. StY *sod – sojdəs* 'secret-s,' *mokəm – məkojməs* 'place-s'). Even the term *lošn-kojdəš*, composed of two HA-origin lexemes, represents an instance of fusion since here *lošn* is reconstructed as a reflex of a TH non-construct (*isolated*) noun, rather than the expected construct form (Jacobs 1991).

Consider the following two examples of morphological fusion which have led to a reanalysis of inherited structure (M. Weinreich 1980: 654–655). Modern Yiddish has the female names *Rivə* and *Jentə*. The former derives from *rivkə* (TH *riβqɔ:*), the latter from Loez-component *jentl* (cf. *gentile*). Since *-l* and *-kə* coincidentally exist as diminutive markers in Yiddish, and are used with personal names, speakers have created the back-forms *rivə* and *jentə* on analogy with base names like *sorə* 'Sarah,' diminutives *sorkə, sorl, sorələ*. Similarly, Yiddish has back-formed a singular *šejmə* 'stray leaf of a Jewish sacred book' from plural *šejməs*, the latter an item inherited from TH *šəmo:θ*. In TH the plural suffix was *-o:θ*, the singular base form *še:m*. Reanalysis in Yiddish was only possible because of a constellation of separate historical developments (within Yiddish, and pre-Yiddish): TH *t* (> *θ*) > *s*, stress shift, weakening of the post-tonic vowel to schwa, and reanalysis of *šejməs* as *šejmə-s*, i.e., a regular (Yiddish) *-s* plural for a schwa-final noun.

The four main components of Yiddish in M. Weinreich's fusion model are: Germanic, Slavic, HA, and Loez. The term "component" is best limited to languages which have had a significant structural impact on Yiddish and which are not confined to lexical borrowings. Concerns about the extremely small number of items from Loez have led to doubts about a "Loez component." Indeed, these are limited to some very few words, e.g., *benčn* 'bless,' *lejənən* 'read,' *o:rn* 'pray' (in WY); some personal names, e.g., *šnejər, fajvuš, jentə, tolcə*, and others. There seems to be no Loez impact on the grammar of Yiddish. We might

16 A similar recourse to "reshuffling" is found in apocopating German dialects as well. However, these developments need not be genetically related.

consider other components in regional varieties of Yiddish, but only to a limited degree. Although there are Lithuanianisms in the Yiddish of Lithuania, Latvia, and Estonia, the influences are mostly lexical, not structural (Lemkhen 1995; Verschik 1999). Thus, it is questionable to posit a "Baltic" component here; to the extent that one exists, it is very marginal. An additional component consists of internationalisms [Intls] – though these for the most part entered Yiddish via Slavic (e.g., *revol'ucjə* 'revolution' [with palatalized l']). Finally, the component cover terms are only general. For example, the numerous NHG loanwords which entered Yiddish in the modern period (e.g., *fragə* 'question' vs. older Yiddish *freg*; *umštand* 'circumstance'; *šprax* 'language') must be distinguished from the original German (MHG) component in Yiddish.

It is important to distinguish among: original fusion (involved in the formation of Yiddish), later externally (contact-) induced change, and Yiddish-internal developments, as well as between the original German component in Yiddish and later NHG elements borrowed into the language. Importantly, these NHG elements show patterning in Yiddish typical of borrowing situations, whereas the earliest German component shows marks of Weinreich's fusion and Thomason and Kaufman's (1988) language shift. However, many other questions remain. For example, Yiddish regularly marks aspectual distinctions. While aspect is present to some degree in German (e.g., *schiessen* 'shoot' vs. *erschiessen* 'shoot dead'), it is much more fully developed in Slavic languages. Yiddish represents an intermediate level of development. What does this mean? Is Yiddish aspect to be seen in terms of genetic linguistics (as an inheritance from German[ic])? In typological terms? In areal terms? On the other hand, a feature such as anticipatory obstruent voicing assimilation (§4.4.3) in NEY is best seen as a contact-induced (Slavic/Baltic) innovation. Thus, discussion of the history of Yiddish must distinguish among substratal, adstratal, structural, and typological prerequisites. Only then can we systematically sort out original fusion from later contact phenomena.

2.4 Proto-Yiddish and the reconstruction of the Proto-Yiddish sound system

The reconstruction of a proto-stage of a language is inherently problematic – it involves an unattested form of the language. The proto-model assumes uniformity, where considerations of original diversity and variation are pushed aside. Nevertheless, reconstruction of proto-languages is a useful tool for describing language history.

Some scholars have argued against the very notion of PY – or at least a single Proto-Yiddish (while not challenging the notion of proto-language in general). In common to all these is an exocentric approach, where Yiddish is seen fundamentally in terms of German. These scholars reject the notion of Western Yiddish, seeing true Yiddish as developing from German only later in contact with Slavic. Marchand (1965, 1987) argues against a single Proto-Yiddish, but suggests that there are perhaps numerous local Proto-Yiddishes, each originating in its own (German-dialect!) locale. Once again, the argumentation is based on German.

The endocentric Yiddish scholarship refutes this view, presenting two important points: (1) no single dialect of German accounts for all the German-component features in any variety of Yiddish; (2) the facts about Yiddish cannot be predicted based only on knowledge of the stock languages (M. Weinreich 1993[1923]: 38). Thus, the reconstruction of PY (or any proto-language) must be founded primarily on investigation of the facts within the language itself; only secondarily do we "check" our preliminary findings by recourse to external data. Problems exist in the reconstruction of Proto-Yiddish as they do in the reconstruction of any proto-language.[17] However, the regularities and patterns found in the Yiddish dialect data – both synchronic and diachronic – offer irrefutable evidence for the feasibility and utility of a reconstruction of Proto-Yiddish.

This section focuses on the reconstruction of the PY sound system. There is overwhelming regularity in diaphoneme[18] patterning across Yiddish dialects, regardless of the component origin of words; e.g., NEY *gejn* 'go,' *sejfər* 'holy book,' *lejənən* 'read' with *ej*, vs. CY *gajn*, *sajfər*, *laj(ə)nən* with *aj* (examples from the German, HA, and Loez components, respectively).

Reconstruction of the PY sound system is thus a methodological task, where the modern dialects constitute the primary point of departure, supplemented, if available, by our knowledge of older stages of the language. As concerns Yiddish, most of the developments have occurred in the vowels. By comparison, the consonantism presents fewer problems. The proto-model must also take into consideration known external facts about the stock languages (but only secondarily). Consider one brief example. We know that early original German monophthongs *i:*, *u:*, *y:* have become diphthongs in the relevant German dialects (the German determinant for Yiddish purposes); cf. StY *dajn* 'your,' *hojz* 'house,' *hajzər* 'houses,' early MHG *dîn*, *hûs*, *hiuser*, and modern StG *dein*, *Haus*, *Häuser*. At the same time, we reconstruct PY long **i:*, **u:* in lexical items from the HA component; cf. WY *di:nim* 'religious laws,' *gvu:rə* 'heroism.' German-component original *i:*, *u:*, *y:* have not merged with HA-component original *i:*, *u:*; the former are PY **aj*, **au*, while the latter are PY **i:*, **u:*. Thus, we must either assume that Yiddish possesses separate component-based phonologies,[19] or that the German-component diphthongization occurred prior to – and thus, external to – the history of Yiddish. While there

[17] Thus, for example, M. Weinreich (1958a) perhaps overemphasizes the role of WY as the parent dialect of later WY and EY.

[18] The term *diaphoneme* refers to the regular modern cross-dialect correspondences of the same historical phoneme, e.g., PY $*u:_{52}$ is regularly *u:-i:-i-u* in, respectively, WY, CY, SEY, NEY.

[19] Consider those varieties of English where the diphthong in indigenous English words like *day*, *take* is realized as [aj]; this change affects loanwords like *nation*, *compensation*, *innate*, as well.

is some evidence of speakers' component consciousness (M. Weinreich 1980: 656–657), the overwhelming cross-component regularity of Yiddish phonology forces us to establish a set of clearly defined phonological prerequisites to the reconstruction of PY – that is, certain developments demonstrably occurred prior to the birth of Yiddish as a linguistic system.[20]

2.4.1 Phonological prerequisites to the pre-history of Yiddish

As a catch-term for locating temporally those developments which are known to have occurred in the stock languages, but which – based on evidence within Yiddish – must have occurred prior to the inception of Yiddish, the term *pre-Yiddish* is used.[21] Sometimes the Yiddish data provide evidence otherwise unavailable in scholarship limited to the stock languages. For example, Semitic linguists have debated whether Tiberian Hebrew actually possessed distinctive vowel length (as opposed to a tense-lax distinction). However, in his analysis of stress placement in HA-component words in Yiddish, Leibel (1965) demonstrated clearly that a systematic length distinction was present in the Hebrew etymons at some stage predating the birth of Yiddish.[22]

Since much is known about the phonology of TH (from the later Masoretes and their pointing system codified in the latter part of the first millennium CE), we may narrow down further our definition of "pre-Yiddish" to a time after the majority of Jews had stopped using Hebrew as their vernacular, but before the birth of Yiddish. Since post-exile Jewish history is continuous, we assume in Jewish diaspora communities a continuous chain of Jewish vernaculars. HA-origin words which survived as integral elements in the chain of Jewish vernacular speech were subject to regular phonological (and other) developments at each vernacular stage along the way. Developments in the HA component found in Yiddish provide evidence for this (see Birnbaum 1979a: 59–66; M. Weinreich 1980: 351ff.; Wexler 1981a; Katz 1985). This is seen most clearly by a component-based contrastive analysis of phonological developments in the history and pre-history of Yiddish.

2.4.2 Pre-Yiddish syllable structure and the nucleus

The TH and German components in Yiddish show a number of parallels which, upon closer examination, must be seen as separate Pre-Yiddish developments

[20] Katz (1982: 135ff., and 263ff.) coined the term "transcomponent reconstruction" which refers to this juxtaposition of Yiddish data based on component origin. The principle has long been used in Yiddish linguistics; see, e.g., M. Weinreich (1973, 1980), Fischer (1936 = Bin-Nun (1973), and others.

[21] M. Weinreich (1954: 87ff.) uses the term *Pre-Ashkenazic*; see also Katz (1993: 71).

[22] It could be argued that vowel length was merely a pre-Yiddish, but post-TH development in a post-Hebrew Jewish vernacular, e.g., Loez. Still, this information becomes available from examination of Yiddish, and not from Hebrew linguistic data alone.

rather than as belonging to the history of Yiddish proper. Prime examples of this are processes of vowel lengthening and shortening according to syllable type – open or closed. Both in the TH component of the pre-Yiddish Jewish vernacular and in (the relevant varieties of) German pre-Yiddish, there occurred a general standardization of quantity [SOQ] in stressed syllables; however, these were independent processes which demonstrably occurred outside the history of Yiddish (Jacobs 1993a).

The basic facts concerning German SOQ are outlined in Prokosch (1939: 140). Early MHG possessed four types of stressed syllable: (1) open-short *ne – men* 'take,' (2) open-long *na: – men* '(they) took,' (3) closed-short *dah – te* 'covered' (NHG *deckte*), (4) closed-long *da:h – te* 'thought.' At the earlier stage, syllable length was measured in terms of vowel length: a syllable was long if it contained a long vowel. At a later stage (in Late MHG) syllable length became measured in terms of the entire rhyme. Quantity (in stressed syllables) was standardized in the new system. Types 2 and 3, above, were unaffected. Types 1 and 4, however, were modified to conform to the new pattern. In type 1, a short vowel was lengthened in open syllable. In type 4, a long vowel was shortened in closed syllable (generally understood here as containing a coda with two or more consonants). There were notable exceptions, such as the coronal appendices; see §4.3.3. Furthermore, this German SOQ was rendered opaque by later analogical lengthening of vowels within a paradigm; thus, older [wek] (originally short vowel) – [we:ge] > [we:k] – [we:ge] 'road-s.'

The (Merged) HA component in Yiddish also shows reflexes of open-syllable lengthening [OSL] and closed-syllable shortening [CSS] (Katz 1977, 1982; Jacobs 1979, 1990a; Lowenstamm 1978, 1979: 114–20). However, the descriptions of these historical processes differ from those in the German component, and they are demonstrably dated outside the history of Yiddish. First, consider reflexes of CSS in the HA component of Yiddish. Unlike the German-component shortening, which generally required two consonants to close the syllable, TH-component CSS required only one consonant; thus: TH (or Pre-Yiddish) **so:ð* 'secret' shortened, whereas German-origin **bro:t* 'bread' remained long; these emerge as StY *sod*, *brojt*. The TH plural form **so:ðo:θ* 'secrets' had initial open syllable, and thus emerges as StY *sojdəs*. Had CSS been a single, unified process within the history of Yiddish proper, we would expect either that both **so:d* and **bro:t* shortened to *sod*, ***brot*, or that neither shortened, yielding StY ***sojd*, *brojt*. Second, consider OSL in the HA component in Yiddish. For example, the first vowel in StY *toxəs* 'backside' traces back to a short vowel in TH *taħaθ*. Yiddish linguists have frequently seen OSL occurring as a parallel process in both the HA and the German component within the history of Yiddish proper, as part of a general "German" process (e.g., Bin-Nun 1973: 278ff.). In this view, both TH *taħaθ* and MHG *sagen* underwent an identical OSL within Yiddish (with subsequent raising/rounding in almost all varieties of Yiddish) > StY *toxəs*, *zogn*, WY *to:xəs, zo:gn*, CY *tuxəs, zugn*, etc. However, I reconstruct *toxəs* as containing PY**ɔ:*, based on consideration of modern Yiddish dialect data. Specifically, in Yiddish in Alsace [AY], lenghtened HA-component original **a* is AY *o:*, while lengthened German-component original **a* emerges as AY *a:*; thus, AY *do:xəs, sa:kə* (Zuckerman 1969). This demonstrates that HA-component OSL (and raising/rounding of this HA lengthened *a*) occurred in pre-Yiddish times.

The German-component OSL must also be placed outside the history of Yiddish, since HA-component words did not undergo the paradigm-based analogical lengthening mentioned above. That is, TH *di:n – di:ni:m* '(Jewish) religious law-s' yield PY **din* (via pre-Yiddish CSS), **di:nim* (no CSS, since open initial syllable). However, within Yiddish, there was no analogical "relengthening" (based on plural form) of **din* > ***di:n*, comparable to the late MHG lengthening of [wek] > [we:k] based on [we:ge] (Jacobs 1990a: 47–48).[23] All Yiddish dialects show reflexes of analogical lengthening in the German component, but none do for the HA component in Yiddish.

A Pre-Yiddish SOQ is posited for what emerged later as the HA component of Yiddish (Jacobs 1993a). In the pre-Yiddish vernacular(s) there was a reorganization such that each stressed syllable came to contain a single branching rhyme. This rhyme could consist either of VC or VV. Thus, the long vowel in the first syllable of TH *so:-ðo:θ* stayed long (rhyme *VV); whereas TH *so:ð* shortened in pre-Yiddish to **sod* (rhyme *VVC > *VC). Short stressed vowels in Pre-Yiddish lengthened in open syllable; thus, TH *ta-ħaθ* > Pre-Yiddish **taa-xas* (and *a:* > [ɔ:]). The requirement that each stressed syllable consist of one and only one branch in the rhyme in Pre-Yiddish (after SOQ) further explains the presence of diphthongs via restructuring in words which originally contained an intervocalic consonant *ayin* (ע) or *alef* (א); cf. TH *maʕăse:, maʔăxɔ:l*, StY *majsə* 'story,' *majxl* '(food) treat.' For early Pre-Yiddish, we assume syllabification **ma-ʕă-se:*, **ma-ʔă-xɔ:l*. However, the loss of *alef* and *ayin* left adjacent **a* -**ă*. Normally, these would coalesce into long *a:* (which then raises and rounds > *ɔ:*).[24] This provides evidence that stress shift occurred in pre-Yiddish times, since this is needed to allow the [ă] to reduce post-tonically to schwa, where it then became linked to the first [a] in a diphthong *aə* (or [aj]). This bimoraic nucleus blocked any further lengthening of the first [a] (to *a:* > *ɔ:*), since the limit was already reached; otherwise, Yiddish forms like ***móəsə*, ***móəxl* would have prevailed (via Pre-Yiddish OSL). Similarly, surface diphthong [aj] did not permit lengthening in TH *ħa-jil* > Pre-Yiddish **xaj-il* > StY *xajəl* 'army.'

[23] Some analogical shortening in the plural forms – especially for nouns ending in /n/ – may have occurred in some varieties of CY; see Bin-Nun (1973: 275).

[24] Actually, raising/rounding may have been an automatic replacement rule: /a/ when short, /ɔ:/ when long. Thus, both Katz (1993) and Jacobs (1990a) question the existence of /a:/ in the pre-Yiddish HA corpus.

By looking at developments in the stock languages and their later reflexes within Yiddish, and by juxtaposing and comparing the diverse components within Yiddish, we can recover relative chronologies, and conclude, for example, that the syllable-based vowel readjustments in German and in the Pre-Ashkenazic Hebrew (component) demonstrably occurred independently, and pre-Yiddish. Stress shift is dated to pre-Yiddish times,[25] as is post-tonic reduction of vowels [PTR].[26] In reconstructing PY, two important points should be emphasized: (1) phonological prerequisites must be determined; (2) the (Merged) Hebrew component in Yiddish derives not directly from TH and/or Judeo-Aramaic, but indirectly, via the intervening pre-Yiddish stages.

Comparison of the components in Yiddish helps to determine relative chronology concerning apocope. In the original German component of Yiddish, historical final schwa is generally absent;[27] cf. StY *kum* '(I) come,' *gas* 'street,' *mid* 'tired,' StG *komme*, *Gasse*, *müde*; though schwa is present where it is a grammatical (adjectival) suffix: *gut-ə* 'good,' *alt-ə* 'old,' *mid-ə* 'tired,' etc.[28] In HA-component items in Yiddish final schwa is present: *tojrə* 'Torah,' *majsə* 'story,' etc. There are two possible scenarios. The first one posits a German determinant in which apocope had already occurred, leaving HA-origin items unaffected within Yiddish. Alternatively, one could argue that at its origins, Yiddish had a German component with final schwa, whereas HA-component items had unstressed final full vowels. Then one could posit apocope of schwa within the history of Yiddish (affecting only German-component words), followed later by reduction of word-final unstressed full vowels to schwa.[29] Both scenarios present problems. There is some evidence that already in pre-Yiddish the HA component underwent PTR to schwa.[30] Furthermore, positing apocope in the German determinant as a pre-Yiddish phenomenon presents problems in the dating of the event within the history of German.

25 Traditionally, this stress shift was seen in Yiddish linguistics as a Yiddish phenomenon; see, e.g., Bin-Nun (1973: 278ff.). More recently, the shifting of stress in the TH-origin items is seen as occurring pre-Yiddish, in terms of two separate metrical processes (Jacobs 1990a); see also Katz (1982). The problem centers around different developments in di- and tri-syllabic words, as described in Leibel (1965).

26 There are other issues of detail; see Katz (1982, 1993); Jacobs (1993a).

27 Dated to the twelfth to thirteenth centuries for Bavarian by Bin-Nun (1973: 248), M. Weinreich (1980: 518ff.).

28 Exceptions in the Gmc component are the words *jidənə* 'Jewish woman,' *mumə* 'aunt,' and possibly *mamə* 'mother,' all with non-apocopated forms. Nevertheless, all three words denote human females; thus, the final vowel may be analyzed as a morpheme.

29 Internationalisms like *ójto* 'car,' *géto* 'ghetto,' entered Yiddish much more recently.

30 This has to do with Pre-Yiddish SOQ, and words like *majsə*, *majxl*; see above. On the other hand, this may be a limited reduction within metrically complex structures; there is otherwise little or no evidence for reduction of post-tonic vowel to schwa in pre-Yiddish (see Jacobs 2004).

2.4.3 Proto-Yiddish vowel system

The PY (stressed) vowel system is reconstructed based on comparison of attested cognate forms in the known dialects. The system generally accepted in Yiddish linguistic scholarship is that developed by M. Weinreich (1960), which is presented here with slight modification. A two-digit numbering system is employed as follows (see Herzog (1965a: 161).[31] The first digit refers to the presumed PY vowel quality: 1- = [a], 2- = [e], 3- = [i], 4- = [o], 5- = [u]. The second digit refers to length or diphthongal quality in PY: -1 = short, -2 = original long monophthong, -3 = original short monophthong, but lengthened very early on within Yiddish, -4 = original diphthong, -5 = special length (for PY **æ:*). Thus, vowel 11 refers to a short **a* in PY, vowel 52 to PY **u:*, etc. By combining a phonetic symbol with a (two-digit) number, we may refer simultaneously to an assumed (or attested) phonetic quality of a given vowel, and to its historical value in the PY system. Thus, SEY o_{11} refers to the same historical vowel as PY $*a_{11}$, current NEY/CY/WY a_{11}, but realized as [o] in SEY, in words such as *[o]ndər* 'other,' *x[o]sənə* 'wedding'; cf. StY *andər*, *xasənə*.[32] SEY o_{11} is distinct from historical $*o_{41}$, which is also realized as [o] in SEY (and universally in Yiddish, e.g., sod_{41} 'secret').

The reconstruction of the PY vowel system is based on Yiddish-internal data, and not on (our knowledge of) developments in the histories of the stock languages (see Katz 1983: 1021–1024; 1993: 49). For example, historical front-rounded vowels present in MHG and modern StG may not be claimed for reconstructed PY, since they are nowhere in Yiddish distinct from their corresponding unrounded front vowels. They are thus not figured into the PY system.[33] This lack (loss?) of front-rounded vowels is thus a phonological fact belonging to the pre-history of Yiddish. Likewise, M. Weinreich's -3 series – with two exceptions – must be dropped from the PY system, since open-syllable lengthening occurred in pre-Yiddish (Katz 1977, 1982: 75; Jacobs 1990a, 1993a). One of the "lengthened" vowels which must be included in the PY system is vowel 13, based on AY, where German-component words have $a{:}_{13}$, e.g., *ta:k* 'day,' *va:s* 'what,' but ou_{12} ($\sim o{:}_{12}$), e.g., *šloufə* 'sleep.' However, in the HA component we find only vowel 12 in AY (TH *taħaθ* > AY *do:xəs*). HA-component OSL was thus a pre-Yiddish development, but the lengthening of vowel 13 is dated

[31] The two-digit numbering system reflects U. Weinreich (1958a), patterned after Haudricourt and Juilland (1949). M. Weinreich uses a notation with one upper-case letter and one subscript number. See also Bin-Nun (1973).

[32] The [o] realization of vowel 11 does not cover the entire SEY territory; see Herzog *et al.* (1992: 64).

[33] On the issue of front-rounded vowels (at least graphemically) in early Yiddish literature, see Haines (1975). The presence of front-rounded diphthong [öy] in Courland represents an innovation. On [y] in border locations between NEY and CY, see below; on [y] in WTCPY, see U. Weinreich (1964).

to Yiddish times. The other "lengthened" vowel is vowel 25. This is based on phonemic contrasts in some dialects; thus, CY *ej*$_{25}$, *e*$_{21}$, *aj*$_{22,24}$; e.g., CY *bejtn*$_{25}$ 'request,' *betn*$_{21}$ 'beds,' *sajfer*$_{22}$ 'Jewish holy book,' *flajš*$_{24}$ 'meat.' Therefore, distinct vowels 13 and 25 must be included in the PY system, even though they have frequently merged with other vowels in the majority of Yiddish dialects; e.g., NEY *betn* means both 'request' (vowel 25) and 'beds' (vowel 21). Vowels 12 and 13 have merged in all EY and much of WY; AY alone provides the basis for positing PY vowel 13.

M. Weinreich (1980: 483ff.) posits PY **ii*$_{34}$, **uu*$_{54}$, as distinct from PY **i:*$_{32}$, **u:*$_{52}$, respectively. This may be an artifact of Weinreich's knowledge of the history of German(ic) (e.g., earlier MHG *dîn*, *hûs*, modern StG *dein* 'your,' *Haus* 'house'). Aware of PY **i:*, **u:* in HA-component words, Weinreich needed to keep these distinct from original German **î*, **û*, but not, as it turns out, from original German *ie*, *uo*, which monophthongized in the relevant German varieties; cf. StG *schiessen* 'shoot,' *Buch* 'book.' In Yiddish, vowels 34 and 54 are universally diphthongs or the reflexes of diphthongs. U. Weinreich (1958a) demonstrated this clearly in his analysis of regional occurrences of *u(:)*$_{54}$ in EY – showing that these were "retrograde sound shifts" (innovations within the history of Yiddish) rather than survivals of an earlier monophthong.[34] He did this by taking into account the entire set of diachronic developments in the vowel systems in the varieties of Yiddish under consideration.

The PY vowel system may be reconstructed from comparison of the four major modern Yiddish dialects – WY, CY, SEY, NEY. Where original distinctions have been lost via mergers in these main dialects, data from vestigial or relic-preserving sub-areas (e.g., Alsace, Courland) will be employed. Based on the modern dialect systems, the Yiddish dialects may be classified in a *stammbaum* framework as follows:[35]

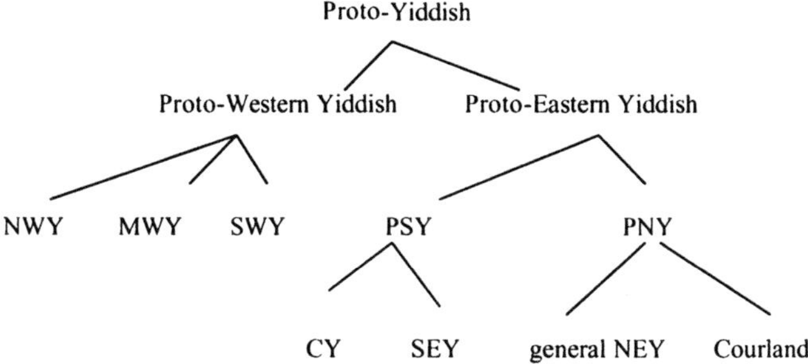

[34] A few lexical items present problems here. For example, StY *gədojərn* 'to last' contains vowel 54; however, regional occurrences of CY *gədi:rn* point to a different source.

[35] See Herzog (1965a: 162), of which the following is a slight modification. For sub-varieties of WY, see Katz (1983, 1993); Herzog (2000). A generalized WY type is given.

Table 2.1. *Vowel systems of the major Yiddish dialects (generalized variants) and StY*

WY	CY	SEY	NEY	StY
i – i: u – u:	i – i: u – u:	i – ɨ u	i u	i u
e – e: o – o:	e –– o ––	e o	e o	e o
a	a	a	a	a
a:	a:			
ej ou (~ au)	ej oj, ou	ej oj	ej oj	ej oj
aj	aj	aj	aj	aj

Any *stammbaum* representation does not take into account the complexity of the dialect map. For general orientation purposes, Table 2.1 provides the vowel system of one generalized variant for each of the four major dialects, along with StY. Table 2.2 provides sample words in StY form, along with the regular vowel realization for each in the major (generalized) dialects and as reconstructed for PY.

The idealized presentation in Table 2.2 largely ignores sub-dialect variation, as well as problems of detail concerning individual word histories and other more general problems (see M. Weinreich 1980: 658–718). Some general points of qualification are as follows. First, transition dialects – which arose via intra-Yiddish dialect contact – do not, by their very nature, allow *stammbaum*-like reconstruction. Second, the timing of some of the developments is crucial. For example, long-mid proto-vowels *$e{:}_{22}$, *$o{:}_{42}$ have diphthongized almost everywhere in Yiddish (including large parts of the WY territory). However, we must still posit these as PY monophthongs to avoid their merger with PY diphthongs *ei_{24}, *ou_{44}, since the latter have remained distinct from 22, 42 in WY (though not in EY). Third, in disagreement with M. Weinreich I posit HA-component long vowels via Pre-Yiddish OSL; here, the AY data ($a{:}_{13}$, $o{:}_{12}$) were crucial. Fourth, methodologically, external sources are ignored in reconstruction. Thus, while the German determinant had long *u:* (historically *uo*) in, e.g., *gut* 'good,' *Mutter* 'mother,' these show universally short vowel in Yiddish (*u-i-ɨ-u*), and, thus, we reconstruct PY short *u_{51} (p. 672). On the other hand, the cognate of NHG *Bruder* is reconstructed with PY long *$u{:}_{52}$ based on the diaphoneme patterning (*u:-i:-i-u*).

Fifth, the Slavic component has not been included in Table 2.2. It is frequently problematic, sometimes participating in regular diaphoneme distributions, e.g., *m[u]čən* ~ *m[i]čən* 'torment,' *p[u]pik* ~ *p[i]pik* 'gizzard'; cf. German-component *k[u]mən* ~ *k[i]mən* 'come,' HA-component *x[u]pə* ~ *x[i]pə* 'wedding canopy,' in other instances, however, not following the patterning. There may be several reasons for this, one of these being the nature of the ongoing contact with Slavic for most EY speakers. Multiple varieties of Slavic served as potential sources of ongoing influence (see U. Weinreich 1963a); cf. *mučən* ~ *mičən* vs. (regional CY) *menčən*. The first pair reflects regular diaphoneme variants of an East Slavic source, the last variant a West Slavic source with nasal vowel.

Sixth, we must distinguish between substrate and adstrate influences as we reconstruct the PY vowel system. The overall consistency of the diaphoneme patterns assists in this. EY has universal *kr[aj]z* 'circle,' *g[aj]st* 'spirit,' rather than normal diaphoneme patterning. These two items are borrowings from NHG in the modern period (M. Weinreich 1980: 695), entering Yiddish long after the major EY isoglosses had crystallized (before *c.* 1700). Similarly, a new loan like *suši* 'sushi' would be expected to have universal [u] in EY. However, there is some evidence of folk-etymologizing of vowels by speakers.[36]

Seventh, there are several problems limited to specific words or morphemes. Thus, suffix קייט *-kejt* '-hood' is [kajt] in both NEY and CY (as well as in StY), in violation of the expected diaphonemic principle (SEY has [kejt]). NEY (and StY) *gram* 'rhyme' contains historical vowel 34 (cf. MHG *gerîm*); however, vowel 34 is regularly WY/NEY [aj], CY [a:], SEY [a]. In this instance, NEY *gram* is a borrowing < CY *gra:m*, subsequently shortened to *gram* in isochronic NEY (M. Weinreich 1980: 694).

Eighth, note instances of dialect-based hypercorrection, reflecting speakers' awareness of the diaphoneme realities; thus, there occur forms like *lutvak* (< *litvak*) 'Lithuanian Jew' among CY speakers who "corrected" their (historically correct in this instance) /i/→/u/, based on the diaphoneme equation: CY /i/ "equals" NEY /u/. Similarly, the term *pajlišə* (*jidn*) 'Polish Jews' arose among NEY speakers aware of the overlapping equations: (1) NEY *ej* = CY *oj*, and (2) NEY *ej* = CY *aj* (cf. StY *pojlišə*).

2.4.4 *Diachronic development of the major Yiddish dialects (stressed vowels)*

A small set of changes in the stressed vowel system encapsulates the *stammbaum* development of the major Yiddish dialects from PY. For discussion, see Herzog 1965a: 161ff.; Katz 1983; Jacobs 1990a: 59–90. Much of the evolution may be seen in terms of chain developments, along with dialect-specific adjustments to these. A major factor has been the maintenance or loss of distinctive vowel length. The main changes have occurred in the long vowels and diphthongs; the original short vowel system has remained less affected by change. Of primary

36 Thus, American Yiddish *lojfər* < English *loafer*. See also Lemkhen (1995), on the "identification" of Lithuanian loan [au] as corresponding to one or the other PY vowel in varieties of NEY.

Table 2.2. *Sample words*[37] *in StY, with vowel realizations in PY and major dialects*

Vowel #	PY value	StY	StY sample words (German component)	StY sample words (HA-component)	WY	CY	SEY	NEY
11	*a	a	*bak* 'cheek,' *vald* 'forest,' *klapn* 'knock'	*kašə* 'porridge,' *daləs* 'poverty,' *ganəf* 'thief'	a	a	o	a
21	*e	e	*betn* 'beds,' *zekl* 'little sock; little sack,' *esn* 'eat'	*eməs* 'truth,' *mekn* 'erase,' *šed* 'demon'	e	e	e	e
31	*i	i	*gəfinən* 'find,' *vidər* 'again,' *zilbər* 'silver'	*gibər* 'hero,' *sinə* 'hatredj' *tfilə* 'prayer'	i	i	ɨ	i
41	*o	o	*obər* 'but,' *odər* 'or,' *zok* 'sock'	*sod* 'secret,' *sonəm* 'enemies,' *jold* 'chump'	o	o	o	o
51	*u	u	*gut* 'good,' *kumən* 'come,' *hunt* 'dog'	*gəulə* 'redemption,' *guzmə* 'exaggeration,' *xupə* 'wedding canopy'	u	i	ɨ	u
12	*ɔ:	o	*blozn* 'blow,' *do* 'here,' *mon* 'poppy seed'	*košər*[38] 'kosher,' *xoləm* 'dream,' *baləbos* 'boss'	o:	u:[39]	u	o
13	*a:	o	*tog* 'day,' *vos* 'what,' *nomən* 'name'	—[40]	o:	u:	u	o
22	*e:	ej	*hejx* 'height,' *frejləx* 'cheerful,' *štejn* 'stand'	*xejn*[41] 'charm,' *šejdəm* 'demons,' *šejgəc* 'gentile lad'	e:	aj	ej	ej
25	*æ:	e	*betn* 'request,' *lebn* 'live,' *štet* 'cities'	*begəd* 'garment,' *šetəx* 'area,' *tevə* 'nature'	e:	ej	ej (~older i:)	e
32	*i:	i	*briv* 'letter,' *hindl* 'little chicken,' *bixər* 'books'	*mədinə* 'country,' *tfisə* 'jail'	i:	i:	i	i
42	*o:	oj	*grojs* 'big,' *štroj* 'straw,' *hojx* 'high'	*sojdəs* 'secrets,' *bojlət* 'conspicuous,' *ojləm* 'audience'	o: (~ou, au)	oj	oj	ej
52	*u:	u	*bux* 'book,' *brudər* 'brother,' *cu* 'to'	*purim*[42] 'Purim,' *lajhudim* 'joy,' *sudə* 'feast'	u:	i:	i	u

24	*ei	ej	*ej* 'egg,' *mejnən* 'to mean,' *flejš* 'meat'	–	a:	aj	ej	ej
34	*ai	aj	*blajbn* 'remain,' *hajzər* 'homes,' *tajx* 'river'	*dajən*[43] 'religious judge,' *xajəl* 'army'	aj	a:	a	aj
44	*ou	oj	*ojg* 'eye,' *bojm* 'tree,' *lojfn* 'run'	–[44]	a:	oj	oj	ej
54	*au	oj	*hojt*[45] 'skin,' *hojz* 'home,' *bojən* 'build'	–[46]	ou	o: (~ou)	ou ~ oj[47] ~ u	oj

[37] Sample words, taken from M. Weinreich (1980: 679ff.), have been selected to show typical realizations for each vowel. For example, part of SEY has o_{11} generally, but not before *r*, *x* (and some other consonants; see Herzog *et al.* 1992: 63); thus, SEY *marx* 'marrow,' *zax* 'thing,' but *lond* 'country'; cf. StY *marx*, *zax*, *land*.

[38] M. Weinreich (1980: 684) claims that there are no examples of the -2 series in the HA component of Yiddish. Jacobs (1990a) differs, as does Katz (1982, 1993: 51). Thus, the examples here are taken from Weinreich's (1980: 689) A3 series.

[39] Often positionally shortened before labial or velar consonant; thus: *zugn* 'say,' *trugn* 'carry,' but *blu:zn* 'blow,' *du:* 'here.' The shortening is, however, somewhat problematic; see below.

[40] None, since Pre-Yiddish OSL already lengthened original TH /a/ > ɔ:, thus: AY *do:xəs* 'backside.'

[41] HA-component examples taken from M. Weinreich's (1980: 690) E3 series.

[42] Examples taken from M. Weinreich's (1980: 692) U3 series.

[43] M. Weinreich (1980: 694) claims that I4 is found only in the German component. However, TH *ajjV* patterns like the diaphoneme vowel 34; see Jacobs (1993a) on HA-component "default diphthongs."

[44] HA did not contribute **ou* to PY, since earlier sequences of TH *owV* > **ovV*; cf. TH *mɔ:weθ*, StY *movəs* 'death.'

[45] Subregional *u(:)* (~ *uj*) 54 in parts of NEY, SEY; see U. Weinreich (1958a).

[46] M. Weinreich (1980: 696) includes Yiddish *goj* 'gentile' as a HA-ism that has fallen into the vowel 54 diaphoneme patterning.

[47] On diffusion of StY oj_{54}, see Jacobs (1994a).

importance seems to be the raising of vowels 12 and 25. These typically have undergone parallel degrees of raising in any given dialect; the differences are attributed to structure-filling needs within a given dialect (Jacobs 1982, 1990b). Furthermore, those Yiddish dialects which maintained phonemic vowel length typically innovated a new /a:/, thus filling a hole in the pattern; this, understandably, is not found in the isochronic systems. The vowel systems of the major Yiddish dialects may be derived from the following sets of changes (based on Herzog 1965a: 159ff., and elaboration of same in Jacobs 1990a: 59–90).

PY > PWY

1. Raising of PY $*ɔ{:}_{12}$ (and 13 outside SWY) and $*æ{:}_{25}$ > PWY $*o{:}_{12}$, $*e{:}_{25}$
2. Monophthongization of PY $*ei_{24}$, $*ou_{44}$ > PWY $*a{:}_{24,44}$
3. Diphthongization of PY $*e{:}_{22}$, $*o{:}_{42}$ in many (though not all) varieties of WY

The most salient indicator of WY generally is the presence of $a{:}_{24,44}$. Vowels 25 and 12 raise to different degrees in regional varieties of WY (Katz 1983, 1993: 51–52). Not all varieties of WY show diphthongization of vowels 22 and 42. Thus, it is unclear whether the development of WY $a{:}_{24,44}$ resulted from a push chain or a drag chain.

PY > PEY

The major changes in the development from PY to PEY are given in Herzog (1965a: 161ff.).[48] As with the development of WY, the starting point is the raising of vowels 12 and 25, and the subsequent chain effects and responses. However, unlike WY, PEY has universal merger of the original mid-vowel long monophthongs with their corresponding diphthongs. In addition, vowels 12 and 13 merged universally in EY. The main changes PY > PEY are:

1. Raising of PY $*ɔ{:}_{12}$ (and $*a{:}_{13}$) > PEY $*o{:}_{12,13}$, and PY $*æ{:}_{25}$ > PEY $*e{:}_{25}$
2. Diphthongization of PY $*e{:}_{22}$, $*o{:}_{42}$, and merger with PY $*ei_{24}$, ou_{44} > PEY $*ej_{22,24}$, $*ou_{42,44}$

PEY > PNEY

A single change is posited for the development from PEY > PNEY: PEY $*ou_{42,44}$ > PNEY $øy_{42,44}$. Herzog (1965a: 164) sees the systems of PEY and PNEY as identical. PNEY is then subdivided into Courland Yiddish [CourlY] and general NEY (called "Stam-Litvish" [SL] in Mark 1951). There are gradations, however, in the transition from SL to CourlY, notably in western Lithuania, Suvalk, etc. (see §3.4.3). The major changes in the development PNEY > general NEY are (Herzog 1965a: 164):

1. Loss of length, resulting in the mergers $i_{31,32}$; $u_{51,52}$; $e_{21,25}$; $o_{12,13,41}$
2. Unrounding of PNEY $*øy_{42,44}$ > *ej*, resulting in general NEY $ej_{22,24,42,44}$

[48] Though I disagree with his positing of $*uu_{54}$, ij_{34} (see above), as well as his positing of PEY $*øy_{42}$ < PY $*o{:}_{42}$. These developments are summarized and modified in Jacobs (1990a: 61ff.).

A third change which might be posited for general NEY is the raising of PNEY $*au_{54}$ > general NEY ou_{54}, followed by the change of the glide from *u* to *j*. However, there is considerable regional variation in vowel 54 in the territory of general NEY: *ou* ~ *oj* ~ *uw*, etc.; furthermore, relics of the older *au* stage are found in intervocalic position, e.g., NEY regional *zavər* 'sour,' StY *zojər* (U. Weinreich 1958a; Herzog *et al.* 1992: 89).

The Courland subregion of NEY generally maintained phonemic vowel length (M. Weinreich 1923):

Vowel System of Courland Yiddish

Short	Long	Diphthongs	
i_{31} — u_{51}	$i{:}_{32}$ — $u{:}_{52}$		
e_{21} — o_{41}	$e{:}_{25}$ – $o{:}_{12,13}$	$ej_{22,24}$	$øy_{42,44}$
a_{11}	$a{:}$[49]	aj_{34}	au_{54}

The vowel system of CourlY is identical with that posited for PNEY, with the exception of /a:/. Significantly, this partial restoration of /a:/ occurs precisely in that subregion of NEY which maintained phonemic vowel length, while no such thing occurs in general NEY. Furthermore, CourlY preserves a rounded glide in $øy_{42,44}$, while general NEY likely does not (see §4.1.4).

PEY > PSY

Herzog (1965a: 164ff.) outlines the development from PEY > PSY as follows (with one modification: I posit PEY $*ou_{42,44}$, where Herzog posits P(N)EY $øy_{42,44}$).

1. Fronting of PEY $*u_{51}$, $*u{:}_{52}$ > PSY $*y_{51}$, $*y{:}_{52}$
2. Unrounding of PSY $*y_{51}$, $*y{:}_{52}$ > PSY $*i_{51}$, $*i{:}_{52}$, resulting in mergers PSY $*i_{31,51}$ and $*i{:}_{32,52}$
3. (Further) raising of PEY $*o{:}_{12,13}$ > PSY $*u(:)_{12,13}$[50]
4. Monophthongization of PEY $*aj_{34}$ > PSY $*a{:}_{34}$

The fronting of vowels 51 and 52 is quite old; Birnbaum (1934) dates it to the middle of the fourteenth century (see also M. Weinreich 1954: 95–98). This fronting was the earliest of the four changes, and is seen as the causal factor in subsequent changes as well (Herzog 1965: 165). Fronting is kept distinct from unrounding, though in almost all instances they are coextensive. In part, this distinction is justified in terms of spellings found in older documents (p. 165). Additionally, however, Braynsk (Polish *Brańsk*), which lies on the border of the *u/i* isogloss dividing NEY from SY, distinguishes $y_{51,52}$ from $i_{31,32}$; thus, *ky*, *ki* 'cow-s.' It is unclear to what extent this represents a survival as opposed to a

[49] Limited; mostly in loans from NHG, Latvian, and Lithuanian. Hence, no diaphoneme number is assigned to this vowel.

[50] It is not justified structurally to mark the raised *u* vowel as phonemically long or short, since there is no length opposition here (vowels 51 and 52 had already fronted/unrounded).

phonetic compromise between [u] and [i], though the distinction here between 51, 52 and 31, 32 points toward $y_{51,52}$ as a survival.[51]

The raising of vowel 12,13 to [u:] in PSY fills a gap created by the fronting of 51 and 52.[52] Significant is the parallelism in the raising of vowels 12 and 25 (Jacobs 1982, 1990a: 69, 1990b; Katz 1982: 79ff., 1983: 1030; Herzog *et al.* 1992: 28). PY $*æ{:}_{25}$, $*ɔ{:}_{12}$ underwent raising universally in both PWY and PEY. The presence of vowel length was a necessary but not sufficient requirement for raising to continue. Thus, two-degree raising to *i:*, *u:* is found in some varieties of WY; however, in other varieties of WY raising halted at *e:*, *o:*. In CourlY raising was halted by the presence of $i{:}_{32}$, $u{:}_{52}$, and thus stopped at $e{:}_{25}$, $o{:}_{12(13)}$; here this filled holes in the pattern vacated by PEY diphthongization of PY $*e{:}_{22}$ > PEY $ej_{22,24}$, and PY $*o{:}_{42}$ > PEY $*ou_{42,44}$ (and subsequently > PNEY $*øy_{42,44}$). In SY, raising continued in ways attributable to pattern-filling needs. PSY $*y_{51}$, $*y{:}_{52}$ > $*i_{51}$, $i{:}_{52}$, thus creating a gap in the *u*-position. Universally in SY, vowel 12(13) has raised all the way to fill that *u*-gap. However, as concerns vowel 25 in CY, raising halted at mid-level, with diphthongization to ej_{25}. Here, this fills a gap, since PEY $*ej_{22,24}$ > CY $aj_{22,24}$ (synchronically, the corresponding back, round long mid-vowel 54 is arguably /o:/ ~ /ou/ in CY). On the other hand, in a portion of what became SEY (the northern portion; see Herzog *et al.* 1992: 28), raising of vowel 25 continued two heights to the *i*-position (presumably via an **e:* stage, since SEY $ej_{22,24}$), and merged with SEY vowel 32,52 or 31,51 (see Herzog 1969: 60–64, 2000: 72). Loss of length occurred only much later (and not everywhere) in SEY. The lexical replacement of SEY i_{25}[53] with [ej] (borrowed from CY) has led to some sporadic hypercorrection as well; thus $[\text{rejfn}]_{52}$ (< PY $*ru{:}fn_{52}$) 'to call' (Herzog 1969: 63ff.).

Monophthongization of PY $*aj_{34}$ > PSY **a:* filled a gap in the PSY system, which had length distinctions at most positions. When SEY lost length, PSY $*a{:}_{34}$ > SEY a_{34}, but this occurred only after (most) $*a_{11}$ > (in a significant sub-area of) SEY o_{11}; thus, SEY man_{34} mon_{11} 'my husband'; cf. CY *ma:n man*; StY *majn man*. This provides additional evidence that SEY lost length relatively late.[54]

[51] On the other hand, if retention of front-rounded $y_{51,52}$ in Braynsk were of structural significance, we might expect retention of front-rounded $øy_{42,44}$. Instead, Braynsk has fully unrounded $ej_{42,44}$, something indicative of general NEY. Thus, Braynsk $y_{51,52}$ may have arisen via diffusion from SY (Herzog 1965a).

[52] Though Braynsk has $o_{12,13}$, leaving the *u* slot unfilled (unless $y_{51,52}$ fills that slot). In general it is preferable to see Braynsk as a contact-transition dialect, and not as part of a linear development of SY. Additionally, Ostrolenke has $i_{51,52}$, and $o_{12,13}$ (Herzog 1965a: 229). These seem to be examples of diffusion of SY fronted 51, 52 into NEY territory.

[53] SEY i_{25} was reported as a feature of "older speakers"; see U. Weinreich (1958b); Herzog *et al.* (1992: 28) call it a receding feature.

[54] There is some evidence that at least some length persisted into the twentieth century; see Jacobs (1995a), citing Gartner (1901). The distinction in SEY between vowels 31, 51 and 32, 52(25) is arguably based on length; see U. Weinreich (1958b).

The four basic changes for deriving PSY > CY are given in Herzog (1965a: 163) in the following chronological order:

1. Lowering of vowel 22,24 **ej* > *aj*
2. Diphthongization of 25 **e:* > *ej*
3. Splitting of vowel 12(13) > CY *u*, *u:*
4. (Regional) monophthongization of vowel 54 *ou* > *o:*

The changes in the development PSY > SEY are as follows:

1. Raising of PSY $*e{:}_{25}$ > SEY $i(:)_{25}$
2. PY/PEY/PSY $*a_{11}$ > SEY[55] o_{11}
3. Loss of length, resulting in mergers $i_{32,52}$ with i_{25} (vs. $ɨ_{31,51}$)

2.4.5 *Consonantism*

The issues concerning the history of Yiddish consonantism are minor compared with the vocalism. Most of the historical changes in the consonantism demonstrably occurred outside the history of Yiddish proper, in pre-Yiddish times. Additionally, fusion plays a role in creating consonantal (including phonotactic) realities unique to Yiddish (that is, not found in the stock languages).

Several developments in TH consonants – in what later became the HA component in Yiddish – date to pre-Yiddish times (or even earlier, to spoken Hebrew times). The task is thus to date a given change either within or outside of the history of Yiddish. One complicating factor is the role of different historical settlement patterns, and different Hebrew pronunciation traditions; another is the role of Hebrew (and Aramaic) as an ongoing source of (adstratal) enrichment. The present discussion concerns those changes in the substratal HA component in Yiddish.

Among the H(A) determinant consonant changes discussed by M. Weinreich (1980: 381–386) are the following. (1) The Hebrew emphatic consonants *ṭ*, *ṣ*, *q* had all changed in pre-Yiddish times. As concerns *ṭ* and *q* this led to merger with the non-spirantized allophones of TH plain /t/ and /k/. The development of TH fricative *ṣ* (צ) is more problematic. In general, it emerges as Yiddish affricate *c*. However, this has left a residue of various mergers with TH /s/ <ס> and ·*s* <שׂ>.[56]

Post-vocalic spirantization of non-emphatic, non-geminate stops *b*, *d*, *g*, *p*, *t*, *k* – the so-called *begedkefet* rule – was a rule of TH (and Judeo-Aramaic) grammar, not of Yiddish. Yiddish generally has spirant reflexes of spirantized TH *ptkb*. Modern Yiddish regularly has non-spirantized *d* and *g* where TH grammar requires spirantized ∂ and γ. However, this likely has to do with a later change of ∂ and γ to stops within the history of Yiddish, since we

[55] In many varieties of SEY; exact phonetic environments blocking the change differ regionally within SEY; see Veynger (1929: 134); Herzog *et al.* (1992: 63–65).

[56] See M. Weinreich (1980: 381) on original apical vs. dorsal articulations.

find residue of the earlier fricative pronunciation; thus, cf. TH *ju:ð* 'yud; tenth letter of the alphabet,' German dialectal (borrowed from Yiddish) *ju(:)s*; cf. Alsatian Yiddish and Swiss Yiddish *jysərlə, ju:zərlə* 'coin with value of ten' (M. Weinreich 1980: 383); TH *lammeð* > Hessian German *lammes* 'thirty.' Further possible evidence that spirants ð and γ were "changed back" to stops *d, g* within Ashkenaz and Yiddish history proper comes from the orthographic rendition (in the oldest extant written sentence in Yiddish from 1272), where <גֿ> may indicate the presence of a fricative [γ] in the older language (here in a German component item realized as [g] in modern Yiddish).[57]

In summary, PY inherited the results of the TH *begedkefet* rule, and made its own changes thereupon. First, former emphatic consonants *ṭ* and *q* did not spirantize post-vocalically. Second, historical non-emphatic stops did not spirantize in morphological environments which normally triggered spirantization in TH; cf. StY *[k]sav* 'writing, script,' *bi[k]sav* 'in writing' vs. TH *[k]əθɔ:β, bi[x]θɔ:β*. Yiddish pronunciation *bi[x]lal* 'in general' (cf. StY *[k]lal* 'rule') is a modern borrowing from Hebrew; older Yiddish (and some modern varieties) have *bi[k]lal*. Yiddish fricatives in *bi[f]rat* 'particularly,' *bə[f]ejrəš* 'explicitly' (cf. StY *[p]rat* 'detail,' *[p]ejrəš* 'commentary') might suggest that spirantization is in fact a productive rule in Yiddish. However, consider StY *vi[b]əfrat* 'and especially' vs. TH *u:[v]ifraṭ*. StY *bəfejrəš*, *bifrat*, *ləfi* 'according to,' *lifnej* 'before' (with [f]) are best considered inherited fossilized forms. Normally, the prefixes *lə-*, *bə/bi-* do not trigger spirantization in Yiddish; StY *[k]ovəd* 'dignity,' *lə[k]ovəd* 'in honor of,' *bə[k]ovədik* 'honorable' provide evidence that Yiddish inherited substratal Hebrew forms, but not Hebrew grammar.[58] Third, German component items do not undergo *begedkefet* spirantization. (The German determinant underwent the Second Sound Shift pre-Yiddish.) Thus, StY *hot* 'has' does not spirantize to ***ho[s]*.

There is evidence from the HA and Loez components of a change **dž* > **j*; thus, a tenth-century Latin-letter transcription of Psalms 45:6 has <*gippolu*> for Hebrew יפלו 'shall fall,' seen as containing initial [dž] < TH /j/ (M. Weinreich 1980: 383). Similarly, the Yiddish personal name *jentə*, discussed above, is of Loez origin; cf. *gentile*, with historical Latin-origin **g* > **dž*. It is uncertain whether **dž* > **j* in Loez times, or within PY itself, since the German component contributed no *dž*. The change did not, however, occur after the introduction of the Slavic component, since here Yiddish has *dž*, e.g., *džobən* 'to peck,' *blondžən* 'to stray'; these did not become ***jobən*, ***blonjən*.

HA-origin approximant ו (*w*) and spirant בֿ are fully merged as Yiddish /v/. The hardening of **w* > [v] must have occurred pre-Yiddish, since words like

[57] Though see Birnbaum (1979a: 149).

[58] Noun (*der*) *lixvojd* 'dedication of a book,' with [x], is from Whole Hebrew; as also evidenced by diphthong *oj*.

מלאך־המות *(maləxa-)movəs* 'angel of death' show PY **ɔ:v*, and do not take part in the development of PY **ou*$_{44}$.

The Hebrew gutturals, *alef* <א> ([ʔ]), *ayin* <ע> ([ʕ]), and voiceless pharyngeal fricative *khes* ח present interesting problems for Yiddish. In TH, *alef* was (positionally) a glottal stop, distinct from *ayin* (presumably a voiced pharyngeal fricative). Already in TH *alef* was realized as Ø in codas. The spirantization rule applied when *alef* was zero; thus, TH חטאתי *ħaṭɔ:Ø-[θ]i:* 'I sinned,' whereas *ayin* in a coda remained, and blocked spirantization: פשעתי *pɔ:šaʕ-[t]i* 'I transgressed.' In Yiddish, *alef* and *ayin* are not consonants, but they leave two types of residue reflecting their earlier presence as consonants. First, they are posited as consonants in pre-Yiddish, since they feed the rule of pre-Yiddish CSS; thus, TH *so:ne:(ʔ), so:nəʔi:m* > Pre-Yiddish **so:ne:*, **so:n-ə-ʔi:m* > **so:n-Ø-ʔi:m* > **son-ʔim* (Pre-Yiddish CSS) > PY **so:nə*, **sonim* > StY *sojnə, sonəm* 'enemy – enemies.' In the Pre-Yiddish plural form the schwa was lost as the weakest *w* in a complex foot (Jacobs 2004), thus creating an environment for CSS. Similarly, *ayin* in Pre-Yiddish feeds CSS, e.g., TH *be:θ-ʕo:lɔ:m* > Pre-Yiddish **be:s-ʕo:lɔ:m* > **bes-ʕo:lɔm* [via CSS] > PY **beso:lɔm* 'Jewish cemetery.' By comparison, vocalized TH <h> did not feed Pre-Yiddish CSS: TH *be:θ-hakkneseθ* > Pre-Yiddish **be:s-Ø-akknesəs*> PY **be:saknesəs*; thus, StY *b[ej]saknesəs* 'synagogue,' but *b[e]sojləm*. As well, contrast TH *so:ne:(ʔ), so:nəʔi:m* (with historical *alef*) vs. *qo:ne:* (with orthographic final <h>), *qo:ni:m* > StY *sojnə, sonəm* vs. *kojnə, kojnəm* 'customer-s.'

The second type of residue of *alef* and *ayin* has to do with nasalized reflexes of TH vowel plus guttural. The geographic distribution of the nasal forms often varies lexically; thus, StY מעשׂה *majsə* 'story' has regional variants *mã:sə, majnsə*, whereas nasalized יעקבֿ *jankəv* 'Jacob' is universal in EY. There is some justification on articulatory grounds for positing a nasal(ized) realization of vowel + *ayin* combinations, and for seeing this as a pre-Ashkenazic development. However, the extension of the nasal pronunciation in Yiddish to words without historical *ayin* suggests that, at some point in pre-Ashkenazic Hebrew, both *ayin* and *alef* had already ceased to be realized as consonants. Thus, consider StY דאגה *dajgə* 'worry,' regionally *dã:gə* ~ *dajŋgə*. Here, nasalization was based on analogy with "the other" zero consonant, *ayin*. Note further CY *jandəs* 'conscience' < TH יהדות *jahădu:θ* 'Judaism'; here, too, another "zero-consonant" (*/h/ realized as zero) opened the door to analogical nasalization.

TH ח (/ħ/) shows various developments in the history and pre-history of Yiddish (M. Weinreich 1958b). M. Weinreich (1980: 384) posits a pre-Ashkenazic development of **ħ* > *h*, merging with preexisting /h/. He sees the identification of ח with *x* (< spirantized TH /k/) as a later sociolinguistic change within Ashkenaz itself, based on competing Hebrew pronunciation traditions. Weinreich attributes Yiddish names (with Ø < *ħ*) like *relə* < רחל 'Rachel,' *simə* < שמחה, *icik* ~ *jicxok* < יצחק to the existence of the two different pronunciation traditions. This has led to the multiple variants across Europe of the name <חנה>: *xanə* ~ *hanə* ~ *Ø-Anna* 'Hannah.' For modern and StY purposes, we have to consider TH *ħ* as merged with *x* (< spirantized TH /k/) in almost all instances. (An exception is *mekn* 'erase'; cf. TH root √mħq). Whatever its complex history, [x] for ח "won out." In summary, the history and pre-history of the HA-component consonants in Yiddish is a combination of linear sound changes and sociolinguistically conditioned realignments.[59]

Consonant degemination in the HA determinant must have occurred at a time after pre-Yiddish CSS and OSL had run their course (M. Weinreich 1980: 386), in light of the evidence from Pre-Yiddish standardization of quantity (Jacobs 1993a). Thus, TH *taħaθ* 'backside' > Pre-Yiddish **tɔ:xas* (via OSL), whereas the short *a* did not lengthen before the geminate *bb* in TH *šabbɔ:θ* 'Sabbath,' thus, PY **t[ɔ:]xəs*, but **š[a]bəs*. It is unclear whether degemination occurred in Pre-Yiddish, or within Yiddish itself; there is only indirect evidence (M. Weinreich 1980: 386–387).

The German component entered into the formation of Yiddish having already undergone (some degree of) the Second Sound Shift, though this is not always evident from the Yiddish data; cf. StY *ferd* 'horse,' *epl* 'apple,' *kop* 'head' vs. StG *Pferd, Apfel, Kopf.* The development OHG /s/ to [z] /_V, > [š]/_C is also dated to pre-Yiddish, since Yiddish contrasts HA-component *stirə* 'contradiction,' *štus* 'nonsense,' *sojnə* 'enemy,' *zojnə* 'prostitute,' *šojtə* 'fool,' etc. While Yiddish probably inherited phonetic [ž] in HA-component words such as StY חשבון [xežbm] 'bill,' *ž* became fully phonemic only after the Slavic component introduced *ž* in all positions, e.g., *žabə* 'frog,' *staž* 'seniority.' Phonemic /l'/, /n'/ in EY derive from the Slavic component (§4.4.5).

Fusion has resulted in Yiddish (from its inception) having consonant clusters not found in any single stock language, e.g., initial clusters with SC – *stirə*, *student* (ruled out in the German determinant); German-component *eršt* 'first,' with *ršt* (not found in TH). In fact, the widespread regional initial clusters in HA-component words like *broxə* 'blessing,' *gnejvə* 'theft,' *ksubə* 'wedding contract' (cf. TH *bərɔ:xɔ:*, *gəne:βɔ:*, *kəθubbɔ:*) may have arisen due to fusion; such clusters are permissible in the German determinant, and this may have allowed elision of schwa to have taken place in the HA-component in Yiddish (M. Weinreich 1980: 379–380). M. Weinreich (p. 435) sees word-final obstruent devoicing as a pre-Yiddish change (in German), inherited into PY. However, there are differences here between Yiddish and German (see King 1980).

[59] Katz (1993: 49) observes the tendency for the survival of sounds which were supported by their presence in the inventories of the coterritorial European vernaculars, as is common in language contact.

2.5 Merged Hebrew vs. Whole Hebrew elements in Yiddish

The HA component in Jewish languages is complex. It includes substratal Merged Hebrew elements and adstratal Whole Hebrew elements. Mark (1958: 124) estimates 12,000–13,000 HA-isms in Yiddish. However, the importance goes beyond mere word count; there are additional principles and details which need to be discussed as concerns the specific Yiddish/Ashkenazic context.

The term *Tiberian Hebrew* refers to the codification of the phonology of the language in the Hebrew Bible by the Tiberian Masoretes in the eighth or ninth century CE. The ten-vowel system of TH is the one generally employed in Yiddish linguistics for reconstruction of the HA component in Yiddish (e.g., M. Weinreich 1954, 1980; Bin-Nun 1973). However, a number of problems pointing to a competing system of Hebrew vocalization led M. Weinreich (1954: 87ff.) to posit an earlier "Palestinian" Hebrew base, later Tiberianized in the middle of the thirteenth century by an influx of Hebrew teachers from the collapsing Yeshiva system in the Middle East. Among the supporting evidence Weinreich cites is the supplanting of the earlier [h]-realization of Hebrew /ħ/ with velar fricative [x]; thus, the doublets like *simə* ~ *simxə*, *icik* ~ *jic[x]ok.*[60] Much of this problem of changing Hebrew models is obviated under recent assumptions of a separate Loter settlement, distinct from the eastern settlements.

The Merged Hebrew component of Yiddish is substratal, the result of continuous oral transmission via the chain of Jewish languages. The systematicity of pre-Yiddish developments like SOQ and CSS bears clear witness to this. Substratal Merged Hebrew component words take part in the regular diaphoneme correspondences across Yiddish dialects; e.g., diaphoneme WY *o:* / CY *u(:)* / SEY *u* / NEY *o*, whether from the HA component *šo:ləm/šu:ləm/šuləm/šoləm* 'peace,' or the German component *bo:dn/bu:dn/budn/bodn* 'bathe.' The cross-dialectal regularity is too overwhelming to assume that these words were borrowed spontaneously from texts into the various Yiddish dialects. Katz (1985: 96) notes that even stronger evidence of the oral transmission analysis is provided by the anomalies – where a word has jumped off its expected historical track, and these then are fully consistent across the Yiddish dialects. Thus, TH *ħe:n* should have emerged as universal vowel $*e_{21}$ in all Yiddish dialects (via pre-Yiddish CSS); however, it has somehow emerged as PY vowel 22, with regular diaphoneme correspondences *ej/aj/ej/ej* (StY *xejn* 'charm').

60 A switch in Whole Hebrew pronunciation norms is not unprecedented; cf. American Hebrew schools in the twentieth century, where, e.g., earlier Eastern Ashkenazic *sìmxəs-tójrə* was consciously replaced with a modified (in the direction of revived, supposedly "Sephardic" spoken Hebrew) *sìmxəs-t[ó(w)]ra*, later supplanted by *simxát-torá* (note two independent lexical 1 stresses, a sign of the markedness/foreignness of the stress pattern in this example for American Ashkenazic Jews). Historically, see also the switch to supposed Sephardic Hebrew by the Berlin *maskilim* of the early nineteenth century.

At the same time, there is a link between that which was orally transmitted (the majority of the forms) and the role played by education and reading of the sacred texts. Birnbaum (1979a: 59) notes that "We need not assume that all SEM[itic] words in Y were orally inherited. Quite a number would have been acquired at school, as in the language of any civilized society." The sacred texts remained a constant presence in Jewish civilization, and thus were constant potential sources of enrichment. In modern times, a limited influence from revived spoken Israeli Hebrew (Ivrit) is to be noted as well; cf. substratal HA-origin *alíjə* 'call to the Torah' vs. *alijá* 'migration to the State of Israel.' The form *alijá* entered Yiddish in modern times, after the historical changes of stress shift and post-tonic vowel reduction had run their course.

Loshn-koydesh and Yiddish exhibit a situation of symbiosis in Ashkenazic civilization. At all linguistic levels – phonology, morphology, syntax, lexicon – the systems of Ashkenazic Whole Hebrew and Yiddish are distinct. However, these systems – in close sociolinguistic proximity to one another – "leak" and exert mutual influences. Furthermore, the boundaries between Ashkenazic Whole Hebrew and the Merged Hebrew component of Yiddish are not always impermeable. There are numerous Yiddish influences on Ashkenazic Whole Hebrew (Mark 1958; Noble 1958). For example, M. Weinreich (1980: 307) cites an occurrence of Ashkenazic Whole Hebrew *hu maxzik es acmoj* 'he considers himself as . . . ' (lit. he-holds- ACC-himself, calqued on Yiddish *er halt zix far a . . .*). Numerous "mistakes" in Ashkenazic Whole Hebrew documents – that is, deviations from Hebrew grammar norms – are understood against the background of Yiddish structure (e.g., the occasional use of definite article *ha* NP-initially with construct nouns: *habalbos* instead of *bal-habajis* 'master of *the* house'; *hašnej cdodim* instead of *šnej hacdodim* 'the two sides'). Conversely, Ashkenazic Whole Hebrew may serve as a source of enrichment in Yiddish – words or whole phrases may be incorporated into a Yiddish context (written or spoken). These may show varying degrees of integration and nativization in Yiddish.

Many HA-isms were created in Yiddish times (Mark 1958). Processes which have lead to the creation of new "Hebrew" forms are productive Yiddish processes only to the extent that these are fully integrated into Yiddish. For example, the *(ə)n* agentive suffix has been employed to create HA-isms not found in Classical Hebrew or even in later rabbinic Hebrew, e.g., *gadlən* 'conceited person,' *lamdn* 'scholar,' *kamcn* 'cheapskate' (Mark 1958; Birnbaum 1979a: 90–91). When such neologisms appear in Ashkenazic Whole Hebrew, they are perhaps best seen as (often) entering via Yiddish. Adding to the complexity, the Yiddish scribal language of the sixteenth to eighteenth centuries employed a type of intentional code switching between Yiddish and Hebrew (§7.7.1). At the boundaries between Ashkenazic Whole Hebrew and Yiddish, sociolinguistic factors such as register, social class, and gender also play a role. For example, while the morphologically regular plural of the Yiddish compound *sejfər-tojrə* 'Torah scroll' is *sejfər-tojrəs*, a reflex of the older Hebrew construct plural, *sifrej tojrə*, may be used in more formal situations within Yiddish speech (Jacobs 1991).

Finally, the phonology of (Ashkenazic) Whole Hebrew presents a set of problems. On the one hand, the sound pattern of Whole Hebrew is not identical with that of the Merged Hebrew component of any variety of Yiddish. On the other hand, the verbalization of Whole Hebrew does not exist independently, unconnected from Yiddish. The pronunciation of Whole Hebrew varies according to the phonology of the Yiddish dialect of the speaker(s). For example, CY speakers who realize vowel 42 as [oj] in, e.g., [brojt] 'bread,' [sojdəs] 'secrets,' have Whole Hebrew [sojdojs], while NEY speakers with ej_{42} have, in addition to Yiddish [brejt], [sejdəs], the Whole Hebrew realization [sejdejs]; similarly, WY varieties with [braut], [saudəs], have Whole Hebrew [saudaus]. The main systematic phonological distinctions between Ashkenazic Whole Hebrew and Merged Hebrew in Yiddish (see Birnbaum 1979a: 60; Katz 1993: 56–60) consist largely in the following. Ashkenazic Whole Hebrew lacks evidence of pre-Yiddish CSS, Stress Shift, and PTR, while these processes are evident in Merged Hebrew. Thus, TH *so:ð*, *so:ðo:θ* 'secret-s' yield CY *sod*, *sojdəs*. However, the Whole Hebrew for CY speakers has *sojd*, *sojdojs*.

How is the relationship between Ashkenazic Whole Hebrew and Yiddish best viewed? The statement that "[e]very traditional Ashkenazi commands two distinct phonologies, one for the Semitic component in his or her Yiddish, the other for Ashkenazic" (Katz 1993: 56) may be too strong. M. Weinreich (1954: 99) writes of "two contiguous systems: they are not identical, but neither are they independent of each other." The two systems share a phonemic inventory, just distributed differently (Birnbaum 1979a: 60). Indeed, while Whole Hebrew is transmitted generationally (and not spontaneously "invented" by each new generation of Ashkenazim), there is nevertheless an interplay wherein Yiddish speakers "map" their (Yiddish) phonology onto the special reading pronunciation of Whole Hebrew. However, the mapping is not one-to-one. In some ways, Whole Hebrew shows a near-lack of foot structure and the reductions which normally (in natural spoken Yiddish) accompany foot formation. Thus, Yiddish speakers, already possessing systematic alternations (in their Yiddish) like *s[o]d – s[oj]dəs* (CY speakers), or *s[o]d – s[ej]dəs* (NEY speakers), have the phonological resources for rendering non-reduced oral reading forms, much as American English speakers may use *divíne – divínity* ([aj] – [i]) as the basis for creating non-standard pronunciations like *[aj]talian* 'Italian,' *[aj]raq* 'Iraq,' etc. Furthermore, forms occur which are phonologically intermediate between Whole Hebrew and Yiddish. Thus, M. Weinreich (1980: 307) notes that the Whole Hebrew pronunciation of the first two words of the benediction are: *bu:rix atu:* 'blessed art thou' by CY speakers, and *borux ato* by NEY speakers. In less careful pronunciation, however, PTR may occur; thus: *bu:rəx, borəx*. Katz (1993: 56–57) posits a "sociolinguistically determined continuum" for the realization of Whole Hebrew, ranging from "Formal Ashkenazic" (most distinct from Yiddish sound patterns) to "Popular Ashkenazic" (most similar to Yiddish). Among the features affected along this continuum are stress placement and the degree of (post-tonic) vowel neutralization (Bin-Nun 1973: 298–301; Birnbaum 1979a: 59–66; M. Weinreich 1980: 307; Katz 1993: 72).

2.6 Periodization of the history of Yiddish

The general contours of a periodization of Yiddish are complicated by sociolinguistic factors affecting written texts from the Old Yiddish period. These often show a written style consciously modeled after German written style norms of the time. In fact, there has been much scholarly debate over whether these texts are Old Yiddish, or merely Middle High German in Jewish letters (see Paper 1954; Frakes 1989). However, these texts often show traits which betray spoken language norms which were distinctly Yiddish, differing from both written and spoken German norms of the time (M. Weinreich 1928, 1931). Thus, great caution must be exercised when basing a periodization of Yiddish on these older documents, especially when venturing beyond the lexicon to the morphology and syntax. For example, older documents give evidence of a preterite form, while modern spoken and written Yiddish do not. However, it is not clear that Jews used the preterite in their speech at that time; it is more likely that they did not.[61] Similarly, as concerns the syntax, along with German-like word order (verb placement) in the older documents, we frequently find in the self-same documents a Yiddish-like word order with proximity of AUX and main verb, as seen in the following examples in Birnbaum (1979a: 151–152): *wil brengen cu ainem guten ende*... 'want to bring to a good conclusion'(dated 1396–1397); *ix bin wordin müde*; *zi zolin wérdin* 'I am become tired; they should become' (dated *c.* end of the fourteenth century CE). Often these early documents show syntactic variation which perhaps betrays Yiddish vernacular norms through the filters of German written models. Thus, in a public apology from the first quarter of the fifteenth century (p. 153): (A) *ix haan gybroxyn di haskoomys di di raboonym haan gymaxt*... 'I have broken the agreements, which the rabbis have made' was followed by (B) *daa ix uufgyxasmut bin* 'since I signed have.' In the preceding, (A) shows proximate AUX and main verb, while (B) shows OV (object-verb) word order in dependent clause. Finally, the early documents show systematic and conscious avoidance of Semitisms, further making them

[61] See, for example, recorded oral testimony in Yiddish, embedded in formal documents written in *Loshn-koydesh* (e.g., Birnbaum 1979a:153, item 9) – these lack a preterite form; compare this, however, to the presence of preterite forms in poems and other literary pieces, often derived from German literary works.

suspect as reliable sources of Yiddish speech of the time (Katz 1985: 97; Frakes 1989; Hutton 1999: 193).

The main divisions in Weinreich's (1980: 719–733) periodization are as follows:

	From		To
Early Yiddish A		–	± 1100
Early Yiddish B	±1100	–	± 1250
Old Yiddish	± 1250	–	± 1500
Middle Yiddish	± 1500	–	± 1700
New Yiddish	±1750		–

Weinreich's chart (p. 733) shows each stage in terms of changing constellations of factors. Written language is presented distinct from spoken language in the chart. The periods are characterized as follows. Early Yiddish A (– ±1100) and Early Yiddish B (±1100–±1250) provide no extant written text. The Early Yiddish period is posited as the time of the (fusion) formation of Yiddish as a Jewish vernacular based on contact with varieties of German. In Weinreich's scenario, Early Yiddish A is characterized by Jewish settlement in compact areas (Loter and Regensburg), and, thus, in contact with a limited number of varieties of German. Weinreich's Early Yiddish B period involves expansion of Jewish settlement into the basins of the Main, Upper Rhine, and Upper Danube, with Jews consequently bringing many more varieties of German into the mix. The recent challenges to Weinreich see the Loter settlement as separate from an initial Jewish settlement to the east (and thus, Yiddish arising on a Bavarian base). However, this would affect the periodization only to the extent that subperiods A and B would no longer be justified, and would conflate into a single period, Early Yiddish.

In the Old Yiddish period (±1250–±1500) Written Language A [WrLg A] develops (on an exclusively WY basis). Weinreich notes that this is the period when the Slavic component "enters into the fusion." However, it may be asked to what extent this event – certainly decisive in the history of EY – may serve as a criterion for a periodization of Yiddish generally, since Yiddish speakers in Ashkenaz I (i.e., WY speakers) of this period were also speakers of Old Yiddish.

The Middle Yiddish period (±1500–±1700) is characterized by the formation and crystallization of the major dialect areas. At the same time, however, WrLg A continues as the written norm (though, increasingly, EY elements appear). The New Yiddish period is dated by Weinreich from ±1750; other sources (e.g., U. Weinreich 1972: 795; Kerler 1999: 15) give the appoximate date 1700.[62] The eighteenth century marked the beginning of a drastic decline of Yiddish in the west, both in speech and in writing. This left a power vacuum

62 See also Kerler (1999: 255–256) on a periodization of Literary Yiddish.

in the east. Written Language B [WrLg B] – based on spoken varieties of EY – emerged in the late eighteenth to early nineteenth century as the new written norm, followed by increasing pressures for a unified, dialect-compromise standardized written language. The modern period sees further tendencies toward dialect consolidation in spoken language: from local to regional, and from regional to pan-regional and/or standard, as well as the expansion of spoken and written Yiddish into new domains of modern European discourse. It is a period in which there is large-scale borrowing of the vocabulary of modernity via NHG and internationalisms.

2.7 The history of written Yiddish: a brief overview

The issue of written Yiddish is a complex one, involving not only Yiddish linguistics and sociolinguistics, but also the cultural history of Ashkenazic Jewry, the history of Yiddish literature, and more (see also §7). Excellent discussions on the origins and development of Yiddish writing are found in Birnbaum (1979a: 145–189); on paleography in Birnbaum (1971); on the history of Yiddish orthography in Schaechter (1999).

2.7.1 Script

Yiddish, like all Jewish languages which have developed a written tradition, is written in the Hebrew alphabet. However, a word of clarification concerning terminology is necessary. The term *Hebrew script* is historically confusing, and Birnbaum (1971: 126) suggests the term *Jewish script*. Basically, what the ancient Hebrews referred to as "Hebrew script" (כתב עברי) was the Paleo-Hebrew script. What is referred to today as "Hebrew script" is the Assyrian/Aramaic alphabet, called אשרית 'Assyrian' in Talmudical sources. At that time, furthermore, the term לשון־הקודש *lswn hqwds* referred to the alphabet as well as the language. Thus, we use the term *Hebrew script* with these qualifications in place, and take into consideration the evolution of Hebrew script, the rise and development of distinct styles, and the interaction of styles with one another.

What is thought of today as the Hebrew square script, used in printing modern Hebrew, modern Yiddish, etc., goes back to the Assyrian/Aramaic-based script. The square script evolved through the centuries to the form as we basically know it today by the tenth century CE (Birnbaum 1971: 174). The square script was used for H-level written functions, e.g, sacred texts. As opposed to this, a cursive style developed for use in less formal situations, e.g., for use in letters, notes, deeds, and other non-literary or ephemeral matters (p. 176). At first, cursive was based on the square script. With time, however, the two styles diverged ever more, and took distinct paleographic evolutionary paths. Birnbaum writes that cursive is old, probably arising with the growth in volume of non-Canonical literature, e.g., commentaries, halakhic, poetic, grammatical, and philosophical works. Later, after the split between formal square script and cursive was already underway, cursive occasionally was used in the writing of more formal texts (e.g., books). This led to the rise of a formal cursive style, which then began evolving down its own path, distinct from the evolution both of non-formal cursive, and of the square script. This new formal, cursive-derived script is called, variously, *mashket* ~ *mesheyt* ~ *mashait*, and, sometimes, "rabbinic" (Birnbaum 1971: 189; M. Weinreich 1980: 275). These distinct styles were used for distinct functions from early on. This predates the rise of Ashkenazic Jewry, and other Jewries employ *mashait/mashket* as well.

The history of Hebrew scripts in Ashkenaz (Birnbaum 1971: 299–312) sheds light not only on the history of writing in Ashkenaz (both *Loshn-koydesh* and Yiddish), but also on sociolinguistic and sociocultural history, as well as on current debates concerning the origins of Ashkenazic Jewry. Thus, for example, the earliest script specimens from Loter are "practically identical with Zarphatic" styles (p. 300), strongly suggesting that at least part of the Ashkenazim came from *Tsorfas* (Jewish "France").

Among Ashkenazim, up until the first decades of the nineteenth century, printing in *Loshn-koydesh* and in Yiddish involved different typefaces in almost all instances (Birnbaum 1971: 310; Fishman 1985).[63] When cursive was used for handwriting, no differentiation was made in font style between *Loshn-koydesh* and Yiddish. The terms *mashket/mesheyt* were used in the sixteenth century; other terms followed later, e.g., *vaybertaytsh*, *taytsh*, *vayberksav*, *ivre-taytsh*, *kleyn-taytsh* (M. Weinreich 1980: 275; Fishman 1985). M. Weinreich (1980: 275) points out that the keeping-separate of *Loshn-koydesh* and Yiddish in pre-modern texts was so clear-cut and thoroughly upheld that "[e]ven single Yiddish phrases and words in Loshn-koydesh texts appeared in the special type" (*mashket*). On the evolution of letter shapes in Ashkenazic *mashket*, Birnbaum (p. 310) writes: "The forms which were reached by roughly the end of the fifteenth century – including some features from the cursive – constitute the basis of the first type cutters' work." Birnbaum (p. 311) notes that the arrival of movable type put an end to the use of *mashket*; books were still often copied by hand – but this was done in cursive. The switch to printed Yiddish in square script (and the consequent end of *mashket*) arose from a constellation of factors: social, sociolinguistic, geographical, and technological (Fishman 1985).

2.7.2 *Development of Yiddish orthography*

Yiddish orthography evolved by adapting traditional Hebrew spelling principles to a non-Semitic language, Yiddish. Thus, Yiddish orthography arose on the basis of (a) older Hebrew and *Loshn-koydesh* norms, and (b) orthographic

[63] Furthermore, *mashket* was used for German language printed in Hebrew characters late into the nineteenth century (Birnbaum 1971: 310).

norms developed in post-*Loshn-koydesh* Jewish languages preceding Yiddish. The primary innovation was to write expressly the vowels in Yiddish. Hebrew had two orthographic traditions – *scriptio defectiva*, where vowels were not written (the pointing system of the Tiberian Masoretes was an attempt to address this lack), and *scriptio plena*, where some vowels were written out by use of the semivowel/glide symbols י and ו. This tradition served as the basis for later orthographic innovations as the Hebrew alphabet was adapted to Jewish vernaculars (Birnbaum 1979a: 112–126). Complementing this was the use of the Hebrew consonant symbols א and ע to represent vowels as well. Orthographic innovations were introduced gradually. Older Yiddish documents have, for example, הנט for /hant/ 'hand,' reflecting the *scriptio defectiva* system. The history of specific orthographic innovations reflects both fine-tuning solutions in the adaptation process, and sociolinguistic macro-issues (Schaechter 1999; §7.7.4).

Yiddish traditionally has maintained the original spelling in words of Hebrew and Aramaic origin in the Merged Hebrew component of Yiddish, as opposed to essentially phonemic spelling for Yiddish words of non-HA origin; thus, StY סוד [sod] 'secret' (< HA), but סאָד [sod] 'orchard' (< Slavic), סודות [sojdəs] 'secrets' (< HA) vs. ברויט [brojt] 'bread' (< Gmc). Occasionally, words have "crossed over" in speakers' perception; thus, חוזק *xojzək* 'mockery' is spelled as if it were of HA origin, though it is likely of Gmc origin. Conversely, HA-origin מעקן *mekn* 'erase' (cf. TH root √mħq) is spelled "phonetically." The orthographic system employed for several decades in the Soviet Union reflected an ideological move to spell all words "phonetically" – including those of HA origin;[64] thus, Soviet Yiddish סאָד, סוידעס 'secret-s.' As a further part of dehebraization in Soviet Yiddish orthography, the final forms ן, ם, ץ, ף, and ך were eliminated (until they were reinstated in 1961).

The Jewish masses in Ashkenaz were well trained in the use of the Hebrew alphabet. Especially the males were literate in Hebrew and Aramaic texts, and, for both males and females, literacy in Yiddish was high. Among the coterritorial Christian populations in Ashkenaz, however, literacy was often limited to the educated elite, especially monks, who were trained (in Western Europe) in Latin, and, hence, the Latin alphabet. The Yiddish term for the Latin-letter alphabet is *galkhes*, created from *galəx* 'monk, priest.' Until the modern period, the Jewish masses (with individual exceptions) could not read *galkhes*. Literate Christians (with individual exceptions) could not read the Hebrew alphabet. Birnbaum (1979a: 108) provides several examples showing that the orthographic system for Old Yiddish was not based on the MHG spelling system. The texts from which Birnbaum draws his examples – the Cambridge manuscript of 1382 – have been the focus of much scholarly debate on whether they are to be

[64] On similar approaches outside the Soviet Union, see Schaechter (1999: 29–30).

seen as examples of MHG in Hebrew letters, or of Old Yiddish. However, even if one views this codex as "German in Hebrew letters," Birnbaum makes clear that Jews did not construct their orthography based on German orthographic norms. Rather, Jewish orthographic norms developed on the basis of earlier Jewish writing norms, e.g., the use of *alef* at the beginning of vowel-initial words. Thus, Old Yiddish has איך corresponding to MHG *ich* 'I.' If Old Yiddish orthography were based on a type of German orthography, Jews would have written this word as **יכה. Even in the wake of the Jewish Enlightenment (late eighteenth to early nineteenth century), when German Jews shifted from Yiddish to German in speech and writing, they continued to use the Hebrew alphabet to write German – at first, exclusively so (based on their earlier Jewish/Yiddish orthographic norms and practices), later, for Jewishly defined purposes (well into the nineteenth century, in some locations into the twentieth; see Lowenstein 1979).[65]

A major change in orthography occurred with the advent of modernity, and the rise of the modern literary language – Written Language B [WrLg B]. Here, non-Jewish orthographic norms (chiefly, German) did influence Yiddish spelling – some features for a longer period, other features for a shorter period. Many of the changes in WrLg B are linked to the ideology and discourse of post-Enlightenment modernity. The orthography in traditionalist Jewish circles, on the contrary, maintains some features identified with traditional Yiddish orthography dating from the pre-modern period; e.g., use of י for schwa in the prefix *gə*: גיזאָגט *gizogt* vs. StY געזאָגט *gəzogt* 'said.'[66] As expected, transitional elements are found in the switch from WrLg A to WrLg B (see Herzog 1965b; Birnbaum 1979a: 145–189; Kerler 1999).

2.7.3 *Written language in Ashkenazic culture*

The issue of written language in Ashkenaz is complex. Traditionally, *Loshn-koydesh* functioned as the acrolectal written language even as Yiddish served as the universal vernacular of Ashkenaz. *Loshn-koydesh* served as the language of sacred and other H-function texts (e.g., commentaries; wedding contracts), whereas the explication of these texts was in Yiddish. Even early on, however, written Yiddish served functions in Ashkenazic civilization.[67] With time the functions of written Yiddish expanded in nature and scope.

[65] On Yiddish in Latin letters in nineteenth-century Germany and elsewhere, see Lowenstein (1979), and §7.7.5.

[66] Though contemporary Hasidic written Yiddish often employs Germanized spelling (Paul Glasser, p.c.).

[67] See M. Weinreich (1980: 247–314; especially Figure 7, p. 279) for schematic representation of oral vs. written language in Ashkenaz.

The earliest evidence of written Yiddish is found in lists of names of Jews of Mainz murdered in the massacre of 1096 (First Crusade); some of these names contain Germanic roots. Yiddish glosses are found in the margins of Hebrew manuscripts from the twelfth century. The earliest known text evidence of an entire sentence in Yiddish is found in the Worms *makhzer* 'holiday prayer book' of 1272 (Sadan 1963). The *makhzer*, in *Loshn-koydesh*, contains a Yiddish rhymed sentence written in small-sized letters inside the large, thick letters of the Hebrew word בדעתו. The Yiddish sentence reads:

גוּט טַק אִים בְּטַגְא שְׁ וַיר דִיש מַחֲזוֹר אִין בֵּית הַכְּנֶסֶת טְרַגְא

This sentence invokes 'A good day unto him occur, who this *makhzer* into the synagogue carry' (*gut tak/im btaḡ?/ s uair dis maħăzor in beis hak:neses̄ traḡ?*). Verbatim testimonies in Yiddish, embedded in *Loshn-koydesh* documents, date from the late fourteenth century. Additionally, we confront the problem of the analysis of texts such as the Cambridge Codex of 1382.

The earliest Yiddish literature was characteristically of two main types (see Max Weinreich 1980): (1) works based on traditional Judaic texts – biblical, talmudical, or midrashic themes, and (2) works which were translations and adaptations for a Jewish readership of European non-Jewish works (e.g., the King Arthur legend; the *Bove-bukh*). In addition, we must consider the development of *taytsh* – the calque language wherein a *Loshn-koydesh* text was calqued into Germanic morphemes, but reflected *Loshn-koydesh* syntax. *Taytsh* was further removed from spoken Yiddish in that HA-origin words – even those used in spoken Yiddish – were systematically avoided. Later, *taytsh* influenced the language of Yiddish texts, serving as a source for stylistic archaisms, expression of holiness in works of a religious nature, and later as a stylistic device in the works of the founders of modern Yiddish literature (Mendele Moykher-Sforim and Perets). The first Yiddish book appeared in 1534 (Kraków): *Mirkevəs ha-mišnə – sejfər rov anšl*; it is a dictionary and concordance of the Hebrew Bible. Other translations of biblical material appear throughout the middle of the sixteenth century. Popular homiletic prose in the form of the צאינה־וראינה *cenə-renə* (a free paraphrasing of the Bible in Yiddish) appeared around the end of the sixteenth century (it continues to be republished to the present day) and had an important archaic stylizing influence on future works as well. The homiletic prose – paraphrases of Bible and other ancient texts – opened new literary doors for the use of Yiddish as a written medium. Yiddish literature also developed an epic tradition as well as fables, from the Cambridge Codex of 1382 onward. The *Bove-bukh* was (indirectly) based on a popular English work, *Sir Bevis of Hampton*. *Tkhines* – prayers of individual and private supplication – appear from the sixteenth century. Thought of characteristically as women's prayers, they might shed valuable light on women's language.

Over the centuries the uses of written Yiddish reflected societal changes in Ashkenaz. Yiddish was used in ever-wider contexts. As with other European vernaculars, Yiddish came to be seen as a language suitable for Bible translation, and as the language of an emerging Yiddish press (dating to 1686 in Amsterdam). In the modern period Yiddish became a full vehicle for literary expression in all domains – poetry, journalism, novels, academic discourse, etc.

2.7.4 *Written languages A and B*

The history of written literary Yiddish breaks into two distinct periods and two distinct models – an earlier period of the first literary language, WrLg A, and a later period of WrLg B. However, there is an extended period of transition. While the beginning of the modern literary language is generally dated to the late eighteenth century, the features of WrLg B began emerging earlier. Furthermore, influences from WrLg A carry on well into the nineteenth century – first as remnants, later as devices of stylistic archaism (Kerler 1999: 25).

WrLg A emerges in the mid fourteenth century as a supraregional form based on WY (M. Weinreich 1980: 727; Kerler 1999: 17). WrLg A served as the model for printed Yiddish up to roughly the beginning of the nineteenth century, whether written by speakers of WY or EY. WrLg A was employed for a pan-Ashkenazic readership. Dialectalisms (including WY dialectalisms) were avoided, since publishers and authors wished to reach as large a readership as possible. In addition, WrLg A was used in a time when, culturally, *Loshn-koydesh* was unquestionably of higher status, used in those texts which – at least publicly – were acknowledged as the most important. One area where Yiddish gained an early and strong foothold for H-status functions was as the language of traditional religious transmission for women and uneducated men (Niger 1913). Written Yiddish occupied a place in pre-modern Ashkenazic expression, and that place was always growing, expanding, and developing. The norm – which even carried into the modern period – was to give *Loshn-koydesh* titles to works (books and pamphlets) written in Yiddish, or at least to give them a twinned *Loshn-koydesh*/Yiddish title. Thus, the first modern Yiddish journal, *Kol mevaser* (Odessa 1862), bears a Hebrew name.[68] The norms, rules, and styles of WrLg A arose to a significant degree out of a synthesis of *Loshn-koydesh* and MHG literary styles, rules, and traditions. The relationship of WrLg A to early spoken Yiddish is problematic (Kerler 1999: 19). However, analogous to the spoken language, WrLg A arose from a type of literary-language fusion, and went on to become a model in its own right for subsequent (and expanding) written expression in Ashkenaz.

WrLg B derives for the most part from spoken EY norms. While elements of EY are found in some documents from the period of WrLg A (Herzog 1965b;

[68] *Kol mevaser* appeared as the Yiddish-language supplement to the Hebrew newspaper *Hameylits*.

Kerler 1999: 26), they are not the base. WrLg B arose out of a constellation of factors, such as: the far-reaching social reorganization of Jewish life in Ashkenaz I (on the way to / during / after the Jewish Enlightenment); the decline of WY, and the related shift to the coterritorial emerging nation-state languages (German, Dutch, etc.); the rise of Yiddish printing centers in the east. While the *Haskole* was transforming Ashkenazic life in the west, the situation was different in Eastern Europe. Here, the conscious development of the vernacular to a national language of *Kultur* was prominent on the Jewish agenda. This included deliberate expansion of the range of functions in which the written vernacular language was now to serve. The new national models arising in Europe often included the conscious development of a written standard and a spoken standard, and the narrowing of the gap between the two. Kerler (1999: 26) writes: "Modern literary Yiddish arose largely from conscious attempts to write in a language primarily based on the contemporary vernacular."

WrLg B arose in the context of general European modernity, where the concerns, goals, and discourse models of modern culture show pan-European commonalities. Much of the tone-setting for modern national movements in Eastern Europe came via the filter of German *Kultur*. For secularizing, modernizing EY, this was a period (late nineteenth / early twentieth century) of massive borrowing of loanwords from NHG, e.g., *fragə* 'question,' *špraxə* 'language' (later nativized to *šprax*), *umštand* 'circumstance.' Furthermore, this was a period when secularizing Yiddish began to copy some NHG spelling norms (Schaechter 1999); e.g., the use of ע and ה as spelling "calques" of devices used to show vowel length in NHG, as in שפּיעל, מעהל; cf. NHG *Spiel*, *Mehl*, StY שפּיל 'play,' מעל 'flour'; the use of double consonants, e.g., אַללע, cf. NHG *alle*, StY אַלע 'all.'

2.8 Names for the Yiddish language

This section is based on M. Weinreich's (1980: 315–327) discussion of the various names used to designate the Yiddish language. He puts the names in their linguistic, historical, and sociological contexts, and considers the following three questions. (1) When did Yiddish come into existence? (2) When was it recognized by Jews and by non-Jews that Yiddish constituted "a linguistic unit in its own right"? (3) When did the present term *Yiddish* come to be applied to this unit?

The name *Yiddish* is much younger than the language itself (M. Weinreich 1980: 315). This is not unusual; the names of languages have often arisen much later than the languages themselves. For example, throughout the Middle Ages, Italian was referred to as *vulgare latinum* ~ *latino vulgare* 'people's Latin,' and the first printed Italian dictionary (sixteenth-century) referred to the language as "tuscan" (p. 320). Weinreich (p. 324) writes: "In general, names of languages are fixed retrospectively." For example, the term "German" begins to take root in the tenth century; prior to that time, we may rightfully only speak of individual tribes; yet scholars today commonly make reference to OHG of the eighth and ninth centuries (p. 324). Similarly, we must exercise caution when basing our claims on names used; these may change. Thus, 'Jews' can be referred to in one period as "Hebrews," in another as "Israelites," but the reference group remains identical.

As concerns a precise nomenclature for varieties of vernaculars, there was, in general, much less concern for this in medieval times as compared with the modern period (M. Weinreich 1980: 316). For Jews, the primary concern was in distinguishing *Loshn-koydesh* from the Yiddish vernacular, which was from early on referred to as *lošn aškənaz* 'the language of Ashkenaz.' In early (*c.* 1290) Hebrew glosses we find *bilšojnejnu* 'in our tongue,' meaning the Jewish vernacular (and not *Loshn-koydesh*). The formula *bilšon aškənaz* 'in the language of Ashkenaz' is found in glosses dating back at least to the thirteenth century, perhaps earlier. Thus, Ashkenazic Jews used the term *lošn aškənaz*[69] in contradistinction to *Loshn-koydesh*. However, the term *lošn aškənaz* also was used occasionally by Jews to refer to the language of the Germans (p. 317). In Nathan Note Hanover's *Sofə bərurə* 'Clear speech' (Prague, 1660), which provides translations of Hebrew words into Yiddish, Italian, and Latin, Hanover writes in the preface: "I have selected the *lošn aškənaz* from the easy language current among us, and very little from the *lošn aškənaz* of the Gentiles that is not found in our language" (cited from pp. 317–318).

That Jewish speech from the outset was not identical to German speech is clear from older documents. Weinreich (p. 319) cites an example of a German court suit (1451, Magdeburg) in which the defendant "speaks like one" (= a Jew). However, extant documents are often vague in distinguishing languages terminologically. For example, medieval German documents use both *(h)ebreisch* and *jüdisch* to refer to 'Hebrew language' (M. Weinreich 1980: 318, referring to an MHG poem from the thirteenth century). A recurring problem is that it is not always clear from the older documents whether the authors intended a clear distinction between script and language; in Jewish documents, *galkhes* is sometimes used to refer to non-Jewish letters, at other times, to refer to the German language.[70]

Weinreich traces the development of the name *Yiddish*. From the beginning of the sixteenth century there appear in Germany works by non-Jewish authors, written in Latin and in German, in which there is not a fixed

[69] Note that *l[o]šn aškənaz*, as with the term *l[o]šn-kojdəš*, represents an innovation; Classical Hebrew grammar would prescribe here a reflex of the construct form, TH *ləšo:n*; see Jacobs (1991).

[70] M. Weinreich (1980: 318) referring to a document from 1698. The term *galkhes* refers to Dutch in a document from 1710, cited in Weinreich (p. 317).

terminology as concerns Yiddish. References to Yiddish are (p. 319): (in Latin) *hebr(a)eae litterae teutonice legendae* 'Hebrew letters to be read in German'; *hebr(a)eo-germanice* 'Hebrew-German'; *jud(a)eo-germanice* 'Jewish-German.' The German-language equivalents are: *hebraisch-teutsch*; *juden-teutsch*; *jüdisch-teutsch*. Wagenseil (1699) referred to Yiddish as *Jüdisch-Teutsch* and, simply, *Teutsch*.

Among Jews, the root *teutsch* (cf. StG *Deutsch*; StY *dajč*) served for many centuries as the base for reference to Yiddish. M. Weinreich (1980: 316–317) notes that the "old name" (for Yiddish) survives in many terms: *tajč-xuməš* 'Yiddish paraphrase of the Pentateuch for women'; *fartajčn* 'translate (into Yiddish);' *ojstajčn* 'interpret;' *arajntajčn* 'read into'; *vos tajč* 'what does it mean?,' *stajč* 'how come? If the necessity arose to differentiate Jewish from non-Jewish speech, the term *jidiš-tajč* could be used. Beginning in the late eighteenth century, the term *pojliš-tajč* is sometimes used to distinguish EY from the WY of German Jews (p. 317).

A shift takes place when the language begins to be referred to by terms meaning 'Jewish.' The term *jidiš* had its beginning as one form competing among several; however, by the eighteenth century it had established itself (M. Weinreich 1980: 320). Weinreich (p. 315) states that the name goes back with certainty at least to the mid seventeenth century (a reference, "spoke Yiddish," in a 1649 text from Amsterdam; a reference to speaking "a Yiddish word" in a text from *c.* 1660). Weinreich (p. 315) provides as well a more ambiguous reference from 1597, wherein a translation is "taken from *galkhes* and rendered into Yiddish." It is unclear whether this refers to script or language. However, it is clear that the meaning 'Jewish' came to be used as a term for the language. Weinreich (pp. 319–320) notes use of the term *jüdische Sprache* in Austrian lands in the late eighteenth century, e.g., in the *Toleranzpatent* of 1781, and cites as well a Czech-language reference from 1581 to *knihy židovské neboližto hebrajské* 'Yiddish or Hebrew books.'

In the late eighteenth century, German *maskilim* (adherents of the Jewish Enlightenment) used the French term *Jargon* to refer to Yiddish. This word had strongly pejorative connotations in French, and this is how it was used by the *maskilim*. Thus, Weinreich (1980: 321) cites Mendelssohn (written in a private letter): "This Jargon contributed no little to the immorality of the common Jews." The term *žargon* diffused from Germany to Eastern Europe. There, at first, the term was mostly neutral, and often associated with positive contexts. The term was used by writers (e.g., Sholem Aleykhem; Dik); in journalism; in the Jewish labor movement, etc. (pp. 321–322). However, it was a term used by the elite; for the Yiddish-speaking masses, the word was "only a book word... never accepted in daily usage" (p. 322). In the early part of the twentieth century the term took on pejorative connotations among EY speakers in the aftermath of the language battles (Hebrew and

Yiddish).[71] The term *jidiš* has emerged as the universal term for the language in Yiddish itself, and has gained increasing acceptance as the term in other languages as well. For example, the common term in American English two generations ago was *Jewish*; the accepted term today is *Yiddish*.

2.9 Summary

In slightly more than one century, modern Yiddish linguistics has made great progress toward an understanding of the history of the Yiddish language. Key to this progress has been the focus on the object of investigation – Yiddish – as the required point of departure. The history of Yiddish presents ongoing challenges for linguists. Languages do not generally lend themselves to evenly flowing, linear histories, without bumps, clashes, and points of relatively sharp discontinuity. Still, as with most languages, the paths of development in the history of Yiddish exhibit overall regularity and systematicity which justify an endocentric investigation of Yiddish, as opposed to exocentric approaches which atomistically look at Yiddish in external terms, and, thus, out of context.

Much progress has been made in refining our understanding of the geographical and linguistic origins of Yiddish. The early view of Weinreich and Birnbaum on a Zarphatic/Loez background and the birth of Yiddish in Loter has given way more recently to a view of Yiddish origins further east. Significantly, scholars from diverse academic backgrounds and perspectives have been converging toward the eastern-origins view. Additionally, there is growing consensus on the (original) distinctness of the Loter Jewish settlement from the eastern Ur-Ashkenazim in ways which clear up some of the problems in the Weinreich/Birnbaum scenarios. Thus, recent scholarship has moved the field forward.

There are desiderata for future research on the history of Yiddish. As with most languages, loose ends remain in the reconstruction of PY; the individual pieces can always be further scrutinized for an ever-tighter fit. The field can address specific challenges expressed by Marchand and others without adopting exocentric and atomized assumptions and methodology. Further, while the fusion model has offered much to Yiddish linguistics, the field is ready for and needs a true contact-linguistics-based description of Yiddish origins.[72] Another

[71] Weinreich (1980: 322) cites the 1908 Tshernovits conference, where the term *žargon* was used negatively by proponents of Hebrew.

[72] In Jacobs (1975) I argued for pidgin/creole origins of Yiddish. Many of the overly bold claims therein were backed up too much by very general arguments, but insufficiently by data which would demonstrate clear evidence for pidgin/creole genesis; see criticism in Fishman (1981a: 3, note 1). More recently, Louden (2000) has addressed pidgin/creole issues in relation to Yiddish origins.

desideratum – though, admittedly, a difficult one – is research directed at clarifying the differences between written and spoken language in the early period. Old Yiddish texts obviously do not reflect the spoken language of the time, yet there are often clues and traces of the latter evident in the former. To the extent possible, these should be systematically collected and analyzed. Furthermore, the field greatly needs systematic investigation of PY historical morphology (King 1987) and syntax. For the latter, insights from typology-based approaches can be of considerable use.

3 Dialectology

3.1 Introduction

This chapter presents an overview of Yiddish dialectology – the investigation of Yiddish in its linguistic geographic dimension. The present focus is on linguistic diversity vs. uniformity in Yiddish from a geographic perspective. To the extent possible, discussion of sociolinguistic variation is deferred to ch. 7. For structured discussion, see M. Weinreich (1939: 23–90, especially p. 71); Herzog (1965a: 1–5; 2000); Katz (1983); U. Weinreich (1991); Herzog *et al.* (1992: 2–3); Sunshine *et al.* (1995).

3.2 History of Yiddish dialectology

Interest in Yiddish dialect variation may be divided into two main periods: pre-modern and modern. The changing foci, goals, and orientations are seen in the larger linguistic contexts of their times. The pre-modern period predated the rise of modern linguistic science, and views of language were thus both essentialist and anecdotal. Some mention of Yiddish regionalisms is noted by Buxtorf (1609); e.g., he cites *enk* 'you' (PL.OBL) as typical for Polish Jews (M. Weinreich 1993[1923]: 215). However, the earliest sustained effort at an overall dialect-based division of Yiddish is found in Carl Wilhelm Friedrich's (1784) work, which presents a classification of four main dialect areas (M. Weinreich 1993[1923]: 195, 214ff.). For the most part, Friedrich's work stands alone in its serious interest in Yiddish dialectology until the twentieth century.[1]

Modern Yiddish dialectology developed in the context of the field of general dialectology. The earlier period of modern Yiddish dialectology focused primarily on establishing a canonical classification of Yiddish dialects, whereas later on both Yiddish and general dialectology began focusing on the problematic

[1] An exception here is Avé-Lallemant's (1858–1862) criticism of Friedrich, which M. Weinreich (1993[1923]: 195–196) shows to be unfounded. Weinreich notes the several errors in Friedrich, but nevertheless sees Friedrich's as the first dialectological work on Yiddish. Weinreich (pp. 215, 221–222) also notes suggestions of regionalisms occasionally found in passing in various works.

data, the interstices, etc.[2] Yiddish dialectology also developed an interest in sociolinguistic pressures and the erosion of dialect (U. Weinreich 1952; Herzog 1964). The earliest dialect research focused on the phonology (and to some degree on the morphology), reflecting early Neogrammarian interests and methodological tools. U. Weinreich (see Herzog *et al.* 1992: 15, note 1) called for the investigation of Yiddish dialect syntax, but that remains an unfulfilled desideratum for the field.[3]

The late nineteenth and early twentieth century saw the blossoming of self-awareness in Yiddish life and literature. In Yiddish linguistic scholarship Yiddish became the focus and point of departure for investigation (M. Weinreich 1993[1923]: 250ff.; Katz 1983: 1019). As with the other national cultures of Europe in the modern period, there emerged an academic interest both in the cultivation of a standard national language of *Kultur*, and in the folk dialects (along with folkways and folklore data) as manifestations of "authentic" folk expression. As concerns Yiddish dialect study, the first stage required the collection and compilation of large amounts of folk-language data, of dialect forms (see Prilutski 1917, 1920) and of folk-sayings, folksongs, etc. The years after the First World War saw the following types of endeavors related to dialect research: (1) continued collection activities, along with the publication of anecdotal notes on various dialect features; (2) more substantial descriptions of the phonology of specific dialects (e.g., Viler 1924 for East-Galician Yiddish; Gutman 1926–1928 for the CY of Lodzh); (3) attempts at systematic classification of the range of Yiddish dialects (for summary, see Herzog 1965a: 1–3). The 1920s saw the rise of the academic institutions of Ashkenaz: the YIVO in Vilnius; the academies in Minsk and Kiev (Baker 1992). These all served as coordinating centers for the next steps in dialect research. Especially the YIVO sought to enlist Ashkenaz-wide participation of the masses in the collection of data.

A fourth type of endeavor consisted of Yiddish linguistic atlas projects, dating back to the 1920s. These show a path of development, from limited to ever-broader geographic focus (the entirety of Continental Ashkenaz), and to integration of linguistic and cultural data. The first Yiddish atlas was begun in the 1920s by Veynger (1925; 1926–1928; 1929); this atlas appeared after Veynger's death as Vilenkin (1931). Unfortunately, this atlas limits itself to phonology, and to Yiddish within the territorial limits of the Soviet Union of 1931 (eastern

[2] See Herzog (1964: 93–94). While the earlier scholars (in the modern period) noted problematic transitional phenomena, Herzog (1965a: 5) credits M. Weinreich (1939: 71) as being the first to clarify the importance of transition dialects in Yiddish dialectology. However, see also Veynger (1929: 20–21).

[3] Veynger (1925) planned to investigate syntactic and morphological variation in Yiddish dialects. That, too, remained unfulfilled. Weinreich's design included the following themes: phonology (vocalism, consonantism), morphology and morphophonemics, vocabulary, and "various" (Sunshine *et al.* 1995: 29). Some syntactic issues were included under "morphology and morphophonemics."

Belorussia and eastern Ukraine) – only a subset of the much larger EY home territory. The next atlas to appear, Jofen (1953), dealt with the entire EY area.[4] Beranek's (1965) atlas, which covered the entire WY area, suffers from serious methodological shortcomings,[5] as well as cartographic vagueness which limits its usefulness. Guggenheim-Grünberg (1973) produced a very useful atlas for a small sub-area of WY (Yiddish spoken in the traditional Alemannic German territory).

The first atlas to cover the entire Ashkenazic home territory is the *Language and Culture Atlas of Ashkenazic Jewry* [*LCAAJ*]. Initiated by U. Weinreich in the 1950s (see U. Weinreich 1995[1960]); Herzog *et al.* 1992: viii–x)[6] – i.e., after the German genocide of the Second World War and the resultant widescale decimation of Jewish life in Europe – the field work was carried out by a research team primarily in the United States and Israel. U. Weinreich (1963b) demonstrated the validity of data collected at a remove from the original source location. Volume I of the *LCAAJ* appeared as Herzog *et al.* (1992), and, subsequently, volumes II (Sunshine *et al.* 1995) and III (Herzog 2000) of a planned eleven volumes have appeared. In its conception and execution the *LCAAJ* deals not only with the entire indigenous Yiddish speech territory,[7] but as well with cultural variation across Ashkenaz. The *LCAAJ* anticipated area-specific dialectological issues in its creation of regional abridgments of the questionnaire (Sunshine *et al.* 1995: 5–7, and Map 1, p. 80). Since the 1960s the *LCAAJ* materials have served as an ongoing source for numerous studies in the field, beginning with Herzog (1964). The digitization of the *LCAAJ* archives currently underway aims to make this material available as an ongoing and dynamic source for new dialectological research.[8]

3.3 Dialect classification

3.3.1 Basis of classification

The major outlines of Yiddish dialect areas were drawn based on systematic differences in the phonetics, and, to a lesser degree, lexical differences. At first,

4 For criticism, see U. Weinreich (1995[1960]: *6).

5 See Katz (1983: 1020); contemporaneous reviews in Guggenheim-Grünberg (1966, 1968).

6 The conceptualization of the *LCAAJ* traces back to the founding of the YIVO in 1925, particularly to Max Weinreich (Herzog *et al.* 1992: viii).

7 The *LCAAJ* also investigated two long-established locations in (and predating) modern Israel – Jerusalem (generally a NEY community) and Safed (generally a SEY community). Also not on the base maps (but given in an inset beginning in volume II) are Estonia and parts of Russia (see Herzog *et al.* 1992: 7). The *LCAAJ* does not, however, cover the later Ashkenazic diaspora, in North and South America, South Africa, Australia. For the most part, these are colonial dialects which do not lend themselves to mapping within the established framework of Yiddish dialects.

8 On digitization of the *LCAAJ* archives and tapes, see Neumann (1995: 14–19) and Kiefer (1997). For longer transcriptions of Yiddish dialect texts, see, e.g., Gartner (1901); Veynger (1929: 142ff.); Kiefer (1995); Geller (2001).

the enterprise was exocentric; thus, Herzog (1965a: 1–2) notes that the earliest modern Yiddish dialectological studies (Şăineanu 1889; Gerzon 1902; Landau 1895; Landau and Wachstein 1911) "explored the possibilities of correlating the several varieties of Yiddish with previously delineated varieties of German." In reaction, endocentric Yiddish dialectological studies arose, with Yiddish as the point of orientation. The Neogrammarian comparative method was applied to the study of Yiddish dialects and to the reconstruction of a uniform proto-Yiddish language (Herzog 1965a: 2).

In the view most widely accepted in Yiddish scholarship, the basic dialect divisions are as follows. The primary cut is between Western Yiddish [WY] and Eastern Yiddish [EY]. EY subdivides into northern and southern branches; of these, Southern Yiddish [SY] subdivides into Central Yiddish [CY] and South-eastern Yiddish [SEY]. Classification is, of course, a matter of interpretation of the dialect data; the linguist's perspective shapes the discussion. Herzog (2000: 21ff.) discusses the ramifications of bi-, tri-, and quadripartite divisions in influencing the classification of Yiddish dialects. Exact dialect boundaries are subjective, since all isoglosses taken in sum show much more gradualness, a more nuanced and less categorical picture. For example, it is generally recognized that a significant isogloss distinguishing CY from SEY is that CY possesses distinctive monophthongal vowel length, which SEY is said to lack. On closer examination, however, we observe the gradual loss of categorical length within CY territory in the sweep from west to east (Jacobs 1996a). Furthermore, residual length (for at least one vowel) has been claimed for SEY (U. Weinreich 1958b). Thus, we operate between two endpoints. At one extreme is categorical classification of dialects; at the other extreme, the linguist despairs of abstracting a set of distinct dialects from the sum of the isoglosses. The most useful approach is that of a middle ground, suggested in Herzog (1965a: 4), which differentiates between varieties which have developed internally via *stammbaum*-origin and differentiation, and varieties which have arisen via contact.

3.3.2 Perceptual dialectology

A desideratum for Yiddish linguistics is a study of the perceptual dialectology (Preston 1999) – an investigation of which features are considered by Yiddish speakers as bellweather indicators of one or the other dialect. There is ample anecdotal mention of folk-awareness of urban speech, regional speech, etc.; e.g., some speakers are stigmatized for *redn mit a rejš* 'speaking with an (alveolar) *r*' (Reyzen 1920: 45; U. Weinreich 1963a: 263). Dialect-based hypercorrection further illustrates a popular awareness of dialect differences.

3.3.3 Settlement history and perceptual geography

Ashkenazic (perceptual) geography is to be examined on its own terms rather than solely in terms of coterritorial peoples. For example, the geographic territory covered in the Yiddish designation *Lite* is not identical with the geography covered by non-Jewish *Lithuania, Litauen, Litwa*, etc. The non-Jewish terms refer to the geographic area within the borders of the Republic of Lithuania. In Ashkenazic geography, *Lite* includes Lithuania, as well as parts of Latvia, Estonia, Belorussia, northern Poland, and northern Ukraine (M. Weinreich 1980: esp. 18, 47, 578; Jacobs 1998). Thus, to yiddophone Jews generally, a speaker of *litviš(ər) jidiš* 'Lithuanian Yiddish,' i.e., NEY, comes from Jewish *Lite*, whereas in the non-Jewish context, s/he may come from Lithuania, Belorussia, Latvia, etc. To take another example, Courland Jews divide their Jewish world into "Courland" and "Zamet." For the rest of Ashkenaz, Zamet is but one region ("Samogitia," adjacent to Courland). For Courland Jews, the term *zamətər* is used to refer generally to any non-Courland Jew (M. Weinreich 1923: 195). Thus, Ashkenazic popular perceptions of regions and regional speech may or may not coincide with the observations of the linguist.

3.3.4 "Age" of the Yiddish dialects

M. Weinreich (1980: 726, 733) dates the rise of the modern Yiddish codialect system (in EY) to the Middle Yiddish period (±1500–±1700). There is a danger in mechanically assigning exact ages to dialects. First, the selection of criterial features is subjective. Second, there can be a tendency to ignore the longstanding coexistence of variant forms within the same speech "type." Furthermore, virtually all of our evidence for a given change in older periods comes from written documents. Thus, we might see the hypercorrect spelling by Polish Jews in writing <u> for etymological <i> as evidence that the historical merger in SY of vowels 51, 31 (and 52, 32) had already taken hold.[9] However, caution must be exercised, since we also encounter spellings such as דער יוד *der jud* 'the Jew' and יודישעס פֿאָלקס-בלאַט *judišəs folks-blat* 'Jewish popular paper' (the names of two newspapers), where the <u> spelling results from conscious imitation of German orthography, and does not correspond to any variety or any period of Yiddish (Schaechter 1999: 2). Thus, the more general formulation is preferable: the modern Yiddish codialect divisions can be dated to the Middle Yiddish period.

If we take M. Weinreich's (1958a) view of WY as the point of departure for the later development of EY, then a number of WY-specific developments must be "held back" until after EY has branched off, e.g., the merger of PY *ei_{24},

[9] Birnbaum (1933, 1934) dates the change to *u* > *y* > *i* to *c.* 1490.

*ou_{44} > WY *a:*$_{24,44}$. M. Weinreich (1980: 41) claims that the main north–south division in EY (the realizations of vowels 12, 51/52) "apparently became stabilized around the seventeenth century." The notion of stabilization is important; variation and coforms existed, and Weinreich attributes a role in this stabilization to the fixing of external state-administrative divisions. U. Weinreich (1972: 794) dates the split between NEY and SY to "before the middle of the 16th century along the dividing line between the Kingdom of Poland and the Grand Duchy of Lithuania" (see map in Bin-Nun 1973; also Jacobs and Loon 1992: 26). U. Weinreich (1963a: 349–350) provides a general historical scenario for EY developments, including the following: 1250–1350 – migration of yiddophone Jews to the Kingdom of Poland; 1350–1500 – movement of Jews (mostly) from Poland into the northern part of the Grand Duchy of Lithuania (= Belorussia, ethnic Lithuania); 1500–1648 – movement of Polish Jews into the Ukraine (especially after 1569); 1300–1675 – migration of Ashkenazic Jews into Hungary; 1350–1600 – continued migration of Jews from Germany and Bohemia-Moravia into Poland.

3.4 Areal phonological differences

3.4.1 Vocalism

The phonological basis for the drawing of the Yiddish dialect map centers primarily on systematic differences in the stressed vowel systems (§2.4.3).[10] The present focus is on how these changes relate to dialectological issues. For a complete list of phonological features tested in the *LCAAJ* design, see Sunshine *et al.* (1995: 29–31).

The history of Yiddish dialect classification shows much basic agreement among the early scholars as to what the major dialects are, and where they are, but some disagreement as to which vowels are to be used diagnostically for classification purposes. Scholars have also proposed different terminologies in providing names for the dialects (see M. Weinreich 1993[1923]: 280–284; Katz 1983: 1020–1023). The four main modern Yiddish dialects – WY, CY, SEY, NEY – may be systematically distinguished by a minimal juxtaposition of stressed-vowel realizations. Generally, scholars have proposed either one or two vowels as diagnostic. The most accepted approach uses two vowels, PY *ei_{24} and *ou_{44}, as sufficient to distinguish the four main dialect areas (Herzog *et al.* 1992: 50, map 1). Thus, using the cognates of StY *kojfn*$_{44}$ 'buy' and *flejš*$_{24}$ 'meat' yields WY *ka:fn fla:š*, CY *kojfn flajš*, SEY *kojfn flejš*, NEY *kejfn flejš*.

In general, the comparative method validates the *stammbaum* approach for classifying the major dialect areas. The primary cut is between WY and EY,

[10] Herzog (2000: 17) notes this in contrast to German, where the consonants play the crucial role.

as proposed by Landau (1895) and Landau and Wachstein (1911); here, WY $a{:}_{24,44}$ serves as the shibboleth.[11] This *stammbaum* cut represents the earliest major division, WY vs. EY, and is supported by closer examination of other features, and by the reconstruction of PY from the synchronic dialects. The *stammbaum* model is also useful concerning many sub-dialect divisions, such as that between general NEY and CourlY. The CourlY distinction between $æi_{24}$ (*flæiš*) and $øy_{44}$ (*køyfn*) is a retention of an older state of affairs; the merger in general NEY to unitary unrounded $ej_{24,44}$ was a later innovation particular to that (geographically larger) sub-area.

Birnbaum (1915: 16), focusing on EY, distinguishes between *u*-dialects and *o*-dialects, vis-à-vis the realization of vowel 12/13; e.g., 'bathe' as northern *bodn* (Courland *o:*) vs. SY *bu(:)dn*. Birnbaum subdivides the *u*-territory according to the realization of PY vowels 22/24 as [ej] or [aj]; e.g., *sejfər/sajfər* 'Jewish holy book,' *gejn/gajn* 'go,' *plejcəs/plajcəs* 'shoulders.' This model is sufficient to make the basic three-way distinction in EY. Katz (1983: 1021) notes the important role of Prilutski (1920: 79) in the shaping of modern Yiddish dialect scholarship. It was Prilutski who endeavored to integrate WY and EY into a single coherent dialect picture.

Veynger's (1929: 55) classification system offers a wealth of subregional data and discussion. Veynger's primary cut, like Birnbaum's, is between *o*- and *u*-dialects (concerning vowel 12/13). Veynger subsequently subdivides the *o*-dialect according to the realization of PY vowel 24: a sub-area with *a:* (our WY), and a sub-area with *ej* (our NEY, encompassing Lithuania, Latvia, Estonia, Belorussia, parts of Ukraine, and more). The ej_{24} sub-area is further subdivided by Veynger into a sub-area with *sabesdiker losn* (= hushing-hissing confusion), and a sub-area lacking *sabesdiker losn* (though not entirely; see §7.5.1). Veynger subdivides the *u*-dialect (i.e., SY) into an *aj*-area (*flajš*) – our CY – and an *ej*-area (*flejš*) – our SEY. Veynger's *aj*-sub-area is located in Crown Poland, western Galicia, Carpathorussia; the *ej*-sub-area encompasses eastern Galicia, Bukovina, Ukraine (excluding the parts of the northern Ukraine in the *o*-dialect territory), Rumania, and Transylvania. Veynger (1929: 56–57) further subdivides the southern *ej*-area according to the realization of historical short $*a_{11}$ (as [a] or [o]) and discusses transitional and mixed dialects. Veynger's classification system is context-sensitive; it distinguishes between the two *ej*-sub-areas (one a subregion of the *o*-dialect; the other of the *u*-dialect). This presents a methodological problem, however, in explaining the similarity of the two contiguous *ej*-sub-areas.[12] Furthermore, Veynger's *o*-dialect, subdivided later according to

[11] The numbering system of diaphonemes is employed here for ease of identification only. The early scholarship did not use this numbering system (though see Bin-Nun 1973).

[12] Birnbaum (1915: 16) suggests a way around this problem by claiming that (our) NEY had /ei/, while (our) SEY had /äi/, thus, phonetically close(r) to (our) CY aj_{24}; see also M. Weinreich (1993[1923]: 281).

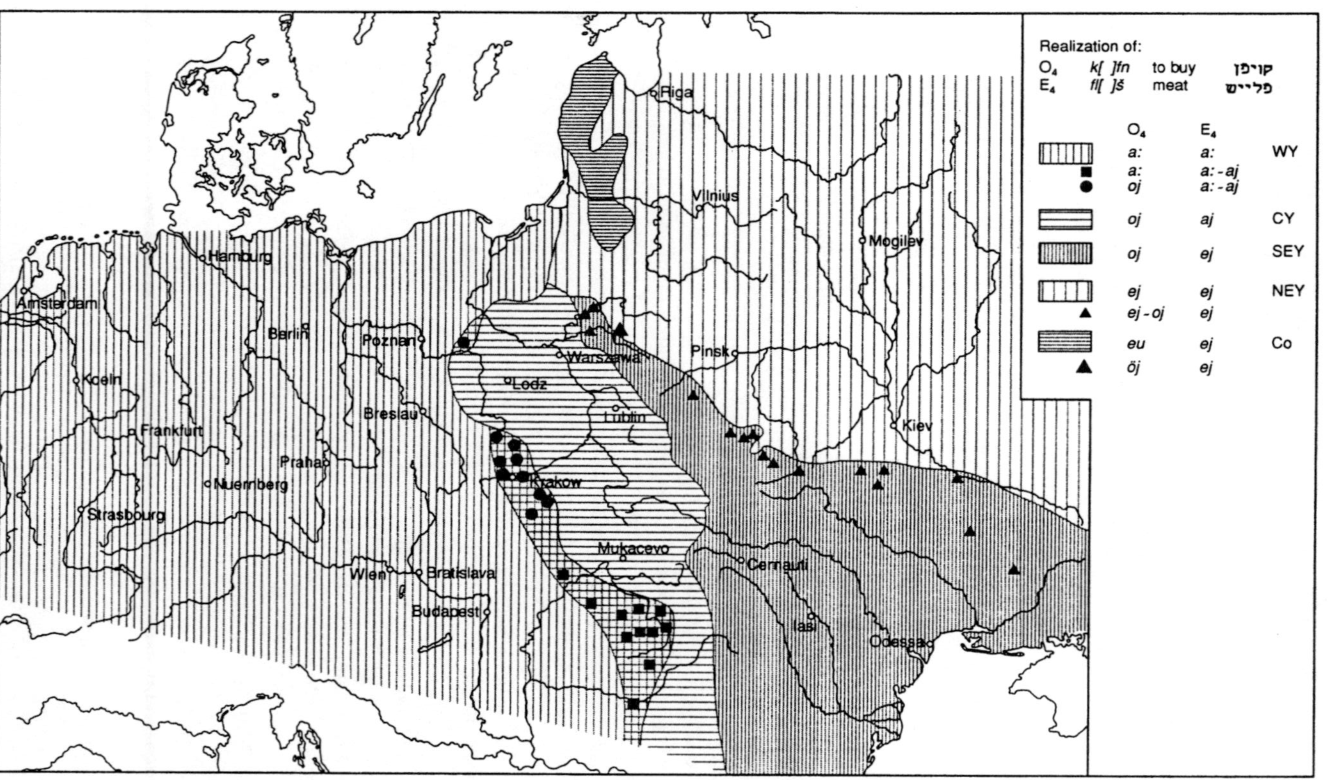

Map 3.1. Map of the major Yiddish dialects, *The Language and Culture Atlas of Ashkenazic Jewry.* Vol. I: *Historical and theoretical foundations*, ed. V. Baviskar, M. Herzog, U. Kiefer, R. Neumann, W. Putschke, A. Sunshine, U. Weinreich (1992: 50). Tübingen: Max Niemeyer Verlag and YIVO Institute for Jewish Research. Reproduced in modified form with permission of the editors and Max Niemeyer Verlag.

(vowel 24 as) *a:* vs. *ej*, might be seen as suggesting a closer link between WY and NEY, to the exclusion of CY and SEY (Herzog 2000: 23, 28; see also M. Weinreich 1923). This perspective sees SY as an area of innovation, while WY and NEY are, relatively speaking, areas of conservatism (Herzog 2000: 26). The task is thus not only one of collecting facts, mapping isoglosses, etc., but rather one of cautiously constructing conclusions and seeing the larger picture.

The visual appearance of the Yiddish dialect map depends on which features are selected as diagnostic, and how we embed those features as structural entailments. For example, if *o*-areas are mapped with horizontal-line filler, and *u*-areas with vertical-line filler, then WY and NEY appear closely linked in one group, CY and SEY in another. However, as additional features are added to the map the subdivisions that emerge are essentially those of the generally accepted (*stammbaum*-based) system of dialects.

Keeping in mind that historical dialect boundaries are in flux, the following general geographic reference information may be given (U. Weinreich 1963a: 337, note 4).[13]

WY – encompassed most of Germany, the Netherlands, Alsace-Lorraine, parts of Switzerland. WY territory once extended further to the east (M. Weinreich 1958a).

CY – Poland proper, western Galicia. Other areas often considered part of CY include Eastern Slovakia, Eastern Hungary, and Carpathorussia; however, these are problematic in that they figure in the southern transitional dialect area (see below).

SEY – Eastern Ukraine (excluding northern Ukraine), Rumania (including Bukovina, Moldavia, Bessarabia), eastern Galicia.[14]

NEY – Belorussia, Lithuania, Latvia, Estonia, parts of northern Poland, northern Ukraine.

3.4.2 *Consonantism*

The following examples represent a subset of issues concerning the consonantism, and should be taken only as general statements; details may vary at specific locations. For more complete discussion, see Prilutski (1917); Herzog *et al.* (1992: 36–44); Sunshine *et al.* (1995: 30–31). Three main

[13] On scholars' motivations for choosing geographic, ethnographic, geopolitical, or neutral dialect names, see Katz (1983: 1020–1022).

[14] Eastern Galicia is traditionally included as part of the SEY territory (see Herzog *et al.* 1992: 39–40). I disagree, and see at least parts of eastern Galician Yiddish (Viler 1924) as belonging to East Central Yiddish [ECY], based on features such as vowel length, $aj_{22,24}$, and devoicing of obstruents word finally; see § 4.1.2.

features in the consonantism are characteristic for entire major dialect areas. They are:

1. *Final devoicing of obstruents*. This is generally seen as characteristic for WY and for CY (Herzog *et al.* 1992: 195, Map 56); e.g., (Sosnovce) CY [lant], [lendɛ] (cf. StY *land – lendər*) 'land-s.'[15] The question arises as to whether final devoicing is a *stammbaum* or areal feature (Louden 2000). U. Weinreich (1963a: 351) suggests the possibility that it was lost in early EY, and restored later in CY under the influence of waves of new immigrants from German lands. Thus, for WY, final devoicing would be seen as a direct inheritance from PY, whereas in CY it would be seen as a feature reintroduced via contact.
2. *Palatalized consonants* arose via contact with Slavic (Bratkowsky 1974: 95ff.), and are thus limited to EY. The details, inventories, and distributions vary across EY dialects. EY generally has phonemic /n'/, /l'/. However, easternmost EY (NEY and SEY) shows subregional /s'/, /t'/, /d'/ as well (U. Weinreich 1958c: 6). There is subregional variation as to extent and degree of integration into the phonological systems of each variety. For example, consider the contextual palatalization of *l* or *n* after velar stops *k*, *g* in varieties of CY (Bratkowsky 1974: 95ff.; Herzog *et al.* 1992: 110–111; Jacobs 1996b). Instructive here is composite map 64, "Palatalization" in Herzog *et al.* (1992: 113), which shows variation in its implementation geographically and phonologically. Excluded from present discussion is the palatal *ç* (and its subregional reflex, *ś̌*) found in much of WY; e.g., WY *šadçn/šadšn*, StY *šadxn* 'marriage broker' (p. 109, map 60). WY *ç* likely arose under influence < StG.
3. *Anticipatory voicing assimilation* – OVA – is characteristic for NEY; e.g., *fu[s] + [b]enkl → fu[zb]enkl* 'foot stool' (see §4.4.3).

Other consonantal features often exhibit geo-patterning, but not always in terms of one or the other dialect; e.g., apical vs. back (velar or uvular) articulation of /r/ (see Herzog 2000: 115–116, map 33).

3.4.3 Sub-areas: phonology

WY may be subdivided – according to phonological criteria – into three (or four) main sub-areas: northern, central, and southern/southwestern (Katz 1983: 1025–1028, and map, p. 1023; Beranek 1965; Herzog 2000: 28). Southern WY has a westernmost subregion in Alsace and parts of Switzerland. The feature most diagnostic of the extreme southwest is *a:*$_{13}$ in, e.g., *ta:k* 'day,' *va:s*

[15] On final devoicing, see U. Weinreich (1963a); King (1980); Stankiewicz (1991: 211); Herzog *et al.* (1992: 36–38).

'what,' contrasting with ou_{12}, e.g., *šloufə* 'sleep,' *do:xəs* (~ *dʊ:xəs*) 'buttocks' (Zuckerman 1969: 46–48).

Katz (1983: 1027) points out that the central WY subregion – in the geographic heartland of the erstwhile WY massif – was the first WY dialect to die out. This is an important point, in that it differentiates between a center and a periphery in the process of WY language death. WY survived longer at the geographic and cultural margins. Geographically, it survived in the extreme south(west) in Alsace and Switzerland, and in the extreme northwest in Holland. Culturally and linguistically, WY survived in areas where the force of emerging StG was not as strong. German dialect speech predominated over StG in Alsace and in Switzerland; Dutch was spoken in the Netherlands. The WY geographic heartland was located in what was emerging as modern Germany proper; here, WY died out the earliest. WY also survived longer at the sociolinguistic periphery (among Jews), in terms of Jewish lexical items and expressions, low-register speech, etc. Katz (1983) provides illustrations of the subregions of WY in their stressed-vowel systems. WY subregional consonantism is given in Herzog *et al.* (1992: 96ff.), in maps 50 (merger/non-merger of initial *t/d*); 47 (*s* or *z* in Gmc-component prevocalic initial position – *zuntik* ~ *suntik* 'Sunday'); 51 (intervocalic fricativization of *b* > *v* – *šabəs* ~ *šavəs* 'Sabbath'); 57 (presence of affricate *pf* in parts of WY under StG influence – *pfilə* 'prayerbook').

NEY may be subdivided into CourlY and general NEY ("Stam-Litvish" [SL]), although, geographically, there is a gradual transition between the varieties (Mark 1951; Lemkhen 1995; Jacobs 2001a). Differences between the two sub-areas include the following: (1) merger of PEY $*øy_{42,44}$ and $*ei_{22,24}$ as SL $ej_{22,24,42,44}$; CourlY keeps these distinct as $øy_{42,44}$ and $æi_{22,24}$. The intervening area between CourlY and SL has $eu_{42,44}$, $ei_{22,24}$. (2) CourlY has preserved earlier vowel length, while SL has lost vowel length.[16] Veynger's (1929: 55) subdivision of NEY (his *o*-dialect, ej_{24} subregion) according to the presence or absence of *sabesdiker losn* is not primarily a *stammbaum* issue, but, rather, a sociolinguistic one (U. Weinreich 1952).

Veynger (1929: 56) subdivides the *u*-dialect (our SY) into sub-areas according to the realization of vowel 24 (*aj* vs. *ej*), as well as "short-*u*-dialects" (SEY) vs. "long-*u*-dialects" (CY). Basically, SEY may be seen as derived from PSY, with subsequent loss of vowel length (Herzog 1965a: 161ff.; Jacobs 1990b: 30–33). However, there remain problematic residues which complicate the picture of SEY as simply a branch of SY. Furthermore, the transition between CY and SEY, and, more specifically, between stressed vowel systems with or without distinctive vowel length is gradual.

16 Vowel length is in collapse in CourlY, under the influence of regional NEY and/or StY; see Jacobs (1994b). On remnants of vowel length in SL for vowel 54 (historically a diphthong), see U. Weinreich (1958a).

SEY may be (*stammbaum*-)sub-divided into areas with o_{11} (*totə* 'father,' *momə* 'mother,' *xosənə* 'wedding') and areas with a_{11} (*tatə, mamə, xasənə*). The o_{11} area shows subregional variation in the degree of generality of the historical change $a_{11} > o_{11}$. For example, in some locations it did not apply /_ŋk, but did apply /_ŋg; thus: *bank*$_{11}$ 'bank,' but *long*$_{11}$ 'long.' This variation can be stated in phonological terms: the rounding rule applies to ever-more general environments in the geographic sweep southward (Herzog *et al.* 1992: 64–65). However, Veynger (1929: 134) notes areas with mixed-dialect forms, where both *long*$_{11}$ and *šlang*$_{11}$ 'snake' co-occur (Alt-Murafe, Vinitser district); similarly, *donk*$_{11}$ 'thanks' and *bank*$_{11}$ (Kamenetsk-Podolsk); regular phonological rules cannot be formulated here. We might be tempted, as well, to subdivide SEY into areas with *i(:)*$_{25}$ vs. *ej*$_{25}$. However, this difference is the result of the sociolinguistically motivated replacement (in the twentieth century) of older *i(:)*$_{25}$ with (< CY) *ej*$_{25}$ (Herzog 1969: 62ff., citing Prilutski 1920: 19, 1921: 258ff.). Not surprisingly, this has led to sporadic hypercorrection, e.g., *rejfn*$_{52}$ 'call' < PY **ru:fn* (Herzog 1969: 67).

Stammbaum classification of the major dialect areas and subregions is useful in constructing the bigger picture of Yiddish in its geographic dimension. It helps us see more clearly other issues of language history, settlement and social history. However, upon closer examination, the subdialects generally show gradual transitions. We can make ever-finer *stammbaum* subclassifications. However, at some point the exercise either becomes pointless, or is disrupted by major discontinuities and the transition-dialect phenomena resulting from the resolution of these discontinuities. M. Weinreich (1965) discusses the "dynamics of Yiddish dialect formation," specifically concerning the chronology of phonological changes; e.g., the realization of vowel 51 before *r* + consonant as in (StY) *kurc* 'short,' regionally, *kurc* ~ *kirc* ~ *korc* ~ *kerc*. Weinreich outlines the chronological order of changes (to obtain *kerc*, we assume fronting first, lowering later; to obtain *korc*, just lowering), but just as importantly includes discussion of sociolinguistic changes in dialect orientation.

3.5 Areal morphological differences

Many items included under the *LCAAJ* rubric "morphology and morphophonemics" (Sunshine *et al.* 1995: 31–33) concern either morphophonemic issues (e.g., the realization of the *-n* suffix after stem-final *m* or *n* [item 451]), or specific lexical items (e.g., the reanalysis of the indefinite article [item 385]; thus, StY *an epl* 'an apple' in some dialects is reanalyzed *a nepl*). Item 458 tests the flexibility of adjectives *andər* 'other,' *bazundər* 'separate'; 459 the flexibility of *jedər* 'each.' These often occur with special inflectional patterns in several varieties of Yiddish. Many maps devoted to gender assignment in NEY focus on individual words. Major morphological rubrics in Herzog (2000: 120–175) are: diminutives; verb morphology; verbal periphrasis (as opposed to regular flexion); noun compounds; noun plurals; feminine derivatives; derivation of adjectives. The following are some morphological issues of geolinguistic interest.

1. *Diminutive suffix*. Geolinguistic variation is found in the type of diminutive suffix employed. Herzog (2000: 120ff.) distinguishes three diminutive-marking systems: *-ḷ*, *-xə(n)* ~ *-çə(n)*, and "mixed systems" (containing both the preceding).[17] Generally speaking, *-ḷ* is seen as EY, and *-çə(n)* as WY. Mixed systems reflect dialect contact, as well as the shifting of historical dialect boundaries. Thus, *-çə(n)* is found contextually in northwestern Poland, parts of NEY, and southwestern Ukraine and Rumania (Herzog 2000: 120). Structurally, the EY mixed system is employed to form diminutives of nouns with stem-final *l*, e.g., StY *mojl* 'mouth,' diminutive *majlxl*. Dialectally, however, the situation is more complex. (Herzog cites EY dialectism *majlxndl*.)
2. *Verbal periphrasis*. Use of a periphrastic construction – HA-component INVARIANT + bleached verb – is typical for the east; use of the HA-origin form as a flexible verb root is typical of the west. Herzog (2000: 136ff.) gives several examples, e.g., EY periphrastic *bojdək-xoməc zajn* vs. WY *xo:məc batlən* 'search for and destroy leaven'; EY *potər vern* vs. WY *patərn* 'get rid of'; EY *sfirə cejln* vs. WY *o(:)mərn* 'ritual counting of days from Passover to Shavuoth; counting the Omer'; EY *malə zajn* vs. WY *maln* 'circumcise.' Again, these are tendencies, rather than absolute divisions; EY certainly contains numerous flexible verbs with HA-origin root, e.g., StY *ganvənən* 'steal,' *hargənən* 'kill,' *tajnən* 'claim.'
3. *Noun pluralization*. Some geo-patterning of plural allomorphs is not the result of structural entailment. For example, *noz* 'nose' has regional plural variants *nez*, *nezər*, *nozn* (U. Weinreich 1960). All three plural variants are plausible, based on analogy with plurals like *štot* – *štet* 'city, cities,' *got* – *getər* 'god-s,' *klog* – *klogn* 'lament-s.' However, sometimes structural entailment is a factor. For example, plurals with suffix *-im* (StY [əm]) frequently co-occur with stress shift, e.g., StY *tálməd* – *talmídəm* 'pupil-s,' *gánəf* – *ganóvəm* 'thief- thieves,' *lúləv* – *lulóvəm* 'palm branch-es' (Herzog 2000: 152ff.). In those varieties of Yiddish with fixed stress, we see the innovation of new (non-etymological) plurals. Thus, several WY locations have *lúləf* – *lúləfs*; those WY varieties which have retained the historical *-im* plural have maintained movable stress as well: *lúləf* – *lulóvim*/*lilúvim*; similarly, fixed stress in other locations (within WY, CY, and SEY) has resulted in reinterpretation of historical (HA-origin) *-im* as a Gmc-origin nasal suffix; e.g., *lúləv[ŋ]*/*líləv[ŋ]*, with regular nasal assimilation (Herzog 2000: 154–155).

[17] On the geography of cognate diminutive suffixes in German dialects, see König (1978: 157).

4. CY permits a clitic form of the masculine pronoun *ejm* 'him' (StY *im*): CY *mítn* 'with him'; cf. StY *mit ím.* This CY development is linked to the shift of phrasal stress to the preposition in CY, something not permitted (except contrastively) in other varieties of Yiddish. The CY development possibly arose on analogy with the general contraction of PREP + definite article *dem.*
5. Characteristic for much NEY speech is the generalized use of *hobn* 'have' as the sole AUX for past tense formation; thus, NEY *ix hob gəšribn* 'I wrote / have written,' *ix hob gəzesn* 'I sat / have sat,' StY *ix hob gəšribn, ix bin gəzesn.*[18] Other regional differences in AUX usage include subjunctive – StY *volt* vs. older regional varieties with *mext, het* (M. Weinreich 1980: 516; U. Weinreich 1964: 254). There are also partly regional differences in the subjunctive as to whether the main verb ends up as an infinitive or past participle.
6. Characteristic for CY and transitional TCPY is the 2P.PL pronoun *ec*$_{[\text{NOM}]}$ - *enk*$_{[\text{DAT/ACC}]}$, and possessive adjective *enkər-*. The verb suffix used with *ec* imperatives is *-c*; thus, CY *gajc* 'go!' *laxc* 'laugh!' CY *ec/enk* is cognate with Bavarian dialectal *ös/önk*, and goes back to an older Gmc dual form. Yiddish *ec/enk* was once found in areas beyond the modern CY territory, but has receded.
7. CY, wTCPY, and parts of SEY (U. Weinreich 1964: 257–258) express the 1P.PL verb by *inc* + verb root + *mə*; e.g., CY *inc zugmə* 'we say,' *inc gajmə* 'we go'; cf. StY *mir zogn, mir gejən.* This seems to be constructed on the basis, historically, of 1.P.PL oblique *inc* (StY *undz* 'us') used here as a type of subject pronoun. The suffix *mə* is the reduced form of *mir* 'we'; cf. widespread colloquial and dialectal German *gemma!* 'let's go!' < formal *gehen wir!* (Herzog 1965a: 147).
8. *Gender.* By far the single most impressive areally defined morphological difference in Yiddish concerns the gender system. Yiddish generally has a three-gender system for singular nouns (M/F/N). NEY innovated a neuterless system, often described as a "two-gender system" (M vs. F). However, the NEY situation is more complex, for a number of reasons. First, the neuter reappears under the sociolinguistic influence of StY. Second, masculine and feminine subdivide in NEY into subtypes (U. Weinreich 1961; Jacobs 1990c). Third, as shown in Wolf (1969), the gender and case systems interact in systematic ways across the entire EY territory. Nevertheless, at some basic level it may be said – sociolinguistic considerations aside – that NEY innovated a system where the historical neuter gender was lost.[19]

[18] Though these relevant varieties of NEY maintain AUX *zajn* for the verbs *zajn* 'to be' and *vern* 'to become' (Mark 1951).

[19] Many varieties of Yiddish seem to be heading toward the erosion of gender distinctions, something that has happened to varying degrees in several Germanic languages (such as English).

9. *Case*. Characteristic for NEY is the collapse of the ACC–DAT distinction in singular NPs. For object pronouns, the dative form has won out; thus, NEY *er zet mir* 'he sees me,' *er helft mir* 'he helps me'; cf. StY *er zet* $mix_{[ACC]}$; *er helft* $mir_{[DAT]}$. For full NP objects, the ACC form has won out; thus, NEY *er zet di altə froj* 'he sees the old woman,' *er helft di altə froj* 'he helps the old woman'; cf. StY *er zet di altə* $froj_{[ACC]}$, *er helft der altər* $froj_{[DAT]}$. In CY the apparent loss-in-progress of case marking is perhaps spurred by phonetic *r*-dropping; thus, definite article *der* [d ɛ] is phonetically similar to *di* ([di] ~ [də]), contributing to the confusion and collapse.

3.6 Lexicon

Certain words are typical for specific regions; thus, the word for 'shop, store' in EY is typically NEY *krom*, CY *gəvelb*, SEY *klejt* (U. Weinreich 1995 [1960]: *3). Lexical items are not generally as tightly bound (in terms of structural entailments) as are phonology and morphology. Nevertheless, some lexical items may be characteristic for a given geographic area. Conversely, an area may be characterized by the absence of a given lexical item otherwise found universally. Furthermore, a given lexical item may be geographically limited in that it signifies a cultural element present in some areas, but absent in others; e.g., typical of WY is the term *ho:ləkra:š* 'naming ceremony for baby girl,' a custom unknown in Eastern Ashkenaz, and, thus, a term not found in EY.

The present section provides some examples of lexical differences across the Yiddish speech territory. Owing to space limitations, we will not deal systematically with semasiological issues (variety in meaning for a given lexical item; e.g., *štub/štib* as 'room' or 'house'; see Herzog 2000, for detailed discussion). Rather, the focus here is on clear-cut onomasiological examples, e.g., WY *o:rn* vs. EY *dav(ə)nən* 'pray.' While the geo-distributions may be clear, the dialectological implications are less so. The examples *krom* ~ *gəvelb* ~ *klejt* illustrate the EY dialect divisions NEY, CY, SEY respectively, while another item, 'chair,' happens to split in EY into a two-way north-south division: *štul* (north) vs. *benkl* (south).

Birnbaum (1979a: 95–99) gives several examples of lexical items typical for given areas, though he does not provide discussion of the dialectological implications, something found in Herzog (2000: eps. 21ff.; see below).[20]

However, the paths to simplification, reorganization, or even loss of gender distinctions in the various Yiddish dialects are distinct, and, thus, to be evaluated separately, in terms of the constellation of developments in each variety.

20 We employ here the traditional dialect terminology rather than Birnbaum's, and do not employ his romanization system. Birnbaum distinguishes the following main dialect areas (traditional terminology follows in parenthesis): Western Yiddish (= WY), Eastern Yiddish

The following words are typical of WY (Birnbaum 1979a: 95–96): *badikn* 'examine the innards of a slaughtered animal,' *bavn* 'drink,' *dormən* 'sleep,' *etə* 'father,' *fra:lə* 'grandmother,' *frimsəliš* 'a certain dish,' *ha:fn* 'pot,' *harlə* 'grandfather,' *ho:ləkra:š* 'name-giving ceremony for girls,' *knoblix* 'garlic,' *ma:n* 'a certain wedding custom,' *mej* 'more,' *memə* 'mother,' *minix* 'pareve,' *nədunjə/nədinjə* 'dowry,' *o:rn* 'say the prayers of the liturgy,' *oumərn* 'count the days between Passover and Shavuoth,' *pilcl* 'servant girl,' *planxənən* 'weep,' *prajən* 'invite,' *ra:m/zɔ:n/šmant* 'cream,' *rozajnən* 'raisins,' *sargənəs* 'shrouds,' *sivlɔ:nəs* 'certain presents exchanged by bride and bridegroom during their engagement,' *ta:čər* 'white Sabbath loaf,' *tečn* 'blow the shofar,' *tfilə/pfilə* 'prayer book,' *tipn* 'pot,' *vešn* 'wash.' Notable for WY is the presence of many more Romance-component words than in EY – e.g., *o:rn*, *bavn*, *dormən*. Furthermore, WY often shows, vis-à-vis EY, a difference in the HA component; e.g., *nədunjə* (< Aramaic) vs. EY *nadn/nədan* (< Hebrew).

Words characteristic for the transitional area between WY and EY[21] are given in Birnbaum (1979a: 96): *cve:bn* 'raisins,' *cvo:rəx/cvu:rəx* 'cottage cheese,' *dejdə* 'grandfather,' *dajgəcn* 'talk about one's worries,' *ejləcn* 'smell of oil,' *libərər* 'grave digger,' *napəcn* 'doze,' *mem* 'mother,' *tet* 'father,' *betropəct* 'dejected,' *tukəcn* 'taste of tallow,' *xoxməcn* 'talk cleverly.'

Words common to both WY and the adjoining transitional area include (Birnbaum 1979a: 96): *barxəs/berxəs* 'challah / festive bread,' *bek* 'baker,' *gejgn* 'against,' *gri:vn* 'cracklings,' *krejn* 'horseradish,' *poršn* 'remove veins and sinews from the meat of slaughtered animals,' *šo:lət* (~ *ša:lət*) 'a certain Sabbath dish,' *trendl* 'teetotum.'

Words characteristically found only in EY include (Birnbaum 1979a: 98): *drejdl* 'teetotum,' *hejvn* 'yeast,' *nadn/nədan* 'dowry,' *ništ* 'not,' *xrejn* 'horseradish' (with initial [x]), and "all the words of Sl[avic] origin."[22]

On the other hand, there are words found in EY and the transitional area, but lacking in WY; Birnbaum (1979a: 98–99) gives, e.g., *badkənən* 'examine the innards of a slaughtered animal,' *cibələ* 'onion,' *dav(ə)nən* 'pray the prayers of the liturgy,' *knobl* 'garlic,' *parəvə* 'food that is neither meat nor dairy,' *sfirə cejln* 'count the days between Passover and Shavuoth,' *sidər* 'prayer book,' *taxrixim* 'shrouds,' *top* 'pot,' *trejbərn* 'remove veins and sinews from meat.'

(= EY) – which sub-divides into northern (= NEY) and southern (SY) dialects; the latter sub-divides into southwestern (= CY) and southeastern (SEY) varieties. Birnbaum labels the transitional area between western and eastern Yiddish "Central Yiddish" (= wTCPY; see below).

21 Herzog's (2000: 26) Southern Transition Area includes both eWY and the wTCPY areas. It is thus larger than Birnbaum's "CY" area and U. Weinreich's (1964) wTCPY area.

22 Actually, a few Slavic-origin words are found in WY, e.g., *nebiš* 'unfortunate.' However, the list is indeed quite limited in WY. On the other hand, the southern transitional area has a more prominent Slavic component, seen in numerous examples in Herzog (2000), e.g., *dejdə* 'grandfather,' *bobə* (and related forms) 'grandmother,' *boxtə* 'a kind of coffee cake.'

The scholarship on areal lexical differences has been advanced considerably in Herzog (2000: maps 63–148, and accompanying discussion). Much of his discussion and maps deal with semasiological and onomasiological differences. Herzog provides numerous examples not dealt with in Birnbaum (1979a), e.g., EY *alijə* vs. WY *micvə* 'call to the Torah' (map 112, p. 279); the terms for 'circumcision': EY *bris*, WY *brìsmílə*, and typical for Herzog's Central Transition Area (including wTcPY) is *sudə*. Furthermore, Herzog maps and discusses the geo-patterning of numerous cultural features. For example, the custom of eating *gefilte fish* is, with minor exceptions, known only in the East and in the Central Transition Area; in WY territory, *gefilte fish* is not eaten, except by immigrants from the East (Herzog 2000: 292–293). For summary of the main types of geo-patterning, see Herzog (2000: 19–38).

3.7 Syntax

A geolinguistic study of syntactic variation remains a desideratum in Yiddish linguistics. The following examples suggest regional variation concerning specific syntactic features. U. Weinreich (1964) notes the following in his discussion of TCPY.

(1) In wTcPY, indirect-object NPs require an accompanying PREP; thus, wTCPY *er helft fər zaj/za:n kind* 'he helps (for) his child'; cf. StY *er helft Ø zajn kind* (U. Weinreich 1964: 258).[23]

(2) Weinreich (1964: 259) notes: *niž vajnc* = not-cry-2P.PL (imperative) 'don't cry.' Several problems here collectively illustrate the mixed-dialect origins (WY and CY) of wTCPY. The realization $[aj]_{24}$ is a CY feature. The *-c* verbal suffix is common to CY and wTCPY. Lexically, *niž* is an easternism; cf. CY *ništ* vs. WY *niks*. However, syntactically, the word order is WY; more typical for EY imperatives is imperative + negative particle.

Examples of features identified with EY (as opposed to WY) are found in U. Weinreich's (1958c) comparison of Yiddish and Colonial German in contact with Slavic. In general, Weinreich notes that Yiddish syntax is much more receptive to Slavic influence than is Colonial German.

(3) Weinreich (1958c: 14–15) notes that constructions like *dos land dos farbotənə* 'the land the forbidden (one)' possibly arose in Yiddish due to Slavic influence. Furthermore, the EY distinction between short-form (base, uninflected) and long-form (inflected) adjectives in predicate position may be due to contact with Slavic; cf. StY short form: *er iz alt* 'he is old' vs. long form: *er iz an altər* 'he is an old (one)'; *zej zajnən alt* 'they are old' vs. *zej*

[23] The requirement of a PREP in wTCPY may reflect regional retention of an older, originally more widespread feature found in older WrLg A texts. This feature is also characteristic of Ashkenazic Jewish Dutch; see §7.8.

zajnən altə 'they are old (ones).' The short form resembles the situation in StG, the long form a Slavic model. EY exploits both patterns to make a semantic distinction.

(4) Weinreich (1958c: 15) also suggests that EY verb-second in subordinate clauses is "reminiscent of the state of things in Slavic."

(5) The construction in "negative purpose clauses" after verbs of fearing is "well established" in EY (U. Weinreich 1958c: 15), e.g., *ix hob mojrə er zol nit kumən*, [I-have-fear-he-should-not-come] 'I'm afraid that he might come' (i.e., 'lest he come'). Weinreich compares this to a similar model in Polish: *boję się żeby nie przyszedł*, ['(I)-fear-REFLEXIVE-that-not-came (3P.SG)].

(6) EY uses *vi* 'how, as' with adverbs in the superlative, e.g., Yiddish *vi cum gixstn*, [as-to-the-fast-superlative] 'as quickly as possible,' a structure similar to Polish *jak* 'how, as' in: *jak naj prędzej* [as-superlative-quick]; cf. StG *möglichst schnell* [possible-superlative-fast] (Weinreich 1958c: 15).

(7) EY expression of comparison with preposition *fun* 'from' is likewise attributed to Slavic influence (Weinreich 1958c: 15–16): EY *gresər fun mir* 'bigger from me'; cf. Polish *większy ode mnie*; StG uses conjunction 'than + NOM': *grösser als ich*.[24]

Mark (1951: 457) notes a regional difference concerning the present participle in gerund constructions, expressing 'while X-ing.' In NEY these may be used to refer either to the subject of a main clause or to the subject of an embedded clause; here, word order is crucial. In non-NEY varieties of EY the present participle may only refer to the subject of the main clause; otherwise, different strategies are required; thus:

NEY							
1.	*gejəndik*	hob	ix	im	gəzen		
	walking	have	I	him	seen		'I saw him (while I was) walking'
2.	ix	hob	im	gəzen	*gejəndik*		
	I	have	him	seen	walking		'I saw him (while he was) walking'
Non-NEY							
3.	*gejəndik*		hob	ix	im	gəzen	
	walking		have	I	him	seen	'I saw him (while I was) walking'
4a.	ix	hob	im	gəzen	*gejn*		
	I	have	him	seen	go (INF)		'I saw him (while he was) walking'
4b.	ix	hob	gəzen,	vi	er	*gejt*[25]	
	I	have	seen	how	he	goes	

[24] Here again it is important to look beyond StG to German dialects for relevant comparison.
[25] NEY employs this circumlocution as well.

3.8 Cultural features

Yiddish dialect research has long focused on the relationship between linguistic and cultural variation throughout Ashkenaz. This approach has been incorporated in the design of the *LCAAJ*, and has borne fruit from early on (e.g., Herzog 1964, 1965a; Schwartz 1969); and has recently been taken considerably further in Herzog (2000). As with linguistic features, the geo-patterning of cultural features reflects historical settlement, contact, and diffusion, and may also be seen in terms of implicational entailments. For example, the major isogloss bundle setting off wWY from all other Yiddish (eWY, and EY),[26] discussed in Wexler (1987, 1991), Herzog (2000: 12–13, 31), and elsewhere, correlates positively with a major cultural division, in synagogue ritual, "religious custom and folkways, liturgical music, traditional foods, Yiddish expressions, etc." (pp. 12, and 31, citing Lowenstein 1995). For example, the eating of *gefilte fish* was an Eastern Ashkenazic tradition "virtually unknown to the west of the Elbe"; "the cake-like שאַלעט *šá:lət* of the West contrasted with the thick soup or stew-like *šó:lət* of eastern Germany and Bohemia-Moravia" (Herzog 2000: 31).

The geo-patterning of cultural features thus reflects the interaction of historical settlement patterns, *stammbaum*-like cultural evolution, and contact. For example, the Slavic component is found in EY; its almost total absence in WY is not something to be "explained away." Similarly, the eating of *gefilte fish* arose in the east, leaving no need to account for its "loss" in the west. Furthermore, just as the linguistic split into the EY subdialects is a later, "EY-internal matter," the isopleth dividing those areas where *gefilte fish* is sweetened or not sweetened is a regional-internal matter (Herzog 2000: 290–291). Similar to the linguistic features, the patterning observable in the cultural features provides strong evidence for a fundamental and original cultural distinction between a westernmost type and an eastern type (which includes speakers of eWY as well). This division is repeatedly borne out linguistically and culturally in the more recent works of scholars with different research agendas (King 1979; Faber and King 1984; Katz 1987a: 54–58; Wexler 1987, 1991; Herzog 2000: 31–33).

Some remarks concerning the diffusion of cultural features are necessary. There can occur "apparent diffusion" of cultural features. For example, eastern traits in eWY are the result of historical shift: a (western) portion of eastern Ashkenazim has shifted linguistically to WY (or, at least, a variety transitional between EY and WY), but retained to a significant degree eastern Ashkenazic cultural patterns (Lowenstein 1995). Cultural traits may become extinct as a result of modernization, urbanization, the spread or non-spread of Hasidism, etc.

[26] Though see Herzog (2000: 31), note 14 on "Jewish" cultural features shared by wWY and EY, but not by eWY.

For example, Herzog (1964: 100, Figure 8) maps the "Forces of modernization from East and West" concerning the eating of tomatoes among Eastern European Jews. Once a forbidden practice, the eating of tomatoes represents an innovation in one respect, but the loss of an earlier feature (prohibition) in another. Rather than merely mapping "yes" vs. "no" areas, Herzog also maps areas where tomatoes are now eaten, but formerly (within informants' memory) were not; he thus provides a view of the direction of diffusion (extinction of the prohibition).

U. Weinreich (1956) provides an example of the inter-connectedness of language, culture, and society in his discussion of the loss of the historical rise-fall intonation contour among a subset of Yiddish speakers in the modern period. The loss of this linguistic feature correlates positively with the adoption of western tonal Jewish liturgical music. The link between the linguistic and the cultural lies in modernization/westernization tendencies. Modernizing Jews were making both their speech (intonation) and music more like the modern non-Jewish society around them. This correlated with other features of modernization in dress, occupational choice, etc.

There are sometimes implicational entailments in the geo-patterning of cultural features. The presence or absence of a given feature, such as the sweetening of *gefilte fish*, would at first not seem to be tightly woven into a system of entailments. On the other hand, cultural features are indeed frequently linked with social conditions, sociolinguistic groupings, and speech communities. Some cultural features correlate positively (or negatively) with dialect areas or subareas (e.g., NEY and non-sweetened *gefilte fish*; CY and the sweetened variety). Other cultural features, however, may show geographic patterns at variance with the known dialect groupings. Even where there is a link, it is sometimes difficult to state this implicationally. For example, Hasidism arose in the southeast, and was historically confined to the SY area (after initial inroads into the NEY area). With the exception of Lubavitch, Hasidism implies vowel $i_{31,51}$ (but not the other way around; there are non-Hasidic CY and SEY speakers). In a larger sense, however, we recognize that Hasidism arose within a specific speech-community subset of Eastern Ashkenaz. This speech community was also a cultural community. How does the eating of sweetened *gefilte fish* fit in with the above? Here, we can perhaps formulate entailment statements such as "Hasidism implies both $i_{31,51}$ and the eating of sweetened *gefilte fish*." However, this is merely formalism which here happens to make correct, rather than incorrect, predictions. In reality, a language/culture subset of Eastern Ashkenaz – where the population had $i_{31,51}$ and ate sweetened fish – was the environment within which a subset of the subset created Hasidism.

It is useful to take a balanced approach, in which the interaction of language and culture is evaluated both at the local level (for each item or feature), as well as in a global-Ashkenazic context. Thus, while the diffusion or non-diffusion of cake-like or stew-like Sabbath food (Herzog 2000: 31) does not necessarily imply restructuring of a whole cultural system in given locales, it nevertheless reflects channels of communication that are real – linguistically, culturally, socially, perhaps economically, religiously, politically, etc. On the other hand, some cultural features are more clearly understood in implicational terms. For example, M. Weinreich (1980: 5) links the custom of eating cabbage soup by WY-speaking Jews at Hoshanah Rabbah to a chance phonetic similarity between Ashkenazic Hebrew *kol mevaser* 'a voice proclaiming' (recited universally by Jews at Hoshanah Rabbah) and (coterritorial) German *Kohl mit Wasser* 'cabbage with water.' This custom does not arise among EY-speakers, where the phonic similarity does not obtain; cf. StY *krojt mit vasər* 'cabbage with water.'

Finally, a culture map of Ashkenaz must focus on the distribution of cultural features, rather than on the distinction of external vs. internal sources. Herzog (2000) provides numerous maps and discussion of customs which are virtually universal across Ashkenaz vs. those which are known in a limited area only, e.g., Map 102 (p. 257) on the preparation of *farfl* 'a kind of noodle' – is it prepared by cutting, grating, chopping, plucking or rubbing, pounding in a mortar, or is this item simply culturally absent in a given area?

3.9 The geolinguistic topography of Yiddish

As opposed to *stammbaum* branchings, the present section focuses precisely on continuity vs. discontinuity, and language contact. Between uniformity (if that indeed ever exists) and abrupt discontinuity where vastly different dialects, or even different languages, abut, we may often observe (in a wide range of languages) a gradualness of change across the dialect map. This gradualness in the geographic sweep across a language territory may be called the *linguistic topography*.[27] It is once again the question of *stammbaum* vs. contact, but viewed here from a different angle. The natural course of *stammbaum* branchings will create more and more diverging speech varieties. At the same time, varieties in contact tend to exert influences upon each other. A leveling and consolidation occurs. The apparent linguistic topography of a language results from the resolution of the dynamic tension between (*stammbaum*) discreteness and contact phenomena (see Levin 1987). Topography is a general characteristic of geolinguistic continua, be it the continuum of east-west within Yiddish, spelled out in depth in Herzog (2000), a Yiddish-German geolinguistic continuum (Kiefer 1990), or the continuum involving particular and/or typological features across different languages in a *Sprachbund* situation.

[27] This term is used here differently than as used (and coined) by Chambers (1994).

3.9.1 Gradualness

As concerns perceptual dialectology, certain features may be valued by speakers as especially important indicators of membership in dialect X or Y. However, as concerns topography, our interest is more in a quantifiable constellation of features and how the constellations vary spatially, i.e. the (types of) elements or units which, collectively, make up the whole, and which, over space, produce the topographical image of gradualness. Topographical variation results from different mixes of elements – in terms of both categorical features (inventory) and processes (structural descriptions of rules). Ultimately, our impression of topography results from variation in the interaction of the two. This may be illustrated by consideration of two features in Yiddish dialects: final devoicing, and vowel length (see King 1988).

In categorical terms, WY and CY have obstruent devoicing in word-final position, whereas NEY and SEY lack this feature. At the categorical level, this is a binary, yes-or-no feature, and the geographic divide is clear and absolute. At the other extreme, one may ignore phonological generalization, and focus on each individual lexical item in isolation. Indeed, anomalies occur, especially at the border areas between the devoicing and non-devoicing varieties, e.g., with *tišəbo[v ~f]* 'Ninth of Av' (Herzog 2000: 96–97). However, between the two extremes of categorical generalization and word-by-word non-generalization lies a middle ground. Thus, Herzog (p. 96, citing Stankiewicz 1991: 211) notes final devoicing as regular and general in WY, but with "considerable fluctuation in CY, where word-class has been proposed as a relevant factor . . . in most CY dialects." What emerges at the macro-level is a topography of final devoicing. This feature is most solid in the west, less so in the geographic middle, and essentially lacking in the easternmost dialects.

As concerns vowel length in Yiddish, the geographic sweep across the Yiddish speech territory shows more monophthongal length distinctions in the west, and progressively fewer as one moves eastward. In terms of categorical phonemes, (most) WY has five distinctions (at the vowel points *i-e-a-o-u*); CY three (at the peripheral points *i-a-u*).[28] The easternmost dialects, NEY and SEY, are typically said to lack vowel length, though both have shown (well into the twentieth century) residual length for at least one vowel position each: *u* vs. *uw* for varieties of NEY (U. Weinreich 1958a), and *i* vs. *i* for SEY (U. Weinreich 1958b). Upon closer examination, however, the generalizations break down. Courland Yiddish, a type of NEY, has largely maintained a rather full set of length distinctions. Still, in the most general terms, the west-to-east topography of vowel length largely holds: 5-3-0(~1)/0(~1).[29]

[28] The phonemicization of /u/ vs. /u:/ is not fully developed in most CY varieties.

[29] Weinreich (1963a: 339–340, note 9) also alludes to a topography of vowel length: "We thus see in Yiddish a remarkable, and so far quite mysterious extension of the pattern discovered in

A closer look reveals even more gradualness in the breakdown of vowel length in the transition from CY to SEY. We may distinguish between wCY and eCY (Viler 1924; Gutman 1926; Bin-Nun 1973; Jacobs 1996a). In categorical terms, both varieties possess phonemic long vowels /i:/, /a:/, /u:/, distinct from short /i/, /a/, /u/. The difference is that eCY "undoes" length in certain contexts, creating short allophones at the least, or, possibly, a morphophonemic alternation long ~ short. Thus, while both varieties have *ti:* '(I) do,' *du:* 'here,' eCY tends to undergo intervocalic gliding and resyllabification; cf. wCY *ti:ər*, eCY *ti-jər* 'doer' (on *r*-vocalization, see §4.1.11). Furthermore, in instances of CY breaking and drawl (§4.1.11), wCY tends to maintain the long vowel even after schwa epenthesis; thus, /bu:d/ 'bath' → wCY [bu:ɛt]. However, eCY intervocalic gliding, along with (re)syllabification, eliminates long monophthongs; thus, eCY [bu-wɛt]. With /a:/, gliding is harder to motivate phonetically. Phonologically, however, note *dra:* 'three,' but *in dra:ən/dra(:)-jən* 'by threes.' Other phonological processes contributing to the contextual elimination of long vowels include shortening of *u:* before (many) labial and velar consonants in CY (PSY **tu:k*, **zu:gn* > CY *tuk* 'day,' *zugn* 'say'), which is generalized further in eCY; thus, wCY *fli:k*, eCY *flik* 'fly' (the insect).

3.9.2 Transitional and mixed dialects

As concerns topography, all dialects (except perhaps for those the linguist designates as "endpoints") may be seen as transitional or mixed. Both transitional and mixed dialects result from contact. Herzog (2000: 25) writes: "Areas designated as 'transitional' generally display the results of prolonged linguistic and cultural contact along relatively fluid 'borders,' and may reflect patterns of settlement and movement of peoples. As such, they may also be viewed as channels of linguistic and cultural innovation." A distinction may be made between the terms *transitional* and *mixed* dialects. Herzog (p. 25) defines a transitional area as one "characterized by one or both of the following: (i) The co-occurrence of features otherwise exclusive to each of its neighbors; (ii) The occurrence of a feature that can reasonably be defined as linguistically (i.e., phonologically, semantically, etc.) transitional between the features that lie on either side." Let us distinguish between transitional and mixed dialects in terms of degree of linguistic integration. In a transitional dialect the features show a greater degree of linguistic integration – a type of internal "leveling." This might be manifested, for example, in an area of contact between a_{11} and o_{11} (in SEY), which arrives at a phonological compromise rule with specific phonetic environments for [a]

German." Weinreich is referring to Zwirner's (1959) study of the gradual reduction in the ratio of duration between long and short vowels in German dialects in the sweep from the north and west to the south and east.

and others for [o]; thus, Veynger (1929: 134) describes locations with a_{11}/_ŋk, but o_{11}/_ŋg. On the other hand, a mixed dialect is also transitional, but here the dialect "contradictions" have not been resolved in terms of structural generalizations. Veynger (p. 134) notes mixed dialects in SEY locations, with, e.g., *donk*$_{11}$ 'thanks' vs. *bank*$_{11}$ 'bank' in Alt-Murafe (Vinitser district); *long*$_{11}$ 'long' vs. *šlang*$_{11}$ 'snake' (Kamenetsk-Podolsk). Here no phonological generalization is possible concerning a_{11} vs. o_{11}. In transitional dialects the mixing is describable in terms of linguistic generalizations; in mixed dialects the mixing has not blended to the point of a generalizable rule. The distinction is one of relative degree along a spectrum, and should be used loosely.

Historical Yiddish dialect borders may shift over time, leaving behind linguistic residue which betrays the earlier dialect situation (M. Weinreich 1958a; Herzog 2000: 26). For example, there is within SEY territory a transitional area. This sub-area shows expected SEY *oj*$_{42,44}$ (as opposed to general NEY *ej*$_{42,44}$). However, this sub-area has *ex*$_{44}$ 'also'; *ex* is the result of a contextual loss of glide before *x*. In this "SEY" sub-area there occurred, historically, a lexical replacement of forms with *ej*$_{44}$ by forms with *oj*$_{44}$; the *ex*$_{44}$ 'also' (< earlier *ejx*) "escaped" this lexical replacement. On the basis of such evidence, there is reason to view this sub-area as having become SEY via the historical dialect shift (= reorientation) of earlier NEY speakers.

Sometimes a dialect border can shift via large-scale in-migration, without the rise of significant transitional or mixed dialects (Veynger 1929: 57; M. Weinreich 1980: 16–17). Here the two dialects may coexist territorially, but have less social interaction. For example, Bendin (Polish *Będzin*) was once part of the historical WY territory. Large-scale in-migration of CY (and other) speakers in the nineteenth century turned Bendin into CY territory. However, WY-isms (WY itself?) survived among the older, poorer Jewish population dwelling in the shacks along the river Przemsza; thus, the newer population had typical CY *štajn*$_{24}$ 'stone,' *kojfn*$_{44}$ 'buy,' while the "original" Jews had typical WY *šta:n*$_{24}$, *ka:fn*$_{44}$ (Lior 1959: 156).

Another example of dialect shift with residue of the earlier dialect is found in Transcarpathian Yiddish [TCPY]. U. Weinreich (1964) divides the area into sub-areas – most importantly, into a western and a non-western type. Weinreich's evidence includes numerous cultural and linguistic features. Weinreich (256–257) sees the wTCPY (Bohemia, Moravia, western Slovakia, western Hungary) speakers as historically eastern Ashkenazim who have shifted to WY. The residue of historical shift and accommodation found in wTCPY makes it, in essence, a transition dialect. The eastern part of Weinreich's area – the Unterland (Hungarian Lowlands, Transylvania, Carpathorussia) – is essentially a mixed dialect (arising via contact between the transitional dialect, wTCPY, and CY). Thus, Weinreich (253) discusses wTCPY in terms of phonology and "grammar," whereas concerning eTCPY he writes (258) "The overriding characteristic of

Yiddish in the Unterland is the profound and fundamentally haphazard mixture of WTCp and CY dialects." Weinreich provides numerous examples of non-generalizable, sporadic dialect mixture in eTCPY, as seen in the following examples from (various) informants: *dajdə* 'grandfather,' showing wTCPY initial /d/, but CY vocalism (*aj*$_{22}$; CY *zajdə*); *vajt*$_{34}$ *fin*$_{51}$ *doj*$_{12}$ 'far from here,' with WY/CY/WY vocalism, respectively; *tojb*$_{44}$ *er is nebəx ta:b*$_{44}$ 'he is deaf, poor thing,' where the speaker has produced CY *oj*$_{44}$ and WY *a:*$_{44}$ for the same word in the same utterance; *špa:bn* 'spit,' with WY /b/, but CY *a:*$_{34}$; the string *niž vajnc* 'don't cry,' with lexical CY-ism *niž*, CY vocalism in *aj*$_{24}$, but WY word order. Further, some speakers have free variation between /y/ ~ /i/; e.g., *cvyšn* ~ *cvišn* 'between,' *gətryknt* ~ *gətriknt* 'dried.' Weinreich (p. 260) sees the Unterland as a "WTCp stratum overrun by speakers of CY." This situation arose much more recently in eTCPY/Unterland than did the rise of wTCPY itself. That eTCPY/Unterland provides evidence of "profound . . . and haphazard mixture" of wTCPY and CY is not unusual; it has not had the time to digest and systematically integrate the conflicting dialect forms.

3.9.3 Major transition areas

The following discussion of the major transition areas is based *in extenso* on Herzog (2000: 25ff.)

1. *North-South transition area* [NST] between NEY and SEY. Herzog sees this as "a reflection of the border between Ukraine and Belorus." Herzog (2000:25) writes: "The vocalic system of the NST is usually perceived as SY, although its underlying features are demonstrably northeastern." Characteristic of the NST are *u*$_{12}$, *ej*$_{22,24,42,44}$. Here we likely have an instance of historical dialect shift (NEY > SEY).
2. *North-South Border* [NSB] consists of North-Central Yiddish [NCY] + the NST. NCY is itself the transition dialect area identified in Herzog (1965a). It is the result of contact and/or dialect shift between CY and NEY. NCY is characterized by the SY fronting/unrounding of original *u(:)* vowels, and the NEY absence of vowel length; thus: *i*$_{31,32,51,52}$. The NSB is thus largely the border between NEY and SY (CY and SEY).[30]
3. *Northern Transition Area* [NTA] and Southern Transition Area [STA] arose via shifts in the historical east-west borders (Herzog, 2000: 26). The STA consists of areas within eWY and the WTCP area. Herzog calls the STA "an

[30] Herzog (2000: 26) also suggests the possibility of viewing all of SEY as a transition area, based on the co-occurrence of *u*$_{12}$ (characteristic of CY, but not of NEY) and *ej*$_{22,24}$ (found in NEY, but not in CY). I disagree with Herzog. That CY developed *aj*$_{22,24}$, leaving SEY with a situation similar to NEY (*ej*$_{22,24}$), is not evidence of a link between NEY and SEY. Birnbaum (1915: 16) noted this problem, and tried to resolve it by positing SEY [æj] vs. NEY [ej], thus linking SEY with CY phonetically.

area of overlap in the E-W border ... defined by the cooccurrence of monophthongal and diphthongal varieties of E4/O4 as well as *ü(:)* (<U1, U2)" (the latter feature being "both geographically and linguistically transitional between WY and CY"). The STA also shows some lexical items lacking both in the west and the east (pp. 236–243, maps 93–96), e.g., *maločə* 'junior member of burial society,' *napəcn* 'to nap.' The STA area is located roughly in Czechoslovakia, Austria, Hungary, and parts of Western Galicia. The NTA runs "East and West along the Polish-East Prussian border, at times incorporating Courland in the Northeast, and crossing westward into WY territory" (pp. 26–27). Characteristic for the NTA is the realization of initial *s* as [c] in HA-origin words (in "northwest Poland and neighboring WY") – e.g., StY *sejxl* 'brains,' *sukə* 'tabernacle' are realized in the NTA with initial [c].

4. *Central Transition Area* [CTA] is discussed by Herzog (2000: 27): "as an area which joins the STA and the NTA ... or as an area delimited by the boundaries of W[estern]m[ost]Y[iddish] and E[astern]m[ost]Y[iddish] ... By definition, the CTA is also the area of overlap created by the eastward extension of definably western features ... and the westward extension of definably eastern features."

3.9.4 External factors in Yiddish dialect topography

External factors play a role in shaping Yiddish dialect topography. Some external factors are non-linguistic: political borders, when and where Jews were permitted to settle, etc. External linguistic factors result from language contact between Yiddish and its coterritorial languages, and are dealt with under the rubric "bilingual dialectology." This section, for reasons of space limitations, focuses on linguistic factors; the fuller picture requires consideration of cultural, historical, and other data. A preliminary word of caution is necessary about the over-eagerness of some scholars to appeal to external causation as sufficient for explanation. The fact that two languages are coterritorial in one period does not imply that such was the case in earlier times. Additionally, the fact that two coterritorial languages share a linguistic feature does not mean that one language necessarily obtained it from the other. The nature, duration, and intensity of contact must be delineated, and we must distinguish between contact-induced change which is structure-affecting vs. non-structure-affecting. In order to understand the ways in which the topography of Yiddish is affected by language contact, we must have a picture of language typology played out areally; of structural issues in Yiddish (varieties); of the linguistic features of the coterritorial languages; and of communication networks – Jewish and general speech, for time and place (U. Weinreich 1952, 1963a; Herzog *et al.* 1992: 1–2).

U. Weinreich (1963a: 336) describes Yiddish bilingual dialectology as "the detailed comparison of isoglosses in Yiddish and in the languages coterritorial with Yiddish."[31] Yiddish in Ashkenaz existed in a situation of virtually universal coterritoriality with other languages. However, the nature and role of language contact vis-à-vis Yiddish has often been misunderstood, overstated, or wrongly stated. All too often in the earlier scholarship (prior to U. Weinreich), scholars (as well as popular writers) were quick to "explain" almost all features in Yiddish in terms of other languages. The task is a much more nuanced one, however, and involves a fuller picture of internal (structural) influences, external contact influences, and the interaction of the two. U. Weinreich focuses on four linguistic features in Yiddish and the coterritorial languages, and notes (336) that there are "significant congruences, but also major discrepancies." The geographic discrepancies between features in Yiddish and the coterritorial languages constitute the "four riddles" which Weinreich attempts to solve.[32] The four features are: (1) presence or absence of phonemic vowel length; (2) presence of word-final voiced obstruents vs. a final devoicing rule; (3) loss of phonemic /h/. (4) confusion of hissing and hushing sibilants. The basic problems with each are as follows.

1. *Vowel length*. CY, TCPY (and WY, which is not part of Weinreich's discussion) are generally described as possessing vowel length, NEY and SEY as lacking this feature (though residue of length is found in both NEY and SEY). The "riddle" is that CY has vowel length while its predominant coterritorial language, Polish, does not. On the other hand, a significant portion of the territory of lengthless NEY is coterritorial with the Baltic languages Lithuanian and Latvian, which have vowel length.
2. *Word-final obstruent devoicing*. Here, too, EY largely disagrees with the coterritorial languages, though CY and Polish share this feature (U. Weinreich 1963a: 341–342).
3. *Loss of phonemic /h/*. U. Weinreich (1963a: 344–348) shows that simplistic references to /h/-loss as deriving from "Slavic" are insufficient. He offers a nuanced discussion of possible scenarios of influences from contact with Slavic, involving confusion in the Yiddish (mis)interpretation of Ukrainian (voiced) *h* as *Ø*, and Belorussian γ as Yiddish *h*.
4. *Confusion of hushing and hissing sibilants*. Weinreich calls this phenomenon in Yiddish, referred to as *sabesdiker losn*, the "most paradoxical" of the four riddles. *Sabesdiker losn* is found in large parts of NEY territory, where the coterritorial Slavic (Belorussian) and Baltic languages for the most part have maintained hushing-hissing distinctions. Weinreich (1963a: 347–348) calls the Yiddish sibilant confusion "structurally analogous" to regional Polish *mazurzenie*, but notes that the Yiddish coterritorial with Polish *mazurzenie* does not have sibilant confusion.

31 For a list and map of coterritorial languages, see Sunshine *et al*. (1995: 83–84).
32 See also King (1988); Louden (2000).

Weinreich's (1963a: 349ff.) overarching approach in dealing with the four riddles is to look to history – known Jewish settlement history, as well as known facts about the external ("coterritorial") languages. He offers a timeline of migrations and events, and fits each of the riddles into this historical context. By way of illustration consider the riddle concerning vowel length. Vowel length is posited for PY and for PEY; Weinreich sees it as exported from Poland in the migrations further east, but subsequently lost there (most of current NEY and SEY territory) in contact with East Slavic.[33] Polish lost vowel length *c.* "turn of the 15th to the 16th century" (p. 342), but coterritorial CY did not. Weinreich claims that vowel length in CY was reinforced by continued migration of Yiddish speakers from Germany, Bohemia, and Moravia.

U. Weinreich (1963a: 357) combines linguistic facts and settlement history to expose the riddles as "artificial riddles"; the geographical disparities arise only within an ahistorical approach. Further, Weinreich notes the importance of taking into account sociolinguistic history. He (351) states that Jewish "coterritoriality" in multilingual areas was often in terms of the language of the towns and cities, not of the rural language(s).

The topography of Yiddish thus may be affected by external factors, taking into account historical context, extralinguistic and sociolinguistic facts. However, as a rule of thumb, we reject the exocentric approach which looks first to external facts to "explain" the presence of features in Yiddish. Rather, internal (Yiddish) factors should be checked first, with appeal to the external only secondarily. Consider, for example, the presence of West-Slavic-origin items in easternmost Yiddish (e.g., *demb* 'oak'). This fact does not require us to posit the presence of West Slavic speech in the easternmost area. Rather, we presume that the item entered Yiddish in the West Slavic area, and was carried further eastward by Yiddish speakers. Conversely, there are East Slavicisms which have diffused westward, beyond the East-West Slavic boundary – in Yiddish, but not in Slavic. Yiddish linguistic geography is not necessarily coterminous with the linguistic geography of the coterritorial languages (see Mark 1951: 447). The differences result from the distinct settlement histories, the nature and degree of communication networks, or paths of diffusion.

We must specify the ways in which contact-induced features in Yiddish function the same or differently in the lender-language and in Yiddish. This helps us

[33] Weinreich (1963a: 350) notes that Lithuanian and Latvian have vowel length, but that this did not reinforce its maintenance in NEY. He points to the "remarkable paucity" there of loanwords from Baltic languages as compared to Slavic-origin words. This leaves a problem with CourlY, however. Weinreich sees vowel length in CourlY as arising secondarily via contact with (Baltic) German. However, Jacobs (1994b) sees this as a retained feature, rather than a contact feature. The implications of this latter view comport well with descriptions of residual length well into the twentieth century for several sub-areas of the NEY territory, and suggest that length was lost more recently in general NEY than previously thought.

toward greater precision in determining internal vs. external causation. For example, it is demonstrably inadequate to attribute the loss of the neuter gender in NEY solely to contact with Baltic languages (U. Weinreich 1961; Herzog 1965a; Wolf 1969; Jacobs 1990c). On the other hand, it may be that NEY intermediate gender arose internally (within NEY) via a syncretism in adjectiveless NPs, which in turn was borrowed from or modeled after an external phenomenon – a syncretism in Slavic (adjectiveless Polish locative NPs). Further, the gender confusion that sometimes arose in Belorussian between feminine and neuter nouns due to a phonological merger of word-final *-o,-a* > *-a* may indeed have contributed to the loss of the neuter in NEY. Thus, it may be that the "simple" explanation – attributing loss of neuter gender in NEY to its absence in Lithuanian and Latvian – is wrong or overly sweeping in its formulation, while at the same time more remote external factors may indeed have played a role.

Once a contact-induced element is part of Yiddish it may or may not diffuse within the grammar of Yiddish, and may or may not diffuse geographically. However, the point is that these are first and foremost now Yiddish-internal issues. Consider two points of illustration.

First, CY has a rule of contextual palatalization of /l/ after *k*, *g* (§4.4.5). The presence of palatalized phonemes /l'/ and /n'/ in EY is attributed to contact with Slavic (Bratkowsky 1974: 95ff.); e.g., StY *l'ul'kə* 'pipe,' *špil'kə* 'pin' reflect a carry-over of Slavic non-dark *l* into Yiddish. However, the CY contextual *l*-palatalization after *k*, *g* is clearly a CY (and partly SEY) phenomenon, which applies even in "violation" of the type of *l* found in the Slavic source. Thus, as expected, general EY has a palatalized *l'* in StY/CY *l'al'kə* 'doll,' and *kl'amkə* 'doorknob' (cf. Polish *lalka*, *klamka*). However, in instances where the Polish source has dark/labialized *ł* after *k* or *g*, StY has non-palatalized *l*, whereas in CY the palatalization rule applies; thus, StY *sklad* 'warehouse,' CY [skl'at]; cf. Polish *skład* ([skwat]). Although CY – like all EY – owes the presence of [l'] to contact with Slavic, how CY defines its occurrence has become an internal matter of CY phonology. It is integrated into the grammar of CY.

Second, consider geographical variation in accentual variants in Slavic-origin words in EY. An interesting observation may be made, based on Green's (1969) discussion of regional Yiddish differences in stress of trisyllabic Slavic loans of the type *kapótə* 'coat,' *podlógə* 'floor.' Some regional tendencies are observable; thus, there is a tendency to initial stress in CY, e.g., *kápətə*, *pódləkə*. However, there are no hard-and-fast phonological generalizations to be made about stress placement in the trisyllabic Slavic loans; thus, EY dialectal variants *póžemkəs* ~ *požómkəs* 'wild strawberries.' Some of the stress variants may be traced to (diachronic and synchronic) differences in the Slavic source dialects (Polish, Belorussian, Ukrainian), or to the lexical diffusion of individual Slavic loanwords from one variety of Yiddish into other Yiddish geographic areas. Phonologically, both stress patterns, *wsw* and *sww*, may be grouped into acceptable foot structures. However, when Slavic (or Baltic) loans contain four syllables, and, thus, cannot be accommodated in a single foot, the basic *sw* Yiddish foot reasserts itself and here we see greater phonological generalization in Yiddish; cf. Baltic loans in NEY *šìmtəkójə* 'centipede,' *šàltənósəs* 'blintzes' < Lithuanian *šimtakõjis, šaltanõšiai* (Jacobs 2001a).[34] Thus, stress differences in polysyllabic Slavic loans in Yiddish often show sociolinguistic or dialectological patterning for trisyllabic words, whereas the patterning is phonologically more predictable in quadrisyllabic words.

The topographic picture should be seen in the context of the overall "soup" in which internal and external factors interact – which languages are found in coterritoriality with a given variety of Yiddish (keeping in mind that "coterritoriality" may be sociolinguistically defined). Thus, some differences between wTCPY and eTCPY are Yiddish-internal, while others may owe to the coterritorial presence of only German in one area vs. the presence of both German and Hungarian in another (U. Weinreich 1964: 247). The topography of the NEY area also reflects the coterritorial "soup" – whether contact was with Baltic languages only, with Baltic and Slavic, or with Slavic only (Jacobs 2001a). Mark (1951: 450) observes that there is much more Slavic influence in the Yiddish of Belorussia (coterritorial with Slavic only) than in the Yiddish of Lithuania, where Yiddish was in contact with a Baltic language (Lithuanian), and with Slavic (mostly Polish). Mark's (1951: 442) main subdivision of NEY is into general or plain NEY (Stam-Litvish [SL]) and Zameter Yiddish [ZY].[35] He gives several examples of a Slavic-origin word in SL corresponding to a German-origin word in ZY; e.g., SL *pastəx* 'shepherd,' *pašə* 'pasture,' *ščur* 'rat,' *pozetskəs* ~ *porzetskəs* (~ *vajmpərləx*) 'currants' vs. ZY *šefər, vajd, rats, vajmpərləx* (only). On the other hand, Mark (439ff.) notes the higher frequency of Lithuanian loans in ZY than in general NEY/SL. In CourlY, *sabesdiker losn* – a characteristic of much of the NEY area – continued to be found in words of non-Germanic origin; e.g., *cepən* 'touch, bother,' *blondzən* 'stray, ramble (having lost one's way),' but the hushing-hissing distinction was restored in words where coterritorial Baltic German provided clear models, e.g., CourlY *vasər* 'water,' *kusn* 'to kiss'; cf. StY *vasər, kušn*, StG *Wasser, küssen* (Jacobs 1994b).

Finally, whatever role external factors (the coterritorial languages) may play, the role of internal Yiddish communication networks must be kept foremost in mind. For example, ZY is seen by Mark (1951: 439ff.) as using a higher frequency of HAisms than does general NEY, and the latter, in turn, higher than in other varieties of EY (= CY, SEY). Thus, the distinctness of ZY from general NEY is not just the result of external contact (see the Slavic- vs. German-origin

[34] Occasional *swww* patterns are found; cf. regional *pílənacəs* 'wild strawberries' (Green 1969: 233, map 4).

[35] Mark also distinguishes a geographically and linguistically intermediate area – Suvalker Yiddish.

examples, above). Rather, it is the result of complex communication networks, and reflects the realities of the internal–external "soup." Similarly, the presence of Slavic-origin words in eWY (such as *de:də/dejdə* 'grandfather') need not be traced to the earlier presence of Slavic speech in the region; rather, it may reflect Jewish historical migration, or the linguistic diffusion of such lexical items within Yiddish via Jewish-internal communication networks.

3.10 Supraregional varieties

This section deals briefly with the role of supraregional spoken varieties which have arisen in the nineteenth and twentieth centuries, and which have served as models and as sources contributing to the extinction of dialect features (see Katz 1983: 1032–1035). Such supraregional tendencies have to be distinguished from local(izable) contact phenomena such as dialect leveling, transitional and mixed dialects. It is useful to use here a framework where we distinguish among local dialect, regional dialect, and standard.[36] To the extent that the same speaker commands and employs multiple varieties, we are dealing with the overlap of dialectology and sociolinguistics.

There is ample evidence of influences from broader regional dialect or StY on local dialect. U. Weinreich (1952) discusses the receding of *sabəsdikər losn* among NEY speakers under the influence of emerging modern StY. Similarly, sporadic hypercorrection by CY speakers resulted in the appearance of short /u/ in, e.g., *šnups* (Sosnovce; Jacobs 1990a: 77), *lutvak* (cf. StY *šnips* 'neck-tie,' *litvak* 'Lithuanian Jew,' both with historical $*i_{31}$). This was based on speakers' knowledge (through contact) of an equation: NEY (or StY) *u* = "our" *i(:)*; e.g., CY *git* 'good,' *šikí:rəm* 'drunks,' *məšígə* 'crazy' "equals" NEY/StY *gut*, *šikúrim*, *məšúgə* (in these words, the historical vowels are $*u_{51}$, $*u{:}_{52}$). Whether this hypercorrection on the part of CY speakers was based on an NEY or an StY model is hard to say here, since the StY vowel system is, with minor modification, essentially identical with that of one NEY variety. CourlY of the early twentieth century provides examples of simultaneous change both toward broader NEY and toward StY (Jacobs 1994b). It is often difficult to determine which is which. Sometimes the situation is best described in terms of sociolinguistically-defined registers.[37]

36 See Wiesinger (1989: 443–444) for German in Austria. He uses a four-level model: primary dialect, regional dialect, colloquial speech, and standard. Wodak-Leodolter and Dressler (1978), in their discussion of Viennese urban German, use a ten-level continuum between deep dialect and Austrian Standard German.

37 The following anecdotal examples serve as illustration. In a one-day public workshop I gave on the structure of Yiddish (Columbus, Ohio, 1989), a participant born and raised in Lancaster, Ohio (*c.* 1915), produced *køyfn* 'to buy.' She then spontaneously added: "I know it's really *kejfn*, but I guess I'm supposed to say *kojfn*" (cf. NEY *kejfn*, StY *kojfn*). Her realizations of this word with

The Yiddophone masses of the nineteenth and twentieth centuries were clearly moving toward the creation of a spoken (and written) standard language. There were, however, differing views on exactly which form the spoken standard should take. The form most widely accepted today is that promulgated by the YIVO Institute, founded in Vilnius in 1925. This push toward a spoken StY was accompanied and followed by the appearance of many publications dealing with codification of StY orthography, grammar, a thesaurus (in 1950), etc. (§7.5.1). Like most standard languages, modern StY represents a number of compromises in terms of dialect features. The phonemic inventory of the vowel system of modern StY is identical to Vilna-region systems:

StY monophthongs			StY diphthongs		
$i_{31,32}$		$u_{51,52}$			
$e_{21,25}$		$o_{12,41}$	$ej_{22,24}$		$oj_{42,44,54}$
	a_{11}			aj_{34}	

The two "concessions" (from the perspective of NEY) are the restoration of a distinction between PEY *$ej_{22,24}$ and PEY *$ou_{42,44}$. In general NEY (excluding Courland and Suvalk), they have merged as $ej_{22,24,42,44}$; StY has $ej_{22,24}$ vs. $oj_{42,44}$. Furthermore, StY merges vowels 42,44 with vowel 54 (a merger which does not occur in NEY); thus, StY $oj_{42,44,54}$: $brojt_{42}$ 'bread,' $kojfn_{44}$ 'buy,' $hojz_{54}$ 'house.'[38] Another NEY phonological feature which may occur (optionally) in StY is anticipatory voicing assimilation of obstruents (§4.4.3).

Katz (1983: 1035) notes the popular perception that StY is a compromise between "southern grammar and northern pronunciation." For example, StY has three genders (masculine, feminine, neuter) – similar to CY and SEY, as opposed to neuterless NEY. On the other hand, there are "grammatical" features found in StY which trace to NEY, e.g., variant neuter vs. masculine gender of *bux* 'book': *dos bux* [N] 'the book,' but *der grojsər vertərbux* [M] *fun der jidišər šprax* 'great dictionary of the Yiddish language' (the official name of the StY dictionary project). Further research on the grammatical lineage of StY needs to look beyond phonology to morphology and syntax. Another desideratum is a systematic examination of regional variation in the emerging spoken standard.

Arguments against a northern pronunciation base for the spoken standard language were based largely on demographics. Thus, Birnbaum questions the need for a spoken standard pronunciation (Birnbaum 1979a: 100–101; see also Gininger 1949: 208–211; Katz 1983: 1035), and, if one is in fact to be chosen, it

historical vowel 44 reflect, respectively, CourlY (possibly, however, Suvalker Yiddish), broader NEY, and StY. Similarly, on another occasion, in personal contact with two other American-born NEY speakers (born 1915 and 1919, respectively) I heard spontaneous examples such as *evər – ejər – ojər* 'ear,' reflecting "deeper" NEY dialect, modified NEY dialect, and StY, respectively.

38 On the differential diffusion of StY oj_{54} in NEY and SEY, respectively, see Jacobs (1994a).

should be southern based, since the overwhelming majority of Yiddish speakers of the interwar period were SY speakers. Finally, Prilutski (1927) argued for a supraregional speech model based on Yiddish theatre pronunciation (see § 7.5). Theatre Yiddish is largely SEY-based, reflecting the place of origin of modern Yiddish theatre in the nineteenth century

4 Phonology

4.1 Vowels

4.1.1 Stressed vowels

The stressed vowel systems of Standard Yiddish and one generalized example from each of the major Yiddish dialects are given in Table 4.1.

The StY stressed vowel system includes eight phonemes: monophthongs *a-e-i-o-u* and diphthongs *ej*, *aj*, *oj*. The distinctiveness of the monophthongs is demonstrated by the examples *nas* 'wet,' *nes* 'miracle,' *nis* '(I) sneeze,' or 'nuts,' *nos* 'sneeze (noun),' *nus* 'nut'; the diphthongs by *vejn* '(I) cry,' *vajn* 'wine,' *vojn* '(I) reside.' Examples for each StY vowel follow:

/a/ *aš* 'ash,' *alt* 'old,' *hant* 'hand; arm,' *ša* 'quiet!' *ganəf* 'thief,' *talməd* 'pupil,' *kašərn* 'prepare (utensils) for Passover,' *mamə* 'mother'

/e/ *es* 'eat!' *epl* 'apple-s,' *hent* 'hands; arms,' *red* '(I) speak,' *betn* 'beds; to request,' *špet* 'late,' *redl* 'small wheel,' *fercn* 'fourteen'

/i/ *ibər* 'over,' *hint* 'dogs,' *šitn* 'pour,' *šisn* 'shoot,' *bin* 'am; bee,' *gvir* 'rich man,' *məlicə* 'florid language,' *zin* 'sons; sense,' *mi* 'effort'

/o/ *odər* 'or,' *bod* 'bath,' *lox* 'hole,' *do* 'here'

/u/ *untər* 'under,' *məšuməd* 'apostate,' *zun* 'son; sun,' *ku* 'cow'

/ej/ *ej* 'egg,' *ejbik* 'eternal,' *rejd* 'discourse,' *gej* 'go!' *šnej* 'snow,' *grejs* 'size,' *sejfər* 'holy book,' *vejn* '(I) cry'

/aj/ *ajx* 'you (PL.OBL),' *ajzn* 'iron,' *majz* 'mice,' *axrajəs* 'responsibility,' *xajəm* 'male anthroponym,' *draj* 'three,' *vajn* 'wine'

/oj/ *ojx* 'also,' *ojšər* 'happiness,' *bojx* 'belly,' *goj* 'non-Jew,' *boj* '(I) build,' *loj* (*mit an aləf*)! 'emphatically not!' *šojmər* 'guard,' *vojn* '(I) reside'

The StY vowel system contains a number of simplifications, as compared with PY and the modern Yiddish dialects.[1] StY shows mergers at every point in

[1] For detailed phonemic analysis of vowel systems in Yiddish dialects, see U. Weinreich (1991: 16ff.).

Table 4.1. *Stressed vowel systems: StY and major dialects (one generalized variant each)*

Standard Yiddish	Western Yiddish	Central Yiddish	Southeastern Yiddish	Northeastern Yiddish
i u	i – i: u – u:	i – i: u – u:	i – ɨ u	i u
e o	e – e: o – o:	e – – o – –	e o	e o
a	a – a:	a – a:	a	a
ej oj	ej ou (~ au)	ej oj, ou	ej oj	ej oj
aj	aj	aj	aj	aj

the PY system except **aj*.[2] The most significant development in the StY system is the loss of historical distinctive vowel length, either through shortening or through diphthongization. StY has the following mergers of PY vowels:

Proto-Yiddish			*Standard Yiddish*	
*i:	*zi:n	'sons'	/i/	zin
*i	*zin	'sense'	/i/	zin
*u:	*zu:n	'son'	/u/	zun
*u	*zun	'sun'	/u/	zun
*e:	*se:fər	'holy book'	/ej/	sejfər
*ei:	*fleiš	'meat'	/ej/	flejš
*o:	*gro:s	'big'	/oj/	grojs
*ou	*koufn	'buy'	/oj/	kojfn
*au	*hauz	'house'	/oj/	hojz
*ɔ:	*bɔ:d	'bath'	/o/	bod
*o	*hot	'has'	/o/	hot
*æ:	*bæ:tn	'request'	/e/	betn
*e	*betn	'beds'	/e/	betn

Based on one feature – retention or loss of distinctive length – a number of other characteristics fall into line, in terms of phoneme inventories and higher-order phonological processes. For example, the long /a:/ position – either lost very early on, or never present, in PY – generally has been filled in length-preserving dialects, though via different historical sources (< **ei* and **ou* in

[2] While the vowel phoneme inventory of StY is identical to at least one variety of NEY, StY has "undone" the merger of PY **e:/*ei* with PY **o:/*ou* found in the relevant NEY varieties.

WY; < **ai* in PSY; Baltic loans in CourlY). Herzog *et al.* (1992: 14ff.) view this as "the pivotal point from which the major differentiation of the Yiddish dialects [would] proceed."

4.1.2 *Vowel length*

The dialect topography of vowel length (§3.9.1) gives a fair picture of the contours of length across the Yiddish speech territory. However, the phonological description of length for any given variety is a complex task. For example, WY is described as possessing a full, five-point set of monophthongal length distinctions. In some WY varieties, however, the short counterpart of /u:/ is front-rounded /ü/. CY contrasts length at the three peripheral positions /i(:)/, /a(:)/, /u(:)/, while short mid-vowels /e/, /o/ contrast with diphthongs *ej*, *ou* (/o:/?). Furthermore, CY /u/ is a recent development, and its phonemic status less established. The loss of length is generally seen as a primary feature of general NEY, yet residual length is found for vowel 54 (as [uw]) in many NEY "lengthless" varieties well into the twentieth century (U. Weinreich 1958a). SEY is also described as lacking distinctive length, but residue of length is found in the distinction between /ɨ/$_{31,51}$ and /i/$_{32,52,(25)}$. Sometimes an appeal is made here to a tense vs. lax distinction, but at an excessive cost to phonological description when a feature is needed for one vowel contrast only.

4.1.3 *Diphthongs and glides*

This section deals with the phonological analysis of diphthongs in Yiddish, either as units, or as sequences of segments. A related question concerns the analysis of glides as vowel or consonant. In U. Weinreich (1991), diphthongs are treated as sequences; these are not included in the inventory of phonemes for the various Yiddish dialects. Viler (1924) views the diphthongal glide as consonantal, limiting the syllable nucleus to one vowel.[3] However, in the synchronic phonology of modern Yiddish dialects, there are arguments for both analyses of the glide.

Phonetically, there are two types of diphthongs in Yiddish: rising and falling. All varieties of Yiddish contain underlying diphthongs consisting of vowel + glide – usually *j* or *w*, in some dialects *y* as well. Additionally, falling diphthongs are found regionally, e.g., CY *i(:)ə*, *u(:)ə*. However, these are not underlying, but, rather, are derived via operation of the processes of *breaking* and *drawl*. A type of possible underlying falling diphthong is found in wTCPY: *xuəsn* 'bridegroom,' *xaruətə* 'regret,' *uətəmən* 'breathe' (U. Weinreich 1992: 25). While all Yiddish dialects possess diphthongs, not all dialects have a round glide.

[3] This is contradicted by his subsequent discussion of syllabification rules; see below.

There is a correlation in Yiddish dialects between the presence of distinctive vowel length and the presence of a round glide. Thus, generalized WY has *ou* and/or *au*, CY has *ou*, whereas modern NEY and SEY generally lack diphthongs with a round glide. Significantly, the conservative Courland subregion of NEY, where vowel length was largely maintained, has round glides *u* ([w]) and *y*. U. Weinreich (p. 19) notes the presence of the *u* glide in all dialects of Yiddish – including the lengthless varieties – "although it is very rare and restricted to onomatopoetic words or fairly recent neologisms in many varieties of Yiddish." It would seem that these "many varieties" are precisely those lacking distinctive vowel length. Weinreich's examples here include [pawzə] 'pause,' [mjawkən] 'meow.'

4.1.4 Glides in NEY

Lack of vowel length is often seen as a defining characteristic of modern NEY (Herzog *et al.* 1992: 14). However, residue of length is found in parts of the NEY "heartland," as well as in the more conservative subregions of Courland and Samogitia. Interestingly, these length-preserving subregions also differ from general NEY in their treatment of historical glides. Consider the following three related phenomena in general NEY: glide hardening, glide substitution, and glide insertion (Jacobs 1994a).

In generalized NEY glide hardening [GH], a round glide *w* (regionally, also *y*) becomes hardened to *v* intervocalically; thus, PEY **zauər* > NEY *zavər* 'sour.' In word-final position the *w* glide generally deletes, e.g., PEY **blou* > NEY *blo* 'blue.' When a vowel-initial inflectional suffix follows, the round glide is not elided, and surfaces as hardened *v*, thus: *blovər*.[4] The simple elimination of the *w* glide in word-final position appears similar to the general loss of monophthongal length in NEY (e.g., PY **ku:* > NEY *ku* 'cow'). In intervocalic position, however, NEY GH creates a consonantal hiatus breaker.

In NEY glide substitution [GS], the unround glide *j* is substituted for the round glides *w/y* (or their hardened reflex *v*). For the most part, GS is found before a consonant; thus: PEY **haut* > NEY *hojt* 'skin.'[5] Substitution of the *j* glide avoids unacceptable phonemic vocalic length ([au]), while maintaining a surface phonetic diphthong. If GH occurred preconsonantally, it would yield ***havt* ([haft]), i.e., a sequence of VCC, rather than a diphthong. In fact, some NEY speakers did associate the sequence *V[v]C* with diphthong + consonant, as evidenced by sporadic occurrences of hypercorrect GS with words

[4] Through paradigm analogy, base forms with *v* arose in some locations in the NEY and SEY areas; thus, regional NEY *blov* 'blue,' *rev* 'raw,' from inflected forms *blovər*, *revər*.

[5] Other NEY regional variants of vowel 54 are [u:], [uw], and [uj]. On the origins of oj_{54} and the other variants of vowel 54, see U. Weinreich (1958a). On the diffusion of [oj] for vowel 54 in NEY and SEY, see Jacobs (1994a).

containing etymological *V[v]C*: *davnən* 'pray,' *bahavnt* 'versed' > *dojnən*, *bahojnt* (U. Weinreich 1958a: 243, note 16). This provides evidence for the association of "hardened glide" (*v*) with the *j* glide, at least in some contexts. For generalized NEY, *j* emerges as the sole glide.

Further evidence of the development of *j* as the generalized glide is found in NEY glide insertion [GI]. General NEY regularly eliminates vowel-vowel sequences by insertion of *j*; cf. StY *toəs* 'mistake,' *rəfuə* 'remedy' vs. NEY *tojəs*, *rəfujə*.[6] GI also occurs across morpheme and word boundaries; thus: NEY /id/ 'Jew,' but *di-j-idn* 'the Jews.' In NEY GI, *j* clearly functions as a consonant which breaks up hiatus.[7]

The crucial feature is the positive correlation of phonemic vowel length and the rounded glide(s). Those conservative subregions of NEY which have maintained some vowel length – Courland and Samogitia – have round glides. Thus, CourlY has *au*$_{54}$: *hauz* 'house,' and glide *y* in *køyfn* 'buy,' *øyər* 'ear,' while general NEY has GS applying in *hojz*, *kejfn*, and GH in *evər*.[8] In summary, lengthless varieties of NEY have eliminated unacceptable vowel length by (various) consonantal means, whereas length-maintaining varieties have not. The several independent processes which have conspired to eliminate glide *w* in general NEY are listed in Jacobs (1994a):

(A) Intervocalic hardening – PY **zawər/*zowər* > NEY *za[v]ər/zo[v]ər* 'sour'; NEY *mevax* 'brain,' *kevax* 'force' < PEY **mowax*, **kowax* < TH *mo:ah*, *ko:ah*.
(B) Positional deletion – *w* is deleted before labial(ized) consonants: **kawm* > *kam* 'hardly,' **mowł* > *mol* 'mouth.'
(C) (Sporadic) hypercorrection, based on heavily labialized NEY *ł*. This occurs / _ C; e.g., **krowt* > *krołt* 'cabbage'; cf. StY *krojt*.
(D) Deletion of last resort – if (A), (B), and (C) above are not available, then simply drop the *w*: **blow* > *blo* 'blue'; cf. StY *bloj*.
(E) Glide Substitution / _ C. PEY **towrə* > Proto-NEY **tøyrə* > NEY *tejrə* 'Torah.'

Historically, GS is assumed to have occurred during a period when intervocalic hardening had not run its course, since GS generally affects sequences of *w* + C, but not sequences of /v/ + C; thus: **towrə* > *tøyrə* > NEY *tejrə* 'Torah,' but **xevrə* > NEY *xevrə* 'gang,' not ***xejrə*.[9]

[6] GI does not occur if the first vowel is schwa; thus: NEY *gəúlə* 'redemption.'
[7] U. Weinreich (1992: 22) also notes that in "many types of NEY, probably where [h] is not phonemic, it appears as an automatic glide in vowel clusters VV [VhV]."
[8] NEY form *ejər* 'ear' is likely a blend of dialectal *evər* with StY *ojər*.
[9] GS might be relabeled "glide unrounding" positing a change *y* > *j*. However, language contact may also have played a role here. In coterritorial Slavic languages we find numerous examples linking *ł* – *w* – *v* –*j*. Recall also the examples *bahojnt*, *dojnən*.

4.1.5 *Diphthongs and glides in SEY*

The situation with diphthongs and glides in the other lengthless dialect, SEY, differs both diachronically and synchronically from that of NEY, largely due to the relatively late retention of vowel length in SEY and to specific historical developments in the phoneme system. In SEY, most instances of historical second-mora *u* were eliminated: PY *$*ou_{42.44}$* > PSY/SEY *oj*; PY *$*u\!:_{52}$* and *$*u_{51}$* fronted/unrounded to PSY **i:*, **i* (> SEY *i*, *ɨ*). The two sources of a (limited) second-mora *u* in SEY derive from PY *$*au_{54}$* and PY *$*ɔ\!:_{12.13}$*. The general development of vowel 54 in SEY was to *u:/uw*, with subsequent shortening to *u*. Vowel 12,13 > PSY **u:*, subsequently shortening as part of the general loss of length in SEY. However, residue of earlier (intervocalic) length remains in SEY glide hardening [GH].

SEY GH is posited for a period in which vowel length was still present in SEY. SEY GH applied generally, to both *j* and *w*. Thus, SEY GH is found with vowel 12,13 in PY **tɔ:əs* 'mistake' > PSY **tu:əs* > **tuuəs* > *tuwəs* > SEY *tuvəs*; similarly, PY **hanɔ:ə* 'enjoyment' > PSY **hanuuə* > **(h)anuwə* > SEY *anuvə*. Vowel 54 shows regional SEY intervocalic hardening, e.g., *zovər* 'sour' (Herzog *et al.* 1992: 33). A parallel situation occurs in SEY with historical second-mora *j* as well. PSY **i:* underwent gliding to *j* intervocalically. In preconsonantal position, and word-finally, PSY **i:* shortens > SEY *i*, thus, PSY **zi:n*, 'son,' **mi:* 'effort' > SEY *zin*, *mi*, analogous to the shortening of vowel 12,13 in SEY *budn* 'bathe,' *du* 'here.' In intervocalic position GH creates a consonantal *j* (analogous to *w* > *v*); cf. PY **rəfu:ə* > (PSY > **rəfy:ə* > **rəfi:ə* > *rəfiiə* >) SEY *rəfijə* 'remedy.'

The descriptions of GH in NEY and SEY differ, owing in large part to the chronology of loss of vocalic length in each dialect. Furthermore, SEY does not have a regular rule of GS, nor a generalized rule of GI. The question remains, however, whether SEY GH is part of the synchronic phonology of SEY, or merely historical residue.

4.1.6 *Glides and gliding in CY*

In CY, which possesses vowel length, there is not a motivation for avoiding V-V sequences. CY has no general rule which simply deletes glides (cf. NEY *blo* < **blow*), nor for inserting glides (though see below for *dra:-j-ən*), nor does CY unambiguously harden glides into consonants, nor does CY substitute the *w* glide with a generalized *j* glide. A type of secondary gliding occurs in CY, but only as one strategy among several for avoiding vocalic overlength (three moras).

As a length dialect, CY maintains both *i* and *u* as second mora. The sources of second-mora *u* in CY are vowels 12/13 and 54. The former is unambiguously analyzed as a long monophthong /u:/ in, e.g., CY *bu:dn* 'bathe,' *du:* 'here,' *šu:ləm* 'peace.' The latter may be analyzed either as a diphthong /ou/ or as a long monophthong /o:/, in, e.g., CY *bo:x* 'belly,' *ho:s* 'house,' *va:ntro:bn* 'grapes,' *aro:s* 'out,' alternatively realized as [bowəx], [howəs], [arowəs]. There are arguments in favor of either analysis (Herzog 1965a: 183–191; Jacobs 1990a: 77–78). I posit underlying diphthong /ou/ in light of the CY processes of breaking and drawl, which apply to a bimoraic nucleus ending in a [+high] element (§4.1.11).

CY breaking and drawl are similar and related processes which insert a schwa-like vowel between a vocalic nucleus and a tautosyllabic consonant (Jacobs 1993b). In both processes the underlying nucleus must be bimoraic. Breaking and drawl thus create three-vowel sequences – a situation of vocalic overlength. In some varieties of CY the middle vocalic element undergoes gliding. There are arguments both for and against classifying CY glides as vowels or consonants. On the one hand, the underlying long monophthong in /štu:t/ → regionally drawled [štuwət] 'city,' creating a new CV syllable structure (wət) as one means of avoiding vocalic overlength (*u:ə* or *uuə*). Similarly, the underlying diphthong in /hojx/ → [hojəx] 'high' via breaking, with syllabification *ho-jəx*. Additionally, a limited instance of *j*-insertion is found in CY, e.g., *in dra:-j-ən* 'by threes' < CY *dra:* 'three.'[10] The common point is the avoidance of vocalic overlength within a single nucleus. However, there is variation in the realization of breaking and drawl across CY varieties:

Underlying	*Regional CY variants*
/bi:x/ 'book'	bi:əx ~ bijəx ~ biəx
/bu:d/ 'bath'	bu:ət ~ buwət ~ buət

How overlength is or is not resolved thus constitutes one of the differences across CY varieties. In eCY, V:ə → Və; the long monophthong simply shortens before the epenthetic schwa. However, underlying diphthongs do not resolve overlength via shortening; the second mora is maintained across the CY map; thus, /hojx/ [hojəx] 'high', never **[hoəx]. The realization of 'skin' either as undrawled [ho:t] ~ [hout], or as drawled *ho-wət*, but not as **[hoət], suggests an analysis of vowel 54 as underlying diphthong in CY. Thus, in CY, glides do not pattern entirely like the second mora of a long monophthong. On the other hand, several points support the analysis of glides as vowels in CY. CY breaking and drawl only operate upon the second mora of a bimoraic

[10] Similar to SEY retention of the glide in word-final position (*cat*$_{34}$ 'time' vs. *naj*$_{34}$ 'new'), some varieties of CY may have [a:j] in word-final position: [ca:t] 'time' vs. *na:* ~ *na:j* 'new,' *dra:* ~ *dra:j* 'three' (Birnbaum 1979a: esp. p. 206). While the *j* is more frequent intervocalically, word-final *j* in variants like *na:j*, *dra:j* does not serve as a hiatus breaker. Perhaps final *j* here owes to paradigm analogy with forms like *na:jə*, *dra:jən*.

nucleus. If the glides were consonants, breaking and drawl could not operate in the first place. In relation to other phenomena as well, *j* clearly functions as a vowel. Thus, *j* does not pattern like a consonant in Viler's (1924: 146–147) syllabification rule of sonorant attraction, or in CY dental deletion (see below). Furthermore, diminutive suffix *-l* may only occur with a form which ends in a consonantal coda; *j* blocks *-l* diminution (§4.4.1). Finally, note the consonantal word-initial *j* in CY *ju:r* 'year,' *jo:x* 'broth,' *jingl* 'lad,' etc.

4.1.7 Other glide issues

U. Weinreich (1991, 1992: 18–19) discusses glides under the topic of syllabicity of *i* and *u*. He is primarily interested in phonemic issues. He describes [j] as a non-vocalic allophone of /i/; [j] occurs when "unstressed in the vicinity of another vowel"; thus "SEY . . . *ió* [jo] 'yes' . . . *ói* [oj] 'ouch' *xáiə* [xajə] 'animal' *góiəm* [gojəm] 'gentiles.'" From a strictly phonemicist framework Weinreich attempts to account for the phonetic contrast in NEY between syllabic and non-syllabic *i*. Syllabic *i* in prevocalic position is found in a number of recent internationalisms: *b[i]ológ* 'biologist,' *v[i]ólə* 'viola,' *h[i]énə* 'hyena,' *d[i]alékt* 'dialect,' etc. These contrast with older *biálə* [bjalə] 'Biały (place name),' *xienə* [xjenə] 'woman's name.' Weinreich (1992: 18–19) posits underlying stress to account for the syllabic [i] in the former group. Similarly, note prevocalic syllabic *u* in recent internationalisms: *tùalét* 'toilet,' *dùalízm* 'dualism.' Prevocalic syllabic *u* does not undergo hardening to [w ~ v].

Regionally restricted varieties of NEY and CY show vocalization of historical *l* > *w* where non-syllabic (Weinreich 1992: 19, 39): *flí* [fwi] 'fly!' vs. *fúj* [fuj] 'phooey.' The phonemic analysis of historical *l* as /l/ or /u/ in such varieties presents some complications for the general description of glides in Yiddish. Note also the regionally restricted occurrence of word-initial phonetic [w] in words like [wozn] for *lozn* 'let' (Bin-Nun 1973: 339). Vocalized /l/ in regional [fwi], [wozn], etc., does not harden to [v].

4.1.8 Nasalized vowels

Herzog *et al.* (1992: 19) write that nasalized vowels "seem to occur in all varieties of Yiddish, under different conditions, but always as a result of a following *n*, whether the consonantal nasal segment is itself phonetically rendered or not. There is therefore no reason to consider nasalization distinctive in any Yiddish dialect." This statement is largely accurate; however, there are a few points which require clarification or qualification. On nasalization in Yiddish see Prilutski (1924, 1940); Viler (1924); Gutman (1926); Herzog *et al.* (1992: 19).

Concerning stressed vowels, Yiddish dialects differ in the precise conditions under which nasalization occurs. Most commonly, a vowel nasalizes when followed by a sequence of nasal consonant plus fricative (Herzog *et al.* 1992: 19). Prilutski (1924: 48ff., 1940: 11–12) formulates it thus: in Yiddish dialects (unclear which) a non-syllabic nasal (*n* or *m*) usually may not occur before a fricative; thus, *dinstik* [dĩstik] 'Tuesday,' *kamf* [kãf] 'battle,' *branžə* [brãžə] 'line of business,' *finf* [fĩf] 'five.' Prilutski provides pairs which demonstrate the synchronic productivity of this nasalization:[11] *ganəf* [ganəf] 'thief' – *ganvənən* [gãvənən] 'steal'; *grin* [grin] 'green' – *grins* [grĩs] 'vegetable.' Nasalization is triggered by this generalized nasal *n*, not by a further-specified nasal consonant. Thus, *kamf*, phonetically [kãf], is analyzed as /kanf/ (see Prilutski 1924: 48, 57; 1940: 12).

As noted, the most general nasalization rule in Yiddish occurs before *n* + fricative.[12] Diverse varieties of Yiddish are consistent in resolving (non-syllabic) *n* + fricative sequences by adopting one of two strategies: (1) nasalization, or (2) oral stop epenthesis. Thus, *ejns* 'one' has the variants [ẽjs][13] ~ [ejnts], *menč* 'person' as [mẽš] ~ [mentš], *ganc* 'entire' as [gãs] ~ [gants], *pinsk* 'Pinsk' as [pĩsk] ~ [pintsk], *vonsəs* 'moustache' as CY [võsəs], NEY [vontsəs], SEY [vontsjəs] ~ [vontšəs] (Herzog *et al.* 1992: 19).

Nasalization of (certain) stressed vowels may also occur without the presence of a following fricative. Herzog *et al.* (1992: 19) generalize a phonological rule for all of CY (and length-distinguishing varieties of SEY) whereby /a:n/ → [ã:] / _ C, including across word boundaries; thus, *za:n ti:r* [zã: ti:r] 'his door,' but *za:n* [za:n] 'his.' In some varieties of CY and adjoining WY any long vowel is nasalized before *n*, with or without subsequent loss of the triggering nasal consonant; thus, regional WY /ba:n/ 'bone' as [bã:n] ~ [bã:], /hi:ndl/ 'chicken' as [hĩ:ndl] ~ [hĩ:dl].[14] If such varieties of WY contrast *šẽ:* < *še:n* 'pretty' and *še:* 'hour,' this would force a choice. Either the nasalized vowel is underlying/phonemic, or it is the result of two processes: vowel nasalization, followed by loss of the nasal consonant. CY [ã:nemə̃] 'to capture' (StY *ajn-nemən)* is /a:n/ + /nemən/, with vowel nasalization and nasal-consonant loss in the prefix, while initial /n/ of *nemən* is unaffected. On nasal vs. oral variants of HA-origin words such as *mã(:)sə* ~ *ma(j)nsə* ~ *majsə* 'story,' *ja(j)nkəf* ~ *je(:)kəf*

[11] StY forms are given here for clarity of presentation, though, strictly speaking, examples should be dialect-specific. Prilutski cites examples from numerous locales. Nasalization is more prevalent in some varieties than in others.

[12] This parallels significantly the situation in Polish, and may constitute a partial rule borrowing.

[13] Herzog *et al.* (1992: 19) mark nasalization over both members of the diphthong. Viler (1924: 28) viewed nasalized diphthongs in his eCY dialect as consisting of oral vowel + nasalized glide; thus: *bronfn* 'distilled spirits' would be [broũfŋ].

[14] Some varieties of WY undergo subsequent denasalization to [ba:], [hi:dl], etc.; see Herzog *et al.* (1992).

'Jacob,' *dã(:)gə* ~ *da(j)ngə* ~ *dajgə* 'worry,' *jã:dəs* ~ *ja(j)ndəs* 'conscience,' see M. Weinreich (1980: 393), Herzog *et al.* (1992: 20), and §2.4.5.

Finally, different Yiddish dialects may show different levels of a nasal "basis of articulation" – that is, some degree of nasality where conditioned nasalization is not at issue. Thus, Gutman (1926: 377) describes the wCY of the Lodzh region as having a general "nasal resonance."

4.1.9 *Nasalization and unstressed vowels*

Herzog *et al.* (1992: 20, 41) describe for most varieties of CY and adjoining varieties of WY word-final *-ən* realized as [ə̃] following a root-final nasal consonant; thus, CY *kimən* [kimə̃] 'come.' They also describe some varieties where word-final *n* in unstressed syllables may be dropped, leading to a situation of free variation: ə ~ ə̃ . Regional loss of *n* also occurs non-word-finally; cf. StY *ganvət* 'steals' vs. *ganvnt* (in Markuze 1790; see Herzog 1965b). The unstable situation has led to sporadic hypercorrect insertion of a nasal (even in stressed position); e.g., *štrundl* < *štrudl* 'strudel,' *angərəs* < *ag(ə)rəs* 'gooseberries' (Herzog 1965a: 225). Note further the regional development of *n* as hiatus breaker in CY /ara:nkimən/, phonetically [arã:kimə̃] 'to come in,' but (*zaj*) [kimə-n-arã:] '(they) come in'; *məlxumə* ~ *məlxumə̃* 'war,' but (*in*) *məlxumə-n-arã:* 'into war'; *ba-n-inc* 'with us' (Herzog *et al.* 1992: 20). In Sosnovce CY a word-final schwa may (with one exception) be realized phonetically as any monophthongal vowel color, and with or without nasalization: *ə*, *ɔ*, *ɔ̃*, *u*, *ɨ*, etc. (Jacobs 1990a: 79–81). The one exception is the vowel [ɛ], which is "reserved" for underlying *ər* (see below).

Finally, Prilutski (1940: 20) mentions CY varieties with nasalization of the liquids *l*, *r*. These varieties have forms like *veksəln* 'exchange (currency),' *zi(:)dəln* 'curse,' *švindəln* 'cheat' (vs. general Yiddish *vekslən*, *zidlən*, *švindlən*. For these varieties Prilutski claims a realization of nasalized syllabic liquid (with loss of consonant *n*), and an analogous development with the /r/ in *Vrŋ* sequences.

4.1.10 *Unstressed vowels*

Two main distinctions are made (at the word level) concerning Yiddish unstressed vowels: (1) pretonic vs. post-tonic position; and (2) underlying vs. derived schwa. Additionally, we must briefly consider destressed vowels – i.e., vowels which have become unstressed via operation of higher-level phonology.

Synchronic Yiddish phonology generally permits a much wider range of vowels in pretonic than in post-tonic position. The following are examples of pretonic vowels in StY; dialect-specific issues will be taken up subsequently.

Pretonic vowel	*StY examples*
i	[i]ndústrijə 'industry,' n[i]gúnəm 'melodies'
e	h[e]fkéjrəs 'neglect,' ekrán 'screen'
a	m[a]pólə 'fall,' [a]ntlójfn 'to run away'
o	k[o]ntáktn 'contacts'
u	k[u]ndéjsəm 'pranksters,' [u]krájnə 'Ukraine'
ə	b[ə]héjmə 'cow,' g[ə]úlə 'redemption,' g[ə]néjvə 'theft'
oj	[oj]fánəm 'ways,' h[oj]dóə 'announcement'
ej	[ej]rópə 'Europe'
aj	m[aj]xóləm '(food) treats,' m[aj]mónəm 'believers'

Thus, StY permits any of its vowel phonemes (including the diphthongs) and schwa to occur in pretonic position. In Yiddish dialects with phonemic vowel length, however, it may be that long monophthongs are not permitted in pretonic position, whereas diphthongs are.[15] For such varieties we might posit a rule that shortens long monophthongs, but which does not apply to diphthongs.

Virtually all examples of pretonic vowel color (other than [a]) in Yiddish derive either from the HA or the Slavic components, or are internationalisms. The fact that Germanic word stress became fixed on the initial root syllable in pre-Yiddish times has meant that the native Germanic words with pretonic vowels are generally limited to ones with (habitually unstressed) inseparable prefixes. The inventory of pretonic vowels in Gmc component words in StY is generally limited to [a], [ə], and possibly [i]:

Prefix	*StY example*
ba-	bakúmən 'receive,' bašrájbn 'cover with writing; describe'
ant-	antlójfn 'run away,' antplékn 'reveal'
far-	farvérn 'forbid,' farkójfn 'sell'
cə-	cəgéjn 'dissipate, dissolve,' cəšpréjtn 'disperse'
der-	dergéjn 'reach by walking,' derlébn 'live to see'
gə- ([gi-]?)	gəzogt 'said (past participle),' gəšén 'happen'
a-	avék 'away,' ahéjm 'homeward'

Compare StY prefixes *ba-*, *ant-*, *a-* with StG *be-*, *ent-* in *bekommen*, *entlaufen*, and MHG *en-* in *enwëc* 'away.' StY generally shows a development in these prefixes of *e* > *a*. (Historical /r/ in StY *far-*, *der-*, and *cə-* is problematic; cf. StG *ver-*, *er-*, *zer-*.) In StY *éntfər* 'answer,' with stress on the historical prefix, the development to /a/ did not occur. The vowel in the prefix *gə-* is generally

15 "Permitted" refers to surface realization. Long vowel can occur underlyingly in length dialects (Glasser 1990: 126). Synchronically, compare syncope in StY *prítsəm* 'landowners' from singular *pórəc*, vs. reduction (but not syncope) in StY *pərúšəm* 'commentaries' from singular *péjrəš*, even though *pr-* is an acceptable initial cluster. Note also the plural variants of *zokn* 'old man': *zəkéjnəm* ~ *skejnəm* 'old men,' with or without syncope (p. 15).

realized as a type of lax [i] in many varieties of Yiddish (though as [ə] in others; see Willer 1915: 408). Katz (1987b: 27) ascribes the *i* pronunciation in [gizókt] 'said' to a general tendency *ə* → *i* in pretonic position. I posit underlying /i/ in the relevant varieties, based on a comparison with the HA-origin adverbializing prefix *bə-/bi-*, in *bifrát* 'in particular,' *bəsód* 'secretly.'[16] The *a* in StY prefix *ba-* is lexical (not derived from underlying *ə*); cf. HA-origin *bəhéjmə* 'cow,' not ***b[i]héjmə* or ***b[a]héjmə*. Developments in the Yiddish dialects differ from StY. For example, many varieties of Yiddish realize the StY prefix *ba-* as [bə], but have [a] in prefix *ant-*. Varieties of NEY have analyzed Gmc-component etymological *ə* as pretonic /u/ in the prefix *cə-*; thus, NEY *cugéjn* 'dissipate' vs. *cúgejn* 'approach'; cf. StY *cəgéjn, cúgejn*. On pretonic vowels in words like *študírn* 'study,' see §4.5.2.

Yiddish dialects tend toward systematic reduction in the inventory of pretonic vowels permitted and toward a general integration into the overall (dialect-specific) synchronic phonology. For example, etymological *o* in Slavic loans containing the prefix *pod-* is often neutralized to *ə*, or to one of the peripheral vowels – *i* or *a* – when unstressed; cf. StY *padéšvə* '(shoe) sole,' dialectal variants *padéšvə, pidéšvə*. Likewise, StY *m[i]lxómə* 'war' (HA component), with etymological [i], shows regional variation: *m[i~a~ə]lxómə*; similarly, the internationalism StY *kapítl* 'chapter' has regional variants *kapítl* ~ *kipítl* (Herzog *et al.* 1992: 34). Variation can occur within a single variety of Yiddish as well; Retín Yiddish *pòdví:rə* (secondary stress on the pretonic vowel) ~ *pədví:rə* 'courtyard' (Bin-Nun 1973: 318).

Yiddish dialects differ concerning maintenance or syncope of a pretonic vowel originally present (in Hebrew); thus, varieties of NEY show [gnéjvə] 'theft,' [mláməd] 'kheyder teacher,' [lvónə] 'moon,' while other NEY varieties have [gənéjvə], [məláməd], [ləvónə] (Herzog *et al.* 1992: 34). Regional syncope thus creates consonant clusters not permitted in other varieties of Yiddish. However, syncope is limited to a pretonic schwa. Where Yiddish has inherited a TH full-color vowel it is generally not dropped; thus: StY *šidúxəm* 'arranged marriages,' *xavéjrəm* 'friends' < Hebrew *šiddu:xi:m, ħăβe:ri:m.*[17] The schwa-dropping NEY varieties have *xavéjrim*, not ***xv-*, even though initial cluster *xv-* is permitted; e.g., *xvaljəs* 'waves.' Presumably, the schwa-dropping varieties will have *[gn]éjvə* 'theft' (< TH *gəne:βɔ:*), but *[gan]óvim* 'thieves' (< TH *gannɔ:βi:m*). The regional syncope in *[gn]éjvə* may reflect a phonological generalization of the (morpheme-internal) pretonic schwa-loss found elsewhere in the HA component in Yiddish; cf. StY *ksúbə* 'marriage contract,' *sfórəm* 'holy

[16] The patterning *i* ~ *ə* was inherited from Hebrew (or at least the HA component of a later Jewish vernacular): [i] / _CC (i.e., in closed syllables), [ə] / _CV (i.e., in open syllables). Note the continuation of this principle when this prefix is combined with a Germanic root, e.g., *b[i]gváld* 'by force.'

[17] Yiddish *xcos* 'midnight' < Hebrew *ħăṣo:θ* is a counterexample.

books,' *cdódəm* 'sides in a dispute' < Hebrew *kəθubbɔ:*, *səfɔ:ri:m*, *ṣəðɔ:ði:m*. Syncope in StY *brojgəz* 'angry' < TH *bəro:ɣe(:)z* may reflect loss of a historical morpheme boundary; cf. regional variants *barojgəz*, *bərojgəz* (Herzog *et al.* 1992: 34). For pretonic vowel deletion to occur, general phonological constraints must prevail. Thus, Yiddish maintains pretonic vowel in closed syllable: *talmídəm* 'pupils,' not ***tlmídəm*. Whether this is due to Yiddish synchronic phonology or to an accident of Hebrew structure is a moot question here; general principles block an unacceptable initial cluster ***tlm-*. Similarly, note the lack of syncope in StY *həkéjfəm* 'scopes,' *nəgídəm* 'rich men,' *jəxídəm* 'individuals' (where unacceptable initial clusters ***hk-*, ***ng-*, ***jx-* would otherwise result) vs. syncope in *pkídəm* 'clerks,' *xsídəm* 'Hasidim' (Glasser 1990: 131–132).

There are often gradations between pretonic syncope and full retention. HA-component pretonic full vowels tend to preserve color before consonant clusters, and to reduce to schwa before a CV sequence, e.g., *muclóxəm* 'successful people,' *mufkórəm* 'libertines' vs. *məšəmódəm* 'apostates from Judaism,' *mətəróføm* 'madmen'; cf. singular forms all with /u/: *múcləx*, *múfkər*, *məšúməd*, *mətúrəf* (Glasser 1990: 110). However, an analysis based on syllable structure must refer to historical geminate consonants (present in Hebrew but not in Yiddish) to explain the pretonic /u/ in, e.g., StY *xumóšəm* 'Pentateuchs,' *musófəm* 'additional morning prayers' (p. 111). Thus, it is not clear whether this particular reduction is part of Yiddish phonology, or is an inheritance of pre-Yiddish developments. Pretonic *u* in open syllable is also maintained in internationalisms, e.g., StY *kuzín* 'male cousin,' *kuzínkə* 'female cousin,' *bufét* 'buffet,' *kurátor* 'curator'; pretonic *o* is maintained in, e.g., *kokét* 'flirt,' *román* 'novel,' *koridór* 'corridor.' While (open-syllable) pretonic vowel in Slavic loans frequently reduces or neutralizes, it may remain, e.g., *ukáz* 'decree.'

All etymological components of Yiddish show tendencies toward reduction of pretonic vowels, though the situation is complex. In part it is the result of differences in style levels; thus, internationalisms often belong to more formal-level discourse, whereas Slavic loans have been embedded into all style levels. A uniform synchronic phonological description evades us; much of the problematic data is inherited from pre-Yiddish developments. Furthermore, synchronic variation may occur within the speech of a single individual. Thus, Bin-Nun (1973) cites Retín CY forms with unstressed schwa-like vowel alternating with secondary-stressed full vowel; from the HA component (p. 297): *ràbú:nəm* ~ *rɒbú:nəm* 'rabbis,' *hòjšá:nə* ~ *həšá:nə* 'Hoshannah'; from the Slavic component (p. 318): *pòdví:rə* ~ *pədví:rə* 'courtyard'; from internationalisms (p. 238): *špətú:l* 'hospital' (cf. StY *špitól* with pretonic [i]).

The phonology of Yiddish post-tonic vowels is much clearer. The main issues are: (1) dialect differences in the realization of post-tonic vowels; (2) underlying schwa versus schwa derived from underlying full vowel; (3) epenthesis and deletion; (4) the vocalic function of syllabic sonorants *l*, *n*, and (limited) *r*.

Yiddish shows a clear tendency to reduce post-tonic vowels – both within a single morpheme and across morpheme boundaries within a phonological word. However, internationalisms, as expected, often show varying degrees of resistance to these neutralizations; cf. Swedish *tema* [a], *eko* [o]; StG *Thema* [a], *Echo* [o]; English *theme* [Ø], *echo* [o(w)]. While Yiddish likewise has maintained a degree of post-tonic vowel color in its non-Germanic vocabulary, the tendency toward a general reduction of all post-tonic vowels is nevertheless considerably stronger than in most other Germanic languages.

Words with neutralization to schwa are felt to be more fully integrated into Yiddish. Glasser (1990: 91–92) provides a number of examples of internationalisms with post-tonic full vowel, including: *dúnam* '.22 acre,' *sérum* 'serum,' *pénis* 'penis,' *ténis* 'tennis,' *tífus* 'typhus,' *módus* '(grammatical) mood,' *mínus* 'disadvantage,' *pátos* 'pathos,' *gúlaš* 'goulash,' *gúmi* 'rubber' (~ *gumə*), *géto* 'ghetto,' *véto* 'veto,' *ójto* 'car,' *móto* 'motto,' *éxo* 'echo,' *sílo* 'silo,' *čélo* 'cello,' *stúdio* 'studio.'

Whereas internationalisms in Yiddish may show divergent behavior in post-tonic position (cf. StY *témə*, *éxo*), Slavic-origin words show generalized schwa; thus, StY *blótə* 'mud,' *káčkə* 'duck,' *kójləč* 'hallah'; cf. Polish *błoto*, *kaczka*, *kołacz*.[18] Likewise, words from the substratal HA-component exhibit (in most dialects) uniform neutralization of post-tonic vowel to schwa: *tójrə* 'Torah,' *tálməd* 'pupil'$_{[M]}$, *talmídə* 'pupil'$_{[F]}$. Examples of Yiddish words with final schwa, from various etymological sources, are as follows:

StY		*Source*	
temə	'theme'	T(h)ema	(source?)
blotə	'mud'	błoto	(Polish)
kačkə	'duck'	kaczka	(Polish)
ózərə	'lake'	ozero	(Slavic)
fragə	'question'	Frage	(NHG)
intonacjə	'intonation'	intonacja	(Polish?)
tojrə	'Torah'	to:rɔ:	(TH)

Nouns ending in ə are regularly assigned feminine gender. Nouns ending in post-tonic full vowel are more marked, are less integrated in Yiddish structure, and are assigned masculine gender (exception: F *géto* 'ghetto'), e.g. (*der*) *sílo* 'silo,' *kíno* 'cinema,' *ójto* 'car.' The notion of integratedness, however, is circular in its formulation. For example, does American Yiddish *péjdə* 'wage' (< English *pay day*) have post-tonic schwa because it is well integrated into American Yiddish, or is it deemed to be well integrated based on the presence of the schwa? In the non-Germanic vocabulary a degree of variation is often

[18] The distinction between Slavic loan and internationalism is not entirely clear-cut, since many internationalisms presumably entered Yiddish via Slavic; e.g., words ending in suffix *-acjə*: *deklaracjə*, *intonacjə*, etc.

permitted, e.g., *gumi* ~ *gumə* 'rubber.' Older toponyms in Yiddish frequently require ə, whereas newer toponyms may allow a full vowel ~ schwa: older *váršə* 'Warsaw,' *krúkə* 'Kraków,' *lítə* '(Jewish) Lithuania' vs. newer *šikágo* ~ *šikágə* 'Chicago.' In toponyms of most recent vintage (in Yiddish) full-vowel retention is more common; e.g., *tókjo* 'Tokyo,' *jokaháma* 'Yokahama.' Acronyms, even when well integrated into the spoken language, tend to retain a degree of (internationalism-)markedness, e.g., *jívo* 'YIVO' (= *Yidisher visnshaftlekher institut*).

Yiddish dialects differ in their phonetic realization of post-tonic vowels. Parts of the NEY area show a tendency to realize a word-final schwa (more accurately, the generalized neutral vowel) as [i] in words like *xálə* 'challah,' *tátə* 'father,' etc., whereas in other geographic areas the general pronunciation of word-final schwa will tend to other vowel qualities. There are, however, differences of deeper systemic importance. For example, some NEY varieties preserve a post-tonic vowel distinction in words from the HA component (Herzog *et al.* 1992: 34): *o* in [éjlɔm] 'public' (< TH *ʕo:lɔ:m*) vs. *e* in [céjlem] 'cross' (< TH *ṣe:lem*), *i* in *dóvid* 'David' (TH *dɔ:wi:ð*) vs. ə in [kóvəd] 'honor' (TH *kɔ:βo:ð*). NEY regularly has [i] in the plural suffix *-im* (< TH *-i:m*): *talmídim* 'pupils,' *kundéjsim* 'pranksters,' *doktéjrim* 'doctors' vs. SY *-əm* in *talmí(:)dəm*, *doktójrəm*, etc. It is unclear whether NEY *im* represents a retention from HA, or regular phonological conditioning, since unstressed vowel before *m* is often [i] even in (Gmc-origin) monomorphemes; e.g., *bézim* ~ *bézəm* 'broom,' *fódəm* ~ *fódim* 'thread' (Herzog *et al.* 1992: 34).

4.1.11 CY breaking and drawl[19]

Varieties of CY commonly distinguish a "plain" schwa from a schwa colored by a following segment. Most often the coloring agent is a velar fricative: /r/ ([ɣ]) or /x/. The exact realization of the colored schwa in CY varies according to region. Thus, in Sosnovce, schwa before *x* is regularly [ɔ], in Retín [ɒ]: CY /talməd/ 'pupil,' /pajsəx/ 'Passover' → (Sosnovce) [talmɛt], [pajsɔx], Retín [talmət], [pajsɒx]. Before /r/, however, Sosnovce regularly has [ɛ], whereas Retín has [ɒ]. The colored schwa is identical before both velar fricatives in Retín, whereas in Sosnovce it is [ɛ] / _ r, [ɔ] / _ x; thus:

Underlying		*Sosnovce*	*Retín*
/bi:x/	'book'	[bi:ɔx]	[bi:ɒx]
/štarkərə/	'stronger'$_{[\text{PL}]}$	[štarkɛrə]	[štarkɒrə][20]

[19] See Jacobs (1990a, 1993b). Sosnovce data are taken from *LCAAJ* tapes and transcripts. Retín data are based on Bin-Nun (1973). Professor Mikhl Herzog first brought the problem of schwa in CY to my attention.

[20] In Bin-Nun's (1973) transcription system, the *a*-colored schwa is [ɒ], whereas "plain" schwa is rendered as [ḷ]. Bin-Nun's plain schwa is given here as ə.

The differences in schwa-coloring become important in light of three other processes in CY: breaking, drawl, and *r*-loss in syllable coda. Consider:

Underlying		*Sosnovce*	*Retín*
/gitə/	'good'$_{[\text{PL}]}$	[gitə]	[gitə]
/gitər/	'good'$_{[\text{M.NOM.SG.}]}$	[gitɛ]	[gitɒ]

The realizations of underlying /gitər/ show the results of schwa coloring and *r*-loss. The *r* is not deleted if it has resyllabified to syllable onset; thus, schwa coloring precedes *r*-loss.[21]

Underlying		*Sosnovce*	*Retín*
/besər/	'better'	[besɛ]	[besɒ]
/besərə]	'better'$_{[\text{PL}]}$	[besɛrə]	[besɒrə]

CY breaking inserts an epenthetic vowel between a long nucleus ending in a [+high] segment and a following tautosyllabic velar fricative. Compare the following forms with and without breaking:

Underlying		*Sosnovce*	*Retín*
/bi:x/	'book'	[bi:ɔx]	[bi:ɒx]
/hojx/	'high'	[hojɔx]	[hojɒx]
/fu:r/	'(I) travel'	[fu:ɛ]	[fu:ɒ]
/fu:rt/	'travels'$_{[\text{3P.SG}]}$	[fu:ɛt]	[fu:ɒt]
/bu:rd/	'beard'	[bu:ɛt]	[bu:ɒt]
/bi:xər/	'books'	[bi: – xɛ]	[bi: – xɒ]
/hojxə/	'high'$_{[\text{PL}]}$	[hoj – xə]	[hoj – xə]
/fu:rn/	'to travel'	[fu: – rŋ]	[fu: – rŋ]

CY breaking feeds the rule of schwa coloring by creating new occurrences of schwa. Breaking must also apply before the rule of *r*-loss in coda.

In CY drawl a vowel is inserted between a long nucleus and a following (dental or palatal) tautosyllabic consonant; thus:

Underlying		*Sosnovce*	*Retín*
/bu:d/	'bath'	[bu:ɛt]	[bu:ət]
/štu:t/	'city'	[štu:ɛt]	[štu:ət]
/hout/	'skin'	[howɛt]	[howət]

Similar to breaking, drawl may not occur when the consonant is not tautosyllabic; thus, /bu:dn̩/ 'bathe' [bu:-dn̩], not **[bu:ə-dn̩]. While diphthongs with glide *j* undergo CY breaking, they do not drawl; thus: *brojt* 'bread,' *bejt* '(I) request.' Unlike breaking, drawl may not apply if more than one consonant

[21] Alternatively, *r*-loss could be formulated as *r*-vocalization, with subsequent degemination of sequences of ə-ə, but leaving other v-ə sequences unaffected; see below.

follows. Thus, /fu:rst/ '(you) travel' breaks to [fu:əst], while /bu:dst/ '(you) bathe' yields [bu:tst], and does not drawl. CY breaking is obligatory, applying whenever the phonological conditions are met.[22] Drawl, on the other hand, is optional; application depends on factors such as speech style and tempo. Drawl may be an incipient generalization of breaking to include other tautosyllabic consonants.

The output of drawl in Retín produces an unstressed vowel [ə] that is phonetically the same as the generalized non-colored schwa in Retín *git[ə]* 'good,' *xásənə* 'wedding,' etc. Thus, Retín Yiddish distinguishes between a single colored schwa [ɒ] and a single general (non-colored) schwa [ə]; [bu:ɒt] < /bu:rd/ 'beard' (via breaking) vs. [bu:ət] < /bu:d/ 'bath' (via drawl). Sosnovce Yiddish, on the other hand, distinguishes three phonetically different types of schwa vowel: (1) [ɔ] before *x*; (2) [ɛ] before r, and non-finally (before [-grave] consonant); and (3) realizations other than [ɔ] and [ɛ]. Thus, in Sosnovce, both /bu:rd/ and /bu:d/ yield [bu:ɛt]. In Sosnovce the contrast in word-final position is between [ɛ] (< *-ər*) and a schwa which may be realized as any vowel but [ɛ]. Thus, /gitər/ is uniquely [gitɛ], whereas /gitə/ may be *gitɒ* ~ *gitɔ* ~ *giti* ~ *gitɔ̃*, etc. Medially, however, Sosnovce realizes the schwa as [ɛ]; thus, *žabə* 'frog' has word-final *ɒ* ~ ɔ̃ ~ *o*, etc., whereas plural *žabəs* has only non-final [ɛ].

The difference in schwa coloring between Sosnovce and Retín reveals the historical presence of an *r* in the second diminutive suffix, StY *-ələ*, as in *tiš* 'table,' 1st DIM *tišl*, 2nd DIM *tišələ*. In StY (orthography) there is no trace of an *r*. In Sosnovce the suffix is realized as *-ɛlə*; the unstressed [ɛ] may be analyzed as regular medial schwa, since no additional internal data for this suffix suggest an underlying /r/. In Retín, however, the suffix is realized as *-ɒlə*. The [ɒ] here is uniquely the result of schwa coloring. Thus, the 2nd DIM suffix is reconstructed as PY **ərlə*, synchronically justified for Retín, but not for Sosnovce.[23]

Consider briefly two other sources of post-tonic schwa: (1) via the rule of post-tonic reduction [PTR], which applies across the Yiddish map (though with dialect-specific differences); (2) special occurrence of a limited vowel epenthesis (not via breaking or drawl) characteristic of CY (and possibly some SEY). Application of PTR reduces an underlying full vowel or diphthong to schwa. The conditions under which PTR applies are governed by the prosodic phonology (stress rules). A schwa produced by PTR patterns phonetically according to the rules of the particular dialect. Thus, in CY, underlying /xavajr/ 'friend,' /talmi:d/, 'pupil,' /tatə/ 'father' → Sosnovce [xávɛ], [tálmɛt], [tátə]

22 A possible exception here are instances involving closely linked structures and fossilized phrases; thus: *ojər* 'ear,' but *in ojər ara:n* [i-noj-ra-ra:n] 'into the ear.'

23 This suffix is commonly *-ɒlə* ~ *ɒli* in NEY, where the [ɒ] may also suggest historical lowering before *r*. The *r* is found in Austro-Bavarian German 2nd DIM as well.

(final ~ ɔ ~ ɔ̃ ~ ɒ, etc), Retín [xávɒ], [tálmət], [tátə]. Similarly, the phonetic realization of an epenthetic schwa not resulting from breaking or drawl follows dialect-specific phonology; thus /milx/ 'milk' → Sosnovce [milɔx], Retín [milɒx].

Sonorants may, under certain conditions, function as (unstressed) vowels, i.e., as syllable nuclei; thus: *tišn̩* 'tables,' *tišl̩* 'table'[1st DIM]. There are differences as to which sonorants may be syllabic – most generally the unmarked nasal /n/ (via assimilation rules, [n], [m], [ŋ]), but less frequently the underlying nasals /m/ or /n'/, and the phoneme /l/. Syllabic /r/ is rare, and is marked as "foreign sounding"; thus, Zaretski (1926: 220) contrasts "Russian" sounding *teátr̩* with nativized *teátər* 'theatre.'

4.1.12 Other segmental processes affecting vowels

The following are some important synchronic processes.

(1) CY shortening of *u:*$_{12}$ before labial or (some) velar consonants; cf., PSY **bu:dn* 'bathe,'**zu:gn* 'say' > CY *bu:dn, zugn*. While this shortening is fairly widespread in CY, there is much residue and complexity across the area. The shortening occurs more in eCY than in wCY; thus, eCY [tuk] vs. wCY [tu:k] 'day' (Bin-Nun 1973: 187). While /r/ patterns with velar fricative /x/ in CY breaking, it does not trigger vowel shortening; thus: wCY/eCY *fu:rn* 'travel.' The /x/ is often problematic as well. Some locations show unexpected contrasts: *šl[u]fn* 'sleep' vs. *štr[u:]fn* 'punish' (Herzog *et al.* 1992: 25). While contextual shortening of *u:* was originally strictly allophonic, it contributes to the incipient restoration of a full /u:/ – /u/ contrast. The three sources for a new short /u/ are: (a) anomalous pairs like *šlufn, štru:fn*; (b) loanwords with short *u* before other than labial or velar consonant: *krulək* 'rabbit' (< Polish *królik*), *revol'ucjə* 'revolution,' etc.; (c) dialect-based hypercorrection; thus: Sosnovce *šnups* 'neck-tie'; cf. StY *šnips*.

(2) eCY shortening of *i:* before /g/; wCY *fli:k* 'fly (insect),' *švi:gɛ* 'mother-in-law,' *fli:gl'* 'wing' vs. eCY *flik, švigɒ*, etc. Bin-Nun (1973: 213) describes eCY *i:* shortening as not fully carried out, and gives variants with long *i:* in his Retín dialect. Whereas *u:* shortening fills a gap in the phonemic system, the fledgling process of *i:* shortening in eCY does not (since eCY contrasts, e.g., *ni:s* '(I) sneeze,' with *nis* 'nut'). Rather, it is a budding generalization of the CY *u:* shortening rule to both high monophthongs.

(3) CY has regional shortening of *ou*$_{54}$ before labial *m*, as in *flom* 'plum' < **floum*; cf. StY *flojm* (Herzog 1965a: 187, 190).

(4) Regionally, CY lengthens /a/ before /r/: CY *na:r, va:rəm*, cf. StY *nar* 'fool,' *varəm* 'warm.'

(5) Short vowel lowering before *r*C or *x*C is common in Yiddish; cf. StY *barg* 'mountain,' StG *Berg*. The degree of lowering may be dialect-specific; thus,

Table 4.2. *Yiddish consonant phonemes*

	Bilabial	Labio-dental	Alveolar (or dental)	Palato-alveolar	Palatal	Velar	Glottal
Stops	p		t		(t')	k	
	b		d		(d')	g	
Fricatives		f	s	š	(s')	x	h
		v	z	ž	(z')	R	
Affricates			c	č			
			(dz)	dž			
Nasals	m		n		n'		
Liquids			l		l'		

StY *fercn* 'fourteen,' Warsaw Yiddish *farcn* < PY *$*i_{31}$* (vs. StY *fir* 'four' < PY *fi:r*$_{32}$). Lowering /_r is one of the key issues in the history of Yiddish dialect formation (M. Weinreich 1965). Similarly, lowering before *x* shows regional variation: *lixt* ~ *lext* ~ *laxt* 'light.'

4.2 Consonants

4.2.1 Consonant phonemes

The consonant phonemes of Yiddish are given in Table 4.2 (see Bin-Nun 1973: 323ff.; Birnbaum 1979a: 222; Prilutski 1940). Largely due to input from the HA and Slavic components, Yiddish possesses a richer consonantism than does (Standard) German – in terms of segmental phonemes, fuller exploitation of features (such as voicing), and phonotactics. Thus, whereas historical German word-initial *s* has become *z* /_v (*sagen* [z] 'say'), and *š* /_c (*slâfan* > *schlafen* [š] 'sleep'), Yiddish contrasts word-initial *s, z, š, ž* in both environments:

sojnə	'enemy'	slup	'pole, post'
zojnə	'prostitute'	zlatə	'fem. anthroponym'
šabəs	'Sabbath'	šlofn	'sleep'
žabəs	'frogs'	žlob	'yokel, hick, boor'

Similarly, Yiddish has inherited non-initial /x/ < German, e.g., *laxn* 'laugh'; word-initially, Gmc **x* > *h*. Yiddish /x/ occurs word-initially as well, due to HA- and Slavic-component input; e.g., *xavər* 'friend,' *xrejn* 'horseradish'; thus, StY contrasts /xojv/ 'debt,' /hojf/ 'courtyard,' /xor/ 'choir,' /hor/ 'hair.'

All EY dialects have palatalized phonemes /l'/, /n'/. The easternmost dialects (NEY, SEY) have regional /s' t' d'/ as well, though their functional load is very low (U. Weinreich 1958c: 6; Herzog *et al.* 1992: 39). Regional problems regarding the phonemic status of consonants shown in Table 4.2 are discussed individually, below.

The obstruents are frequently classified in terms of an opposition lenis vs. fortis, or voiced vs. voiceless. A regionally limited three-way distinction is sometimes made in some germanized WY dialects: voiceless (fortis or lenis) vs. voiced (lenis only) (Herzog *et al.* 1992: 36). The voiceless oral stops are unaspirated in EY. The series /t d n/ are realized regionally as either alveolar or dental. Prilutski (1940: 31) describes the articulation of /s/ and /z/ as apico-alveolar (articulated with tongue tip at the lower-teeth alveoli). There is regional variation in the base pronunciation of /l/, in addition to strong conditioning by phonetic environment. Thus, NEY generally is described as having a very dark *l*, with regional velarization as [ɫ], or even vocalization to [w]; parts of CY have positional [w] as well. On the other hand, a light *l* is reported for CourlY, probably a result of contact with Baltic German.

The phoneme /r/ in Yiddish is generally a trill – either apical [r], or uvular [R]. Unless otherwise specified, the symbol <r> is used generally to represent /r/ throughout the present work. Although a trill, /r/ frequently functions as part of a natural class with the velar fricative /x/ in regional phonological processes (e.g., CY breaking and schwa-coloring; NEY obstruent voicing assimilation). Prilutski (1940: 17) gives [r] as the norm for Poland Major, certain Ukrainian varieties, some Lithuanian varieties, Bessarabia, and Old Rumania. He describes a heavily rolled *r* as especially characteristic for Bessarabia, as well as for inhabitants of small settlements and villages. He further writes that urban Yiddish speakers usually produce an *r* with fewer trills – even realized as a single tap. The [R] articulation is commonly found in many CY varieties, throughout Galicia, and in some varieties at the periphery of former Congress Poland, in Volhynia and Podolia in a strip along Galicia. A further realization of /r/ as [ʁ] – more like a true velar fricative – is found in certain Ukrainian Yiddish dialects, as well as in many Lithuanian Yiddish dialects (p. 19). Thus, it is hard to draw a clear synchronic map of front vs. back /r/ in Yiddish dialects.

The following sample words illustrate consonant phoneme distinctions in StY. The most obvious contrasts (*p* vs. *b*, *m* vs. *n*, etc.) are given. The oppositions hold generally; e.g., *pajn* 'anguish,' *dajn* 'your,' *šajn* 'shine,' *zajn* 'be,' *fajn* 'fine.'

	Initial		*Medial*		*Final*	
/p/	pux	'down, fluff'	kapórə	'fowl'	rip	'rib'
/b/	bux	'book'	kabólə	'receipt'	rib	'rape (vegetable)'
/t/	tajnə	'contention'	ejtər	'pus'	mit	'with'
/d/	dajnə	'your' (PL)	ejdər	'before'	mid	'tired'

/t'/	t'oxkən	'throb'	mot'ə	'man's name'	–	
/d'/	d'egəxts	'tar'	god'ə[24]	'man's name'	–	
/k/	kelt	'cold'	akər	'plow'	zok	'sock'
/g/	gelt	'money'	ogər	'stallion'	zog	'(I) say'
/f/	fajn	'fine'	rojfə	'Jewish physician'	ruf	'(I) call'
/v/	vajn	'wine'	tojvə	'(a) favor'	pruv	'(I) try'
/s/	sojnə	'enemy'	xosər (gejn)	'go to waste'	bis	'bite'
/z/	zojnə	'prostitute'	xazər	'pig'	biz	'until'
/s'/	s'erp	'scythe'	–[25]		–	
/š/	šabəs	'Sabbath'	bušə	'shame'	aš	'ash'
/ž/	žabəs	'frogs'	kalúžə	'puddle'	až	'as much as'
/x/	xet	'sin'	štexn	'to prick'	štex	'(I) prick'
/r/	ret	'speaks'	štern	'to disturb'	šter	'(I) disturb'
/h/	hojx	'high'	bahávnt	'well-versed'	–	
Ø	ojx	'also'	ba-Ø-ávlən	'mourn'	–	
/m/	majn	'my'	bimə	'almemar'	šojm	'scum'
/n/	najn	'nine'	binə	'stage'	šojn	'already'
/n'/	n'an'ə	'governess'	pin'ə	'man's name'	pen'	'stump'
/l/	lojz	'loose'	gojləm	'dummy'	dil	'floor'
/r/	rojz	'rose'	gojrəm	'factor'	dir	'you'[DAT]
/l'/	l'ul'kə	'pipe'	kal'ə	'spoiled'	mol'	'moth'

Palatalized consonant phonemes play a role in Yiddish phonology, however (near-)minimal pairs are very hard to come by: *nit* 'not' vs. *n'it* 'brownness (of baked crust),' *polkə* 'drumstick (of fowl)' vs. *pol'kə* 'Polish woman.' The problem is largely one of analysis – should the palatalized consonants *l'*, *n'* (and regional *s'*, *t'*, *d'*) be analyzed as distinct phonemes or as derived from underlying $l + j$, $n + j$, etc. Ultimately, scholars have opted for the underlying solution, based on the cost of the competing solution to the overall phonology of Yiddish. The palatal phonemes clearly occupy a marginal position in Yiddish phonology (see Bratkowsky 1974).

There is considerable dialect variation as concerns palatalized *l'* and *n'*. The case for phonemic /l'/, /n'/ (as opposed to sequence analysis) is based on pairs like: *pen* 'pen' vs. *pen'* 'stump,' *mol* 'time occurrence' vs. *mol'* 'moth.' U. Weinreich (1958c: 6) contrasts *kal'e* 'spoiled' ([kal'ə]) with *italjə* 'Italy' (cf. also *kalə* 'bride'), and *man'e* 'woman's name' ([man'ə]) vs. *manjə* ([manjə]) 'mania.' Weinreich (p. 6, 1968: xxiii–xxiv) claims that the palatalized

24 See U. Weinreich (1958c: 6) on possible oppositions /d'/ vs. /dj/, /l'/ vs. /lj/, etc. Weinreich contrasts /d'/ in *god'ə* 'man's name' with sequence /dj/ in *melodjə* 'melody.'

25 See Herzog *et al.* (1992: 39) on the paucity of words with palatalized consonants.

consonants are pronounced with simultaneous coarticulation, as opposed to a sequential articulation in *lj*, *nj*, *sj*, etc. However, other analyses cannot be ruled out here. Weinreich contrasts, for example, the syllabification *az-ját* 'Asian' with *ka-z'ónə* 'hackneyed'; thus, presumably also the syllabifications *ka-l'ə* vs. *itál-jə*. Palatal consonants might thus be analyzed as sequences of C and tautosyllabic *j*. M. Weinreich (1939: 75) cites *bin-jomən* (syllable boundary between *n* and *j*) 'Benjamin' vs. hypocoristic form *n'omə*, with palatalized *n'*. A similar argument based on tautosyllabic (coronal) consonant + *j* could be made for all the hypocoristic forms of proper names well-discussed in the literature: *do-d'ə* < *dovəd*, *pi-n'ə* < *pinxəs*, *pe-s'ə*, etc.[26] Further complicating unit- vs. sequence-analysis for palatalized coronals is the general tendency in many varieties of Yiddish to a more palatalized articulation in the proximity of front vowels; e.g., the *l* is lighter in *lign* 'lie' than in *lozn* 'let.' In pairs such as *kal'ə/italjə*, *man'ə/manjə*, the sequence analysis may appeal to syllabification strategies for support. However, word-initial position poses a greater problem. If sequences are posited in [l'ul'kə] 'tobacco pipe,' [l'al'kə] 'doll,' [l'arəm] 'noise,' [n'an'ə] 'governess,' [d'egəxts] 'tar,' then reference to underlying stress is necessary in *dìalékt* 'dialect' in order to prevent ***d'alékt*.

Whereas plain *n* assimilates to place of articulation of a following *k* in, e.g., /bankn/ 'banks' [ŋk], palatal *n'* does not; thus: /ban'kəs/ [n'k] 'cupping glasses.' This feature (palatalization) is sociolinguistically marked (U. Weinreich 1958c: 6; Stankiewicz 1985; Herzog *et al.* 1992: 36); thus, some Yiddish speakers use the feature to create "phonological pseudo-Slavicisms": *l'axən* 'guffaw' < *laxn* 'laugh,' *kn'akər* 'big shot' < *knakər* (a big shot, but less conceited). Many recent internationalisms have a palatalized *l'*, even in the absence of a triggering *j*; thus: *revol'ucjə* 'revolution,' *hotel'*, *rol'ə* 'role'; there is, however, noticeable individual and regional variation ([l'] vs. [l]). Thus, *l'* and *n'* are phonemes in EY, but only marginally so.

4.2.2 Affricates

Yiddish scholarship is unclear on how to handle the phonemic status of affricates. Falkovitsh (1966: 602) lists only two (both voiceless): *c* [ts] and *č* [tš]. U. Weinreich (1968) lists only one clear affricate, *c* [ts]. Perhaps not coincidentally, this is the only affricate represented by a single graph <צ>. In Weinreich's list of letters and sounds (p. xxi), *č* and *dž* are not listed, since they may be automatically derived from their component sounds/symbols.

[26] Non-coronal consonant + *j* is unambiguously a sequence (*pj*, *bj*, *mj*) in U. Weinreich (1958c: 6).

Phonetically, Yiddish has the homorganic affricates *c*, *č*, [dž], and [dz] (contextually limited).[27] Other stop-fricative sequences, uncontroversially sequences, are ignored in the following discussion; thus, [tx] in *šadxn* 'marriage broker'; cf. *šidəx* 'arranged match'; similarly, *ps-* in *psixológjə* 'psychology,' *pš-* in *pšorə* 'compromise,' *ks-* in *ksilofón* 'xylophone.'

The distribution of affricates throughout the language is not symmetrical. Weinreich's dictionary (1968) contains numerous examples with initial *c* and *č*, a few with initial *dž*, and none with initial *dz*. In initial position affricates may contrast with either of their component parts:

c	cejln 'count'	tejln 'parts'	sejfər 'holy book'
č	čepən 'bother'	tepər 'potter'	šepn 'derive'
dž	džobən 'to peck'	dobrə 'woman's name'	žabə 'frog'

While [dz] does not occur in initial position (except in parts of NEY), both of its segmental components do: *[d]ajn* 'your,' *[z]ajn* 'be,' but not ***[dz]ajn*. Examples of affricates in non-initial position include:

-c-	məlicə 'florid language'	zic '(I) sit'
-č-	mučən 'torment'	jungač 'brat, rascal'
-dž-	lodžər 'of/from city of Lodzh'	lodž 'Lodzh' (toponym)

Surface phonetic affricates are frequently found between consonants *l*, *n*, and a following sibilant, though this might be seen as a historical process:

*Pre-form	StY	
*menš	men[t]š	'person'
*gans	gan[d]z	'goose'
*hals	hal[d]z	'neck, throat'
*falš	fal[t]š (regional)	'false'

The historical epenthesis of a dental stop has given rise to the fourth homorganic affricate, *dz* (and created new instances of *č*, *c*, and *dž*). Thus, *dz* is limited, occurring after *l* or *n*; *dz* is found in codas (*haldz*, *gandz*), as well as in onsets following syllabification processes: *hel-dzə-lə* 'little throat,' *gen-dzə-lə* 'little goose.' Finally, note the following two points, the first of which argues for a sequence analysis, the second for a unit analysis. As part of the variation between [nasalized vowel + fricative] ~ [oral vowel + nasal stop + oral stop + fricative] (*mẽš* ~ *mentš*), the *t/d* clearly functions as a separate stop consonant, epenthetically inserted. Furthermore, affricates tend to function as heavy codas (see below). On the other hand, consider the hushing assimilation of *s-š* → *šš* → *š* (degemination); e.g., *es-šisl* → [ešisl] 'eating bowl.' Zaretski (1926: 224)

[27] Affricate [pf] is found in varieties of WY; thus, *pfilə* 'prayerbook' < *tfilə* (Herzog *et al.* 1992: 38).

gives an example of *s* → *š* / _ *č* (or *tš*): *vos čepət er zix* 'why is he being annoying?' with [šč]. This suggests a unit analysis for *č*, since a sequence *tš* would presumably not trigger hushing assimilation across an oral stop. As with many other languages, the issues concerning affricates in Yiddish are rather clear, but an exclusive analysis is not.

4.2.3 Nasal assimilation

Yiddish has three nasal phonemes: /m/, /n/, and /n'/. For the most part, nasal assimilation to place of articulation of an adjacent consonant is limited to the unmarked nasal /n/. There are some differences according to whether /n/ precedes or follows the conditioning consonant; additionally, prosodic structure may play a role. Consider first assimilation to a preceding consonant. Nasal assimilation occurs within a morpheme, e.g., /lign/ [ligŋ] 'lie' (untruth), and across morpheme boundaries, e.g., /leb-n/ [lebm] 'live.' Since nasal assimilation applies to forms generated post-cyclically by a rule of lexical schwa deletion [LSD], it is also a post-cyclic rule.

Underlying (StY)	Post- LSD	Nasal assimilation	
/zokejn/	zokn	[zokŋ]	'old man'; cf. pl. [skejnəm]
/lamdon/	lamdn	[lamdn]	'learned man'
/korbon/	korbn	[korbm]	'victim'; cf. pl [korbónəs]
/gətrofən/	gətrofn	[gətrofɱ]	'met'
/šrajbən/	šrajbn	[šrajbm]	'write'
/gəšribən/	gəšribn	[gəšribm]	'written'
/gərotən/	gərotn	[gərotn]	'successful'
/faršvigən/	faršvign	[faršvigŋ]	'silenced'

When a vowel intervenes, *n* does not undergo assimilation, thus: *(on)gəšribə[n]ə*, *korbo[n]əs*, etc. In varieties of Yiddish with back [R], /n/ → [ŋ]; e.g., CY *fu:rn* [fu:Rŋ] 'travel.' For the most part Yiddish [ŋ] is clearly allophonic, since a conditioning velar consonant is always present; e.g., StY *zing* [ziŋg] '(I) sing,' *zogn* [zogŋ] 'say.' However, a special problem is presented in those Poland Major dialects where word-final /ng/ is realized as [ŋ], rather than the more common [ŋg]; thus, *zing* [ziŋ] (Prilutski 1940: 24). Phonemic /ŋ/ is also claimed for Samogitia and CourlY by Herzog *et al.* (1992: 41).

It is the "syllabic n" which assimilates post-consonantally (Prilutski 1940: esp. p. 24; Herzog *et al.* 1992: 41), non-syllabic *n* does not; thus, cf. *drob[n]ə* 'petite,' *lig[n]ər* 'liar.' Underlying /m/ in post-consonantal, final position usually requires an intervening vowel (and thus is neither syllabic, nor positionally open to assimilation); cf., *otəmən* 'breathe,' and *rexənən* 'reckon,' in 1P.SG: *otəm* ([əm]) vs. *rexn* ([ŋ]); similarly, Yiddish *fodəm* 'thread,' *bojdəm* 'attic.'

Before obstruents, *n* assimilates both within a morpheme and across morpheme boundaries: /n/ → [ŋ] in *ba[ŋ]k* 'bank'; historical **n* > [m] in *kimpət* < **kin(d)bet* 'childbirth.' The nasals /m/ and /n'/ resist assimilation to a following obstruent: *ku[m]kən* 'say "come,"' *za[m]d* 'sand,' *ba[n']kə* 'cupping glass.' Note also retention of *l'* / _C in *pol'kə* 'Polish woman' vs. *polkə* 'drumstick,' *vil'nə* 'fluffy' vs. *vilnə* 'Vilnius.'

Across word boundaries *n* assimilation is more complex; in normal (rapid) speech (Bin-Nun 1973: 344): *in bet* → *i[m]bet* 'in bed,' *fun gold* → *fu[ŋ]gold* 'of gold.' However, the status of many elements, especially verb particles ending in *n* (*in, arajn, ahin, ajn*), must receive special attention (Prilutski 1937). The definite article *dem* regularly contracts to *n* after a preposition; e.g., *mit dem* → *mitn*. However, the status of nasal assimilation is unclear here: *af* + *dem* → *afn*. Similarly, CY unstressed clitic *-n* 'him' (stressed form *ejm*) does not seem to assimilate to the following velar /g/ in CY *rot-n gəzéjn* < *er hot ejm gəzej(ə)n* 'he saw him' (Gutman 1926: 386).

4.2.4 *Contextual palatalization*

All varieties of Yiddish tend to have a lighter timbre of /l/ in the vicinity of a front vowel, though the exact conditions vary regionally (Herzog *et al.* 1992: 39–41). In varieties of CY, /l/ → [l'] before *i, e*; after *i*; sometimes after the *j* glide in a diphthong; and after *k* or *g*. Contextual palatalization of other consonants occurs regionally, e.g., sub-phonemic palatalization of dentals and velars before front vowels in varieties of NEY and SEY (U. Weinreich 1958c: 5–6). Some speakers of NEY and SEY palatalize all consonants before /i/ and /e/ (Herzog *et al.* 1992: 40). However, U. Weinreich (1958c: 6) analyzes words with labials, like *pjatə* '(foot) sole,' as containing sequence /pj/.

Harder to classify are instances of *s', t', d', z'* which occur in environments where non-palatalized *s, t, d, z* occur as well; thus, *kit'kə* 'type of hallah' vs. *mitə* 'stretcher (for a corpse),' *s'erp* 'scythe' vs. *sejxl* 'brains' (Herzog *et al.* 1992: 39). The functional load is so low in those varieties of Yiddish that one is reluctant to call these phonemes. The instability of these palatalized apical consonants is illustrated by the tendency of *t', d'* to become affricates (in varieties of NEY); e.g., *tir* 'door' as [t'ir] ~ [čir], *dir* 'you'$_{[\text{DAT.SG}]}$ as [d'ir] ~ [džir]. Regional mergers occur between the palatalized *t', d', s', z'* and underlying fricatives and affricates, though often with different outcomes (p. 41, note 50).

4.2.5 h-*sounds*

StY /h/ contrasts with zero and with /x/, e.g., *hojlə* 'hollow'$_{[\text{PL}]}$ – *ojlə* '(Jewish) pilgrim' – *xojlə* 'ill person.' However, in a large swath covering significant parts of the NEY and SEY territory, an /h/ phoneme is lacking, and phonetic [h] occurs only automatically or optionally in hiatus (U. Weinreich 1958b: 224); thus, regional SEY /naít/ → [na(h)ít] 'peas'; /di ont/ → [di hont] 'the arm,' but /mit der ont/ → [mit der ont] 'with the arm.' Additionally, some areas may have a limited three-way opposition by the presence of a voiced [ɦ] in (Ukrainian) loans: *buɦaj* ~ *buhaj* 'bull.'

4.2.6 *Final devoicing*

CY (along with WY) is generally described as neutralizing the voicing opposition for obstruents in word-final position; thus, /grojs/, /grojsə/ → [grojs], [grojsə] 'big,' but /lojz/, /lojzə/ → [lojs], [lojzə] 'loose.' However, there are a number of complications. Devoicing does not occur before a vowel in close constructions. Thus, CY devoices /tug/ → [tuk] 'day,' but not in the expression /tug in naxt/ → [tugənaxt] 'day and night.' Furthermore, parts of CY devoice a final obstruent in nouns and adjectives, but not in the 1P.SG of verbs; thus, /tug/ → [tuk], but /zug/ → [zug] '(I) say' (Stankiewicz 1991: 211).

4.2.7 *Initial clusters*

In large part owing to fusion, Yiddish has a much richer list of permissible consonant clusters than do other Germanic languages. The following discussion is based on an expansion and modification of Birnbaum (1979a: 222–223). Sample words are given in StY form. For purposes of the following discussion, the affricates are treated as unit phonemes (complex segments), not as sequences (= clusters); thus, the list does not include words like *cu* 'to,' *čapkə* 'cap,' *džobən* 'peck.' On voicing conflict in clusters *kd-*, *sd-*, *cd-*, see below.

Two consonants

	Voiceless		Voiced
pt-	ptirə 'death, demise'	bd-	bdikə 'inspection'
pl-	plit 'raft'	bl-	blat 'leaf, sheet of paper'
pr-	prat 'detail'	br-	brudər 'brother'
pn-	pnímiəs 'inwardness'		
ps-	psurə 'message'		
pš-	pšat 'literal meaning'		
px-	pxor 'first-born son'		
pl'-	pl'us 'plus sign'		
pk-	pkidəm 'officials'	bg-	bgodəm 'garments'

tr-	trinkən 'to drink'	dl-	dlonjə 'palm (of hand)'
tm-	tmixə 'support'	dn-	dno 'bottom'
tn-	tnaj 'condition, provision'	dr-	draj 'three'
tl-	tliə 'gallows'		
tk-	tkufə 'epoch, era'		
tv-	tvuə 'grain, cereal'	dv-	dvojrə 'Deborah'
tf-	tfilə 'prayer'		
tx-	txojər 'coward'		
kn-	knakər 'big shot'	gn-	gnod 'mercy'
kt-	– ??	gl-	gloz 'glass'
kd-	kdušə 'sanctity, saintliness'	gr-	grin 'green'
kl-	klejn 'small'	gv-	gvurə 'heroism'
ks-	ksenofobjə 'xenophobia'	gz-	gzejrə 'edict'
kr-	krojt 'cabbage'		
kv-	kvurə 'burial'		
fl-	flojm 'plum'	vl-	vlad 'fetus'
fr-	fraj 'free'	vr-	vrak 'wreckage'
sm-	smolə 'tar, resin'	zm-	zman 'semester'
sf-	sforəm 'holy books'	zn-	znus 'prostitution'
sv-	svivə 'environment'	zg-	zgal 'species, kind'
sn-	snop 'beam (of light)'	zr-	zriə 'seed'
st-	staž 'seniority'	zl-	zlidnə 'annoying'
sd-	sdorəm 'orders, arrangements'	zb-	zborovski 'Zborowski' (surname)
sk-	skarbovə 'commonplace'		
sp-	spontán 'spontaneous'		
sx-	sxojrə 'ware(s)'		
sr-	srejfə 'fire'		
sl-	slup 'pole, post'		
šm-	šmekn 'to smell'	žm-	žmenjə 'handful'
šv-	švigər 'mother-in-law'	žl-	žlob 'yokel, hick, boor'
šf-	šfixəs-doməm 'aggravation'	žl'-	žl'ok 'gulp'
šn-	šnurəvən 'to lace (shoes)'		
št-	šteln 'to put, set'		
šp-	špet 'late'		

šk-	škarmúc 'paper bag'	
šx-	šxejnəm 'neighbors'	
šr-	šrajbn 'to write'	
šl-	šlofn 'sleep'	
šl'-	šl'ax 'unpaved road'	
šč	ščav 'sorrel'	
xm-	xmarə 'threatening cloud'	
xv-	xvatiš 'dapper'	
xš-	xšad 'suspicion'	
xs-	xsidiš 'Hasidic'	
xl-	xlor 'chlorine'	
xk-	xkirə 'speculation'	
xc-	xcos 'midnight'	
xn(')-	xn'ok 'unreasonable conservative'	
xr-	xropən 'to snore'	
cl-	clomәm 'clubs (in cards)'	
cn-	cníəs 'chastity'	
cd-	cdodəm 'sides in a dispute'	
cv-	cvišn 'between'	
čv-	čvok 'nail'	
mr-	mrakən 'to drizzle'	
ml-	mloxəm 'kings'	

Initial clusters: Three consonants

špr-	šprax 'language'	spr-	spravən 'to manage, acquit'
štr-	štrik 'rope'	str-	strunə 'string (of an instrument)'
škr-	škrobən 'scrape'	skr-	skrupl 'scruple'
špl-	– ??	spl-	– ??
škl-	šklaf 'slave'	skl-	sklad 'warehouse'

Some dialects permit clusters in HA-origin words such as *gnejvə* 'theft,' whereas other dialects require a vowel: *gənejvə* (Herzog *et al.* 1992: 34). However, it should be seen whether the latter dialects also break up the cluster in Gmc-component words like *gnod* 'grace.' Initial clusters containing three consonants consist of sibilant + stop + liquid. There seem to be no systemic reasons for lack of initial *špl-*, *spl-*.

4.2.8 *Final clusters*

Two consonants

-pt	xapt 'grabs'	-ts[28]	gots 'God's'	-ks	biks 'rifle'
-ps	ojps 'fruit'	-tš[29]	?? (see *č*)	-kt	mekt 'erases'
-pš	hipš 'considerable'			-kš	lokš 'noodle'
		-čt	pačt 'slaps'		
		-ct	zict 'sits'		
-ft	klugšaft 'wisdom'	-št	kušt 'kisses'	-xt	maxt 'power'
-fc	lefc 'lip'	-st	bajst 'bites'	-xc	krexc '(I) moan'
-fs	ganəfs 'of the thief'	-sp	vesp 'wasp'	-xs	nojəxs 'Noah's'
		-sk	pisk 'animal mouth'		
-mp	lomp 'lamp'	-nt	hant 'hand, arm'		
-mb	demb 'oak'	-nd	land 'country'		
-md	zamd 'sand'	-nk	bank 'bank'		
-mt	amt 'office'	-ng	lang 'long'		
-mš[30]	–??	-ns	románs 'romance'		
-ms	ejdəms 'sons-in-law'	-nc	ganc 'entirely'		
		-ndz	gandz 'goose'		
		-nč	menč 'person'		
		-nš[31]	??		

-lp	zalp 'salvo'	-rp	karp 'carp'
-lb	halb 'half'	-rf	dorf 'village'
-lc	zalc 'salt'	-rt	kort 'card'
-lt	alt 'old'	-rd	bord 'beard'
-ld	jold 'chump'	-rb	harb 'difficult, severe'
-ldz	haldz 'neck, throat'	-rk	štark 'strong'
-lk	melk '(I) milk'	-rg	karg 'stingy'
-lg	folg (mix a gang) 'that's a stretch'	-rm	farm 'farm' [American Yiddish]
-lš	falš 'false'	-rs	mars 'Mars'
-lz	belz 'Belz (toponym)'	-rš	karš 'cherry'

[28] Here, *ts* rather than *c* is used because of the morpheme boundary.

[29] Under unit analysis of affricates, *č* in, e.g., *pač* is not a cluster. Needed here is a word with root-final /t/ followed by a morphemic /š/. This is the case for *dajč* 'German' historically, but not synchronically.

[30] Theoretically possible is *ejdəmš* 'son-in-law-ish,' e.g., *an ejdəmš tišl* 'a son-in-law's (type of) little table.' However, it is unclear if such forms are attested.

[31] Theoretically possible is *goldmanš* 'Goldman-ish,' e.g., *a goldmanš tišl* 'a Goldmanian (type of) little table.' However, it is unclear if such forms are attested.

-lx	milx 'milk'	-rc	harc 'heart'
-lf	helf '(I) help'	-rx	marx 'marrow'

Three consonants

-psk	vitepsk 'Vitebsk'			-kst	badékst 'you cover'
-pst	xapst '(you) grab'				
-pts	gəxapts 'caught'				
-fst	kojfst '(you) buy'	-šst	kušst '(you) kiss'[32]	-xst	hexst 'extremely'
-fts	gəšrifts 'writ'			-xts	ajngəmaxts 'jam'
-fct	zifct 'sighs'				
-mst	kumst '(you) come'	-ngt	brengt 'brings'[33]		
-mts	gəgramts 'rhymed'	-nkt	trinkt 'drinks'		
		-nks	kranks 'sick'		
		-nts	frajnts 'friend's'		
		-nčt	benčt 'blesses'		
		-nst	gəfinst '(you) find'		
		-nct	tanct 'dances'		
		-nsk	brajnsk 'Braynsk'		
-lst	tejlst '(you) share'	-rst	herst '(you) hear'		
-lšt	farfalšt 'forges'	-rxt	horxt 'obeys'		
-lct	zalct 'adds salt'	-lks	folks 'of the people'		
-lkt	melkt 'milks'				

Four consonants
All codas containing four consonants have a coronal appendix (see below); e.g., *harpst* 'autumn,' *farštarkst* '(you) strengthen,' *brengst* '(you) bring.'

Most of the permissible three-consonant clusters in final position involve a morpheme boundary and a following suffix containing voiceless coronal consonants: *t*, *s*, *st* (and dialectal *-c*). Obstruent voicing oppositions are neutralized where these suffixes are added; e.g., /g/ in /trogn/ 'carry' → [k] in [trokst] '(you) carry.' Examples of final clusters with a post-consonantal sonorant are not included above, since these automatically syllabify: *ti-šl*, *ti-šn*, *tro-gŋ*, *šraj-bm*, *komuni-zm*. An exception here is the monosyllabic American Yiddish loan *farm* 'farm.' Left for separate discussion (below) is the regional vowel epenthesis which breaks up final clusters *-r*C or *-l*C. Several consonant

[32] Likely simplified to [št]. [33] Voicing resolution to [ŋkt].

phonemes apparently do not occur in final clusters; thus, whereas *l'* and *n'* occur in *mol'*, *pen'*, it is questionable whether they occur within final clusters; thus, compare StY toponym *Brajnsk* [nsk] with Polish *Brańsk* [n'sk]. As expected, *h* does not occur word-finally, neither alone, nor as part of a cluster. Finally, the unit or sequence analysis of affricates does not matter here, since they are all coronal in Yiddish, and, thus, may function as appendices.

Medial position permits several more clusters not allowed in final position, e.g., *vd* in *ivdə* (vox) 'next (week),' *nx* in *planxənən* 'bawl,' *ndž* in *blondžən* 'stray.' This is partly due to the "stacked deck" of voiceless suffixes (in final position), and partly to syllabification possibilities available medially, but not word-finally. The number of permissible final clusters is greatly reduced in CY, due to final devoicing.

Finally, there is a sense of the centrality or marginality of specific clusters to the core phonology of Yiddish. Thus, whereas onsets *tl-*, *dl-* occur in Yiddish, they are not preferred. Prilutski (1940: 48) notes that certain speakers change *dl* medial clusters in toponyms – after resyllabification – to a more preferred onset *gl*; thus: Polish toponym *Jedlińsk* → Yiddish *Jegli(:)nsk*; also, dialect evidence from Ukrainian and Lithuanian Yiddish areas where (StY) *antlojfn* 'run away' resyllabifies *an $ klojfn*. Bin-Nun (1973: 392–394) notes a tendency in Yiddish to simplify complex clusters in Slavic loans.

4.2.9 *Voicing resolution in obstruent clusters*

There is a strong general tendency in Yiddish to resolve [±voice] in obstruent clusters via regressive (anticipatory) assimilation within a simplex word; e.g., before verb suffixes *-t*, *-st*, /xapt/ 'grabs' and /šrajbt/ 'writes' → [xapt], [šrajpt]; /rufst/ '(you) call' and /pruvst/ '(you) try' → [rufst], [prufst]. This is not simply a (final) devoicing, but, rather, a regressive assimilation, as evidenced by morpheme-internal resolution; thus, StY *ši[d]əx* 'match' – *ša[t]xn* 'matchmaker,' *[z]okn* 'old man' – *[s]kejnəm* 'old men,' *[s]kejnə* 'old woman'; similarly, TH *bəsu:rɔ:*, *səɣullɔ:* > StY *[p]surə* 'message,' [z]*gulə* 'remedy, solution';[34] StY [g] for orthographic <k> (TH <ק>); thus, *[k]ojdəš* 'holy,' but *bejsamí[g]dəš* 'Holy Temple (in Jerusalem).'

Boundary types play a crucial role in dialect differences in voicing assimilation. For example, CY does not voice the *s* across word boundary in *dus bi:x* 'the book,' whereas the historical *š* is voiced morpheme-internally in CY *xe[ž]bm* 'bill.'

[34] Why U. Weinreich's (1968) dictionary lists *[s]ejdər –*, *[s]dorim* 'order-s' is unclear to me, since he has *[z]gulə*.

Sonorants do not play a role in Yiddish voicing resolution (thus, both *[d]raj* 'three' and *[t]rinkən* 'drink,' *[s]molə* 'tar, pitch' and *[z]man* 'semester'). However, parts of NEY have a harshly fricative *r* which patterns (preconsonantally) with velar fricative *x* in voicing assimilations (Herzog *et al.* 1992: 38); thus: NEY regional *štexn* 'to prick,' *štern* 'to disturb' yield NEY *(er) šte[x]t* '(he) pricks = disturbs,' *(ix) šte[ɣ] dir* '(I) prick = disturb you.' There are some apparent exceptions to morpheme-internal voicing resolution, especially as concerns /v/: *s[v]ivə* 'environment,' *t[v]uə* 'grain,' *š[v]uə* 'oath' vs. *s[f]orəm* 'holy books,' *t[f]ilə* 'prayer,' *d[v]ojrə* 'Deborah.'

4.2.10 Regional vowel epenthesis and consonant clusters

In much of CY a limited epenthesis[35] breaks up final clusters with *r*C (where C = velar obstruents /k/, /g/, /x/): /štark/ 'strong,' /barg/ 'mountain' → [štarək], [barək]; /milx/ 'milk' → [miləx]. However, the epenthesis does not occur when a vowel follows; thus, [štarkə] 'strong' [PL], [bergɛ] 'mountains,' [milxik] 'dairy,' etc. This epenthesis is best described in terms of syllable structure. Widespread in CY, SEY, parts of NEY (Herzog *et al.* 1992: 24) are [finəf] 'five,' [eləf] 'eleven,' [cveləf] 'twelve'; these are best viewed as lexicalized forms, since these same dialects have [(h)elf] '(I) help,' not **[(h)eləf].

4.3 Syllable structure

4.3.1 The syllable in metrical phonology

The syllable (σ) may be represented metrically as follows: (optional) onset (O) containing zero to n consonants, obligatory nucleus (N), and optional coda (C); nucleus and coda together are dominated by a common node, rhyme (R):

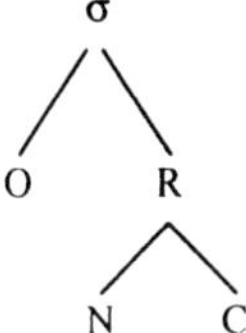

The segmental make-up of onsets, nuclei, and codas is governed by general universal principles (based on sonority hierarchy and language-specific

[35] For similar epenthesis in adjacent varieties of WY, see Herzog *et al.* (1992: 23–24).

constraints). The general sonority hierarchy, presented in terms of a Sonority Sequencing Generalization (SSG) in Booij (1995: 24),[36] is:

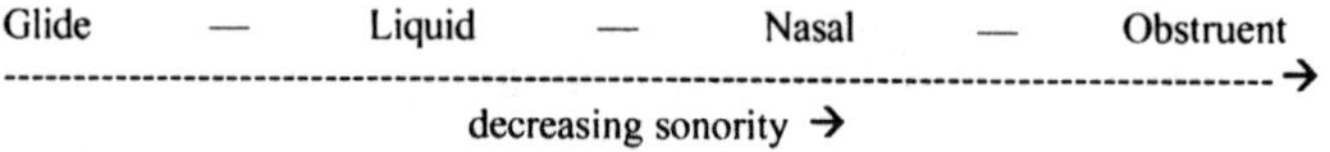

Booij writes that the SSG "restricts the co-occurrence of segments in onsets and codas, and also explains the mirror-image effects in these constraints." Booij gives examples from Dutch where the order of identical segments is constrained, depending on whether they occur in onset or coda: *kl-*, *sl-* may be onsets in Dutch (*klem* 'grip,' *slop* 'slum'), but not codas (***mekl*, ***posl*). Similarly, *-lk* and *-ls* occur in codas (*melk* 'milk,' *pols* 'wrist'), but not in onsets (***lsop*, ***lkem*). However, the mirror-image effect is not absolute. Some of this has to do with well-known problems concerning sibilants. Thus, English has onset *st-* (*stop*), mirror coda *-ts* (*pots*), coda *-st* (*post*), but no mirror onset *ts-*. However, this is certainly not a universal constraint; within Germanic it is a constraint of English, Dutch, or Swedish, but not of Yiddish or German.

The Yiddish syllable of course conforms to universal constraints. Phonotactically, the permissible consonant clusters in Yiddish vastly outnumber those of other Germanic languages. However, it will be shown that the Yiddish prosodic syllable in its essence conforms to the basic Germanic pattern.

4.3.2 *Stressed-syllable onset*

Consonantal onset is optional in Yiddish stressed syllables. Furthermore, there is little evidence for a strong glottal stop in vowel-initial words in Yiddish (King 1990b).[37] This is especially evident in resyllabification across word boundaries; Yiddish is thus less like StG, and more like dialects of Bavarian, as well as Dutch and English. Zero-onsets word-initially occur in words from all etymological components (HA, Slavic, Germanic, etc.). Examples include: (with stressed vowel) *épl* 'apple,' *árbət* 'work,' *ójcər* 'treasure,' *ózərə* 'lake'; (with unstressed vowel) *avéjrə* 'sin,' *ekrán* 'screen,' *avék* 'away,' *atén* 'Athens,' *ukáz* 'decree.'

In onsets consisting of a single consonant, any Yiddish consonant may occur – even word-initially (except for regionally limited *dz*). Onsets of two consonants

[36] Based on other works as well; Booij is cited for convenience.

[37] Reyzen (1920: 45) mentions a weak glottal stop before a stressed vowel word-internally. U. Weinreich (1954: 10) calls initial glottal stop in Yiddish "entirely sporadic."

may consist of the following orders:

Stop-Fricative	*pšat* ‘meaning,’ *ksenofobjə* ‘xenophobia,’ *tfilə* ‘prayer’
Stop-Sonorant	*tnaj* ‘provision,’ *krojt* ‘cabbage,’ *plit* ‘raft,’ *tliə* ‘gallows,’ *brudər* ‘brother,’ *tmixə* ‘support’
Stop-Stop	*tkufə* ‘epoch,’ *ptirə* ‘demise’
Fricative-Stop	*skarbovə* ‘trite,’ *zgulə* ‘remedy,’ *xkirə* ‘speculation,’ *staž* ‘seniority’
Fricative-Fricative	*svivə* ‘environment,’ *sxojrə* ‘ware(s),’ *švarc* ‘black,’ *xvat* ‘dapper person’ *sforəm* ‘(Jewish) holy books’
Fricative-Sonorant	*zman* ‘semester,’ *vlad* ‘fetus,’ *fraj* ‘free,’ *žmen’ə* ‘hand-ful,’ *slup* ‘pole,’ *šnur* ‘daughter-in-law,’ *xmarə* ‘threatening cloud,’ *xropən* ‘snore’
Sonorant-Sonorant	*mloxəm* ‘kings’
Affricate-Fricative	*čvok* ‘nail’
Affricate-Sonorant	*cloməm* ‘clubs (in cards)’
Fricative-Affricate	*xcos* ‘midnight,’ *ščerbik* ‘jagged’

Affricates will usually come first in two-consonant onsets: *cloməm*, *čvok*. The type *xcos* seems much rarer. Slavic loans with [šč] (< Polish) are frequently simplified in Yiddish (Stankiewicz 1965). Sonorant-sonorant onsets are rare, and are frequently broken up by a vowel; e.g., regional *m(a)lóxəm* ‘kings.’

The data suggest that if an onset consists of three consonants, the first one must be a sibilant: *s* or *š*, the second one an oral stop, and the third one a liquid *l* or *r*, but not a nasal. The absence of initial *spl-/špl-* in U. Weinreich (1968) seems accidental. Yiddish speakers likely would have no problem with a toponym like *Split*, or an NHG loan like *šplitər* ‘splinter.’ The parallel three-consonant onsets with voiced sibilants *z*, *ž* appear to be lacking: ***zbr-*, ***žbr-*.

Evidence for the onset as a prosodic unit is provided by, among other things, the dismissive onset *šm-*, which systematically replaces an underlying onset (including a zero-onset) as part of a rhyming couplet; e.g., *epl-šmepl*, *lerər-šmerər*, *gvirəm-šmirəm*.

4.3.3 *Stressed-syllable rhyme*

A major exception to the general limit on rhyme weight in SoQ-varieties of Germanic is the coronal appendix (Booij 1995: 26ff.). With very few exceptions, the overlong syllables in modern Germanic SoQ-dialects are limited to those ending in one or more coronal consonants; e.g., English *hands*, *lunch* (*tš*), *find* [ajnd]), *finds* [ajndz]; German *Kunst* ‘art,’ *schreibst* ‘you write,’ *spielt* (VVCC) ‘plays’ vs. *mild* [milt] (VCC) ‘mild’; Swedish *fint* (VVCC) ‘fine’$_{[\text{N.SG.}]}$, (*till*) *hands* (VCCC) 'available'; Dutch *gepoogd* (VVCC) 'attempted', *Bargoens* (VVCC) 'thieves' cant'. Particularly problematic – though much rarer – are overlong syllables ending in a non-coronal. Thus, a sequence analysis of affricate *pf* in German *Kampf* 'battle' yields a structure VCCC, with non-coronal final /f/, whereas a unit-analysis yields structure VCC (*du kämpfst* 'you battle' has non-problematic coronal appendix). Similarly, English *joined*, *finds* (with VVCC, VVCCC) are non-problematic; but, presumably, *oink* is a problem.

Yiddish stressed syllables by and large conform to general Germanic syllable structure constraints, including overlong syllables with coronal appendix; e.g., StY *šrajbst* '(you) write,' *benčt* 'blesses,' *kranks* 'sick (one),' *horxt* 'obeys,' *horxst* '(you) obey,' *melkt* 'milks,' *harpst* 'autumn.' Exceptional *-(s)k* occurs in toponyms *vitepsk*, *brajnsk*, etc.[38]

Using StY as a point of departure, the following rhymes are permitted in stressed syllables (V = vowel, C = consonant, G = glide [j is the only glide in StY]):

-V	*do* 'here,' *ku* 'cow,' *ze* '(I) see,' *ša* 'quiet!' *mi* 'effort'
-VG	*gej* 'go!' *draj* 'three,' *goj* 'non-Jew'
-VC	*bod* 'bath,' *gram* 'rhyme,' *xap* 'grab!' *šif* 'ship'
-VCC	*karp* 'carp,' *zamd* 'sand,' *helf* 'help,' *kost* 'costs,' *lang* 'long,' *vesp* 'wasp'
-VGC	*šrajb* 'write!' *šojn* 'already,' *grejs* 'size'
-VGCC	*lajxt* 'light,' *rajxs* 'rich,' *bojst* '(you) build,' *fajnt* 'enemy,' *gejst* '(you) go'
-VGCCC	*šrajbst* '(you) write,' *tejlst* '(you) share,' *brajnsk* 'toponym'
-VCCC	*melkt* 'milks,' *vitépsk* 'toponym,' *trinkt* 'drinks,' *badékst* '(you) cover'
-VCCCC	*brengst* '(you) bring,' *zinkst* '(you) sink,' *farštarkst* '(you) strengthen,' *melkst* '(you) milk'

The basic maximal Germanic limit to three slots in a rhyme generally holds: diphthongs occur before zero or one consonant, short vowels are followed by two or more consonants. The exception is the coronal appendix; thus, *gejst*, *šrajbst*, *brengst*; even monomorphemes *trejst* 'comfort,' *ojps* 'fruit' have a coronal appendix.[39]

The vocalic length distinction is phonologically important in certain varieties of Yiddish. StY lacks long monophthongs. In the length dialects, long monophthongs (VV) pattern like diphthongs (VG); thus, CY *boj* 'build' *gaj* '(I) go,' are of

[38] Note similar non-coronal overlength with *sk* in Swedish, e.g., *dansk* 'Danish (adj.).'

[39] The rhyme simplification which deletes the coronal *t*, resulting in Yiddish *ojps* 'fruit,' *mark* 'marketplace,' *kunc* 'trick' is historical (cf. StG *Obst*, *Markt*, *Kunst*), and not part of Yiddish synchronic phonology. Thus, StY also has *kunst* 'art' < NHG *Kunst*.

the same type as *du:* 'here,' *ki:* 'cow,' *mi:* 'effort' – with long nucleus and zero coda. CY VV and VG both occur before maximally one C, coronal appendices excepted: *fi:lst* '(you) feel,' *fi:lt* 'feels,' *šra:bt* 'writes,' *kojfst* '(you) buy.' In CY a stressed syllable rhyme may consist of a long vowel and zero coda: *ki:*, *du:*, *dra:* 'three,' or a diphthong: *gaj*, *boj*. NEY, lacking long monophthongs, also lacks syllable rhyme **VV, though it does have VG rhymes. Both NEY and CY have identical stressed syllable *kna-* in *knakər* 'big shot' < root *knak* + suffix *ər*. However, in CY, stressed short rhyme (V) occurs only in derived environments, whereas in NEY, it may occur underlyingly (*ku*, *mi*, *do*).[40] In metrical terms, (underlying) stressed syllables in CY must have at least one branching node: either the nucleus, N → VV or VG, or the rhyme, R → VC. NEY permits non-branching N → V with zero coda. CY non-branching stressed rhymes occur only in derived environments.

Generally, VV or VG occur only if followed by a maximum of one consonant, plus a maximum of two coronal consonants in an appendix. Thus, the maximal rhyme in Yiddish is generally limited to five segments: e.g., StY *šrajbst*, *kemfst*, *harpst*, CY *šra:bst*. NEY diphthongization of *e*, *a* / _ *ŋ* leads to surface forms [brejŋgst] '(you) bring,' [badajŋkst] '(you) thank,' with six segments in the rhyme. However, the *j* glide is predictable, and, thus, might be considered phonologically "invisible" here.

4.3.4 Syllabification

Viler (1924: 147) spells out general syllabification rules for the East Galician Yiddish [EGalY] of Lemberg as follows.

(1) General syllabification:
   (a) a string ... VCV ... will syllabify V $ CV; e.g., /besər/ → *be* $ *sɒ* 'better';
   (b) a string ... V$C_i C_{ii}$V ... will syllabify ... VC_i $ C_{ii}V ... e.g., /altə/ → *al* $ *tə* 'old.'

   However, Viler lists two exceptions to general syllabification:

(2) Sibilant clustering: if, in a string ... V$C_i C_{ii}$V ..., C_i = *s* or *š*, and C_{ii} = voiceless stop (*p,t,k*), then sibilant C_i syllabifies with C_{ii} in the second syllable; e.g., EGalY /e:štn̩s/ → *e:* $ *štn̩s* 'first of all,' /fɒšprajt/ → *fɒ* $ *šprajt* 'spread out.'[41]

(3) Sonorant attraction: if C_{ii} is a sonorant, then C_i syllabifies with C_{ii}, e.g., EGalY *vi* $ *klən* 'wrap,' *ba:* $ *tn̩* 'change,' *maj* $ *dl̩* 'girl.'

[40] CY *ša* 'quiet!' if short, may be an exception. On shortening of destressed vowels in CY, see below.

[41] Prilutski (1940: 49) adds the sequence *ks* to this group, syllabifying *vaksn* → *va* $ *ksn̩* 'grow.' This is supported by internationalisms with initial *ks-*, e.g., *ksenofóbjə* 'xenophobia,' *ksilofón* 'xylophone.' However, this is not sibilant clustering per se.

Sonorant attraction creates onsets which are permissible in Yiddish generally, including word-initially, as seen in the following StY examples:

Sonorant cluster	*StY via sonorant attraction*	*StY word-initially*
kl	vi $ klən 'wrap'	klejn 'small'
tn	ku $ tnər 'from Kutne'	tnaj 'condition'
dl	mej $ dləx 'girls'	dlonjə 'palm (of hand)'
tl	šte $ tləx 'market towns'	tliə 'gallows'
kr	pri $ krə 'embarrassing'	krojt 'cabbage'

There are some asymmetries in the application of sonorant attraction. For example, it is questionable with nasal *n* (and *m*?). The main question is whether there are created any derived onsets which do not occur lexically. Syllabifications *mej* $ *dləx, ku* $ *tnər* are assumed, based on *dlonjə, tnaj*, etc. However, *drobnə* 'petite' presents a problem: *dro* $ *bnə* or *drob* $ *nə*? There is no word-initial ***bn-*. Finally, CY broken and drawled variants of /boux/ 'belly,' /štu:t/ 'city' syllabify *bo* $ *wəx, štu(:)* $ *wət*; thus, with a syllable onset ([w]) which does not occur word-initially.

Automatic syllabification (and postlexical resyllabification across word boundaries) creates more preferred syllables – ones with, rather than without, onsets. Automatic syllabification word-internally occurs both with stressed and unstressed syllables, as seen by addition of the following vowel-initial suffixes:

Unstressed				
-ər	arbət + ər	→	ar – bə – tər	'worker'
	špil + ər	→	špi – lər	'player'
-ə	gut + ə	→	gu – tə	'good'[PL]
	alt + ə	→	al – tə	'old'[PL]
	kligst + ə	→	klig – stə	'smartest'[PL]
-əm	talmid + əm	→	tal – mi – dəm	'pupils'
-iš	lomd + iš	→	lom – diš	'scholarly'

Stressed				
-ánt	aspir + ánt	→	a – spi – ránt	'research student'
-ál	fundament + ál	→	fun-da-men-tál	'fundamental'
-ír(n)	romans + ír(n)	→	ro – man – sírn	'to romance'
-íst	komun + íst	→	ko-mu-níst	'communist'

Automatic syllabification also occurs morpheme-internally: *ga-nəf* 'thief,' *o-zə-rə* 'lake,' *bo-tl* 'void.' Thus, morpheme-internal zero onsets are very rare; they seem limited to two types: (1) recent internationalisms, e.g., *po-émə* '(long) poem,' *po-étiš* 'poetic,' *ne-ologízm* 'neologism,' *di-alóg* 'dialogue,' *te-átər* 'theater'; (2) HA-origin words which historically had intervocalic consonant *alef* or *ayin*; e.g., StY *to-əs* 'mistake,' *məšá-ər* (*zajn*) 'assume,' *rəfú-ə* 'remedy,' *hanó-ə* 'pleasure.' These StY examples contain a medial syllable with zero onset. Yiddish dialects, however, have usually resolved this non-preferred structure in one way or other; e.g., via NEY glide insertion, NEY and SEY glide hardening. NEY glide insertion creates a preferred syllable structure with onset (*j*): *rəfu-jə*, *to-jəs*, *məša-jər*. Analogously, CY breaking and drawl – to the extent that glides are created – creates word-internal onsets: [štu(:)-wət], [bo-wəx], rather than ***štu(:)-Øət*, ***bo:-Øəx*.

4.4 Cyclic and lexical phonology

4.4.1 Dental epenthesis

Yiddish has numerous examples of the phonologically conditioned insertion of a dental stop *t* or *d*, as compared with StG; thus, StY *haldz* 'neck,' *gandz* 'goose,' *menč* ([tš]) 'person' vs. StG *Hals*, *Gans*, *Mensch*. Yiddish also has several words with a dental stop not derivable via regular phonological processes: *demolt* 'then,' *gəvejnləx* ~ *gəvejntləx* 'usual,' *denstmol* 'then'; cf. StG *damals*, *gewöhnlich* (see also Reyzen 1920: 91–94). Likewise, there are words where Yiddish has lost a *t* still present in German: StY *ojps* 'fruit,' *mark* 'marketplace,' *kunc* 'trick' vs. StG *Obst*, *Markt*, *Kunst*. Many of these examples belong to the phonological (pre-)history of Yiddish, and are thus not part of Yiddish synchronic phonology.[42] The following two examples focus on insertion of dental stops in the synchronic phonology of Yiddish.

In regular diminutive formation (Jacobs 1995b), a syllabic *l̩* is suffixed to a nominal form containing a consonantal coda; thus: *tiš* + *l̩* → *tišl̩* 'small table,' *bank* + *l̩* → *benkl̩* 'stool,' *kop* + *l̩* → *kepl̩* 'headline.' However, there is no 1st DIM of *froj* 'woman,' *ku* 'cow,' *tatə* 'father,' since they end in a zero coda. When the base ends in /n/ (either syllabic or non-syllabic), there is epenthesis of oral stop *d*: *bejn* 'bone,' *nign̩* 'melody,' *šejn* 'pretty'+ *l̩* → *bejndl̩*, *nign̩dl̩*, *šejndl̩*.

The *d*-epenthesis breaks up sequences of *nl*. However, mere linear adjacency does not trigger *d*-epenthesis; thus: *finland* 'Finland,' *dajn land* 'your country,' not ***fin[d]land*, ** *dajn [d] land*. Compare 1st DIM plural *bejndləx* 'small bones' with the adjective *pajnləx* 'painful' < *pajn* + *ləx*. The former shows epenthesis, whereas the latter lacks it. The difference is explained through the cyclic phonology, where *d* is inserted only when *n* and *l* are (temporarily) in the same syllable. Thus, *bejn* + *l̩* automatically syllabifies *bej* – *nl̩*, creating

[42] The Yiddish linguistic literature has much discussion of presence or absence of *t/d* (see, e.g., Reyzen 1920; Viler 1924; Gutman 1926; Zaretski 1926; Prilutski 1940). However, these often mix synchronic and diachronic issues.

an unacceptable sequence which is resolved via *d*-epenthesis to *bejndl̩*, which syllabifies acceptably as *bejn – dl̩*. In the next cycle, the plural suffix -*əx* is added; *l̩* becomes [-syllabic] since it is now adjacent to a vowel; thus, surface form *bejn – dləx*. The adjective *pajnləx* is formed by adding suffix -*ləx* to *pajn*; thus, even in the first cycle, *n* and *l* are not tautosyllabic, and no *d* is inserted: *pajn – ləx*. A *d* inserted in the first cycle (*bejndl̩*) remains after application of the second cycle, since there is no operative rule deleting it, thus, *bejndləx*. Non-epenthetic (etymological) *d* remains as well, e.g., *handl* + *ən* → *handlən* 'deal in,' *mandl* + *ən* 'almonds.'

Further evidence that *d*-epenthesis is cyclic is seen in 2nd degree diminution, realized as the discontinuous morpheme *ə* . . . *ə* around 1st DIM suffix *l̩*: *tišələ*, *kepələ*. The 2nd DIM is derived from the 1st DIM, rather than directly from the base form of the noun; thus: *bejndələ*, even though *n* and *l* are no longer adjacent. Where *d*-epenthesis is blocked in the first cycle, it "stays" blocked in the second cycle: *dinə* 'Dinah' → *dinələ*; base form *dinə* may not undergo 1st DIM since it ends in a vowel. When a pseudo-2nd DIM applies in the second cycle, it is too late for *d*-epenthesis to apply. Similarly, the umlaut accompanying 1st DIM is cyclic: *kop* + *l̩* → *kepl̩*; 2nd DIM *kepələ*; whereas *tatə* 'father' misses 1st DIM and, thus, misses umlaut: *tatələ*.[43] Thus, Yiddish *d*-epenthesis between *n* and *l* is a cyclic rule, and sensitive to syllable structure.[44]

A second type of dental stop epenthesis is found between sonorants *n* or *l* and a following sibilant; thus: StY *gandz* 'goose,' *haldz* 'neck, throat,' *mentš* 'person,' regional *faltš* 'false'; cf. StG *Gans*, *Hals*, *Mensch*, *falsch*. Sibilant-triggered epenthesis is largely morpheme-internal, and is arguably historical. Sibilant-triggered epenthesis creates new instances of permissible syllables containing coronal appendices (-*ndz*, -*ldz*, -*ntš*, -*ltš*); cf. StY *zalts* 'salt,' with etymological /t/. Furthermore, subsequent resyllabification creates additional instances of the acceptable onsets: *ts*- (*c*), *tš*- (*č*). The one phonological addition is the occurrence of the affricate *dz* as an onset: *hel-dzl̩*. This epenthesis is cyclic. Thus, epenthetic /t/ in *faltš* remains after later resyllabification: *fal – tšə*, *vel-t-šənə nis* 'walnuts' (cyclically, from [vel-t-š]), whereas no epenthesis in periphrastic verb root *malšən* (*zajn*) 'slander,' where *l* and *š* were never tautosyllabic.

4.4.2 *Dental deletion*

Viler (1924: 14) notes the lack of epenthetic *t* after *l* when two (or more?) consonants follow; thus: *vilst* '(you) want' is phonetically [vilst], not ***viltst* (see also Zaretski 1926: 224). This is best described as a rhyme constraint.

43 Though *ku* 'cow,' with no 1st DIM (since vowel-final), but 2nd DIM is umlauted *kiələ*.

44 The rule must be formulated differently for those dialects which insert *d* in *en-ləx* [endləx] 'similar,' homophonous with *end-ləx* 'finally.'

Compare the following StY forms (deletions indicated by Ø):

/vil-st/	[vilst]	(no epenthesis)	'(you) want'
/volt-st/	[vol-Ø-st]	(t-deletion)	'(you) would'
/get-st/	[getst]	(no deletion)	'(you) divorce'
/bajt-st/	[bajtst]	(no deletion)	'(you) change'
/traxt-st/	[trax-Ø-st]	(t-deletion)	'(you) think'
/max-st/	[maxst]	(no epenthesis)	'(you) make'

The dental stop deletes as part of coda simplification: c*t*cc → c-Ø-cc. CY does not have an /l/ in *voltst*; thus, the *t* does not delete: [votst]. This deletion does not occur after *r* or *n*; thus: *švarts-t* 'blackens,' *bentš-t* 'blesses.'[45]

Dental stop deletion is cyclic. Thus, when the superlative suffix *-st* is added to *gəšikt* 'skillful,' deletion yields *gəšik-Ø-st*. In the next cycle, when an inflectional suffix is added, resyllabification makes the /st/ the onset of the following syllable, but the root-final /t/ has already been deleted: *gəšik-Ø-stə*. If resyllabification preceded deletion, there would have been no reason to delete the underlying /t/ of *gəšikt*.[46]

The cyclic approach to *t*-deletion also presents a solution to a problem noted by Zaretski (1926: 224). He claims that when verb suffix *-st* is added to a verb with root-final /st/ one *-st-* is "lost"; thus: /koststl/ → /kost/ '(you) cost.' In the cyclic approach: *kost* + *st* → *kos-Ø-st* (*t*-deletion) → *kos-Ø-Ø-t* (degemination) → [kost]. Likewise, superlatives of adjectives with root-final /st/ would be homophonous with their base adjectives: *ernst* + *st* + *ə* and *ernst* + *ə* are both realized as [ernstə] '(most) serious,' *bavust* + *st* + *ə* and *bavust* + *ə* as [bavustə] '(most) eminent.' Tellingly, Zaretski notes: "one writes *ernststər*, *bavuststər*... but these are avoided in the spoken language."

4.4.3 Obstruent voicing assimilation

Dialects differ in the application of anticipatory voicing assimilation in obstruents [OVA]. In all dialects, OVA applies within a morpheme (called voicing resolution, above: *xe[ž]bm* 'bill' < TH *ħešbo:n*), as well as within a word consisting of root + inflection (*šrajb* + *t* → [šrajpt]). In NEY, OVA is so pervasive that it can be described as a linear rule, applying cyclically, post-cyclically, and post-lexically; thus: NEY *dos bux* 'the book,' *štex dir* 'prick you,' *fest* + *gəštelt* 'confirmed' → *do[z] bux*, *šte[γ] dir*, *fe[z(d)]gəštelt*. On the surface it appears that OVA is lacking in CY and SEY, e.g., CY *du[s] bi:əx*; cf. compound StY

[45] In both instances other factors may play a role: *r* within a rhyme frequently patterns like a vowel; with *n*, there is the variation between nasalized vowel + sibilant vs. V*n* + sibilant, noted above.

[46] Yiddish superlatives generally occur in inflected form only. Thus, *t*-deletion in this example provides evidence for the reality of cyclic phonology.

fusbenkl 'bench,' CY *fi:[s]benkl*, NEY *fu[z]bejnkl*. Herzog *et al.* (1992: 38, citing Gutman 1928) state that CY has a "German" sandhi type (all obstruents are voiceless in word-final position), whereas NEY has an "Eastern Slavic" sandhi type (with OVA). Thus, SEY may prove particularly interesting, since it lacks final devoicing, yet does not seem to show OVA. In a compound such as *tog-student* 'day student,' *g* → *k* / _ *s* in NEY via OVA; it devoices to [k] via final devoicing in CY, but remains voiced in SEY. However, in words such as *kligstə* 'most intelligent (inflected),' the /g/ presumably devoices in all Yiddish dialects due to the cycle with /kligst/, in which /g/ and /st/ were tautosyllabic. SEY thus might have *tu[g]-student*, but *kli[k]stə*. After the inflectional suffix -ə is added, resyllabification occurs: *klik – stə*, but the devoicing *k* < *g* is not undone. OVA is clearly not post-lexical in CY and SEY (*xap grojsə* 'catch big . . . '), whereas it applies post-lexically in NEY (*xa[b] grejsə*).

However, the situation in CY and SEY is more complex. Elements of the "Eastern Slavic sandhi type" are found under certain (varying) conditions. Thus, Bin-Nun's (1973: 331) Retín *ouzugn* 'divulge' can only arise via degemination after OVA: *ous* + *zugn* → **ou[z]zugn* → *ou-Ø-zugn*. Although OVA in CY generally is not linear (or post-lexical), it does seem to occur in more closely linked constructions, as well as in quicker speech. Bin-Nun (p. 331) cites *rikn* 'move,' but *ri[g] dɒx* 'move yourself,' *gib a ri:[f]* 'call' (singulative aspect) vs. *ɒri:[v] gəgein* 'called' (singulative aspect). Note also OVA where a historical word boundary has been lost in the surname *li[f]šits*, *li[p]šits* (< **v*, **b*). Finally, true clitics (as opposed to full pronoun objects) do not trigger OVA, even in NEY; thus, NEY *hot zəx* [(h)otsəx] 'has + self' vs. *hot zilbər* [(h)od zilbər] 'has silver.'

4.4.4 Degemination

Yiddish lacks geminate consonants. Historical morpheme-internal geminates were eliminated in Pre-Yiddish or PY (StY *šabəs* 'Sabbath' < TH *šabbɔ:θ*). However, Yiddish synchronically creates and eliminates new geminates.[47] Yiddish degemination is persistent, occurring both within a word, and across word boundaries; thus: StY *gəhit* + *t* + ə [gəhitə] 'cautious,' *ojs* + *sejdərn* [ojsejdərn] 'put in order,' *on* + *nemən* [onemən] 'accept,' *vil laxn* [vilaxŋ] 'wants to laugh'; Bin-Nun (1973: 334) gives Retín *a bejt tin* [ɒbejti:n] 'request' (singulative aspect). Other processes feed degemination, e.g., after voicing assimilation: *gəred* + *t* + ə → [gəretə] 'spoken' (inflected), *avek* + *gejn* → [avegejn] 'go away,' *op* + *brengən* → [obreŋgən] 'bring back'; after sibilant assimilation: *ojs* + *šisn* → *oj[šš]isn* → [ojšisn] 'go off; fire.' Thus, homophones

[47] Bin-Nun (1973: 334) notes gemination in fast speech: *zenən* → [zenn] 'are.' However, the second *n* is likely syllabic: [zenn̩]. Viler (1924: 146–147) claims "the only gemination in Yiddish" is intervocalic -*jj*- in, e.g., eCY *oj-jɒ* 'ear.'

arise with the abstract noun suffix *kajt* in *grin* 'green' + *kajt* → [griŋkajt] 'greenness' (n → ŋ/_k), and *gring* 'simple' + *kajt* → *griŋgkajt* → *griŋkkajt* (*g* → k / _ k) → [griŋkajt] 'simplicity' (degemination). Note also that geminate /nn/ is avoided in CY dialects where verb particle /u:n/ (StY *on*) is realized as [ũ:]: /u:nnejmən/ [ũ:nejmə] 'accept.'

Examples of apparent gemination may be accounted for prosodically. Whereas *l* + *l* → *l* (*vil laxn* → *vilaxn* 'wants to laugh'), consider the compound noun *hengḷ-lajxtər* 'chandelier.' Syllabic *ḷ* in *hengḷ* functions as the nucleus of the syllable *gḷ*, whereas initial *l* in *lajxtər* is a consonantal onset. Thus, because of their roles within the prosodic syllable structure, *ḷ* + *l* do not undergo degemination (see Viler 1924: 146). Furthermore, although syllabic *ḷ* automatically becomes [-syllabic] when a vowel is added cyclically (*pekḷ* + *əx* → *peklәx* 'parcels'), *ḷ* remains syllabic when followed by a vowel post-lexically: *bejgḷ* + *esər* → *bejgḷ-esər* 'bagel-eater,' not ***bejglesər*; likewise, *in štetḷ arajn* 'into town,' not ***in šte[tla] rajn*. This suggests that syllabification and syllable structure are cyclic in Yiddish. Thus, cyclic *mit-nemər* 'person who takes something along' has three syllables, *mit – ne – mər*, while post-cyclic *mitn emər* 'with the bucket' has four syllables: *mi-tṇ – e – mər*. The *n* of *mitn*, made vocalic by the prosodic phonology, does not then undergo normal consonant resyllabification, while a consonantal *n* does: *an emər* → *a $ ne – mər* 'a bucket,' but *mi – tṇ – e – mər*. Thus, consonant degemination in Yiddish applies after cyclic syllable structure has assigned C or V status.

4.4.5 *CY* l*-palatalization*

Many varieties of CY and SEY have contextual palatalization of *l*, alongside underlying /l'/ (see Bratkowsky 1974). The phenomenon is more widespread in CY, occurring in three main environments (Bin-Nun 1973: 339–342): after *k*/*g*; before front vowels *i*, *e*; after *i*. Of present interest are the occurrences after *k*/*g*, and where these fit in the phonology (Jacobs 1996b). The process occurs morpheme-internally– CY /glu:z/ 'glass,' /klajn/ 'small' → [gl'u:əs], [kl'ajn] – as well as across morpheme boundaries: *ring* + *ḷ* → [riŋgḷ'] 'little ring,' *pak* + *ḷ* → *pekḷ'* 'parcel.' Palatalized *ḷ'* remains in 1st DIM plurals (it becomes, automatically, [-syllabic]): *riŋgl'əx*, *pekl'əx*. However, in 2nd DIM, *l* is not palatalized: *riŋgɒlə*, *pekɒlə*. Furthermore, CY *l*-palatalization does not apply across word boundaries: *aveklajgn* 'put down' is *ɒ-ve-[kl]ajgn*, not **[kl'] (cf. present indicative *ix lajg avek*). Thus, the process is not post-lexical. Proposing that it is cyclic would require a special rule which depalatalizes *ringḷ'*, *pekḷ'* in the 2nd DIM cycle: *ringɒlə*, *pekɒlə*; similarly, presumably CY *miškḷ'* – *miškú:ləm* (prosodic) 'meter-s.' However, underlying /l'/ in, e.g., *l'al'kə* 'doll,' *l'ul'kə* 'pipe,' *revol'ucjə* 'revolution', does not depalatalize. Therefore, CY *l*-palatalization is likely a post-cyclic rule which applies to /l/ in the appropriate environments, but which has no effect on underlying /l'/. After post-lexical resyllabification /l/ remains non-palatalized in *aveklajgn̩*, *aveklojfn̩*, etc., while underlying [l'] word-internally remains; e.g., *dekl'aracjə* (Bin-Nun 1973: 321).

4.4.6 *Final devoicing of obstruents in CY*

WY and CY are generally described as possessing word-final obstruent devoicing. The present discussion is on devoicing in CY. The situation is complex, both phonologically and geographically. Some of the complexity has to do with the related problem of OVA and the two main sandhi types mentioned above ("German" vs. "Eastern Slavic"). Ideally, the areas of OVA (identified with NEY) and devoicing (identified with CY) do not overlap. However, even in CY, devoicing seems blocked in close juncture with a voiced sound; thus, Bin-Nun (1973: 331) notes for the verb *laign̩* 'lay': *laik* '(I) lay,' but *laigəs* 'lay it,' *laig ništ* 'don't lay'; *gip* '(I) give,' but *gib ɪm* 'give him'; Viler (1924: 33) gives *klu[g] žə* 'complain then'; CY *ri:f* 'call' (underlying /f/) > *a ri:[v] gɪgein* 'gave a call' (Bin-Nun 1973: 331). Thus, we distinguish between close-juncture voicing assimilation in CY (*f* → *v* in *a ri:[v] gɪgein*) vs. the non-application of devoicing before vowel or sonorant consonant: *gi[b] əm* 'give him' (vs. *xa[p] əm* 'catch him'). Further, Stankiewicz (1991: 211) has suggested that CY devoicing does not apply to verbs and adjectives; thus: CY /tug/ [k] 'day' vs. /zug/ [g] '(I) say.' Herzog *et al.* (1992: 38) contrast (*ix*) *red* '(I) speak' with (*er*) *ret* '(he) speaks.' Thus, either Bin-Nun (1973) is wrong in claiming devoicing in 1P.SG verb forms like [gip] (< /gib/), [lajk] (< /lajg/), or there is geographic variation in CY.

Devoicing operates in the post-cyclic phonology; otherwise, there would be no way to retrieve the underlying /d/ in CY *lant* 'country' for plural *lendər* without voicing an underlying /t/ as well (plural of *blat* 'leaf' is *bletər*, not ***ble[d]ər*); similarly, the devoicing of underlying /d/ in CY [mojt] 'maiden,' since 1st DIM shows the [d]: *majdl̩*.[48] Devoicing is also distinct from the cyclic (thus, word-internal) devoicing that occurs as part of voicing resolution. Viler (1924: 33) compares imperative singular [zi:d ouəs] (/zi:d o:s/ 'boil!') with [d] vs. imperative plural [zi:ts ouəs] (/zi:d-ts o:s/) with voiceless [ts]. In the former, close juncture with the V-initial verb particle allows maintenance of the [d]. In the latter, root /d/ devoices cyclically (via voicing resolution) before suffix [ts]. The cyclically devoiced consonant is not restorable to an underlying voiced /d/.

[48] One exception is given in Bin-Nun (1973: 331): *bi:tl̩*, a 1st DIM of /bu:d/ [bu:ət] 'bath'; with plural [beidɒ].

4.4.7 Schwa deletion in the prosodic phonology

Discussion of lexical schwa deletion [LSD] in Yiddish (Jacobs 1990a: 92–97) concerns the fleeting schwa in, e.g., *ejdl̩ – ejdələr* 'refined,' *ongəšribn̩ – ongəšribənər* 'written'; that is, syllabic sonorant versus schwa + sonorant. Basically, the conditioning environment is whether or not a vowel follows the sonorant. Two analyses are possible: either an underlying vowel is deleted [LSD], or there is a rule of vowel epenthesis. Several points justify the LSD analysis. First, compare the inflected form of the adjective *jung* 'young' + nasal suffix: *jungn̩* ([juŋgŋ̩]) vs. plural of noun *jung* 'unmarried male': *jungən*. Verbs and nouns require a schwa to separate root-final nasal consonants *n*, *m*, or clusters *ng* and *nk* from a nasal suffix; cf. infinitives *kumən* 'come,' *zingən* 'sing' vs. *šrajbn̩* 'write,' *drukn̩* 'print.' However, with adjectives this holds only for root-final *n* and *m*: *šejn-əm* 'pretty,' *frum-ən* 'pious,' but *lang-n̩* 'long.' Thus, we posit underlying adjective suffix /n/, and underlying noun-plural suffix /ən/ (*jungn̩* vs. *jungən*). Positing underlying /n/ for both, along with a general rule of vowel epenthesis, would yield identical surface forms (*jungən*). Similarly, positing underlying /ən/ for both, followed by a general LSD, would also lead to homophony, either by application of LSD (*jungn* in both instances), or by a special blocking of LSD, based on the cluster *ng* (*jungən* in both instances). LSD is formulated as follows: ə → Ø / C _ n,l (C) $.

	no vowel follows	*vowel follows*	
1.	ejdl̩	ejdələ	'refined'
	ongəšribn̩	ongəšribənə	'written'
	nign̩	nigúnim	'melody'
	rexn̩	rexənən	'reckon'
2.	handl̩	handlən	'deal in'
	lign̩ 'lie' (noun)	lignər	'liar'
	–	drobnə	'petite'
	–	nudnə	'boring'
	–	nudnik	'pest, bore'

The forms in 1 contain an underlying vowel, which deletes when the conditions of LSD are met (*ejdl̩, rexn̩*), but which is not deleted when a vowel follows the sonorant (*ejdələ, nigúnim*). The forms in 2 lack an underlying vowel; none is deleted, and none is inserted. Thus, Yiddish has a general rule of LSD, but no general rule of vowel epenthesis. A nasal suffix is used to form adjectives out of many nouns designating materials, metals, etc. The plural forms of the adjectives are *goldənə* 'golden,' *štolənə* 'of steel,' *blajənə* 'leaden,' etc.; see Zaretski (1926: 73); cf. English *golden*, *silken*, *wooden*, etc. For foot-based considerations, the suffix is realized as *n* after an unstressed syllable; thus: *zílbərnə* 'of silver,' *xéjləvnə* 'of tallow.' Where stress is on the immediately preceding syllable, schwa before *n* occurs: *papírənə* 'of paper.'

LSD is post-cyclic. If LSD were a cyclic rule, then schwa would delete in /ongəšribən/, /ejdəl/ → *ongəšribṇ*, *ejdḷ* in the first cycle. Since there is no general rule of vowel epenthesis, there would be no way to restore the schwa in a later cycle when a vowel-initial suffix is added, without at the same time inserting a schwa in words like *lignər*, *handlən*. Furthermore, LSD is not post-lexical, since no schwa is found in, e.g., *er hot ongəšribṇ a briv* 'he wrote a letter'; not *ongəšrib[**ə]n a briv*.

LSD is confronted with a problem vis-à-vis diminutive formation [DIMFORM]. DIMFORM is a cyclic rule, LSD a post-cyclic rule. DIMFORM requires that its base noun end in a consonant coda. Application of DIMFORM is blocked after a syllable nucleus; thus, no 1st DIM of *ku* 'cow,' *tatə* 'father,' *froj* 'woman.' Furthermore, whereas a special 1st DIM occurs after consonantal /l/ (*mil* 'mill,' *mojl* 'mouth' → *milxl*, *majlxl*), no 1st DIM may be formed after a syllabic *ḷ*, in, e.g., *fojgḷ* 'bird,' *mojḷ* 'ritual circumciser.' Presumably this is so because the SSA has already specified this noun-final syllabic *ḷ* as a nucleus, and DIMFORM may not apply after a nucleus. Presumably, the SSA specifies noun-final *ṇ* as a nucleus as well, and 1st DIMFORM should be blocked here. Instead, we find *nigṇ* → *nigṇdḷ* 'little melody.' Positing underlying /nigun/, based on plural /nigunim/, yields consonantal, non-syllabic /n/ and permits regular application of 1st DIMFORM. Since LSD is post-cyclic, some sort of vowel (*u* or *ə*) before the /n/ would still be present throughout the cyclic phonology. However, there remains a troublesome list of nouns with syllabic *ṇ* and no support for positing an underlying vowel. According to the SSA, such an *ṇ* would be assigned nucleus status, and block 1st DIMFORM. In fact, Yiddish speakers have shown their awareness of this problem by treating this class of nouns in ways which try – by one strategy or another – simply to avoid the problem. Thus, from *zibṇ* 'seven' obtains *zibələ* 'premature baby'; *gortṇ* 'garden' yields doublets: SY *gurtṇdḷ* ~ *gertṇdḷ*, NEY *gertḷ*; *kastṇ* 'box' → *kestḷ* ~ *kastṇdḷ*. For *nigṇ*, alongside a largely SY *nigṇdḷ* is NEY *nigələ*. Some nouns show a clearer tendency to generalize one strategy; thus, *štekṇ* 'stick' → *štekḷ*. In the Ukraine we find plural *ligínim* of singular *ligṇ* 'lie,' presumably on analogy with SY *nigṇ* – *nigí(:)nim* (Mordkhe Schaechter, p.c.). Thus, by various means, Yiddish speakers have tried strategies to overcome the problem syllabic *ṇ* poses for the prosodic phonology, either by eliding it (NEY *nigələ*, *gertḷ*), or by treating it like a coda of an LSD-reduced syllable (Ukrainian Yiddish *ligṇ* – *ligínim*).

4.4.8 *Resyllabification*

Yiddish has general post-lexical resyllabification: *zet alə* 'sees all [PL]' → *ze $ ta $ lə*; *est epl* 'eats apples' → *e $ ste $ pl*; *avek-lojfn* 'run away' → *a $ ve*

$ kloj $ fn. Thus, resyllabification comes later in the phonology than CY final devoicing; cf. compound *tu[k]-arbətər* 'day-laborer,' syllabifying as *tu $ kar $ bə $ tər* (though *tu[g]ṇnaxt*).

4.5 Stress and relative prominence

In the metrical approach only one element within a linguistic unit may emerge with primary stress; other levels of stress are derived hierarchically or rhythmically; thus, *refórm, jídiš, fírn, bíxər*, but *reformírn, jidišíst, ónfirn, tógbixər*. The main treatment of Yiddish word stress to date is U. Weinreich (1954); see also Wolf (1977) and Glasser (1990). Many of the examples in the present discussion are taken from these works. Weinreich's main concern was the unambiguous delineation of the word in Yiddish according to structuralist methodology. The present discussion assumes the metrical word (ω) as a basic unit in phonological processes. Present points of disagreement with Weinreich's analysis derive largely from the theoretical approaches employed here, just as Weinreich's observations were shaped by the structuralist framework. For example, Weinreich (1954: 4) is quick to reject secondary stress in compounds like *xúpə-klèjd* 'wedding dress,' whereas the metrical approach sees secondary stress as a regular by-product of the process of compounding. Similarly, Weinreich (p. 3) sees the secondary stress in *kàrosérjə* '(automobile) body' as the result of the higher sonority of [a] over [o], whereas the metrical approach describes this in terms of foot-formation rules.

4.5.1 Word stress: general

The statements most commonly made about Yiddish word stress may be summarized as follows. (1) In the Germanic component stress is fixed on the initial root syllable, e.g., *lébn* 'live,' *lébədik* 'lively,' *balébn* 'animate,' *árbət* 'work,' *gəárbət* 'worked,' *árbətndik* 'working.' (2) In internationalisms, stress falls on the suffix, e.g., *komuníst, internacjonál, internacjonalízm, aspiránt* 'research student.' (3) There is a type of stress shift within the root in many HA-component nouns and adjectives: *tálməd-talmídəm* 'pupil-s,' *gánəf-ganóvəm* 'thief-thieves,' *séjfər-sfórəm* 'holy book-s,' *lámdṇ-lamdónəm* 'scholar-s,' adjective *lamdóniš* 'scholarly.' (4) Penultimate stress is the default stress in Yiddish; that is, assume penultimate stress unless otherwise indicated.

However, the situation is more complex than these common generalizations would indicate. For (1) note the main stress in complex verbs like *avékgèjn* 'go away,' *ónšràjbn* 'finish writing.' For (2) note non-final stress in *komunístišə, aspirántn*. For (3) note that stress shifts in some non-HA-origin nouns like *klímat-klimátn* 'climate-s,' *lítvak-litvákəs* 'Lithuanian Jew-s,' *kózak-kozákn* 'Cossack-s,' *bóčan-bočánəs* 'stork-s' (Glasser 1990: 93). For (4), note ultimate stress in *kontákt, ekspórt, bagáž, submarín, samovár, garderób, kanibál, alfabét*; thus, *klímat* vs. *špinát* 'spinach' requires explanation, as does the penultimate stress in *kapótə* 'kaftan,' *torpédə* 'torpedo,' when compared to the antepenultimate stress in *xásənə* 'wedding,' *pérənə* 'featherbed,' *glóbusn* 'globes.' While many of the problems in stress location can be explained historically (Leibel 1965; Green 1969), the task at hand is to provide a synchronic phonological account for the disparate facts of Yiddish stress.

Glasser (1990) provides detailed discussion of canonical shapes, and posits (p. 88) abstract underlying representations (see also Wolf 1977; Lowenstamm 1979), which may be summarized as follows.

Fixed stress

(a) Monosyllabic base noun – root syllable keeps stress in plural: *tiš-tíšn̩* 'table-s,' *sod-sójdəs* 'secret-s,' *šed-šéjdəm* 'ghost-s,' *slup-slúpəs* 'pole-s,' *bild-bíldər* 'picture-s.'

(b) Base noun ends in a vowel – stress remains fixed in plural: *šo-šóən* 'hour-s,' *tójrə-tójrəs* 'Torah-s,' *žábə-žábəs* 'frog-s,' *frágə-frágəs* 'question-s,' *géto-gétos* 'ghetto-s'; *bjuró-bjuróən* 'office-s,' *talmídə -talmídəs* '(female) pupil-s.' A class of exceptions requires abstract underlying representations: *ílə-ilúəm* 'child prodigy, -ies,' *gábə-gabóəm* 'synagogue trustee-s' (Glasser 1990: 105).

(c) Base noun has ultimate stress, and the stress remains fixed on that syllable: *konflíkt-n* 'conflict-s,' *internát-n* 'college dormitory,-ies,' *ekspórt-n* 'export-s,' *jəríd-əm* 'fair-s,' *samovár-n* 'samovar-s,' *garderób-n* 'cloak room-s.' This holds as well for adjectives derived from ultimate-stress nouns or verbs: *socjalíst-iš* 'socialistic,' *socjalizír-ungən* 'socializations.'

(d) Base noun has fixed initial stress: *kórpus-n* 'corpus-es', *módus-n* 'mode-s,' *pénis-n* 'penis-es,' *pátos-n* 'pathos,' *gúlaš-n* 'gulash-es.' The examples (Glasser 1990: 91–92) mostly contain a non-productive quasi-morphemic (unstressable) ending: *-um/-is/-us*, etc. To this class may be added Gmc-component nouns with consonant-final second syllable (whether root or suffix): *árbət-ər* 'worker,' *šrájbung-ən* 'writings.'

Two problems remain concerning the location of lexical stress. First, there is regional stress variation in Slavicisms in Yiddish dialects, e.g., *kápətə* ~ *kapótə* 'kaftan,' *káləžə* ~ *kalúžə* 'puddle.' Green (1969) showed that stress for a given word in a given dialect location had to do with (a) the historical phonology of Yiddish and the relevant Slavic source dialects; (b) sociolinguistically determined diffusion of forms across Yiddish dialects. The variation occurs in words of three or more syllables (p. 219). There is no way to predict synchronically *kápətə* or *kapótə* based on factors such as weight of penult syllable (thus: *truskáfkə* '(cultivated) strawberry,' *podéšvə* '(shoe) sole' have heavy penults, but so do dialect variants *póžəmkəs* ~ *požómkəs* 'wild strawberries,' *mógilkə*

~ *mahílkə* 'non-Jewish cemetery). Thus, for trisyllabic words, stress is on the first or second syllable if the (base/non-derived) word ends in a vowel;[49] ultimate stress if C-final (*samovár*). The exceptions to the latter occur with the "latinate" quasi-suffixes in, e.g., *máksimum, mínimum, édipus*, etc. Non-final stress in variant *revólvər* (~ *revolvér*) 'revolver' may reflect analysis by some speakers of a root *revólv* + suffix *ər*.

The second problem concerns words with movable root stress [MRS]: *tálməd - talmídəm, klímat - klimátn, bóčan - bočánəs*, 'stork-s', *lítvak - litvákəs, lámdn - lamdónəm.*[50] These contain C-final disyllabic base. (Trisyllabic bases have fixed stress; cf. above: *talmídə-s, garderób-n.*) C-final disyllabics with ultimate stress keep fixed stress: *kontákt-n, jəríd-əm, špinát-n, bagáž-n.* Thus, the concern is with stress in types *tálməd-talmídəm, lámdn-lamdónəm*, and *klímat-klimátn, ádres-adrésn* 'address-es', along with why PTR/LSD occur in the former (*tálm[ə]d, lamd-Ø-n*), but not in the latter (*klím*[a]*t*).

I posit underlying stress differences in /špinát/ vs. /klímat/, and a cyclic rule of stress backing [SB] for trisyllabic plurals; thus: *klimátn*; SB applies vacuously in *špinátn*. Again, the type *kórpus* resists SB; the exceptions all involve word-final *-us/-is/-os/-um/-aš* (Glasser 1990: 91–92). The problem lies with HA-component words. Following Wolf (1977), Lowenstamm (1979), and Glasser (1990), we must resort to abstract underlying representations. Positing underlying /gánOv/, /lámdOn/ (on abstract representation of vowel /O/, see below), with initial stress, and SB in plurals *ganóvəm, lamdónəm* creates a problem for adjective derivation, where suffix *-iš* does not generally affect stress: *šrájbəriš* 'writerly,' but *lamdóniš* 'scholarly,' not ***lámdniš*. Thus, distinct from cyclic stress assignment, I posit a post-cyclic rule of stress fronting [SF], which applies to abstract forms (with underlying final stress) /lamdÓn/, /talmÍd/ → [lámdn], [tálməd], yet does not apply to *bagáž, špinát*. This claim is supported by diverse data. First, the canonic shape of the vocalism in SF words patterns distinctly from non-SF words (Glasser 1990). Second, post-tonic vowel reduction [PTR] applies only to vowels destressed by SF, but not to underlyingly unstressed vowels (*tálm[ə]d*, but *klím[a]t*). Furthermore, vowels destressed cyclically (including rhythmically) maintain vowel color: *socjál, sòcj[a]líst, cvuják, cvùj[a]kízm* 'hypocrisy,' *kantón, kànt[o]níst, absólv, àbs[o]lvént*; thus: *tálməd* < /talmúd/, but *tàlm[u]díst*. Finally, consideration of level 1 and level 2 affixes (below) shows that allomorph selection is cyclic, and is sensitive to abstract

[49] Green (1969: 216) notes ultimate-stressed Slavicism *čepuxá* 'nonsense' as a non-integrated foreignism.

[50] The two main approaches to MRS have been (a) diachronic (Katz 1977, 1982; Jacobs 1979, 1990a), and (b) appeal to separate lexicons (Birnbaum 1979a). Synchronic description of HA-component MRS via abstract representations is found in Wolf (1977); Lowenstamm (1979); Glasser (1990).

structures which are not etymologically based, but, rather, apply in the language generally.

Plural allomorphs frequently provide evidence for the underlying abstract vowel; for StY /i/ in *tálməd*, /ej/ in *xávər*, /u/ in *šídəx*, /o/ in *məšúməd*, based on plurals *talmídəm* 'pupils,' *xavéjrəm* 'friends,' *šidúxəm* 'matches,' *məšəmódəm* 'apostates.' HA-component nouns like StY *sójfər* 'scribe,' *séjfər* 'holy book' (which happen to end in [ər]), are best seen from the perspective of their plural forms, *sófrəm*, *sfórəm*. If the underlying form were based on the singular, there would be no way to distinguish these from nouns like *šrájbər(-s)* 'writer-s.'[51] Similarly, words like *gábə*, *ílə* require abstract representations based on their plurals *gabóəm*, *ilúəm*; otherwise, regular *-s* plurals would be generated.

Word stress in the HA-origin elements is formulated as follows. (1) The underlying form is based on the plural, including specification of the location of stress; thus, singulars /lamdÓn/, /talmÍd/, based on plurals *lamdónəm*, *talmídəm*.[52] (2) There is a special post-cyclic stress-fronting rule [SF] limited specifically to these disyllabics (with the exception that schwa may not carry stress: *jəríd*). (3) SF applies vacuously in Yiddish *šójmər* 'guard,' since the plural already has initial stress: *šómrəm*.[53] Wolf (1977: 135) notes that this forces underlying abstract /sejfÓr/ 'holy book,' plural /sejfÓrəm/, in order to obtain both singular *séjfər* and plural *sfórəm*. Adjective derivation provides additional evidence for abstract underlying forms; cf. StY *gazlóniš* 'murderous,' *talmúdiš* 'Talmudic,' *lamdóniš* 'scholarly.' Adjective *baləbátiš* 'well-to-do' clearly is derived from noun plural *baləbátəm*, not singular *baləbós* 'owner.'

Consider MRS in *klímat – klimátn* vs. fixed stress in *špinát – špinátn*. Applying a stress-fronting rule like the one applying in HA-component nouns, to obtain *klímat* < **/klimát/ would likewise yield initially stressed ***špínat*. Thus, underlying initial stress is posited for *klímat*, *ádres* 'address,' *bóčan* 'stork,' *kózak* 'Cossack,' *lítvak* 'Lithuanian Jew,' *dólar* 'dollar,' *vóron* 'raven,' *rótor* 'rotor,' which undergo stress-backing [SB] to obtain penultimate stress in *klimátn*, *adrésn*, *bočánəs*, etc.[54] SB applies vacuously in *kontákt-n*, *ekspórt-n*, etc. The phonological case can be made, but it must resort to a degree of abstractness. The role of morphological environments should be kept in mind. The SF-words show specific suffixes: plural *-əm*, abstract-noun *-əs*. SB words have

[51] A Yiddish loan in German provides external evidence for the plural as the base form: singular *Ganóve* 'thief' < plural *Ganóven*.

[52] Capital letters are used here to hedge the exact representation. Glasser and Wolf posit long vowels, which corresponds to the historical Hebrew situation, and to length varieties of Yiddish. However, I hesitate to posit underlying long vowels for Yiddish varieties in which no long vowels surface.

[53] The alternation *oj* (in open syllable) vs. *o* (in closed syllable) is synchronically morphophonemic.

[54] Glasser (1990: 94) calls these nouns foreign-like in the singular, native-like in their plural forms. Here he is referring to the presence of a morpheme-internal non-reduced post-tonic vowel in the singular forms. See also Zaretski (1926: 229).

plural suffixes *-n* or *-əs*. Words with quasi-morphemic unstressable "latinate" endings *-us/-os/-is/-um/-aš* do not undergo SB.

4.5.2 *Suffixation and word stress*

For Yiddish we must distinguish among: (1) suffixes which are never stressed; (2) suffixes which may receive a type of secondary stress; (3) suffixes which demand primary word stress (which can reduce in a later phonological cycle); (4) elements which are popularly perceived as suffixes, but which behave phonologically as a separate word.

Unstressable suffixes – type (1) – include[55] adjective suffixes *-ə*, *-ər*, *-n*, (~ *-ən*, *-əm*), *-iš*, *-ləx*, *-ik*; verb suffixes *-ən*, *-əvə*, *-kə*; noun suffixes: *-ḷ*, *-ələ*, *-kə*, *-tə*, *-jə*, *-əs*, *-əm*, *-šə*, *-əxts*. These suffixes normally (non-contrastively) may not receive stress. However, their presence may allow underlying stress to surface on another root syllable or suffix: *or* in *profésor* stresses in plural *profesórn* 'professors,' *profesóriš* 'professorial.' This is best described in terms of underlying stress for the element *or*, since an unstressable element remains unstressed before plural *-n*: *kórpus-n*. Thus, type (1) suffixes in general do not change overall word stress: *gút-ə*, *šrájbər-iš*, *bésər-ə*, *árbət-ər*, *šnájd-ər-kə*. In HA-origin nouns like *lámdn*, *šídəx*, initial stress arises via the rule of SF; the underlying stress is /lamdÓn/; thus, adjective suffix *-iš* does not affect stress in *lamdóniš*.

Type 1 suffixes frequently contain a schwa vowel. Unstressed suffixes with a full vowel might arguably be assigned to class 2, which bear underlying (secondary) stress. StY does not provide evidence to support or refute this claim. However, some dialects regularly reduce the vowel in suffixes *-ik*, *-iš* to [ə]; thus, regional *(j)ídəš* 'Yiddish.' In these dialects, the schwa remains when a following syllable is added: *j(í)dəšə*, and the underlying representations of these particular suffixes are /ək/, /əš/. However, in other varieties, some "unstressed" suffixes emerge with (optional) secondary stress when non-final; thus Retín CY regularly shows *šábəsd[ə]k* vs. *šábəsd[ì]kə* 'Sabbath; festive.' Here, *-dik* has underlying stress.

The allomorphy of certain suffixes – *(ə)niš*, *-(ə)dik*, *-(ə)nju*, CY *(ə)ši* – suggests a rhythmic strategy for maintaining vowel color. The strong syllable of the suffix distances itself from a preceding stressed syllable via schwa; cf. *badérf-əniš* 'need,' *gəšé-əniš* 'event' vs. *fínstər-niš* 'darkness'; *léb-ədik* 'lively' vs. *šábəs-dik* 'Sabbath; festive,' *prótəm-dik* 'detailed,' *péjsəx-dik* 'fit for Passover'; *tróg-ədik* 'pregnant,' but *trógn-dik* 'carrying,' *trogəv-dik* 'carriable'; the endearing address forms *gót-ənju* 'God,' *zún-ənju* 'son' vs. *tatə-nju* 'Dad,'

[55] Ignored here are suffixes which lack any (potentially) syllabic element; e.g., verb suffix *-t*.

bóbə-nju 'Grandma,' *brúdər-nju* 'brother.' However, we must be cautious in equating vowel color with underlying stress. Morpheme-internal post-tonic vowels in a simplex word are not necessarily schwa (*klímat* 'climate,' *vóron* 'raven,' *róman* 'man's name'), and the unstressed suffix *-[u]ng* also maintains color (*farbetung* 'invitation'). Furthermore, varieties of NEY preserve post-tonic vowel color where StY has schwa: NEY *éjl[ɔ]m* 'audience' vs. *éjl[i]m* 'pilgrims.'

It was claimed above that SF in the HA-component disyllabics is post-cyclic. Thus, singulars *jóntəv* 'holiday,' *mázl* 'luck' are posited as underlying /jontójv/, /mazÓl/ based on plural forms *jontójvəm,mazóləs* 'astrological signs.' However, the adjective forms are *jóntəvdik,mázldik*, with initial stress, and apparently based on the singular forms. We might expect ***mazól-ədik*, ***jontójv-ədik*. The apparent exceptions all seem to consist of strings which are open to (re-) interpretation as morphemes in Yiddish: *-əv* in *jóntəvdik* (cf. *trog-əv-dik*), *-l̩* in *mázldik* (cf. *bix-l̩-dik* 'bookish'); note also *xávər-iš* 'friendly,' *xázər-iš* 'piggish,' where both nouns end in morpheme-like root *ər*. These are apparent exceptions since SF is post-cyclic, and the cyclic application of *-(ə)dik* should presumably bleed SF. Note that the trisyllabic word *sakónə-s* 'danger-s' yields *sakónə-dik* ~ *sakónəs-dik* 'dangerous.' Both variants provide a final unstressed syllable; thus, the adjective allomorph predictably is *-dik*. We would predict that /lamdÓn/ would yield adjective ***lamdónədik*; however, this does not obtain. Rather, an intervening abstract-noun suffix typically occurs with this type of root; thus, *raxmón-əs-dik* 'merciful,' but neither ***ráxmən-dik* nor ***raxmónə-dik*. Taken together with the type *mázldik*, it may be a conspiracy at play here, with various morphological strategies conspiring toward solutions to a phonological problem.

Suffixes which demand word stress – type 3 – are most frequently found in, e.g., internationalisms like *aspir-ánt, nacjon-ál, socjal-íst*; Slavic-component pejorative suffixes, e.g., *šnajdər-úk* 'bad tailor,' *jung-áč* 'rascal'; the toponym suffix *-ín* in *Bendín, Volín*, etc. The Gmc-component adverbializer *-ərhéjt*, depending on analysis, might be regarded as a stress-attracting suffix: *gəzúnt* + *ərhéjt* → *gəzùntərhéjt* 'in a healthy manner.' The stress-demanding suffixes are all of non-HA origin, but may combine with HA-origin nouns: /talmúd/ + /íst/ → *talmudíst* 'Talmudist.'

Stress-demanding suffixes are added cyclically, and thus may lose prominence in subsequent cycles: *fundamént, fundamentál, fundamentalíst*. Suffixes which take main word stress include: *-ánt, -ént, -át, -ácjə, -íst, -ízm, -ér* (*miljonér*), *-ín, -úk, -(əv)átə, -áč, -(j)ák, -ár, -éc, -əráj*, possibly *-ərhéjt*. Unstressed suffixes may follow cyclically, with no movement of main stress: *socjalístišə, anglicízmən, socjalizírungən, šnajdərúkəs*. The suffix *-or* only shows main stress if followed by an unstressed suffix, e.g., *profésor, profesórn, profesóriš*.

4.5.3 *The foot*

The preferred foot in Yiddish is a disyllabic trochee (sw). Where *ws* feet exist, they are often marked, e.g., the first syllable contains ə (*jəríd* 'fair'), or morphological considerations intervene. Syllable weight played a historical role in foot formation, and has left residue, but it is not directly part of synchronic Yiddish phonology.[56] Consider the following disyllabic words:

1a. *frágə* 'question,' *úvdə* 'task,' *káčkə* 'duck'
1b. *jəríd* 'fair,' *gəzógt* 'said'
2. *véto* 'veto,' *géto* 'ghetto,' *gúmi* 'rubber'
3. *bjuró* 'office,' *trikó* 'leotard,' *kupé* '(railroad) compartment'
4a. *vóron* 'raven'
4b. *žetón* 'badge'

Predictably, type (1a) is *sw*, and 1(b) is *ws*, since a single schwa syllable is unstressable. However, types (2) and (3) (both V-final) do not allow prediction. Types (2), (3), and (4) are often considered "foreign," though for different reasons: types (2) and (4a) because of post-tonic full vowel, type (3) because of an iambic stress pattern *ws* in a vowel-final word, types (3) and (4b) for a stress pattern *ws*, in which *w* dominates a full vowel.

Stress is thus, strictly speaking, unpredictable in non-derived, disyllabic words. However, non-derived words (typically, internationalisms) of three syllables pattern according to (historical) weight of their final syllable; C-final words have ultimate stress – *samovár*, *garderób*, *kanibál* – while V-final words do not: *dómino*, *kapótə*. Geller (1994: 171) notes the variants *papugáj* ~ *papúgə* 'parrot'; here, the diphthong *aj* could be seen as VC. However, there is also a class of "French-like" final stress in words like *kabaré* 'cabaret,' which must be seen as exceptional. Green (1969: 216) notes that *čepuxá* 'nonsense' (< Slavic) "sounds very 'foreign'." Trisyllabic words which pick up a consonantal coda cyclically do not "become" heavy: *dómino-s*, *kapótə-s*; thus, contrast *religjéz* 'religious' with *relígjə-s* 'religion-s.' However, when a syllable is added cyclically to words of two syllables or longer, predictable penultimate stress emerges; thus, stress in disyllabics *klímat*, *ádres*, *vóron*, *lítvak* contrasts with *špinát*, *kontákt*, *bagáž*, etc., whereas stress is regularized in plurals *klimátn*, *adrésn*, *vorónəs*, *litvákəs*, *špinátn*, *kontáktn*, *bagážn*; also, *garderóbn*, *samovárn*, etc. (Glasser 1990: 93). Furthermore, the (cyclic) addition of stress-demanding suffixes overrides earlier stress assignment; thus: *magístər*, *magistr-át*, *magistr-ál*; *fundamént*, *fundament-ál*, etc. Thus, final stress in cyclically derived words like *aspiránt*, *socjalíst* has to do with stress-demanding suffixes, rather than with canonic shape (as in *garderób*). Trisyllabics arising via cyclic phonology do not "count" as concerns stress in trisyllabic words; e.g., *šábəs-dik* 'Sabbath;

[56] On the diachronic evolution of foot structure in Yiddish poetic meter, see U. Weinreich (1955).

festive,' *norvég-iš* 'Norwegian.' There is a small class of words with initial stress: *mínimum, máksimum, léksikon, édipus*. These all have light penults and "latinate" suffixes *-on/-um/-us*. Penultimate stress in *majóntik* 'manor; a fortune' (< Slavic) is due either to final-syllable [ə] or based on a perceived morpheme boundary between a root + suffix (*-ik*); cf. plural: *majontkəs*. Finally, while stress is not predictable in *klímat* vs. *špinát*, C-final disyllabics with "extra heavy" final syllable will (mostly) have predictable final stress: *kontákt, baláns*, etc.; however, *íncest* 'incest.' Thus, disyllabics are treated differently from words with more than two syllables.

In its most general form, (synchronic) Yiddish constructs left-headed feet of the type *sw*, from right to left. Thus, a stressed final syllable will form a single-node final strong foot, (*samo*)-*vár*. If an unstressed syllable is added in a later cycle, the more general *sw* foot reasserts itself: (*samo*)-*várn*, (*šnajdər*)-*úkəs*.

Non-derived words of four syllables typically will form two *sw* feet: *bàləmúčə-* 'procrastinate,' *kàləmútnə* 'gloomy,' *kùkəríku* 'cock-a-doodle-do,' regional NEY *šìmtəkójə* 'centipede,' *šàltənósə* 'blintz.' In derived words with four syllables, footing depends on the nature of the suffix, since footing proceeds from right to left; cf. *fundamént-n* vs. *fundament-ál*, with the structures:

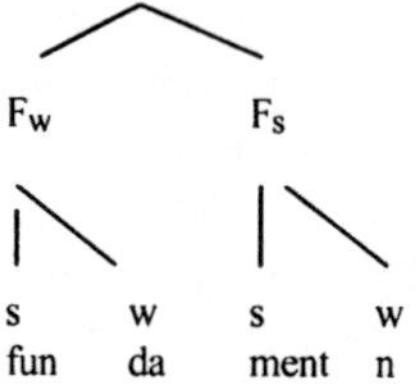

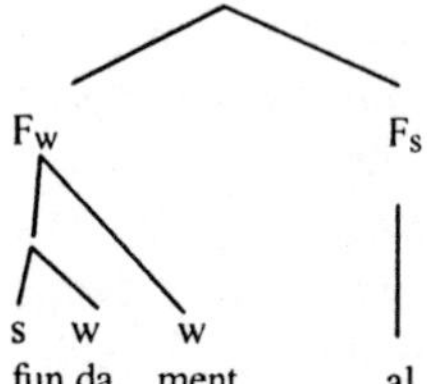

Generally, the rightmost foot in the word is strong, and thus receives main word stress.[57] In non-derived trisyllabic words with final stress, the structure is exemplified as follows:

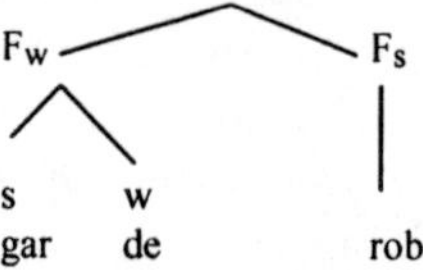

This also accounts for the secondary stress in *sàmovár, gàrderób, sùbmarín*, since *samo-*, *garde-*, *subma-* are forced to form their own feet. A rhythm rule resolves stress clash in derived words like *absólv* + *ént* → *àbsolvént*; *subjékt* + *ív* → *sùbjektív*, etc. Furthermore, rhythmic secondary stress is foot-based. In

57 This is the formulation for the word-stress rule for German as well (Wiese 1996: 282).

məšúgə 'crazy,' *mə* is stray-adjoined to the only foot in the word. However, the plural *məšəgóəm* has a rhythmically induced secondary stress (possibly [mì]); similarly, noun *mìšəgás* 'craziness.'

There are certain foot-related problems which arise in connection with the "Dreisilbengesetz" (Kiparsky 1966: 69). Basically, Yiddish shows much evidence for a limit of foot length to *sww*. Mark (1978: 186) gives examples where 1st DIM (suffix *-l̩*) and 2nd DIM (*- ələ*) are blocked if resulting main stress would be more than three syllables from the end of the word. Thus, whereas *káčkə* 'duck' has a diminutive *káčkələ*, there is no (2nd) DIM allowed for *jídənə* 'Jewish woman,' *lópətə* 'shovel.' Mark claims that whereas *cájtung* + *l̩* is permitted, a diminutive of *réxənung* 'calculation' is not; similarly, no 2nd DIM of *królik* 'rabbit' + *ələ* → ***królikələ*. Examples where 1st DIM occurs, but 2nd DIM does not, include: *hántəx* 'towel,' *mólcàjt* 'meal' (a compound!), *ministérjum*, *pórəc* 'landowner,' *xúməš* 'Pentateuch,' *məlámǝd* 'kheyder teacher,' *švéstər* 'sister,' *gútskajt* 'goodness.' The variant pronunciations of *revólvər*-***ələ* ~ *revolvérələ* pattern predictably. The constraint is based on number of unstressed syllables, and not on morpheme boundaries; *núd-nik* 'pest' undergoes 1st DIM → *núdnikl̩*, but not 2nd DIM ***núdnikələ*; *teátərnik* 'theatre person,' *vóxərnik* 'usurer' may not undergo 1st DIM.

However, consider initial stress in noun *teátərnicə* 'theatre person' (*nicə* = feminine of agent suffix *nik*), or inflected adjectives *lébədikə*, *jídišləxə*, all with *swww*, presumably an illegal foot. Thus, the three-syllable restriction applies with certain types of affixes, but not with others. Basically, it seems to permit inflectional endings, but not noun derivations; thus, derived *gəhéjm-əniš* 'secret,' *fínstər-niš* 'darkness' (sww) are permitted, but presumably not ***majóntək-əniš* (**swww). However, once the noun is (acceptably) derived, pluralization with *-n* is permitted: *gəhéjm-əniš-n*; thus, *swww*. Assigning separate foot status for the suffix *(ə)dik* would yield two feet in *lebədikə*: *lébə* and *dìkə*, but this would then violate the word rule, which says that the rightmost foot in ω is strong. Thus, we are forced to admit a morphologically based distinction. Derivation is permitted where it does not violate foot limits. However, once a (legal) derivational suffix is added, inflections are permitted, even where these create feet otherwise blocked. Thus, 1st DIM ***teátərnikl̩* is blocked, but feminine *teátərnicə* is permitted, as an extension of *teátərnik*.[58] However, whereas *vísnšaft-n* 'science-s' (swww) is permitted as inflectional (< *vísnšaft*, sww), the derived adjective *vísnšaftləx* (swww) presumably should be blocked (though, once allowed, inflected *vísnšaftləxə* is permitted). This remains a problem, since foot-status for *šaft* would create a violation of the word-stress rule.

58 Mark notes sporadic exceptions: *šnájdərkələ* 'woman tailor,' *bašéfəništ̩* 'creature,' and others. I question Mark's disallowing of 1st DIM in *kimpətórn* 'woman in childbirth,' since presumably *-órn* demands word stress.

I posit foot status for a weak initial syllable which contains a full vowel in, e.g., *kòntákt, bàgáž, bjùró*, but no foot status when the vowel is schwa: *gəzógt, jəríd* – here the initial syllable is stray-adjoined. There is some limited evidence for foot status of a weak initial heavy syllable. Consider first dental epenthesis between *l* and a following sibilant. This is syllable-based: /falš/ → [faltš] 'false'; the *t* remains after syllabification in subsequent cycles: *fal – tšə, fal – tšn̩*. However, *málšən zajn* 'slander' lacks epenthesis, since *l* and *š* are in no cycle in the same syllable. On the other hand, dental epenthesis between *n* and a following sibilant appears to be foot-based; not only *gans, vunš* > StY *gandz* 'goose,' *vuntš* 'wish,' but *fénstər* > StY *fénctər* 'window' (cf. StY *indzl̩* vs. StG *Insel* 'island'), since the *n* and the sibilant are in the same foot. However, *konsérv* (*kon* + *serv*) 'can (of food)' contrasts with *koncért* 'concert.' In both, the second syllable starts a foot. By assigning separate foot status for *kon*, we can account for lack of dental epenthesis in *konsérv*; the dental stop in *koncért* ([nts]) is thus underlying. Presumably *románs* 'romance' has [nts], but *romansírn* [ns], again, due to foot structure. A problem is *konservírn*, which ends in strong foot *vírn*; presumably *konserv* forms a weak *sw* foot. Note the lack of epenthesis in compounding: $[[\text{ón}]_\omega\ [\text{zóg}]_\omega] \rightarrow$ *ónzòg* 'message,' presumably since independent foot structure is maintained.

Finally, foot structure may play a role in the rule of PTR – if not an absolute one, at least as a tendency. Dialects with initial stress in trisyllabic Slavicisms tend to reduce both post-tonic vowels: CY *kápətə, pódləkə* vs. StY *kapótə* 'kaftan,' *padlógə* 'floor.' This seems foot-based.

Whether we wish to define the light weak syllable *ka* in *kapótə* as an independent foot or a stray syllable is open to debate. However, in *kápətə* only one foot structure is possible, and PTR applies across the entire foot.

4.5.4 *Rhythm*

The rhythmic alternation of strong and weak stresses may be represented metrically. Whereas *mə* is unstressed in *məšúgə* 'crazy,' *məšúməd* 'apostate,' it has secondary stress in *mə̀šəgóəm, mə̀šəgás, mə̀šəmódəm* (regionally, [mì]). In Retín, rhythmic secondary stress preserves vowel color: *šábəsd[ì]kə*, while the vowel is regularly reduced to schwa in *šábəsd[ə]k*. Though the vowel-color retention here seems related to foot structure, whether this qualifies as a full foot is debatable (in light of the word-stress rule). A rhythm rule [RR] resolves stress clash of two adjacent *s* (along with cyclic reduction from primary to secondary stress): *absólv* + *ént* → *àbsolvént* 'graduate,' *socjál* + *íst* → *sòcjalíst* 'socialist.' There is no stress clash in *gəzúnt* + *ərhéjt* → *gəzùntərhéjt* 'in a healthy manner,' *šnájdər* + *úk* → *šnàjdərúk* 'tailor' (pejorative), since the two *s* are separated by a syllable. However, the rhythm rule does not just count linear syllables. Thus, when *-ál* is suffixed to *fundamént*, RR resolves the stress clash by moving stress to the syllable *fùn*, not to ***dà*: *fùndamentál*. Stress clash is thus resolved at the prosodic level. The RR does not apply in compounding; thus, [arо́p] + [gáng] → *arópgàng* 'descent,' not ***ároрgàng*. However, there is resolution of rhythm in phrases (see below).

4.5.5 *Prefixed words*

The six productive verb prefixes *ba-*, *far-*, *ant-*, *cə-*, *der-*, *gə-* do not affect word stress.[59] Generally, they require an immediately following (primary) stressed syllable; thus, *gánvənən*, *zógn* form their past participles with *gə-* – *gəgánvət*, *gəzógt* – whereas verbs *bàləmúčən* 'procrastinate,' *àbonírn* 'subscribe' do not.[60] Other unstressed prefixes also do not affect word stress: *bə-sód* 'secretly,' *bə-kícər* 'in short.' The stress pattern which emerges here is *ws*; however, it is arguable whether this is a *ws* foot, or a stray syllable adjoined to a foot. I have not found implications for one analysis over the other.[61]

The verb particles are phonological words (rather than prefixes) in Yiddish, and together with their verb (or deverbal noun), share a number of characteristics with compounds on the one hand, and with phrases on the other. The verb particles are always strong in relation to the verb, which shows secondary stress, e.g. *ójstrìnkən* 'drink up,' *ónšràjbn* 'finish writing,' even when the syntax places it after the verb: *er trìnkt ójs*.[62] Deverbal nouns with a verb particle maintain the stress pattern of the complex verb: *ónzògn* 'announce,' (*der*) *ónzòg* 'message.' Periphrastic verbs function similarly in that the invariant receives the primary stress; however, it is possible that the carrier verbs 'have' and 'be' lose their

59 Nor do the less-productive prefixes *de(z)-* 'dis-,' *za-* in *dezinfecírn* 'disinfect,' *začépən* 'brush against.'

60 Rhythmic secondary stress in (*bàləmútšən*, *àbonírn*) is not enough to support prefixation of *gə*; however, cf. *far-notírn* 'jot down,' *far-registrírn* 'put down in writing.'

61 Marginal double-prefix *šəbə* in, e.g., *kéləv šəbəklóvəm* 'despicable scoundrel,' would create an illegal foot if adjoined to a word with non-initial stress; presumably, *gánəf šəbəgunóvəm* 'lowest of thieves' is not allowed.'

62 Thus, Yiddish does not have the stress contrast found in StG *übersetzen 'put something across'* vs. *übersétzen* 'translate.' U. Weinreich (1954: 8) claims equal primary stresses in *úm-gəvášn* '(with hands) unwashed.' I posit secondary stress in the verb element.

secondary stress: *xásənə hobn* 'get married,' *bójdək zajn* 'check'; *er hot xásənə* 'he marries,' *er iz bójdək* 'he checks.'

4.5.6 Compounding

Compounding occupies an intermediate ground involving phonology, morphology, and syntax. Yiddish has two types of compounds, based on a "Germanic model" and a "Hebrew model" – though these terms are only partially satisfactory (Jacobs 1991). In the Gmc-type compounds, the order of elements is modifier – head [MOD-HEAD]. Main stress is on the MOD, thus, the stress pattern is *sw*. Gender, adjective agreement, and plural are based on the final element, the HEAD. Thus: M *tog* 'day' + N *bux* 'book' → *tógbùx* 'diary,' which is neuter; plural is based on the final element (HEAD): *tógbìxər*. In this type of compound, the MOD is typically stripped of morphological markings sometimes evident in (varieties of) German, e.g., *Tagblatt* ~ *Tageblatt* ~ *Tageszeitung* vs. Yiddish *togblat*, *togcajtung*, etc.[63]

The "Hebrew-model" compounds in Yiddish have the order HEAD-MOD, main stress on the MOD, and thus stress pattern *ws*. Gender, adjective agreement, and pluralization are based on the MOD (as opposed to Hebrew, where these were based on the HEAD of construct constructions). This appears to be a compromise; the order of elements and overall stress pattern are similar to Hebrew, but there is partial adaptation to the Germanic model in that the final element is used to determine gender, adjective agreement, and plural form.

While the Germanic model compound is least marked in Yiddish, both models are highly productive in the language, and not limited etymologically, as seen in the following:

Source	*Gmc model (MÓD-HÈAD)*	*Hebrew model (HÈAD-MÓD)*
Gmc + Gmc	tóg – bùx 'diary'	ònhejb jór 'beginning of the year'
Gmc + H	špráx – xùš 'language sense'	blàt gəmórə 'page of Talmud'
H + Gmc	sóf – zàc 'final sentence'	sòf zác 'end of the sentence'
H + H	jəšívə – bòxər 'Yeshiva student'	ksàv jád 'manuscript'

In basic unmarked Germanic-model MOD-HEAD compounds, main stress is on the first element of an [AB] compound, where A and B are each phonological words. However, tripartite compounds yield different parsings. U. Weinreich (1954: 6) uses the words *folk* 'people,' *šprax* 'language,' and *xuš* 'sense, feeling' to contrast [[[folk][šprax]][xuš]] 'sense for the popular language' (= [[AB][C]]) with [[folk] [[šprax][xuš]]] (= [[A][BC]]) 'popular sense of the language.' In

63 Interesting is StY *brivntregər* 'postman,' with an *n* which cannot be attributed to case, gender, number; cf. Yiddish *briv* 'letter-s'; see §5.7.

line with general metrical analysis of compound stress, I assume that in a compound, AB, main stress is on A, unless B is branching at the word level; thus, *[fólk-šprax]xùš* vs. *fòlk[šprax-xuš]*.[64]

Coordinative compounds are right-strong: *tatə-mámə* 'parents,' *xosn-kálə* 'bride and groom,' *xanə-léjə* 'woman's name,' *arjə-léjb* 'man's name,' *punkt-kómə* 'semicolon' (U. Weinreich 1954: 8). Weinreich (p. 8) claims equal primary stresses on the A and B elements in certain compound-like constructions (for differing analysis, see below), e.g., *úm-gəvášn* 'with hands unwashed,' *ánti-komuníst* 'anti-Communist,' *pró-arábiš* 'pro-Arab,' *túnkl-blój* 'dark blue,' *dráj-un-cvántsik* 'twenty three,' *éngliš-dájč* 'English-German'; in reduplication: *vájt-vájt* 'very far.'

Yiddish does not seem to manifest compounding to the same degree found in German. Thus, U. Weinreich (1954: 7) calls extended compounding "a possibility, largely in theory, of making up constructions of the third or even higher degrees." He makes up an example: *[məluxə=šul-jontəv][gasn-parad]* 'state school-holiday street parade.' However, such examples seem to be questionable in Yiddish.

The Hebrew-model compounds fall into two groups: true compounds, and pseudo-compounds of syntactic convenience. The true compounds are fully fused. Modifiers are placed in relation to the entire compound, either before or after, e.g., *der altər ksàv-jád* 'the old manuscript,' *a ksàv-jád, an altər* 'a manuscript – an old one.' The pseudo-compounds are only apparent surface compounds of the *ws* stress type: *ònhejb-jór* 'beginning of the year.' As soon as an adjective is added, the pseudo-compound reveals its nature as a partitive construction: *ònhejb fun(əm) najəm jór* 'beginning of the new year'; *der langər sóf-zàc* 'the long final sentence' vs. *der sof fun(əm) langn zác* 'the end of the long sentence.' Thus, true compound *másn-arèstn* 'mass arrests' contrasts with pseudo-compound *màsn-aréstn* 'masses of arrests.' The *ws* stress in true compounds (*ksàv-jád*) is one productive type of compound stress, whereas the *ws* stress in pseudo-compounds is phrasal. Further evidence for this is seen in quantitative constructions (Mark 1978: 180–184), where *ws* phrasal stress is accompanied by a pause: *a vànt* [pause] *zéjgərs* 'a wall [pause = "of"] clocks' vs. compound noun *vánt-zèjgərs* 'wall clocks,' with *sw* stress.

4.5.7 *Stress in foreignisms*

Descriptions of a given language often deal with foreignisms, and the degree to which these have/have not been nativized, that is, conformed to the etymologically "native" grammar. However, it becomes increasingly difficult to

64 U. Weinreich (1954: 8) assumes that all compounds have main stress on the A element, irrespective of whether or not B is (word-)branching.

demarcate foreign words from native the more the borrowed elements are part of productive patterns in the borrowing language. Thus, while *študirn, fundamentalist, aspirant* are identifiable as internationalisms in Yiddish, they exhibit morphological and phonological features that are clearly productive in Yiddish grammar. To a certain extent, simplex words with post-tonic full vowel are seen as non-native: *véto, géto, gúmi*, as are polysyllabic V-final words with ultimate stress: *čepuxá, bjuró, trikó, alijá, kupé*. However, the large corpus of such words patterns into regular classes (Glasser 1990). At some point their "foreignness" must be questioned; any language which has integrated the residue of contact may be called a "fusion language."

For Yiddish, however, we might speak of a highly developed fusion, where the boundaries of component sources have been blurred to a larger degree than in many other languages. While we might view words like *glóbus, véto, ténis* as marked or less native in Yiddish, the fact is that speakers spontaneously create forms like *jívo* (~ *jivó*) 'YIVO,' and treat these as regular words (thus, predictable masculine gender: *der jívo*). Stress placement can also be used stylistically; some SEY speakers produce *xazérnik* (instead of *xázərnik*) 'piggish person' for ironic effect (M. Schaechter, p.c.). Looking objectively at the productive patternings in Yiddish as a whole, rather than solely etymologically ("Germanic" vs. "non-Germanic" components), has implications for how we formulate our descriptive grammar. If *vét[o]* and *vór[o]n* are "native," then we must rethink our formulation of the PTR rule. Still, there is a sense that post-tonic schwa is more "native"; older Yiddish toponyms consistently have schwa: *váršə* 'Warsaw,' *krúkə* 'Cracow'; newer ones may sometimes vary: *šikág[o ~ ə]* 'Chicago'; newest or least-integrated ones will tend to have full vowel: *tókj[o]* 'Tokyo.' Finally, even marked foreignisms tend to become more integrated via application of the cyclic phonology/morphology. Thus, whereas *klím[a]t, bóč[a]n* are somewhat marked in Yiddish, their plurals *klim[á]tn, boč[á]nəs* are less so (Glasser 1990: 94).

4.5.8 Phrasal stress

There is very little literature on phrasal stress in Yiddish. U. Weinreich (1954) touches on it briefly; Zaretski (1926) deals with it systematically, but subsumed as part of his (scattered) remarks on intonation. As a nuclear stress rule [NSR] for Yiddish is presented, below, it is important to keep in mind that normal phrasal stress can be affected/overridden by issues of sentence focus, contrastive stress, etc. – as these interact with word order. Zaretski (p. 162) writes: "A syntagma with a logical accent often comes not in its usual place, but it is difficult to give rules here."

NSR is formulated as follows. In a construction [AB], main stress is on B if $[AB]_P$ is a phrase. This contrasts with one type of compound (*tógbùx*), represented here as $[AB]_C$. Thus, the phrase *grin blát* 'green léaf' contrasts with *grínblat* 'proper name.' Phrasal stress is most commonly phrase-final: *der gútər* 'the góod (one),' *der gutər mán* 'the good mán.' This holds regardless of syntax-governed case assignment: *dem gútn, dem gutn mán*. It holds for verbs as well: *vil géjn* 'wants to gó,' *vil gejn ésn* 'wants to go éat.' As phrases are combined into larger units (e.g., sentences), NSR operates at each successive level. Again, the final element normally receives main stress (unless otherwise marked). Zaretski (1926: 162) gives the examples:

1. ix gib dem xavər a búx	'I give the friend a book'
2. ix gib a bux dem xávər	'I give a book (to) the friend'
3. ix gib es dem xávər	'I give it (to) the friend'
4. ix gib dem xavər **és	'I give the friend **ít'

In 1, 2, 3, the final word in the sentence-final phrase receives main stress. Thus, phrasal stress is final in both *di zilbərnə matbéjə* 'the silver coin' and *di matbejəfun zílbər* 'the coin of silver.' Pronouns, however, may not receive (non-contrastive) phrasal stress; thus, 4 is blocked. When pronouns occur sentence-finally by default, they are not stressed: *ix gíb es* 'I give it,' *er léjənt es* 'he reads it.' Further examples of phrasal stress are:

ADJ – N	a šejnər tóg 'a pretty day'
V – NP	er lejənt a cájtung 'he reads a newspaper'
ADV – ADJ	šojn gút 'already good'
NP – VP	mojšə trínkt 'Moyshe drinks'
NP – VP	mojšə trinkt vájn 'Moyshe drinks wine'
N – PP	der man mitn špígl 'the man with the mirror'
Possessive – N	der altər frojs búx 'the old woman's book'
NP-NP Partitives	štikl brójt 'piece of bread'

In summary, phrasal stress generally operates blindly, stressing the final word in the phrase, and, subsequently, the sentence. The syntax dictates what elements may or may not (normally) occur in final position.[65]

4.5.9 Rhythm and stress in phrases

In paired adjectives of the type *tùnkl-blój* 'dark-blue,' *hàlb-grín* 'half-green,' *špògl-náj* 'brand-new' (with stress pattern *ws*), there is stress adjustment within

[65] Zaretski (1926: 185) provides a hierarchy of main stress in a construction, in the following descending order: object of the verb, verb particle or other invariant, adverb, participle or infinitive in a compound verb, conjugated verb. As a result, he states that normally unaccented are: subjects, adjectives, possessives, number words, auxiliaries, and pronouns. Note, however, that a topicalized subject may occur sentence-finally (p. 162): *in štot treft im a bakántər* 'An acquaintance meets him in town.'

the phrase when a noun with initial stress follows: *tùnkl-bloj búx* 'dark-blue book,' *špògl-naj hítl* 'brand-new hat.' However, stress adjustment is based on metrical structure, not linear counting of syllables. Thus, *špògl-najə árbət* 'brand-new work' is represented:

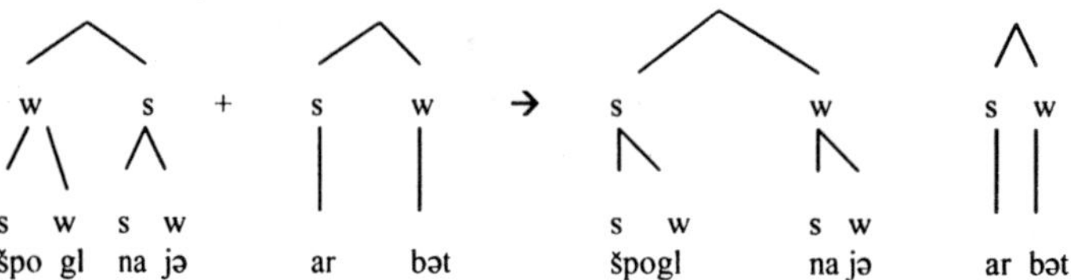

The two highest-level *s* are adjacent metrically, but not linearly; stress clash is resolved in spite of unstressed syllable *jə* intervening between *na-* and *ar-*. Interestingly, the Hebrew-model compounds, which are *ws*, give further evidence that stress clash is resolved across word boundaries (here, though, within a compound, rather than a phrase). Thus, *xílək-xilúkəm* 'difference-s,' but *xìlukə-déjəs* 'difference of opinion,' not ***xilùkə-déjəs*; however, *xanùkəs-(h)abájəs* 'housewarming,' where there is no stress clash, since *(h)abájəs* is *ws*.

Stress clash in Germanic-model compounds and NPs is not resolved in Yiddish as it is in German. Wiese (1996: 306) gives the examples for StG:

1 2	1 3 2	1 2	1 3 2	2 1	2 3 1
Ausfall –	Stromausfall	sichtbar –	unsichtbar	Paderborn –	Paderborner Uni

However, Yiddish appears not to reduce the secondary stress here; thus: *ónzòg* [12] 'message,' but *héjm-ònzog* [123?] 'home message,' *váld-gèto* 'forest-ghetto' [123?], not *váld-**getò*; *hójz-àdres* 'house address' [123], not **[132] (M. Schaechter, p.c.). Thus, as concerns stress in AB constructions, Germanic-model compounds in Yiddish show systematic metrical reduction of stress [12], but do not further resolve stress clash rhythmically (as does German). However, interestingly, the Hebrew model compounds, with *ws* stress, are treated to some extent as phrasal stress and undergo rhythmic stress adjustment.

4.5.10 Phrasal foot

Just as syllables pattern into feet within a word, there is an echo of this beyond the word level. The phrasal foot is similar to the formal foot of word-level phonology, but it is not identical, and it is not subject to the same limits as the formal foot.[66] The phrasal foot consists of a strong stress followed by zero to *n*

[66] Prilutski (1940: 55ff.) combines the formal foot and the phrasal foot under the single term *redtakt*. The two are distinguished in the present work in conformity both with theory constraints (violation of strict ordering) and empirical constraints (the two feet are, finally, different).

unstressed syllables, until the next-occurring strong stress. Thus, the number of phrasal feet will tend to reduce in fast speech, increase in slow speech. Prilutski (1940: 55) divides the sentence: *ix hob dix šojn ništ lib* 'I don't like you' into two phrasal feet: *xódəxšuniš*, and *líb*. Prilutski's phrasal foot may consist of only part of a word; thus *ix hob dir dox šojn gəzogt* 'I already told you' divides into *xódərdəxšngə*, and *zógt*. Here, the first phrasal foot consists of an *s* followed by four *w*, something not allowed in a word-level foot.

Both the formal foot and the phrasal foot show similar patterning in the tendency to reduce post-tonic vowels within a foot to schwa. Thus, within a word, *sàmo-vár* is in Retín *sàm[ə]vár*; similarly, within the phrasal foot: *nem dir dos kind* 'take (unto) you the child' → *némdərs-kínd* (Prilutski 1940: 54). Consider the metanalysis of indefinite article *a(n)* + V-initial noun, which has led to forms such as *nepl* 'apple' < *an epl* 'an apple.' Some speakers have *avéjrə* 'transgression,' *agúnə* 'abandoned woman,' but *anəvéjrə*, *anəgúnə*, presumably treating these as foot-like, with a foot *ána* → *ánə* (p. 57). This reanalysis is only possible with words with unstressed initial vowel; thus, there is no reduction to schwa in [anádres] 'an address,' [anól] 'an awl.'

4.6 Intonation

There has hitherto not been a systematic investigation of the intonational system of Yiddish. The current discussion is based on scattered remarks in Zaretski (1926), as well as U. Weinreich (1956). Intonation does not operate in isolation, but rather it interacts with syntax, morphology, and phonology. Zaretski (1926: 34) calls intonation the "fourth carrier of meaning." The following is a brief outline of the major points concerning intonation in Yiddish.

Intonation is seen not in terms of absolute pitch, but, rather, in terms of patterns of pitch variation. For notational ease the following references are used to describe intonation: H for high pitch, L for low pitch. Transitions may be inferred; thus, LH is rising, HL falling, LHL the rise-fall contour. Under normal conditions, a stressed syllable in Yiddish will be produced with a higher pitch than an unstressed syllable, and a stressed syllable begins with a higher pitch, which falls; thus: *gut* [HL], *gu* (H) – *tə* [L]. Function within larger syntactic units plays a role. Thus, in isolation, *cvéj* 'two' is [HL]. However, in the NP *cvej bíxər* 'two books,' *cvej* – being less prominent – does not receive the same height of pitch. If stressed contrastively in the same NP, *cvej* will again be [HL]. Within longer syntactic or discourse units intonational patterns emerge which reflect structure. Thus, in *der man trinkt vájn* 'the man drinks wine,' the main stress, and highest H, will normally be on *vájn*; however, the pitch on *man* (most prominent member in its NP) will be higher than on *der*.

Normal declarative statements generally have a final HL falling intonation, realized over the final foot of the utterance:

(1)	er trinkt vájn [HL]	'he drinks wine'
(2)	zi lejənt bí- [H] xər [L]	'she reads books'
(3)	mojšə iz an aspir-ránt [HL]	'Moyshe is a doctoral student'
(4)	zej zenən aspi-rán- [H] tn [L]	'they are doctoral students'
(5)	du kojfst cáj- [H] tungən [LL]	'you buy newspapers'

Yes/no questions are characterized by a rising final contour, manifested on the final foot, e.g., *(ci) trinkt er vájn* [LH] 'does he drink wine?'; *(ci) zenən zej aspi-rán* [L] *tn* [H] 'are they doctoral students?' The rising contour is also employed with declarative word order to make yes/no questions: *er trinkt vájn* [LH] 'does he drink wine?' Questions formed with question-words exhibit declarative contour: *ven iz péjsəx* [HL] 'when is Passover?'; *farvos hostu lib foneémən* [HL] 'why do you like phonemes?'; *ver vet kojfn a búx* [HL] 'who is going to buy a book?'

Zaretski (1926: 184) states that indirect questions generally have declarative [HL] contour; e.g., *x'vejs nit, funvanən iz er gəkumən* 'I don't know where he came from'; however, frequently speakers turn the non-question into a question, with accompanying rising intonation. This occurs not only with indirect questions, but with clear non-questions: *ze, vi du bist blas?* (LH), literally, 'Look how pale you are!' Rising intonation turns it into a type of question, 'Do you see how pale you are?' Zaretski (p. 184) also provides an example of rising intonation to express a wish or command: *dust ojfhern šrajən?* 'Are you going to stop yelling?' = 'Stop yelling, already!'

A marked higher than normal tone is found in the examples of fronting and verb-drop listed by Zaretski (1926: 136), e.g., *frúm* [HL] *–Ø– der tatə* 'Father is pious'; *réjn* [HL] *–Ø– der himl* 'the sky is clear.' Linguistic asides and parenthetical remarks are characterized by overall lower pitch, flatter intonation, quicker tempo, and marked pauses at both ends of the aside (pp. 176–177), as seen in the following cited from Sholem Aleykhem: *orəmə kindər zoln nit arumgejn – (ix bet ibər ajər kovəd) – mit di pupkəs indrojsn* 'poor children should not go around – (please excuse me) – with their belly buttons hanging out.'

Intonation is used to signal the linking of phrases. Thus, U. Weinreich (1956: 634) gives: *az s'iz gəvorn tog* [H], *hot er derzén dem xurbn arum zix* 'when day broke he saw the devastation around him.' Weinreich calls this "unmarked transition," characterized by a level H tone in *tog*. Compare this with the normal HL falling contour in *s'iz gəvorn tog* [HL] 'day broke.' The level contour (non-falling) signals the transition – that something will follow, and that it is linked to *tog*.

Weinreich's example is part of his larger discussion of the rise-fall intonation contour in Yiddish. As with the other contours, the rise-fall contour is manifested over the final (phrasal) foot. It is characterized by a rise from L to H, followed by a distinct fall (Weinreich 1956: 633). The L is on the primary stress in the foot, and the transition to H and the subsequent fall both follow. Thus, an utterance ending in a monosyllabic foot will realize the entire LHL rise-fall on that syllable. Where the final primary stress is followed by one or more unstressed syllables, the rise and fall are manifested on these.

Weinreich (1956: 634ff.) discusses three main functions of the rise-fall contour in Yiddish. The first signals dramatic transition between phrases. Using the identical string *az s'iz gəvorn tog hot er derzén dem xurbn arum zix*, Weinreich describes the following: (a) *tog* with level [H] intonation – this is unmarked transition, glossed as 'when day broke he saw the devastation around him'; (b) *tog* with partial rising stress [LH] – this is a marked transition, corresponding to a comma in written form, 'when day broke, he saw the devastation around him'; (c) *tog* using the rise-fall contour – signaling a dramatized transition, '[All night he wasn't aware of a thing, but] when day broke – [then] he saw the devastation around him.'

The second function of the rise-fall contour is to signal an incredulous question. Weinreich gives the string: *hajnt iz a tónəs*; (a) falling contour for a simple declarative 'today is a fast day'; (b) rising contour for a yes/no question 'Is today a fast day?'; (c) rise-fall contour: 'Today isn't a fast day, is it?' The third function of the rise-fall contour is found in echo questions; thus: *vu iz ér* [LHL] 'where is hé, did you say?'

U. Weinreich suggests pre-Ashkenazic Jewish sources for the rise-fall contour, including the role of Talmudic chant employed in traditional learning. Weinreich found no evidence of direct influences from coterritorial languages in the development or use of the rise-fall contour in Yiddish. Though the rise-fall contour began dying out in conjunction with modernization/westernization, remnants of it are found in post-Yiddish Ashkenazic speech (§7.8).

5 Morphology

5.1 Approaches to Yiddish morphology

This chapter presents a basic outline of Yiddish morphology: (1) the major classes and categories (root, affix, noun, verb, inflection vs. derivation, etc.); (2) the function-morphemes, and their main allomorphs; (3) the major processes, and related problems. The main sources of data and examples are Zaretski (1926), Mark (1978), Birnbaum (1979a); for handy overview, see U. Weinreich (1949). Zaretski provides the most insightful, thorough, and theoretically informed discussion to date of Yiddish morphology. Mark presents a prescriptive grammar of StY. This discussion refers to a generalized Yiddish – roughly, StY – except where otherwise specified.

5.2 Basic nouns

The rubric *noun* includes diverse phenomena: base nouns vs. derived nouns, nominalizations, diminutives, pejoratives, etc. Zaretski (1926: 38) divides Yiddish nouns into two main groups: actual (basic) nouns vs. nominalizations. Basic nouns are further sub-divided into those with and without affixes. Yiddish nouns generally do not mark grammatical case on the noun, but, rather, on the NP. Gender is generally not formally marked on affixless nouns; thus: *tiš* 'table'$_{[\text{M}]}$, *šprax* 'language'$_{[\text{F}]}$, *land* 'country'$_{[\text{N}]}$. Base nouns are generally formally unmarked for other categories as well, such as animacy vs. inanimacy (e.g., *man* 'man, husband' vs. *plan* 'plan').

There are problematic nouns which reside somewhere between intrinsic basic noun and affixed basic noun. Thus, while final ə may be analyzed as a feminine suffix in *talmidə* 'female pupil' (cf. *talməd* 'male pupil'), its status is less clear in *mamə* 'mother,' *fragə* 'question.' Furthermore, base nouns *tatə* 'father,' *sojnə* 'enemy' are masculine, which complicates the analysis of the ə as a feminine marker. There are no underlying related forms ***tat*, ***mam*, ***so(j)n*, ***frag*. Are words like *tenis* 'tennis,' *globus* 'globe,' *serum* 'serum,' monomorphemic in Yiddish? On the one hand, *globus* relates to *global* 'global,' suggestive that *-us* is a morpheme. On the other hand, *-us*, *-is*, *-um* do not behave phonologically as morphemes (§4.5.1). Many speakers have reinterpreted historical neuter *dos ojər* 'ear,' feminine *di mojər* 'wall' as masculines, based on the surface similarity of root-final [ər] with the masculine agentive suffix *-ər*, suggesting confusion at points where morphology and phonology collide. Furthermore, base nouns ending in syllabic *n̩* are predictably masculine: (*der*) *vogn* 'cart,' *balkn* 'ceiling,' *volkn* 'cloud,' while nominalized verb infinitives are consistently neuter in StY: (*dos*) *esn* 'eating,' *trinkən* 'drinking,' etc. This suggests that speakers are aware of the nominalization process for verb infinitives, but does not tell us whether they also perceive the *-n* in *vogn* as a suffix.

5.3 Derived nouns

5.3.1 Nominalized roots

Zaretski sees two types of nominalization which do not employ affixation (but which may use root-internal modification).[1] First, C-final verb roots may be used as nouns, based on either the infinitive/present or past participle. The root is unchangeable in weak verbs; thus: nouns (*der*) *kuk* 'look,' *pač* 'slap' (verbs: *kukn, gəkukt*; *pačn, gəpačt*). However, most strong verbs show a root-internal difference between infinitive/present tense and past-participle forms: *brexn, gəbroxn* 'break,' *trinkən, gətrunkən* 'drink,' *gejn, gəgangən* 'go'; here the noun is based on the past participle: (*der*) *brox, trunk, gang*, etc. However, the noun (*der*) *bavajz* 'demonstration' (verb: *bavajzn – bavizn* 'show') is clearly not based on the past participle. This nominalization process is distinct from base nouns which have a related verb root, e.g., verb *gebn – gib – gəgebn* 'give' vs. noun *gob*; *bašlus* 'decision,' but verb *bašlisn – bašlosn* 'decide.' Irregular verbs are problematic; cf. *ton* ~ *tun* 'to do,' present root *tu-*, past participle *gəton* ~ *gətuən*, nominalized as (*der*) (*ojf*)*tu* 'accomplishment,' pointing to a present-tense base. Nominalized verb roots are regularly assigned masculine gender[2] – (*der*) *dank* 'thanks,' *kuš* 'kiss,' *trunk* 'drink' – even when containing a prefix (*der bazux* 'visit') or verb particle (*der onzog* 'message'). Verb-root nominalization is quite productive, pushing out older forms containing abstract noun suffix *-ung*, e.g., *ojslejg* over older *ojslejgung* 'spelling'; cf. verb *ojslejgn* 'spell.'

Second, adjective roots may be nominalized to express a quality. Since historical umlaut applies here (where possible), these forms are arguably root + zero affix → modified root; e.g., *hojx* 'high,' *hejx* 'height'; *grojs* 'big,' *grejs* 'size'; *lang* 'long,' *leng* 'length.' Where umlaut is not possible, the adjective

1 Discussion and examples derive largely from Zaretski (1926: 38ff.), and Mark (1978).
2 However, note StY *di* ~ *dos špil* 'the game; play' < verb *špiln*.

and the abstract noun are identical: *brejt* 'broad; breadth,' *tif* 'deep; depth.' These nouns are assigned feminine gender: (*di*) *leng*, *tif*, *hejx*, *grejs*.

5.3.2 *Derivational suffixes*

The list in Table 5.1 is a modified compilation from Zaretski (1926: 40–43), Mark (1978), and Birnbaum (1979a: 231ff.). Suffixes demanding word stress are indicated. Gender in StY follows suffix.

Several Latinate (or internationalism) suffixes which preserve paradigmatic relationships in Yiddish suggest a possible analysis of StY *-izacjə* into *iz* + *at* + *cjə*; thus: *kolonizacjə* 'colonization,' *emigracjə* 'emigration,' but also *stancjə* 'station,' *redakcjə* 'editorship.' Thus, *organizator* 'organizer' and *organizacjə* 'organization' may be analyzed: *organ* + *iz* + *at* + *or* for the agent; for the abstract noun the suffix *-or* is dropped, and *-cjə* is added (along with degemination of *tt* → *t*). How far we wish to carry the sub-analysis is a matter of preference, to the extent it is supported by the data and is synchronically productive. Thus, both *–izm* and *-ist* in *socjalizm*, *socjalist* could be analyzed to a single morpheme /iz/, followed by abstract noun suffix /m/, or agent suffix /t/. However, both of these seem unsupported by the rest of the language. Finally, the productivity of suffixes *-énc*, *-ánt*, etc., may be questioned. These suffixes are limited mostly to clearly identifiable internationalisms.

5.3.3 *Prefixed nouns*

Prefixation as a means of noun derivation is of limited productivity in Yiddish. The two prefixes relevant to noun derivation listed in Zaretski (1926: 39) and Birnbaum (1979a: 232) are *gə-* and *um-*. However, only *gə-* functions in the grammar as a prefix. Nouns with *gə-* express collectiveness, and are neuter. It is prefixed to a verb root, with frequent modification (umlaut) of the root vowel. It usually denotes an action, e.g., (with umlaut) *der gəhilf* 'helper,' *gəjeg* 'hunting,' *gəšleg* 'fight' (cf. verbs *helfn*, *jogn*, *šlogn*); (without umlaut[3]) *gəzang* 'singing,' *gədank* 'thought,' *gəvejn* 'crying.' Prefix *gə-* coupled with suffix *-ts* seems to be added to nouns (rather than to verbs). The element *um-* 'un-; not' is not a prefix, but, rather, has a more limited function as a noun extender, since it is added (in noun derivation) to one type of word – nouns only, and behaves unlike a prefix phonologically. Likewise, *pro-*, *anti-*, *neo-*, behave phonologically as words rather than as prefixes. Nouns such as *bašefəniš* 'creature,' *antviklung* 'development,' *dercejlung* 'tale' contain prefixes, but are derived from prefixed verbs (*bašafn*, *antviklen*, *dercejlen*), not from nouns.

[3] The prefixed nouns without umlaut either contain vowels which may not umlaut, or reflect ablaut.

Table 5.1. *Noun suffixes (modified from Zaretski 1926: 40–43)*

Suffix	Basic meaning	Affixed to	Examples
-átor[4] (M)	agent	verbs with *-ir*	*operátor* 'operator' *organizátor* 'organizer'
-hajt[5] (F)	quality	adjectives, nouns	*šejnhajt* 'beauty' *kindhajt* 'childhood'
-ung (F)	result of action	verbs	*antviklung* 'development' *hofənung* 'hope'
-varg (N)	collection	adjectives; nouns	*rojvarg* 'raw material' *jungvarg* 'youth'
-tum (N)	'-dom'	adjectives; plural nouns	*hejliktum* 'shrine' *jidntum* 'Jewry'
-tl, *-stl*[6] (N)	'fraction of'	numbers (with modification of root)	*fertl* 'one quarter' *cvancikstl* 'one twentieth'
-ízm (M)	'-ism'	nouns; proper nouns; adjectives, including non-free-occurring roots	*anarkízm* 'anarchy' *ateízm* 'atheism'
-íst (M)	'-ist'; follower of an -ism	nouns; proper nouns; non-free-occurring roots; adjectives	*altruíst* 'altruist' *bundíst* 'Bundist'
-ər (M)	agent	verbs; numbers; nouns	*šnajdər* 'tailor' *kremər* 'shopkeeper' *finfər* '5-er'
-áj (F, N)[7]	craft; long-lasting action; venture	mostly from nominalized verbs via *-ər* suffixation	*bekəráj* 'bakery; baking' *farbəráj* 'dye-shop; dyeing'
-nik (M)	agent	nouns; invariants, especially < HA component	*laməd-vovnik* 'one of the 36 Good Men' *nudnik* 'pest; bore'
-l̩ (various genders)	tool; apparatus for an action	verbs	*šlisl̩* 'key' *fligl̩* 'wing' *drejdl̩* 'teetotum'
-kajt (F)	abstract nouns; quality	adjectives; past participles	*klejnkajt* 'smallness' *ojsgəhaltnkajt* 'consistency'
-(ə)niš (N, F)	abstract nouns; result of action[8]	present/infinitive of verb	*bajsəniš* 'itch' *brexəniš* 'breaking'[9]
-šaft (F)	abstractness; quality	adjectives; nouns	*klugšaft* 'prudence' *krojvəšaft* 'kinship'
-(j)ə[10] (various genders)	various meanings, including simple noun status	non-free-occurring roots; geographic names	*mamə* 'mother,' *tatə* 'father' *m(ə)loxə* 'craft' *geografjə* 'geography'
-əxts (N)	abstract action; sometimes pejorative	verbs (present/infinitive root)	*gejəxts* 'going' *tuəxts* 'task' *špajəxts* 'saliva'
gə- + [root] + *-ts*[11] (N)	collection of items within a body of items	nouns	*gəšrifts* 'writ'
-ən (plurals)[12]	groups by number	numbers; quantifiers	*cvejən* 'twos' *drajən* 'threes' *asaxən* 'many'

Table 5.1 (*cont.*)

Suffix	Basic meaning	Affixed to	Examples
-énc (F)[13]	result of action?	verbs with *-ir*	*konferénc* 'conference'
-ént (M)	agent	verbs with *-ir*	*absolvént* 'graduate'
-ánt (M)	agent	verbs with *-ir*; nouns	*aspiránt* 'research student' *fabrikánt* 'manufacturer'
-ár (M)	agent or state	nouns	*misjonár* 'missionary' *bibliotekár* 'librarian'
-or (M)	agent	verbs with *-ir* (> nouns with *-at*)	*redáktor* 'editor' *profésor* 'professor' *kompensátor* 'compensator'
-ér (M)	agent or state	usually with internationalisms; nouns; non-free-occurring roots	*miljonér* 'millionaire' *pionér* 'pioneer'
-n[14] (M)	agent	nouns	*šadxn* 'matchmaker' *paxdn* 'coward'
-əs (N)	abstract nouns, mostly < HA component	nouns	*lamdónəs* 'learnedness' *xsidəs* 'Hasidism'
-s (N)	action or result of action	verb infinitive or past participle	(*dos*) *badékns* 'bride veiling' (*dos*) *gəbrótns* 'roast meat'
-ling (M)	agent?		*cendling* 'ten-score'
-ik (F)	field of learning or research	adjectives and nouns; includes non-free-occurring roots	*lingvístik* 'linguistics' *problemátik* 'problematics' *botánik* 'botany'
-át (M)	agent or place	verbs with -ir?	*delegát* 'delegate' *internát* 'dormitory' *magistrát* 'magistrate'
-itét (M, F)			*universitét* 'university' *ojtoritét* 'authority'

4 Analyzable as *-at* + *or*; see below.

5 In CY, abstract noun suffixes *-hajt*, *-ung*, *-əniš*, *-šaft* take neuter gender.

6 Suffix *-stl* for numbers twenty and higher might be analyzed as genitive *-s* + *tl*; however, this is fossilized, not synchronically productive.

7 Zaretski (1926: 43) notes the gender distinction between the place where the action occurs, and the nominalization of the action itself; thus: *di bekəraj*$_{[F]}$, 'bakery (the place)' vs. *dos bekəraj*$_{[N]}$ 'bakery/baking.' The second meaning may often be accompanied by prefix *gə-*, e.g., *gəzingəraj* 'singing.'

8 Zaretski (1926: 43) treats this as equivalent to *-əraj*.

9 Zaretski (1926: 43) notes occasional modification of the root (via umlaut): *baheltəniš* 'hide-out,' but *haltəniš* 'view'; cf. verb *halt-n* 'hold.'

10 This is a problematic wastebasket which includes both word-final underlying schwa (*mamə-s*, *tatə-s*, *mloxə-s*) and underlying full vowel contextually realized as schwa (*gábə* - *gabóəm* 'synagogue trustee-s,' *ílə* - *ilúəm* 'child prodigy, -ies'). Basically, underlying /ə/ is a feminine suffix, except where semantic maleness is involved.

11 The suffix may be analyzed as two morphemes, *t* + *s*, and thus is given as *ts* rather than *c*.

12 This plural suffix is listed here among derivational affixes (rather than inflectional) solely because it transforms number-words into (plural) nouns.

13 Perhaps linked to *-ánc* (masculine gender), e.g., (*der*) *instánc* 'agency.'

14 In some HA-component nouns; cf. cognate nouns *šidəx* 'match'; *paxəd* 'fear'; not productive for new creations.

5.4 Noun inflections and extenders

Whereas noun derivation applies variously to different categories of bases (nouns, verbs, adjectives), noun inflections apply only to nouns. Noun inflections do not "create" nouns, but, rather, do something systematic to nouns.

5.4.1 Feminine forms

In addition to semantically female nouns like *froj* 'woman,' *mamə* 'mother,' Yiddish contains feminine extensions based on a masculine or unmarked base noun. These denote female agents or female of a species (from Zaretski 1926: 44; Mark 1978: 192ff.; Birnbaum 1979a: 232ff.):

-in[15]	*lerərin* 'teacher'$_{[F]}$, *virtin* 'hostess'$_{[F]}$, *kimpətórin* 'woman in childbirth'[16]
-kə	*šnajdərke* 'tailor'$_{[F]}$, *lerərkə* 'teacher'$_{[F]}$
-tə	*xavərtə* 'friend'$_{[F]}$, *kojnətə* 'customer'$_{[F]}$ (< HA-component)
-intə[17]	*harintə* 'proprietress'
-nicə	*nudnicə* 'bore'$_{[F]}$, *məfúnicə* 'fastidious woman'[18]
-icə	*kalbicə* 'calf'$_{[F]}$ (feminine of animals)
-ínə	*frajndínə* 'friend'$_{[F]}$, *kejsərínə* 'empress,' *balərínə* 'ballerina'
-ənə	*jidənə* 'Jewess'
-cn	*rebicn* 'rabbi's wife' (probably unique to this word)
-šə	*sekretáršə* 'secretary'$_{[F]}$, *dóktəršə* 'doctor'$_{[F]}$
-ə	*talmídə* 'pupil'$_{[F]}$
-ixə	*játixə* 'gal,' *léjbixə* 'lion-ess,' *barónixə* 'baroness' (pejorative)
-íxə	*zalmənixə* 'wife of Zalmen,' *goldbergíxə* 'wife of Goldberg'
-əs/-is	*xojlánis* 'sick woman,' *cadéjkəs* 'saintly woman' (rare; < HA component)
-ésə	*baronésə* 'baroness,' *poetésə* 'poetess' (limited; internationalisms)

With the exception of two suffixes (syllabic *ņ*; *-əs/-is*) all the feminine suffixes end in [ə] (*rebicn* is analyzed as *rebə* + *icə* + *in*). While *-in* and *-kə* have rather identical meanings (*-in* is somewhat more formal), there is sometimes also a (lexically idiosyncratic) nuance difference. Thus, *šnajdərkə* may be either a

[15] Pronounced as syllabic [ņ].

[16] This function is restricted to women, yet the feminine form is based on a never-used masculine form.

[17] Likely a double feminine suffix: *-in* + *tə*.

[18] Suffix *nicə* is feminine agent, corresponding to masculine *-nik*, e.g., *nudnik*; *məfunicə* arose via analogy from Hebrew-origin masculine *məfunək*, which happened to end in a string phonetically similar to agentive *-nik*.

female tailor or the tailor's wife, whereas *šnajdərin* is only a female tailor (Mark 1978: 192–193).

The most common feminine suffixes are *-in* and *-kə*.[19] Suffix *-tə* (< Aramaic), while frequent, is found almost exclusively with HA-component nouns. Feminine suffixes may attach to a base noun (*virt-in*) or to a derived masculine agent noun (*šnajd-ər-in, šnajd-ər-kə*). Suffix *-intə* is a double feminine suffix: *-in* + *tə*.[20] Similarly doubly marked are nouns with *-ín-ə*, *-és-ə*, *-ən-ə*, and *-icə-in* (*rebicn*). The stress difference in *léjbixə* vs. *goldbergíxə* is interesting, but hard to comment on morphologically.

5.4.2 *Emotives*

Both endearment and pejoration may be expressed by regular processes of suffixation (Zaretski 1926: 46–47; Mark 1978: 190–192). Except for *-ələ*, all the suffixes are (from Mark 1978) of Slavic origin. The endearment suffixes are:

Suffix	*Examples*
-inkə	*léjbinkə, mójšinkə, sórinkə, tátinkə, zúpinkə, fúsinkə*
-(ə)nju	*léjbənju, mójšənju, gótənju, brúdərnju*
-ši	*zéjdəši, máməši, bóxərši, méjdlši*
-čə	*avrémčə, sórčə, róxčə, fájvčə*
-čik	*avrémčik, fájvčik*
-kə	*dovədkə, ruvkə, brudərkə, švestərkə*
-ələ	*lejbələ, fisələ*

Mark notes that suffix *-inkə* is widespread. It is used with proper nouns and with common nouns (and with verbs and adjectives; see below). Whereas 2nd DIM suffix *-ələ* used with a proper name refers to a child, e.g., *lejbələ*, the form *lejbinkə* may refer endearingly to an adult. With common nouns, *-inkə* is characteristic of child talk (though not exclusively so); thus, *gotinkə, gib brojtinkə* 'dear God, give bread.' The suffixes *-inkə* and *-ələ* may not create words ending in three unstressed syllables (= they must follow a stressed syllable); thus, no ***dóvədinkə*, ***fótərələ*, etc. Stem-final schwa deletes, permitting suffixation: *tátə* + *inkə* → *tátinkə*.

Also widespread are endearment suffixes *-(ə)nju* and *-ši* referring to a person (or to God). Suffix *-(ə)nju* may attach to personal names, e.g., *lejbənju, sorənju, gotənju*, and to class-names: *zejdənju* 'grandpa,' *bobənju* 'grandma,' etc. Allomorph *-nju* occurs after unstressed syllable: *bobə* + *nju*, *brudər* + *nju*.

[19] Suffix *-kə* is also used as a gender-neutral diminutive marker for proper nouns, especially in NEY.

[20] The *-in* may be for rhythmic purposes; cf. unstressed syllable preceding *-tə* in *ganəftə* 'thief$_{[F]}$,' *xavərtə* 'friend$_{[F]}$.'

Suffix *–ši*, which is more frequent in CY, is more limited to class names: *zejdəši, maməši, mejdlši, boxərši*, and is less frequent with proper names.

Suffixes *-čə/-čik* are less common. As with *-inkə*, *-(ə)nju*, *-ši*, these suffixes usually do not trigger umlaut in the root. Root-final syllabic ə, n̩, l̩ is dropped: *ruvčə/ruvčik* < *ruvn* 'Reuben'; *sorčə* < *sorə* 'Sarah'; *roxčə* < *roxl* 'Rachel.' The forms with umlaut *avrémčə/avrémčik* < *avróm* 'Abraham' are probably relexified from 1st DIM *avréml*. The 2nd DIM suffix *-ələ* is used to express endearment. Suffix *-kə* is used in several functions (endearment; female agent; diminution), e.g., *ruvkə, mojškə, brudərkə.*

Pejorative suffixes – all primary-stressed – are suffixed to nouns, or to nominalized adjectives. The pejorative suffixes are (from Mark 1978):

-áč	*frumáč* 'hypocritically pious' < *frum* 'pious'; *furmáč* < *furman* 'drayman'
-ák	*frumák* 'hypocritically pious,' *prosták* 'coarse man,' *cvu(j)ák* 'hypocrite'
-ún	*kargún* 'cheapskate,' *kabcún* (< *kabcn* 'pauper'), *dajčún* 'German'
-éc	*boxəréc* 'brat,' *gojéc* 'gentile,' *mojdéc* 'womanizer'
-úk	*šnajdərúk* 'bad tailor,' *mamzərúk* 'bastard'
-úč	*lignúč* 'dirty liar,' *parxúč* 'rotten person'
-úrə	*lignúrə* 'dirty liar,' *porəcúrə* < *porec* 'landowner'

In certain situations the *l*-diminutives may be used to express contempt or belittlement. The feminine of the pejoratives is formed by adding *-kə*: *frumáčkə* (*-ák*>*-ač* / _*-kə*). Pejoration may, in certain instances, be expressed by a pseudo-application of stress shift (only with plurals): *ojgánəs* 'peepers' (vs. *ojgn* 'eyes'), *šrajbárəs* 'bad writers' (vs. *šrajbərs* 'writers'). Zaretski (1926: 47) also lists enlargement as a means of pejoration: *mojdrílə* 'woman (pejorative).' Agentive suffix *-nik* may be used pejoratively.

5.4.3 Case marking on nouns

Yiddish nouns are not marked for case, with three exceptions. (1) Adjectives may be used as nouns. (2) Personal names, including close family terms, and a few words such as *jid* 'Jew,' *menč* 'person,' and *rebə* 'rabbi' (Birnbaum 1979a: 225–226) may be marked in the oblique with suffix *-n*; thus, proper names *vajnrajxn, zareckin, mojšən, rivkən, avremlən* in accusative or dative. Terms for male family members may receive *-n* in both accusative and dative: *tatn, zejdn*. Female family terms receive *-n* in the dative (*bobn, mamən*), but not in the accusative. Possessive forms are *dem tatns, dem zejdns*, but *der bobəs, der maməs*. The last element of the personal name receives the marker: *mit fraklinən* 'with Franklin,' *mit rozeveltn* 'with Roosevelt,' *mit franklin rozeveltn* 'with Franklin Roosevelt.' When preceded by a title, e.g., *xavər(tə)* 'comrade,' *prezident* 'president,' *profesor* 'professor,' oblique *-n* is not used: *mit prezident franklin rozevelt-Ø*. The oblique marker is optional with *jid* 'Jew': *dem jid(n)*. Some family member terms may also be used as proper names; thus: *mitn tatn* 'with my father,' *mit tatən* (no LSD) 'with Dad.' (3) Fossilized case markers are found in some idioms, e.g., *zin* 'sense,' *luft* 'air' → *hobn in zinən* 'have in mind,' *in der luftn* 'in the air.'

5.4.4 Diminutives

The most common means of diminutive formation is via suffix *l̩*. Two degrees of diminution occur: *l̩* (1st DIM) and *-ələ* (2nd DIM). In general, 1st DIM expresses diminution, 2nd DIM endearment. The former may not apply to nouns ending in a vowel/diphthong,[21] or syllabic *l̩*. Epenthetic *d* occurs in nouns with final *n*; if noun ends in non-syllabic [l], epenthetic [x] occurs; thus:

Gloss	*Base*	*1st DIM*
foot; city; bench	fus; štot; bank	fisl; štetl; benkl
bone; son	bejn; zun	bejndl; zindl
father; woman; cow	tatə; froj; ku	No 1st DIM
bird; key	fojgl̩; šlisl̩	No 1st DIM
mill; mouth	mil; mojl	milxl; majlxl

Umlaut of the noun root (where possible) is regularly triggered by 1st DIM, if the syllable immediately preceding the 1st DIM suffix is stressed: *fus* 'foot,' *pšat* 'literal meaning,' *mojz* 'mouse,' *baləbós* 'proprietor' → 1st DIM *fisl, pšetl, majzl, baləbésl*. Note, however, exceptions, e.g., *fur-furl* 'cart,' *jat-jatl* 'guy.' When an unstressed syllable intervenes, forms with and without umlaut occur: *boxər-boxərl* 'lad,' *sojxər-sojxərl* 'merchant,' *xosəd-xosədl* 'Hasid,' *doktər-doktərl* 'doctor'; but: *ponəm-penəml* 'face,' *toxtər-textərl* 'daughter'; *volkn* 'cloud'-*v[o]lkndl, kastn* 'box'-*kastndl* ~ *kestl̩* (with *n*-dropping). Note *vasər* 'water'-*vasərl* 'creek' vs. *vesərl* 'drink remedy.'

The 2nd DIM is derived cyclically from 1st DIM, not from the base noun; thus, epenthetic *d, x* from first cycle remain in the 2nd DIM, although the conditioning environment is no longer present: *bejn* 'bone' – *bejndl̩* – *bejndələ*; *mil* 'mill' – *milxl̩* – *milxələ*. Synchronically, we might posit the 2nd DIM suffix as discontinuous ə . . . ə. However, the string *ələ* also occurs in words which blocked 1st DIM, at which cycle the *l* ostensibly was affixed; thus: *tatə – tatələ, ku – kiələ, fojgl – fejgələ*. In these instances the 2nd DIM form is used to express simple

[21] Exceptions to this are personal names with final schwa which may be truncated, and thus 1st DIM applies: *fejgə, šejnə* → *fejgl, šejndl*. Note, however, the name *dínə*, where ə may not be truncated. This may provide some evidence of a distinction between root vs. stem schwa.

(1st-degree) diminution, rather than endearment. The affixation of *-ələ* comes as a "package"; thus, proper name *dinə* → *dinələ*, not ***din[d]ələ*.

Where a sequence of more than two unstressed syllables would result, 2nd DIM is blocked; thus: *kastndḷ*, but not ***kastndələ* (alternate form *kestəle* is acceptable); similarly, *toxtər-textərḷ*, but not ***textərələ* (§4.5.3). In StY, 1st and 2nd DIM nouns in the singular receive neuter gender; thus: *der fus*, *di bank*, *dos bux* → *(dos) fisḷ*, *benkḷ*, *bixḷ*. Nouns with syllabic *ḷ* as part of the root/stem are masculine: *der šlisḷ*, *fojgḷ*, etc. Remarkable are the diminutive plurals of many nouns with HA-origin roots: *xosədḷ-xsidəmləx* 'Hasid-im,' *begədḷ-bgodəmləx* 'garment-s'; cf. also *kindərləx* 'children' < Gmc component. These are formed by adding the diminutive suffixes (*ḷ* + *əx*) onto the plural of the base noun rather than from the 1st DIM form (see Perlmutter 1988).[22]

5.5 Pluralization

Yiddish generally marks noun plurals via suffixation, modification of the root, or a combination of the two. A limited class of nouns has zero-allomorph for the plural; for these, reference to the entire NP, or to subject-verb agreement is necessary. While Yiddish has remnants of the Hebrew dual (e.g., StY *jodájəm* 'hands' [pejorative]), the dual is not a systematic part of Yiddish grammar. Collective nouns pattern partly like singulars, partly like plurals.

The allomorphs of the plural marker are given below. While many clear patterns exist, the following should be kept in mind. (1) There is often no way to predict the plural form based solely on the canonic shape of the singular (or vice versa); thus, StY *hant-hent* 'hand-s' but *land-lendər* 'land-s'; *vajb-vajbər* 'wife-wives' but *tajx-tajxn* 'river-s.' (2) There is significant regional variation in plural form, e.g., *noz* 'nose' – StY *nezər*, dialectal *nez*, *nozn* (U. Weinreich 1960b). (3) Semantic factors may play a role; thus, *man* 'man; husband,' but *menər* 'men,' *manən* 'husbands.' (4) Certain plural affixes are frequently associated with the gender of the base noun. (5) To some extent etymology is taken into account. Thus, many C-final nouns from the Slavic component take the *-əs* plural, e.g., *slup-əs* 'pole-s,' *nudnik-əs* 'bore-s.'

Zaretski (1926: 47) lists the following classes of plurals in Yiddish: (1) *-(ə)n*; (2) *(ə)s*; (3) *-ər* (with umlaut); (4) *-(ə)m* (possible stress shift and/or vowel change); (5) *-(ə)x*; (6) just umlaut; (7) zero-affix plurals, which are distinguished from (8) mass nouns, which do not take a plural; (9) irregular plurals.

[22] Dutch slang cognate loanword *gawriimpjes* shows the same exceptional structure as *xavərl-xavejrimləx* 'friend-s.' This also violates regular Dutch rules for diminutive plurals (Hans den Besten, p.c.). German shows this type of structure in the diminutive plurals *Kinderchen* 'little children,' *Wägelchen* 'small cart.' Zaretski (1926: 52) remarks that this structure (*xavejrimləx*) shows some tendency toward regularization in structure; thus: *xazərləx* 'little pigs' (presumably alongside *xazéjrəmləx*). However, this innovation is not the norm in StY.

A number of (imperfect) generalizations may be made. Derived nouns – with few exceptions – take the *(ə)n* plural; thus: *bundist-n* 'Bundist-s,' *delegat-n* 'delegate-s,' *universitet-n* 'university, -ies,' *baderfəniš-n* 'need-s,' *profesor-n* 'professor-s,' *špajəxts-n*[23] 'saliva-s,' *klejnikajt-n* 'trifle-s,' *bekəraj-ən* 'bakery, -ies,'[24] etc. This group includes nominalized C-final verb roots, e.g., *trunk-ən* 'drink-s,' *kuš-n* 'kiss-es.'[25] C-final nouns derived via prefixation also generally show the *n* plural – *gədank-ən* 'thought-s,' *gəšleg-n* 'fight-s,' *gəšrifts-n* 'writ-s,'[26] – as do nouns derived from adjectives: *leng-ən* 'length-s,' *hejx-n* 'height-s.'

Other generalizations include the following. (1) Nominalized verb infinitives – if they may be pluralized – take the *-s* plural: *dos lebn-di lebns* 'life-lives,' patterning like non-derived nouns with final syllabic *n̩* (*vogn-s*). Nouns containing the latinate "quasi-suffixes" show consistent *-n* plural: *globus-n* 'globe-s,' *gulaš-n* 'gulash-es'. (2) If *(j)ə* is considered a derivational affix, it nevertheless takes a phonologically predictable *-s* plural: *redakcjə-s* 'editorship-s.' Likewise, even if pejoratives are considered derivational, schwa-final nouns take predictable *s* plurals, e.g., *mojdúrə-s* 'women [pejorative].' (3) Semantics plays a role; derived nouns with agent suffix *-ər* take *-s* plural: StY *zingər-s* 'singer-s.'[27] Suffix *-ər* when referring to geographical proper names takes a zero plural: *bostonər-Ø* 'Bostonian-s'; however, there is reason to view these geography words as adjectives used in noun function: *bostonər* (*jidn*, *lingvistn*, etc.). (4) Abstract nouns formed with *-varg*, and often with *-tum*, generally do not take a plural: *jungvarg* 'the youth, young people,' *jidntum* 'Jewry,' though Zaretski cites *ejgntum - ejgntimər* 'possession-s.' Abstract nouns formed with suffix *-əs* take *-n* plural: *hisnagdəs-n* 'opposition-s.' (5) The *l*-diminutives take plural *-(ə)x*, e.g. 1st DIM *štetl-əx* 'market towns,' 2nd DIM *štetələ-x*. Morphology takes precedence over phonology in diminutive plurals; nouns with (synchronic) root-final *l̩* take the *n* plural, e.g., *šlisl̩*, *šlislən* 'key-s.' (6) The emotive suffixes are of Slavic origin, and take plural allomorph *-əs* after consonants (*-s* after schwa); e.g., *frumák-əs*, *šnajdərúk-əs*, *kargún-əs*, *avrémčik-əs*; and with agent suffix *nik*: *nudnik-əs*.[28] Nouns ending in *-ik* (both stressed and unstressed) are problematic; it may be part of the root, e.g., *fabrík-n* 'factory, -ies,' or a suffix: *gráfik-n* 'graph-s' (cf. *fotografjə* 'photograph'), *gramátik-əs* 'grammar-s' (cf. *gramát-iš* 'grammatical'). Its status is unclear in *cendlik-ər* 'ten score-s' (~ *cendling*). (7) Nouns ending in unstressed vowel generally take the *-s* plural:

[23] CY uses the *-ər* plural for nouns with suffix *əxts*.

[24] Plural of the place; nominalized verbal action (*dos bekəraj*) does not take a plural.

[25] Zaretski (1926: 47) lists exceptions: *tanc - tenc* 'dance-s,' *pač - peč* 'slap-s,' *klap - klep* 'blow-s,' *štox - štex* 'sting-s,' *gang - geng* 'method-s.'

[26] *Dos gəšlext - di gəšlextər* 'gender-s' is a problem. Perhaps it is non-derived; there is no related form ***šlext*.

[27] Masculine *-ər* agentives often take the zero plural in Yiddish dialects.

[28] An apparent exception is given in U. Weinreich (1968): *boxəréc-n* 'brat-s.'

fragə-s 'question-s,' *tatə-s* 'father-s,' *tojrə-s* 'Torah-s,' *géto-s* 'ghetto-s,' *kíno-s* 'cinema-s.' Words like *gábə-gabóəm, ílə-ilúəm* are problematic (§4.5.1), as are schwa-final *kojnə-kojnəm* 'customer-s,' *sojnə-sonəm* 'enemy, -ies.' (8) Nouns ending in syllabic *-n̩* take *-s* plural, unless they are of HA-origin (where the plural form serves as the best source of the underlying form); thus: *lebn-s* 'life-lives,' *vogn-s* 'cart-s,'[29] but HA-origin *nígn-nigúnəm* 'melody, -ies.' (9) Nouns ending in stressed vowel take *-ən* plural: *bjuró-ən* 'office-s,' *trikó-ən* 'leotard-s.' (10) C-final polysyllabic nouns with final stress generally take *n* plural: *kontákt-n* 'contact-s,' *konflíkt-n* 'conflict-s,' *samovár-n* 'samovar-s,' *garderób-n* 'wardrobe-s' (however: *jəsód-jəsójdəs* 'basis-bases'). These mostly involve stressed derivational suffixes: *aspir-ánt-n* 'research student-s,' *deriv-át-n* 'derivative-s,' *jidiš-íst-n* 'Yiddishist-s.' (11) Plural suffix *-əm* is used with HA-origin nouns, and has been extended analogically in some instances to non-HA-origin nouns. Several noun classes with *-əm* plural may be described, based on canonic shape (Zaretski 1926; Glasser 1990; Wolf 1977), e.g., /CACCO:n-/ in *lámdn-lamdónəm* 'scholar-s,' /CICUC-/ in *šídəx-šidúxəm* 'match-es.' Furthermore, to what "classes" do analogical plurals *kundéjsəm* 'urchins,' *doktójrəm* 'doctors' belong? For the most part the *əm* nouns consist of two syllables, are C-final (though *kojnə-kojnəm, sojnə-sonəm*), and have initial stress (in the singular). However, there are also monosyllables like *šed-šejdəm* 'ghost-s,' *prat-protəm* 'detail-s' (with vowel change), or even *din-dinəm* 'religious law-s,' *xuš-xušəm* 'feeling-s' (with no vowel change in StY). Most often the *əm* nouns preserve the original Hebrew plural, though not always: StY *šábəs-šabósəm* 'Sabbath-s' (TH *šabbɔ:θo:θ)*. These often undergo stress shift – *gánəf-ganóvəm* 'thief-thieves,' *lámdn-lamdónəm*, – though not always: *šójmər-šómrəm* 'guard-s'; also: *pójər-pójərəm* 'farmer-s' (< Gmc). Polysyllabic C-final words with ultimate stress are not eligible for the *əm* plural: *kontákt* is not open to analogy here, whereas initially stressed *kúndəs, dóktər* are.

What remain are the nouns that appear unmarked in their canonical shape, and untouched by morphological processes. These mostly have unpredictable plural marker. Many nouns of Slavic origin take *-əs*: *slup-əs* 'pole-s,' *demb-əs* 'oak-s' (~ *demb-n*), *pisk-əs* '(animal) mouth-s,' *čvok-čvek-əs* (exceptionally with umlaut) '(metal) nail-s.' Perhaps the model for these were HA-component C-final nouns like *sod-sojdəs* 'secret-s,' *mokəm-məkójməs* 'place-s,' *xojv-xojvəs* 'obligation-s,' *lóšn-ləšójnəs* 'language-s.' Not all (C-final) Slavic-origin nouns have *-əs* plural; e.g., *parénč-n* 'railing-s.' C-final nouns with *-əs* plural are lexically marked in Yiddish.

This remaining corpus of unmarked nouns is often fair game for one of the following three plural devices (all of Gmc origin): (1) -*(ə)n*; (2) *ər* (+ umlaut); (3) umlaut. Selection is not synchronically predictable, and there is

[29] Note regional plurals *vegənər, vegn.*

dialect variation (*nez* ~ *nezər* ~ *nozn* 'noses'); cf. StY *mojz-majz* 'mouse-mice,' *hojz-hajzər* 'house-s,' *rojz-rojzn* 'rose-s,' *bojm-bejmər* 'tree-s'; *tog-teg* 'day-s,' *bod-bedər* 'bath-s.' Synchronically in Yiddish the classes are morphological and fixed, and often do not correspond to the StG patterns; cf. StG *Tisch-e*, *Zunge-n*, *Ort-e*, StY *tiš-n* 'table-s,' *cung* ~ *cungən* ~ *cingər* 'tongue-s,' *ort-ertər* 'place-s.'

The corpus of daytshmerisms adds evidence of the reality of Yiddish pluralization rules. Alongside colloquial *fragə-fragn* 'question-s,' *grupə-grupn* 'group-s,' *ufgabə-ufgabn* 'task-s,' is an ongoing tendency for nativization to StY *fragə-s*, *grupə-s*, *ufgabə-s* (Zaretski 1926: 48); similarly, cf. colloquial *umštand-umštendn* 'circumstance-s' (possibly from NHG dative plural *Umständen*) ~ StY plural *umštandn*; important here is that the (German) *-e* plural (StG *Umstände*) is unavailable in Yiddish grammar.

The class of nouns with zero-allomorph plural markers is distinct from nouns which simply do not occur in the plural. Zaretski (1926: 52) gives examples of the former: *epl* 'apple-s,' *ejdəs* 'witness-es,' *arbl* 'sleeve-s,' *bejgl* 'bagel-s,' *briv* 'letter-s,' *hor* 'hair-s,' *hering* 'herring-s,' *verk* 'work-s,' *ferd* 'horse-s,' *rext* 'right-s,' *lixt* 'light-s.' These behave as true plural nouns in NP agreement, and in subject-verb agreement.

Nouns occurring only in the singular include substances, e.g., *gold* 'gold,' *zilbər* 'silver,' *putər* 'butter'; abstract nouns like *jugnt* 'youth,' *raxmonəs* 'pity'; exhaustive collectives, e.g., *jidntum* 'Jewry,' *menčhajt* 'humanity,' *dos gutə* ~ *guts* 'goodness.' Zaretski (1926: 53) notes, however, that nouns of this class may be used in a special marked sense, e.g. *di cvej jidišn* 'the two Yiddishes' (i.e., two types of Yiddish).

Zaretski (1926: 51) discusses irregular plurals, e.g., *orəmán-orəməlájt* 'poor man/men,' *jungərmán-jungəlájt* 'young man/men.' I see these rather as NPs on the way to becoming compounds; thus, NOM *der jungərmán*, ACC/DAT *dem jungnmán*. He also calls irregular the contempt plurals like *ojgánəs* 'peepers,' *šrajbárəs* 'bad writers,' etc. I disagree; they follow a phonologically describable pattern. Truly irregular is *íšə-nóšəm* 'female-s,' and perhaps *bes-medrəš–botə-medrošəm* 'small orthodox synagogue-s.'

5.6 Noun gender

StY has a three-gender system in the singular: masculine, feminine, neuter. The system is mixed, reflecting an interplay of phonology, morphology, and semantics. However, gender is also inherent for "empty" nouns which lack formal or semantic motivation for gender assignment. Thus, gender must be learned along with the noun. Frequently, the only evidence for noun gender is from the definite article and/or adjectives. Plural NPs show no gender differences for definite article and adjectives. For a summary of scholarship on Yiddish gender, see Glasser (1990: 35ff.).

Consider first non-derived nouns. In the StY system, semantics often overrides morphology/phonology. Thus, *tatə* 'father' (final -ə) is masculine, since it denotes a male. Similarly, *švestər* (final *ər*) 'sister' is female, thus grammatically feminine. Sometimes formal marking overrules semantics. Diminutives are assigned neuter gender in StY, even when referring to males or females: *dos jingl* 'boy,' *dos mejdl* 'girl.' Sometimes pressure from the semantics has led to a change of historical gender: StY *mitglid* 'member' is masculine, though *glid* 'limb' is neuter. Note also variation in StY *dos* ~ *di vajb* 'wife,' historically a neuter.

The gender of non-derived nouns may relate to canonic shape. There is a general tendency for base nouns ending in syllabic sonorants *l̩*, *n̩* (or *əm*) to take masculine gender: *(der) fligl* 'wing,' *vogn* 'cart,' *bojdəm* 'attic.'[30] Non-derived C-final nouns from the HA component are regularly masculine: e.g., *(der) sod* 'secret,' *mokəm* 'place,' *din* 'religious law.' Nouns ending in root [ər] tend to be(come) masculine, based on the similarity to derivational masculine agent suffix *ər*; thus, *der putər* 'butter,' *dos* ~ *der ojər* 'ear,' *di* ~ *der mojər* 'wall' (historically, feminine, neuter, and feminine, respectively). Non-derived nouns with final ə are regularly feminine (unless semantically a male).

For StY derived and inflected nouns, gender assignment is more regular, as follows. (1) Nouns with suffixes which refer specifically to males or females receive the respective gender; e.g., masculine *šrajb-ər* 'writer,' *nud - nik* 'bore,' *komun-ist* 'communist,' *miljon-ér* 'millionaire,' *sekret-ár* 'secretary'; feminine *šrajb-ər-in, nudnicə, komunist-kə, sekretár-šə*. Phonology alone does not determine the masculine suffixes, cf. suffixes *-nik*$_{[M]}$, *-ik*$_{[F]}$. (2) 1st and 2nd DIM singular is assigned neuter gender in StY. (3) Derived nouns ending in a schwa-final derivational suffix take feminine gender: *organizacjə* 'organization.'[31] (4) C-final nominalized verb roots are masculine: *der trunk* 'the drink.' Nominalized verb infinitives are neuter: *dos trinkən* 'the drinking.' Adjectives > nouns (with umlaut where possible) are feminine: *hojx* 'high' > *di hejx* 'height.' (5) For derivational suffixes which do not refer to animate, gendered beings, but, rather, to abstract situations, events, actions, results of actions, etc. – the gender in StY must simply be learned. Generally, nouns denoting abstract state, situation, or place are feminine in StY, while those denoting action, result of action, or collectivity are neuter. Abstract nouns with suffix *-əs* are neuter in StY. C-final Intl suffixes with primary word stress mostly steer masculine gender: *institút, internát*, etc. (but *di konferénc* 'conference'; also *universitét*$_{[m]}$ 'university' vs.

[30] Noun *di varəm* 'warmth' is feminine since it is derived from adjective *varəm* 'warm.'

[31] An exception is StY *dos rebistvə* 'tenure of Hasidic rabbi.' On nominalized adjectives (*dos gutə*), see below.

ojtorítét$_{[F]}$ 'authority'). In CY, abstract nouns with suffixes *šaft*, *ung*, *əniš*, etc., regularly take neuter gender.

The NEY gender system – where historical neuter has been lost – has been the focus of much attention (U. Weinreich 1961; Herzog 1965a; Wolf 1969; Jacobs 1990c). Much of this has to do with the NP (see below). NEY diminutives (both animate and inanimate) receive the gender of their base noun; thus: NEY *der tiš* 'table,' *di bet* 'bed' → *der tišl, di betl.*

5.7 Compound nouns

In subordinating compounds one element is the head [HEAD], the other(s) the modifier [MOD]. In coordinating compounds both elements are equally HEAD. In many languages, the order of MOD and HEAD often relates to language-typology universals. In Yiddish, however, historical fusion has resulted in both orders being productive means of compounding. However, etymology alone is not explanatory, since both types of compounds ("Hebrew" and "German") show examples with words from outside the home components (§4.5.6). Present discussion of the various noun compound types in Yiddish follows Zaretski (1926: 55ff.).

Noun + noun These divide into (1) Gmc type (MOD-HEAD; *sw* stress): *tógbux* 'diary' < *tog*$_{[MOD]}$ 'day' + *bux*$_{[HEAD]}$ 'book' – a type of book, not a type of day; *zéjfnbloz* 'bubble'; *ájznban* 'railway'; (2) Hebrew type (HEAD-MOD; *ws* stress): *ksav-jád* 'manuscript' – a type of *ksav* 'script,' not a type of *jad* 'hand.'[32] There are also noun-noun coordinating compounds (with *ws* stress). These sub-divide into: (a) parallelisms, where A is a HEAD, modified by B: 'A [who is] B,' as in *dovəd haméjləx* 'King David,' i.e., 'David [who is the] King'; not **David of the King; *arbətər-komisár* 'worker-commissar'; (b) coordinating HEAD-HEAD; these may take an intervening 'and' – *un* (< Gmc), or *ve-* (< HA) – *xosn-kálə* 'groom-bride,' *tatə-mámə* 'parents' (lit. 'father-mother'), *tint-un-pen* 'ink and pén,' *sosn-və-símxə* 'joy and jubilation.' This sub-type is more like a fixed phrase than a true compound; cf. English phrasal stress in *pen-and-ínk*, *mother-and-fáther*, *vim-and-vígor* (vs. *dóghouse*, *fáther-figure*, etc.).

Adjective + noun Zaretski treats this under two distinct rubrics: "adverb + noun," and "adjective + noun" (reflecting his view of uninflected adjectives as adverbs). The former are true compounds, and have *sw* stress: *hálbjor* 'half year,' *grójsštot* 'metropolis,' *zójərmilx* 'sour (curdled) milk' (vs. phrasal stress

[32] The "Hebrew-type" compounds are almost exclusively noun + noun, and thus are more limited than the Germanic type. For examples of Hebrew-origin compounds with B element as inflected adjective, see Zaretski (1926: 57); e.g., *odər šéjni* 'second month of Adar.' These are best seen as fossilized Whole Hebrew.

in NPs *di grojsə štót; di zojərə mílx*), *éltərzejdə* 'great-grandfather' (vs. *der eltərər zéjde* 'the older grandfather').[33] For adjective + noun, Zaretski gives, e.g., *gutərfrájnt* 'close friend,' *grobərjúng* 'ruffian,' etc. These inflect like NPS (cf. ACC/DAT *dem gutnfrájnt, grobnjúng*), and have phrasal stress. Thus, their status as true compounds is weak.

Verb root + noun These are MÓD-HEAD, *sw* stress; examples: *léjənzal* 'reading room,' *hákmesər* 'cleaver,' *šrájbtiš* 'desk,' *abonír-gelt* 'subscription money.'

Cardinal number + noun MÓD-HEAD, *sw* stress; e.g., *drájek* 'triangle,' *drájfus* 'tripod.' The examples *tarjag mícvəs* 'the 613 commandments,' *esər mákəs* 'the ten plagues' (both with *ws* stress) are fossilized Whole Hebraisms (see Zaretski 1926: 57).

Invariant + noun MÓD-HEAD, *sw* stress. This category includes diverse types of invariant elements, e.g., (1) preposition: *cvíšn-minutn* 'intervening minutes,' *mítmenč* 'fellow human being'; (2) adverb: *éjnmol-mojše* 'the one-and-only Moyshe.' Zaretski excludes here compounds formed with verb particles, saying these are derived from verbs (that is, complex verb formation precedes nominalization), e.g., *úntərgang* 'decline,' *ónfal* 'attack.' However, it is not altogether clear that Zaretski's claim holds. Thus, *(der) gang* 'method; gait' exists as a simplex noun, before creation of complex nouns *untərgang, arojsgang*, etc.; furthermore, cf. nominalized infinitives: *dos gejn* 'the going,' *dos arojsgejn* 'exiting,' *avekgejn* 'leaving,' etc. Consider also invariant *cuzamən* 'together,' which functions in Yiddish more like an adverb than like a verb particle; cf. StY *mir forn cuzamən* 'we travel together,' *mir zajnən gəforn cuzamən* 'we went together' (cf. StG *zusammengefahren*). Furthermore, how is StY *cuzamənfor* 'convention' to be analyzed?

Internationalism-based compounds These involve elements which have morpheme status in Yiddish. When occurring before a main noun, these often pattern as quasi-words within a compound (Zaretski 1926: 57), e.g., *anti-, vicə-, demo-, xrono-, neo-, kvazi-, antropo-*. However, the basic stress pattern here is *ws*: *antisemít* 'anti-Semite,' *xronolόgjə* 'chronology,' *vicə-prezidént* 'vice-president,' *psixo-lingvíst* 'psycholinguist.' Thus, these remain problematic, residing somewhere between compounds and NPs.

Compound + noun Complex compounds have hierarchical structure [AB]C or A[BC] (see §4.5.6). Mark (1978) mostly disallows complex compounding as (prescriptively) illegitimate for StY. Yiddish – along with most other Germanic languages – does not seem to manifest complex compounding to the same

[33] Zaretski includes in this group *orəmán* 'poor man' (< *orəm* 'poor' + *man* 'man'). This is an instance of haplology; cf. (inflected) plural *orəməlájt*. Note also *ws* stress pattern for both.

extent as does StG. Albeit limited, Yiddish does have structure-sensitive complex compounding; cf. [folk][šprax-xuš] 'linguistic sensitivity of the people' (A[BC]), vs. [folk-šprax][xuš] 'a feeling for the colloquial language ([AB]C).'

Phrase + noun Yiddish treats [phrase + noun] compounds as MÓD-HEAD, with *sw* stress; e.g., *zajt-mir-mójxl menčn* 'Excúse-me people' (i.e., people whose nature it is to apologize); *ven-ix-bin-gəven-júng majsələx* 'when-I-was-yóung stories,' etc. This type represents simple compounding rather than complex compounding, since, structurally, the phrase functions as A in an AB compound. Within this A element, normal rules of phrasal stress assignment apply.

Generally, in both the German and Hebrew stock languages, gender, adjective agreement, and plural allomorph are based on the HEAD element. In Yiddish, these are based on the final element in the compound. The Hebrew-type compounds, however, show partial adaptation to the Germanic pattern (Jacobs 1991). The original HEAD-MOD order, and stress pattern *ws*, remain; however, gender, adjective agreement, and pluralization are based on the final element; thus: *der* (~ *dos*) *sejfər* 'the Jewish holy book,' *di tojrə* 'the Torah,' but compound *di sejfər-tójrə*$_{[F]}$ 'the Torah scroll'; NP *di altə sejfər-tojrə*. The plural of *sejfər* is *sforəm*, but *sejfər-tojrə* → *sejfər-tojrəs*. The separation from Hebrew is often complete; thus, *der ezrəs-nóšəm* 'women's section of the synagogue' is a masculine singular compound in Yiddish, and takes predictable *s* plural: *di ezrəs-nóšəms*. In Hebrew, the first element was a (construct case) feminine singular, the second element a feminine plural.[34]

Yiddish noun-noun compounds may show internal morphological structure, mostly in terms of singular vs. plural marking; thus, *kindər-jorn* 'childhood (= children's) years,' *vertər-ojcər* 'vocabulary' (lit., 'words-treasure'), but *vort-koncert* 'poetry reading' (lit. 'word concert'). However, Yiddish noun-noun compounds do not show internal case structure (except in the type *grobərjúng*, *gutərfrájnt*; see above). Whereas varieties of German have *Tag(e)blatt*, or *Tageszeitung*, Yiddish has only *tog-blat*, *tog-cajtung* for 'daily newspaper,' with no internal suffixation. In Yiddish, the occurrence of compound-internal -*s* or -*n* is semantically and morphologically empty. These are solely connective elements (though they trace historically to plural -*n* and possessive -*s*). The connectives are employed for ease of articulation and rhythmic purposes, though some individual lexical variation is found (Mark 1978: 208ff.). In addition, the various rule-like tendencies may contradict each other. The connectives are

[34] Style levels play a role in degree of divergence from Hebrew structure. In everyday speech the plural of *sejfər-tojrə* is *sejfər-tojrəs*. However, in higher-register speech, the Whole Hebrew construct plural *sifrej-tojrə* may occur.

restricted to "German-type" MOD-HEAD, *sw* compounds, but not necessarily in the same patterns as in German.

The more frequent connective is *s*, e.g., *dorf-s-jid* 'village Jew.' Mark (1978: 208–209) describes this *s* (in one respect) as breaking up consonant gemination occasioned by compounding; thus: *dorf-s-fur* 'village cart,' *šafung-s-gajst* 'spirit of creativity,' *blut-s-tropn* 'drop of blood'; however: *bank-Ø-kvečər* 'bookworm.' The *s* connective is mostly blocked: (a) after dentals *t*, *d*, or *st* (except where needed to break up a geminate; cf. *blut-s-tropn*); thus: *luft-Ø-menč* 'person without a definite occupation,' *bet-Ø-gəvant* 'bedding,' *post-Ø-kartl* 'post card'; (b) after vowel or diphthong: *xanəkə-Ø-lomp* 'Hanukkah menorah'; *gumi-Ø-klepəxts* 'rubber adhesive'; (c) after connective *n*: *briv-n-tregər* 'postman'; (d) before or after a sibilant or sibilant cluster/affricate: *lebn-s-frejd* 'conviviality' but *lebn-Ø-standard* 'standard of living'; *šlos-Ø-mexanizm* 'locking mechanism'; *folk-Ø-šul* 'public school' vs. *folk-s-lid* 'folksong'; *blic-Ø-lomp* 'flashlight.'

Connective *n* might possibly be analyzed as a plural marker in: *vox-n-blat* 'weekly newspaper'; cf. *vox-n* 'week-s'; *karš-n-bojm* 'cherry tree'; cf. *karš-n* 'cherry-cherries.' However, connective *n* frequently contradicts expected plural forms; thus: *briv-n-tregər* but *briv-Ø* 'letter-s,' *ferd-n-štal* 'horse stable,' but *ferd-Ø* 'horse-s', *nus-n-bojm* 'nut tree,' but *nus-nis* 'nut-s.'

5.8 Nouns via clipping, abbreviation, etc.

Nouns may be formed via clipping, abbreviation, and similar processes (Zaretski 1926: 58–59); e.g., *ojto* < *ojtomobil* 'car,' *kilo* < *kilogram*. Zaretski's example *der jugnt* < *der jugntfarband* 'youth association,' with masculine gender (< *der farband*), contrasts with F *di jugnt* 'youth.' Zaretski discusses three main types of nouns formed via abbreviation or combination of (parts of) more than one word. (1) Whole portions (usually syllables) of words may be combined into a single word: *folkombild* < *folk-komisarjat far bildung* 'people's commissariat for education'; *gezérd* < *gəzelšaft far erd-ajnordənung fun jidn* 'society for the agrarianization of Jews.' (2) A portion of the first word (an adjective) is affixed to the (entire) second word: *jidišə sekcjə* → *jidsekcjə* 'Jewish section (of the Communist Party of the USSR)'; *komunistišə partej* → *kompartej*. (3) Nouns may be formed from initial letters: *ceká* < *central-komitet* 'Central Committee.' These are essentially sequential lists of letters (with *ws* stress); cf. English FBÍ, KGB, LÁ 'Los Angeles.' The Yiddish versions are based on names of Latin, not Jewish, letters; thus, *ceká*, not ***cadik-kúf*. Zaretski's examples for the most part reflect Soviet (or at least non-traditionally Jewish) methods of abbreviation. More traditionally Jewish is the creation of words based on initial letters (but not letter-names): *Rashi* רש״י from Rabbi Shlomo ben Yitshaq; the name *Katz* from כהן־צדיק 'Koyen Tsadik'; *tarjag* '613 commandments' from the letters

Table 5.2. *StY Definite article + adjective + noun*

	Masculine	*Feminine*	*Neuter*	*Plural*
NOM	der gut-ər man	di gut-ə froj	dos gut-ə kind	di gut-ə menər/frojən/kindər
ACC	dem gut-n man	di gut-ə froj	dos gut-ə kind	di gut-ə menər/frojən/kindər
DAT	dem gut-n man	der gut-ər froj	dem gut-n kind	di gut-ə menər/frojən/kindər
POSS	dem gut-n mans	der gut-ər frojs	dem gut-n kinds	[Rarely used]

comprising the numerical equivalent of 613. This is a productive process in newer words, e.g., *jivo* 'YIVO' < *jidišər visnšaftləxər institut* 'Jewish Scientific Institute.'

5.9 The NP

5.9.1 Article and adjective

Within the NP, definite article and adjective inflect in most situations for number (singular or plural) and, if singular, gender and case. There are three active cases: nominative, accusative, dative, and marginally a fourth – the possessive, which is formed on the basis of the dative NP (Birnbaum 1979a: 241–242).

The StY definite article and attributive adjective are given in Table 5.2, using the adjective *gut* 'good,' plus nouns *man* 'man,' *froj* 'woman,' *kind* 'child.' The indefinite article is *a* before C-initial word, *an* before V-initial word. The indefinite article is realized as Ø in plural NP: *Ø gutə kindər* 'good children.' After the indefinite article, adjective inflection remains unaltered, except for the neuter singular, which takes a zero-suffix;[35] thus, NOM *a gutər man*; *a gutə froj*; *a gut kind*; *gutə menər*.

Four basic inflectional suffixes fill out the matrix: *-ə*, *-ər*, *-n*, and zero (*-Ø*). Suffix *-n* is realized as *-ən* after root-final /m/: *frum-ən* 'pious,' *-əm* after root-final /n/: *šejn-əm* 'pretty.' After root-final obstruents, nasal assimilation occurs: *klug*[ŋ] 'clever,' *grob*[m] 'coarse.' Unlike the situation with verbs and nouns, the adjective nasal suffix does not require an intervening vowel after velar nasal clusters *ng*, *nk*; thus: *jung-n* [juŋgŋ] 'young' vs. *jung-ən* [juŋgən] 'youths.' After stressed vowel or diphthong *-ən* occurs: *fraj-ən* 'free,' *fri-ən*

[35] Optionally, in some varieties, the nasal suffix occurs: *a gutn kind* (ACC/DAT), *a gutn kinds* (POSS).

Table 5.3. *Nominal inflection of adjectives*

	Masculine	*Feminine*	*Neuter*	*Plural*
NOM	gutər	gutə	guts	gutə
ACC	gutn	gutə	guts	gutə
DAT	gutn	gutər	gutn (~guts)	gutə
POSS	gutns	gutərs	gutns	–

'early.' Allomorph -*əm* is exceptional in *naj-əm* 'new,' *gənoj-əm* 'exact.' Suffix -*s* occurs with nominalized adjective in a possessive construction, regardless of gender – *dem altns, der altərs*, etc. – and with nominalized predicate adjectives in indefinite neuter NP: *dos kind iz a guts*. Thus, -*s* is a nominal suffix, not adjectival. Adjectives with root-final schwa are inflected normally, though geminate schwa is resolved; e.g., *prikrə* 'embarrassing' → *prikrən, prikrər*; base form *nudnə* 'boring' → *nudnər, nudnə-Ø, nudnəm* (/əm/ on analogy with *n*-final adjectives). The adjective *grojs* 'big,' when used before an abstract noun – and when there is no article – occurs in the short form – *(mit) grojs frejd* '(with) great joy' – but: *di grojsə frejd* 'the great joy.'

In NPs lacking a noun, adjectives are used as nouns, taking the following forms (Table 5.3, adapted from Birnbaum 1979a: 81). Nominalized F.SG and (all) PL subjects appear identical in form, and are distinguished via subject-verb agreement, e.g., *di klugə hobn lib lingvistik* 'the clever (people) like linguistics' vs. *di klugə hot lib lingvistik* 'the clever (woman) likes linguistics.'

Normally, adjectives are inflected in attributive position but not as a bare predicate, unless they are used as nouns. The nominal declension is used in the predicate to distinguish:

Predicate adjective	*Nominalized* ADJ
er iz alt 'he is old'	er iz an altər 'he is an old one'
mir zajnən alt 'we are old'	mir zajnən altə 'we are old ones'
dos bux iz gut 'the book is good'	dos bux iz a guts 'the book is a good one'

Mark (1978: 214–215) notes that this strategy is often used to distinguish temporally limited vs. non-limited conditions: *er iz gliklәx* 'he is happy (now)' vs. *er iz a gliklәxәr* 'he is happy (by nature).'

5.9.2 Use of articles

The definite article signals that the noun referred to is known to the interlocutors. It is not used with an unmodified personal name in the singular, but occurs in the plural in referring to members of a family, e.g., *di vajnrajxs*. The definite article may be used with a proper name if an adjective precedes; thus: (***der*) *mojšə*, but *der klugər mojšə* 'the smart Moyshe'; *finland*, but *dos šejnə finland* '(the) beautiful Finland.' Some geographic names require a definite article: *der dnjepər* 'the Dnieper,' *di dardaneln* 'the Dardanelles.' Both indefinite and definite article may be used to refer generally to an inclusive class. Zaretski (1926: 61) gives the following equivalent sentences, all meaning '(the) elephant(s) live(s) a long time': *der helfant lebt lang* ~ *di helfantn lebn lang* ~ *a helfant lebt lang* ~ *helfantn lebn lang*. The definite article is used with nominalized adjectives in neuter gender to show a general quality: *dos gutə* 'good.'[36] It is also used in colloquial speech with female personal names with *íxə* derived from masculine names: *di bregmaníxə* 'Mrs. Bregman.' When stressed, the definite article has the meaning 'this/these.'

The indefinite article *a(n)* expresses indefiniteness: *a bux* 'a/any book' vs. *dos bux* 'the book.' When *a(n)* is used with unmodified personal or geographic names it denotes 'any; some sort of': *a mojšə hot ongəklungən* '(some guy / some sort of guy named) Moyshe telephoned.' The indefinite article may be used similarly in: *ot nemt, a štejgər, a dajčland, a pojln – vos zeən mir dortn?* 'Take, for example, a Germany, a Poland – what do we see there?' (Zaretski 1926: 63). A homophonous particle *a* is used to express approximateness; *a hundərt bixər* 'about 100 books.' However, this is not the indefinite article, since it also occurs with plural amounts and does not have the variant *an* before V-initial words: *a axcik bixər* 'about eighty books.' Neither article may co-occur with a possessive adjective: (***a*/***dos*) *majn bux* '(**a/**the) my book' (§6.3.3). No article is used when a common noun is personified and functions as a personal name. Nouns used vocatively occur without an article: *Štot!* 'Oh, City!' (p. 63).

The unstressed definite article *dem* regularly undergoes contraction to *n* and attaches enclitically to the preposition; e.g., *mit dem gutn man* → *mitn gutn man* 'with the good man.' After prepositions ending in /n/, contraction patterns as follows. Monosyllabic nasal prepositions *fun* 'from; of,' *in* 'in; to' + *dem* → *funəm* ~ *fun-Ø*, *inəm* ~ *in-Ø*; thus, *in klas* 'in the class,' *fun farlegər* 'from the publisher.' With disyllabic nasal prepositions, e.g., *vegn* 'about,' *lebn* 'next to' + *dem*, only the zero allomorph occurs: *vegn-Ø*, *lebn-Ø*. Non-contracted *fun dém farlegər* expresses 'from thís publisher'; similarly, *vegn altn man* 'about the old man,' *vegn dém altn man* 'about thís old man.' Note *in nox-milxomədikn pojln* 'in post-war Poland,' where an underlying *dem* has undergone contraction and deletion. Preposition *on* 'without' seems to permit only a non-contracted form of the definite article: *on dem man* 'without the man,' not ***on-Ø man*. However, with abstract and non-count nouns, no definite article is required: *on gelt* 'without money.' After V-final preposition, *dem* → *-m*: *baj* + *dem* → *bajm* [ba(:)m] (regional [ba(:)n], with *-n*); *cu* + *dem* → *cum*. It is not clear

[36] Nominalized *-s* form of the adjective in this meaning may occur with or without the definite article: (*dos*) *guts*.

whether speakers permit contraction with prepositions ending in unstressed vowel: *ləgábə* 'compared to' + *dem* → ***ləgábən*(?), *pázə* 'along' + *dem* → *pázən*(?). It is also questionable whether contraction occurs with longer and/or stylistically marked (H-register) prepositions, e.g., *lətojvəs* 'on behalf of,' *micád* 'on the part of,' *məkojəx* 'about.'[37]

5.9.3 Negative article

Yiddish possesses a negative article *kejn* (when unstressed [kn̩]). It is used in conjunction with the negative particle *ni(š)t*. *Kejn* requires an indefinite NP, and thus is not normally used to negate NPs containing a proper name, definite article, pronoun, or possessive adjective. When *kejn* is added, the indefinite article *a(n)* is deleted. *Kejn* is an invariant, and is not inflected for number, gender, or case (on inflected nominal use, see below). Compare the following positive sentences and their negation:

Positive	Negative	
1. ix lejən	ix lejən nit	'I (don't) read'
2. ix lejən dos bux	ix lejən nit dos bux	'I (don't) read the book'
3. ix lejən a bux	ix lejən nit kejn bux	'I (don't) read a book'
4. ix lejən es	ix lejən es nit	'I (don't) read it'
5. dos iz a bux	dos iz nit kejn bux	'this is (not) a book'
6. dos zajnən bixər	dos zajnən nit kejn bixər	'these are (not) books'
7. dos iz majn bux	dos iz nit majn bux	'this is (not) my book'
8. ix ze bendin	ix ze nit bendin	'I (don't) see Będzin'

When used with a personal name, *kejn* conveys the meaning 'not any': *ix ken nit kejn mojšə* 'I don't know any Moyshe (anybody named Moyshe).' In instances of topicalization, *kejn* moves with its NP: *ix lejən nit kejn bux* → *kejn bux lejən ix nit*.

5.10 Adjectives

5.10.1 Base adjectives

Base adjectives are underlying, not created via a derivational process; e.g., *brojn* 'brown,' *klor* 'clear,' *alt* 'old,' *šejn* 'pretty,' *xošəv* 'distinguished.' An adjective like *gəzunt* 'healthy' is problematic, since it may derive via adjectivization of noun *gəzunt* 'health.' (The historical prefix *gə-* is not of synchronic interest; there is no ***zunt* in Yiddish.)

[37] Stylistically marked prepositions also show marked NP behavior; e.g., after *al-pi* the definite article is usually omitted: *al-pi din* 'according to religious law,' *al-pi rov* 'according to the majority.'

5.10.2 *Derived adjectives*

Some adjectives are derived from other parts of speech, with no overt affixation or modification of the root.[38] For example, the noun *eməs* 'truth' adjectivizes → *eməs*, in *der eməsər lingvist* 'the true linguist'; adverb *gor* 'extremely' in *di gorə velt* 'the whole world.' Here, adjectivization creates adjectives with no overt marking of the process. Rather, it is inferred from syntactic and morphological patterning. Most derived adjectives in Yiddish, however, show overt signs of derivation. Derived adjectives may be divided into main types: (1) adjectives derived from non-adjectives; (2) adjectives derived via compounding of distinct words. Dealt with separately from the derived adjectives are processes of intensity modification: comparative, superlative, adjective "softeners", and endearment. These lie somewhere between derivation and inflection. They apply systematically to adjectives, rather than create them. However, they add or change meaning, much like derivational affixes.

Past participles may be adjectivized, after which they inflect normally; e.g., from weak verbs: *gəkojft-ər* 'purchased,' *abonirt-ər* 'subscribed'; with inseparable prefix: *farkojft-n*, 'sold'; with verb particle: *ibərgəlejənt-ə* 'read'; from strong verb: *gətrogən-əm* 'carried.' With the infinitive root, the most common adjectivizing suffix is some variant of *dik* ~ *ik*.

Most general is the gerund suffix *(ə)ndik*; e.g., root *lax-* 'laugh' yields *laxndik* 'laughing': *laxndik trinkt er dem vajn* '(while) laughing he drinks the wine.'[39] The gerund may occur as an inflected adjective: *der laxndikər man trinkt dem vajn* 'the laughing man drinks the wine.'

Distinct from *(ə)ndik* is the suffix *-ədik*, which denotes 'that which does X.' The distinction is partly aspectual. Thus, Mark (1978: 228) compares *a štejəndikər lomp* 'a standing lamp' (at the moment) vs. *a štejədikər lomp* 'a standing lamp' (a lamp built to stand rather than hang from the ceiling, or attach to the wall); *a štejədikər lomp* can thus, at any given moment, be packed away horizontally in a box and still be *štejədik*. Other examples include: *trog-* 'carry' → *trogndik* 'while carrying,' vs. *trogədik* 'pregnant'; *kum-* 'come'→ *kuməndik* 'while coming' vs. *kumədik* 'future' (*kumədikə cajt* 'future tense'). A related suffix complex is *-əvdik*. The *-əv* adds a meaning of inherent characteristic; thus: *trogəvdik* 'carriable'; from *špirn* 'feel,' *špirəvdik* 'sensitive'; *bejgn* 'bend,' *bejgəvdik* 'flexible.' These suffixes may be analyzed further as *(ə)n*, *ə*, or *əv*, followed by a single suffix *-dik*. With nouns we find, e.g., *šabəs-dik* 'Sabbath; festive,' *mojrə-dik* 'fearful,' *sejxl-dik* 'logical,' *sakonəs-dik* ~ *sakonə-dik* 'dangerous,' all with noun-final unstressed syllable, followed

[38] Discussion is taken largely from Zaretski (1926: 68ff.).

[39] It could be argued that these forms are based on the verb infinitive plus *-dik*, thus: *laxn-dik*. However, this leaves unexplained *zajəndik* 'being,' *gejəndik* 'walking,' *štejəndik* 'standing' vs. infinitives *zajn*, *gejn*, *štejn*. Zaretski (1926: 68) notes older literature had forms like *gejənd*, *der gejəndər*, conscious copies of German models; these forms became increasingly avoided in the modern language.

by *-dik*; note also noun *xejn* 'charm,' adjective *xejnəvdik*. This suggests an analysis: *trog + n + dik* and *trog + əv + dik*, whereas *trog + dik* undergoes default schwa insertion: *trogədik*. However, selection may in part be morphological rather than phonological, at least in some Yiddish varieties; cf. *milx-ik* 'dairy' ~ regional *milx-ədik*. Most frequent is adjectivization with *(ə)ndik* – this may occur with any verb. The other suffixes are lexically limited; thus: *trogəvdik*, *špirəvdik*, but not ***zajəvdik*.

Two suffixes otherwise associated with adjectivization from nouns are also used in verb > adjective derivation (Mark 1978: 223ff) *-ik*, and *-ləx*; e.g., *flis-ik* 'fluent' (*flis-n* 'flow'), *arumnemik* 'encompassing' (< *arumnemən* 'comprise'); *dergrejxləx* 'attainable' (< *dergrejx-n* 'reach'). A third suffix, *-bar* – a daytshmerism – is used in limited instances in the function generally expressed with *-ləx*; e.g., *dankbar* 'thankful.'

Mark's (1978: 223) analysis of *ik* ~ *dik* as allomorphs of a single morpheme is problematic. The distribution is as follows: (1) *-ik* requires preceding stress (*mílx-ik* 'dairy,' *dervájl-ik* 'temporary'); (2) stress is calculated metrically; thus, in compounded adjectives (see below): *cvéj-tràf-ik* 'disyllabic,' *éjn-mòl-ik* 'onetime,' *frémd-špràx-ik* 'foreign-language'; (3) *ik* is parallel to *dik* in some words with final *-ər*: *vasərik* ~ *vasərdik* 'watery,' *gədojər(d)ik* 'lasting'; however, most general is *-dik* (*vintərdik* 'wintery,' *lexərdik* 'full of holes,' *bejnərdik* 'boney'); *hungərik* 'hungry' is an exception; (4) suffix *-ik* occurs with unstressed V-final base: *slinə + ik* → *slin-Ø-ik* 'of saliva.' However, in V-final HA-origin words, *-dik* is common: *corə-dik* 'lamentable,' *xarotə-dik* 'regretful.' (5) Syllabic *n̩* disappears before *-ik*: *faraxtogn* 'last week' → *faraxtogik* 'last week's'; *farcvejvoxn* 'two weeks ago' → *farcvejvoxik* 'of two weeks ago.' It drops as well from a root: *frimorgn* 'early morning' → *frimorg-Ø-ik*; however: *volkn* 'cloud' → *volkndik* 'cloudy,' not ***volkik*. (On *-ik* in adjective diminution, see below.)

Suffix *-iš* is frequent in derivation of adjectives from nouns. It has two allomorphs: *iš* and *š* (Mark 1978: 225–226). Allomorph *iš* generally occurs after stressed syllable: *jídiš* 'Yiddish,' *lamdóniš* 'scholarly,' *xsídiš* 'Hasidic,' *ejropéiš* 'European,' *gójiš* 'non-Jewish.' Root- (or stem-) final unstressed vowel deletes before *iš*: *məlúxə* 'state,' *aprióri* 'a priori,' *histórjə* 'history' + *iš* → *məlúxiš*, *aprióriš*, *históriš*. After syllabic *l̩*, *š* occurs; e.g., *himlš* 'heavenly,' *mejdlš* 'girl-like,' *jinglš* 'boy-like.' For nouns ending in *-ər*, we find two situations. After agentive suffix *-ər*, allomorph *-iš* occurs: *šrajb-ər-iš* 'writerly,' *mit-cajt-lər-iš* 'contemporary.' However, after non-derivational [ər] (whether plural suffix or part of the root), *-š* ~ *-iš* (p. 226); e.g. (< singular): *pojər-š* 'farmerly,' *mamzər-š* 'bastardly'; (< plural): *kindər-š* 'children's,' *bixər-š* 'bookish.'[40]

[40] Mark (1978: 226) lists as possible exceptions adjectives derived from frequently occurring agentive nouns: *šnajdər-š*, *šustər-š* 'tailor-s' 'shoemaker-s.' I. B. Singer uses *šrajbər-š* for

Suffix *-iš* also occurs immediately following a stressed syllable in internationalisms; thus, nouns *logik* 'logic,' *gramátik* 'grammar,' *xáos* 'chaos,' *elíps* 'ellipse,' *legéndə* 'legend,' *sistém* 'system' have corresponding adjectives *lógiš, gramátiš, xaótiš, elíptiš, legendáriš, sistemátiš*. The modifications to the base forms suggest that Yiddish acquired the nouns and adjectives ready-made from the lending language(s), since these modifications are limited to the internationalisms (Mark 1978: 226).

A nasal suffix /ən/ is used to create adjectives from nouns denoting materials or substances: *štol – štolənər* 'of steel,' *zilbər – zilbərnər* 'of silver.' With some nouns, the string *-ərn* is found, e.g., *gloz-glezərnər* 'of glass,' *hilcərnər* 'wooden.' Zaretski (1926: 72–73) posits a suffix *-ərn*. I posit a regular "materials" suffix *(ə)n* added to noun-plural forms (*glezər*; though *hilcər-* is adjectival). After a stressed vowel, the schwa remains: *papírənər* 'of paper,' *metálənər* 'of metal.' Material-name adjectives with *-(ə)n* may not occur as uninflected predicate adjectives: *der zilbərnər tiš* 'the silver table,' but not *der tiš iz* ***zilbərn*. Here, a circumlocution is required: *der tiš iz fun zilbər*. However, inflectional zero is permitted: *a zilbərn-Ø bux* 'a silver book.'

Suffix *-nə* is found in derived adjectives of Slavic origin; e.g., *zapasnə* 'spare,' *kapriznə* 'fickle' < nouns *zapas* 'reserve,' *kapriz* 'whim.' I posit suffix *-nə*. Zaretski (1926: 72–73) posits suffix *-n* (but does not explain the ə which follows). He claims that it attaches to Slavic-origin nouns. However, *nudnə* 'boring' is probably derived from a verb *nudjən*; cf. also *modnə* 'strange'; there are not corresponding nouns ***nud* (though, *nudnik*), ***mod*.[41]

Other suffixes occurring in adjective derivation < nouns include (Mark 1978: 227):

- *-ik* competes to some extent with more general *-dik*. The former attaches to nouns (and to verb roots; see above): *flejšik* 'of meat,' *farbik* 'colorful,' *blutik* 'bloody.' It also attaches to invariants: *hajntik* 'contemporary,' *ictik* 'current.'
- *-ləx* is not to be confused with the homophonous adjective softener *-ləx* (the latter is non-derivational, and only attaches to existing adjectives). Derivational *-ləx* attaches to nouns and to verb roots: *glik* 'happiness,' *pajn* 'anguish,' *krist* 'Christ' → *glikləx* 'happy,' *pajnləx* 'painful,' *kristləx* 'Christian.' With nouns, umlaut occurs if the final syllable is stressed: *tog* 'day,' *gəfór* 'danger' → *tegləx* 'daily,' *gəférləx* 'dangerous.' Examples with verb roots include: *trinkləx* 'drinkable,' *farbajtləx* 'changeable,' *opkojfləx* 'purchasable'; note lack of umlaut in *vašləx* 'washable' < *vaš-n* 'wash.'

'writerly' (David Neal Miller, p.c.). On nuance distinctions such as *kindiš* vs. *kindəriš*, see Mark (1978: 225).

41 Mark (1978: 214) notes that this type of *-nə* adjective from Slavic was indeclinable until approximately the end of the nineteenth century: *der/dem nudnə man* 'the boring man.' Zaretski (1926: 72–73) writes that the suffix is often felt to be non-native, and is often exchanged for native suffixes like *iš*.

Mark notes the following suffixes are marked; they occur with specific components of the lexicon.

- *-ál/-él* with internationalisms:[42] *teatrál* 'theatrical,' *kulturél* 'cultural,' *racjonál* ~ *racjonél* 'rational,' *liberál* 'liberal.'
- *-(j)éz* with internationalisms *religjéz* 'religious,' *nervéz* 'nervous.'
- *-átə* with a limited group of Slavic-origin nouns: *pisk-átə* 'mouthy,' *horb-átə* 'hunched.'
- *-əvátə* related to *-átə*, is from Slavic, but is much more productive in Yiddish. It conveys the meaning 'X-like, X-ish,' and, thus, softens the adjective; it occurs with Slavic-origin bases, e.g., *suk(əv)átə* 'gnarled,' *šmatəvátə* 'rag-like'; also with non-Slavic bases: Gmc *narišəvátə* 'foolish,' HA *taməvátə* 'foolish,' *məšugəvátə* 'crazy.'
- *-loz* is rare, and marked as heavily daytshmerish; examples in modern StY: *maxtloz* 'powerless,' *cvekloz* 'purposeless,' *arbətloz* 'unemployed,' *bodnloz* 'homeless.'[43]
- *-bar* and *-zam* are also daytshmerisms, and, not productive (Mark 1978: 228). Individual words accepted in StY include: *dankbar* 'thankful,' *gangbar* 'current,' and perhaps *ummitlbar* 'immediate'; *-zam* in *ajnzam* 'lonely,' *arbətzam* 'industrious,' *ojfmerkzam* 'attentive.'
- *-haft(ik)*: *mustərhaft(ik)* 'exemplary,' *vorhaftik* 'truthful,' *štandhaft(ik)* 'durable.'
- derivational suffix *-ər* in adjectives based on geographic names is distinct from noun agentive suffix *-ər*. Geographical *-ər* adjectives are indeclinable, e.g., *der/dem nju-jorkər lerər* 'the New York teacher,' *nju-jorkər cajtungən* 'New York newspapers'; in nominalized function: *der/di bostonər hot/hobn lib bejsbol* 'the Bostonian(s) like(s) baseball.' Note also *amerikə-amerikánər* 'America-n,' *varšə-varšəvər* 'Warsaw – Warsovian.' Not all geographic adjectives take this suffix; thus: *ejropə-ejropéiš* 'European,' *ejropeišə bixər* 'European books' vs. *amerikanər bixər* 'American books.'
- *-ərlej* means 'kinds/types of.' It can be indeclinable: *cvejərlej* 'two-faceted,' *drajərlej* 'three-faceted,' *kolərlej* (~ *alərlej*) 'all kinds of': *kolərlej altə bixər* 'all kinds of old books.' However, with singular nouns, it receives suffix *-ik* and inflects: *a cvejərlejikər plan* 'a two-faceted plan.'

5.10.3 Compound adjectives

Compound adjectives are treated like a single adjective as concerns inflections. They fall into some main types (Zaretski 1926: 68ff.; Mark 1978: 231–233). One type involves compounding first, followed by adjectivization: [*gut-brudər*]*-iš*

42 Mark (1978: 229) notes that where both *-él* and *-ál* forms are available, *-él* is used for adjectives, *-ál* for nouns: *der intelektuélər man* 'the intellectual man,' *der intelektuál* 'the intellectual.'

43 This illustrates clearly daytshmerish origins; cf. cognates StG *Boden*, StY *bojdəm* 'attic.'

'comradely,' [*zibn-un-cvancik*]-*stər* 'twenty-seventh,' [*klejn-birgər*]-*ləx* 'petit bourgeois.' In the other type, the second element is already an adjective before compounding takes place. Zaretski's examples of several sub-types of the second type include the following.

NOUN + ADJ These are structured MOD-HEAD, with stress on the A element; examples: *lúləv-trukn* 'dry as a lulav,' *mójər-hojx* 'high as a wall,' *cúkər-zis* 'sugar-sweet,' *lébns-feik* 'capable of living,' *práxtful* 'splendid,' *planmesik* 'according to plan.' These function very much like (Germanic-model) compound nouns.

Another type of compound adjective has stress on the B element. These subdivide into two types: MOD-HEAD and HEAD-HEAD. Examples of MOD-HEAD are *tunkl-blój* 'dark blue,' *hel-grín* 'light green,' *špogl-náj* 'brand new.'[44] HEAD-HEAD consists of two coordinated adjectives, expressing "both A and B"; however, inflection follows only the B element: *a socjalistiš-utopistišər plan* 'socialist (and) utopian plan'; *dos jidiš-švedišə vertərbux* 'the Yiddish-Swedish dictionary.'

INVARIANT + ADJ – structurally, MOD-HEAD, with stress on the HEAD. These involve adjectivization of phrases, or groups of words; examples: *azoj-gərúfn* 'so-called,' *nit-dervárt* 'unexpected.'

Evidence that -*(d)ik* is the default suffix for adjective formation is provided by phrases used adjectivally: *funzixdik* 'in and of itself,' *cvej-xadošəmdik* 'bi-monthly'; *azoj-fun-alcding-cu-bisləxdik vi megləx* 'thus from everything as gradually as possible' (Zaretski 1926: 76). This would be similar to English "Chomsky-and-Halle-Sound-Pattern-of-Englishly approached." Zaretski (1926: 76) notes *nit-rusiš-špraxik* 'non-Russian-speaking.' There is no adjective ***špraxik*; it cannot stand alone (thus, *cvej-špraxik* 'bilingual'), nor is there something like ***nit-rusiš-šprax* 'non-Russian language.' The adjective *rusiš-špraxik* serves as the base to which the negative particle *nit* may then be compounded.

Some elements – often independent words in their own right – occur frequently enough to be considered as forming regular classes of B elements in compound adjectives: -*ful* 'full': *ojsdrukful* 'full of expression,' *praxtful* 'splendid'; -*rajx* 'rich': *inhaltrajx* 'full of meaning,' *idéjən-rajx* 'rich in ideas.'

5.10.4 Adjectival prefixes

The so-called "adjectival prefixes" pattern phonologically mostly like independent words. The most productive of these is *um* (Mark 1978: 229–231), which usually negates: *(um)gliklǝx* '(un)happy.' The *um* occurs with roots from various components, e.g., Gmc *umgliklǝx*; Slavic *umplidnǝ* 'infertile' (referring

44 Zaretski claims these have stress on the A element; U. Weinreich (1954) claims A and B have equal stress. I posit primary stress on the B element (subject to rhythmic modification; see §4.5.10).

to an animal)'; HA *umkóvədik* 'derogatory'; internationalisms: *umdemokratiš* 'undemocratic.' The *um* may also occur with a past participle; though here with a more specialized meaning: *umgəgesn* means 'not yet having eaten,' rather than **'uneaten.'[45] Not all adjectives may take *um*; thus, no ***umgrojs* 'un-big,' ***um-mogər* 'un-thin,' ***um-zis* 'un-sweet.' Mark (p. 230) observes that this limitation tends to concern adjectives which have clear lexical antonyms available: *grojs* 'big' vs. *klejn* 'small'; *zis* 'sweet' vs. *bitər* 'bitter.' He further notes a nuance difference between *um* and *nit*: *umcajtik* 'immature' vs. *nit-cajtik* 'not mature.'

The prefix *on* (< preposition *on* 'without') has the meaning 'lacking'; thus: *onzunik* 'unsunny,' *onbejnərdik* 'boneless.' This is not as frequent as *um*, and is considered newer, having gained ground during the twentieth century (Mark 1978: 231). In the spread of StY, *on* began replacing: (1) daytshmerish *-loz*: *maxtloz* > *onmaxtik* 'powerless'; (2) Slavic prefix *bez-* in calques based on Slavic semantic models: *onbordik* 'beardless,' *ontalantik* 'talentless,' *onbušədik* 'shameless.'

Also widespread is adjective compounding with negative particle *nit*: *nit-šejn* 'not nice,' *nit-košər* 'not kosher,' *nit-simetriš* 'non-symmetrical.' However, these may also occur unlinked: *nit šejn*. This compounding softens the negation somewhat (Mark 1978: 231).

Mark (1978: 232) lists a number of otherwise independent words which occur frequently enough in adjective-compounding processes that they verge on quasi-prefix status:

fil- 'many' *filzajtik* 'many-sided,' *filtrafik* 'poly-syllabic'
ful- 'full' *fulštendik* 'complete,' *fulvertik* 'full-valued'
ejgn- 'self' *ejgnartik* 'peculiar,' *ejgnmaxtik* 'self-powered'
glajx- 'same' *glajxcajtik* 'simultaneous,' *glajxvertik* 'of equal value'
faršejdn- 'varied' *faršejdn-farbik* 'of varied colors,' *faršejdn-minik* 'diverse'
lang- 'long' *langvajlik* 'boring,' *langjorik* 'of many years'
kurc- 'short' *kurcvajlik* 'of short duration,' *kurczixtik* 'near-sighted'
vajt- 'far' *vajtzixtik* 'far-sighted,' *vajt-bestər* 'best by far'
gut- 'good' *gutmutik* 'good natured,' *gut-šxejniš* 'good-neighborly'
vojl- 'well' *vojl-kenəvdik* 'erudite,' *vojltetik* 'beneficial'
grojs- 'big' *grojsštotiš* 'metropolitan,' *grojsmutik* 'generous'
brejt- 'broad' *brejtharcik* 'generous,' *brejtzinik* 'broad-minded'
klejn- 'small' *klejnštetldik* 'provincial,' *klejnbirgərləx* 'petit bourgeois'

To these may be added *halb-* 'half,' *psevdo-* 'pseudo-,' *neo-* 'neo-,' *anti-* 'anti-,' *pro-* 'pro-,' etc.; also: *eltər-* in the sense 'great-': *eltər-zejdə* 'great-grandfather'; *ur-* in *urejnikl* 'great-grandchild.' As well, Mark notes the

45 It is not clear that these are adjectives; see discussion on verbal aspect, below.

numbers *ejn-*, *cvej-*, *draj-*, in, e.g.: *ejntrafik* 'monosyllabic,' *cvej-voxik* 'lasting two weeks,' *draj-perzonik* 'for three persons.'

5.10.5 Softeners

Yiddish possesses morphological means of modifying adjectives for degrees of intensity. In addition to the common (for Germanic languages) hardeners – comparative and superlative – Yiddish marks relative degrees of softening, even endearment. The following are softeners; they do not trigger umlaut (from Mark 1978: 227–228).

- *-ləx* is the most productive adjective softener; e.g., *rojtləx* 'reddish,' *langləx* 'somewhat long.' Adjectives with final /l/ take allomorph *-bləx*: *gel* 'yellow,' *gelbləx* 'yellowish.'
- *-əvátə* is of Slavic origin; used with Slavic-, Gmc-, and HA-component bases; *šmatəváte* 'ragged,' *taməvátə* 'foolish,' *narišəvátə* 'foolish.'
- *-(d)ik* is most commonly used to derive adjectives from other word classes, e.g., verbs – *flis-ik* 'fluent,' – or nouns – *mut-ik* 'courageous'; when used derivationally, it is not a softener. However, *-(d)ik* also functions as a softener when applied to existing adjectives: *mid* 'tired,' *midik* 'somewhat tired'; *hejmiš* 'cozy,' *hejmišdik* 'somewhat cozy.'
- *-ink*, *-ičk*, *-čink* all express endearment from the speaker toward the thing described; examples: *vajsinkər* < *vajs* 'white,' *junginkər* < *jung* 'young,' *nidəričkər* < *nidərik* 'lowly,' *najinkər* < *naj* 'new.'

Softeners take regular inflectional endings; thus: *der rojtləxər komunist* 'the sort-of-reddish communist,' *di midikə lojfərs* 'the somewhat-tired runners,' *afn vajsinkn tišələ* 'on the (dear little) white table.' Final schwa in *-əvátə* deletes before inflection *n*: *mitn taməvatn filosof* 'with the foolish philosopher.' Suffixes *-ink*, *-ičk*, *-čink* may not appear in the short form (for example, in predicate adjective position); thus: *di fon iz rojtləx* 'the flag is reddish,' but not *di fon iz* ***vajsink*.

5.10.6 Hardeners: comparative and superlative

The most productive suffix of comparison is *-ər*, occurring with most types of adjectives, e.g., *fajn-ər* 'finer,' *elektriš-ər* 'more electric,' *gərotənər* 'more successful,' *sejxldik-ər* 'more logical,' *jidišləx-ər* 'more Jewish-like.' Comparison frequently (but not always) triggers umlaut: *alt-eltər* 'old-er,' *grojs-gresər* 'big-ger,' *klejn-klenər* 'small-er,' *klug-kligər* 'smart-er,' *gəzunt-gəzintər* 'healthy, -ier'; however: *oft-eftər* ~ *oftər* '(more) often,' *xošəv-xešəvər* ~ *xošəvər* '(more) distinguished.' Sometimes the absence of umlaut is predictable from the phonetic environment, e.g., frequently before *r*, *x*: *švax-švaxər* 'weak-er,' *štark-štarkər* 'strong-er,' *varəm-varəmər* 'warm-er.' Sometimes a semantic distinction is made: *klor* 'clear'-*klorər* 'clearer (abstract)' vs. *klerər* 'clearer (concrete),' *grob* 'fat; thick; coarse'-*grebər* 'fatter' vs. *grobər* 'coarser' (Mark

1978: 221). There is some suppletion: *gut-besər* 'good – better,' *šlext-ergər* 'bad – worse.'

Comparative adjectives may occur in their short or long (inflected) form; thus (inflected): *der gresərər tiš/dem gresərn tiš* 'the bigger table,' *di kligəre froj* 'the smarter woman'; (short form in predicate adjective) *di froj iz kligər* 'the woman is smarter'; (nominal inflection) *dos kind iz a kligərs* 'the child is a smarter one.'

Linking in comparison is either via the prepositions *far* or *fun* + dative, or the conjunctions *vi/ejder/vidər* + nominative. Thus, 'he is richer than the man' may be expressed: *er iz rajxər far/fun dem man*$_{[\text{DAT}]}$ or *er iz rajxər ejdər/vi/vidər der man*$_{[\text{NOM}]}$. Use of *als* + nominative for comparison is considered daytshmerish.

The superlative is formed from the comparative of the adjective, minus the -*ər* suffix; e.g., *klug – kligər – (der) kligstər* '(the) smartest'; *gərotn-gərotənər-(di) gərotnstə* '(the) most successful'; *gut-besər-(der) bestər* '(the) best.' Superlatives receive normal adjective inflections. They may not occur in the short form; thus: *er iz klug – er iz kligər*, but *er iz der kligstər*; *zej zajnən di kligstə*, etc.

The superlative may also be expressed by *samə* + base form of the adjective (+ inflection): *di samə grojsə štot* = *di grestə štot* 'the biggest city.' When *samə* is used with the superlative form of the adjective it functions as an intensifier: *di samə grestə štot* 'the very biggest city.'

5.10.7 *Possessive adjectives*

The base forms of the possessive adjective are as follows:

	Singular	Plural
1P	majn	undzər
2P	dajn	ajər[46]
3P	zajn$_{[\text{M}]}$, ir$_{[\text{F}]}$, zajn$_{[\text{N}]}$	zejər

Possessive adjectives in attributive position are not inflected for gender or case with nouns in the singular; with noun plurals they receive uniform -*ə* suffix: *majnə*, *undzərə*, etc. All remaining adjectives in the NP are unaffected: *der gutər xavər* → *majn gutər xavər* 'the/my good friend'; *a gutə xavərtə* → *majn gutə xavərtə* 'a/my good (female) friend'; *dem gutn xavər* → *majn gutn xavər*; *gutə xavejrim* → *majnə gutə xavejrim*. Only with N.SG nouns is this an issue. Here the possessive adjective acts like the indefinite article – the zero suffix is found with nominative and accusative: *majn gut-Ø kind* 'my good child'; with DAT/POSS we find *majn gut-Ø kind(s)* ~ *majn gutn kind(s)*, echoing the variation found in general: *mit a gut-Ø* (~ *gut-n*) *kind* 'with a good child.'

46 Characteristic for varieties of CY (and at one time over a larger area) is the possessive adjective *enkər*-, corresponding to the 2P.PL pronoun *ec*$_{[\text{NOM}]}$ - *enk*$_{[\text{ACC/DAT}]}$.

Following a noun, or when used as a noun, possessive adjectives inflect for number, gender, and case; e.g., *der brudər majnər, mitn brudər majnəm* '(with) my brother'; *di švestər majnə, mit der švestər majnər* '(with) my sister,' *di bridər majnə* 'my brothers.' Postposed possessive adjective after neuter singular noun shows nominal inflection *-s* in the nominative and accusative: *dos jingəle majns* 'this boy of mine'; in dative: *mitn jingələ majns* ~ *majnəm*. In an NP without other nominal(ized) element, the possessive adjective is nominalized; e.g., *majn tiš iz gut* → *majnər iz gut* 'my table / mine is good.' Constructions like *majnər a xavər* 'a friend of mine' consist of two separate NPS (§6.3.3).

Possessive adjectives pattern partly like adjectives, partly like nouns. There is historical residue where they function as full pronouns; cf. older Yiddish *potər vern* + *majnər, dajnər*, etc., 'get rid of X,' where X is historically a pronoun in the genitive case.[47] Modern Yiddish lacks a formal genitive case, and expresses this analytically: *potər vern fun X* 'get rid of X.' Inflection of the number *ejn* 'one' follows the pattern of possessive adjectives: *ejn jid iz gəblibn in dorf* 'one Jew remained in the village'; *ejnər iz gəblibn in dorf* 'one (guy) remained in the village.'

Possession is expressed in several ways in Yiddish. Possessive adjectives tend to be omitted where possession is clear from the context; thus: *der tatə* 'my father,' *di mamə* 'my mother' (lit., 'the father,' 'the mother'). The possessive adjective is used here contrastively: *májn tatə* 'my father (and not yours)'; where possession is contextually less clear: *majn tiš* is non-contrastively 'my table.' The possessive "case" – dative NP + *-s* – is mostly limited to human or anthropomorphized possessors: *dem altn mans bux* 'the old man's book,' *mojšəs fedər* 'Moyshe's pen,' etc. More general is the use of preposition *fun*, e.g., *dos bux fun(əm) altn man*; *di fedər fun mojšən*. For plural possessors the one option allowed by Mark is analytic: *dos bux fun di studentn* 'the book of the students' [= 'the students' book'].

5.11 Pronouns

5.11.1 General pronouns

In NEY the ACC/DAT distinction in pronouns has collapsed in favor of the historical dative forms: *du zest mir* 'you see me' (StY *mix*$_{[\text{ACC}]}$),' *du helfst mir* 'you help me' (StY *mir*$_{[\text{DAT}]}$).' See Wolf (1969) on regional variation in Yiddish case and gender. Discussion is based on Mark (1978).

In StY, the reflexive pronoun is *zix* for all persons, singular and plural: *ix ze zix, du zest zix, er zet zix, mir zeən zix*, etc., 'X sees X.' It is used in both

[47] Out of use by the latter part of the nineteenth century (Mark 1978: 240).

Table 5.4. *StY Personal Pronouns*

	Singular					Plural		
	1P	2P	3P.M	3P.F	3P.N	1P	2P	3P
NOM	ix	du	er	zi	es	mir	ir	zej
ACC	mix	dix	im	zi	es	undz	ajx	zej
DAT	mir	dir	im	ir	im	undz	ajx	zej

accusative and dative.[48] CY expresses the reflexive by the appropriate accusative or dative pronoun for 1/2P, *zix* for 3P.SG/PL. The four main uses of *zix* are: (1) as a true reflexive, i.e., when X does some action to X (self); (2) reciprocal action, e.g., *avrom un ix trefn zix* 'Avrom and I meet' (= Avrom meets me and I meet Avrom), extended to *mir trefn zix* 'we meet'[49]; (3) inherently reflexive verbs; e.g., *špiln zix* 'play': *di kindər špiln zix in park* 'the children are playing in the park'; (4) benefactives: *ix gej zix špacirn* 'I go (for me) for a walk.'[50]

Yiddish uses *alejn* 'alone' to emphasize the actor; English employs a pseudo-reflexive (or the word 'even'): *du zogst alejn az du zingst nit šejn* 'you yourself (= even you) say that you don't sing nicely.' This *alejn* is not a pronoun.

The impersonal pronoun *men* expresses 'one; they; people,' and occurs only as a subject. It is used in active sentences to express passive meaning: *vu redt men jidiš* 'where do they (does one; do people) speak Yiddish?' = 'where is Yiddish spoken?' The *men* requires 3P.SG verb agreement. Before the finite verb, *men* is realized as [me], or even as proclitic *m*: *me nict a sax jidišə vertər in holendiš* 'they use a lot of Yiddish words in Dutch.'

The form *jedər* 'each; every' refers to a noun in the singular. When no other nominal element is in the NP, *jedər-* inflects like a nominalized element, and functions as a pronoun, referring to a male or a female:

	Masculine	Feminine
NOM	jedərər	jedərə
ACC	jedərn	jedərə
DAT	jedərn	jedərər
POSS	jedərns	jedərərs

Examples: *jedərər vet hanoə hobn ojf der simxə* 'everyone$_{[M]}$ will enjoy the party'; *jedərərs iz besər fun dajn disertacjə* 'everyone's$_{[F]}$ is better than your

48 Historically, *zix* is a 3P reflexive which has been generalized, perhaps under the influence of Slavic (cf. also generalized reflexive in Viennese German dialect).

49 To emphasize the reciprocal meaning, Yiddish may employ *ejnər dem cvejtn* 'one another.'

50 Note *zaj mir gəzunt* '(you) be (for me) well,' with non-reflexive *mir*, reflecting a different recipient relationship.

dissertation' (= the dissertation of each and every female in group X is better than your dissertation).

If an adjective or noun follows in the NP, *jedər* is not a pronoun, but rather, a qualifier: *jedər gutər man* 'each good man.' StY (optionally) invariant *jedər* is used for all genders and cases: *jedər gutər man, jedər gutə froj, jedər gutn man, jedər gutn mans*, etc. On the other hand, StY also has a root *jed-* which inflects: *jedər (gutər) man, jedn (gutn) man, jedə (gutə) froj*. Thus, StY permits both *jedər* ~ *jedəs jingl* 'each boy$_{[N]}$.' An interesting problem arises when an adjective follows invariant *jedər* with a neuter noun (since the invariant comes from NEY, which lacks neuter gender): *jedər gut-(Ø?/ə?/s?) kind*? This is non-problematic with inflected *jed-*: *jedəs gutə kind* 'each good child.' Intensification of *jedər* is expressed via inflected *ejn-* 'one': *jedər ejnər, jedn ejnəm* 'each/every one'; alternatively, *ajedər* or *jedər ejncikər* 'each one.'

Similar in meaning to *jedər* is *jetvidər*, which is invariant for gender in the nominative, but shows oblique inflectional *-n, -ər*. Adjectival pronoun *itləx-* is similar (and also only occurs with singular): *itləxər* 'each one$_{[M]}$,' *itləx kind* 'each child$_{[N]}$'; *itləx-* may be nominalized: *itləxs fun di kindər* 'each of the children.'

Demonstratives (proximate and distant) occur in both singular and plural. When stressed, the definite articles *der, di, dos, dem* function as proximate demonstratives 'this/these'; e.g., *der mán* 'the man,' *dér man* 'this man.' The proximate demonstratives may be intensified through use of particles *ot* ~ *ot-o* before the demonstrative, or *-o* after it: *ot der gutər man* ~ *ot-o der gutər man* ~ *der-o gutər man* 'this good man.' Additionally, an inflected form of *dozik-* may follow the definite article: *der dozikər, dem dozikn, di dozikə, dos dozikə*; *dozik-* may co-occur with preposed *ot(o)*: *ot(o) di dozikə froj* 'this woman.' Proximate and distant demonstratives may occur alone in their NPs: *dós iz alt* 'this is old.'

Inflected root *jen-* expresses distant demonstratives 'that/those':

	MASCULINE	FEMININE	NEUTER	PLURAL
NOM	jenər	jenə	jenc	jenə
ACC	jenəm	jenə	jenc	jenə
DAT	jenəm	jenər	jenəm	jenə

When *jen-* stands alone in a possessive, *-s* is affixed, e.g., *jenəms gortn* 'that one's$_{[M]}$ garden,' *jenərs gortn* 'that one's$_{[F]}$ garden.' Compare *jenəm mans bux* 'that man's book' vs. *jenəms bux* 'that one's book'; in the latter, *jenəms* stands alone in its possessive NP, and therefore has the nominal *-s* suffix.

The adjective *andər* denotes 'other,' 'the other one(s)': *ejnər trinkt milx, andərə trinkən bir* 'one (person) drinks milk, others drink beer.' 'The same' is expressed by definite article + inflected *zelb(ik)-*, e.g., *der zelbikər man* 'the same man.' A synonym is *ejgn-*: *der ejgənər man* 'the same man.'

Other demonstrative pronouns include: uninflected *azá* 'such (a)': *azá majsə* 'such a story.' Before V-initial word it is realized as *azán*: *azán altə majsə* 'such an old story.' Mark (1978: 244) further gives a nominal inflection for reference to a neuter noun: *a kind azás* 'a child like that one.' Also meaning 'such' are the inflected demonstratives *azojn-* and *azelx-*: *azojnə* ~ *azelxə majsəs* 'stories of that kind'; nominalized N.SG: *azojns/azelxs* ~ *azelxəs.*

Demonstratives may occur as (human) possessors: *dems bux* 'this one's$_{\text{[M]}}$ book,' *jenərs bux* 'this one's$_{\text{[F]}}$ book,' *dem zelbikns bux* 'the same one's$_{\text{[M]}}$ book,' *dem doziknṡ bux* 'this one's book,' *dem anderns* 'the other one's.'

'Someone, somebody' is expressed by *eməc(ər)*: *eməc* ~ *eməcər hot ongəklungən* 'somebody telephoned.' It is masculine in form, and takes oblique suffix *-n*: *eməcn*; possessive: *eməcns (bux)* 'someone's (book).' If the someone is known to be a female, then there is a preference among speakers to use a generic female reference, e.g., *a froj hot ongəklungən* 'someone (lit. a woman) called.' 'Something' is expressed by *epəs*; *er zet epəs* 'he sees something.'

The negative pronoun for animates is an inflected form of *kejn-*, accompanied by negative particle *nit*: *ix ken do kejnəm nit* 'I don't know anybody (= nobody) here'; *kejnər*$_{\text{[M]}}$/ *kejnə*$_{\text{[F]}}$ *zingt nit* 'nobody is singing'; *dos iz kejnəms nit* 'that is nobody's' (= belongs to no one); *kejns*$_{\text{[N]}}$ *fun di kindər kukt nit* 'none of the children is looking.' Inanimate nouns are represented pronominally by *kejn zax nit*, lit., 'no thing not'; here, *kejn* is invariant. Additionally, the adverb *gorni(š)t* may be used pronominally as 'nothing': *er hot gornit* 'he has nothing.'

Inanimate 'everything' is expressed by the invariant *alc*: *alc iz in der hejm* 'everything is at home'; *er hot alc opgəgesn* 'he ate everything up.' Alternatively, (invariants) *alcding* ~ *aldosding* ~ *alding* may be used. The form *aldos* is used with abstract nouns in NOM/ACC: *aldos guts* ~ *aldos gutə* 'everything good'; in DAT *aldos guts* ~ *aləm gutn.*

'Everything' and 'everyone' referring to an all-inclusive group of more than one is expressed by *alə*: *alə zingən* 'everyone is singing'; *alə bixər zajnən tajər* 'all books are expensive.' When denoting inanimate objects, *alə* is invariant: *ix halt fun alə* 'I like all' (e.g., all the books). When designating humans, the ACC/DAT of *alə* is *aləmən* (if no noun follows): *er hot lib aləmən* 'he likes everyone / them all$_{\text{[ACC]}}$' (vs. *er hot lib alə menčn* 'he likes all [the] people'); the possessive is *aləməns*. Pronoun *alə* is made proximate with *dí*: *dí alə* 'all these.'

'Several' is expressed by *etləxə*, which only occurs in the plural: *etləxə studentn* 'several students,' *etləxə bixər* 'several books'; nominalized: *etləxə* 'several (ones).'

5.11.2 Interrogative pronouns

The interrogative pronoun for a person or persons is NOM *ver* 'who,' ACC/DAT *vemən* 'whom,' POSS *veməns* 'whose.' Interrogative pronoun *vos* 'what' is invariant. As subjects, *ver* and *vos* steer 3P.SG verb agreement. The interrogative adjective *vosər* 'which' is uninflected in the singular for all genders and cases; it is *vosərə* in the plural: *vosər šprax iz dos?* 'which language is that?'; *vosər man helfstu?* 'which man are you helping?'; *vosərə bixər lejənt zi* 'which books is she reading?' The form *vosər(ə)* developed from the synchronically still viable *vos far a* 'what kind of a' (lit. 'what for a'), which is lexicalized, since it occurs with both singular and plural nouns: *vos far a bux iz dos? / vos far a bixər zenən dos* 'what kind of book(s) is/are that?' Also deriving from this is *sara* 'what kind of,' which also occurs with both singular and plural nouns.[51] An inflected form of *velx* 'which' may be used adjectivally or pronominally to refer to specific or delimited groups: *velxər brudər kumt hajnt* 'which brother is coming today?'; *velxn fun di cvej ojtos hot ir farkojft?* 'which of the two cars did you sell?'; *velxs (~velxəs) kind iz dos?* 'which child is that?'

5.11.3 Relative pronouns

The unmarked relative marker is invariant *vos* 'what,' which may refer to animates and inanimates, in both singular and plural: *der man vos ix ze / di menər vos ix ze* 'the man/men which/that/whom I see.' When the relative pronoun is the subject of its embedded sentence, a resumptive anaphoric pronoun may optionally be added: *di froj vos zi lejənt dos bux iz a lerərin* 'the woman who-she is reading the book is a teacher.' The resumptive pronoun does not occur when the relative pronoun is a bare object: *der man, vos ix helf, iz a šnajdər* 'the man whom.DAT I am helping is a tailor.' However, when the relative pronoun is headed by a preposition, *vos* + PREP + PRONOUN occurs: *di froj vos mit ir bistu gəgangən in klas, hot a heft* 'the woman with whom you went to class has a notebook.' Similarly, relative possessives show a resumptive construction: *der man vos zajn bux lejən ix vojnt in kalifornjə* 'the man whose book I'm reading lives in California.'

Relative constructions with *ver* 'who' are possible, using *es* 'it': *ver es hot di mejə – hot di dejə* 'he who has the money has the say' (Mark 1978: 245). Also found is inflected form of *velx-*: *der man mit velxn ix hob gəredt, iz zejər rajx* 'the man with whom I spoke is very rich.'

5.11.4 Clitics

Cliticization involves the bonding of an element X (generally identified as a word) onto another word, Y, in such a way that X is no longer phonologically an

[51] Mark (1978: 244) claims that *sara* "does not occur in dative."

independent word. Cliticization thus differs from compounding, where phonological ω is not lost. Clitics must also be distinguished from fast-speech phenomena. This task is made more difficult since clitics frequently are "undone" in slower, emphatic speech; e.g., *vos lejənstu* 'what are you reading?' vs. *vos lejənst dú* 'what are yóu reading?' Conversely, unstressed words within a discourse (phrasal) foot will regularly reduce in fast speech, but are not clitics; e.g., *šojn* 'already' reduces to [šən] (Prilutski 1940: 55–57). Yiddish clitics mainly involve the definite article, some finite auxiliary verbs, pronouns (especially in the dialects), and some prepositions and adverbs. Yiddish clitics are either proclitic or enclitic, and tend to be words with weak semantic baggage (p. 56). Yiddish clitics are never stressed phonologically, nor topicalized syntactically.

An enclitic corresponding to the definite article *dem* occurs after a preposition, e.g., *mitn, bejsn* < *mit dem, bejs dem* 'with/during the.' Only an unstressed article may undergo contraction: *mit dem man* → *mitn man* 'with the man' vs. *mit dém man* 'with thís man.'

Subject pronoun *du* is enclitic when immediately following the conjugated verb; this occurs also in the orthography as well: דו שרײַבסט אַ בריוו *du šrajbst a briv* 'you write a letter' vs. וואָס שרײַבסטו *vos šrajbstu* 'what are you writing?' However, the arguments for enclitic status are not just based on orthography – they are phonological. For example, NEY OVA does not apply with cliticized *du*. Thus, in NEY *du kejfst dem bux* 'you buy the book,' the sequence /fst/ → [vzd] / _ *d* of *dem*; however, *vos kejfstu*, 'what are you buying?' not ***kejvzdu*.

Generally, object pronouns may be cliticized: NEY *vos hert zix* [hertsax] 'what's happening?' vs. *ver hert zaxn* [herdzaxŋ] 'who hears things?' The voiced [z] in *zix* devoices, opposite of the regular OVA process in NEY. CY generally has neither OVA nor regressive voicing assimilation: *du[s b]i:x* 'the book,' not **[zb]/**[sp]. However, clitics behave differently in CY; thus: *hotsə* may be the realization of both *hot zi* 'has her' and *hot zaj* 'has them' (Prilutski 1940: 56). Similarly, for eCY Bin-Nun (1973: 331) distinguishes between object full-pronoun *deiɒx* vs. clitic *dɒx* 'you'; the former does not trigger OVA, the clitic does.

CY also shows (historical?) cliticization of the 1P.PL subject pronoun after the verb – *esmər* 'we eat' (cf. StY *esn mir*), with loss of the original verb suffix *-(ə)n*: *esn* + *mir* → *es-Ø-mər*. Clitic *mər* reduced further to a new 1PPL inflectional ending, and a new subject pronoun is introduced; thus, *mesmər* (= *mir es-mir*) 'we eat,' *məzugmər* (= *mir zug-mir*) 'we say.'[52] This suffix triggers nasal assimilation: (*mə*) *kemər* 'we can' < *ken-mər* (cf. StY *mir kenən*).

[52] Some varieties of CY use *inc* (StY ACC/DAT *undz*) as the subject form of the pronoun: *inc zugmər* 'we say.'

Future AUX 'shall' may attach enclitically to a preceding subject pronoun, as shown in the following examples using 'shall eat':

full form	*clitic form*
ix vel esn	íxl/xel esn
du vest esn	dust esn
er/zi/es vet esn	er(ə)t, zi(ə)t, es(ə)t esn
mir veln esn	mirn esn
ir vet esn	ir(ə)t esn
zej veln esn	zej(ə)n esn

Prilutski (1940: 56) cites the clitic forms as frequent in NEY. These are enclitics attached to the pronoun, and not proclitics to the infinitive (*esn*), since an inserted adverb will intervene: *mirn bald esn* 'we shall eat soon.' When another element is topicalized, V-2 reasserts itself, and the verbal clitic forms are blocked: *bald veln mir esn* 'soon we shall eat,' not *bald **n-mir esn*.

Generally, Yiddish PPs have stress pattern *ws*, whether with full or pronoun NP, e.g., *mit rívkən* 'with Rivke,' *mit der frój* 'with the woman,' *mit ím* 'with him.' In CY, however, pronoun *ejm* 'him' contracts after a PREP (similar to general Yiddish PREP + article *dem* contraction): *mit* + *ejm* → *mítn*. Here, the PREP is metrical *s*, something not permitted in other Yiddish varieties. CY further permits pronoun *ejm* to attach enclitically to the preceding finite verb: *ròtn gəzéjn* (StY *er hot im gəzén*) 'he saw him.'

The verb *hobn* 'have' (CY infinitive *ubn*), when used as an AUX, may behave phonologically differently from full verbs. Thus, /b/ is lost in, e.g., CY *omər* < *ob-mər* '(we) have,' but not in *šra:b-mər* '(we) write.' Similarly, verb *lozn* 'let' serves as the historical source for StY *lomər* 'let's,' *lomax* 'let me' (cf. English *lemme*). Thus, *lozn*, like *hobn*, behaves here differently than most verbs.[53]

It is unclear whether subject pronouns which reduce preverbally are really clitics, or merely reduced in fast speech. It is common for *ix* → *x-* preverbally: *x-šrajb* 'I write,' *x-es* 'I eat,' *x-vel* < *ix vel* 'I shall,' etc. Impersonal pronoun *me(n)* may reduce to *m-* in quicker speech: StY *márbət* < *me arbət* 'one works'; CY *motsə* < *me hot zi/zaj* 'one has her/them' (Prilutski 1940: 56). CY *ec* 'you 2P.PL$_{[NOM]}$' reduces: *cot* < *ec (h)ot* 'you have.' The common reduced preverbal forms of subject pronouns are: *ix* → *x-*; *er* → *r-*; *es* → *s-*;[54] *me(n)* → *m-*. A further candidate for proclitic status is *s* < neuter definite article *dos*: *slebn* < *dos lebn* '(the) life.' Thus, varieties of NEY (where the historical neuter has been lost) have *di skind* 'the child'; the *s* here has been reinterpreted as part of the root. However, this is lexically quite limited. Prilutski's (p. 57) example (CY) *nemdirskind* < *nem dir dus kind* 'take the child' is a general fast-speech reduction, not lexically limited to specific nouns.

53 In *lomər*, furthermore, the case is wrong: *mir* is a nominative.

54 The variant *se* occurs for ease of articulation, rhythm, etc.; *s-nemt* 'it takes' vs. *se-zict* 'it sits.'

5.11.5 Question words

The question words have various functions: as PRO elements, as pseudo-relatives, as conjunctions, etc. These are taken up in the appropriate sections in this chapter. The question words are: *ver* 'who' (ACC/DAT *vemən*); *vos* 'what,' *far vos* 'why,' *vi* 'how,' *ven* 'when,' *vu* 'where' (*fun vanən* ~ *fun vanət* 'from where'; *vuhín* 'where to').

5.12 Cardinals and ordinals

The system of cardinal numbers is represented as follows for numbers 1–20 (0 = *nul*):

1 ejn(s)	6 zeks	11 elf	16 zexcn
2 cvej	7 zibn	12 cvelf	17 zibəcn
3 draj	8 axt	13 drajcn	18 axcn
4 fir	9 najn	14 fercn	19 najncn
5 fin(ə)f	10 cen	15 fufcn	20 cvancik

Form *ejns* is used in counting; *ejn* occurs before other elements in the NP. Numbers not exact tenscore are created on the formula '1 and 20,' '2 and 20,' etc.; e.g., *ejn-un-cvancik*, *cvej-un-cvancik*, etc. Categories higher than 20 are:

30 drajsik	80 axcik
40 fercik	90 najncik
50 fufcik	100 hundərt
60 zexcik	1,000 tojznt
70 zibəcik	1,000,000 miljón

In attributive position the cardinal number is an invariant adjective: *draj bixər* '3 books,' *zibəcn kačkəs* '17 ducks.' Generally, the presence of the cardinal number does not affect other adjectives in the NP: *draj gutə bixər* '3 good books'; *ejn gutər man*$_{[\text{NOM}]}$ '1 good man,' *mit ejn gutn man*$_{[\text{DAT}]}$ 'with 1 good man'; *(mit) ejn gut-Ø bux* '(with) 1 good book.' Numerically specified multiples of hundred, thousand, million are given in the singular: *draj hundərt* '300,' *finf tojznt* '5,000,' *zeks miljon* '6 million'; thus: *zeks tojznt cvej hundərt draj-un-drajsik* '6,233'; *ejn miljon finf hundərt draj-un-axcik tojznt fir hundərt zibn-un-drajsik* '1,583,437.' Nouns which denote quantities, amounts, units of measure occur in the singular after a cardinal number: *finf funt* '5 pound(s),' *cvej kilometər* '2 kilometer(s),' *cen dolar* '10 dollar(s).' Thus, *finf hundərt man* '500 men' ('man' in singular) contrasts with *finf hundərt bavofntə menər* '500 armed men' – in the latter, each individual is the focus (Mark 1978: 235). Units ending in schwa use the plural form: *cen kopikə-s* '10 kopecks,' *draj lirə-s*

'3 lira.' With time units use of singular or plural is idiosyncratic; with singular: *finf minut/šo/jor/meslés/mol* '5 minutes/hours/years/24-hour periods/times' (vs. *di minutn, šoən, jorn* 'the minutes, hours, years'); with plural: *finf xadošim* '5 months' (but synonym: *finf monat* in singular), *finf teg* '5 days' (but idiom: *ibər axt tog* 'a week from today'; lit., 'over 8 day'), *finf voxn* '5 weeks,' *finf sekundə-s* '5 seconds.' The noun plural is used when the cardinal number appears with a plural suffix *-ər* in the meaning 'X-s of': *hundərt jor* '100 year(s),' but *hundərtər jorn* 'hundreds of years.'

Freestanding cardinal numbers may nominalize. With the exception of *ejn-*, nominalized cardinal numbers are invariant; e.g., *ix hob zibn ojtos* 'I have 7 cars' vs. *ix hob zibn* 'I have 7 (cars).' Freestanding *ejn* 'one' inflects like nominalized adjectives; thus: M.SG *ix hob ejn tiš* → *ix hob ejnəm* 'I have 1 (table)'; N.SG: *ix hob ejn bux* → *ix hob ejns* 'I have 1 (book).' Cardinal numbers may be explicitly nominalized via suffixation of *-ər* in money units: *finfər* 'five-spot'; *finf-un-cvancikər* 'twenty-fiver.' These take a regular *-s* plural: *špogl-najə finfərs* 'brand-new fivers'; *draj finfərs* 'three five-spots.' Time expressions with *a zejgər* 'o'clock' (*ejns a zejgər* '1 o'clock,' *cvej a zejgər* '2 o'clock') have colloquial variants *ejnsə, cvejə*, etc.

Ordinals are adjectives, formed via suffixation of *-t* (for numbers less than 20), *-st* (20 or higher) to a root (possibly modified from its cardinal form). The following ordinals are given in M.SG.NOM form.

1st erštər	6th zekstər	11th elftər	16th zexcntər
2nd cvejtər	7th zibətər	12th cvelftər	17th zibəcntər
3rd dritər	8th axtər	13th drajcntər	18th axcntər
4th fertər	9th najntər	14th fercntər	19th najncntər
5th fi(n)ftər	10th centər	15th fufcntər	20th cvancikstər

Ordinal units with suffix *-st* occur with unmodified cardinal roots: *drajsik-stər, fercik-stər, hundərt-stər*, etc. Uneven amounts (24th, 89th) are thus formed: *fir-un-cvancikstər, najn-un-axcikstər*, etc. Ordinals may not occur in the short (uninflected) form; they must be inflected – *der cvejtər, di dritə, dem fertn*, though neuter NP Ø inflection is permited: *a cvejt-Ø bux* 'a second book.'

Though not part of Yiddish grammar proper, note the longstanding Jewish tradition of using the letters of the alphabet numerically: א = 1, ב = 2, ג = 3, etc. Yiddish *laməd-vovnik* 'one of the 36 righteous men' is based on ל '30' + ו '6.' In addition to Jewish professional jargons, this practice has left its mark on non-Jewish varieties of German and Dutch slang. In the latter, for example, a *joetje* is '10-guilder note,' a *heitje* '25-cent coin' (from five times a basic five unit), based on י and ה (the tenth and fifth letters).

Fractions are nouns. Synchronically, they derive from the ordinal stem + suffix *l*; e.g., *drit* + *l*, *fert* + *l*, *cvancikst* + *l* → *dritl, fertl, cvancikstl*

(U. Weinreich 1949: 314). In a differing analysis, Mark (1978: 235) posits fractions as containing a single suffix *-(s)tl*. A diachronic analysis posits the suffix *-(s)tl* developing from **tejl* 'part'; thus, *dritl* '(a) third' < *drit* + *tl*; *zibətl* '(a) seventh' < *zibət* + *tl* (degemination *tt* → *t*). However, both analyses assume ordinal bases; thus, synchronically, *cvancikstl* < *cvancikst* + *l* '(a) twentieth.' The fraction one-half is idiosyncratic: *halb*; '1-and-one-half' is *ondərhalbn* ~ *ondərtalbn*; '2 and a half' *cvejthalbn*, etc. Fractions behave like other quantity nouns after a cardinal number – the denominator occurs in the singular; e.g., *cvej dritl* 'two-thirds,' *zibn cvancikstl* 'seven-twentieths.' When occurring without a numerical quantifier (numerator), the denominator is pluralized: *in dritlən, nit in fertlən!* 'in thirds, not in fourths!'

The element *zalbə-* is used with (the short form of) ordinals to express quantities adverbially: *zalbəcvejt/zalbədrit* 'in a group of 2/3,' etc.; e.g., *s'iz gut cu zingən duetn zalbəcvejt* 'it's good to sing duets as a twosome.' Sentence adverbials formed from the ordinals use a nominalized possessive: *erštns* 'first of all,' *cvejtns* 'second of all,' *dritns* 'thirdly,' etc.

5.13 Adverbs

Adverbs stand apart as somewhat autonomous.[55] They are invariant, not inflected for noun number, gender, or case, nor for person or number of the verb. This fact led Zaretski (1926) to call the uninflected adjective an "adverb," which only became an adjective when inflected. Zaretski (pp. 117ff.) contrasts the word *šejn* used adjectivally and adverbially. As an adverb, *šejn* is not inflected: *šejn zingən* 'sing nicely,' *šejn gəzungən* 'nicely sung,' *er zingt šejn* 'he sings nicely.' As an adjective it inflects regularly: *der šejnər gəzang, dem šejnəm gəzang* 'the pretty singing.' The same holds true for adjectives derived from past participles. When used adverbially, they are invariant: *er kukt farvundərt* 'he looks in amazement' vs. *a farvundərtər kuk* 'an amazed look.' An adverb may also modify a nominalized verb: *dos zingən šejn* '(the) singing nicely' vs. inflected adjective *dos šejnə zingən* 'the pretty singing' (p. 118). The adverb(ial)s are best described in terms of their syntactic function, rather than in absolute terms of morpholexical class. Thus, *frajtik* 'Friday' functions as a noun in *arbətərs in amerikə hobn lib frajtik* 'workers in America like Friday(s),' but as an adverb in *er vet kumən frajtik* 'he's coming (on) Friday.' As opposed to Zaretski's stricter stance (treating all uninflected adjectives as adverbs), Mark points out that a short-form predicate adjective is easily changed to an inflected nominal form: *dos kind iz šejn, der man iz šejn* 'the child/man is pretty' → *dos kind iz a šejns, der man iz a šejnər*. A true adverb here, however, remains invariant: *dos kind zingt šejn* 'the child sings nicely.'

[55] This is further seen concerning intonation; see Mark (1978: 355ff.).

Mark distinguishes between true adverbs and pro-adverbs. However, the distinction is often one of degree. True adverbs include, e.g., *bald* 'soon,' *ict* 'now,' *šojn* 'already,' *bazundərš* 'especially.' Pro-adverbs include, e.g., *azoj* 'thus(ly),' *do* 'here,' *dort(n)* 'there.' Frequently, pro-adverbs stand in for sentence adverbials of time, place, or manner, e.g., *vu iz zi?* 'where is she?' answered with phrases such as *baj der arbət* 'at work,' *in di bahamas* 'in the Bahamas,' or via pro-adverbs *do, dortn*, etc. Thus, pro-adverbs are easily substituted by more specific strings, such as prepositional phrases or NPs. However, the same may be said (though to a lesser degree) for the true adverbs, e.g., (*zi kumt*) *bald* '(she's coming) soon' → *in finf minut arum* 'in five minutes' or *in a kurcər cajt arum* 'in a short time'; the true adverb *hajnt* 'today' by *dém tog* 'this day'; *demolt* 'then' by *bejs der erštər velt-milxomə* 'during the First World War.' These substitutions for the true adverbs are lexically and semantically quite specific. On the other hand, the pro-adverbs typically consist of semantically bleached elements, and are thus much more general, e.g., *der-* in *derfár* 'therefore,' *dernóx* 'afterwards,' *dervajl(ə)* 'in the meantime.' Together, true adverbs and pro-adverbs constitute a rather closed, finite set. The syntactic adverbs are essentially an open-ended set comprising (morphologically) diverse elements used adverbially.

5.13.1 Adjective base

The base form of an adjective may be used adverbially; e.g., adjectives *gut* 'good,' *farvundərt* 'amazed,' in *zej zingən gut, un der ojləm hert zix cu farvundərt* 'they sing $[\text{well}]_{\text{ADV}}$, and the audience listens $[\text{in amazement}]_{\text{ADV}}$.' However, there are constraints on the use of past participles as adverbs. Generally, most past participles may be used as adjectives; e.g., *gəredt* → *di gəredtə šprax* 'the spoken language.' However, only a few past participles occur "as is" in adverbial function, e.g., *fartraxt* 'lost in thought' → *er zict fartraxt* 'he sits lost in thought,' *antojšt* 'disappointed' → *er fort avek antojšt* 'he goes away disappointed.' These examples are easily converted into inflected adjective forms: *er zict a fartraxtər; er fort avek an antojštər.* Most interestingly, all of Mark's examples contain either a verbal prefix – *far-*, *ant-*, *cə-*, *der-*, *ba-* – or a verb particle, e.g., *ajn-*, *ojs-*, *on-*. A bare past participle (with prefix *gə-*) occurs only rarely here; thus, perhaps, *der lerər lejənt gəpajnikt di šlextə esejən* 'the teacher reads tormentedly the bad essays.' Mostly, however, a prefix is needed, even when the verb itself normally does not require one;[56] thus, *er lejənt ojfgərudərt di esejən* 'he reads excitedly the essays,' *er gejt deršlogn in klas* 'he goes dejectedly to class,' all with prefixes. This suggests something aspectual about the semantics of (most) adverbs.

[56] Similarly, cf. German verb *wundern sich* 'be amazed,' but adverb: *verwundert* (Wolfgang Wölck, p.c.).

On the other hand, bare past participles may be used more generally in syntactic constructions which look like adverbs, but which function like past-tense gerunds: *gəlofn in park, gejt er ahejm* 'having run in the park, he goes home'; *gəzen di probleman, zuxt er an andər metod* 'having seen the problems, he looks for another method.' Use of bare past participle is permitted; however, there is a strong tendency to use (aspectually) a prefix. This suggests a relationship to systematically reduced VPs: *ojsgətrunkən dos bir hejbt er on trinkən dem vajn* '(having) drunk up the beer, he begins drinking the wine.' These are syntactically less strongly linked to the main sentence and are less adverbial in their function.

The present gerund similarly appears to function adverbially, but, again, in a way which suggests that it has more to do with syntactically reduced structures than with adverbs. Thus, for sentences like *laxndik zingt er dos lid* 'laughing, he sings the song,' Zaretski (1926: 118) notes that these almost always have a double connection: to the verb and to the subject. Adverbial present gerund may easily derive from the verb of an embedded sentence: *laxndik est der man dos brojt* 'laughing, the man eats the bread' < (1) *der man est dos brojt* 'the man eats the bread,' and (2) *der man laxt* 'the man laughs.'

5.13.2 Adverbs from nouns

Nouns designating temporal concepts may be used as adverbs. When used adverbially, they generally occur without article or preposition: *(der) jontəv* '(the) holiday' → *er kumt jontəv* 'he's coming (at) holiday-time'; *(der) zumər* '(the) summer' → *zumər fort er in kanadə* 'he's going to Canada (in the) summer(s).' These adverbs may be modified by a demonstrative: *er fort dém zumər in kanadə* 'he's going to Canada thís summer.' There is idiomatic use of *um* with Judaism-specific time terminology when used adverbially: *um šabəs* 'on Sabbath,' *um pejsəx* 'at Passover,' etc.

5.13.3 Adverbial suffixes

In addition to the present gerund form, there are several other adverb-forming suffixes.

-ərhéjt is very productive (see Mark 1978: 351). It attaches to root adjectives – *gəzùnt-ərhéjt* 'in good health,' *àlt-ərhéjt* 'in old age,' *štìl-ərhéjt* 'silently' – and to derived adjectives: *dervàksən-ərhéjt* 'in adulthood.' Mark notes that the suffix *-(d)ik* usually blocks *ərhejt* in StY, but that it is frequent in colloquial speech (though often limited to specific lexical items), e.g., *blutikərhejt* 'bloodily,' *lixtikərhejt* 'while lit.' Likewise, the adjectives with derivational suffix *-ləx* which allow adverbial *-ərhejt* are very limited; e.g., *gliklax-ərhejt* 'happily,' *vunderləx-ərhejt* 'wonderfully.' However, when *-ləx* is the adjective softener, *-ərhejt* is blocked: *švarc-ərhejt* 'blackly, in

a black condition,' but not ****švarcləx-ərhejt.** Adjective suffixes *-iš*, *-n*, and *-ərn* also block *-ərhejt*; thus, *xazəriš* 'piggish,' but no ****xazərišərhejt**; as does suffix *-əvatə* (exception: *taməvatərhejt* 'naively'). Adverbial *-ərhejt* may occur with adjective endearment suffixes *-ink-*, *-ičk-*, etc., e.g., *altinkərhejt* 'while old,' *frumičkərhejt* 'piously.' Adverbial *-ərhejt* is fully productive with (de)verbal elements. It attaches freely to gerund forms: *laxndikərhejt* 'while laughing,' *esndikərhejt* 'while eating.' As with gerunds in general, *-ərhejt* may attach to gerunds with prefixes or verb particles, e.g., *bašrajbndikərhejt* 'while describing,' *arojsgejəndikərhejt* 'while going out.' The semantic distinction between a gerund used adverbially and gerund + *-ərhejt* is very small. Mark (p. 351) gives the example: *er est štejəndik* vs. *er est štejəndikərhejt* 'he eats while standing.' The first sentence points to a concrete occurrence, whereas the second describes an ongoing nature or characteristic. The second form permits an aspectual distinction: secondary forms with schwa instead of the nasal suffix denote ongoing duration (e.g., *štejədikərhejt*, *laxədikərhejt*). Likewise, *-ərhejt* attaches generally and productively with past participles. There is a strong tendency toward perfectivity in adverbs describing most past action. Thus, Mark's examples all contain perfectivizing prefixes or verb particles, e.g., *cərisənərhejt* 'in a ripped-up manner,' *batraxtərhejt* 'in a deliberate manner,' *ojfgərudərtərhejt* 'excitedly.'

-vajz is productive, though less so than *-ərhejt*. *-vajz* generally attaches to nouns, most frequently to plurals, e.g., *štikərvajz* 'by piece(s),' *bisləxvajz* 'bit-by-bit,' *šoənvajz* 'by the hour,' *madrejgəsvajz* 'by increments,' *pornvajz* 'by pairs,' though also to noun singulars, e.g., *kindvajz* 'as a child,' *tejlvajz* 'partly,' *jinglvajz* 'as a lad.' Adverbs with *-vajz* may undergo adjectivization: *a tejlvajzər analiz* 'a partial analysis' (Mark 1978: 352).

-(n)s Mark (1978: 352) calls this suffix synchronically non-productive, though it occurs in several examples. This suffix is perhaps better separated into *n* + *s* (*-s* is more general than *-ns*). The *s* alone occurs in, e.g., *fartogs* 'at the crack of dawn,' *frajtik-cu-naxts* 'Friday night,' *pavolinkə-s* 'slowly'; *-ns* is found in, e.g., *cufusns* 'at the foot of,' *cukopns* 'at the head (of bed),' *fun der vajtns* 'from afar,' *untərvegns* (~ *untərvegs*) 'underway.' It is clear from *cufusns*, *cukopns* that the *-n* here is not a plural marker (cf. plurals *fis* 'feet,' *kep* 'heads'). To some extent, the *-n* can be linked to adjectives (e.g., *fun der vajtns*). It also occurs with some nouns (*cufusns*, *cukopns*, *untərvegns*), though not with all nouns (*fartogs*, *-cunaxts*). Not all adjectives get the *-n* before adverbial *-s*, e.g., adverbs *link-s* 'left,'

rext-s 'right' (adjective roots *link-*, *rext-*). With ordinal numbers used adverbially, *-ns* is generalized: *erštns* 'firstly,' *cvejtns* 'secondly,' etc.

-n alone is synchronically a non-productive adverb marker,[57] found chiefly with certain lexicalized prepositional phrases; e.g., *in der luftn* 'in the air,' *ojf der eməsn* ~ *in der eməsn* ~ *ojf an eməsn* 'in truth; truly'; optionally with *anumlt* ~ *anumltn* 'recently.' These fossilized PPs do not permit an intervening adjective: *in der (**gancər) eməsn.*

-t, -tn, -ər, -ərt. There are variants of many adverbs (and some verb particles and conjunctions) which may take a type of optional "extra" suffix; e.g., *ict* ~ *ictər(t)* 'now,' *anumlt(n)* 'recently,' *ojx(ət)* 'also,' *friər(t)* 'earlier.' The distribution is often regional. In some respects the extra suffix is used for rhythmic purposes; cf. verb particle *arojs* in *er gejt arojs(ət)* 'he goes out' vs. infinitive *(er vet) arojsgejn*, not *arojs(** ət)gejn.*[58]

5.13.4 *Adverbializing prefixes*

Mark (1978: 354–355) notes the following adverbial prefixes:

a- in, e.g., *aponəm* 'apparently,' *ahejm* 'homeward,' *aštejgər* 'for example,' contrast with NP consisting of indefinite article + noun: *a ponəm* 'a face,' *a hejm* 'a home,' *a štejgər* 'a manner.' The NPs allow adjective insertion: *a šejn ponəm* 'a pretty face,' *a gutə hejm* 'a good home,' the adverbs do not.

bə-/bi- of HA origin, where it has the basic meaning 'in,' and could be used to form adverbial constructions. Its primary function in Yiddish is adverbial; thus, StY *sod* 'secret,' *bəsod* 'secretly'; *kovəd* 'honor,' *bəkovəd* 'honorably'; *ksav* 'writ,' *biksav* 'in writing.'[59] This prefix has extended to some non-HA-origin elements, e.g., *bigvald* 'by force,' *bənatur* 'by nature.' Some adverbs with *bə-* may adjectivize, e.g., *bəkovədik* 'honorable.'

lə- is of HA origin (meaning 'to'). It is of limited (lexicalized) productivity in Yiddish; e.g., *sof* 'end,' *ləsof* 'finally'; *rov* 'majority,' *lərov* 'mostly.' It has extended to some Gmc-origin elements, e.g., *ləšpetər* 'until later,' *ləvajtər* 'until further.'

57 A fossilized F.OBL noun marker; cf. adverb *in dər eməsn* 'in truth; truly' < *eməs* 'truth,' which is masculine in modern Yiddish, but feminine in older Yiddish and in Hebrew (Mark 1978: 353).

58 Some sort of "extra" coronal suffix is found in various Germanic languages; e.g., adverbial *-t* in Swedish; a type of adverbial *-t* in varieties of midwestern American English: *once-t, twice-t, across-t*; English variants *among(st), while* ~ *whilst, anyway(s)*, etc.

59 The allomorphy [bə] /_CV, [bi] /_CCV goes back to TH phonology.

mə- HA clitic form for 'from'; occurs in Yiddish mostly in a few fossilized and formulaic expressions 'from X to Y,' e.g., *məšabəs ləšabəs* 'from Sabbath to Sabbath,' as well as in some fully lexicalized elements, where the meaning of *mə-* has been lost: *məkolškn* 'all the more so.'

kə- HA origin; meaning 'as'; limited productivity in Yiddish; thus, *sejdər* 'order,' *kəsejdər* 'continually'; *kəjadúə* 'as is known'; with Gmc-origin elements: *kə-opgəredt* 'as agreed,' *kə-bacolt* 'as paid' (Mark 1978: 355).

5.13.5 *Adverbial comparative and superlative*

Comparative adjective short forms may be used adverbially, e.g., *besər* 'better,' *gresər* 'bigger': *er šrajbt besər/gresər fun dir* 'he writes better/bigger than you (do).' Note *afriərt* 'earlier,' with prefix *a-* and optional coronal suffix *-t* added to the comparative *fri-ər*.

For superlative adverbs the prescribed StY construction is *cum* + superlative + *n*: *cum gringstn* 'most easily.' Colloquially, constructions like *am bestn*, *am gringstn* are found, but this is considered daytshmerish, and outside StY usage. Exceptionally, *hexst-* 'highest' is used adverbially, but has detached from its adjectival meaning; *hexst interesant* 'most interesting.' Additionally, HA-origin *šəbə-* may be used adverbially in limited expressions: *gut-šəbə-gut* 'very most good' (= 'very best').

5.13.6 *Complex adverbs*

Three main types of complex adverbs may be distinguished, though the boundaries between the types are not always sharp. Discussion is based on Mark (1978: 357ff.).

Type 1 consists of fossilized compounds in which the constituent parts cannot be analyzed synchronically, or where the meaning of the whole is not identical with the meaning of the individual parts. Mark (1978: 358) cites *fundestvegn* 'nevertheless,' where modern Yiddish has no word ***dest*, and the two elements (ordinarily prepositions) *fun* and *vegn* here have lost their regular meanings. Included here are the "fused" adverbs formed with *der-*: *dermit*, *deruntər*, *derfun*, *dercu*, etc.[60] These are pro-adverbs; thus: *mojšə vil zicn ojf zajn štul, obər di kac šloft derojf* 'Moyshe wants to sit on his chair, but the cat is sleeping thereupon' (= *ojf zajn štul*). Fused adverbs show loss of specific lexical meaning, e.g., *untəranand* 'between one another,' *cuzamən* 'together.' *Der ikər* 'above all' is written as two words, but functions as an invariant adverb

[60] Mark (1978: 358) also notes pleonastic forms in colloquial speech, e.g., *cudercu*, *mitdermit*, *dernoxdem*.

(the definite article *der* is constant); similarly, the adverb *der hojpt* 'mainly'; thus: [*der ikər*]$_{ADV}$ *farštejt er nit* [*dem ikər*]$_{ACC}$ 'mainly, he doesn't understand the principle.' Type 1 also includes forms like *durxojs* 'absolutely,' *forojs* 'forward.'[61]

Type 2 compound adverbs maintain the meanings of their constituents, the meaning of the whole is derivable from the meaning of the parts, and the compounding process is productive. Mark (1978: 358–359) cites: *kejnmol* 'never,' *andəršvu* 'elsewhere,' *jorn-lang* 'lasting for years,' *majln-vajt* 'miles away'; cf. *kejn* 'none,' *mol* 'time occurrence,' *andərš* 'otherwise,' *vu* 'where,' *jorn* 'years,' *lang* 'long,' *majln* 'miles,' *vajt* 'far.' Various elements may combine: nouns, adverbs, adjectives, etc. Type 2 is productive, since new forms may be created: *voxn-lang, šoən-lang, jorhundərtər-lang* 'lasting for weeks/hours/centuries.'

Type 1 generally shows stress pattern *ws*: *dermít, der íkər, cuzámən*, etc.; *fundéstvegn* is probably best seen synchronically as [fun] + [déstvegn]. Type 2 normally has the pattern *sw*, and the structure MOD-HEAD. However, several problems remain. For example, what is the structure of type 2 compound adverbs with a final (postposed) *-cu*, and stress pattern *ws*, e.g., *aruntərcú* 'downward,' *ahincú* 'thither?' These seem structurally distinct from compound adverbs with first element *cu* + nominal element: *cumól* 'intermittently.' The examples given of types 1 and 2 all show hierarchical structure. There is, furthermore, a coordinating-compound sub-type with equal stress: *xáp-láp* 'haphazardly,' *kídər-vídər* 'at odds,' *mér-véjnik* 'more or less.'

Type 3 consists of phrases, often PPs. Type 3 is the most productive, arising from the communication needs of the moment, whereas types 1 and 2 are more lexicalized.[62] Thus: *in klas* 'in the class,' *untər der hašgoxə fun* 'under the religious supervision of,' *bejsn xurbn* 'during the Holocaust,' *mit di bixər* 'with the books,' *on a fedər* 'without a pen.'[63] These permit insertion of an adjective: *on a grinər fedər* 'without a green pen.' A preposition may also combine with an adverb to form a (new) adverb: *fun amol* 'from then (that time)'; *ojf curik* 'reversedly.' Type 3 also includes adverbial expressions formed with various words (e.g., question words, conjunctions) followed by an adverb: *vos mér* 'all the more,' *vi azój* 'how (so),' *alc mér* 'ever more,' *cufíl* 'much too,' *cufrí* 'too early'; *abi vén* 'whenever,' *abi vú* 'wherever'; *cum bestn* 'best' (Mark 1978: 359). All of these seem to have *ws* phrasal stress. Mark (p. 360) argues for a slight distinction between a PP used adverbially, and merely as a PP, citing differences in intonation. Furthermore, the meaning of the adverbial PP is more figurative, not precisely the sum of its parts.

61 These are difficult to analyze. Is *durx* a preposition? Is *ojs* a fossilized preposition, just an adverb, or a verb particle? Is *for* a preposition? Probably not, since it is not elsewhere a preposition in Yiddish; it is found as a daytshmerish verb particle in, e.g., *forkumən*,'occur'; cf. StG,*vorkommen*.

62 Some PP adverbials have become lexicalized idioms, e.g., (*kumən*) *ojfn zejgər* '(arrive) on time,' *ojf kaporəs* 'good for nothing' (Mark 1978: 360).

63 Adverbs *ojfsnaj, funsnaj* 'anew' are fossilized.

5.14 Prepositions

Providing a canonic list of prepositions in a language is difficult, since non-prepositions may, in certain situations, function syntactically like prepositions. Problems also arise at the boundaries between prepositions and other lexical categories, specifically: conjunctions, verb particles, prefixes. The following discussion distinguishes simple prepositions, complex prepositions, and co-occurring prepositions. The list is adapted and expanded from Mark (1978) and Zaretski (1926).

5.14.1 Simple prepositions

adank	'thanks to'	bejs	'during'	maxməs	'because of'
axuc	'besides'	bimkojm	'instead of'	mit	'with'
ojs	'(derived) from'[64]	bənəgejə	'concerning'	micad	'on the part of'
ojsər	'besides'	durx [~dialectal adurx]	'through'	məkojəx	'about'
untər	'under'	hintər [~dialectal ahintər]	'behind'	nox	'after'
ibər	'over'	vegn	'about'	erəv	'on the eve of'
in	'in, to'	vedlik	'according to'	pazə	'along'
inmitn	'during, in the middle of'	zint [~zajt] ~cajt]	'since'	far	'for; before'
on	'connecting X and Y; without'	troc	'regardless of'	farbaj	'gone, past'
antkegn ~ akegn ~ kegn	'(as) against'	lojt	'according to'	fun	'from, of'
anštot ([~onštot])	'instead of'	lebn[65]	'next to'	cu	'to, toward'
ojf ([af])	'on'	ləgabə	'in relation to'	cvišn	'between, among'
arum	'around; concerning/about'	lətojvəs	'on behalf of'	culib	'because of'
baj ([ba(:)])	'by, at'	ləkovəd	'in honor of'	kejn	'toward'
biz (~bizkl)	'until'	leng-ojs	'along'	kegnibər	'opposite of'
bəšas	'during'	ləšém	'for the sake of'		

The following marginal prepositions are listed by Mark (1978): (a) *vidər* 'against'; this is archaic; (b) *um* 'at the time of'; Mark considers this an archaic preposition, used in Judaism-specific expressions; however, Zaretski argues

[64] Archaic; found in WY, regional CY; replaced in the twentieth century by *fun*.
[65] Some authorities accept variant *nebn*, others do not.

against *um* as a preposition (see below); (c) *mank* 'among, between'; archaic, as well as dialectal; (d) *məxuc* 'besides' (variant of *axuc*, *xuc*); (e) *kəfí* 'pursuant to'; (f) *klapej* 'vis-à-vis'; (f) *ləfí* 'according to'; (g) *ləroə* 'to the detriment of';[66] (h) *kənegəd* 'versus.' In StY, prepositions steer the dative case.[67]

The semantic fields covered by the prepositions are discussed in detail in Mark (1978: 251ff.).[68] Some prepositions have more than one meaning, and have extended metaphorically; thus, *ibər* 'over' may be used to mean 'because of': *ibər a hitl* 'because of a hat.' The preposition *fun* is the most frequent preposition in Yiddish (p. 251), and often serves as the default preposition when a prepositionless constituent is transformed into a PP. Many verbs require a PP object, where selection of the PREP is lexically specified, e.g., *dermonən on X* 'remember X,' *fargesn on X* 'forget X,' *vartn ojf X* 'wait for X.' There is a tendency for object-PREP selection to mirror the cognate verb particle, when present: *mitnemən mit*, *cugejn cu*, *ojfšrajbn* ([*uf*]) *ojf* ([*af*]), etc.

5.14.2 Complex and co-occurring prepositions

The term complex preposition encompasses several grammatically diverse phenomena: PREP + PP; [[PREP + [NP + ADV]]$_{ADV}$; fossilized expressions. Additionally, some prepositions co-occur in formulaic pairs; however, these are not complex prepositions.

Examples of PREP + PP involve preposition *fun*; e.g., *fun untərn tiš* 'from under the table,' *fun far der milxomə* 'from before the war' (Zaretski 1926: 133). These may be analyzed either as compound preposition or as *fun* + PP.

A second type involves prepositions *fun* or *in* + NP + adverbial element (frequently a verb particle): *fun klas arojs* 'from out of the class,' *in gortn arajn* 'into the garden,' *in draj šo arum* 'three hours from now,' *fun tiš arop* 'down from the table.' These all are PPs consisting of PREP + NP + postposed adverbial modifier. Yet these may involve separate phenomena; *mit ... curik* 'ago' is an idiomatically fixed pair; *arop* in *fun tiš arop* is likely a verb particle remaining after deletion of a verb (*aropfaln fun tiš*). A special problem is posed by *fun* in combination with the preposition *vegn* in fossilized possessive constructions.

[66] U. Weinreich's (1968) dictionary calls *ləfi* (+ additional element) and *ləroə* adverbs.

[67] The situation in older Yiddish is more complex, with text evidence for prepositions steering accusative or dative; thus, *afsnaj* 'anew' presumably arose from PREP *af* + (*dos*$_{ACC}$ >)-*s* + *naj*. However, modern StY would require a dative in, e.g., *afn najəm (X)* 'on the new (X).' In StY the connectors *vi* 'as, like,' *tojrəs* 'the law/rule of,' *majsə* 'like, in the manner of' occur with a nominative complement.

[68] Considerable caution – here and elsewhere – should be exercised by people with a knowledge of German (but not of Yiddish). The uses of the cognate prepositions often vary significantly in the two languages. Thus, while StG *nach* is cognate with StY *nox*, StY *nox* is not used for spatial approach: cf. StG *Ich fahre nach Boston*, StY *ix for kejn boston*. In Yiddish, *ix for nox boston* 'I shall travel after Boston,' i.e., after temporally defined event(s) taking place in Boston.

These consist of *fun* + possessive NP + postposed *vegn*: *fun di klejnə kindərs vegn* 'for the sake of the small children'; cf. similarly fossilized genitive forms like *majntvegn, dajntvegn* (the genitive forms *majnt-* 'my,' *dajnt-* 'your' are not found elsewhere) with postposed *-vegn*. There is a tendency to regularize these to complex prepositions + dative NP: *fun vegn di klejnə kindər*.

Sometimes mistakenly grouped with complex prepositions are formulaic constructions involving two separate but linked PPS: *fun X cu Y*: *fun cajt cu cajt* 'from time to time,' *fun hajnt biz morgn* 'from today until tomorrow.' Additionally, there are constructions which, though not strictly prepositions, are used prepositionally, e.g., *vos šajəx* 'as concerns' + NP in dative: *vos šajəx der erštər fragə* 'as concerns the first question.' To these may be added *in mešəx fun* 'in the course of' = 'during,' *inmitn (fun)* 'in the middle of.'

5.14.3 Functional distinctions of prepositions

Zaretski (1926: 128–133) provides a synchronic analysis of prepositions in Yiddish, based on their function. Prepositions may be distinguished from homophonous verb particles based on intonational cues and/or syntax; thus, with *mit*: *x'nem mít* [*a lefl*]$_{[ACC]}$ 'I bring along a spoon' (< *mítnemən* 'take along') vs. *x'nem* [*mit a lefl*]$_{[PP]}$ 'I take with (= by using) a spoon.' In the present tense only stress helps disambiguate the two sentences. However, the distinction is clear from the syntax in the past tense: *xob mítgənumən* [*a lefl*]$_{[ACC]}$ 'I took along a spoon' vs. *xob gənumən* [*mit a lefl*]$_{[PP]}$ 'I took with (= by using) a spoon.'

Zaretski (1926: 130) gives examples showing that prefixes do not permit insertion of additional material, whereas prepositions do. Unfortunately, Zaretski uses here as examples of "prepositions" a verb particle, *on*: *ónfal* 'attack' (cf. verb *ónfaln*, past participle *óngəfaln*). His point is that "prefixed" noun *ónfal* allows no insertion of other material, whereas preposition *on* + noun *fal* do: *on a fal* 'without a case,' *on dem fal* 'without this case.' A better argument is Zaretski's claim against preposition status for *um* and *am*, since neither permits insertion: *um šabəs* 'on the Sabbath,' but not *um* ***hajntikn šabəs* 'on the current Sabbath'; *am bestn* 'best (of all),' but not *am* ***samə bestn*.

Prepositions govern a dative NP, whereas conjunctions have no relation to case, and, thus, any case may follow a conjunction; e.g., after PREP: *ix mit – dir, der froj, dem man* (all in DAT); after conjunction: *ix un du* (NOM), *mir un dir* (DAT), *mix un dix* (ACC).

5.15 Conjunctions

Conjunctions are primarily syntactic traffic directors which link words, groups of words, or sentences. The conjunctions state the terms of the linkage: inclusion, exclusion, restriction, etc. They form a class of words and are typically presented as such; hence their inclusion in a morphology chapter. However, this class presents a number of problems – morphological, in that other classes of words (e.g., prepositions and adverbs) may function as conjunctions, and syntactic, in that elements commonly classified as conjunctions may sometimes elicit differing syntactic behavior. The present discussion mainly follows Mark (1978: 89–107), who provides lists, and describes idiomatic usage. Zaretski (1926) for the most part focuses on syntactic discussion of phrasal linkages – subordination, coordination, etc.; he is thus less concerned with the enumeration of a list. Zaretski's approach pares down Mark's overgenerous list. In Yiddish, a conjunction (whether coordinating or subordinating) generally has a zero-value in terms of sentence unit, and thus does not trigger V-2 movement, whether in main clause or dependent clause. On syntactic grounds, Zaretski distinguishes conjunctions ("meaningless" elements) from conjunctives (meaning-bearing elements which count as sentence units); see Kahan-Newman (1983: 130–136). Mark divides Yiddish conjunctions into types, based on semantic field (conjunction, disjunction, comparison, purpose/goal/condition/assumption, temporal, conclusion/summary). He does not, however, provide an overarching framework according to syntactic type (coordinating vs. subordinating).

5.15.1 Coordinating conjunctions

un 'and'	hen . . . hen 'both X and Y'	ojx 'also'
i . . . i 'both X and Y'	saj . . . saj 'both X and Y'	

This type combines two elements. The most general is *un*, which may link whole sentences – *er lejənt un zi šrajbt* 'he reads and she writes' – or smaller units such as NPs – *ix lejən a cajtung un a bux* 'I read a newspaper and a book'; *der man un dos kind lejənən* 'the man and the child read.' Conjunction *un* also occurs with ellipsis, for example, when AUX deletes: *er vet esn un AUX-Ø trinkən* 'he shall eat and (shall-Ø) drink.' The relationship of conjunctions to ellipsis is more general. Thus: *er vil nit šrajbn, nor zingən* derives from: *er vil nit šrajbn, nor* [*er vil*] *zingən* 'he doesn't want to write, but (he wants to) sing.'[69]

The doubled conjunctions *i . . . i, hen . . . hen, saj . . . saj* signal intensification of the linking; e.g., *i der lerər i di talmidəm hobn lib jontojvəm* 'both the teacher and the pupils like holidays.' Mark mentions some limited use of a single *i*

[69] On uses of *un* see Mark (1978: 90–93). Particularly interesting is the use of a narrative s-initial *un* which carries over from Biblical Hebrew *və-* into the Ashkenazic translation tradition. From there it spread into Yiddish popular literature until the end of the nineteenth century (pp. 90–91).

'and.' The word *ojx* 'also' is problematic in that it is also an adverb. Mark claims that *ojx* may be used as a conjunction; however, it tends to avoid S-initial position. The pair *nit nor ... nor ojx* 'not only ... but also' is also problematic. Here, the if-portion is excluding/disjunctive, but the whole construction ends up functioning as a coordinating conjunction by virtue of the *ojx*. For the most part the paired conjunctions in Yiddish show parallelism in their elements.[70] Of the 'both X and Y' pairs, *i ... i* is most general, occurring with S, NP, VP, adverbs, etc.; *saj ... saj* seems to occur less with S. The pair *hen ... hen* is of HA origin, and is limited to (Jewish) scholarly usage; *i ... i* is of Slavic origin, as is the synonymous *to ... to*, used by writers from Ukraine (Mark 1978: 96).

5.15.2 Disjunctive conjunctions

obər 'but'	*nor* '(but) rather'	*sajdn* 'unless'
odər 'or'	*najərt* 'rather'	*(a)xíbə* 'unless'
odər ... odər 'either X or Y'	*abí* 'as long as'	*ci* 'or'
obər ... obər 'either X or Y'	*kol-zman* 'as long as'	*afílə* 'even'
entfər / entvidər / entvedər ... odər 'either X or Y'	*dox* 'yet; still'	*nit nor ... nor ojx* 'not only ... but also'
	fort 'yet; still; nevertheless'	
	blojz 'merely'[71]	

Prepositions used as disjunctive conjunctions include:

anštot 'instead (of)'	*xuc/məxuc* 'except for; besides'
ojsər 'except (for)'	*fundéstvegn* 'nevertheless; yet; still'

The true disjunctive conjunctions tend to occur with S, as well as with smaller units (often derived from S via ellipsis), e.g., *obər* + S: *er redt engliš, obər er ken es nit lejənən* 'he speaks English, but he cannot read it'; *obər* + NP (< S): *najn rabonəm kenən kejn minjən nit maxn, obər cen šustərs jo* 'nine rabbis cannot form a minyan, but ten shoemakers (can) indeed' (Mark 1978: 100). The synonym to *obər* – *nor* – occurs with S or NP: *er vil kojfn a grojs hojz, nor er hot nit gənug gelt* 'he wants to buy a big house, but he doen't have enough money'; *er hot nit kejn fedər, nor a blajər* 'he doen't have a pen, but rather, a

[70] As opposed to StG, e.g., *nicht nur ... sondern auch*; *sowohl ... als auch*; *entweder ... oder*; *weder ... noch*.

[71] Mark calls *dox, fort, blojz* conjunctions. However, in most of his examples they do not occur S-initially; they frequently occur almost as adverbs (as in U. Weinreich 1968). Perhaps *dox* triggers V-2 inversion: *ix hob gəvolt kumən cu der cajt, dox hob ix faršpetikt* 'I wanted to come on time, but I was late.'

pencil.' The conjunction *najərt*, seen as an alternate of *nor*, made its way in the early twentieth century from orthodox usage to educated secular use (p. 101).

Disjunctive conjunctions *abí, sajdn, afílə* occur with S or NP. They do not trigger V-2 inversion. The prepositions which Mark lists as functioning as disjunctive conjunctions – *anštot, ojsər, (mə)xuc* – only do so with S (including infinitival S), and there is no V-2 inversion, e.g., with S: *anštot du zolst es alejn ton* ... 'instead of you doing it yourself...; with infinitival S: *anštot cu trinkən bir, trinkt er vajn* 'instead of drinking beer he drinks wine.' When attached to an NP, they are prepositions. Mark discusses *fundéstvegn* as an adverb which may function as a conjunction; however, in his example it triggers V-2 inversion, and is thus less conjunction-like, and more adverb-like (weight-bearing).

The pair *odər... odər* adds emphasis, from 'or' to 'either-or': *odər der tatə odər di mamə darf cugrejtn dos esn* 'either father or mother must prepare the food.' Regionally, *obər... obər* may be used for 'either-or'; variants *entfər* ~ *entvidər* ~ *entvedər... odər* are considered even more intensified. The construction *nit nor... nor ojx* presents a problem of classification. An alternative to *odər* is *ci*, e.g., *vilst trinkən kavə ci tej* '(you) want to drink coffee or tea?' It also occurs as a weight-bearing trigger to yes/no direct questions (§6.2.3).

5.15.3 Conjunctions of comparison

Conjunctions expressing comparison, roughly 'like; than; as,' constitute a border area between conjunctions and prepositions. The most common conjunction of comparison is *vi* (or as modified in *azoj vi, punkt vi, glajx vi, akurat vi*, all roughly 'just like'). When comparison is expressed with PREP (*fun, far*), the PREP heads a dative NP: *er iz eltər fun dir* 'he's older than you.' When conjunction *vi* is used, it may head S or smaller unit; thus, *ix red francejziš punkt vi er redt engliš* 'I speak French just like he speaks English.' With NPs the conjunctions are case-neutral; thus: *der tatə*$_{[NOM]}$ *iz eltər vi di mamə*$_{[NOM]}$ 'Father is older than Mother'; *ix hob lib dos bux*$_{[ACC]}$ *azoj vi dem film*$_{[ACC]}$ 'I like the book just like the movie.' The word *majsə* 'in the manner of' may be used like *azoj vi*; however, it seems only to occur with NP, and thus might be seen as a (unique) preposition which steers the nominative case: *majsə gəvinər* 'like a winner,' *majsə der rajxstər* 'as the richest (man).' The conjunction *ejdər* 'before' normally occurs with S: *ix vil onklingən ejdər der klas hejbt zix on* 'I want to call before class starts' (vs. PREP + NP: *far-n klas* 'before the class'). However, *ejdər* may also be used in comparison for 'than,' and here it may head S (including infinitival S), NP, VP, or adverb: *besər špetər ejdər kejnmol* 'better later than never'; *er iz mer xoxəm ejdər du mejnst* 'he's smarter than you think' (< Mark 1978); *zi vil hobn a ganəf ejdər a məlaməd* 'she wants a thief rather than a teacher.' The word *vidər* used in comparison is archaic: *ergər vidər ix* 'worse than I.'

5.15.4 Subordinating conjunctions

Subordinating conjunctions, which introduce subordinate clauses, divide into two main types: those with semantic content, and those which primarily serve a syntactic function. A major group of subordinating conjunctions are those denoting purpose, goal, condition, assumption. These include: *vajl* 'because,' *vorəm* ~ *vorn* 'because,' *maxməs* 'because,' *xoč* 'although,' *hagám* 'although,' *vivójl* 'although,' *kədéj* ~ *bikdéj* 'in order that/to.' These all require a following S, and do not trigger V-2 inversion, illustrated as follows:

1. *er ken nit šlofn, vajl di šxejnəm zingən* 'he can't sleep because the neighbors are singing'
2. *zi lernt zix italjeniš, kədej zi zol kenən zingən opərə* 'she's learning Italian, in order to be able to sing opera'
3. *zi lernt zix italjeniš, kədej cu kenən zingən opərə* 'she's learning Italian in order to be able to sing opera'
4. *hagam er iz a rajxər, iz er a kargər* 'although he's a rich (man), he's a stingy (man)'
5. *vajl di šxejnəm zingən, ken er nit šlofn* 'because the neighbors are singing, he can't sleep.'

When *kədej* heads an infinitival S (3), *cu* is obligatory.[72] Dependent S may frequently occur first, as in (5), however, not with *vorəm/vorn* (Mark 1978: 103). Mark lists several words as subordinating conjunctions which are not; e.g., the adverbs *derfar* 'therefore,' *derfun* 'therefrom.' These are weight-bearing adverbs which trigger V-2 inversion. The status of *lemáj* ~ *hal(ə)máj* 'why; what for; how come' is unclear; Mark's (p. 103) examples exhibit both presence and absence of V-2 inversion.

Mark's (1978) discussion of conjunctions of time includes many prepositions and adverbs used as conjunctions. With the prepositions the situation is essentially PREP + S (instead of PREP + NP), e.g., *er darf blajbn, biz er vet ojstrinkən di milx* 'he must stay until he finishes drinking the milk'; *bəšas er lejənt di cajtung, šlofn di andərə menčn* 'while he reads the paper, the other people sleep.' The use of PREP as conjunction extends the domain of PP from [PREP + NP] to [PREP + S], while the S remains a type of indivisible whole in which V-2 inversion does not occur.

Wh- words do not trigger V-2 inversion when they function as syntactic conjunctions; i.e., they relate S and S. When they are content-bearing, they are adverbs which trigger V-2 inversion (§6.2.3).

72 Use of *um ... cu* 'in order to' is archaic; it reflects germanizing tendencies in early WrLg A.

Other subordinating conjunctions are: *az* 'that,' *ojb* 'if,' *beím* 'if,' *aní(š)t* 'if not' (= *ojb nit*). The most general of these is *az*, which derives from two distinct historical sources: **daz* and **als* (cf. StG *daß*, *als*). This merger complicates description. Most basically, *az* links a COMP S with a main clause, especially with verbs like *zogn* 'say,' *mejnən* 'opine,' *traxtn* 'think,' *visn* 'know,' *hern* 'hear.' Other uses of *az* are: as a replacement for relative pronoun *vos* – *mitn bašlus vos/az* 'with the decision that'; in colloquial speech in comparison – *ix bin erləxər az du* 'I'm more honest than you;' and elsewhere. The *az* is used as the default conjunction in dependent clauses, e.g., in expressions of emotionality – *az der tajvl zol es nemən*! 'to hell with it!' (lit. 'that-the-devil-should-it-take') – as well as in formal register, e.g., in official resolutions expressing 'whereas': *zeəndik az*... 'whereas, seeing...' Synonymous with this latter use is conjunction *hejojs (vi)* 'being that; inasmuch as.'

5.16 Fillers

There are several filler words which function to raise or lower the intensity of an utterance, to color it, etc. (Matisoff 1979). These include, e.g., *jo* 'yes; indeed,' *dox* 'yet; still,' *avadə* 'of course.' Some fillers may trigger V-2 inversion, while others do not: *er iz avadə a mumxə* 'of course he is an expert!' → *avadə iz-er a mumxə* [inversion]; but: *er iz jó a mumxə* 'yes he ís an expert' → *jo, er iz a mumxə* [no inversion] 'yes, he is an expert.' Sometimes whole expressions or even S may function as a filler: *majnə cvej zin – (zoln zej mir zajn gəzunt) – hobn fajnt fiš* 'my two sons – (they should be for me healthy) – hate fish.' Other fillers of this type are, e.g., [Person]$_{[\text{DAT}]}$ *cu langə jor* 'may X live a long time,' *mircəšem* 'God willing.' The element *žə* functions semantically like a filler, but formally like an enclitic. It may occur as a softener of verb imperatives: *kum(t)žə!* 'come!'; *zaj(t)-žə mojxl!* 'excuse me!' It also attaches to *wh-* question words, functioning as an intensifier: *vos-žə* ([vožə]) 'what (then),' *ver-žə* 'who (then).'

5.17 Verb formation and verb types

Yiddish has the following types of verbs:[73] (1) root (non-derived) verbs; (2) verbs derived from adjective or noun; (3) verbs derived via regular processes of suffixation; (4) verbs derived via regular processes of prefixation; (5) verbs derived via regular addition of an invariant element.

Type 1. Basic root verbs. This class includes verbs like *es-n* 'eat,' *kuš-n* 'kiss,' *šlof-n* 'sleep' which basically describe an action. The corresponding nouns (*der*) *kuš*, *šlof*, etc., are deverbal nouns derived

[73] Discussion and many examples are based on Zaretski (1926) and Mark (1978).

from these verb roots. On the other hand, verb roots like *farb-n* 'to color,' *mišpət-n* 'to judge' are derived via verbalization, since their base meaning here is a thing or quality: *di farb* 'the color,' *der mišpət* 'the trial.' Thus, the verb *kašər-n* 'make kosher' is basic, not derived from adjective *košər*. Similarly, the verb root in *ganvə(n)-ən* 'to steal' is basic; cf. nouns *ganəf* 'thief,' *gnejvə* 'theft.'

Type 2. Derived verbs. This catch-all category includes verbs derived from nouns, adjectives, or other verbs. When derived from nouns, the noun root may remain unchanged – as in *tog* 'day' → *togn* 'to become day,' *xoləm* 'dream' → *xoləmən* 'to dream' – or may show umlaut: *kop* 'head' → *kepn* 'to behead,' *vunč* 'wish' → *vinčn* 'to wish.' Some verbs are formed from a noun singular (e.g., *tog-n*; cf. *teg* 'days'), others from the plural: *blat* – *bletər* 'leaf-leaves,' *bletərn* 'to leaf through.' Verbs derived from adjectives generally umlaut (where possible), and are based either on the base form or the comparative of the adjective; from base form: *jidiš* 'Jewish,' *jidišn* (*a kind*) 'circumcise (a child)'; *grojs* 'big,' *grejsn zix* 'to pride oneself'; *krum* 'crooked,' *farkrimən* 'distort'; from comparative: *gring(ər)* 'simple(r),' *fargringərn* 'facilitate'; *gut* 'good,' *besər* 'better,' *farbesərn* 'to improve.' Concerning verbs derived from verbs, the historical relationship in pairs such as *lign* 'lie' – *lejgn* 'lay,' *zicn* 'sit' – *zecn* 'set' pre-dates Yiddish, and is synchronically non-productive. While verbs such as *šlofinkən* or *faršlofn* are derived from the base verb *šlofn*, these are dealt with separately under the rubrics of suffixation and prefixation. To this category may be added the marginal verbalization of some nouns in the spoken language, noted by Zaretski (1926: 79), e.g., *tišn a tiš* 'to set (= table) a table'; *gəlerərt* 'teachered,' a past participle based on *lerər* 'teacher.'

Type 3. Suffixation. This is productive in deriving verbs from nouns, adjectives, and other verbs. Zaretski (1926: 77) lists the following suffixes:

- *-ik* with nouns: *end-ikn* 'to end'; adjectives: *rejn-ikn* 'to clean.'
- *-ir* based on nouns (usually internationalisms): *datírn*, *telefonírn*, *maršírn*, *fabrikírn* ~ *fabricírn*, *registrírn*; cf. nouns: *datə* 'date,' *telefon* 'telephone,' *marš* 'march,' *fabrik* 'factory,' *registər* 'register.' With certain noun forms, *-izír* is added: *kolonjə* 'colony,' *nacjə* 'nation' → *kolonizirn* 'colonize,' *nacjonalizirn* 'nationalize.'
- *-l* with adjective: *rojt* 'red' → *rejtlən zix* 'blush'; noun: *kind* 'child' → *kindlən* 'have children.'
- *-əvə* from Slavic imperfective suffix; occurs with many Slavic-origin verb roots, e.g., *žaləvən* 'economize.' It is also used with

non-Slavic-origin verbs, e.g., with nouns (often based on plural): *zixrojnəvən* 'to reminisce,' based on *zixrójnəs* 'memoirs' (historically cognate with singular: *zikórn* 'memory'); *baləbátəvən* 'to keep house, manage,' based on plural *bal(ə)bátəm* 'proprietors,' not singular *bal(ə)bós*; with adjective: *vildəvən* 'to rage' < *vild* 'wild'; with verb root (with pejorative meaning): *šrajbəvən* 'to write (in a low-quality manner).'

- *-ər* Zaretski treats this as a verbalizing suffix. I see it rather as part of the noun plural, since it only occurs in verbs derived from those nouns which normally take *-ər* plurals, e.g., *glid-ər* 'limb-s' –> *glidərn* 'to segment'; *gajst-ər* 'spirit-s' → *bagajstərn* 'inspire.' Thus, the *-ər* suffix is not a part of a general process of verb morphology, but, rather, is a fact of noun morphology.
- *-kə* denotes onomatopoeic verbs, or refers to the sound-gestalt of the verb; e.g., *ojkən* 'say "oy,"' *mekən* 'bleat,' *havkən* 'bark' (in Yiddish, goats/sheep say *me*, dogs say *hav-hav*); *kumkən* '(repeatedly) say *kum* (come)'; *šakən* 'say *sha* (quiet)!'
- *-ink* may be used as an endearment form in verbs (it does not trigger umlaut): *šlof-inkən*, *es-inkən*, etc. Its use is restricted to infinitives.[74]

Type 4. Prefixation. It is misleading to say that prefixation "creates" verbs, but it often accompanies verb derivation; thus, adjectives *krum* 'crooked,' *tif* 'deep,' *gresər* 'bigger' → verbs *farkrimən* 'distort,' *fartifn* (*zix*) 'delve into,' *fargresərn* 'enlarge.' More commonly, however, the prefixes add concrete and/or aspectual meaning to preexisting verbs, and thus, do not derive verbs from non-verbs. The verbal prefixes are unstressed and inseparable from the verb root. The verbal prefixes, along with some frequent meanings, are:

- *far-* has several meanings, including verbalization, intensification, or making opposite; e.g., *farkojfn* 'sell' (cf. *kojfn* 'buy'), *faršrajbn* 'register,' *farfirn* 'mislead.'
- *cə-* Apart, dissolve, diffuse movement; e.g., *cəgejn* 'dissolve,' *cəštern* 'destroy'; used aspectually with *zix* denotes sudden commencement of action: *cəzingən zix* 'burst out singing.'
- *gə-* collective (non-productive, lexicalized); *gəfinen* 'find,' *gədojərn* 'last,' *gəvinən* 'win.'
- *ant-* away from; *antlojfn* 'run away,' *antšuldikn* 'forgive' (< *šuld* 'guilt').
- *ba-* makes verbs transitive: *baglikn* 'bestow happiness' (<*glik*), *bašrajbn* 'describe; cover with writing'; *baganvənən* 'rob (someone)' vs. *ganvənən* 'steal.'

74 Zaretski (1926: 78) also notes *-ələ* as a verbal endearment form: *vejnələn* < *vejnən* 'cry.'

- *der-* completed action; *dergejn* 'arrive (on foot)'; *deršisn* 'shoot dead'
- *de(z)-* dis- (*dez-* /_V, *de-* /_C). This prefix is not usually included in descriptions of the six Germanic-origin suffixes listed above. Zaretski (1926: 78) includes it on the grounds that it patterns like the other prefixes: it is unstressed, and it blocks *gə-* in past participles. This suffix is limited to a corpus of internationalisms, e.g., *dezinfecirn* 'disinfect,' *denacjonalizirn* 'denationalize.'

Type 5. Verb + invariant. This type conflates two categories: (1) complex verbs consisting of verb + verb particle, and (2) periphrastic verbs consisting of verb + invariant. The former contains the class of "separable prefixes" (called in Yiddish *konverbn*), a finite set of adverb- or preposition-like elements which may be linked to a semantically full verb to add concrete or aspectual meaning. The second type consists of a meaning-bearing invariant (often a nominal) plus a semantically bleached verb. In both sub-types the main stress is on the invariant, which behaves phonologically as a separate word. The two types are grouped together as a single class for phonological and syntactic reasons.[75] The invariant occurs before non-finite forms of the verb, but after finite forms and imperatives; thus, with verb particle: infinitive *arójsgèjn* 'go out,' past participle *arojsgəgangən*, gerund *arojsgejəndik*, conjugated form *ix gej arojs*, *du gejst arojs*, etc. Since the verb particle is phonologically a separate word, past participle prefix *gə-* is added (cyclically) where applicable: *arojs-gəgangən*, *on-gəšribn*; however, *er hot mit-(**gə-) organizírt* 'he co-organized' (since non-initial word stress in *organizírn*). The verb particles in Yiddish are as follows:

(a)durx	on	nox
ahín	anídər	funándər [fanándər]
ahér	op	for → forójs, afér
avék	aróp	cu
ojs	arójs	cuzámən
um	arúm	curík
untər	arójf	afér ~ afír
ojf [uf]	aríbər	arúntər
antkégn ~ akégn ~ kegn	arájn	farbáj
ibər	baj	forójs
ajn	mit	fir

[75] This extends to the passives; see Zaretski (1926: 82); den Besten and Moed-van Walraven (1986); § 6.2.6.

Additionally, there are some idiomatic constructions which function like verb particles; e.g., *cufridnzajn* 'to be satisfied,' *er iz cufridn* 'he is satisfied'; however, past tense *er iz cufridn gəven* ~ *gəven cufridn*. Mark (1978: 301) notes that (almost) all verb particles stem from prepositions or adverbs (exceptions: *ajn, um*). There are limited occurrences of verb particle + prefixed verb: *(untər)bavofənən* 'supply with arms,' *(ajn)derkučən* 'pester,' *(ojs)dercejln* 'tell fully.' However, there are no instances of verb particle + verb particle + verb; thus, *ojstrogn cuzamən* 'endure together,' making it clear that *cuzamən* is an adverb (p. 302).

In periphrastic verbs the invariant [INV] patterns like a verb particle. It occurs before non-finite forms: infinitive, past participle, gerund; it occurs after finite forms and the imperative. Morphologically, both the verb particle and the INV of the periphrastic are invariant. Both receive primary stress. However, the verb particles constitute to a higher degree a finite set of grammaticalized elements. With periphrastics it is the verb itself which is one of a limited set of bleached verbs, whereas the invariant elements are essentially unlimited. Zaretski (1926: 80–83) and Mark (1978: 311–315) distinguish classes of periphrastic verbs. The classes differ semantically and syntactically.

Class 1 consists of (primarily HA-origin) INV + *zajn* 'be,' e.g., *xojšəd zajn* 'suspect,' *mojxl zajn* 'forgive,' *maskəm zajn* 'agree'; present tense: *ix bin xojšəd* 'I suspect,' *du bist mojxl* 'you forgive,' *mir zajnən maskəm* 'we agree.' These have active meaning (not passive); *zajn* is merely a verbal vehicle for conveying the meaning of the INV. The INV may itself be complex, e.g., *məkabl-ponəm zajn* 'welcome; greet,' where *məkabl-ponəm* < Hebrew 'receiving face.' Class 1 includes some constructions with INV of non-HA origin, e.g., *ojsn zajn* 'intend,' *visn zajn* 'be aware of,' though these are problematic, and limited as to which tenses may occur (Zaretski 1926: 80; Mark 1978: 313).

Class 2 contains the verb *vern* 'become,' used generally to create passive constructions, e.g., *gəšribn vern* 'to be written.' However, many periphrastic verbs with partly passive meaning simply require *vern* as their verbal vehicle; e.g., *potər vern* 'get rid of' (= 'be rid of'); *kaljə vern* 'become spoiled.' Thus, the INV in *məkujəm vern* 'be fulfilled' is from a TH passive form, whereas the INV in *məkajəm zajn* 'fulfill' (Class 1) is based on a TH active form. As opposed to Class 1, the Class 2 periphrastics are more open to INVs of non-HA origin (as long as they fit semantically); e.g., *ajngəzunkən vern* 'become submerged,' *gəvo(j)r vern* 'find out,' *antšlofn vern* 'fall asleep.' These are not passives, since they have no corresponding active form, e.g., ***ix antšlof emicn* **'I fall asleep someone' (Zaretski 1926: 81).

Class 3 consists of INV + *hobn* 'to have.' The INV may be of HA- or non-HA origin, e.g., *xasənə hobn* 'get married,' *mojrə hobn* 'be afraid,' *lib hobn* 'like/love,' *fajnt hobn* 'hate.' These are lexicalized verbs rather than verb + ACC COMP. Thus, while *xasənə* 'wedding' is a noun, cf. *er hot nit xasənə* 'he isn't getting married' vs. *er hot nit kejn xasənə* 'he doesn't have a wedding.'

Class 4 is a grammatical category denoting (singulative) aspect, rather than a morpholexical category. However, Zaretski includes these since they pattern on the surface like periphrastics. This class consists of an INV deverbal root + verbal vehicle *ton* 'do' or *gebn* 'give,' e.g., *a kuš ton* 'give a kiss,' *a lax ton* 'let out a laugh.' Various other verbal vehicles conveying semantic definiteness and non-durational meaning include: *derlangən* (*a klap*) 'give (a hit),' *xapn (a kuk)* 'grab (a look),' *maxn (a štarb)* 'perform (a die)'; consider also: *tfilə ton* 'pray' (lit., 'do a prayer'), *čuvə ton* 'repent,' *micvə ton* 'perform a commandment' (Zaretski 1926: 81). These reside somewhere between periphrasis and idiomatic expressions containing verb + ACC COMP.

Class 5 is used by Mark as a catch-all category for various idiomatic expressions which look like periphrastic verbs; e.g., *xasənə maxn* 'marry off (someone),' *xojzək maxn* 'make fun of.' The verbal elements are semantically varied; the INV is a COMP which may even be a PP, e.g., *ojf kidəš-hašem gejn* 'die a Jewish martyr's death.' These have become idiomatically lexicalized, and pattern partly like periphrastic verbs.

5.18 Non-finite verb forms

5.18.1 Infinitives and gerunds

The infinitive is marked by /ən/, which is suffixed to the verb stem. The allomorphs of the infinitive marker are [ən] and [n̩], depending on the shape of the verb stem: [ən] after stressed vowel or diphthong, nasal consonant *n*, *m*, cluster *ng* or *nk*, or syllabic *l̩*; thus: *flí-ən* 'fly,' *ru-ən* 'rest,' *bój-ən* 'build,' *fardín-ən* 'earn,' *kum-ən* 'come,' *zing-ən* 'sing,' *trink-ən* 'drink,' *handl̩-ən* 'purchase.'[76] Exceptions include *gej-n* 'go,' *štej-n* 'stand,' *to-n* 'do.' Allomorph *-n* occurs after unstressed vowel, consonant (except those listed above), including suffixes: *zog-n* 'say,' *mučə-n* 'torment,' *mest-n* 'measure,' *benč-n* 'bless,' *rejnik-n* 'clean,' *organizír-n* 'organize.'

In regular verbs the infinitive is based on the present-tense form of the root/stem. For weak verbs the root is identical in the infinitive, present, and past participle; e.g., *zog-n* 'say,' *gə-zog-t*. With strong verbs, a distinction may or may not be apparent, e.g., *trinkən* 'drink'-*gətrunkən*, but *forn* 'travel'-*gəforn*. The irregular verbs are few: *ton* 'do'-*tu-gəton*; *gebn* 'give'-*gib* (*gist, git*)-*gəgebn*; *visn* 'know'-*vejs-gəvust*; *zajn* 'be'-*bin* (*bist, iz*, etc.)-*gəvén*; *hobn* 'have'-*hob* (*host, hot*)-*gəhat*; *veln-vil-gəvolt* 'want'; sometimes also *brengən-breng-gəbraxt* (~ *gəbrengt*) 'bring.'[77] The irregular verbs provide

[76] Syllabic *l̩* becomes [-syllabic] before suffix vowel.

[77] The term "irregular" refers here to verb roots which differ in their infinitive and finite forms. Not included here are verbs with consonant changes in the past participle, due historically to application of Verner's Law; e.g., *šnajdn* - *gəšnitn* 'cut,' which is otherwise a regular Germanic class 1 strong verb.

the only evidence that the so-called tautological infinitives are only pseudo-infinitives; thus, *šrajbn šrajbt er a briv* 'as concerns writing, he is writing a letter'; but infinitive *zajn* 'to be,' *visn* 'to know' vs. *izn (**zajn) iz er a šnajdər* 'what he is is a tailor,' *vejsn (**visn) vejst er alc* 'as far as knowing, he knows everything.'

Some verbs do not occur in all forms, e.g., the future tense marker (*vel, vest, vet, veln, vet, veln*) occurs only in the conjugated form, and has no infinitive or past participle. Similarly, the verb used to signal past habitual action, *flegn*, does not occur in the past participle.[78]

Verbs with a thematic vowel are generally of Slavic or HA origin; e.g., < Slavic: *mučə-n* 'torment,' *čepə-n* 'bother'; < HA: *tajnə-n* 'argue,' *xkirə-n zix* 'speculate.' The HA-component thematic verbs either derive from nouns, or trace back to pre-Ashkenazic nominal forms (Stankiewicz 1993: 7; Jacobs 1989).

For infinitives of prefixed verbs (*bakumən, antlojfn*, etc.) no other element may be inserted between prefix and root. The verb particle occurs before non-finite verb forms, but other elements may be inserted; thus, *ojs-trinkən, ojs-gətrunkən, ojs-cu-trinkən*.

The present participle (gerund) of regular verbs is based on the infinitive / present root: *trink-ən-dik* 'drinking,' *zog-n-dik* 'saying.' After stressed vowel / diphthong, the suffix shows expected schwa – *štej-əndik* 'standing,' *gej-əndik* 'going' – suggesting an underlying finite form of the verb (cf. infinitive *štejn* vs. 1/3PL *štejən*). For irregular verbs the infinitive form often serves as the base; thus, from: *veln* (*ix vil*) → *velndik* 'wanting' (not ***vilndik*); *gebn* (*ix gib*) → *gebndik* 'giving,' ***gibndik*; *zajn* (*ix bin*) → *zajəndik* 'being'; however, *ton* (*ix tu*) → *túəndik* 'doing.' Prefixes and verb particles precede the verb root in gerunds: *bašrajbndik, arojsgejəndik*.

5.18.2 *Past participles*

The past participle is formed via affixation of prefix *gə-* and a suffix, either *-(ə)n* or *-t*. Prefix *gə-* is blocked in StY if the verb root does not have initial primary stress (an unstressed inseparable prefix thus blocks past participle prefix *gə-*); e.g., *šrajbn – gəšribn*, but *bašrájbn – bašríbn*. Non-prefixed *organizírn* 'organize,' *baləbátəvən* 'keep house' have no *gə-* in their past participles, since they have non-initial stress.[79] The past participle of verbs with verb particle take prefix *gə*. The verb particle has overall primary stress, and is phonologically a separate word: [[ón][šràjbn]], [[ón][gəšrìbn]]. In periphrastic verbs and passives

[78] Except in parts of CY, which use *hobn* + *gəflegt*, but do not use the finite form (Paul Glasser, p.c.).

[79] Zaretski (1926: 90–91) notes dialectal *gətelefonírt* 'telephoned,' *gəfantazírt* 'fantasized,' and the rare occurrence of past participle with verb particle + *gə-* + prefix + root: *on-gə-dercejlt* 'told.'

the verbal element takes *gə-* in the past participle: *bójdək gəven* 'checked,' *xásənə gəhat* 'married,' *antšlófn gəvorn* 'fell asleep.'

The past participle dental suffix is more frequent than the nasal suffix. It occurs with (1) all verbs with thematic vowel or syllabic consonant (including *ər, əm*): *gəčepət* 'bothered,' *gəhandlt* 'purchased'; (2) all derived verbs, whether via suffixation – *organizirt* 'organized,' *gərejnikt* 'cleaned,' *gəojket* 'said "oy"' – or simply derived,[80] e.g., *gətogt* 'became day' < noun *tog*; *gəgrint* 'greened' < adjective *grin*; from noun plurals: *gəglidərt* 'segmented,' *bagajstərt* 'inspired'; from comparative form of adjective: *fargresərt* 'made bigger';[81] (3) all modals: *darfn - gədarft, zoln - gəzolt*, etc., including irregular *veln - gəvolt.*

The nasal suffix occurs with historically strong verbs. For most of the strong verb classes the nasal suffix is accompanied by a vowel change in the verb root, e.g., *trinkən - gətrunkən*. However, this is not always the case (*forn - gəforn, gebn - gəgebn*); here, the description is opaque.[82] Furthermore, irregular verbs *visn-gəvust, veln-gəvolt, brengən-gəbraxt* have root vowel change but dental suffix. Some verbs show historical change from strong to weak, with corresponding shift to the dental suffix; e.g., *šajnən* 'shine'-*gəšajnt* (historically a class 1 ablaut verb). Sometimes doublets have arisen with semantic differentiation, e.g., *glajxn* → *gəglixn* 'compared,' *gəglajxt* 'resembled.' Since strong verbs are historically a Germanic development, the past participles with nasal suffix are almost exclusively of Germanic origin; a notable exception is HA-origin *šextn-gəšoxtn* 'ritually slaughter.' All verbs specified for past tense AUX *zajn* 'be' take the nasal suffix.

Zaretski (1926: 91ff.) describes the following strong verb classes in Yiddish. As elsewhere in his book, Zaretski's point of departure is Yiddish structure rather than traditional external categories. Thus, these classes do not correspond to the traditional ablaut series given in historical grammars of Germanic.

1st class: no vowel change in root

a – a	*haltn - gəhaltn* 'hold'; *vašn - gəvašn* 'wash'
o – o	*grobn - gəgrobn* 'dig'; *forn - gəforn* 'travel'
oj – oj	*štojsn - gəštojsn* 'push'
e – e	*gebn - gəgebn* 'give'; *fargesn - fargesn* 'forget'
ej – ej	*hejsn - gəhejsn* 'be called'
u – u	*kumən - gəkumən* 'come'; *rufn - gərufn* 'call'

80 Addition of prefix or verb particle is thus not considered derivation.

81 Note, however, noun *zalc* 'salt' > verb: *zalcn - gəzalct* ~ *gəzalcn*. For *vinčn - gəvunčn* 'wish-ed' vs. noun (*der*) *vunč* '(the) wish,' the noun derives from the past root of the verb.

82 Since modern Yiddish lacks the preterite form; cf. StG *fahren - fuhr - gefahren, geben - gab - gegeben.*

2nd class: vowel change; past participle root with [o]

e – o	*helfn* - *gəholfn* 'help'; *šenkən* - *gəšonkən* 'give'; *meldn* - *gəmoldn* 'announce'
i – o	*nisn* - *gənosn* 'sneeze'; *krixn* - *gəkroxn* 'crawl'
a – o	*varfn* - *gəvorfn* 'throw'; *vaksn* - *gəvoksn* (~ *gəvaksn*) 'grow'
oj – o	*lojfn* - *gəlofn* 'run'
aj – o	(*untər*)*štrajxn* - (*untər*)*gəštroxn* 'emphasize'

3rd class: past participle with [u]

i – u	*bindn* - *gəbundn* 'tie'; *zingən* - *gəzungən* 'sing'; *vinčn* - *gəvunčn* 'wish'
e – u (limited)	*nemən* - *gənumən* 'take'

4th class: past participle with [i]

aj – i	*bajtn* - *gəbitn* 'change'; *blajbn* - *gəblibn* 'stay'; *šnajdn* - *gəšnitn* 'cut'

5th class: past participle with oj (~ o before /r/)

e – o(j)	*švern* - *gəšvo(j)rn* 'swear'
i – o(j)	*farlirn* - *farlo(j)rn* 'lose'; *fliən* - *gəflojgn* 'fly'
ej – oj	*bejgn* - *gəbojgn* 'bend'
aj – oj	*lajxtn* - *gəlojxtn* (~ *gəlajxt*) 'shine'

6th class: various and irregular
gejn - *gəgangən* 'go'; *zajn* - *gəve(z)n* 'be'; *zicn* - *gəzesn* 'sit'; *lign* - *gəlegn* 'lie'; *štejn* - *gəštanən* 'stand'; *šrajən* - *gəšrign* (~ *gəšriən*) 'shout'

5.19 Finite form of the verb

Two forms of the verb inflect: conjugated ("present tense") forms, and imperatives. There is one basic set of conjugational inflections (with one modification for modals). Conjugated verbs inflect for person and number. The inflectional suffixes are:

	Singular	Plural
1P	-Ø	-(ə)n
2P	-st	-t
3P	-t	-(ə)n

The verb *šrajbn* 'write' conjugates: *ix šrajb*, *du šrajbst*, *er šrajbt*, *mir šrajbn*, *ir šrajbt*, *zej šrajbn*. Thematic root vowel remains in conjugated forms: *ix čepə-Ø*, *du čepə-st*, *er čepə-t*, *mir čepə-n* 'bother,' as does vowel in a suffix, e.g., *er oj-kə-t* 'he says "oh."'

Unlike StG, which shows vowel change in the 2/3P.SG of strong verbs (*sehen, du siehst, er sieht*), Yiddish regular verbs remain unchanged: *zen* 'see': *du zest, er zet*, etc. Irregular verbs take regular inflectional endings; thus: *ton* 'to do,' *ix tu-Ø, du tu-st, er tu-t, mir tu-ən*. Degemination occurs with stem-final C and inflectional suffix: /hejs-st/ → הייסט *hejst*; /arbət-t/ → אַרבעט *arbət*. Root-final /z/ devoices and degeminates phonetically (but not orthographically) before suffix *-st*: /muz/ + /st/ → מוזסט [must]; likewise, root-final /d/ before suffix *-t*: *red* + *t* → רעדט [ret]. Root-final /st/ plus suffix *-st* surface as a single sequence of /st/: *mest-n* 'to measure' → (דו) מעסט (*du*) *mest* 'you measure' (§4.4.2).

StY finite forms of irregular verbs

	zajn[83] 'be'	*hobn* 'have'	*gebn* 'give'	*visn* 'know'	*ton* 'do'
1P.SG.	bin	hob	gib	vejs	tu
2P.SG.	bist	host	gist	vejst	tust
3P.SG.	iz	hot	git	vejst	tut
1P.PL.	zajnən	hobn	gibn	vejsn	tuən
2P.PL.	zajt	hot	git	vejst	tut
3P.PL.	zajnən	hobn	gibn	vejsn	tuən

Conjugated forms of the future marker, for which there is no infinitive, are: 1P.SG *vel*, 2P.SG *vest*, 3P.SG *vet*, 1P.PL. *veln*, 2P.PL *vet*, 3P.PL *veln*.

The imperative inflects, and verb particle or INV occurs after it. The suffixes are -Ø when addressing one person (familiar), *-t* for more than one person, or politeness (any number of persons). The imperative of regular verbs is based on a non-past stem; thus: *šrajb(t)* 'write!'; *čepə(t) nit* 'don't touch!' The imperative is based on the finite form, rather than the infinitive; thus, infinitive *ton*, imperative *tu(t)*. The plural imperatives of *gebn* and *hobn* are *git, hot*; they are not based on the singular imperative forms *gib, hob*; but, exceptionally, on the indicative forms. The imperative of *zajn* is *zaj(t)*; prefixed verb: *bašrajb(t)*; verb-particle verb: *šrajb(t) on*; periphrastic verb: *zaj(t) bojdək*.

The Yiddish modals are: *kenən* 'can,' *zoln* 'should,' *megn* 'may,' *torn* + *nit* 'may not,' *darfn* 'must,' *muzn* 'must' (stronger), *veln* 'want.' Except for *veln* (present root *vil-*, past participle *gəvolt*) all the modals are regular, with unchanged root, and *-t* suffix in the past participle. The modals lack 3P.SG suffix *-t*, thus, *er darf-Ø* 'he must.' In some varieties *flegn* 'used to' is treated as a modal: *er fleg-Ø*; also, the verb *gəhern* ~ *kern* 'to belong to,' when used in modal meaning 'ought; might; may,' has -Ø suffix in 3P.SG; StY 3P.SG *er vejs-t* 'he knows' ~ *vejs-Ø* (probably an influence from NHG *er weiß*). Exceptional use of *-t* suffix with a modal is found in the construction *es vil-t zix* (+ DAT *mir, dir*, etc.) 'I/you/etc. want,' a calque from Slavic; however, this is limited to this verb and this expression. Yiddish *kenən* corresponds to two historical verbs

83 Alternate plural forms are *zenən-zent-zenən* in colloquial speech. Some varieties of NEY have regularized singular forms based on 1P.SG *bin* → 2P. SG *binst*.

(cf. StG *können* 'can,' *kennen* 'know'; 3P.SG *er kann-Ø* 'he can,' *er kenn-t* 'he knows'); in Yiddish the verb inflects like a modal for both meanings.

5.20 Tense

Except for the simple present tense, all tenses, moods, and aspects are constructed with a finite AUX or modal plus a non-finite form of the main verb. The past tense consists of AUX (conjugated form of *hobn* or *zajn*) + past participle. There is no preterite in modern Yiddish; thus, StY *ix hob gənumən* 'I took / have taken.' Examples of a past tense for base verb, prefixed verb, verb-particle verb, and periphrastic verb are as follows:

Present tense	*Past tense*	
ix šrajb	ix hob gəšribn	'I write / wrote / have written'
ix blajb	ix bin gəblibn	'I remain(ed)'
ix bašrajb	ix hob bašribn	'I cover(ed) with writing'
ix šrajb on	ix hob ongəšribn	'I complete(d) writing'
ix bin bojdək	ix hob bojdək gəven	'I check(ed)'
ix hob lib	ix hob lib gəhat	'I like(d)'

Most verbs take AUX *hobn*. The verbs with AUX *zajn* involve motion, whole-body movement or state, and the like.[84] Verbs taking AUX *zajn* are intransitive, and take nasal suffix in the past participle (Zaretski 1926: 84):

blajbn-gəblibn 'stay'	*tretn-gətrotn* 'step'	*fliən-gəflojgn* 'fly'
gejn-gəgangən 'go'	*lojfn-gəlofn* 'run'	*frirn-gəfrojrn* 'freeze'
gəlingən-gəlungən 'succeed'	*šlofn-gəšlofn* 'sleep'	*kumən-gəkumən* 'come'
gərotn-gərotn 'turn out'	*špringən-gəšprungən* 'jump'	*krixn-gəkroxn* 'crawl'
gəšen-gəšen 'happen'	*štejn-gəštanən* 'stand'	*rajtn-gəritn* 'ride'
hangən-gəhongən 'hang'	*lign-gəlegn* 'lie'	*rinən-gərunən* 'leak'
vaksn-gəvaksn ~ *gəvoksn* 'grow'	*deršajnən-deršinən* 'appear'	*švimən-gəšvumən* 'swim'
vern-gəvorn 'become'	*faln-gəfaln* 'fall'	*štarbn-gəštorbn* 'die'
zajn-gəven 'be'	*forn-gəforn* 'travel, go'	*štajgn-gəštign* 'ascend'
zinkən-gəzunkən 'sink'	*faršvindən-faršvundən* 'disappear'	
zicn-gəzesn 'sit'	*flisn-gəflosn* 'flow'	

[84] Characteristic for NEY is generalization of AUX *hobn*; e.g., *ix hob gəkumən, gəblibn*.

Periphrastic verbs formed with AUX *zajn* show a mixed construction in the past tense: AUX *hobn* + past participle *gəven*, thus, *er hot bojdək gəven*. When a *zajn* verb becomes transitive, it may take AUX *hobn*: *ix hob faršlofn di lekcjə* 'I overslept the lesson'; *hot bakumən* 'received'; however, note AUX *zajn* in *er iz bagangən alejn-mord* 'he committed suicide.'

A complex VP contains only one finite verb: *du vilst esn* 'you want to eat'; *er gejt šlofn* 'he goes to sleep.' Thus, addition of the past-tense AUX triggers finite verb → past participle, but leaves an infinitive untouched: *du host gəvolt esn* 'you wanted to eat,' *er iz gəgangən šlofn* 'he went to sleep.'

The Yiddish pluperfect occurs more in literary language. It is formed by adding an invariant *gəhat* (past participle of *hobn*) or *gəven* (~ *gəvest*)[85] to the past tense: *er hot gətrunkən* 'he drank / has drunk' → pluperfect: *er hot gəhat gətrunkən* 'he had drunk.' The pluperfect of *zajn* verbs is problematic. Thus, Mark (1978) distinguishes: (1) in NEY (and isolated islands elsewhere) a "normal" pluperfect: *ix bin gəven gəforn* 'I had gone,' *er iz gəven gəkumen* 'he had come,' etc.;[86] (2) a "mixed" form in literary Yiddish, and in all of Poland – either *iz gəhat* + past participle, or *hot gəven* + past participle, e.g., *er iz gəhat gəštanən* 'he had stood.' The pluperfect of *zajn* verbs is thus muddled, and frequently simply avoided by speakers.

The future tense is formed by future AUX + infinitive: *ix šrajb* → *ix vel šrajbn* 'I shall write'; *er ken redn jidiš* → *er vet kenən redn jidiš* 'he will be able to speak Yiddish.' Verb particle and INV occur before the infinitive: *er trinkt ojs* → *er vet ojstrinkən* 'he will drink up'; *er iz bojdək* → *er vet bojdək zajn* 'he will check.'

The future perfect is formed by future AUX + *hobn* [infinitive] + past participle of the main verb: *er vet hobn gəredt* 'he will have spoken.' Because of the aspectual nature of the future perfect, many past participles here require perfective markers (see Rockowitz 1979).

5.21 Mood

The four moods are: indicative, imperative, conditional, and subjunctive. The indicative is the unmarked mood, and contains the basic constructions outlined above. In contast, the other moods express speakers' attitudes, deference, or impose overall reality conditions or constraints. Tense distinctions are expressed via the indicative (Zaretski 1926: 90; Kahan-Newman 1983: 73).

85 The former is the past participle of *zajn*; *gəvest* is not found elsewhere in Yiddish.
86 How does this square with the NEY tendency to generalized past tense AUX *hobn*? Perhaps this comes from the literary language.

5.21.1 Imperative

The imperative is expressed morphologically only in the 2P.SG/PL However, the imperative mood may be expressed for all persons, as follows:

	Singular	*Plural*
1P	*lomix* + infinitive	*lomir* + infinitive
2P	present root + -Ø	present root + *-t*
3P	*zol* + 3P.SG.NOM + infinitive	*zoln* +3P.PL.NOM + infinitive

Constructions with 1P contain traces of the verb *lozn* 'let'; *lomix* < **loz* + *mix*$_{[\text{ACC}]}$ 'let me,' whereas *lomir* < **loz* + *mir*$_{[\text{NOM}]}$ 'let we.' In 3P.SG/PL, the pronouns accompanying *zol(n)* are nominatives, 's/he should,' 'they should.' In imperative meaning, 3P.SG present indicative + V-1 word order is also used: *xapt im der ruəx* lit., 'grabs him the devil,' i.e., 'to hell with him!'

5.21.2 Conditional

The conditional is formed with AUX *volt-* (which has no infinitive) + past participle.[87] The conditional most frequently involves if-then propositions. The conjunctions *ojb, az, ven* occur here, and *volt-* occurs in both clauses: *ven ix volt gəhat gənug gelt, volt ix gəforn in palongə* 'if I had (= would have) enough money (then) I would go to Palonga.' The construction *volt-* + infinitive is used to express deference in commands: *ix volt ajx betn . . .* 'I would ask you . . . '

The pluperfect conditional is formed with INV *gəhat*: *ven ix volt gəhat gəzen dem film, volt ix gəhat gəkojft dos bux* 'if I had seen the film, I would have bought the book.' As with the indicative, the pluperfect conditional of *zajn* verbs presents problems: [??]*volt gəhat/gəven gəgangən* 'would have gone.'

Zaretski (1926: 88) describes a special "regret" sub-category (also used for "polite advice"), formed with INV + past participle ~ infinitive. The INVs are *nexáj* ~ *xaj, xájbi, nexájbi*; *xaj* + *volt* may reduce to *xolt* ~ *xajlt* ~ *halt*; e.g., *xalt ix hobn gelt* 'if only I had money'; *nexáj volt dos šojn gəven* 'if only it were already so.'

5.21.3 Subjunctive/mixed mood

Often linked to the conditional under the term "*subjunctive*," the mixed mood (*konyunktiv*) expresses several meanings (Zaretski 1926: 89-90), among them: (1) doubt: *er zol hobn a grojsn ojto*, lit. 'he should have a big car,' i.e., 'he is said to have a big car'; (2) counterfactual: *zol šojn kumən di gəulə* 'redemption

[87] For both *hobn* and *zajn* verbs. Note regional *volt-* + past participle ~ infinitive; as well, regional AUX *het, mext* + infinitive.

should come already' (it has not yet done so). Counterfactual and imperative *zoln* thus overlap. Doubt may be expressed for past action via a perfect construction: *zol(n) hobn* + past participle – *er zol hobn gəholfn di menčn* 'he is said to have helped the people.'

5.22 Passive voice

Most sentences with a transitive verb may be transformed into passive voice. In the passive, the recipient of the action is the subject, and the agent of the action is expressed in a dative PP. The active verb becomes a past participle INV, and the verb *vern* is used as an AUX; active: *di froj kojft dem tiš* 'the woman buys the table'; passive: *der tiš vert gəkojft durx der froj* 'the table is bought by the woman.' As with periphrastic and verb-particle verbs, the invariant element – here, the passivized past participle – follows finite forms of AUX *vern*, but precedes non-finite forms of *vern*; thus: *der tiš muz gəkojft vern* 'the table must be bought'; *der tiš vet gəkojft vern* 'the table will be bought'; *der tiš iz gəkojft gəvorn* 'the table has been bought.'

Periphrastic verbs formed with INV + *vern* are problematic (e.g., *neləm vern* 'vanish,' *antšlofn vern* 'fall asleep'), in that they straddle the border between lexicalized periphrastic verbs (with passive meaning) and syntactic passives. Certain verbs regularly block the passive; there is no passive of intransitives, nor of verb *hobn*, nor of periphrastic verbs (Zaretski 1926: 83). Neither may the singulative aspect undergo passivization; this provides evidence that occurrences with this are not merely VPs with an accusative complement, but, rather, complex verbs.

Passive meaning may be expressed by two other means: (1) an active sentence using *me(n)* 'one' as a non-specific subject (verb in 3P.SG); thus: *švediš vert gəredt in švedn* ~ *me(n) redt švediš in švedn* 'Swedish is spoken in Sweden'; (2) use of reflexive pronoun *zix*: *der tekst lejənt zix azoj*, lit. 'the text reads itself thusly,' i.e., 'the text is (to be) read like this.'

5.23 Reflexives

StY *zix* is the generalized reflexive pronoun for all persons, genders, and numbers.[88] In some ways, *zix* functions as an independent word, and thus, may move in the syntax: *er zet zix* 'he sees himself' → *er vet zix zen* 'he will see himself.' On the other hand, it exhibits clitic-like characteristics.[89] Because of its patterning, Zaretski (1926: 80) treats (some instances of) *zix* as a particle.

[88] Many regional varieties inflect the reflexive pronoun for person and number.

[89] Note also regional NEY gerund form *bodnzixdik* vs. StY *bodndik zix* 'while bathing (oneself)' (Mark 1951; Lemkhen 1995; Jacobs 2001a).

The following uses of *zix* are noted: (1) a true, syntactically generated reflexive object pronoun, where agent = recipient, e.g., *mojšə zet zix* 'Moyshe sees himself'; (2) a type of passive: *der tekst lejənt zix azoj* 'the text is read thusly' = 'reads itself.' Here, agent is not identical with recipient, since the text is not performing the act of reading; (3) lexicalized verbs with *zix*: *špiln zix* 'to play,' *lernən zix* 'to learn.' When *špiln* has a concrete object, the *zix* deletes: *er špilt zix* 'he is playing' vs. *er špilt bejsbol* 'he is playing baseball,' though *zix* co-occurs with a direct object in *er lernt zix jidiš* 'he is learning Yiddish'; note also *er špilt zix in kort(n)* 'he is playing$_{[\text{REFLEXIVE}]}$ [in] cards'; (4) reciprocals; thus, the first meaning of *kartər un brežnev kušn zix* is reciprocal 'Carter and Brezhnev kiss one another.' A forced reflexive reading is possible: Carter kisses Carter, and Brezhnev kisses Brezhnev; (5) the ethical dative is sensitive to semantic structure; thus, *er gejt zix špacirn* 'he goes (for himself; self-benefit) for a walk,' but *zol er mir zajn gəzunt* 'he should be [for] me well,' with dative pronoun *mir*.

5.24 Aspect

Aspect refers to how an action is performed: complete vs. incomplete; one-time vs. repeated action; continual vs. sudden action; intensity of action. The degree to which grammatical aspect is exploited in Yiddish lies somewhere between the fully developed systems found in many Slavic languages, and its slight presence in modern German (see Schaechter 1951; Aronson 1985; Rothstein 1990). Yiddish aspect is expressed in a variety of ways, including the use of verbal prefixes, verb particles, or specific AUX + verb constructions. The following discussion is based on Zaretski (1926), Mark (1978), and Birnbaum (1979a).

The perfective aspect may be marked by use of a prefix or a verb particle. Selection is often idiosyncratic; thus, perfective verbs *der-gejn* 'arrive,' *far-endikn* 'complete,' *ojs-trinkən* 'drink up,' *op-esn* 'eat up,' *ibər-lejənən* 'read entirely,' *on-šrajbn* 'write to completion.' Furthermore, dialects may differ in marker selection, or even whether or not a particular verb generally takes an aspectual marker. Perfective expresses completed action; thus, *zi lejənt ibər di cajtung* 'she reads the newspaper (in its entirety).' Note that *ibər* is not a preposition; *di cajtung* is accusative, not the dative complement of a preposition.

The inchoative aspect expresses commencement of an action of (unspecified) duration. This is expressed by *nemən* 'take' or *nemən zix* + the action: *er nemt arbətn* 'he begins working'; *er nemt zix cum arbətn*. Birnbaum (1979a: 272) allows *nemən zix* + infinitive. Mark's examples have *nemən* + infinitive, or *nemən zix* + nominalized verb infinitive – *er nemt zix cum arbətn* – ~ NP with non-verbal noun: *er nemt zix cu der arbət*.

The iterative aspect expresses ongoing non-interrupted or repetitive action. It is expressed by verb *haltn* + *in* + infinitive: *er halt in esn* 'he is engaged in eating'; *zi halt in lernən zix rusiš* 'she's in the process of learning Russian.' This may be intensified by insertion of *ejn*: *zi halt in ejn lernən zix rusiš* 'she is taken up (exclusively) with learning Russian.'

Similar to iterative is the habitual aspect (Birnbaum 1979a): *ton* + infinitive – *er tut šrajbn* 'he writes (as a regular activity),' with the emphasis on the repetitiveness. Mark (1978: 293) says this is rare; it is found in popular poetry, and was more common in earlier spoken language.

Habitual past action is expressed by *flegn* + INF. In StY *flegn* is used only in the present tense, but refers to past action; e.g., *ix fleg lejənən pojlišə cajtungən* 'I used to read Polish newspapers.' Regionally (CY), the past tense (*hobn* + *gəflegt* + INF) is used instead.

One-time action without ongoing duration – which Birnbaum calls "singulative aspect" – is expressed by verb *ton* or *gebn* + deverbal root: *er tut a kuk* 'he gives a glance' vs. *er kukt* 'he looks' (activity continues for some duration). The singulative aspect straddles syntax and morphology. On the one hand, the verb root is a deverbal nominal; thus, an inflected adjective may be added: *a bejzn kuk ton* 'to give an angry glance.' Further, the nominalized root may undergo diminution: *a kukələ ton*. On the other hand, it exhibits non-noun-like characteristics as well; thus, *an eməsn cəhuljə ton* 'to have a real fling'; here, untypically, a schwa-final noun is masculine. Furthermore, particle verbs in the singulative aspect do not behave like their corresponding nouns. Thus, from complex verb *onzogn* 'divulge' obtains noun (*der*) *onzog* 'message'; however, singulative aspect generates *er tut a zòg-ón*.

Sudden commencement of an action is expressed by the prefix *cə-* + verb + *zix*, e.g., *er cəlaxt zix* 'he bursts out laughing.'

Aspect and tense have many points of overlap in Yiddish. For example, many verbs in the future perfect and pluperfect demand a perfectivizing prefix or verb particle. With the exception of habitual past action (with *flegn*), the aspects outlined above may occur in future or past tense; thus: *er halt in šrajbn*, *er hot gəhaltn in šrajbn*; *er hot gənumən arbətn*; *er hot zix cəlaxt*; *er hot ojsgətrunkən di milx*; *er vet ojstrinkən dos bir*; *er hot gəton šrajbn*. Note also: *er hot a zog-ojs gəton* 'he revealed'; gerund *a kuk-gebndik* 'giving a glance.'

6 Syntax

6.1 Introduction

There exist several works which deal with Yiddish syntax,[1] typically as part of normative reference grammars (e.g., Mark 1978; Birnbaum 1979a; Katz 1987b), or school grammars (e.g., Ferdman 1958). However, these generally have little concern with syntactic issues of interest to general linguists, i.e., with precise description of constituents, clauses, movement processes, and the like. The one exceptional attempt at a general and comprehensive theory-based description of Yiddish syntax is Zaretski (1926). Kahan-Newman (1983) provides discussion both of Zaretski's theoretical approach and of his analysis of data within that approach, and relates much of this to more current syntactic frameworks. Hall's (1967) dissertation applies then-current generative-transformational apparatus to Yiddish syntax. More recent theory-oriented works on Yiddish syntax have focused on single issues or sets of related issues (Lowenstamm 1977; den Besten and Moed-van Walraven 1986; Prince 1989; Diesing 1990, 2003; Santorini 1994). An overview of Yiddish syntax is found in Jacobs, Prince, and van der Auwera [JPA] (1994). Many of the examples in the present chapter are taken or derived from Zaretski (1926) and Mark (1978). For further data the reader is referred to Zaretski (1926), and to more recent works containing longer corpora of free spoken Yiddish (e.g., *LCAAJ* archives and tapes; Dyhr and Zint 1988; Kiefer 1995; Geller 2001).

6.2 Clause types

6.2.1 Declarative clauses

It is worth noting briefly the "general knowledge" about basic Yiddish sentences, as noted in prescriptive grammars, and taught in language classes. The unmarked order in declarative main (and subordinate) clauses is SVO: *der man lejənt*

[1] For discussion of general syntactic issues, the reader is referred to works such as Borsley (1999).

dos bux 'the man reads the book.'[2] V-2 is predominant in Yiddish; thus: *dos bux*$_{\text{[DirObj]}}$ *lejənt*$_{\text{[V]}}$ *der man*$_{\text{[Subj]}}$ 'it's the book that the man is reading,' with direct object topicalized, triggering reassertion of V-2, and the local switch of subject and verb. Similarly, interrogative clauses trigger *wh*-fronting, but remain V-2: *di froj*$_{\text{[Subj]}}$ *lejənt*$_{\text{[V]}}$ *dos bux*$_{\text{[Obj]}}$ 'the woman reads the book,' but *di froj lejənt vos* 'the woman reads what?' undergoes *wh*-fronting → *vos*$_{\text{[Obj]}}$*lejənt di froj* (likewise, *ver*$_{\text{[Subj]}}$*lejənt dos bux* 'who reads the book?').

Topicalization is extremely common in Yiddish, occurring with direct objects, indirect objects, adverbials – thus, almost any constituent may, in principle, be topicalized (see Waletzky 1980). The topicalized constituent fronts to initial position, with V-2 reasserting itself. Marked word order (with marked intonation) signals the topicalization. Consider:

(1)	Der lerər	šrajbt	di zacn	mit krajd	afn tovl.
	The teacher	writes	the sentences	with chalk	on the blackboard.

This yields a series of permutations with different topicalized constituent, e.g., *di zacn šrajbt der lerər mit krajd afn tovl* 'it's the *sentences* [not mathematical equations] that the teacher is writing with chalk on the blackboard'; *mit krajd šrajbt der lerər afn tovl* 'with *chalk* (not with a crayon) . . . '; *afn tovl šrajbt der lerər* . . . 'it's on the *blackboard* [not the notepad] that the teacher is writing . . . ' Non-counting elements may precede the subject or a topicalized constituent: *(nejn,) ix trink nit dém vajn* '(No,) I don't drink this wine' → *(nejn,) dém vajn trink ix nit.*

Since the unmarked order in declarative main clauses is SVO, an alternative strategy is needed to topicalize a subject.[3] This may be achieved through use of a dummy *es* 'it' in initial (subject) position. This blocks any other constituent from opportunistically occupying this position, where it could be perceived as topicalized; thus: *es šrajbt di zacn afn tovl der lerər* 'it's the teacher [not the student] who is writing the sentences on the blackboard' ~ *es šrajbt der lerər di zacn afn tovl.*[4] The indefinite subject *men* 'one' may not be topicalized, but may occur in sentence-final position as a result of V-2 when another element is topicalized; thus: *vajn trinkt men* 'it's wine that one drinks,' but not ***es trinkt vajn men.*

Finite verb topicalization presents a special problem, since fronting to initial position would violate V-2. What occurs is a copy of the stem of the finite

[2] On deeper representations of the sentence (S), and whether the subject originates there, or outside S, see, e.g., den Besten and Moed-van Walraven (1986); JPA (1994).

[3] For reasons of space limitation, distinctions between topicalization and focus are not considered here. On subject position and topicalization, see Prince (1989, 1993).

[4] JPA (1994: 414) note that "prepositional phrases may and clauses must be extraposed beyond the postposed subject"; thus: *cum šenstn baləbos fun štot iz gəkumən a šadxn redn a šidəx dem baləbos' toxtər* 'to the finest gentleman in town came a matchmaker to arrange a marriage for the gentleman's daughter.'

verb + infinitive suffix into initial field, creating a pseudo-infinitive; thus, *er trinkt nor milx* 'he only drinks milk' → *trinkən trinkt er nor milx* 'as far as concerns drinking, he only drinks milk.' Since almost all Yiddish verbs have an identical stem in their infinitive and finite forms, the pseudo-infinitive is mostly indistinguishable from a true infinitive. However, when the present and infinitive stems differ, the use of the present stem is clear; e.g., *visn* 'know,' present stem *vejs-*, thus: *er vejst alc* 'he knows everything' → *vejsn* (***visn*) *vejst er alc* 'as far as knowing (things), he knows everything.' Note fully irregular verb *zajn* 'be': *binən bin ix a kalifornjər* 'as for what I am – I'm a Californian'; *izn iz er a kamcn* 'as to what he is – he's a cheapskate.'

Thus, Yiddish declarative clauses are both SVO and verb-second. The initial field is obligatorily filled (JPA 1994: 412). The default filler is the Subject. If initial field is empty, expletive *es* is employed.[5]

(2) Es iz mir kalt un nas.
it is me cold and wet
'I'm cold and wet.'

If the recipient *mir* is fronted to initial field, *es* deletes: *mir iz* (***es*) *kalt un nas*. Expletive *es* also does not occur if initial field is occupied by an entire clause: *es regnt šojn a gancn tog, iz* (***es*) *mir kalt un nas* 'it rains already a whole day, (so) I'm cold and wet.' Similarly, existential sentences expressing 'there is/are' employ an expletive *es*:

(3) Es iz do a bux afn tiš.
'There is a book on the table.'
(4) Es zajnən do bixər afn tiš.
'There are books on the table.'

However, expletive *es* is deleted if something else comes to occupy initial field, for example, with topicalization:

(5) A bux iz (**es) do afn tiš.
(6) Bixər zajnən (**es) do afn tiš.
(7) Afn tiš iz (**es) do a bux.
(8) Ci iz do a bux afn tiš?
'Is there a book on the table?'[6]

When *es* serves as a full pronoun (rather than as an expletive), it does not delete when bumped out of initial position: *es iz an alt hojz* 'it is an old house' → *vos*

[5] "[M]erely a place-holder and not a dummy subject" (JPA 1994: 412). Most of the following observations concerning clause types are taken from or based on Prince's syntax section in JPA.

[6] For interrogative existential sentences, the yes/no trigger *ci* appears to be obligatory rather than optional if no other element precedes the verb (*iz/zajnən*), i.e., in which no topicalization occurs. See below.

iz es? 'what is it?'; *an alt hojz iz es* 'it's (indeed) an old house.' Mark (1978: 375) distinguishes the various uses of *es* as follows. A "real" subject *es* does not delete when not in initial position:

(9) Es vet bald regənən.
'It's going to rain soon.'
(10) Bald vet es regənən.
'Soon it's going to rain.'

A fictive subject *es* is absent when initial position is otherwise filled:

(11) Es tut mir vej der fus.
'My foot hurts.' (lit. it-does-me-hurt-the-foot)
(12) Mir tut vej der fus.
'My foot hurts.' (lit. me-does-hurt-the-foot)
(13) Der fus tut mir vej.
'My foot hurts.' (lit. the-foot-does-me-hurt)

Fictive *es* is also used in initial position as a device to enable movement and thus topicalization of the subject (p. 373):

(14) Es iz der student gəkumən cu zajnə eltərn ojf pejsəx.
'The STUDENT came to his parents for Passover.'

Mark (p. 375) notes that when the true subject is a personal pronoun, use of fictive *es* is not permitted; thus: *der lerər iz gəkumən* 'the teacher came' → *es iz gəkumən der lerər*; *er iz gəkumən* 'he came,' but not: ***es iz er gəkumən*; similarly, *er iz do* 'he is here,' but not ***es iz do er*. Finally, there is a use of *es* or *dos* in predicates as a type of expletive or intensifier (see Birnbaum 1979a: 303): *der tatə iz es der bal-simxə* 'Father is the party host'; similarly: *er šrajbt es* (~ *dos*) *a briv* 'he writes a letter.'

6.2.2 *Imperative clauses*

Imperative clauses are V-initial, and initial field is empty or non-existent (JPA 1994: 412). The most basic imperative clause, directed at 2P, occurs as follows:

(15)	Ø	trink (-t)	di milx!	'(You) drink the milk!'
	[INITIAL FIELD]	drink$_{[IMP]}$	the milk$_{[DIR.OBJ]}$	

Informal 2P.SG imperative form of the verb takes a special zero-inflection (vs. normal 2PSG inflection *-st*). For 2P.PL/formal, the verb suffix *-t* is added: *trink-t di milx*! – here, identical in form to the conjugated form (*ir trink-t*). Evidence that the imperative is a finite form is seen by the position of the verb particle relative to the verb, and with the invariant in periphrastic verbs; thus, *ojs-trinkən* 'drink up/entirely,' *bojdək zajn* 'check' → imperatives *trink*(*t*) *ojs*! 'drink up!'; *zaj*(*t*) *bojdək*! 'check!' (see below).

Examples of marked filling of initial field in imperatives are given in JPA (1994: 412). A subject may be explicitly expressed contrastively; thus: *du nem un lojf, un ix vel mir gejn pameləx* 'you start running and I'll walk slowly.' Other elements may be topicalized as well – particle *to* 'then': *to kuš mix nit in kop* 'then don't kiss me on the head'; adverb *dernox* 'afterwards; then': *dernox gej bavajz az du bist nit kejn ber*! 'then go and prove that you're not a bear!'

Two types of imperatives occur involving verbs of coming or going followed by a second verb. The first type has the 'come'/'go' verb + infinitive, e.g., *gej*(*t*) *šlofn* 'go to sleep!' Here, *šlofn* is a type of complement of imperative *gej*(*t*). In the second type both verbs occur in the imperative form, e.g., *gej*(*t*) *bavajz*(*t*) 'go and prove!'; *kum*(*t*) *es*(*t*) 'come and eat!' These function as coordinating imperatives as opposed to the complementizing/subordinating type in *gej*(*t*) *šlofn*.

When the imperative is directed to the third person, the subject is explicitly expressed. The clause is V-initial here as well, with Subject following the verb *zoln* 'should,' and preceding the main verb infinitive: *zol er trinkən kavə* 'he should/let him drink coffee'; *zoln zej esn kuxn* 'they should/let them eat cake!' As with general 2P imperatives, a topicalized element may be (markedly) inserted into the empty initial field: *to zol er gejn* 'then (consequently) he should go.'

An imperative directed to 1P uses a letive construction, consisting of (a frozen form etymologically related to *lozn* 'let'): *lomix* 'let me' or *lomir* 'let's' (lit. 'let' + 'we'$_{[NOM]}$, rather than 'let us'$_{[ACC]}$) + infinitive of the main verb (JPA 1994: 413) – *lomir esn zup* 'let's eat soup.' The verbal status of the frozen form *lomix*/*lomir* is demonstrated by its attraction of negative particle *nit*, thus: *lomir nit gejn* 'let's not go'; as well as of pronoun objects: *lomir im helfn* 'let's help him' (vs. full NP object in *lomir helfn dem man* 'let's help the man'). Letives may also be preceded by a particle: *to lomir gejn* 'so let's go.' Since the default order in imperative clauses is V-first, the element *to* is inserted in imperative subordinate clauses where ambiguity might otherwise arise (where it might be confused with the V-first order found in narrative contexts; see §6.6.6). Thus, the *to* is used to disambiguate: *dos bux iz majns, to gib mir es!* 'the book is mine, (so) give it to me!'; *mir hobn šojn gəgesn, to lomir gejn!* 'we already ate, (so) let's go!' (U. Weinreich 1949: 332).

6.2.3 *Interrogative clauses*

Direct questions, which occur in main clauses, solicit an answer. They are of two types: constituent and yes/no. The constituent questions are typically formed with a *wh*-word, which stands in as a PRO-form for the item about which the speaker wishes information. Consider the basic sentence:

(16) Di froj lejənt di cajtung hajnt in park.
The woman reads the newspaper today in (the) park.

One may ask what the woman is reading, where she is reading, when, etc. The *wh*-word is a PRO form for the whole constituent, and is, in direct questions, obligatorily fronted to initial position, where it counts as a sentence unit, triggering V-2 inversion.

(17) Vos lejənt di froj hajnt in park?
what reads the woman today in (the) park
'What is the woman reading today in the park?'

(18) Vu lejənt di froj di cajtung hajnt?
where reads the woman the newspaper today
'Where is the woman reading the newspaper today?'

(19) Ven lejənt di froj di cajtung in park?
when reads the woman the newspaper in (the) park
'When does the woman read the newspaper in the park?'

(20) Ver lejənt di cajtung hajnt in park?
who reads the newspaper today in (the) park
'Who's reading the newspaper in the park today?'

A constituent question may be asked about an entire sentence, e.g.,

(21) Far vos lejənt di froj di cajtung hajnt in park?
why reads the woman the newspaper today in (the) park
'Why is the woman reading the newspaper in the park today?'

(22) Vi lejənt di froj di cajtung hajnt in park?
how reads the woman the newspaper today in (the) park
'How does the woman read the paper in the park today?'

As seen in (20), a *wh*-Subject also occurs in surface initial position. In traditional descriptions, initial *wh*-Subjects are seen as basic (e.g., Birnbaum 1979a: 304). However, theory-based approaches see Yiddish main-clause interrogatives as verb-initial clauses, with the *wh*- in the complementizer position rather than in the clause proper; the *wh*-Subject then fronts via an operation (JPA 1994: 413). In this view, both yes/no questions and constituent questions are verb-initial:

(23) Zajnən zej məšugə?
are they crazy
'Are they crazy?'

(24)

Vu žə	iz	di cvejtə polkə?
where-then	is	the second drumstick

'Where then is the other drumstick?'

Interrogatives may be preceded by a topicalized element or particle. However, if an interrogative complementizer is present, the particle or topicalizing element precedes it, "indicating that the clause is in fact verb initial" (p. 413):

(25)

To	far vos	gejst	du	on	hojzn?
then	why	go	you	without	pants

'Then/so why are you going around without pants?'

If the optional element *ci* is used with a main-clause yes/no question, it occurs in initial position, followed by finite verb and Subject:

(26)

(Ci)	farštejt	er	španiš?
(yes/no)	understands	he	Spanish

'Does he understand Spanish?'

When another element is fronted to initial position, *ci* may not occur elsewhere in the sentence. Alternative word orders may occur with direct questions, however they are all – in one way or another – marked. Thus, a yes/no question using declarative word order (and no *ci*) has a marked (rising) interrogative intonation:

(27)

Er	farštejt	španiš?
he	understands	Spanish

'Does he understand Spanish?'

It might be claimed that use of declarative word order with marked rising intonation can be extended to constituent questions as well:

(28)

Di froj	lejənt	di cajtung	vú?
the woman	reads	the newspaper	where

'The woman is reading the newspaper WHERE?'

Here, the intonation, the stress, and the lack of *wh*-fronting are marked. Birnbaum (1979a: 304) notes *du ver bist* 'you-who are YOU?' saying that "[s]pecial emphasis is effected by placing the subject before the interrogative." Diesing (p.c.) suggests that this is more likely the placement of the topic (rather than the subject) to the left of the *wh*-phrase, citing examples like *in vald – ver fun ajx vet gejn*? 'Into the woods – who of you shall go?' where *in vald* is a topicalized adverbial.

In contrast to direct questions, *wh*-words in indirect constituent questions do not trigger V-2, even though they are fronted:

(29)	Ix	vejs	nit	vos	di froj	lejənt.
	I	know	not	what	the woman	reads

'I don't know what the woman is reading.'

Similarly, indirect yes/no questions do not show V-2:

(30)	Ix	vejs	nit	ci	er	farštejt	španiš.
	I	know	not	whether	he	understands	Spanish

'I don't know if he understands Spanish.'

In (30), *ci* is obligatory, but – as with *wh*-words in indirect questions – does not trigger V-2. Either *ci* is a weight-bearing sentence unit (similar to *wh*-words) in main clauses, and a conjunction in subordinate clauses; or it indeed is like a *wh*-word, and main and subordinate clauses in Yiddish differ in their basic structures. Note that Yiddish permits topicalization with indirect questions, but not with direct questions (examples from Diesing 1990: 50):

Direct questions:

(31)	Ver	hot gəgesn	dos brojt?
	'Who	ate	the bread?'
(32)	**Ver	dos brojt	hot gəgesn?
	**'Who	the bread	ate?'

(33)	**Ver	hajnt	hot gəgesn	dos brojt?
	**'Who	today	ate	the bread?'

Indirect questions:

(34)	Ix	vejs	vos	baj mir	tut	zix.
	I	know	what	by me	does	REFL

'I know what goes on with me.'

(35)	Zi	iz gəkumən	zen	ver	friər	vet	končən.
	she	is come	see	who	earlier	shall	finish

'She came to see who would finish earlier.'

Furthermore, when the pronominal *wh*-word is the subject of the embedded clause, the element *es* is inserted, provided no other topicalized element occurs in the position after the subject (Birnbaum 1979a: 307):

(36)	Er	vejst	nit,	ver es	vet	blajbn	in park.
	he	knows	not	who-IT	shall	stay	in the park
(37)	Er	vejst	nit,	ver (**es)	in park	vet	blajbn.
	he	knows	not	who	in the park	shall	stay

Note also: (*ci vejst er den ništ*) *vos do tut zix* '(Doesn't he know) what's happening here?' (p. 304). Here the underlying subordinate clause is: *es tut zix do vos*. The obligatory *wh*-fronting does not by itself trigger loss of the *es*. However, topicalization of *do* does.

Diesing (2003) discusses multiple *wh*-fronting in Yiddish. It is important to note some significant dialect differences. Multiple *wh*-fronting does not occur in WY or NEY; in CY it is limited to indirect questions; in SEY it is permitted in both direct and indirect questions (pp. 55–56).[7] Diesing (pp. 53–54) provides examples (from Mark 1978 and Zaretski 1929):

(38) Ver vuhin vet gejn mit ajx?
who where will go with you
'Who will go where with you?'

(39) Ver vos hot gəkojft?
who what has bought
'Who bought what?'

(40) Ver vuhin gejt?
who where goes
'Who is going where?'

These are basically combinations of two separate questions into a single question; cf. also:

(41) Far vos un vi azoj hot er es gəton?
why and how did he it done
'Why and how did he do it?'

Consider multiple *wh*-fronting in indirect questions (JPA 1994: 414):

(42) (Hot zi nit gəkent farštejn) ver mit vemən es šlogt zix.
(so she couldn't understand) who with whom it hits REFL
'(So she couldn't understand) who was fighting with whom.'

Thus, multiple *wh*-fronting alone does not trigger deletion of expletive *es*; consider also (from Diesing 2003: 55):

(43) Lomir gejn, ver vuhin es gejt.
let's go who where EXPL goes
'Let's go, where(ever) who(ever) is going.'

[7] Diesing's data suggest an interesting dialect-geographical scenario wherein multiple fronting – typologically un-Germanic, and not part of PY – arose in CY, where it was limited to indirect questions. Its generalization in SEY may be due to the history of SEY itself – essentially, a newer contact dialect where CY and NEY speakers mixed. The former NEY speakers – lacking any multiple *wh*-fronting, but now in contact with CY speakers – possibly overgeneralized the limited CY *wh*-fronting.

However, when a non-subject is topicalized in the indirect question, expletive *es* deletes (p. 55):

(44) Lomir gejn, ver vuhin hajnt gejt.
let's go who where today goes
'Let's go, where(ever) who(ever) is going TODAY.'

Note also retention of the *es* in exclamatory expressions, e.g., *vi es lajxtn di štern*! 'how the stars do shine!' (Birnbaum 1979a: 307).

Zaretski and Mark note instances of special emphasis, exclamation, poetic language, etc., with finite verb in third position, and a marked intonation, e.g., *vos er hot ibərgəlebt*! 'what he has experienced!'; *in vald – ver fun ajx vet gejn*? 'to the forest – which of you shall go?' This word order emphasizes either the first or second element.

The word order in echo questions suggests an underlying (= pragmatically determined) subordinate-clause structure:

(45) Far vemən hot duk snajdər gəšpilt?
for whom has Duke Snider played
'For whom did Duke Snider play?'

(46) (Du vilst visn) far vemən duk snajdər hot gəšpilt?
(you want to know) for whom Duke Snider has played
'(You want to know) for whom Duke Snider played?'

Finally, Yiddish does not permit preposition stranding; the preposition fronts with its object *wh*-word (or NP): *mit vos šrajbt er?* 'what does he write with?' – not ***vos šrajbt er mit?*

6.2.4 Subordinate clauses

Subordinate clauses in Yiddish are – like main clauses – SVO. Zaretski (1926: 163ff.) discusses "some rules" about word order in "compound linkages." He notes that conjunctions do not count as sentence units. Thus, main and subordinate clauses show identical structures in the following examples, with, respectively, unmarked SVO order, topicalization of the adverbial, and subject postposing.

(47) (Ix vejs, az) mojšə kumt morgn.
'(I know that) Moyshe is coming tomorrow.'

(48) (Ix vejs, az) morgn kumt mojšə.
'(I know that) it's tomorrow that Moyshe is coming.'

(49) (Ix vejs, az) es kumt morgn mojšə.
'(I know that) it's Moyshe that's coming tomorrow.'

Zaretski (p. 168) notes that *es* in (50) is optional in a main clause, but obligatory in subordinate clause; thus:

(50) (S') kumt cu gejn an altər man.
(51) X'ze vi s'kumt cu gejn an altər man.
(52) **x'ze vi Ø kumt cu gejn an altər man

The verb-initial variant of the main clause in (50) shows pragmatically related consecutive word order, with implied 'so'; thus, the finite verb occupies second position at some higher discourse level. Comparison of (51) and (52) shows that *es* is required, suggesting that a conjunction – which signals the start of the subordinate clause – pragmatically "pushes the reset button," ruling out the verb occurring first.

The conjunction introducing a subordinate clause may in some instances be optionally deleted, with word order unaffected: *Zi mejnt, (az) ix bin məšugə gəvorn* 'She thinks (that) I have gone crazy' (Birnbaum 1979a: 306).

Wh-words in subordinate clauses have an intermediate status (Kahan-Newman 1983: 135–136). Generally, they do not trigger inversion, even when they are object pronouns:

(53) Ix vejs nit vemən du host gəzen.
'I know not whom you have seen.'
(54) Ix vejs nit vos du host gəzen.
'I know not what you have seen.'

There is likewise no inversion when the *wh*-word in the relative clause is a subject:

(55) Ix vejs nit ver es hot gətrunkən di milx.
'I know not who [it] has drunk the milk.'
(56) Ix vejs nit vos es ligt afn tiš.
'I know not what [it] lies on the table.'

When another constituent gets topicalized, the *es* is not present (except with multiple *wh*-fronting; see above):

(57) Ix vejs nit ver (**es) DI MILX hot gətrunkən.
'I don't know who drank THE MILK.'
(58) Ix vejs nit ver (**es) HAJNT vet kumən.
'I don't know who TODAY is coming.'

In the following examples, the *wh*-word appears to trigger inversion in a subordinate clause (Kahan-Newman 1983: 135–136):

(59)

X'gədenk	nit	ven	hob	ix	gəlejənt	ostvaldn.
I remember	not	when	have	I	read	Ostvald

'I don't remember when I read Ostvald.'

(60) Ix farštej nit far vos gejt er.[8]
'I understand not why goes he'
'I don't understand why he's going.'

This creates a problem for most analyses of *wh*-words in subordinate clauses. Kahan-Newman suggests that the reason for the inversion lies in the semantics of the sentences; both have a negative matrix. The corresponding affirmative sentences would disallow inversion:

(61) **x'gədenk ven hob ix gəlejənt ostvaldn
(62) **x'farštej far vos gejt er

She writes: "the negation of the matrix verbs . . . creates a doubtful state of affairs, and the *wh* word of the subordinate clause that follows then assumes a question-like quality. So instead of fixed boundaries between question words and relation words, there is a range of increasing degree; *wh* words that follow negative matrix verbs become question-like and therefore trigger inversion."

6.2.5 Relative clauses

Relative clauses in Yiddish present several complications, including defective relative-pronoun paradigms, overlapping use of *vos* as a relative pronoun and a subordinating conjunction, other optional fronting processes, resumptive pronouns, and varying types of pronoun deletion (see Lowenstamm 1977). Generally, the interrogative *wh*-words are used as relative markers. However, their syntactic function as relatives differs from that in interrogative clauses. The main relative markers are uninflected *vos*, and inflected *velx-*. The other *wh*-words may be used in relative function as well, e.g., *der zumər, ven mir zenən gəforn in kolorado, iz gəven a hejsər* 'the summer when we went to Colorado was a hot one.'

In its most unrestricted usage, *vos* may be used as a generalized relative marker for animate (including human) and inanimate nouns, for singular and plural, and in nominative, accusative, and dative cases:

(63) Der jid vos trinkt dem tej iz majn xavər.
'The guy who$_{[\text{NOM}]}$ is drinking the tea is my friend.'
(64) Der jid vos du host gəzen iz majn xavər.
'The guy whom$_{[\text{ACC}]}$ you saw is my friend.'
(65) Di kindər vos du host gəholfn hobn lib bejsbol.
'the children whom$_{[\text{DAT}]}$ you helped like baseball.'
(66) Dos bux vos ligt afn tiš iz alt.
'The book which$_{[\text{NOM}]}$ is lying on the table is old.'

[8] Some native speakers surveyed spontaneously produced "normal" subordinate-clause word order: *ix farštej nit far vos er gejt*. On "embedded direct questions" in Yiddish, see Santorini (1995).

(67) Dos bux vos er lejənt iz alt.
'the book which$_{[ACC]}$ he is reading is old.'

The more specified relative pronoun *velx-* is often, though not entirely, interchangeable with *vos*. It inflects for number, gender, and case.[9]

(68) der jid, velxər trinkt dem tej . . .
'the guy who$_{[NOM]}$ is drinking the tea . . . '

(69) der jid, velxn du host gəzen . . .
'the guy whom$_{[ACC]}$ you saw . . . '

(70) di froj, velxər mir hobn gəholfn
'the woman whom$_{[DAT]}$ we helped . . . '

Generalized relative *vos* may not co-occur with a more specified relative pronoun, e.g.,

(71) der jid, **[vos velxn] du host gəzen . . .

The status of *vos* as a pronoun breaks down in several ways. First, the distinction between animate and inanimate referent plays a role. Oblique animates may take the relative *vemən* 'whom,' while oblique inanimates may not; thus:

(72) der man vos/velxn/vemən du host gəzen
'the man that/which/whom you saw . . . '

(73) der tiš vos/velxn/**vemən du host gəzen
'the table that/which/**whom you saw . . . '

Furthermore, *vos* may not be the object of a preposition when referring to humans; here, a specified relative pronoun must be used (Lowenstamm 1977: 200):

(74) di temə af vos er redt . . .
'the subject on which he is speaking . . . '

(75) **der jid af vos ix farloz zix . . .
'the guy on whom I depend . . . '

(76) der jid af velxn/af vemən ix farloz zix . . .
'the guy on whom I depend . . . '

Lowenstamm (pp. 200ff.) shows that *vos* is in fact a relative pronoun only when it stands for a non-human noun, and that in "all other cases, it is a conjunction of subordination." This is of relevance to several processes, such as optional frontings and deletions (see below).

9 There is some variation as concerns the inflected form of *velx-* for N.SG nouns; see Lowenstamm (1977: 199); Mark (1978: 244–245); Katz (1987b: 246).

As seen above, relative clauses by themselves do not trigger subject-verb inversion. This also is so with a bare possessive relative:

(77) di froj veməns bux ix hob [**hob ix] gəlejənt...
'the woman whose book I read...'

In this respect, relative clauses resemble indirect-question subordinate clauses. However, there are some crucial differences between indirect questions and relative clauses, discussed in Prince (1989: 406ff.). Most of these differences have to do with the fact that *vos* functions not as a true relative pronoun, but, rather, as a subordinating conjunction. For example, *vos*- relative clauses optionally permit a resumptive subject pronoun, whereas indirect questions do not:

(78) Der jid vos (er) zict dortn iz duk snajdər.
'The guy who (he) is sitting there is Duke Snider.'

(79) Ix vejs, ver [**er][10] zict dortn.
'I know who (**he) is sitting there.'

However, with a specific relative pronoun, the resumptive pronoun does not occur:

(80) Der jid velxər [**er] zict dortn iz duk snajdər.
'The guy who (**he) is sitting there is Duke Snider.'

Furthermore, as Prince (1989: 406) observes, the intensifier particle *-žə* may cliticize onto *wh*-pronouns in free relatives, indirect questions, and direct questions, but not in relative clauses:

(81) (Ix vil visn) ver žə es ligt dortn!
'(I want to know) who the hell is lying there!'

(82) **der jid vos-žə/velxər-žə ligt dortn (zol pejgərn!)
**'the guy who the hell is lying there (should croak!)'

To summarize, subject-verb inversion does not occur in basic relative clauses, whether they have a bare *wh*-relative pronoun, or one headed by a preposition. As expected, inversion also does not occur when *vos* functions as a subordinating conjunction. The conjunction *vos* may head a whole S COMP:

(83) Ix bin gliklәx vos du host gəkrogn di stipendjə.
'I'm happy that you got the fellowship.'

[10] The resumptive pronoun is specific (for number and gender), and is not to be confused with the expletive *es* which does, in fact, remain in (non-topicalized) indirect questions, e.g., *ix vejs, ver es zict dortn* 'I know who is sitting there.'

The status of *vos* as a conjunction further explains the presence of "resumptive" pronouns in *vos*-headed clauses (Lowenstamm 1977: 206):

(84) di froj vos ix ze zi . . .
'the woman that I see her . . . '

(85) der jid vos ix farloz zix af im . . .
'the guy that I depend on him . . . '

Relative clauses permit topicalization, which then triggers subject-verb inversion (Diesing 1990: 64–65):

(86)	der jid	vos	xajəm	vet	zen	šabəs	baj naxt . . .
	the guy	that	Khayim	shall	see	Saturday	at night

'the guy that Khayim will see Saturday at night . . . '

(87) der jid vos šabəs baj naxt vet xajəm zen . . .

Here, *vos* functions not as a relative pronoun, but, rather, as a conjunction. Subject-verb inversion occurs only if another sentence unit is present in "topic" position. Use of conjunction *vos* requires that the PP contain a regular pronoun, not a relative pronoun (*velxn*, *veman*). This "regular" PP then functions as a topicalized unit triggering inversion (Lowenstamm 1977: 214).

(88)	Der jid,	mit vemən	er	hot gəredt,	iz	majn šoxn.
	the guy	with whom	he	has spoken	is	my neighbor

'The guy with whom he spoke is my neighbor.'

(89) der jid, vos mit im hot er gəredt, iz majn šoxn

Similarly, consider the following possessive relative clauses:

(90)	der jid,	vemən s	hojz	mir	hobn	gəkojft . . .
	the guy	whose	house	we	have	bought

'the guy whose house we bought . . . '

(91)	der jid,	vos	zajn hojz	hobn	mir	gəkojft . . .
	the guy	what	his house	have	we	bought

'the guy whose house we bought . . . '

When the bare possessive relative NP *vemans hojz* occurs alone, subject-verb inversion does not occur. However, inversion does occur with conjunction *vos* + topicalized NP *zajn hojz*.

Finally, relative clauses permit deletion of the "resumptive" pronoun under certain conditions. Consider the following (from Lowenstamm 1977: 211–212):

(92) der jid vos mir hobn im gəzen in boston iz a grojsər lamdn
the guy that we have him seen in Boston is a great scholar

(93) der jid vos mir hobn Ø gəzen in boston . . .

The object pronoun may optionally delete. However, if another element is topicalized within the relative clause, the deletion may not occur:

(94) der jid vos in boston hobn mir im gəzen....
(95) der jid vos in boston hobn mir **Ø gəzen...

Additionally, Yiddish relative clauses may optionally delete bare *wh*-words, but not *wh*-words headed by a preposition (Lowenstamm 1977: 214; Hall 1967: 167):

(96) der man vemən ix ze → der man Ø ix ze
'the man (whom) I see'
(97) der man mit vemən/velxn ix red → der man mit **Ø ix red
'the man with **Ø I speak'

If the *wh*-relative pronoun is not deleted, *vos* may not co-occur. Lowenstamm (1977: 215) posits an optional rule of *vos*-insertion which may only apply if optional *wh*-deletion has already occurred: *der boxər vemən ix ze → der boxər Ø ix ze → der boxər vos ix ze* 'the lad that I see.'

Finally, Yiddish permits infinitival free relatives (JPA 1994: 416): *zi hot nit vos cu esn* 'she doesn't have anything (lit. what) to eat.'

6.2.6 OV features

The SVO structure of Yiddish, in both main and subordinate clauses, is typically pointed out as noteworthy in respect to German. German is classified as SOV, with a rule which fronts the inflected verb in main clause, but not in subordinate clause. However, Yiddish exhibits some features typical for OV languages. Among these are diverse phenomena concerning the syntax of verbs, including: passives; the order of verb particle and verb; periphrastic verbs (den Besten and Moed-van Walraven 1986). In all three instances, the complement precedes the non-inflected verb, something typical of OV languages.

Yiddish passives are formed by the verb *vern* 'become' plus a deverbalized past participle of the semantically main verb. If *vern* is inflected, it is moved in front of its complement; uninflected (infinitive or past participle) it follows its complement; e.g., with *gəkojft vern* 'to be bought':

(98) Dos hojz vert gəkojft.
the house becomes bought
'The house is bought.'
(99) Dos hojz muz gəkojft vern.
the house must bought become
'The house must be bought.'

(100) Dos hojz iz gəkojft gəvorn.
the house is bought become
'The house was bought.'

Similarly, a verb particle precedes the non-inflected verb; e.g., *avek-šikn* 'send away' (den Besten and Moed-van Walraven 1986: 118–119):

(101) Er šikt avek dem briv.
he sends away the letter
'He sends off the letter.'

(102) Er vet avek-šikn dem briv.
he shall away-send the letter
'He will send off the letter.'

(103) Er hot avek-gəšikt dem briv.
he has away sent the letter
'He sent off the letter.'

The periphrastic verbs (whether containing a complement of Germanic or HA origin) pattern similarly: *lib hobn* 'like' → *er hot lib* 'he likes'; *er vet lib hobn* 'he shall like'; *er hot lib gəhat* 'he liked'; *məgazəm zajn* 'exaggerate' → *er iz məgazəm* 'he exaggerates'; *er vet məgazəm zajn* 'he shall exaggerate'; *er hot məgazəm gəven* 'he exaggerated.' For all of the above, imperatives pattern syntactically as inflected verbs: *ver ufgəgesn durx a hunt*! 'get eaten up by a dog!'; *šik avek dem briv*! 'send the letter!'; *zaj nit məgazəm*! 'don't exaggerate!'

Sadock (1998) makes the case for seeing certain phenomena in Yiddish as vestiges of earlier OV syntax. He does not dispute that Yiddish is, synchronically, SVO in both main and subordinate clauses. Rather, it is in a piece of highly circumscribed behavior (concerning constraints on gapping) where a vestige of earlier verb-final syntax has managed to "sneak by" and survive.[11] JPA (1994: 411) also suggest possible OV vestiges in Yiddish as concerns clitic floating/climbing.

6.3 Constituent structures

6.3.1 *Noun phrases*

A full NP consists minimally of a HEAD – usually a noun, but sometimes a nominalized element (see below). The HEAD noun may be preceded by determiner [DET] and modifiers. The order of the elements in full NPs is largely fixed

[11] Sadock (1998: 225) notes that Slavic languages pattern in the relevant constructions differently from Yiddish, and that since Slavic languages never had verb-final word order, "we have to reject the idea that Yiddish arose by relexifying a Slavic language like Sorbian with Germanic words." Sadock thus argues against Wexler's (1987, 1991) hypothesis; see §2.1.6.

(Mark 1978: 390–393): DET + Adj + Noun, e.g., *di altə štot* 'the old city,' *a gutər plan* 'a good plan.' The rubric DET may include either an article or a possessive adjective – they may not co-occur:[12] *di altə štot* 'the old city,' *majn altə štot* 'my old city,' but not ***di majn*/***majn di altə štot*. The quantifier *alə* 'all' precedes the entire rest of the NP: *alə (dajnə) gutə fragəs* 'all (your) good questions.' Before the definite article, however, it occurs as *al*: *al di gutə fragəs* 'all the good questions,' *al dos guts* 'all the best.' Thus, *al-* inflects for the plural NP before a possessive adjective, but not before a definite article. In some ways, *al-di* is exceptional from the other quantifiers – *jedər* 'each, every,' *itləx* 'each,' *etləxə* 'several.' These may not co-occur with an article or a possessive adjective within an NP.

Yiddish NP structure may be represented in hierarchical tree form, where at each level the modifying element appears to the left of its head:

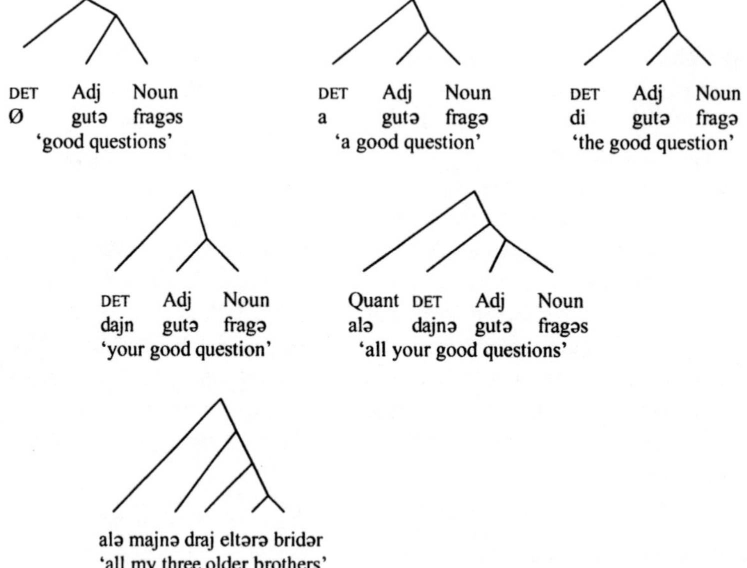

Note two points of variability in the order of elements in an NP. First, intensifier *o(t)* may occur before or after the DET it intensifies; thus, *ot der man* ~ *der-o man, ot dem man* ~ *dem-o man* 'this man.' Second, adverb *zejər* 'very' may only occur after the definite article; however, it may optionally move to before the indefinite article: *a zejər altər man* ~ *zejər an altər man* 'a very old man.'

[12] Commonly dealt with under the rubric SPEC in some recent approaches.

Mark (1978: 391) gives: *di najə cvejgorndikə hilcərnə hajzər* 'the new two-story wooden houses,' and claims that the order is fixed, with only one interpretation of structure possible (adapted from Mark):

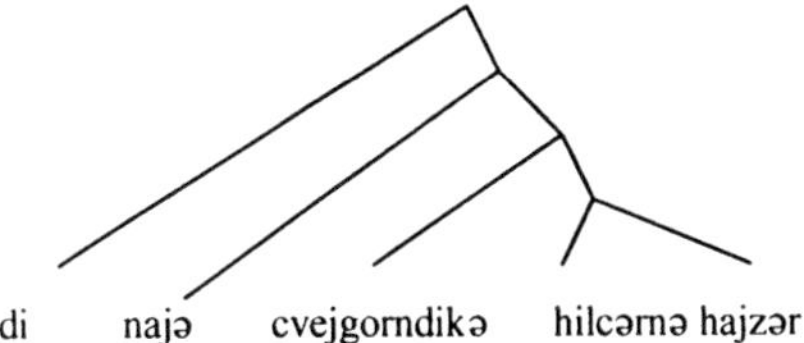

In a series of adjectival modifiers, the one closest to the noun is primary. Thus, Mark (p. 391) contrasts: *dos klejnə vajsə cigələ* 'the little *white* kid/goat' vs. *dos vajsə klejnə cigələ* 'the white *little* kid/goat.'

Adverbs or other elements modifying an adjective occur to the left of the adjective; thus: *der gut gəšribənər tekst* 'the well-written text'; *der zejər gutər vajn* 'the very good wine'; *di dervajl*$_{\text{[Adv]}}$ *nox*$_{\text{[Adv]}}$ *vajtə hilf* 'the in-the-meantime still distant help.' In *der gut gəšribənər tekst*, *gut* is unambiguously an adverb, and is fixed as to word order. If it were used as an (inflected) adjective, it could occur (contrastively) either before or after *gəšribənər*.

In predicate position, a base form of the adjective may occur as a complement of semantically light verbs of the type 'be,' 'become,' etc. The adjective is uninflected for number or gender: *der man/di froj/dos kind iz gliklәx* 'the man/woman/child is happy'; *di menčn zajnən gliklәx* 'the people are happy.' Zaretski (1926) views these uninflected forms as "adverbs," since they do not function here within an NP. In this regard, adverbs may regularly occur as complements of most verbs (not just in semantically light verbs), e.g., *er zingt gut* 'he sings well,' *mir gejən štilinkərhejt* 'we go silently.'

On the other hand, Yiddish regularly permits inflected predicate adjectives when they are part of an NP, e.g., *der man iz a gliklәxər, di froj iz a gliklәxə* 'the man/woman is a happy one,' *di menčn zajnən gliklәxə* 'the people are happy ones.' When a predicate adjective refers to a neuter noun, a special nominal suffix *-s* occurs: *dos kind iz a gliklәxs* 'the child is a happy one' (vs. *dos kind iz gliklәx* 'the child is happy'). When the predicate NP refers to an earlier object NP, the expected case inflections occur: *ix hob im gəfunən a gliklәxn* 'I found him a happy one.' In instances of oblique rather than nominative predicate adjectives, Yiddish appears not to allow a bare predicate adjective, but, rather, requires an NP; thus: *ix hob gəfunən dem man a gliklәxn* (***gliklәx*).

6.3.2 *Possessive adjectives and the* NP

Possessive adjectives pattern in some respects like adjectives, in other respects like a DET. They inflect like regular adjectives when occurring after their head noun: *der brudər majnər, dem brudər majnəm, di švestər majnə, mit der švestər majnər, dos bux majns*, etc. Possessive adjectives in attributive position take the -ə suffix before plural nouns, but take a zero inflection or no inflection in attributive position before singular nouns, irrespective of gender or case: *majn brudər, mit majn švestər, in majn bux.*

However, in several crucial respects, possessive adjectives pattern like a DET. First, they do not co-occur with another DET within an NP (with the exception of *al-ə*). Second, determiners may not occur in predicate position "alone"; rather, they must come as part of a larger NP package; thus: *der tiš iz alt* 'the table is old,' but not *der tiš iz **majn* 'the table is **my' (nor *majn tiš iz **der* 'my table is **the/that/this'). To the extent that possessive DETs occur alone in predicate NPs, they must pick up an NP inflection: *der tiš iz majnər, dos bux iz dajns*, etc. With a definite article DET, an empty nominal/adjectival element is inserted to carry the necessary inflection: *majn tiš iz der dozikər* 'my table is this/that one.' When an adjective is present, it carries the NP inflection, and insertion of the empty element *dozik-* is not needed: *majn tiš iz der (**dozikər) altər* 'my table is the old (one)'; likewise, *der tiš iz majn-Ø altər* 'the table is my old (one).' A post-nominal possessive adjective DET is in its own separate NP: *der brudər majnər*. This is what allows the apparent co-occurrence of definite article and possessive adjective, since they are in separate NPs in apposition, similar to separate full NPs in apposition, e.g., *a mejdl a šejns* 'a girl – a pretty one,' *a park a šejnər* 'a park – a pretty one.' When possessive NPs occur before their head NP, they behave as a DET, and thus block a separate DET in the head NP: *der bobəs/mojšəs (**dos) bux* 'grandma's/Moyshe's (**the) book.' When a possessive NP follows its head NP, it must occur in a PP: *dos bux fun der bobn / fun mojšən.*

6.3.3 NP-NP constructions

Yiddish has hierarchical NP-NP constructions, where one NP is a modifier or complement of the other. In *majn brudər/švestər/bux* 'my brother/sister/book,' the *majn* is in the same NP as the head noun. However, consider:

(104) majnər a brudər
'one of my brothers'

(105) majnə a švestər
'one of my sisters'

(106) majns a bux
'one of my books'

Here, *majnər/majnə/majns* occurs alone in a separate NP, and is fully inflected, even in the singular; thus, *mit majnəm a brudər* 'with one of my brothers,' *mit majnər a švestər* 'with one of my sisters.' The inflected *majn-* occurs adjacent to a DET (the indefinite article), something which may not occur within a single

NP. The occurrence of strings like *majns a brudər* 'one of my brothers,' with *-s* (*brudər* is masculine, not neuter) instead of expected *majnər a brudər* suggests possibly a development-in-progress toward uniform *-s* inflection when the possessive form stands alone in an NP; thus, even after a preposition there can occur: *mit majnəm* ~ *majns a brudər* 'with one of my brothers.' Note also full possessive NP: *dem rovs an ejnikl* 'one of the rabbi's grandchildren.'

Another example of NP-NP involves partitive constructions, e.g., *a gloz tej* 'a glass (of) tea,' *najn mos rejd* 'nine measures of speech,' *štikər holc* 'pieces (of) wood,' *a bintl briv* 'a bundle (of) letters.' Here, the second NP stands in modifying relationship to the first. The first NP may take both a DET and an adjective: *a grojs gloz gutər tej*. The second NP in partitive constructions may take an adjective, but not a DET; thus: *a gloz gutər tej* 'a glass of good tea,' *a bintl altə briv* 'a bundle of old letters.' However, when a DET occurs in the second NP, a PP with preposition *fun* is required: *a gloz fun majn/dem gutn tej* 'a glass of my/the good tea'; *a bintl fun dajnə/di altə briv* 'a bundle of your/the old letters.' Addition of a possessive NP creates NP-NP-NP constructions, e.g., *mojšəs bintl briv* 'Moyshe's bundle of letters', *dem zejdns gloz gutər tej* 'grandfather's glass of good tea.' Note also: *a bintl altə briv dajnə* 'a bundle of old letters of yours.'

A few units of time which normally have a regular plural form will use their singular form after numerical quantifiers; thus: *dos jor – di jorn* 'the year-s,' *di šo – di šoən* 'the hour-s,' but *draj jor* 'three years,' *mit draj šo curik* 'three hours ago' (vs. *draj xadošəm* 'three months,' *draj voxn* 'three weeks,' etc., with plural form of the noun).[13] Contrast: *hundərt jor* '(one) hundred years' vs. *hundərtər jorn* 'hundreds of years.' The latter is a partitive construction, where *hundərtər* and *jorn* are in separate NPs; thus, *jorn* takes its regular plural form.

The relationship between the NPs in NP-NP constructions, while semantically clear, presents problems in terms of morphological description. Consider:

(107) [a gloz] [gutər tej]
'a glass (of) good tea'

(108) [a tog] [šverə arbət]
'a day (of) hard work'

In Yiddish the two NPs in a partitive construction are assigned a single grammatical case. Thus, post-prepositionally, we find dative: *mit a gloz gutn tej* 'with a glass (of) good tea,' *nox a tog šverər arbət* 'after a day (of) hard work.' As a direct object, the accusative is found in both NPs: (*ix hob lib*) *a gloz gutn tej* / *a tog šverə arbət* '(I like) a glass (of) good tea / a day (of) hard work.' The absence of a regular genitive case in Yiddish likely contributes to the situation;

[13] Singular or plural with non-numerical quantifiers needs further examination; cf. *a sax jorn* 'many years' vs. *etləxə jor* 'several years.' It may be that *a sax* 'many' is somehow felt by speakers to be part of a partitive construction, lit. 'a-sum-of' + X, thus permitting plural form *jorn*.

there is simply no case-marking strategy (other than possessive *-s* for human possessors) available to show a hierarchical relationship. Compare with StG, where the second NP is in the genitive case, regardless of the case of the first NP: NOM *ein Glas / eine Tasse guten Tees, ein Tag schwerer Arbeit*; DAT *einem Glas / einer Tasse guten Tees*; ACC *einen Tag schwerer Arbeit.*

In both Yiddish and German these NP-NP constructions break down under pressure, though in structurally distinct ways. In Yiddish, if the second NP contains a DET, the full PP with PREP *fun* must be used: [a gloz] [fun dem/dajn gutn tej] 'a glass of the/your good tea'; *hundərtər bixər*, but *hundərtər fun undzəre bixər* 'hundreds of our books'; also permissible is *hundərtər bixər undzəre* 'hundreds of books of ours.' In German, problems arise for some speakers when an adjective is inserted in the second NP in, e.g., [eine Flasche] [Wein] 'a bottle (of) wine.' For most speakers, *eine Flasche Wein* is unproblematic. However, many (educated) speakers hesitate or vacillate when an adjective is added: *eine Flasche deutschen Weins*$_{[GEN]}$ ~ *deutschen Wein*$_{[ACC]}$, the latter based on the pragmatic assumption that *deutschen Wein* is the direct object of what they are ordering in a restaurant (thus, this is similar to Yiddish). However, the second NP in German *ein* (~ *einen* ~ *einem*) *Tag schwerer Arbeit* seems unproblematically genitive. Also seemingly unproblematic in StG is when the second NP contains a DET; thus: *eine Flasche des deutschen Weins*; *der Besuch meines guten Freundes* 'the visit of my good friend' (or with a PP: *eine Flasche von dem deutschen Wein*; *der Besuch von meinem guten Freund*).

Another limit on NP-NP constructions in Yiddish concerns the type containing a reduced embedded sentence. JPA (1994: 408) write: "any noun phrase may in fact occur in second position, whether it contains an adjective or not, so long as it can be understood predicatively"; thus: *ejnər a jid* 'one (who is) a Jew/guy'; *a məlaməd a kabcn* 'a teacher (who is) a pauper'; *ejnər a jid a məlaməd* 'one (who is a) Jew/guy (who is) a teacher.' On the surface, these look like appositives. There seem to be limits on this type of condensing, whereby only one NP in the set may contain an adjective: *ejnər an altər jid* 'one old guy'; *ejnər a jid an altər məlaməd* 'one guy who is an old teacher'; but not: ***ejnər an altər jid a gutər məlaməd*. The question arises as to whether it is only the final NP which may take the adjective or other COMP. Thus, *ejnər a jid a məlaməd fun varšə* 'one guy – a teacher from Warsaw,' but not ***ejnər a jid [**fun varšə] a məlaməd*.

The negative particle *kejn* is blocked from occurring in an indefinite NP, if that NP is itself part of a larger NP-NP construction. Compare the negated forms of the following:

(109) er iz [a xavər] 'he is a friend' → er iz nit kejn xavər
(110) er is [majnər] [a xavər] 'he's one of my friends' → er iz nit majnər a xavər

Here, *kejn* is blocked: *er iz nit majnər a [**kejn] xavər*. For the negation of super-NPs speakers will frequently resort to circumlocutions such as: *er iz nit fun majnə xavejrəm*, lit. 'he is not from my friends,' or *er iz mir nit kejn xavər*, lit. 'he is (for) me not any friend,' or simply, *er iz nit kejn xavər majnər*.

6.3.4 NP and PP

A PP COMP of an NP will immediately follow its head NP: *der məlaməd fun varšə hot gəkojft a bux* 'the teacher from Warsaw bought a book.' The PP [fun varšə] follows its head [der məlaməd]. Similarly, in *der məlaməd hot gəkojft a bux fun varšə*, the PP [fun varšə] modifies [a bux]. When there is more than one PP COMP of an NP, a hierarchical relationship is reflected in the syntax. A PP with *fun*, expressing a genitive relationship, will immediately follow its head NP, ahead of sentence-adverbial PP; thus, Mark (1978: 392) gives:

(111)	di foršungən	[fun di lectə jorn]	[vegn der atomišər energjə]
	the researches	of the recent years	about the atomic energy

Differing orders reflect differing relationships/meanings (p. 392):

(112)	di haxonəs	[fun gancn hojzgəzind]	[cum jontəv]
	the preparations	of the whole household	to the holiday
(113)	di haxonəs	[cum jontəv]	[fun gancn hojzgəzind]
	the preparations	to the holiday	of the whole household

In (112), the PP [fun gancn hojzgəzind] tells us what kind of preparations these are; in the latter example, the PP is a COMP of the PP [cum jontəv], and thus tells us what kind of a holiday it is. Furthermore, one must distinguish between PPs which modify nouns and those which are true complements of nouns. A true COMP PP will strongly tend to be adjacent to the noun it associates with, while placement of a modifier PP is freer (M. Diesing, p.c.); thus, in *der libhobər fun bejsbol* 'the fan of baseball,' *fun bejsbol* is a complement/argument deriving from 'like baseball.' However, in *der libhobər fun bruklin* 'the fan from Brooklyn,' the PP modifies the NP. When both PPs occur here, the true argument will occur closer to the NP: *der libhobər fun bejsbol fun bruklin* 'the fan of baseball from Brooklyn,' not ***der libhobər fun bruklin fun bejsbol* **the fan from Brooklyn of baseball.'

6.3.5 NP + S-COMP

Similar to NP + PP-COMP is NP + S-COMP. The S-COMP follows its head NP, forming a single sentence unit, which is then followed by the finite verb; thus:

(114) Der fakt [vos du host nit kejn gelt] iz nit vixtik.
'The fact [that you have no money] is not important.'

6.3.6 *Verb phrases*

The VP consists of the verbal group and any NP arguments required by the main verb, as well as adverbials of time, manner, and place. The verbal group contains the verb(s) and verb particles. Constituents may be further modified by adverbs. Our interest here is in the basic order of constituents within the VP. Certain movements within the VP are discussed here because they are fundamental and necessary for description of the VP. However, outright movement processes concerning all or part of the VP are held for §6.4.

A simple VP consists maximally of one finite verb (including here imperatives). All tenses and aspects are formed with an AUX verb; thus, in all forms other than the present indicative, the main verb will occur in a non-finite form (infinitive or past participle).[14] The AUX (as well as modal verbs) precedes the main verb, both in main and subordinate clauses, e.g., *ix hob*$_{[\text{AUX}]}$ *gəvust*$_{[\text{MAIN VERB}]}$, *az er vet*$_{[\text{AUX}]}$ *zingən* $_{[\text{MAIN VERB}]}$ *dos lid* 'I knew that he was going to sing the song.' As a new verb – AUX or modal – is added, it picks up the conjugation, and changes the previously finite verb to the appropriately triggered non-finite form; thus:

(115) Du zingst.
'You sing.'
(116) Du kenst zingən.
'You can sing.'
(117) Du vilst kenən zingən.
'You want to be able to sing.'
(118) Du host gəvolt kenən zingən.
'You wanted to be able to sing.'
(119) Du vest veln kenən zingən.
'You are going to want to be able to sing.'

However we wish to represent the formal structure of tense, aspect, mood, and the passive, the order of the elements relative to each other is: tense (AUX) – modal(s) – main verb; thus:

(120) Du zingst.
'You sing.'
(121) Du vest zingən.
'You will sing.'
(122) Du vest kenən zingən.
'You will be able to sing.'

[14] One possible exception to this is the singulative aspect (see below).

(123) Du vest darfn kenən zingən.
'You will have to be able to sing.'

(124) Du host gədarft kenən zingən.
'You had to be able to sing.'

The future perfect is formed by using the conjugated future marker + infinitive *hobn* + past participle of the main verb: *du vest hobn gəzungən* 'you will have sung.' Whereas the verb *hobn* is generally seen as a primary AUX for (past) tense formation, here it is pushed out of its finite form by introduction of the future marker. In the future perfect *hobn* functions aspectually, rather than as a tense marker. Similarly, the future marker and modals may occur with passive constructions:

(125) Dos lid vert gəzungən.
'The song is sung.'

(126) Dos lid vet gəzungən vern.
'The song will be sung.'

(127) Dos lid ken gəzungən vern.
'The song can be sung.'

Generally, a main verb is pushed to the infinitive by introduction of a new verb into the VP. The two main exceptions are the past-tense AUX (*hobn* and *zajn*) and the subjunctivizer *volt-*; these generally trigger the past participle.[15] This triggering is automatic; thus, the "mixed modes" noted by Zaretski (1926: 89–90): *zol hobn gəšribn* 'has supposedly written,' *hobn gəzolt šrajbn* 'were supposed to write.'

The diverse phenomena where the verbal element consists of two verbal heads (den Besten and Moed-van Walraven 1986; and §5.17) all concern an element which occurs before non-finite forms of their associated verb, but after the finite forms; cf. periphrastic verbs (*bojdək zajn* 'check' – *er iz bojdək* 'he checks'); passives (*gəšribn vern* 'be written' – *es vert gəšribn* 'it is/becomes written'); verb particle verbs (*ojs-trinkən* 'drink up' – *er trinkt ojs dos bir* 'he drinks up [all] the beer').

The singulative aspect presents a special problem (see also Taube 1987; Diesing 1998, 2000). It is formed with a bleached verb *gebn* 'give' ~ *ton* 'do' + deverbalized main-verb root; e.g., *er tut/git a lax* 'he lets out a laugh,' *er tut a kuk* 'he gives a glance.' The problem concerns main verbs which contain a separable verb particle, e.g., *uf-esn* 'eat up entirely,' *on-šrajbn* 'write to completion,' *arojs-špringən* 'jump out.' Consider: *er git an es-uf dem epl* 'he gobbles up the apple.' If a simple verbal group is limited to a single finite

[15] Some varieties of Yiddish use infinitive form of the main verb in *volt*-constructions.

verb – here, *git* – then presumably the main verb should not be a finite form. It is here a deverbalized verb root. Yet it is not fully nominalized, since in nouns derived from such verbs the particle always precedes the root: *on-zogn* > *der onzog* 'message.' Thus, there is something still verbal about the main verb root in the singulative construction. Further evidence of this is provided by the strong verbs, which here use the non-past participle root: *er tut a špring arojs* 'he gives a quick jump out,' *er tut a trink ojs dem vajn* 'he gulps down the wine' (whereas the nouns are based on the past-participle root: *der trunk* 'the drink,' *der šprung* 'the leap').

The pluperfect is marked by the use of an "extra" *gəhat* (past participle of *hobn*); thus: *er hot gəzen dem film* 'he saw/has seen the film,' *er hot gəhat gəzen dem film* 'he had seen the film.' The *gəhat* is placed syntactically like a verb particle, preceding the main verb (past participle), since the pronoun object and the negativizer *nit* occur after the conjugated verb and before the *gəhat*: *er hot im nit gəhat gəzen* 'he hadn't seen him.'

The unmarked order of constituents in the VP is: verbal group – indirect object – direct object – time adverbial – place and manner adverbial.[16] However, many things may intervene, causing different orders. A PRO form will normally occur before a full-form constituent. Thus, as full object NPs, the DAT precedes the ACC in (Birnbaum 1979a: 295): *di mamə git dem kind*$_{[DAT]}$ *dos bux*$_{[ACC]}$ 'the mother gives the child the book'; however, with a PRO-form: *di mamə git es*$_{[ACC]}$ *dem kind*$_{[DAT]}$; *di mamə git im*$_{[DAT]}$ *dos bux*$_{[ACC]}$. If both objects are pronouns, the order ACC – DAT may occur: *zi zogt es*$_{[ACC]}$ *im*$_{[DAT]}$ 'she tells it (to) him.' Here, rhythm, emphasis, or pragmatic factors may play a role. A DAT PP will regularly come after the ACC: *er zingt a lid far zajn hunt* 'he sings a song for his dog.' Similarly, a PP adverbial will occur after a plain adverbial: *er iz gəgangən dem gancn tog mit zajn hunt* 'he walked all day with his dog.'

The unmarked situation is for a pronoun object to follow immediately the finite verb in complex verb groups: *di talmidəm hobn gəlejənt dos bux* → *di talmidəm hobn es gəlejənt* 'the pupils read the book / it'; *ix vil zen di menčn* → *ix vil zej zen* 'I want to see the people / them.' However, in clauses with topicalization of another element, V-2 will put PRO-subject after the verb, and before the PRO-object:

(128) Ix vel im zen morgn.
'I shall see him tomorrow.'

(129) Morgn vel ix im zen.
'It's tomorrow that I'll see him.'

[16] Reference grammars are in agreement that time adverbials normally come first. However, I have been unable to find any further statement concerning place and manner adverbials, suggesting perhaps a freedom in the relative order of the two.

If, however, the subject is a full NP, and the object a pronoun, then the PRO-object occurs before the subject in instances of topicalization:

(130) Der sojxər vet zen dem kojnə morgn.
'The merchant will see the customer tomorrow.'

(131) Morgn vet der sojxər zen dem kojnə.
'Tomorrow the merchant will see the customer.'

(132) Morgn vet im zen der sojxər.
'Tomorrow the merchant will see him.'

Likewise, reflexive pronoun *zix* follows the finite verb, unless V-2 inversion puts a PRO-subject after the verb:

(133) Engliš lernt er zix.
'It's English that he's studying.'

(134) Engliš lernt zix der man.
'It's English that the man is studying.'

As opposed to a full adverbial (including PP adverbials), a PRO form of an adverb may also move (non-contrastively) into the verb complex:

(135) Mir veln zingən dem erštn maj.
'We are going to sing on May Day.'

(136) Mir veln zingən um šabəs.
'We are going to sing on the Sabbath.'

(137) Mir veln bald zingən.
'We are going to sing soon.'

Thus, the PRO-adverb intervenes in the verb complex in: *er meg dortn blajbn* 'he may stay there,' but not in *er meg blajbn in park* 'he may stay in the park.' In marked order putting the PRO-adverb after the verb complex conveys emphasis (and receives special stress): *der tatə vet bald kumən* vs. *der tatə vet kumən báld* 'Father will come soon' (Mark 1978: 389).

With complex verbs there is some freedom concerning PRO-object placement (including reflexive *zix*), as a device for emphasis. Mark (1978: 382–383) gives all the following as acceptable:

(138) Zi hot mit im zix gətrofn cvej mol a tog.
she has with him REFL met two times per day
'She met (with) him twice a day.'

(139) Zi hot zix mit im gətrofn cvej mol a tog.
'She met (with) him twice a day.'

(140) Zi hot amol šojn gəhat zix gətrofn mit im.
'She had already met (with) him.'

(141) Zi hot zix šojn amol gəhat gətrofn mit im.
'She had already met (with) him.'

However, Mark (1978: 382) states that the *zix* may not be "too far" from the main verb; he gives as ungrammatical: ***di kindər hobn zix noxn plucəmdikn tojt fun zejər mutər nit gəhat vu ahincuton* 'the children didn't have [**REFL] anywhere to turn after the sudden death of their mother.' The reflexive pronoun *zix* relates here to the verb *ahinton*. By "too far" Mark presumably means actual length of the intervening string of elements, since an object pronoun may be extracted out of its infinitival S (see climbing, §6.6.1). However, structural factors are also at play. Mark (p. 382) claims that *zix* cannot be separated from its verb by a non-AUX verb; thus, he disallows the following:

(142)	**alə	zajnə	frajnd	zajnən	zix	gəkumən	gəzegənən	mit im
	all	his	friends	are	REFL	come	part	from him

Here, *zix* is the COMP of verb *gəzegənen*, and is constrained from raising to the main-clause VP containing the verb complex AUX + *gəkumən*. However, just such a raising occurs in climbing (§6.6.1): *ix hob ajx fargesn cu zogn*, lit. 'I-have-you-forgotten-to-say' 'I forgot to tell you.' Thus, Mark's restriction may be prescriptive rather than descriptive. Furthermore, there may be a distinction between *zix* in truly reflexive verbs such as *lernən zix* 'learn,' *špiln zix* 'play' vs. reflexive pronouns which are true object pronouns transformed into reflexive forms by the syntax; cf. *er hot zix gəvolt šlogn* 'he wanted to hit himself' (< verb *šlogn* 'hit') vs. *er hot gəvolt zix šlogn* 'he wanted to fight / be combative' (< reflexive verb *šlogn zix*).[17]

The *zix* may precede or follow its nominalized infinitive (or past participle or gerund form); thus Mark (1978: 383) allows both – *trefn zix mit im/zix trefn mit im hob ix šojn opgəredt* 'I already arranged to meet with him' – though Mark prefers the latter option, *zix trefn*. However, when the definite article precedes the nominalized infinitive, *zix* obligatorily occurs afterward: *dos trefn zix* (p. 383). Furthermore, Mark cautions against use (in StY!) of *zix* in sentence-final position when the sentence contains more than a single simple verb; thus: *mir kumən zix gəzegənən* lit. 'we-come-REFL-part' 'we come to say goodbye (to each other),' not ***mir kumən gəzegənən zix*. The prescriptivist caution against this in StY likely reflects the fact that many speakers were, in fact, using *zix* here post-verbally, probably based on contact influence from reflexive verbs in Slavic (Mordkhe Schaechter, p.c.).

A nominalized inifinitive may function as the object COMP of a verb (Birnbaum 1979a: 294): *ix hejb on cu farštejn* 'I begin to understand.' When the verb infinitive is the object COMP of a (non-modal) verb, *cu* 'to' is

[17] See also Wolf (1974: 27–28).

inserted.[18] The infinitival object may itself take an object: *ix hejb on cu farštejn dos ejsək* 'I begin to understand the matter.'

Verb particles present some problems for the syntax. Most often they behave like COMPs of the verb. A PRO object intercedes between verb and verb particle (*er trinkt ojs dos bir* → *er trinkt es ojs* 'he drinks up the beer / drinks it up'). However, there are fuzzy areas between verb particle and PRO adverbs. Mark (1978: 372) gives several examples with *ahejm* 'homeward.' In some examples, *ahejm* patterns like a verb particle, in others, like an adverb (see §5.17, discussion on *cuzamən*). Some of the fuzziness reflects semantic differences. Zaretski (1926: 127) contrasts *arop* in *er kúkt aróp* (two independent stresses), vs. compound-word stress in *er kùkt aróp* (one main stress), in the past tense: *er hot gəkúkt aróp* 'he looked down' contrasts with *er hot arópgəkùkt* 'he lowered his eyes'; similarly, infinitives: *arópkùkn* 'lower one's eyes' vs. *kúkn aróp* 'look down.'

Some of the placement issues are best seen in terms of regional tendencies. Thus, Mark (1978: 381) gives all of the following as grammatical renditions of 'I'll come to you (= your home) soon': *ix kum bald arajn cu dir in štub* ~ *ix kum bald cu dir in štub arajn* ~ *ix kum bald cu dir arajn in štub*. Mark says that for NEY speakers the verb particle tends to be closer to its matrix verb, whereas for CY/SEY speakers it tends to be further away, or in final position.[19] Even here, the fuzziness of the boundary between true verb particle and adverb is apparent. Thus, there is a tendency among CY/SEY speakers (M. Schaechter, p.c.) to doubled *arajn* (given here in StY form): *ix vel arajnforn in štot arajn* 'I'll travel into town.' Here, it might be argued that *in štot arajn* is a PP with a two-part PREP *in ... arajn* (similar to *mit ... curik* 'ago,' *in ... arum* 'from now'); in this view, PREP *arajn* would thus be distinct from verb particle *arajn*. However, rhythmic factors may play a role here; there is perhaps less of a tendency to use double *arajn* with a finite matrix verb; e.g., *ix kum* (***arajn*) *in štot arajn* ~ or *ix kum arajn in štot*, but not *ix kum arajn in štot* (***arajn*).[20]

6.3.7 Negation

The position of the negative particle *ni(š)t* depends on several factors (Mark 1978: 393–394). The unmarked or neutral position is after the finite verb; here, it generally serves to negate the whole clause. Elsewhere, the *nit* is marked

[18] There can be some variation as to how obligatory *cu*-insertion is with certain verbs; e.g., with *gejn* 'go' there is no *cu*-insertion: *er gejt šlofn* 'he goes (**to) sleep'; see Birnbaum (1979a: 294).

[19] For StY, Mark (1978: 382) recommends a middle ground, i.e., after the verb, but before the adverbial(s).

[20] A perhaps comparable use of doubled forms occurs among NEY speakers: *mit ... dermit*, *cu ... dercu*, etc. (M. Schaechter, p.c.).

and serves to emphasize that constituent which it immediately precedes. Thus, Mark gives:

(143) Er kumt nit hajnt cu mir.
'He isn't coming to me today.'
(144) Nit er kumt hajnt cu mir.
(= someone else is coming)
(145) Er kumt hajnt nit cu mir.
(= he's visiting someone else, not me)
(146) Nit hajnt kumt er cu mir.
(= he's coming another day)

A contrastive use of *nit* may be expressed by marked intonation as well (Zaretski 1926: 161).

When the verb complex contains an AUX or modal + infinitive or past participle, Mark (1978: 394) notes a tendency to a difference between written and spoken style. In spoken language, *nit* occurs right after the finite verb; for formal written language, *nit* precedes the infinitive / past participle; thus, spoken *er vet nit morgn in der fri kumən cu undz* vs. written *er vet morgn in der fri nit kumən cu undz* 'he will not come to us tomorrow morning.' When a PRO-object or PRO-adverb intervenes, the placement of *nit* differs. However, this may be due to differences in the movement of the PRO element. Note also the position of *nit* relative to the pluperfect marker *gəhat*: *er hot nit gəhat gəzungən* 'he hadn't sung.'

Yiddish negative concord spans the negative clause (JPA 1994: 417): *kejnər darf zix kejnmol nit ajln* 'no-one should ever hurry' (lit. 'no-one-shouldn't-ever-not-hurry'). Negative concord (use of *kejn*) is blocked by definiteness: a definite article, possessive adjective, or proper name ('a non-referring argument'; p. 417); thus: *er hot nit gəzungən kejn lid* 'he didn't sing any song,' but *er hot nit gəzungən dos lid* 'he didn't sing the song.' Negative concord is not a local or linear rule. This is seen when a constituent is topicalized: *er zingt nit kejn lid* 'he isn't singing any song' → *kejn lid zingt er nit*. Not using the *kejn* where it is otherwise appropriate (unmarked) is a means of expressing emphasis (Mark 1978: 394): *du bist mir nit kejn frajnd* 'you're not a friend of mine' vs. *du bist mir nit a frajnd* 'you're no friend to me.' Similarly, marked use of *kejn* where it is normally blocked (by definiteness) expresses emphasis: *ix ken nit mojšə(n)* 'I don't know Moyshe' vs. *ix ken nit kejn mojšə* 'I don't know any (anybody named) Moyshe.' Negative concord illustrates the distinction of true arguments from verb particles ("complements of periphrastic verbs"): *er hot nit xasənə gəhat* 'he didn't get married' vs. *er hot nit gəhat kejn xasənə* 'he didn't have a wedding' (JPA 1994: 417).

Note the syntactic implications of short vs. long form predicate adjectives as concerns negation. With the short form, NP negation particle *kejn* may not attach; with the long form it does apply; thus, StY *er iz nit* [**kejn] *alt* 'he is not [**kejn] old'; *er iz nit kejn altər* 'he is not an (=no) old (one).'

6.4 Sub-categorization

It is commonly observed for language in general that verbs may differ in their basic properties as to what kinds of COMPS they may take, whether the COMPS are obligatory or optional, etc. This in turn affects the formal structural description, and defines the constraints on specific movement rules. For example, verbs like *esn* 'eat,' *lejənən* 'read' are described as regularly taking a direct-object COMP, while (ditransitive) verbs like *dercejln* 'tell,' *brengən* 'bring' regularly, and, in some sense, basically, have two argument COMPS, a direct object "what" and an indirect object "to/for whom." For some verbs the filling of the COMP slot is obligatory, for others it is optional. The verb *helfn* 'help' regularly has only a dative object, while an adjunct PP may tell us "with what": *er helft mir* (*mit matəmatik*) 'he helps $me_{[DAT]}$ (with $math_{[PP]}$).' For a verb such as *lejənən* 'read' or *zingən* 'sing' the accusative COMP is basic, and a dative COMP is less necessary: *er zingt mir a lid* 'he sings $me_{[DAT]}$ a $song_{[ACC]}$,' where solely an ACC COMP is grammatical – *er zingt a lid* while solely a DAT COMP is less so: ??***er zingt mir*. A few verbs such as *lernən* 'teach,' *kostn* 'cost' are exceptional in that they inherently take two ACC COMPS (Birnbaum 1979a: 294): *er lernt mix derəx-erəc* 'he teaches $me_{[ACC]}$ $respect_{[ACC]}$.' The verb *betn* 'ask (= request)' takes an ACC object, but when a second object is added, the original object undergoes a circumlocution to a PP (U. Weinreich 1949: 100):

(147) Bet di $\check{s}vest\partial r_{[ACC]}$.
'Ask (= request of) your sister.'

(148) Bet dos bux baj der švestər.
ask the book at the sister.
'Ask your sister for the book.'

Similarly, the verb *fregn* 'ask (= inquire)' may take two ACC objects. When it does, however, one of the objects is often closely semantically linked to *fregn* itself – it is a noun denoting a type of question: *fragə* ~ *kašə* ~ *šajlə*, etc., or indefinite *epəs* 'something'; thus:

(149) Er fregt $mix_{[ACC]}$ a $frag\partial_{[ACC]}$ / $ep\partial s_{[ACC]}$.
'he asks me a question / something.'

This differs from the sub-categorization of *šteln* 'place; put,' where *fragə* then is a true object, and the human recipient is in the dative:

(150) Er štelt $mir_{[DAT]}$ a $frag\partial_{[ACC]}$.
'He asks me a question.'

The description of bleached verbs used to form the singulative aspect differs from that of their full-verb counterparts *ton* 'do' and *gebn* 'give.' The full verb *gebn* has its recipient in the DAT, the thing being given in the ACC:

(151) Er git der froj$_{[DAT]}$ a kuš$_{[ACC]}$.
'He gives the woman$_{[DAT]}$ a kiss$_{[ACC]}$.'

However, in the singulative aspect, *gebn* is bleached, and the recipient – here, the woman – is the accusative object of the verb *kušn* 'to kiss':

(152) Er git a kuš di froj$_{[ACC]}$
'He quickly kisses the woman.'

Finally, there is a class of verbs which typically govern an S-COMP; these are usually verbs of knowing, telling, thinking, believing, etc. (Hall 1967: 81–83). We may also speak of verbs with strongly vs. weakly governed (ACC) objects; only the former may undergo passivization (Kahan-Newman 1983: 82–83).

6.5 Grammatical functions

This section deals with the main grammatical functions: subjects, direct and indirect objects, and adverbials (see also Kahan-Newman 1983: 80–129). Solely looking at structural categories (NP, VP, etc.) is sometimes insufficient. Consider, for example, the situation of V-2. The unmarked position of the finite verb in declarative clauses is "second sentence unit." However, consider: *a štikl brojt ligt af dajn telər* 'a piece (of) bread is on your plate.' Here, the subject 'a piece (of) bread' consists of two NPS: [a štikl] and [brojt]. It could be argued that such NP-NP constructions are joined into a single higher-level NP which thus serves as a single sentence unit. However, consider:

(153) Der man fun bendin hot gəšikt a briv.
the man from Będzin has sent a letter
'The man from Będzin sent a letter.'

(154) Der man hot gəšikt a briv fun bendin.
the man has sent a letter from Będzin
'The man sent a letter from Będzin.'

Clearly, the placement of the PP tells us which NP it modifies. In the first example, it tells us that the man is from Będzin, in the second example, that the letter was sent from Będzin. This is describable in terms of phrase structures. However, when the PP is ambiguously either a COMP of an NP, or an adverbial, then we resort to our notions of grammatical functions. Consider: *ix hob gəzen dem hunt fun park* 'I saw the dog from the park.' If the PP *fun park* is a COMP of the NP, it may not be separated or extracted from its NP in topicalization: *dem hunt fun park hob ix gəzen* 'It's the dog from the park that I saw'; ungrammatical are both: ***dem hunt hob ix gəzen fun park*; ***fun park hob ix gəzen dem hunt* (if we are talking about the dog from the park). On the other hand, if it is an adverbial of place, *fun park* 'from the park' – which relates to the clause as a whole – then it may be topicalized: *fun park hob ix gəzen dem hunt*, in the meaning 'I saw the dog (while I was) in the park.'

Similarly, we must appeal to grammatical functions to distinguish the two meanings of: *er molt zeltn šejn*; either (a) 'he rarely draws nicely,' or (b) 'he draws very nicely.' In the first meaning, *zeltn* is a sentence adverbial; in (b), *zeltn* is an adverb modifying only the verb *molt* (Kahan-Newman 1983: 105–106).

The unmarked position in declarative clauses for both subject and topic is initial position. The fact that the two are often – but not always – coterminous sometimes leads to ambiguities and problems. Typically, the subject consists of a nominal of some sort – NP, pronoun, proper name, PP, or nominalized non-finite verb form. When a finite verb is topicalized, it takes a deverbalized pseudo-infinitive form which then fills a sentence-unit slot and triggers V-2 (§6.2.1). Other constituents may also fill the topic role, e.g., an adverbial: *gix lojft er* 'It's quickly that he runs' (Kahan-Newman 1983: 123ff.).

The overlap between subject and topic is further seen from consideration of the fictive subject *es*. It is deleted as soon as another element becomes topicalized. Furthermore, the finite verb is not subject to the same strict requirements of agreement as when linked to a true subject: *es kumt a student* 'there's a student coming' vs. *es kumən studentn* 'there are students coming.' In existential sentences with *es iz do / es zajnən do* 'there is / there are' some speakers have a tendency to use the singular form of the verb with a plural (true subject) NP: *es iz do azojnə* 'there is$_{[SG]}$ such ones.' Prince (1989: 407) notes non-agreement and subject postposing; thus: *es zenən / iz gəkumən di baləbatəm* 'the elders came,' but *di baləbatəm zenən/**iz gəkumən*. When the *es* is a true subject it does not delete when not in topic position, and agreement obtains: *bald vet es regənən* 'soon it will$_{[SG]}$ rain.'

When the topicalized constituent fills the role of subject (i.e., it is not identified as a sentence adverbial or object), and, at the same time, it is not specified as a noun or NP, it is generally treated as a singular concept, e.g., *zingən štert undz* 'singing bothers us.' The subject role may be filled by complex structures which contain COMPS, dependent clauses, etc.: *zajn zingən lidər vos er gədenkt fun cvejtn klas štert undz* 'his singing songs which he remembers from second grade bothers us.' In general, a non-specific subject steers 3P.SG verb agreement. Evidence for this is seen in the use of *iz* 'is' as a "topic marker which occurs when the topic of the sentence and the subject of the sentence are not identical" (Kahan-Newman 1983: 124). This usually occurs in longer sentences as a strategy for re-establishing the sense that a finite verb is indeed to be found in second position; thus Kahan-Newman (p. 124) cites Zaretski's (1926: 157) example:

(155) In frankrajx iz, di heldn matrosn, velxə hobn zix opgəzogt arojscutretn kegn der arbetər-pojərišər rusland, matərn zix nox alc in tfisə.

'In France, is, the hero sailors, who have REFL refused to come out against worker-peasant Russia, suffer REFL still yet in jail.'

This cumbersome sentence derives from a more basic structure: *in frankrajx matərn zix nox di heldn matrosn velxə* . . . 'In France suffer REFL the hero sailors who . . . ' The marked foregrounding of two weight-bearing constituents – the locative adverbial *in frankrajx*, and the true subject *di heldn matrosn* – forces a situation where a dummy *iz* is inserted as a temporary stop-gap until the true verb (in agreement with the true subject) occurs (Kahan-Newman 1983: 124–125).

Consider the element *dos* in: *dos iz der brudər* 'this is the brother' (Kahan-Newman 1983: 81–82). A problem arises here in determining which is the subject – *dos* or *der brudər*, since the verb *iz* could agree with either. However, this is disambiguated when considering *dos bin ix* lit. 'this-am-I' 'it's me'; *dos zajnən altə cajtungən* 'these are old newspapers.' The verb agrees with the true subjects, *ix* and *altə cajtungən*.

In many instances we have to go beyond the syntax, and resort to the semantics, in order to get closer to determining the subject of a sentence. For example, in: *es kumt dir a šejnəm dank* 'it comes $\text{you}_{[\text{DAT}]}$ a nice $\text{thanks}_{[\text{ACC}]}$' (= 'you deserve a lot of thanks'), the thing you deserve, a nice thanks, appears as an accusative object. However, in: *es kumt dir a gutər man* 'it comes $\text{you}_{[\text{DAT}]}$ a good $\text{husband}_{[\text{NOM}]}$' (= 'you deserve a good husband'), the thing you deserve – a good husband – is in the nominative case. The difference here may be that *a gutər man* is capable of being an agent, while 'a nice / lot of thanks' less so.[21]

Another problem with subject-verb agreement concerns group referents in which conjunction *un* 'and' has been replaced with PREP *mit* 'with,' as part of a phenomenon of "pseudo-subordination of NPS" (Yuasa and Sadock 2002: 100ff.). Here, semantics plays a crucial role. This replacement of coordinating conjunction *un* with (subordinating) preposition *mit* is limited to logical members of a pair or set; thus, contrast: *der tatə mit der mamən zingən* 'Father and Mother sing[3P.PL]' vs. *der rebə mitn hunt zingt* 'the rabbi with the dog sings[3P.SG].' Yuasa and Sadock (p. 100) call the first example "pseudo-subordination," where the members may be reversed in order without change in reference; thus, "*der tat[ə] mit der mam[ə]n* refers to the same individuals as

[21] Laurie Maynell (p.c.). It may be that *es kumt dir a šejnəm dank* is produced by native speakers, but not allowed in the prescriptive grammar.

di mam[ə] mit dem tatn," whereas "*der reb[ə] mitn hunt* refers to a particular rabbi while *der hunt mit dem rebn* refers to a particular dog." They further write: "verb agreement with pseudo-subordinate subjects is plural . . . while . . . simple subordination is singular. In this case, then, the agreement is determined by the semantic form rather than the syntactic form."

In non-problematic data a specific case generally is associated with subjects (NOM), direct objects (ACC), and indirect objects (DAT). However, several problems are to be found, which force issues of sub-categorization of verbs (see Kahan-Newman 1983: 82–92).

6.6 Movements, transformations, and deletions

6.6.1 *Floating and climbing*

Yiddish permits – and under certain conditions requires – fronting of constituents to clitic position after the finite verb. JPA (1994: 411) discuss floating (movement within the VP) and climbing (movement from an embedded infinitival clause).[22] With a full NP or with a PP, floating and climbing are stylistic options; thus:

(Floating)
(156) Er hot ufgəgesn dem epl → er hot dem epl ufgəgesn.
'He ate up the apple.'

(Climbing)
(157) Ir megt zix farlozn ojf mir. → ir megt zix ojf mir farlozn
'You may depend on me.'

With a bare pronoun object, however, floating and climbing are normally obligatory; thus: (floating) *mir hobn zej gəzen* 'we saw them' (***gəzen zej*); (climbing) *ix hob ajx fargesn cu zogn* 'I forgot to tell you' (***cu zogn ajx*). Climbing also occurs with a pronoun raised from an embedded clause in subject-to-object raising:

(158) Ix hob im gərufn esn.
'I called him to eat.'

This derives from an embedded infinitival S [he eat]. Thus, the sentence *ix hejs im šisn*, lit. 'I-order-him-shoot' is ambiguous; the meaning 'I order him to be shot' is an instance of floating; the meaning 'I order him to shoot' is an instance of climbing.

[22] In current theoretical terms, "floating" is roughly equivalent to the terms "object shift" or "short scrambling"; "climbing" corresponds to the term "scrambling."

6.6.2 *Infinitival complements, raising, and control*

The situation with infinitival complements and raising is quite constrained in Yiddish – basically limited to modals and aspectuals (JPA 1994: 415). Rather, Yiddish employs constructions with a conjunction (most commonly, *az, vos, vi*) and subordinate clause. Thus, where English permits raising sentences like "You seem to be happy," and "I believe him to be happy," Yiddish has subordinate-clause constructions: *daxt zix, az du bist gliklǝx*, lit. 'Ø-seems-REFL-that-you-are-happy,' and *ix mejn, az er iz gliklǝx*, lit. 'I-think-that-he-is-happy.'

However, the movement of embedded subject to main-clause object position occurs in some very limited circumstances, typically with main-clause verbs having to do with observing, permitting, or commanding. Thus, all of the following have a surface object *im* 'him' which is an underlying subject in the embedded infinitival clause (see Zaretski 1926: 146; Kahan-Newman 1983: 103):

(159) Ix her im zingǝn.
'I hear him sing.'
(160) Ix loz im gejn.
'I let him go.'
(161) Ix ruf im esn.
'I call him to eat.'
(162) Ix hejs im šisn.
'I order him to shoot.'

The last example above contrasts with the same surface form in the meaning 'I order him to be shot,' where the surface object *im* is also underlyingly an object (of *šisn*). Similarly, Zaretski (1926: 146) contrasts: *ix ruf im esn* with *ix pruv im ajnredn*, lit. 'I-attempt-him-convince,' 'I try to convince him.' In the former, the object *im* is underlyingly the subject of the embedded infinitival clause, whereas, in the latter, the raised *im* is a true underlying object.

In instances of subject-to-object raising there is no deletion of identical subjects; rather, a reflexive pronoun is generated; thus: *ix her zix zingǝn, du herst zix zingǝn* 'I/you-hear-REFL-sing,' etc. However, this deletion does occur in constructions with the verb *veln* 'want to'; thus: *X vil X gejn* 'X wants X to go' → *X vil gejn* 'X wants Ø (to) go.' When the two subjects are not identical, Yiddish resorts to the default situation of S-COMP (with deletion of the complementizer *az*): *du vilst, er zol gejn* lit. 'you-want-he-should-go' 'you want him to go.'

The default status of S-COMP is further seen when a verb which normally requires an explicit object lacks one. Thus, *rufn* 'call' usually requires an explicit object. This triggers the subject-to-object raising in examples like *ix ruf im esn*. However, if an explicit object is not present, a default S-COMP would seem to be required:

(163) ??Ix ruf, (az) er zol esn.
'I call out (in general), that he should eat.'

Note further the dialect differences discussed above (§3.7) concerning gerund constructions like: *ix hob im gəzen gejəndik* lit. 'I-have-him-seen-going.' For most varieties of Yiddish the gerund form may only refer to the subject of the main clause; thus, 'I saw him (while I was) walking.' To refer to the subject of the embedded clause, either subject-to-object raising or an S-COMP construction is employed: *ix hob im gəzen gejn* lit. 'I-have-him-seen-(to) go' ~ *ix hob gəzen, vi er gejt* lit. 'I-have-seen-how-he-goes.' NEY permits a gerund to refer to either a main-clause or embedded-clause subject; however, here the gerund may not be moved out of its home clause.

6.6.3 Passivization

The three basic means for expressing the passive voice (§5.22) are: (1) passive formed with AUX *vern* + past participle of main verb, with conversion of ACC object → formal subject, and agent subject to a PP COMP; (2) active sentences with *me(n)* 'one' in passive meaning; (3) reflexives used in passive meaning. Of present concern is only the first type, which may be described in terms of a transformation. There are several limitations on which verbs may undergo this passive transformation (Wolf 1974). In general, it requires a transitive verb with a strongly governed ACC object. Modals and aspectuals, as well as periphrastic verbs, may not undergo passivization. However, a modal may dominate a passive VP: *der epl muz [gəgesn vern]* 'the apple must [be eaten].' There is no "double passivization" – that is, type 2 and type 3 passives may not undergo further *vern*-passivization.

Passivization with *vern* does not require the creation of an explicit PP COMP; thus: *lidər vern gəzungən* lit. 'songs-become-sung' 'songs are sung.' Normal topicalization is permitted; thus:

(164) Lidər vern gəzungən durx di studentn in klas.
'Songs are sung by the students in class.'
(165) Durx di studentn vern lidər gəzungən in klas.
(166) In klas vern lidər gəzungən durx di studentn.

Subjectless passives with a dummy subject *es* are permitted:[23]

(167) Es vert gəzungən.
it-becomes-sung
'There's singing going on.'

As in active sentences, the dummy *es* in passives deletes when another constituent is topicalized:

(168) Es vert gəzungən in park.
'Singing is happening in the park.'
(169) In park vert (**es) gəzungən.

It is unclear whether a passive sentence may undergo subject postposing:

(170) ??es vern gəzungən in park di lidər

6.6.4 *VP movement*

Under normal topicalization a constituent may be extracted out of a VP and moved to topic position:

(171) Der man est an epl.
'The man eats an apple.'
(172) Der man vil esn an epl.
'The man wants to eat an apple.'
(173) An epl est der man.
'It's an apple that the man is eating.'
(174) An epl vil der man esn.
'It's an apple that the man wants to eat.'

An entire VP (minus the tensed verb – AUX, modal, etc.) may be fronted:

(175) Esn an epl vil der man.
eat-an-apple-wants-the-man
'To eat an apple is what the man wants.'
(176) Gəgesn an epl hot der man.
eaten-an-apple-has-the-man
'Ate an apple is what the man did.'

In the following examples the non-finite verb may not be extracted without its object COMP (see Zaretski 1926):

(177) Me tor nit ojfvekn dos kind.
'One may not wake up the child.'

[23] However, it is questionable whether a subjectless passive with dummy *es* may also contain a 'by'-phrase.

(178) [ojfvekn dos kind] tor men nit
(179) **[ojfvekn] tor men nit [dos kind]

However, Mark (1978: 383–384), citing Sholem Aleykhem, gives:

(180)	(az)	gəredt	hot	er	ojf jidiš
	(that)	spoken	has	he	in Yiddish
(181)	gəgangən	iz	er	on	a hitl
	gone	is	he	without	a hat

Mark's examples all contain a PP COMP. Santorini (1993: 233) gives examples with a direct object, e.g., [*gəfinən*] *veln zej im baj mir* '(As concerns finding) they will find him with me.' This perhaps suggests that the non-finite verb(s) may leave behind a pronoun COMP, but not a full NP; thus: *me meg im ojfvekn* →*??ojfvekn meg men im*, but not ***ojfvekn meg men dem man*. Perhaps this has to do with the bracketing situation in Yiddish (vs. German); cf. acceptability in German of *Aufwecken darf man das Kind*. Perhaps the presence of negation adds a complicating factor constraining the fronting of the finite verb in *me tor nit ojfvekn dos kind* (M. Diesing, p.c.).

6.6.5 Subject pro-drop and object pro-drop

Both subject- and object-pronouns may optionally delete, though the two processes differ in terms of frequency, conditions, and style-level. In both instances the deleted pronoun must be inferrable from the context. JPA (1994: 408) write that in colloquial StY "salient main clause initial subjects can be deleted"; thus *Ø iz in štub* '(he) is in the house' may be given as a response to the question *vu iz der menč* 'where is the person?' Non-initial subjects, as well as subjects in subordinate clauses, may also delete, though less frequently:

(182) Efšər volst Ø mir gəkent lajən a finf rubl.
'Maybe (you) could loan me about five rubles.'
(183) Trink nit di kavə, vorəm Ø vest nit kenən šlofn.
'Don't drink the coffee, because (you) won't be able to sleep.'

Subject pro-drop may occur even when referring to an earlier non-subject (Birnbaum 1979a: 304):

(184)	Es vert	ir	eng	in štub	un	Ø	vil arojs.
	it becomes	$\text{her}_{[\text{DAT}]}$	tight	in (the) house	and	(she)	wants out

'She feels constricted in the house and Ø wants to get out.'

Object pro-drop is more widespread, occurring in "all varieties of Standard Yiddish, formal as well as colloquial," in both main and subordinate clauses (JPA 1994: 408):

(185) Er hot gəkojft an epl un hot ufgəgesn Ø afn ort.
'He bought an apple and devoured it on the spot.'

(186) Zogt der policmejstər, az ven der rov farštejt dajč, vet er ojx farštejn Ø.
'So the police sergeant says that if the rabbi understands German, he'll also understand (it).'

Subject- and object pro-drop may co-occur in a single clause (p. 408): *vu iz di flaš vajn? Ø host šojn ojsgətrunkən Ø?* 'Where is the bottle of wine? (You) drank (it) up already?'

6.6.6 *Consecutive word order*

Yiddish employs the strategy of "consecutive word order" – finite verb in clause-initial position – for declaratives which follow as a consequence of another clause, and thus convey a meaning of 'so' or 'as a result': ($_{[A]}$ *Du host ojsgətrunkən dos bir.*) $_{[B]}$ *Trink ix dem vajn.* '(You drank up the beer.) [So] I'll drink the wine.' The A clause serves as a type of sentence unit, with the finite verb then following in a "second" position. Consecutive word order may be employed without an A clause, as a narrative device to convey that what is said follows from some previous (specified or not) circumstances: *gej ix!* 'So I'm outta here!'

Consecutive word order clauses are underlyingly SVO, and the occurrence of the finite verb in clause-initial position is thus a marked strategy to convey a larger discourse context, where an earlier proposition (whether explicit or implicit) serves to fill initial field. Therefore, they may not be preceded by subordinating or coordinating conjunctions, since these "push the reset button" and trigger SVO order afresh.

6.6.7 *Gapping and* VP *deletion*

Under certain conditions optional deletion of a finite verb (gapping) or of a VP may occur (JPA 1994: 410). Both types of deletion have to do with conjoined clauses, and the deleted element must be inferrable; thus: *zi gejt arajn un er (gejt) arojs* 'she goes in and he goes out.' Deletion of an AUX may occur, even when it differs from the AUX in the linked clause (Birnbaum 1988: 57–69): *mir zenən gəkumən . . . un (hobn) gəgesn* lit. 'we-are-come . . . and- (have) -eaten' 'we have come . . . and (have) eaten'; *di fejgl hobn gəzungən . . . un (zajnən) avekgəflojgn* lit. 'the-birds-have-sung . . . and- (are)-away-flown' 'the birds have sung . . . and (have) flown away.' Especially open to gapping are finite forms of *zajn* 'be' in *vos*-clauses, even when another instance of this verb is not present in the conjoined clauses: *vos Ø gəven iz gəven* lit. 'what-Ø-been-is-been' 'what was, was'; also: *der dojərkajt vos efšər Ø zej bašert* 'the posterity that (is) perhaps destined to them' (examples from JPA 1994: 409). Finally, a 3P finite form of *zajn* may be deleted, and replaced by a special intonation on the topicalized predicate adjective (Zaretski 1926: 136; see §4.6): *der tatə iz frum* 'Father is pious' → *frum Ø der tatə*.

Gapping is blocked if the syntax otherwise dictates that the clause would normally be verb-initial, e.g., in consecutive declaratives, and when a subordinate clause precedes the clause in question (JPA 1994: 410). Thus, gapping is blocked in the second clause in: *zi gejt arajn, gejt er arojs* 'she goes in, (so) he goes out.' Here, the finite verb is needed for the purpose of being put into marked position, and may thus not be deleted. However, in VP deletion, another finite verb (AUX or modal) is available to fill the positional requirements. Thus, VP deletion may occur in coordinated independent clauses, and/or when a subordinate clause precedes: *zi trinkt a gloz vajn un er vil (trinkən a gloz vajn) ojx* 'she drinks a glass of wine and he wants to (drink a glass of wine) also'; *az er vet forn in kanadə, veln zej (forn in kanadə) ojx* 'if he will go to Canada, they will (go to Canada) also.'

7 Sociolinguistics

7.1 Introduction

Much has been written on the sociology of Yiddish (see Fishman 1981a), relatively little on the sociolinguistics *senso stricto*. The present chapter aims to provide a general picture of the Yiddish sociolinguistic milieu. This milieu is a complex one, involving differences in spoken and written language, social groups, time and space and multilingualism. The specifics of the Yiddish situation – universal coterritoriality with other languages, internal and external bilingualism and/or diglossia – make it difficult to provide a "sociolinguistic road map" of Yiddish in the traditional sense of modern sociolinguistic studies.

7.2 Language attitudes and language ideology: general issues

Speakers' attitudes about language may be distinguished in terms of those attitudes which relate specifically to language use (e.g., what types/forms of speech are considered "good," "bad," "refined," "uneducated"), and those attitudes which relate to macro- or meta-issues such as: is our linguistic medium a "language"? A dialect? What is a dialect? What are the relationships of our speech to other types of speech? For Yiddish speakers this has been an intriguing and complex playing field, owing to several factors, including: (1) the surface similarity of Yiddish to German, and Yiddish speakers' overt awareness of this; (2) internal Jewish bilingualism (M. Weinreich 1980: 247–314) and the traditional valorization of written and spoken *Loshn-koydesh* [LK] (as against the Jewish vernacular); (3) the role of external Jewish bi-/multilingualism; (4) Yiddish speakers' component consciousness. Speakers' attitudes can also play a role in shaping the sociolinguistic playing field.

Modern sociolinguistic works on specific languages commonly begin with questions like: "what is language X" or "who speaks X" (as opposed to genetically related speech varieties called "not X"; e.g., "German" vs. "Dutch"). One may ask why Swiss German is still called "German," even though it is often less comprehensible to more StG speakers than is Dutch. Ultimately, the classifications are based on extra-linguistic factors such as political boundaries, religious or ethnic differences (e.g., Hindi and Urdu, Serbian and Croatian). The fact that Yiddish has lacked the geopolitical boundaries and the authority-apparatus of a modern nation-state has, of course, had its sociolinguistic repercussions. No less importantly, this lack has often proved to be a formidable conceptual obstacle for those linguists and others who focus on language fundamentally through the looking-glass of nation-state legitimation (Fishman 1981b: 7).

What does it mean to say that person/group X "speak(s) Yiddish"? Our point of departure is endocentric, based on the internal dynamics of the speech community itself, and (the use of) the language in question. Thus, for example, we are not interested here in Eckardt's (1911) appropriation of Yiddish speakers in Riga as a part (the sociolinguistic dregs) of the Baltic German speech community (Jacobs 1994b) and other such appropriations of Yiddish "as" German. More relevant to our current interest are the times, places, and conditions under which Ashkenazim possibly viewed their vernacular (Yiddish) as – or as not – a type of German.[1] In terms of how this has played out sociolinguistically, the data often reveal a more accurate picture of what is happening, one sometimes at variance with speakers' expressed attitudes and opinions. In principle, then, we reject external measuring devices in delineating the Yiddish speech community. For example, German linguistic scholarship has often had trouble distinguishing systematically between Yiddish per se, and Jewish ethnolects of German which arose via language shift (< Yiddish) among German Jews in the eighteenth and nineteenth centuries (Jacobs 1996c). At the same time, directly relevant to our discussion are the ways and extent to which nineteenth and twentieth-century Yiddish speakers recognized and distinguished Germanized Yiddish from Jewishly spoken German, and how the Yiddish speech community contextualized each of the above (Fishman 1981a: 57).

We may ask what it means when Yiddish speakers, individually and collectively, identify someone as speaking Yiddish as opposed to speaking something else. Similarly, one sometimes hears of someone: *er redt jidiš vi a goj* 'he speaks Yiddish non-natively / like an outsider.' What does this mean in sociolinguistic terms? On the flip side of the same coin, what does it mean to speak Yiddish like an insider? This is a complex question which goes beyond grammatical structure. The answers will depend as well on factors such as age, gender, region, traditional vs. modern orientation, Hasidic vs. non-Hasidic, time and geography. For example, the threat of a tidal wave of Slavic loans into nineteenth century EY is not perceived of as a threat in America after the Second World War. While much testifies to the overall unity of the Yiddish speech community, it is to no surprise a diverse one.

Varieties of Yiddish should be seen within their larger complex social, political, and cultural contexts. For example, StY arose in a general modern European

[1] See Szajkowski (1981); Frakes (1989); Strauch (1990).

milieu which valorized standard language as against dialect speech. This milieu was linked to emerging paradigms of nation, and notions of *Kultur* and *Kultursprache*. The shared discourse on nation, culture, and language transcended ethnic and national boundaries. Not surprisingly, the emerging modern European standard languages developed significant (shared) vocabularies reflecting this (shared) ideological orientation.

The relationship between spoken and written language among Ashkenazim has defined itself differently in different periods. Varying types, styles, and indeed languages, have been employed over the centuries as the written medium of Yiddish-speaking Jewry. These written varieties have all interacted with spoken Yiddish, and there have been mutual influences. On the respective roles (both written and spoken) of LK and Yiddish in traditional Ashkenazic society, see M. Weinreich (1972, 1980).

7.3 Language contact, bi-/multilingualism, and diglossia

7.3.1 Internal Jewish bilingualism

Jewish civilizations are seen structurally in terms of the interaction of vertical (unbroken chain of Jewish existence) and horizontal (external, non-Jewish) patterns. Each Jewish diaspora civilization is a unique, creative synthesis, as is each Jewish diaspora language. The latter arose via language shift, where the pre-existing Jewish vernacular leaves its imprint on the new Jewish speech form supplanting it. The Jewish vernacular precursors to Yiddish affected the structure of what emerged as Yiddish; similarly, the structure of Yiddish shaped, in part, what emerged as the post-Yiddish Jewish ethnolects of, e.g., German, Dutch, English, Polish, and modern Israeli Hebrew.

"Vertical legitimation" (M. Weinreich 1980: 206–210) refers to Jewish points of reference and authority drawn from chronologically antecedent Jewish sources. This notion applies to language as well. The languages of the sacred texts – written in Hebrew and Judeo-Aramaic (collectively, LK) – remained as ongoing sources of enrichment and innovation within the linguistic milieu of Jewish diaspora communities. M. Weinreich (pp. 247–314) devotes a chapter to the topic of internal Jewish bilingualism – "within the Jewish community . . . the symbiosis of Yiddish and Loshn-koydesh throughout the entire history of Ashkenaz and the position of each of these languages in the cultural system of Ashkenazic Jewry" (p. 247). Internal Jewish bilingualism was an integral part of traditional Ashkenazic civilization. The relationships between Yiddish and LK were complex. While Yiddish was the universal vernacular in traditional Ashkenaz, the presence of LK was formidable and fundamental. Virtually every male child was schooled in Hebrew. There existed a fairly intact division of labor between Yiddish and LK, but with fuzzy areas of overlap (p. 279).

Spoken LK was employed in certain intra-Ashkenazic situations, and as a lingua franca with non-Ashkenazic Jews. LK was the ostensible language of writing, yet even here a nuanced discussion is necessary (§7.7). LK served as the language of sacred texts and prayer. However, written Yiddish occurred as well in circumscribed contexts. Thus, while official legal documents such as divorce decrees were written in LK, these contained verbatim testimony in Yiddish. Public proclamations were in a mixed LK-Yiddish (p. 256). Furthermore, Yiddish encroached onto the domain of oral prayer. For the period preceding the upheavals of modernity, Fishman (1965: 3–4) gives the primary functions for Yiddish within Ashkenazic society as: (1) the vernacular "of all Ashkenazic social groupings . . . spoken by both men and women, by both rich and poor, by both scholars and illiterates, by merchants and artisans"; (2) the vehicle of entertainment literature (*Bove-bukh*, *Shmuel bukh*, *Maase-bukh*, etc.); (3) the vehicle of popular religious education or indoctrination (for those less literate in Hebrew). Thus, the relationships between Yiddish and LK as written and spoken media in traditional Ashkenazic society were defined socially.[2]

7.3.2 *External bi-/multilingualism*

In addition to internal Jewish bilingualism, Yiddish has been spoken in a situation of universal contact with other languages. Often this contact is with coterritorial languages: Polish, Lithuanian, Latvian, Hungarian, German, Dutch, etc.[3] Care must be taken to specify the facts, nature, and extent of contact, and the varieties of languages involved. For example, Jewish linguistic "coterritoriality" was often with the urban languages, not the rural languages of the area. Mark (1951: 465ff.) describes the social environment of contact between Yiddish and Lithuanian. He distinguishes between Jewish–Lithuanian contact in villages (Jews with Lithuanian farmers), and in towns (with town-dwelling Lithuanians, and with farmers on market days). Furthermore, the existence of non-Jewish Slavic-speaking nannies may have played a role in shaping the Slavic component in Yiddish, and the perception of its emotive function.

Significant contact has at times been with extra-territorial (or at least supra-regional) languages, e.g., German and Russian at different times in Warsaw (Geller 2001: 30ff.). Furthermore, especially in the development of modern Yiddish, German played both overt and covert roles (Schaechter 1969; and below). Thus, the contact between Jewish and non-Jewish languages must be specified socially and geographically, in addition to linguistically. The nature of the Jewish bilingualism must be specified. How well did Jews (comprising what

2 For full discussion of the sociology of Yiddish, see Fishman (1981a).

3 For a list and map of coterritorial languages in continental Ashkenaz, see Sunshine *et al.* (1995: 83–84).

percentage of that Jewish population) know the language(s) in question? How stable was the bilingualism? What varieties of these languages were involved? In which social situations was the external language used? Was there any compartmentalization by domain – e.g., the identification of Slavic as "earthy" or "emotional"? Furthermore, to what extent did specifically Jewish varieties of the "external" language serve as the contact models? In such an instance, contact between, for example, Yiddish and Polish might be: (1) mediated (with Jewish-Polish), (2) unmediated (with non-Jewish Polish), or (3) both.

The nature or extent of (external) language contact is often reflected in the types and degrees of contact influences observed in Yiddish. Thus, contact with Lithuanian resulted mostly in lexical influences. Minor surface phonetic influences from coterritorial languages are found in many varieties of Yiddish (e.g., timbre of /l/ and /r/). On the other hand, contact with Slavic has resulted in deep and profound influences in EY: the development of a broad system of aspectual distinctions, palatalized phonemes, stress, and other grammatical features. This presumably reflects more extensive, deeper contact with Slavic than with Lithuanian. In more superficial contact the influences are usually limited to loanwords; with more extensive contact some morphological influences may occur (Thomason and Kaufman 1988; van Coetsem 1988). Miller (1955: 120) distinguishes for American Yiddish between English loanwords (which he considers acceptable) and system-affecting influences from English (to be avoided). For the latter, discussion concerns the use of prepositions in Yiddish based on their cognate use in English, counter to earlier Yiddish usage, e.g., *gejn cu a koncert* 'go to a concert'; cf. general Yiddish *gejn af a koncert.*

7.3.3 Diglossia

While the term *diglossia* has been used in various (often contradictory) ways, all approaches recognize a functional division of linguistic labor within a speech community, where language/variety/dialect X is used in certain socially defined contexts, variety Y in others. Though diglossia, by definition, involves two (or more) languages or varieties, the terms diglossia and bi-/multilingualism are not coterminous. Fishman (1967) distinguishes situations of: (1) diglossia with bilingualism; (2) diglossia without bilingualism; (3) bilingualism without diglossia; (4) neither diglossia nor bilingualism.

Type 1 covers the "normal" situation of diglossia, where the intragroup tasks of communication are divided functionally; language X is used in everyday situations, while language Y is used in formal situations, writing, etc. Diglossia is often discussed in terms of H(igh) and L(ow) varieties. Fishman (1967: 31–32) writes that type 1 typically involves: "a fairly large and complex speech community in which the members have available to them both a range of *compartmentalized* roles as well as *access* to these roles." There may be multiple overlapping communities. For example, we recognize a broader (general American) English speech community in the United States, of which Jewish bilinguals are a part. At the same time, Jewish bilinguals are members of (1) a Yiddish speech community, (2) a speech community of Yiddish-English bilinguals, (3) a broad speech community of Jews (both bilinguals and monolinguals). There is furthermore a Jewish speech community of English monolinguals who consider themselves as such, interact as such. This situation is distinct from the Yiddish-English diglossic community, though the latter may have extensive and regular interaction with the former (for example, the generation of bilingual parents with a generation of English monolingual children). This interaction plays a significant role in the rise of post-Yiddish Jewish ethnolects.

Type 2 – diglossia without bilingualism (Fishman 1967: 33–34) – concerns situations wherein two separate speech communities happen to cohabitate the same geographical, political, religious, or economic unit. Thus, this is diglossia by "default." Frequently, one language is identified as the language of an elite, another language as that of the masses. Type 3 – bilingualism without diglossia – is used by Fishman (pp. 34–36) to describe situations where bilingualism occurs at the level of "individual linguistic behavior," but is not incorporated into a super-system of compartmentalized functions. Fishman (p. 35) speaks of "[d]islocated immigrants and their children" who

> use their mother tongue and other tongue for intragroup communication in seemingly random fashion . . . Since the formerly separate roles of the home domain, the school domain and the work domain are all disturbed by the massive dislocation of values and norms that result from simultaneous immigration and industrialization, the language of work (and of the school) comes to be used at home.

However, the situation in Ashknenaz was different from the above. The Ashkenazic community typically possessed (varying degrees of) knowledge of coterritorial languages, and used these languages in regular, definable social situations, e.g., Lithuanian with farmers on market day in *shtetlekh* in Lithuania. Language contact left its mark in terms of loanwords and other influences; however, this was not diglossia. In traditional Ashkenaz, Jews generally did not have regularly defined intragroup functions for Lithuanian, Ukrainian, Rumanian, etc.

Within the diglossic situation a continuum of intermediate forms may arise. For example, in addition to the distinction between Merged Hebrew and Whole Hebrew, Yiddish speakers may exhibit a continuum of speech styles in Whole Hebraisms, ranging from "formal Ashkenazic" to colloquial (Katz 1993: 76–78). This range of styles may be found in pronunciation, syntax, morphology, etc. Whether these Whole Hebraisms are seen as code-switching (within a

Yiddish frame), or as H linguistic markers within Yiddish, depends on numerous factors in context, as well as the linguist's analysis (Fishman 1981c: 744). Similarly, diglossia with German at the beginning of the modern period led to a spectrum of levels of germanized Yiddish – from individual loanwords to almost fully (syntactically) germanized Yiddish.[4] Thus, the distinction I make here between diglossia and bilingualism is a qualitative one. Diglossia involves a superstructure within which system-governed interactions occur. In bilingualism (without diglossia) a linguistic superstructure is lacking, and the contact influences are sporadic. When a Yiddish speaker uses a higher amount of germanized speech, or a higher amount of formal Whole Hebrew terms (and formal Ashkenazic pronunciation), the audience is likely to perceive a style/register shift (the speaker is speaking "fancier" Yiddish) rather than code-switching. On the other hand, if the same speaker begins inserting Ukrainianisms, Latvianisms, etc. (beyond the norm), the audience is likely to perceive this as macaronic speech, code or language switching, or something else, but not as activity within the recognized diglossic playing field of Ashkenazic discourse.

The make-up of the diglossic mix may change over time and place. Thus, in Poland following the First World War, Polish for the first time entered into the diglossic mix for many yiddophone Jews. Likewise, for many modern secularized Ashkenazim, LK dropped out of the diglossic mix; it was reduced to residue status – individual lexical items, morphemes (e.g., plural suffix *-im*), fossilized idiomatic expressions (e.g., *mazltov*) – Yiddish elements which happen to be of HA origin. In spite of the legacy of daytshmerish, modern German is no longer part of the diglossic mix for Yiddish speakers of the late twentieth century. Similarly, the Holocaust has removed Polish as an active part of the diglossic mix, even though individual elements of Polish origin live on in Yiddish.

The functions of both written and spoken Yiddish have also changed over time. For example, early on in the modern period Yiddish began to be printed in the square script previously the exclusive domain of the H language in Ashkenaz – LK. This reflects a rise in the status of Yiddish in this period (Fishman 1985). Yiddish increasingly came to be used for H functions in Ashkenazic society, eventually assuming the role of a Jewish national language.

Thus, we are concerned with the complex social situations of Yiddish-speaking Jewry as these are manifested linguistically and sociolinguistically, as they operate in an overall diglossic (and bilingual) mix which we may call the sociolinguistic "soup." The effects of the "soup" may be seen, for example, in the differences in the dialect topography of NEY based on whether the

[4] See Fishman (1981a: 11, note 4) on a late nineteenth century admonition concerning sending one's children to a yeshiva with a secularized rabbi "who easily abandons and changes the Yiddish language to German."

coterritorial language contact is with Slavic alone, or with Slavic + Baltic (§3.8.4). Yiddish language contact must be elaborated precisely in its specific historical and social contexts for each variety under investigation, and not simply for the language "as a whole." For example, Geller (2001: 24–33) provides an overview of the complex sociolinguistic history of Warsaw Yiddish. While this included a period of significant (Jewish) Yiddish–Polish bilingualism, the period after the First World War marked a qualitative change, with the rise of Polish to the status of official language, and the rise of a diglossic situation (Yiddish–Polish) among the younger generation of Yiddish speakers. The list of languages present in the "soup" remained the same, while the "recipe" changed.

In fact, it may be claimed that watershed linguistic changes among Ashkenazim coincide with alteration of the soup – or even that the former resulted from the latter. In traditional Ashkenaz there was a diglossic (or triglossic) situation: Yiddish + Hebrew (+Aramaic). This was reinforced at several levels: in the language employed in traditional learning (*lernen*), in the use of LK for official documents, etc. Hoge (1991) connects the decline/death of WY not solely to the acquisition of German by WY speakers, but also to the disruption of the traditional di-/triglossia in western Ashkenaz. Modernity has had a major linguistic impact on Ashkenazic Jewry, both in terms of language choice, and in the overall language milieu. Thus, Birnbaum (1930, 1979a: 14) is correct in claiming that the rise of the new secular Yiddishist Yiddish leads it onto an ever-widening fork away from the Yiddish of tradition-oriented Ashkenazim. The differences, at least in the initial stages, lie primarily not in grammatical features, but, rather, in sociolinguistic and sociological issues, orientations, and in the diglossic soup. Traditional Ashkenaz maintained strong bonds not only to LK as a language, but also to its discourse world. Likewise, secular Yiddishist Yiddish has strong links to the discourse world of modern political movements (socialism, communism, various forms of Jewish nationalism). Thus, secularized Yiddish not surprisingly includes a flood of internationalisms (e.g., *proletarjat, socjalizm, revolucjə*), sometimes via specific languages (e.g., *bavegung* 'political movement' via German). However, the division into traditionalist vs. secularist Yiddish is not absolute. Whole Hebrew continued to be a source of stylistic enrichment even in secularist Yiddishist circles. Furthermore, the discourse of European modernity and *Kultur* had its influences on both secular and traditional Yiddish. Daytshmerish is found in both. As well, secularist Yiddish made itself felt even in the Yiddish of traditionalist circles (Berliner 1981).

7.3.4 Code-switching, style, and register

Given the complex linguistic milieu in which Yiddish has existed, it is not surprising to find this linguistic heterogeneity put to use by speakers as part of a supersystem in which code-switching, style and register variation all interact regularly. Traditional Ashkenazic internal bilingualism (and specifically, the *lernen* tradition) provided a model for codified, regularized, systematic code-switching. In *lernen* situations, a portion of a Hebrew or Aramaic text is read aloud, followed by discussion in Yiddish. The Yiddish discussions could regularly contain embedded strings of LK, the latter showing varying degrees of integration into Yiddish. The boundaries are thus fuzzy between what constituted code-switching (Yiddish–LK), and what developed into H-register Yiddish. Whether code-switching, or register, the conscious switch to ever-more HAisms had a formalizing effect in yiddophone exchanges (Noble 1958).

Macaronic language – the conscious mixing of two or more languages – should also be considered in a discussion of code-switching. M. Weinreich (1972: 284) sees the rise of the macaronic scribal language as "a compromise between the necessity to record in Hebrew and the urge to express oneself in Yiddish." Also relevant is the use of macaronic language (Yiddish and Slavic) in numerous Yiddish folksongs (Rubin 1979: 147–148). Its use is marked, often used pointedly to create rhymes. However, both scribal language and macaronic folksongs are consciously performed linguistic activities, and do not represent the (unmarked) norm of everyday speech.[5]

The distinction between code-switching and register variation is further made more difficult by the diversity of contexts of Ashkenazic speech. While use of words like *maxməs* 'because of,' *hejojs* 'whereas,' etc., are seen as instances of code-switching within the scribal language, they are arguably style markers within spoken Yiddish. Merged Hebrew words like *mafsək zajn* 'interrupt' are seen as Yiddish words, and not as instances of code-switching. This raises the whole question of what is native vs. foreign lexicon (and in which contexts). Modern Yiddish borrowed both *šprax* 'language' and *fragə* 'question' from NHG; cf. StG *Sprache*, *Frage*. Many older Germanic-component words in Yiddish show the results of historical apocope; cf. StY *gas* 'street,' *mid* 'tired,' StG *Gasse*, *müde*. StY *šprax* was originally borrowed as *špraxə* in the nineteenth century. Is it therefore "more nativized" than is StY *fragə*? Furthermore, the word *fragə* often takes colloquial plural *fragn* (cf. StG *Frage-n*); StY has normalized this to *fragə-s*, in line with regular schwa-final nouns. While apocope in *šprax* represents one strategy of nativization, other nativization strategies are available.

Many anglicisms in American Yiddish (e.g., *flor* 'floor,' *vində* 'window') were initially foreignisms, later increasingly integrated/nativized. Thus, American Yiddish *pejdə* 'wage' represents phonological integration of borrowed English *pay day*; likewise, American Yiddish *biznə* (plural: *biznəs*) is a

[5] On performative code-switching in Jewish cabaret, see Jacobs (2003).

reanalysis of English *business*, while other anglicisms retain non-native structure in Yiddish: *troks* 'trucks,' *rezolts* 'results.'[6] American Yiddish has *gla(j)xn* 'to like' based on English *to like*; cf. general Yiddish meanings of *glajx* 'same,' *glajxn* 'compare; liken.'

The Yiddish of American Hasidim in Brooklyn regularly includes several types of code-switching.[7] Females frequently speak English to one another, but switch to Yiddish when speaking to their children, or to adult males. The Yiddish speech of both males and females shows frequent code-switching containing longer English strings. In some instances, this is situational (e.g., prompted by reference to a course on computers), sometimes metaphorical. In addition, there is frequent lexical-level activity which is harder to classify. For example, in a commercially sold cassette tape of stories for children, the storyteller uses the word *kar* 'car' with an American [r], repeated a few seconds later with a Yiddish [R] (or vocalized). He also renders *dobl-parkt* 'double-parked,' again with American English pronunciation. On the other hand, the expression 'all of a sudden' is produced in a (more) Yiddish accent. Sometimes the proximity of an American-accented anglicism influences a nearby Yiddish word, e.g., *dort* 'there' with American *r* (otherwise, [R]). In general, American Hasidic Yiddish uses many American English loans, e.g. (from recent newspaper ads), *drajvn* 'drive (a car),' *fir-rumigə* 'four-room(ed),' *bejbisitn* 'baby-sit,' as well as significant calquing, e.g., *in a veg* 'in a way (manner)' (cf. StY *ojf an ojfn*).

Code-switching is found in other Yiddish-speaking communities. Thus, Peltz (1990: 71) cites the string: *The ofis iz geven, aj ges in somwonz hom... Er hot geven sekreteri for cvej un drasik jor* 'the office was, I guess in someone's home... He was secretary for thirty-two years.' In addition to noticeable English influences – e.g., preposition *for*, where the influence is both lexical and syntactic – we find the English definite article in *the ofis*, as well as a whole phrase in English. From another informant, Peltz (p. 66) cites: *Omaj gad, bot e – ix gedenk...* 'Oh, my God, but uh – I remember...' Code-switching among modern Orthodox Jews presents an especially valuable area of investigation, since this often involves traditionalist Jews speaking languages other than Yiddish in a "soup" that includes LK, and frequently Yiddish (Heilman 1981). On language choice and code-switching in storytelling, see Kirshenblatt-Gimblett (1972: 330–384).

[6] Examples taken from various Yiddish newspapers dating from the 1930s to the present. A single advertisement in a recent Hasidic newspaper contained both *selfons* and *selfonən* 'cell phones.' On anglicisms in Amercian Yiddish, see Mark (1938a).

[7] Based on personal observation in June 2001, and June 2002, in Williamsburg, New York. The speakers were mostly members of the Satmar community. On generational differences in language preference among Lubavitch Hasidim, see Jochnowitz (1981: 732ff.).

Many Yiddish speakers have an acute awareness of the etymological origins of elements in Yiddish. This awareness, referred to as component consciousness (M. Weinreich 1980: esp. 656–657), is reinforced from many sources: on the one hand, by internal Jewish bilingualism, the *taytsh* tradition, etc.; on the other hand, by pervasive external bilingualism. Yiddish speakers commonly deconstruct their language according to component origin, identifying words as "Hebrew," "German," "Polish," etc. – even when they are sometimes (historically) wrong in their identifications. For example, *xojzək* 'ridicule,' likely of Germanic origin, was (mis)identified by Yiddish speakers as being of Semitic origin, and, thus, given "etymological" Hebrew spelling חוזק in StY (p. 308). However, the role played by component consciousness is not an absolute one; otherwise, fusion would not have been productive in Yiddish, and it would be difficult to account for instances where etymology has been overridden, as in the use of Hebrew-origin plural suffix *-im* with non-Hebrew roots: *doktər-doktojrəm* 'doctor-s,' *kundəs-kundejsəm* 'prankster-s,' or the Gmc-origin plural suffix in *ksav-jadn* 'manuscripts.' Still, speakers' component consciousness does permit some component-based stylistic nuancing. Furthermore, the more (traditionally) learned the individual, the more likely that the individual will know the Whole Hebrew forms.

The relationship between Hebrew and Yiddish within Ashkenazic internal bilingualism is a dynamic one, and the boundaries between the languages themselves are often fuzzy and fluid. Some Merged Hebrew forms created within the Yiddish environment have filtered back into Ashkenazic Whole Hebrew; e.g., *taləs-talejsəm* vs. *talijos* 'prayer shawl-s' (M. Weinreich 1980: 310). M. Weinreich (p. 310) cites forms which "at first glance are Loshn-koydesh, but that are not found in Loshn-koydesh sources"; e.g., *ləmanašem* 'for God's sake,' *majsə sojxər* 'businesslike.' Further, Ashkenazic Whole Hebrew documents at times show calquing from Yiddish, e.g., *hu maxzik es acmoj* 'he thinks highly of himself' < Yiddish *er halt fun zix* (p. 307), as well as syntactic influences.

M. Weinreich (1980: 229ff.) discusses linguistic styles of specific groups. Thus, a Hasidic style of speech arose, wherein certain words took on specialized intragroup meanings; e.g., *tikn* 'a drink of whiskey' < 'brandy drunk at someone's anniversary of death' (< 'purification of the soul'); *zic* 'meeting' (< verb 'sit'; among Lubavitch Hasidim, 'meeting' is *farbrengən*, which generally means 'enjoyment'). Similarly, there arose specialized lexicons and styles for various professions (see below). Shlomo Noble observed a style of delicate speech among the *šejnə jidn* 'distinguished Jews' (M. Weinreich 1980: 230), where many words and expressions viewed as coarse were habitually substituted with more refined terms; e.g., *bod* 'bathhouse' and *gatkəs* 'underwear' are replaced by (Hebrew-origin) *merxəc*, *taxtojnəm*; *esn* 'eat' is replaced by *nemən epəs in mojl arajn* 'take something into the mouth.'

7.4 Spoken Yiddish

7.4.1 Spoken Yiddish in the pre-modern period

Spoken Yiddish in pre-modern times existed within a traditional Ashkenazic framework: Yiddish and LK in a diglossic relationship, coupled with moderate (but less crucial) knowledge of external languages. As concerns the spoken language, daytshmerish was not the controversial issue it became in modern times. We have no direct record of Yiddish speech in the Old Yiddish period (with the exception of short verbatim quotes within LK documents). The records are via the filter of the written language of the times, which was largely based on German written norms and models. Furthermore, the relationship between spoken and written language does not remain constant at all historical times. The earliest WrLg A texts showed a tendency to supraregionality. Whether the same was also true for the spoken language is unknown. However, there are hints that, for Jews, spoken supraregionality was indeed at play. Thus, no variety of Yiddish may be reconstructed back to a single German dialect. From the outset, the emerging Yiddish speech community had communication networks distinct from (and often broader than) the corresponding German ones. The Amsterdam Yiddish newspaper *Kurantin* (1686–1687) strove for a supraregional Yiddish, comprehensible to a pan-Ashkenazic readership; use of local Dutch Yiddishisms was held to a minimum.

The rise and crystallization of the major Yiddish dialects (WY, NEY, SEY, CY) is also dated to the pre-modern period – no later than the end of the seventeenth century (M. Weinreich 1980: 733). It could be argued that this represents fragmentation into smaller regional units. However, looked at differently, the crystallization represents local dialect beginning to give way to broader (supra)regional dialect. This might be linked to the emergence of an introspective awareness of dialect speech as such; i.e., an awareness by speakers of what constitutes local, regional, and supraregional speech. This, in turn, supported and was supported by the rise of supraregional written varieties, as in the Amsterdam *Kurantin* of this period, in Yiddish bible translations, etc. (S. Wolitz, p.c.).

7.4.2 Spoken Yiddish in the modern period

The field of Yiddish linguistics has mostly lacked studies of spoken Yiddish beyond the largely phonological and lexical regional variation which constituted the foci of dialect atlases (Fishman 1981a: 63; Peltz 1998). Fishman (1981a: 61) writes: "least examined but closest to the heart of the entire sociolinguistic enterprise is the topic of 'oral' functional variation in (or partially in) Yiddish." There exist numerous descriptions of the "language" of professions, locales, etc. – but these almost exclusively focus on words, idioms, and expressions. Recent works have begun to examine longer spoken passages (e.g., Dyhr and Zint 1988; Kiefer 1995; Geller 2001). The next step for the field is to record and analyze natural dialogue and conversation. This will be the pathway to a true sociolinguistics of Yiddish, and will encompass, as well, an ethnography of Ashkenazic speech.

The lack of such studies is understandable in its sociological and political context. Fishman (1981a: 62–63) notes that the stigma of "corruption," and the real threat of language shift (away from Yiddish) long steered Yiddish linguists and Yiddishists away from looking at variety switch within Yiddish, and cross-language code-switching. Fishman (p. 63) notes as well the very "meager studied recognition of the differences between spoken and written (i.e. printed) language and of the separate standards that these might pursue." Thus, the study of spoken Yiddish in its full discourse context is in its infancy, even if specific points in isolation have been studied (e.g., several points in Zaretski 1926).

The following discussion focuses on variation in spoken styles, registers, etc. To the extent possible, dialect variation is excluded from consideration; it is relevant insofar as it resurfaces as sociolinguistic variation, i.e., in the tension between dialect and standard speech. Typically, speakers possess a repertoire of competence in more than one style, and vary sociolinguistically in their usage. Formal style often reflects attempts by speakers to approximate the written language. Finally, this discussion should be seen in the context of movement toward a tacitly and/or overtly accepted spoken standard. The competing models for a spoken standard have often served rather distinct speech communities, but also have exerted mutual influences. It is in this milieu that activist language planning emerged as well.

7.4.3 Styles of spoken Yiddish

Though often taken as concrete realities, terms such as style, register, etc., are difficult to define precisely, and often overlap. As used here, they refer loosely to a cluster of things. Certain varieties of speech are frequently identified with particular sub-sets of the larger speech community, e.g., Hasidim, women, musicians. This often has to do with specific lexical items, and less with core linguistic structure. Other sociolinguistic issues concern linguistic register, fast speech phenomena, dialect and standard, etc.

One cannot easily compare apples and oranges across the speech styles of different groups. For example, Hasidic style uses familiar 2P.SG pronoun *du* more often than it uses the formal *ir*. The conceptual space of *du* vs. *ir* is different for Hasidic speech as opposed to that of other Yiddish speech. To take another example, the use of a daytshmerism may be marked in the speech of one group, but (have become) unmarked in another. Fishman (1981a: 57, note 20) notes that the use of "more or less German was a stylistic functional variant in the linguistic repertoire of many Yiddish speakers." Other linguistic features may seem less immediate on the surface, yet may be indicative of overall social and linguistic orientation. Thus, U. Weinreich (1956) notes the ongoing loss of the rise-fall intonation contour among westernizing/modernizing Yiddish speakers. This, too, is a signal of solidarity within a specific group. In summary, various styles may be identified, but these are not hermetically sealed units. Rather, they exist in multidimensional space with multiple interacting axes.

7.4.4 Male and female speech

A typical assumption made is that male speech will reflect the higher exposure to LK (through formal education). M. Weinreich (1980: 290) notes that LK is "so much more associated with the male world." Lévy (1924) provides several examples where the male and female responses in certain formulaic exchanges differ precisely in that the male response contains or consists entirely of an Ashkenazic Whole Hebrew expression. For example, upon someone else sneezing, a male response is *asisə* (< Aramaic), a female response is *cə gəzint* (< German component). In warding off bad events, a male will utter (HA-origin) *loj alejxəm* 'not upon you,' a female *ništ far a:x gəzugt* 'not for you said' (< German component).

The lower facility in LK by females is frequently noted as a factor in the rise of Yiddish literature – as help-material for "women and less-educated men" (M. Weinreich 1980: 274–278). However, the fact remains that the specialized calque language, *taytsh*, did develop, and was used by men as well. Mark (1951: 439ff.) notes that women's speech in NEY showed a higher frequency of use of HAisms than in SY, and higher frequency in the ZY sub-region than in other parts of NEY.[8] Thus, we must be cautious in overgeneralizing concerning the HA component and female speech. Future research concerning gender-based differences in spoken language must go beyond the lexical to check for differences in the frequency of linguistic forms selected, in specific features, and concerning larger questions of code-switching, language choice, etc. Rothstein (1998: 25) notes a gender-based difference in Jewish professional argot, where a layer of obscene vocabulary "is a purely masculine argot."

7.4.5 "Refined" speech; euphemism; taboo avoidance

Speech communities commonly categorize particular words or expressions as "delicate," "appropriate," or "refined," and others as "coarse," "vulgar," or

[8] Mark (1951) actually notes that both men's and women's speech in NEY showed a higher frequency of HAisms than in other EY areas. See also Shtif (1929: 16).

"inappropriate." Furthermore, certain concepts may be taboo to utter directly, and require circumlocution in culturally appropriate speech. (The specifics may vary among sub-groups of the larger speech community.) For example, in traditional Ashkenaz, names for God used in prayer and sacred situations were typically avoided or altered in everyday speech; thus, *adənoj* > *adəšem*; *elojhejnu* > *elojkejnu*, etc. In Hasidic speech the word *šabəs* 'Sabbath' is not uttered in a bathhouse; rather, it is replaced by a euphemism: *der zibətər* 'the seventh' (M. Weinreich 1980: 422).

The speech style of *šejnə jidn* 'prominent, distinguished Jews' involves a conscious distancing from direct reference, which is seen as unrefined (M. Weinreich 1980: 230, referring to Shlomo Noble's observations). Thus, instead of referring to a woman as *trogədik* or *məuberəs* 'pregnant,' one says *ojf der cajt* 'at the time' (cf. English *with child*). Instead of *er iz krank* 'he is sick,' M. Weinreich (p. 230) notes that Vilna Yiddish frequently used *er iz nit gəzunt* 'he is not healthy.'[9] In general, this is a speech style of modesty, achieved through a relatively high frequency of euphemisms. M. Weinreich (p. 193) notes that the specific vocabulary of this language of modesty is a Jewish-internal innovation, since the match between the modes of euphemistic expression in German and Yiddish is "not overly close."

Also avoided are utterances which could be seen as inviting misfortune. Thus, NEY speakers created *vu frejt ir zix*? 'where do you rejoice?' as a replacement for *vu vojnt* ([vejnt]) *ir* 'where do you live?' since vowel mergers in NEY (24, 42) have created a homonym *vejnən* 'cry; dwell.' Rather than possibly ask "where do you cry?" a euphemistic opposite is consciously employed. Another conscious replacement is *dos gutə ojg* 'the good eye' for *dos bejzə ojg* 'the evil eye.'

Traditional Ashkenazic culture employs a system of formulaic utterances for warding off, invoking, etc. (Matisoff 1979). For example, in counting inanimate objects, one merely counts: *ejns*, *cvej*, *draj*, etc. When counting people, in order to ward off the evil eye, traditional Ashkenazim count *ništ ejns*, *ništ cvej* 'not one, not two,' etc. Traditionalist Yiddish is similarly replete with expressions such as *mircəšem* 'God willing' for actions desired or planned for the future; *xasvəxolilə* 'God forbid,' etc. While many of these formulaic expressions have remained in modern secularist Yiddish, they likely occur less frequently there than in the Yiddish of traditionalist circles.[10]

Linguistic taboos must be defined for the specific group(s) in which they apply. For example, a longstanding taboo in the baseball world was to mention aloud that a pitcher had a "no-hitter" in progress, lest it jinx the chances of

[9] Note similarly Polish *on nie żyje* 'he lives not,' considered more delicate than *on umarł* 'he died'; cf. Yiddish *er lebt nit* 'he lives not.'

[10] As concerns written language, secular newspapers rarely print formulas like 'God willing,' 'thank God,' etc.; such expressions are frequent in current Hasidic newspapers.

achieving the no-hitter. Slavic culture traditionally considered direct mention of the bear as taboo, and developed the euphemism 'honey-eater': Russian *medved'*, Ukrainian *vedmid'*; cf. also Germanic references to 'the brown one.' Public buildings in the United States frequently skip over the thirteenth floor in numbering floors, reflecting a Christian taboo avoidance.

A type of taboo avoidance in traditional Ashkenazic culture concerns the mentioning of two things within a single context when they should be kept apart. When nevertheless linked in a single context, they may be reseparated by insertion of the word *ləhavdl* 'make a distinction (between sacred and profane).' An aspect of distinction (found more in traditional culture) involves reference to Jewish vs. non-Jewish people, things, actions. This has led to a number of separate words, e.g., *jontəv* '(Jewish) holiday' vs. *xogə* 'non-Jewish holiday,' *besojləm* ~ *besalmən* 'Jewish cemetery' vs. *cvintər* 'non-Jewish cemetery' (M. Weinreich 1980: 193–195). In modern secular Yiddish this has largely faded out; thus, Soviet Yiddish may refer to May 1 as *der jontəv funəm proletarjat* 'the holiday of the proletariat.'

7.4.6 *"Secret languages" and professional jargons*

Members of a profession, occupation, lifestyle, hobby, etc., typically develop a specialized set of vocabulary, used primarily to set off insiders from outsiders. These speech styles are frequently referred to as "secret languages."[11] However, they are not languages per se, with independent grammatical structures. Rather, they are specialized jargons used within the structure of the vernacular. For example, M. Weinreich (1980: 181) describes the rise of a linguistic style within the Yiddish speech community involving conscious use of HA lexical material (not normally found in regular Yiddish) within a Yiddish frame as a way for Jews – a minority in a precarious position – to block access by German-speaking outsiders. This style is sometimes referred to as *jəhudi bəloj!* 'Jew, beware!' M. Weinreich (p. 181) gives the example: *zaj šomea vos der orl iz magid!* 'listen to what the Gentile is saying!' which was less comprehensible to German speakers than normal Yiddish *her vos der goj zogt!* This speech style thus employed "secret" words which the insiders believed to be inaccessible to the outsiders.[12]

In the European context the notion "secret language" is often used to refer to many distinct, though often overlapping, phenomena: professional jargons (e.g., of musicians or cattle dealers), thieves' cant (including related categories such as prisoners, prostitutes and pimps), vagabonds, etc. These groups have in common that they are at the margins of dominant society. These various

11 A better term might be "solidarity" speech; see Rothstein (1998: 24). On European notions of the "hidden language of the Jews," see Gilman (1986).

12 This contrasts with the conscious use of HAisms in Yiddish scribal language, where the goal was stylistic rather than cryptic, and the whole discourse took place intragroup.

specialized jargons are often confused with one another by outsiders, who see them as variants of a single phenomenon. Much of this confusion arises from the fact that these general (non-Jewish) European specialized jargons contain significant HA-origin vocabularies. Further feeding the general misconceptions, many of the same HA-origin lexical items are found in several or most of the specialized jargons, e.g., in specialized jargons as supposedly diverse as nineteenth-century Polish soldiers' slang, and Bargoens, the Dutch-based underworld slang. Sometimes a single term is used to refer to several different phenomena (e.g., Rotwelsch), sometimes a single phenomenon is known by a variety of names (see Wexler 1988; Siewert 1996). Much of the historical German interest in Yiddish arose in the context of the study of specialized jargons of the underworld (e.g., Avé-Lallemant 1858–1862). The present discussion considers non-Jewish specialized jargons only insofar as they touch upon Ashkenazic linguistic concerns.

We must distinguish between Jewish- and non-Jewish specialized jargons. Jewish thieves, cattle dealers, etc., were distinct from their non-Jewish counterparts (Glanz 1968). However, social – and thus, linguistic – contact did occur. Matras (1996: 48) asks about the nature of the relationship between Jewish cattle dealers' language and, on the one hand, Jewish vernacular speech (Yiddish and/or Jewish ethnolects of German), and, on the other hand, other (non-Jewish) specialized jargons (in German lands). He points out that the majority of HA-origin items in Rotwelsch also occur in the Jewish cattle dealers' language. He adds, however, that it is a one-way relationship: the Jewish cattle dealers' language served as one source for the general (non-Jewish) specialized jargon, but not the reverse. The Jewish cattle dealers' language of the region and the Rotwelsch of the region (here: Rexingen) share a common lexicon of HA origin, but not the main part of their specialized lexicon of non-HA origin. The Jewish cattle dealers' language contains – HAisms aside – hardly any other element of specialized Rotwelsch vocabulary (p. 53).

The nature of the HA element differs in the specialized jargons and in Yiddish (or its successor lect, Jewish-German). Matras (1996: 48–49) traces the source of the innovative HAisms in both Jewish and non-Jewish specialized jargons to the Jewish specialized jargon. These HAisms originated neither from Hebrew texts, nor from everyday Jewish vernacular speech, but, rather, were innovations created within the Jewish specialized jargon, and follow Germanic grammatical patterns rather than Hebrew ones; thus: *schochamajim* 'coffee,' lit. 'black' + 'water' (Hebrew grammar would require noun + adjective: *majim šxojrim*); *seifelbajis* 'toilet' < *seifela* 'urinate' (vulgar) + *bajis* 'house' – the normal Hebrew construction would be 'house of X' (p. 55). Differences are found at other levels of the grammar as well. In the phonology, HAisms with initial /x/ in Jewish specialized jargons frequently have initial /k/ in the non-Jewish jargons (< TH *ħ*); e.g., Jewish cattle dealers' language *chulef* 'milk,' *chassir* 'pig,' *choufes* 'debts' vs. non-Jewish *kuhlef, kassir, koufes* (pp. 55–56). In morphology, note Viennese underworld slang *Kalches* 'priest' (Burnadz 1966). The suffix *-es* traces back to TH *-u:θ*; in Yiddish, this is a marker of abstract nouns; cf. Yiddish *galxəs* 'Latin letters' (i.e., the written matter of Catholic monks) vs. *galəx – galoxəm* 'priest-s.'

Thus, the sociolinguistic "soup" differed for Jewish and non-Jewish marginal groups. While Jewish cattle dealers could create HAisms counter to Hebrew grammatical norms, they also, as Jews, had access to spoken Yiddish, and to Whole Hebrew (M. Weinreich 1980: 256). For Jewish specialized jargons the innovative HAisms stood in contrast to those HAisms resulting from continuous oral transmission in the chain of Jewish vernaculars. The non-Jews did not have direct access to LK as a source of raw materials from which to innovate; thus, the innovative HAisms came as "ready-made packages." Furthermore, the communication networks of the groups differed. Contact among non-Jewish groups permitted diffusion along those channels (see, e.g., Spangenberg 1996a, 1996b, on non-Jewish musicians' language). This holds for thieves' cant as well; Jewish thieves' bands were distinct from non-Jewish ones, and so were their sociolinguistic situations (Glanz 1968). Thus, the meanings of HAisms often differed among Jews and non-Jews (Matras 1996).

The task remains to distinguish between the vocabulary of various Jewish specialized jargons and that vocabulary which is part of general Yiddish slang. The boundaries are not always clear. Rothstein (1998: 24) distinguishes professional argot from slang according to "relative size of the group that uses it: typically small and more specialized in the case of the former, larger and more general (e.g., speakers of certain generations) in the latter." Thus, Yitskhok Varshavski[13] (1944) describes several words in the language of a Yiddish-speaking Warsaw thief; however, Noyman's (1947) response disputes several of Varshavski's words (e.g., *kifn* 'hit,' *cipn a štejn* 'throw a stone'), claiming that several of the words are not limited to thieves' jargon. Likewise, several of the words frequently listed for klezmer jargon are common to other (Jewish and non-Jewish) jargons as well. Investigation of slang and jargons must take into account that individuals and groups operate in multiply complex sociolinguistic milieus. Yiddish scholarship contains many descriptions of Jewish professional jargons (see Trivaks 1923; Dushman 1928; Elzet [= Zlotnik] 1920; Landau 1913; see also Bratkowsky 1988: esp. 152–154, for several bibliographic references): butcher shop speech (Zamet 1967); yiddophone dentists in Bialystok (Yunin 1972); shoemakers in Grodno (Sheskin 1965), etc. Blumental, in several articles from 1959 to 1964 in the journal *Yidishe Shprakh*, described specialized Yiddish terminology and expressions which arose during the Holocaust. While there can be local variation in vocabulary lists, there is

[13] One of several pseudonyms of future (1978) Nobel laureate Isaac Bashevis Singer.

frequently a commonality across regions. Consider briefly examples from the Yiddish professional jargons of musicians and horse/cattle dealers.

Bernshteyn (1959) discusses the specialized jargon of *klezmorim* 'musicians.' He focuses on vocabulary, and provides a summary of scholarship on the subject. *Klezmorim* (~ *klezmers*) were at the margins of mainstream society. Bernshteyn (p. 22) situates *klezmer-loshn* between professional jargon and underworld slang; many of the items occur in both (e.g., *baš* 'money'). Some klezmer terminology has crossed into modern Yiddish literature.

Bernshteyn cites six existing studies on *klezmer-loshn*, containing collectively approximately 1,000 vocabulary items of special interest.[14] Bernshteyn (1959: 23) points out that many of these words are common to other Yiddish specialized jargons: marriage brokers, cantors, waiters, entertainers, synagogue choirboys, and especially actors, and notes the links between these professions. He devotes specific discussion to words found in the memoirs of a Bessarabian Jewish musician. Where possible, Bernshteyn identifies the source for the given words, whether borrowed from a non-Jewish language, or via internal innovation. Sometimes he notes that a word is found in *klezmer-loshn* of other regions. Selected items from Bernshteyn's list, along with his explications, follow.

ukril – 'bread'; source?; StY *brojt*

bacamblən – 'pay'; < Yiddish *bacoln* 'pay' + *cimbl* 'cymbal'

baš – 'money'; < initials ב"ש for *Bankschilling*; the term referred to is external, while the strategy of creating a vocalized word from Hebrew initials is an internal Jewish tradition (cf. StY *jaš* 'booze' < the initials of *jajin sorəf* 'burned/distilled wine')

berjən – 'eat'; extension of meaning; cf. StY *berjən zix* 'manage (under difficult circumstances)'

dojl – 'chump'; perhaps a type of reverse slang, based on *jold* (same meaning)

žikrəcn – 'eyes'; source?

žečəs – 'things'; borrowing from Polish *rzecz* – *rzeczy* 'thing-s'; noteworthy is that this term is found in Bessarabia

tretərs – 'shoes'; cf. StY *tretn* 'tread'; Bernshteyn notes this is a widespread term, used beyond *klezmer-loshn*

lobən – 'play theatre'; agent form *labešnik* 'klezmer or actor'

motrə – 'look'; < Slavic, with *s*- prefix deleted; cf. Yiddish *smotrən*; Russian *smotret'*

mojšə – 'audience; public'; common to actors' jargon; < name *Mojšə* 'Moses'

štekər – 'pocket'; cf. StY *štekn* 'to stick'

14 More recently, Rothstein (1998: 28, note 5) refers to a compiled list of over 600 lexical items.

klivəcə 'pretty (woman)'; Bernshteyn claims a Czech source; cf. thieves' cant *kliv(ə)* 'pretty; good; smart'

Bernshteyn (1959: 24–25) discusses klezmer terminology used for the playing of dominos during free time; terms for tile faces include:

šestjorək – 'six'; < Slavic word for 'six'; *klezmer-loshn* also uses *šustər* 'shoemaker,' based on phonic similarity with this term

pitorək – 'five'; < Slavic; also: *fajf* < English *five*

frak – 'four'; source?

širək – 'three'; cf. *šurək*, name of a TH vowel pointing consisting of three dots

šejvə – 'two'; from the name for TH schwa, a symbol consisting of two dots

xirək – 'one'; based on TH *ḥiriq*, a symbol consisting of one dot

nakətər tof – 'blank,' lit. 'naked (letter) tof'; i.e., the letter without a dot; normally in Yiddish that letter (ת) is called *sof*

While the words are specific to the professional jargon, the grammar remains Yiddish. Bernshteyn (pp. 24–25) gives examples of sentences in *klezmer-loshn* which demonstrate that the syntax, morphology, and phonology are general Yiddish.

In a more recent discussion of *klezmer-loshn*, Rothstein (1998) provides numerous examples of specialized vocabulary (including a longer passage from Sholem Aleykhem's *Stempenyu*), as well as a categorization into types and semantic fields. He notes (p. 25) some words shared by *klezmer-loshn* and *ganovim-loshn* 'thieves' cant': *baš* 'money,' *tokn* 'give,' *matrən* 'look,' *klift* 'coat,' *krel* 'bread,'[15] *švaljər* 'ruble,' *drižblən* 'sleep; have sex' (only the latter meaning in *ganovim-loshn*). Rothstein (p. 25) discusses some semantic fields well-represented in *klezmer-loshn*, but notes that "[s]urprisingly, musical terminology is not prominent." However, he provides some examples: *fojal* 'clarinet,' *šojfər/čanik* 'trumpet,' *štolpər* 'flute,' *čekal/čikal* 'drum,' *varpljə/verpljə/verfli* 'violin,' *verbl* 'drum; bass,' *voršt* 'clarinet' (general Yiddish *voršt* 'sausage'); *lejənən blat* 'read music' (< 'read a page of Talmud'). Rothstein (p. 25) notes that there are many terms for money and numerals, e.g., *baker* 'two,' *baker baker* 'four,' *baker baker spen* 'nine,' and for food, professions, and body parts. Rothstein (p. 25) cites Trivaks' (1923) observation that obscene terminology was characteristic of male argot. Also noteworthy are the numerous words created via a type of reverse slang, where the position of consonants is changed within an existing word, e.g., *gejzər* 'watch' < *zejgər*; *xamən* 'make' < *maxn*; *xat* 'eight' < *axt*; *lakl* 'bride' < *kalə* (Rothstein 1998: 29, note 11). He also notes structural play with Slavic-origin etyma in *klezmer-loshn*.

[15] From Slavic; attested variants include *kril*, *krel*, *okril*, *okrel* and *ukril*; also: *krelik* 'a roll,' probably the source of *krelikəs* 'female breasts' (Robert Rothstein, p.c.).

The jargon of horse and cattle dealers constitutes another important area of investigation. Jews were long prominent in these trades, especially in that part of Ashkenaz comprising Switzerland, Germany, and Alsace. Guggenheim-Grünberg (1954: 49) calls this trade "one of the most important business specialties of German and Swiss Jews in the seventeenth and eighteenth centuries." Heavy Jewish presence in this trade continued into the twentieth century.

Guggenheim-Grünberg (1954: 49–50) describes the horse and cattle dealers' language (in Switzerland) as follows. They were (originally) WY speakers, who fashioned a professional technical vocabulary "adapted mostly from Hebrew." This also served as a "secret language of the trade" – as concerns both non-Jews and Yiddish-speaking Jews.[16] The very high frequency of HAisms included some items taken from the Merged Hebrew component of Yiddish, others taken directly from Hebrew (and not generally found in Yiddish).[17] More significantly, these HAisms are subject to productive processes within Swiss Yiddish grammar. Thus, the horse/cattle dealer term *kanjənə* ~ *kinjənə* 'buy' (cf. Hebrew root √qnh 'buy') yields *fərkanjənə* 'sell,' based on the model *kaufen* 'buy'-*verkaufen* 'sell'; similarly, *fəroumədə* 'understand' (cf. Hebrew root √ʕmd 'stand'), a calque of *ver* + *stehen*; *abšef* 'spavin,' based on German *Absatz*; here, prefix *ab* + *šef* (cf. Hebrew √šb 'sit').

This jargon included use of Hebrew letters in counting.[18] Additionally, many of the structural models for the integration of HAisms in this jargon are, not surprisingly, those found in Yiddish. Thus, newly innovated verbs containing an HA-origin root are either conjugated regularly, e.g., *xelkənə* 'divide,' *ge:šəmə* 'rain,' or occur as periphrastic verbs, e.g., *makir saĩ* 'know,' *siç məhanə saĩ* 'enjoy' (see Herzog 2000: 134–145). Guggenheim-Grünberg provides running dialogue (1954: 54–55), as well as an extensive glossary of those words (pp. 55–62) in the dialogue which she says "would not be intelligible to readers with a knowledge of standard Yiddish or German." Here she overstates, for many of the words are in fact found in many varieties of Yiddish, including StY. However, the list does include many words specific to the trade jargon. Some of these words are found in thieves' cant (and German slang) as well, e.g., *məlɔ:xənə* 'work.' Thus, this trade jargon is not hermetically sealed off from the broader, complex linguistic milieu.

[16] Over time, non-Jewish horse/cattle dealers acquired this specialized vocabulary. Conscious efforts to do so are documented as early as Wolf E. von Reizenstein (1764), where a chapter is devoted to this specific Jewish vocabulary.

[17] All the while, local Swiss Yiddish was undergoing a dehebraicization – replacing HA-component items with German words. There was also adaptation to some local Alemannic German features.

[18] Guggenheim-Grünberg (1954: 50, note 11) discusses whether this usage was an innovation or traces to earlier Jewish practice.

7.4.7 *"Style" vs. "register"*

To speak in a style identifiable with being, say, a musician, shoemaker, or dentist is often linked to the social status of these professions within the society as a whole. This tilts the scales in how certain speech is evaluated along register levels. For certain speakers at certain times, the use of a higher number of daytshmerisms may be linked to higher-register speech; in another time and place, polonisms may serve a similar function (Geller 2001: 30ff.). In much of the history of Ashkenazic Jewry, Whole Hebrew served as a source for register-elevation (Fishman 1981c: 744).

Complicating matters for the modern period is that language choice was often linked to socioeconomic class. Many middle- and upper-class Jews opted out of Yiddish and into reigning non-Jewish vernaculars of the locale (German, Dutch, Polish, French, etc.), leaving Yiddish as the language (of) "der ungebildeten Juden" (Liptsin 1944), lower socioeconomic classes, etc. However, this is a culturally loaded perspective, which bases evaluation in terms of dominant-society norms of what constitutes *Bildung*, status and success. The rise of modern European standard languages (and the attendant ideology) put particular models of language in a favored position, and subordinated other varieties according to how they differed from the favored models. As concerns Yiddish in the modern period, "register" seems linked to the rise of Yiddishism, and to the emergence of a notion of standard language, or at least of tacitly recognized norms of "correct" speech.

7.5 Models

Some important models of spoken Yiddish emerged in the modern period. These models were overarching varieties, seen by significant segments of the yiddophone population as idealized targets; an aspired-to, or at least tacitly acknowledged, "standard" (though not all groups aspired to an official standard). The models discussed below are: Theatre Yiddish, Standard Yiddish (the "YIVO variety"), Soviet Yiddish, and Hasidic Yiddish. Spoken variation is seen against the backdrop of these models, in terms of the dynamic tension between more intimate and/or local varieties in interplay with the broader-based models, as well as with speech styles. Discussion focuses on description of some characteristic grammatical features.

The construct employed below follows much recent scholarship on European languages, where scholars have set up categories: local dialect – regional dialect – colloquial language – standard language (e.g., Wiesinger 1989). These typically coexist in a supersystem, and constitute a continuum. Colloquial language is often seen as a type of modified standard. Frequently, scholars speak as well of regional varieties of the standard language. The general model is only partly accurate for the Yiddish situation as concerns the development of recognized regional varieties of the standard language. Clearly, though, models of Yiddish exist in the modern period, and with them a tendency toward consensus and consolidation of speech toward the model accepted by the particular group. Whether this involves conscious adoption of a standard language ideology (secular and Soviet Yiddish), or an unstated, tacit movement toward a set of canonized norms (Hasidic Yiddish), the pressure toward consolidation is clear.

The division into the specific models discussed below is both justifiable and arbitrary. The models are describable in terms of features, and evidence from speech variation by individuals shows the reality of these models as abstract target systems. At the same time, these models are not self-contained, or sealed off from other models, styles, and real-world social complexities.

7.5.1 Standard Yiddish

The term "standard (Yiddish) language" is itself problematic (Schaechter 2001).[19] The term *klal-šprax* 'standard language' dates to Yudl Mark (1938b); earlier, terms like *literarišə šprax* 'literary language' were used. The term *klal-šprax* never entered Soviet Yiddish usage; more often, one finds reference to "uniform" grammar, pronunciation, and spelling. Later, M. Weinreich (1950) distinguished between *klal-šprax* and *kultur-šprax* 'language of culture.'

The notion of modern spoken Standard Yiddish belongs largely in the context of a modern (as opposed to traditionalist) sub-set of yiddophone Jewry, and thus is often linked with secular Ashkenazic Jewry. Modern StY arose from an interplay of forces: internal (Jewish), and external (European-modern); see also Katz (1994). Schaechter (2001) speaks of the development of three main "regional standard languages" at the end of the nineteenth-century – in Podolye (SEY based), Poland (CY based), and Lite (NEY based). These in turn played a role in the shaping of the various twentieth-century models. The overall climate was ripe for the rise and acceptance of a standard language. Schaechter also mentions a precursor, namely, maskilic Yiddish, which marked the beginnings of a self-conscious awareness of Yiddish language usage.

Which variety was to serve as the pronunciation base for the standard language was still a matter of contention during the interwar period – the blossoming time of modern Yiddish scholarship and cultural activity. Thus, Prilutski (1927) argued that the standard language – a necessity for any cultivated people – should be based on Theatre Yiddish. Theatre Yiddish is based on a variety of SEY (Podolye), since, historically, it was in that dialect region that modern Yiddish theatre arose in the latter part of the nineteenth century. Prilutski's

[19] Much of the following discussion derives from a public lecture by Dr. Mordkhe Schaechter, June 27, 2001, at a seminar at the Jewish Theological Seminary, New York.

argumentation was based on the following. The stage pronunciation played a significant role in the rise of modern StG norms (*Bühnenaussprache*). Furthermore, Theatre Yiddish is particularly well suited, since it was SY based (the overwhelming majority of Yiddish speakers was SY-speaking), and, importantly, there had already occurred a significant leveling within Theatre Yiddish, since actors had to align their speech varieties on stage for cohesiveness within the play, as well as make their language understandable to audiences in all regions. Theatre Yiddish pronunciation largely refers to the use of a slightly modified SEY (Podolye) vowel system, with elimination of those features most identifiable as local-regional (Katz 1994: 213): (1) Podolye o_{11} (so-called "*totə-momə lušn*") is "restored" to [a]; (2) i_{25} ("*xirik lušn*") > [ej] (a CY feature!). Thus, Theatre Yiddish maintains features common to SY in general (*i* corresponding to PY $*u_{51}$, $*u{:}_{52}$; *u* corresponding to PY vowel 12), but "undoes" features specific to smaller sub-areas. Things turned out differently, however, as concerns the historical path taken in the development of modern StY, in spite of Prilutski, and in spite of the SY-speaking majority. Modern StY has emerged in two main varieties, neither of which is based on Theatre Yiddish.

The "YIVO" standard is often seen as having a NEY base. This perception is likely due to features such as e_{25}, and non-fronted $u_{51,52}$. In truth, however, YIVO StY is a compromise dialect containing features found in NEY, SEY, and CY (Schaechter 2001). Mark (1978: 17) calls the base of StY pronunciation a "modified NEY pronunciation." The StY vowel system consists of an inventory which is identical with one variety of NEY – that of the Vilna intelligentsia (M. Weinreich 1973: I, 308; Katz 1994: 207) – but differs in the distribution of historical vowels within that system. The most identifiable regional features have been dropped in StY, including the undoing of several mergers, e.g., the (general) NEY merger of vowels 22,24 with 42,44 as [ej]; thus, StY *sejfər*$_{22}$ 'holy book,' *brejt*$_{24}$ 'broad,' *brojt*$_{42}$ 'bread,' *kojfn*$_{44}$ 'buy,' vs. general NEY [ej] in all these examples. Lacking as well in StY is the SY merger of the historical *i* and *u* series. StY also lacks other regionally marked features, e.g., NEY *sabesdiker losn*; CY word-final devoicing; NEY hiatus-*j*. Regional u_{54} (present in sub-regions of both NEY and SEY) has given way to StY *oj*$_{54}$ (Jacobs 1994a). Outside the phonology, StY also eschews (Schaechter 1969) (largely) CY pronouns *ec*/*enk* 'you'; and NEY generalized past tense AUX *hobn*; StY uses the three-gender system, not the neuterless NEY system.

The tendency toward supraregionalism in the spoken language goes back at least to the nineteenth century (a century earlier for the modern literary language). This is observable at both the popular and the intellectual levels. Katz (1994: 208) points out Borokhov's (1913) observation that, in the emerging secular Yiddish world, the NEY intelligentsia were avoiding NEY *ej*$_{42,44}$, and that SEY intelligentsia in the Ukraine were moving toward NEY vocalism (and away from S[E]Y). Similarly, Geller (2001: 32) notes the esteem of Warsaw

CY speakers for NEY. At the popular level, dialect-based hypercorrection (both systematic and sporadic) is found; thus, *šn[u]ps* 'neck-tie' in Sosnovce CY (Jacobs 1990a: 77); *r[ej]fn* 'to call' widespread in SEY (Herzog 1969: 67); *p[aj]liš* 'Polish' in NEY; cf. StY *šnips*$_{31}$, *rufn*$_{52}$, *pojliš*$_{42}$.

Yiddish supraregionalism in Eastern Ashkenaz was part of a hierarchical construct: local dialect – broader regional dialect – standard/supraregional variety. Like other emerging national languages in Europe, the standard variety was linked to the literary language. Recall the anecdotal evidence (§3.9), where American-born native speakers spontaneously produced *evər* > *ejər* > *ojər* 'ear,' reflecting deeper NEY dialect, broader NEY (a hybrid form between NEY and StY?), and StY, respectively; likewise, the spontaneous production of *køyfn* > *kejfn* > *kojfn* 'buy' reflecting, respectively, CourlY, general NEY, and StY. Dialect speech was giving way to waves of modernization (Herzog 1964). Where dialect did not die out completely, or immediately, the most stereotypical dialect features were becoming increasingly stigmatized, and most subject to elimination, e.g., *sabesdiker losn* in NEY (U. Weinreich 1952). However, the disappearance of dialect speech occurred along a multidimensional continuum. Thus, CourlY in the twentieth century could move simultaneously both toward broader NEY and toward emerging StY. The emerging consensus-based standard pronunciation "undid" the most identifiable regional features, and was "felt" to be (i.e., identified as) "*litvish*."[20] This process of standardization of pronunciation could take different paths in different areas. For example, StY *oj*$_{54}$ spread into the NEY and SEY areas by different means (Jacobs 1994a); in (many sub-regions of) NEY, it diffused phonologically, as part of an adjustment in the overall vowel system; in SEY, it diffused lexically.

7.5.2 *Soviet Yiddish*

Yiddish linguists in the Soviet Union also showed a keen interest in the cultivation of a standard Yiddish language, though not using the term "standard" itself (Erlich 1981). As with the emerging YIVO standard, the Soviet consensus Yiddish language had, at first glance, an NEY caste (based largely on the NEY of Belorussia), along with some features of SEY of the Ukraine (Birnbaum 1979b; Schaechter 2001). There was considerable activity in the 1920s and 1930s in the research centers in Minsk and Kiev. Some of this interest was purely dialectological (primarily in Minsk; see Veynger 1925, 1929; Vilenkin 1931). However, there was also much interest in normative language usage, and the normalization of orthography. Much of this was heavily ideological; Yiddish (along with other Soviet national minority languages) was to be the

[20] The prestige of *Lite*, and NEY, especially for the emerging secular and politicized circles played a significant role in this perception; see M. Weinreich (1980); Katz (1994).

medium of the progressive proletarian elite of the new Soviet order (Erlich 1981: 706–707).

Considerable discussion concerned the HA component in Yiddish. It was seen as serving outmoded and discredited bourgeois and clericalist class interests, and needing to be systematically expunged from progressive Yiddish (Shtif 1929).[21] Dehebraization efforts included the orthographic reforms, i.e., the "naturalized" spelling of HA-origin Yiddish words,[22] and the elimination of word-final ם, ן, ך, ץ, ף. Such moves attempted to distance Yiddish from association with Hebrew, and LK traditions. However, the proponents of dehebraization differentiated between HAisms which were firmly part of everyday Yiddish, and those which were part of a conscious LK layer (see Shtif 1929). In spite of such efforts, dehebraization was "not very successful" (Erlich 1981: 704).

Zaretski (1931) *Far a proletarisher shprakh* ('In favor of a proletarian language') is a collection of essays concerned with, among other things, the nature of newspaper Yiddish vocabulary and its relationship to its readership; dehebraization; questions of internationalisms in Yiddish. The essay *Yidish! Yidish!* deals with debates over what constitutes authentic Yiddish, and makes a distinction between folk-language and culture language. Zaretski enters into stylistic debates on whether certain constructions, such as the passive (p. 105), are properly part of the authentic folk-language. In summary, Soviet Yiddish linguistics of the 1920s/1930s was very concerned with the cultivation of Yiddish as a language for all the needs of modern discourse in an emerging progressive Soviet society. As such, the language required a firmly normalized orthography, based on scientific principles. Much of the scholarship attempted to wrap itself in the general theoretical linguistic frameworks of the time. Zaretski's grammar (1926) stands out even today as the best attempt at a comprehensive, theory-based grammar of Yiddish.[23]

Birnbaum's (1979b) discussion of Soviet Yiddish is based on written sources – the monthly *Sovetish Heymland*; the daily *Birobidzhaner Shtern*. The topics covered include: gender; plurals; (dialect-based) variants; alphabet and spelling. The largest portion is reserved for the etymological components – Semitic, German, and Slavic. Concerning gender Birnbaum (p. 30) notes variation for the same noun, e.g., *der* ~ *dos kol* 'the voice,' reflecting neuterless N(E)Y vs. three-gender SY. Birnbaum also notes the regularized use of feminine gender with abstract noun suffixes *-əs*, *-iš*, *-kajt* (vs. neuter gender in CY). He (p. 30) discusses choice of lexical variants: *nit* over *ništ* 'not'; *rejdn* over *redn* 'speak'; *ton* over *tun* 'do,' etc. Birnbaum (pp. 32–33)

[21] For response to Shtif, see M. Weinreich (1931).

[22] On support for naturalized spelling outside the Soviet Union, see Erlich (1981: 701).

[23] Under increasingly oppressive political pressure in the late 1920s, Zaretski – attacked for being overly formalistic in his grammatical approach – retreated from some stances in his 1929 second edition; see Kahan Newman (1983: 2–5).

notes the regular integratedness of the HA component in Yiddish (even in the Soviet Union); often, however, "words of Semitic origin have been replaced by German ones – an inheritance from the Enlightenment of the nineteenth and twentieth centuries" and the old and new words are "used side by side," e.g., *šilər* ~ *talmid* 'pupil,' *erə* ~ *kovəd* 'honor,' *farflixtung* ~ *hisxajvəs* 'obligation.' Concerning the German component, Birnbaum (p. 34) discusses naturalization – the conscious nativization of recent borrowings, e.g., borrowed German *Erfolg* 'success' > Yiddish *derfolg* (a process common in much of literary Yiddish and literary-language-influenced spoken Yiddish of the modern period in Eastern Europe). Birnbaum's discussion of the Slavic component (pp. 37–39) concerns Russification. The pre-Revolution Russian influence on Yiddish was very minor. In the Soviet period, Russian influence on Yiddish (and other national minority languages) grew considerably. Birnbaum's examples include: the names of months, e.g., *janvar* 'January,' *fevral* 'February' (cf. StY *januar, februar*); calquing, e.g., *derlernən* 'study' < Russian *izučat'*, *ojsfiln* 'carry out (a duty)' < Russian *ispoln'at'*. Additionally, Soviet Yiddish adopted Soviet (Russian-)style abbreviations and officialese (see also Estraikh 1994: 7ff. 1999: 45ff.): *kom* < *komitet* 'committee' in *ojsfirkom* 'executive committee,' *gegntkom* 'regional committee'; the use of *al-*: *alveltləx* 'universal,' *alfolkiš* 'of all peoples' (cf. Russian use of *vs'e-* 'all'); 'class' as (invariant) adjective in *di klasovə linjə* 'the class line/policy' vs. nominal-based modifier *klasn-* in non-Soviet Yiddish (Estraikh 1994: 5).

7.5.3 Dynamic tension between standard and dialect

The new sociolinguistic superstructure created a dynamic tension between the Yiddish of H-functions and the Yiddish of L-functions. Dialect speech increasingly became viewed as non-H and stigmatized. This is even to be observed in traditionalist circles, which generally eschewed the mostly secularist-based standard language ideology. For example, Berliner (1981) complains of the encroaching influences emanating from secularist Vilna Yiddish, which corrupted the good (CY-based) Yiddish of the Beys-Yankev religious schools of Poland. Berliner laments that the "Litvak" pronunciation was creeping into the speech of pupils and teachers alike; and that good, authentic CY/SY speakers were opting for this inauthentic southern riff on northern Yiddish when speaking in public. Further examples are seen in Jochnowitz (1981) on Yiddish among Lubavitch Hasidim in America. He notes the increasingly frequent use of back [R], in line with general trends in Yiddish, even though Lubavitch historically (NEY speakers from Belorussia) had apical [r]. Jochnowitz (p. 732) claims that there was little or no StY influence among his informants, "although the elimination of rare lexical items necessarily favors standard forms," e.g., *drejdl* 'teetotum' has begun pushing out the inherited regional form *gor*; similarly, a generational shift from inherited regional *holt hobn* > *lib hobn* 'like; love' (the latter is more widespread, and used in StY as well). Jochnowitz further notes that *sabesdiker losn* was already dead in the parents' generation. Thus, traditionalist – even Hasidic – speech was not immune to what was happening in the broader Yiddish sociolinguistic milieu of the modern period.

The recession of dialect speech is thus seen in the contexts of modernization, urbanization, and westernization.[24] The emerging new social, political, and economic networks laid the ground for the "systematic extinction" of Yiddish dialects (Herzog 1964), leaving in their wake a continuum of speech varieties along a standard–dialect spectrum. The Yiddish scholarly literature is replete with examples. For example, Peltz (1990: 65–68) notes the presence of dialect doublets, where an SEY speaker has (expected) o_{11} alternating with a_{11}, sometimes in the same lexical item. We observe frequent "anomalies" in dialect speech, where an informant generally produces the expected regional pronunciation of a given stressed vowel, but for specific words will consistently have another realization.

That speakers had implicit knowledge of a hierarchical supersystem is evident from the examples given above, such as *køyfn* (CourlY) ~ *kejfn* (general NEY) ~ *kojfn* (StY) 'buy,' *evər* > *ejər* > *ojər* (StY) 'ear,' as well as from dialect-based hypercorrection, which most typically was unidirectional in its intent – i.e., toward the perceived H- or standard language, away from dialect. Fishman (1981c: 741–743) notes that among a group of SEY speakers in his personal social circle certain SEY features were used in intragroup intimate speech. However, when "outsiders" (non-SEY speakers) were present, the S(E)Y features in question were dropped in favor of the more general, less localized realizations; thus: *o* > *a* (*totə* 'father,' *momə* 'mother,' *kolt* 'cold'> *tatə, mamə, kalt*); *i* > *u* (*pitər* 'butter,' *mitər* 'mother,' *šviəs* 'Shavuoth'> *putər, mutər, švuəs*); *Ø* > *h* / #_ (*olb* 'half,' *amər* 'hammer,' *ejs* 'hot' > *halb, hamər, hejs*). Fishman notes "no such transitions seem to occur" (or, occur much less frequently) for *u* > *o* (vowel 12/13: *zugn/zogn* 'say'), or *ej* > *e* (vowel 25; *lejbn/lebn* 'live'). In summary, stigmatized dialect features tended to recede in the emerging sociolinguistic milieu. When dialect features remained, they often did so as covariants in the repertoire of individual speakers. Further examples are found in Gutmans' (1958) analysis of spoken Yiddish on the radio, and Prince's (1987) discussion of the songs of folksinger Sarah Gorby.

7.5.4 Model without a standard language: contemporary Hasidic Yiddish

The following discussion is based on my observations (June 2001) of Hasidic Yiddish in New York, and does not take into consideration Hasidic Yiddish in

[24] M. Weinreich (1980: 318) notes that "[t]he very concept of dialect is a product of modern times."

Europe, Israel, and elsewhere, and ignores as well differences between Hasidic groups (Jochnowitz 1981; Isaacs 1999). Although written and spoken language are distinct phenomena, there is overlap between the two. For example, current Hasidic newspapers contain – in addition to frequent formulaic LKisms – many anglicisms (lexical and syntactic) which reflect the spoken language. Code-switching – both situational and metaphorical – is a regular, integral part of American Hasidic speech, with clear differences between male and female speech. Much of the research on Hasidic speech thus must necessarily focus on language contact, bilingualism, language choice, code-switching, and the nature of the linguistic competence of speakers in this speech community.

The Hasidim generally have not taken part in the rise of a secular StY. Yet there are generalizations to be made about a model for Hasidic spoken Yiddish. First, it is SY/CY-based; Hasidism arose and was centered in SY territory.[25] Still, encroachments from the broader Yiddish speech community occur, including from secularist (St)Y (Berliner 1981; Jochnowitz 1981). The following data are taken from one recent issue of each of three New York Hasidic newspapers.[26] The newspaper examples focus on items which reflect spoken language.

The three newspapers regularly show a single undifferentiated case for F.SG nouns, even after prepositions, e.g., (*mit*) *di hilf* '(with) the help,' (*mit*) *di perzenlixə batejligung* '(with) the personal participation.' However, this likely reflects something beyond a simple collapse of case distinctions for F.SG nouns. More likely is an ongoing collapse of the overall case and gender system in the spoken language, with a tendency toward generalized definite article [de ~ də ~ di ~ da]. However, it is a collapse in progress, with synchronic instability in the system. The same noun may be coupled with different definite articles within the same paragraph of a newspaper article. There is also frequent gender assignment counter to prevailing gender in most varieties of Yiddish, e.g., *der konferenc* vs. StY *di konferenc* (see Jochnowitz 1981: 729–730). Other examples found in the newspapers suggest that the case and gender collapse in the spoken language has been filtered through the written language, and has forced gender-assignment decisions that the spoken language cannot support. Thus, one finds examples such as *mit der fotər* 'with the father,' where *fotər* is masculine, but the expected dative (or at least oblique) definite article is *dem*; similarly, *far unzər jidiš-ər ganəf* 'for our Jewish thief'; *culib dos stabilkajt* 'because of the stability,' where N.SG definite article *dos* remains unchanged after preposition *culib*. One finds NPs with total mixing and haphazard case and gender markings,

25 After initial inroads into NEY territory (*Lite*) Hasidism was opposed and banned there. The exception is the presence of Lubavitch Hasidism, which is NEY-based. CY/SY is also the base of traditionalist Yiddish of the Beys-Yankev schools of interwar Poland (Berliner 1981; Birnbaum 1981).

26 The three newspapers are *Der Yid*; *Der Blat*; *Di Tsaytung*. For convenience, the transliterations use StY values, e.g., here, vowel *ej*$_{24}$ (CY has [aj]). Note further that the orthography in these newspapers uses <"> both for vowel 22,24 and for vowel 34.

e.g., a classified advertisement asks: *darft ir a hejmiš-ə farleslix-ər drajvər* 'do you need a [Hasidic] reliable driver.' This likely reflects a spoken language situation with uniform suffix [ə] in both instances.

The frequent influences from English are of several different types. There is outright code-switching, where a whole English phrase is used.[27] Among numerous English loanwords are, e.g., *džab* 'job,' *elektrišon* 'electrician,' *drajvər* 'driver,' *ofis furnitšər* 'office furniture.' Sometimes these retain English inflections, e.g., *selfoun-s* 'cellphone-s.'[28] Other times there is some integration into Yiddish structure, e.g., nouns *bejbisitər* 'babysitter,' *drajvər* 'driver' have led to verbs *bejbisitn* 'babysit,' *drajvn* 'drive.' Sometimes, a loanword will remain uninflected, e.g., *ojf a konfidenšal-Ø ojfn* 'in a confidential$_{\text{[uninflected]}}$ manner'; *zuxt an ekspiriensd-Ø fond reizer* 'seeks an experienced-Ø fundraiser'; however, grammatical integration also occurs in: *bestə gəfit cum sajz* 'best fit to the size.' Calques are frequent; thus: *prubirt ojs* < 'tries out'; *ojgust dem 5-tn* 'August the fifth,' *dem fertn fun juli* 'the 4th of July,' *noxn zajn farxapt <far> 14 štundn* 'after being kidnapped <for> 14 hours'; *fun ejn zajt <fun> vald* 'from one side of the woods' is likely a calque of the English structure (cf. StY partitive construction: *fun ejn zajt vald*); *in a veg vos štert dos drajvn* 'in a way which disturbs driving' (cf. StY *ojf an ojfn* 'in a way'); a clothing ad featuring two cartoon figures in dialogue has one saying *dopəlt di prajz* < 'double THE price,' the second replying: . . . *gəcolt hob ix helft prajz* 'I paid HALF PRICE.' Noteworthy in the phonology is the spelling <אָו> in English loans, e.g., באַנגאַלאָו *bongolou* 'bungalow,' סעלפֿאָונס *selfouns* 'cellphones.' Difficult to characterize is *biz cum di endə* 'until the end'; perhaps *biz cum* has been reinterpreted as a single preposition modeled after English *until*. Also noteworthy is the frequent use of sentence-initial *ojx* 'also' as a weight-bearing sentence unit triggering v-2, e.g., *ojx hobn mir ofis furnitšər* 'we also have office furniture.'

7.6 Other features

Fishman (1981c: 747) writes: "Almost every sociolinguistic consideration of Yiddish is bound to be in the context of multilingualism." That is perhaps overstated. Some phenomena concerning style, register, and tempo may be looked at internally. The following provides a few examples, along with suggestions for future investigation.

Pronoun *mir* 'we' often reduces > *mə* when following the verb; thus – in careful, slower, or formal speech – (*brojt*) *esn mir* '(it's bread that) we eat' reduces

[27] The code-switching works in both directions. Thus, there is a furniture ad entirely in English, except for the inclusion of <היימישע עולם> (*hejmišə ojləm*) 'reliable people.' Another ad in English (all Latin letters) includes: "We will toivel and deliver" (cf. StY *tojvl zajn* 'immerse'); "Join the list of kallahs" ('brides').

[28] Note Yiddish plural *s*, not the phonetic [z] dictated by English grammar; conversely, Yiddish loans in English, e.g., *latke-s* 'potato pancake-s,' take plural marker [z] from English grammar.

to (*brojt*) *esnmə* in faster or more casual speech. Reduced *mə* is a clitic;[29] it may be that clitics typically occur in certain speech styles. Certain verbs, especially an AUX like *hobn* 'have,' lend themselves to the creation of exceptional forms which go beyond mere cliticization; thus, in non-formal speech: *homə* < hobn *mir* 'we have'; *xob* < *ix hob* 'I have.' Note also the casual-speech clitic forms for the future AUX: *xvel* ~ *ixl* ~ *xel* < *ix vel* 'I shall'; *dust* < *du vest* 'you will'; *ert* < *er vet* 'he will'; *mirn* < *mir veln* 'we shall,' etc. Non-auxiliary verb *veln* 'boil (milk)' permits fast-speech clitic form *xvel* 'I boil (milk),' but not ***xel*, ***ixl*, etc. Reduced *s* (< *dos*) in *nemdirskind* < *nem dir dos kind* 'take (unto you) the child' might be considered a clitic used only in fast speech.

Also related to speech tempo are phenomena such as CY drawl (§4.1.11). CY /štu:t/ 'city' is more likely to be drawled in slower speech, undrawled in faster speech. It would be interesting to investigate the relationship, if any, between speech tempo and styles according to region, occupation, gender, generation, and other variables. Other features meriting a closer look for sociolinguistic patterning include: subject PRO-DROP, e.g., (±*du*) *bist a šrajbər* '(you) are a writer'; the distribution of the *ir* vs. *du* form among different groups of Yiddish speakers (Slobin 1981); and the widespread tendency to produce a *z*-less form of past tense AUX *iz*, e.g., *er i(z) gəgangən* 'he went.' In more careful speech the form with [z] is more common, perhaps a "reading pronunciation." It would be worthwhile to set up a scale of style levels for Yiddish, and determine, for example, if *z*-less past tense AUX *i* implies clitics, that is, if *i gəkumən* implies *esn-mə*, or the opposite, or if AUX *iz* implies non-reduced subject pronouns.

7.7 Written Yiddish

The relationship between written and spoken Yiddish is complex, and has varied over time. Fishman (1981a: 63) notes the very "meager studied recognition of the differences between spoken and written (i.e., printed) language and of the separate standards that these might pursue." In the pre-modern period the dominant role of LK as the language of writing in Ashkenaz was clear, and largely uncontested. M. Weinreich (1980: 255–256) notes that LK, in addition to being "firmly linked" with the sacred texts, was used in a variety of established functions. Thus, "as a matter of course," rabbis conducted oral discussion in Yiddish, and, just as self-evidently, wrote about the discussion in LK. LK was the language of general recording, as well as for family notices on the flyleaf of a festival prayerbook, in business and general letters, etc. Gender-based differences are evident; LK was "so much more associated with the male world" in traditional Ashkenaz (p. 270). Typically, the letter of a yeshiva student to his father was written in LK, with a few lines to his mother added in Yiddish

29 It has become regularized as the 1P.PL verb suffix in CY.

(p. 256). Letters written by women typically contained an opening salutation and a closing embellishment in LK, but switched to Yiddish for the body of the letter (p. 256). However, the line between male and female written style is not always as clearcut as sometimes claimed. Thus, the memoirs of Glikl of Hamel (recorded between 1691 and 1715) show frequent use of stylistic LKisms within the Yiddish, and frequent use of code-switching to Whole Hebrew passages throughout the text (Landau 1901).[30] Yiddish nevertheless developed a set of circumscribed written roles. Official LK documents such as divorce decrees, legal testimony, etc., contain verbatim quotes in Yiddish, and posted public proclamations could be in a mixed LK/Yiddish (M. Weinreich 1980: 255–256). Furthermore, the boundaries (in both directions) between LK and Yiddish could be fluid; one frequently encounters Yiddish influences in Ashkenazic Whole Hebrew texts (Noble 1958). Finally, there evolved over time an increasing use of Yiddish in the liturgy, both oral and written (M. Weinreich 1980: 258ff.).

7.7.1 Taytsh *and Yiddish scribal language*

In addition to Whole Hebrew and Yiddish, two other important written media arose in Ashkenaz: the *taytsh* tradition, and the Yiddish scribal language. While neither variety in itself constitutes written Yiddish, both have had an impact on modern Yiddish stylistics.

The term *taytsh* refers to the calque language which originated as a practical aid for translation of the bible and prayers.[31] The calque tradition for practical bible translation is found in many Jewish culture areas, e.g., the written Ladino of the Sefardim (as opposed to their vernacular, Judezmo). This phenomenon has antecedents in Jewish tradition (and, hence, vertical legitimation), tracing back to the practice of reading aloud both the Hebrew original (twice) and the (Judeo-)Aramaic *targum* (once); see M. Weinreich (1980: 68–69). *Taytsh* consists of a systematic morpheme-by-morpheme translation. The result is an artificial calque language which does not follow Yiddish syntax, illustrated here using the first sentence in the bible:

AshkH	bə-rejšis	boro	elojhim	es hašomajim	vəes	hoorec
Taytsh	in onfang	hot bašafn	got	Ø di himlen	un Ø	di erd
Gloss	in beginning	created	God	[ACC] the skies	and	[ACC] the earth

Taytsh differs here from Yiddish word order; cf. StY *in onhejb hot got bašafn dem himl un di erd*. In Yiddish, the topicalized adverbial 'in the beginning'

30 For analysis of the language and style of letter writing in Ashkenaz, see Sunshine (1991).
31 On use of the term *taytsh* simply as the name for Yiddish, see M. Weinreich (1980: 316–317).

triggers regular movement of the finite AUX *hot* ahead of the subject *got* 'God.' In *taytsh*, the whole verbal group *hot bašafn* occurs before subject *got*, reflecting not a movement, but, rather, a calquing of the original Hebrew.

A further characteristic of *taytsh* is the systematic avoidance of HA-origin words, even if these happen to occur as everyday (Merged Hebrew) words in spoken Yiddish. Thus, the normal word for 'inheritance' in Yiddish is *jərušə* (< TH *jəru:šɔ:*); however, *taytsh* avoids this, using instead *arb* (cf. StG *Erbe*). A rare HAism which made its way into *taytsh* is *mekn* 'erase'; cf. TH √mħq. Noble (1939, 1943) provides thorough discussion of *taytsh*, and of the *taytsh* legacy in later Yiddish. Because of its canonized use in bible translation, *taytsh* came to acquire an identifiable cachet, and was used later within modern Yiddish literature as a device for archaizing stylistic effect.

The Yiddish scribal language [ScrY] is a macaronic style of writing employed by communal and organizational scribes. M. Weinreich (1980: 257) suggests that ScrY arose originally as "individual stylistic caprice" which gained wider currency. ScrY was "used by Yiddish scribes in both Western and Eastern Europe between the 16th–18th centuries" (Kahan-Newman 1990: 35; M. Weinreich 1980: 307ff.). ScrY involves repeated switching (within a text) back and forth between Whole Hebrew and Yiddish. It thus differs both from Yiddish texts which contain Merged Hebrew elements, and from Yiddish texts, such as correspondence, which happen to contain Whole Hebrew salutations or embellishments. ScrY exhibits a number of significant patterns worthy of linguistic description and analysis. Kahan-Newman (pp. 36–37) provides ten introductory sample strings of ScrY (along with their putative Rabbinic Hebrew equivalents, and English glosses) from a text from 1676. Two examples are given here:[32]

(1)	RbcH	kaašer	ejze balbos	mexujev lešalem	sxar limud	leejze melamed
		A	B	C	D	E
	ScrY	ven	ejze balbos	leejze melamed	sxar limud	šuldig ver
		A	B	E	D	C
	gloss	'[A] when	[B] some man	[C] owes	[D] tuition	[E] to a teacher'
(2)	RbcH	ad	še-hu	jerace	es hamelamed horišon	
		A	B	C	D	
	ScrY	biz	er	hamelamed horišon	cufridn štelt	
		A	B	D	C	
	gloss	'[A] till	[B] he	[C] molifies	[D] the first teacher'	

Kahan-Newman (p. 38) generalizes regarding the examples: "It is apparent that although the majority of the units in these ten scribal Yiddish passages are Hebrew, they largely follow Yiddish word order. It is as though the scribes

[32] Kahan-Newman's romanization is followed here. See also U. Weinreich (1958d) on ScrY.

were using a Hebrew norm to generate the number of morphological units and a Yiddish norm to place these units within the sentence." Both of the examples given above are dependent clauses, and ScrY shows finite verb in final position, something more typical of (German-influenced) WrLg A than of modern Yiddish. Kahan-Newman also notes the ScrY tendency to "provide a Yiddish morph for each Hebrew morph" (p. 38). Kahan-Newman discusses constraints on the shape of ScrY; e.g., a Hebrew verb may not co-occur with a Yiddish subject (p. 38). ScrY had an effect on written Yiddish; "[t]hrough the scribe's hybrid register, Yiddish gained the possibilities of a stiffened chancery style" (M. Weinreich 1980: 258), including many of the H-register conjunctions.

7.7.2 Yiddish literary language

The first literary Yiddish language (WrLg A) arose in the Old Yiddish period. WrLg A was based on WY, and was supraregional, with "regional angularities . . . polished off" (M. Weinreich 1980: 727). WrLg A served as the pan-Ashkenazic literary norm until its decline at the cusp of modern times. Before the emergence of WrLg B, even books written and published in Eastern Europe conformed to the WrLg A model. This was in part market-driven, as seen, for example, in the conscious avoidance of (Dutch Yiddish) localisms in the Amsterdam newspaper *Kurantin* (1686–1687). The decline of WY resulted from a constellation of factors – *Haskole*, acculturation to German, Dutch, etc., and the shift away from Yiddish as the vernacular of Western Ashkenazic Jewry.

WrLg B – based on spoken EY – largely emerged in the nineteenth century. However, the transition began earlier, as Yiddish texts produced in Eastern Europe began showing some EY elements; thus, see Herzog (1965b) on Markuze's *Seyfer refues* (1790). Kerler (1999) provides analysis of some key texts which illustrate the movement from WrLg A > WrLg B. Kerler (p. 25) distinguishes between *transition* and *shift*. He defines transition as "the reprinting, re-editing, and linguistic revision of old Yiddish literary works that began in the late eighteenth century," often "updated," i.e., modified toward EY norms. He uses the term *shift* to refer to "the linguistic characteristics of the earliest Eastern Yiddish books from the last three decades of the eighteenth century," including "entirely new translations, one new Eastern Yiddish version of an older literary work, as well as two original works written in Eastern Yiddish."

Fishman (1985) addresses the macro-sociological question of "Why did Yiddish change?" in the modern period. WY had started disappearing in Germany, Holland, etc., further undercutting the power base for WY-based WrLg A. The emergence and crystallization of the EY dialects created speech varieties that were even more distant from WrLg A. Long before the emergence of the new literary language, EYisms had been sporadically creeping into WrLg A texts produced in Eastern Ashkenaz. The social changes of this watershed time were major as well. Fishman notes that, with rare exceptions, no pre-modern Yiddish publication used the square script font for Yiddish (square script was reserved for printed LK).[33] Yiddish publications after 1800 regularly did so, switching from earlier *mashket* (§2.7.1). Culture-internally, this was part of the struggle for increased (H-)functions of Yiddish in modernizing Ashkenazic society. In general European terms, it parallels the struggles of other European vernaculars to be elevated to languages of *Kultur*, national literature and discourse, worthy of standardization. The subsequent language battles between Yiddish and (revived spoken) Hebrew for recognition as the emerging language of Jewish national culture were battles between contenders within a common modern framework.

7.7.3 Contemporary written Yiddish

The interplay of often competing forces gave rise to various styles of written Yiddish in the contemporary period (twentieth century). Our focus is on widely used and accepted norms within the mainstream(s) of Yiddish written discourse: personal, literary, journalistic, etc.[34] The forces of general European modernity resulted in an influx of influences from NHG, as well as from internationalisms. Emerging modes of political discourse – nationalism, internationalism, socialism, etc. – had their impact(s) on Yiddish discourse styles and vocabulary. Still, tradition and continuity remained part of the equation. WrLg A and earlier forms of Yiddish literature made themselves felt in the nascent modern written language. As well, internal Jewish bilingualism (even as this was changing or eroding among large numbers of secularizing Jews) meant that a considerable arsenal of LKisms continued to be available for stylistic enrichment within written Yiddish. Likewise, the modern written language could draw from *taytsh* and ScrY as sources of enrichment: *taytsh* for archaic effect; ScrY for the emerging chancery and formal spoken style (M. Weinreich 1980: 258).

Schaechter (1969: 284–285) distinguishes three main types of contemporary written Yiddish: (1) Standard Yiddish [StY] – which he defines generally as the literary language conforming to "the orthographic, grammatical, and stylistic norms" of the YIVO, and of the reference manuals;[35] (2) Non-Standard Yiddish [Non-StY] – "those varieties of the written language – primarily the journalistic

[33] The notable exception is *Liblikhe tfile oder kreftige artsnay far guf un neshome*, by Aaron ben Shmuel Hergershausen (1709); see M. Weinreich (1980: 262–263).

[34] Principally ignored here are phenomena such as nineteenth-century romanized dialect texts for amusement in Germany (Lowenstein 1979).

[35] See *Takones* in Schaechter (1999), U. Weinreich (1949, 1968), Stutshkov (1950), Schaechter and Weinreich (1961).

prose of the daily Yiddish press – which have lagged behind in adopting the more modern standards"; (3) Written Yiddish [WritY] – encompasses both StY and Non-StY. Central to his discussion, Schaechter defines daytshmerish as "the tendency to appeal to Standard German . . . as a model of 'correctness' for the Yiddish language." Schaechter's thesis is that many features of contemporary WritY can be attributed to a "hidden standard" – "the unconscious preference for those linguistic forms that coincide with Standard German (NHG)," as opposed to spoken regional varieties of Yiddish. Schaechter (p. 285) summarizes the susceptibility of WritY to NHG influence as follows: StY (*belle lettres*) – relatively immune; StY (non-belletristic prose) – selectively resistant; Non-StY[36] – highly susceptible.

German influence has fluctuated in the history of WritY. Schaechter (1969: 285) writes: "The First Literary Language . . . was based on . . . WY . . . dialects of the pre-nineteenth century period. Patterned on the . . . MHG . . . model, it adopted not only the imagery of the non-Jewish literature of the period . . . but many of its standards of linguistic correctness as well." Schaechter contrasts this with the Second Literary Language (WrLg B), "Modern Yiddish," which is "marked by a more or less conscious turning away from WY towards the spoken Yiddish of Eastern Europe." Here, dating from the second half of the nineteenth century, "a new trend became apparent . . . the more or less explicit application of criteria derived from NHG linguistic material to determine the acceptability of Yiddish forms for literary usage" (p. 286).

Where Yiddish dialects were not unanimous, StY appealed to NHG norms (Schaechter 1969: 287). For example, where Yiddish dialects show gender variation in *dos* ~ *der ferd* 'horse,' *dos* ~ *di gloz* 'glass,' StY *dos ferd*, *dos gloz* show agreement with StG (*das Pferd*, *das Glas*). Where there is full dialectal agreement across the Yiddish dialects, StY generally follows this, and not NHG; thus, StY *der tovl* 'blackboard'; cf. StG *die Tafel*. Schaechter provides detailed discussion and data where the emerging modern Yiddish literary language has standardized neither the majority Yiddish form, nor a form current in a minority dialect, but has adopted instead an NHG-based form, including, e.g.,

- *šotn* vs. *sotn* 'shadow'; the majority of Yiddish dialects have hisser [s] (~ regional [c]); StY prefers *šotn*, closer to NHG *Schatten*
- *im* vs. *e(j)m* 'him'; the *em* territory is "by far" the majority form (NEY, CY, WY), and was also common in WrLgA; cf. StY *im*, StG *ihm*
- *mer* vs. *mejn* 'more'; *mejn* occurs in most of CY and SEY, and a small part of NEY; cf. StY *mer*, StG *mehr*
- *krik* vs. *curik* 'back'; (variants based on) *krik* are widespread in all Yiddish dialects; WritY has *curik*; cf. StG *zurück*

36 Schaechter (1969: 285) distinguishes Non-StY of the Yiddish daily press from non-standard written Yiddish dialect, noting that Non-StY is "furthest from the dialects, while StY . . . best reflects the uniqueness of various dialects."

- StY feminine suffix is written *-in* <ין>, though universally pronounced as syllabic [n̩] in Yiddish; cf. StG *-in*
- Yiddish dialect variants such as *štivl* ~ *štibl* 'boots,' *borvəs* ~ *borbəs* 'barefoot,' *ojvn* ~ *ojbn* 'above,' *hejvn* ~ *hejbn* 'midwife' are resolved in StY based on the NHG model: StY *štivl, borvəs, ojbn, hejbam*; cf. StG *Stiefel, barfuss, oben, Hebamme*. However, where Yiddish differs universally from NHG, the universal feature (fricative or stop) prevails in StY. Thus, the epenthetic vowel found in all Yiddish dialects remains in StY *vorəm* 'worm,' *turəm* 'tower,' *zenəft* 'mustard' (cf. StG *Wurm, Turm, Senf*); however, the regionally limited epenthetic vowel in CY *barik* 'mountain,' *miləx* 'milk,' *hojəx* 'high' does not make it into StY *barg, milx, hojx* (cf. StG *Berg, Milch, hoch*).

Yiddish spoken dialects show widespread drastic reduction in the case system; thus, CY/NEY show syncretism of nominative/dative/accusative F.SG nouns – even after a preposition (Schaechter 1969: 296). This is found in written Non-StY as well, e.g., *(nox) di milxomə* '(after) the war.' Written StY maintains much more of the system of case distinctions: *di milxomə, nox der milxomə*. Perhaps this reflects the generally more conservative nature of written language, or, perhaps, NHG influence. Written Hasidic Yiddish also frequently shows this case syncretism of feminine nouns, but has not gone along with written StY in following the NHG "hidden standard." At the same time, written Hasidic Yiddish frequently exhibits daytshmerish features of its own. At times the "hidden standard" was not all that hidden, for example, in Yiddish publications containing (German) features which are foreign to Yiddish, e.g., the name of the publication *judišəs folks-blat* (Schaechter 1999: 2, note 3). Furthermore, two newspapers appearing in mid nineteenth-century Galicia were written in a consciously mixed (Yiddish and German) language, the explicit motivation being to strike a balance between German, seen as the high language of culture, and Yiddish, the still less-valued vernacular of the readership (Jacobs 1996c: 208).

The intellectual counterweight against daytshmerish was led by Yiddish linguists, normative grammarians, and major literary figures such as Mendele Moykher-Sforim and Sholem-Aleykhem (Schaechter 1969: 286). In this climate, for example, the borrowed (from NHG) adjective suffixes *-bar, -haft, -zam* came to be perceived as "too obviously foreign" and were rejected; the present participle suffix *-ənd*, common in the Yiddish press of the late nineteenth and early twentieth century, generally disappeared in contemporary StY; daytshmerish spellings adopted earlier were now eliminated. Thus, StY arose in a complex milieu involving both the external influences of the "hidden standard" and the system-internal consolidation of StY, yielding all of the following: NHG loan *špraxə* nativized via apocope to *šprax*; NHG loans *fragə* 'question,' *grupə* 'group' did not undergo apocope, but innovated nativized plurals in StY *fragə-s, grupə-s* (alongside non-StY *fragə-fragn, grupə-grupn*); similarly, for

NHG loan *Umstand* (PL. *Umstände*), StY has a nativized plural *umštand-n* 'circumstance-s,' while Non-StY has *umštand-umštendn*, with the plural possibly deriving from StG DAT plural *Umständen*, but more likely a compromise, since Yiddish lacks the *-e* plural suffix.

7.7.4 *The development of StY orthography*

The following discussion derives from Schaechter's (1999) comprehensive history of Yiddish orthography.[37] Schaechter (p. 1) traces the historical interest in Yiddish orthography back at least to Boeschenstein (1514). This interest continued in many of the basic grammars of Yiddish which appeared in Germany during the sixteenth and seventeenth centuries. These early descriptive works were concerned with WrLgA. While the orthography of WrLgA showed great variation and inconsistency, it nevertheless exhibits principled norms (see Timm 1987).[38] The shift from WrLg A to WrLg B involved a major change in orthography – not just, for example, in the change from WY-based to EY-based vocalism, but in a whole constellation of orthographic norms, e.g., the symbols used to represent unstressed vowels. This time of upheaval saw as well the revolutionary shift from *mashket* > square letters in Yiddish printing.

Modern Yiddish orthography developed against the backdrop of complex and changing social and linguistic contexts. As with other emerging European standard languages, concern about suitably codified orthography took on a new urgency. Schaechter (1999: 1–2) notes the two main opposing tendencies driving much subsequent orthographic debate and reform in Yiddish: (1) phoneticization of Yiddish orthography, and (2) maskilic influences, which pushed toward germanizing Yiddish orthography. Debates over the appropriate degree of phoneticization continued into the twentieth century. An early proponent of radical phonetic spelling was Mendl Lefin-Satanover (1819), who pushed phonetic spelling to the point of disrupting morphophonemic identity within a morpheme; thus, twentieth-century Yiddish linguists such as Birnbaum, Gininger, and Joffe wrote the past participle *gəredt* [gəret] 'spoken' as גערעט; cf. StY גערעדט (Schaechter 1999: 2). On the other hand, the maskilic/daytshmerish tendency led to spelling with ה and ע to indicate vowel length (e.g., ליעב; cf. StG *Lieb*); and the use of double consonants (e.g., אַללע, עססען; cf. StG *alle*, *essen*).

As the modernization of large segments of Jewish life hit full stride in the mid nineteenth century, there was a reaction against German-modeled spelling on the one hand, and the "somewhat chaotic" manner of spelling on the other.

37 See also the very useful Introduction (in English) to this work by Glasser (1999).

38 Glasser (1999: v) notes that for earlier Yiddish, like "other languages in their pre-standardization period, Yiddish spelling was remarkably inconsistent until the twentieth century."

This spurred conscious and serious attempts at orthographic reform (Schaechter 1999: 4). The major breakthrough came in the lexicographic work of Lifshits (1867, 1869, 1876). The impact of Lifshits was significant in setting the direction of future orthographic reform. Among Lifshits' specific innovations, Schaechter (1999: 4) cites: the *rofe* diacritic on /f/ פֿ to distinguish it from /p/ פּ; syllabic ל *l* (vs. daytshmerish על *-el*), e.g., הימל *himl* 'sky'; svarabhakti vowel, e.g., באַדערפֿעניש *baderf-ə-niš* 'need' (cf. StG *Bedürf-Ø-nis*); suffixes עך, לעך (vs. daytshmerish spelling יך, ליך; cf. StG *-ich*, *-lich*); dropping of silent ע in, e.g., *lib*, *fil* (vs. daytshmerish ליעב, פֿיעל; cf. StG *Lieb*, *viel*); use of · to indicate palatalized consonants ל·אַדע /l'adə/ 'any,' ל·אַרעם /l'arəm/ 'noise'; word-final ט (*tes*) replacing daytshmerish ד, thus: האַנט 'hand; arm,' ווינט 'wind,' געלט 'money' (cf. StG *Hand*, *Wind*, *Geld*).

In general, the history of StY orthography involves an ongoing process to free itself from daytshmerish orthography, and to base Yiddish orthography on Yiddish-internal considerations (phonetic/phonological, and morphological). This process is seen in those orthographic reformers who came after Lifshits. Sholem Aleykhem (1888) had an orthographic system which was innovative yet contained daytshmerish elements (Schaechter, 1999: 5),[39] e.g., in his proposal to differentiate שטיין 'stone' from שטעהן 'stand' (based on StG *Stein*, *stehen*). Later sources in which daytshmerish spelling is found include (p. 5): (early on) Yiddish grammar books, the first modern Yiddish journal *Der Yud* (1899–1902), and, later, *Der Fraynd* (1903–1914).

The major twentieth-century figures associated with orthographic reform – Borokhov, Yofe, Prilutski, Birnbaum, and Soviet Yiddish linguists – to varying degrees all adopted Lifshits' approach (Schaechter, 1999: 9). The emerging yiddophone intelligentsia increasingly saw orthographic normalcy as important and necessary for the Yiddish-based national agenda (pp. 9–10); thus, see Borokhov (1913). Even in orthodox traditionalist circles, orthographic reform became an issue (Schaechter 1999: 32–33). The interwar period saw the formalization of two major secularist orthographic schools – the Soviet version, and the YIVO/Tsisho version. Both versions developed from a common source (pp. 11–26), especially the Kiev-based (in independent Ukraine, 1917–1919) commission for the "new orthography." The Kiev commission not only developed a system (with sixty orthographic rules), but also succeeded in having it adopted by a major Yiddish daily newspaper (p. 10).

StY orthographic debates in recent decades have largely involved fine-tuning, for example, on use of diacritics vs. silent *alef* in וואו vs. וו· /vu/ 'where.' With some exceptions, the YIVO StY orthography has gained ground in recent decades, and even publications with longstanding orthographic traditions of

[39] Schaechter notes that in matters of lexicon, Sholem Aleykhem was strongly anti-daytshmerish.

their own (such as the newspaper *Der Forverts*, founded 1897) have recently switched to StY orthography.

7.7.5 *Romanization systems*

The orthography debates also included calls for romanization – the writing of Yiddish in Latin letters (for internal use within the Yiddish speech community). Serious early calls for romanization came from prominent figures: Nathan Birnbaum (in his early years), the convener of the 1908 Tshernovits conference; Ludwig Zamenhof; Zaretski; Zhitlovski; Yofe; and others (Schaechter 1999: 16). The earliest such voice was likely Dr. Philip Mansch (1888–1890). Overwhelmingly, however, there was a strong negative reaction to romanization, though some short-lived romanized publications did appear (Schaechter 1999: 16): *Unzer Shrift* (1912; New York), *Der Unhojb* (1923; Vienna), as well as some Holocaust-survivor publications (1945–1947; Germany and Austria). Language ideology carries over into romanization as well. Orthographic distance from German – a notion which had gained support in modern Yiddishist circles – carries over into Max Weinreich's principled system of romanization for transliteration purposes – e.g., *sh* for ש, thus, graphically distinct from German-based *sch*; or *kh* vs. German *ch* for [x] (Frakes 1993: xviii–xix).

7.8 Post-Yiddish Ashkenazic speech

Under the impact of modernization, segments of the yiddophone Ashkenazic population (in differing times and places under somewhat differing circumstances) ceased using Yiddish as their dominant vernacular, giving rise to Jewish ethnolects of German, Dutch, English, revived Hebrew, etc. The newly created post-Yiddish ethnolects shared many common features. One may thus speak of Ashkenazic speech in its broadest sense; the post-Yiddish ethnolects are successor lects to Yiddish, arising via language shift.[40]

WY largely died out among western Ashkenazim, who shifted to the new vernaculars (German, Dutch, French, etc.) asssociated with modernity, emancipation, and acculturation. However, Yiddish in the west survived into the modern period in two main ways. First, it survived at the geographic margins (Alsace, Switzerland, etc.) well into the twentieth century. Second, it survived in socially circumscribed contexts, serving a more limited range of functions than it did some few generations earlier. Speakers in a given generation might use WY in conversations with their grandparents, but German with their parents. Additionally, vestiges of Yiddish could be used in intragroup Jewish German or Jewish Dutch; these are mainly vocabulary words (Weinberg 1969; Beem

[40] Comparative Jewish German and Jewish Dutch is addressed in Jacobs (1999).

1967). Even where knowledge of Yiddish continued, it was increasingly not as the dominant language. Hoge (1991) links the death of WY to the disruption of a traditional triglossic situation.

For some speakers of EY in America, one may describe a situation of incomplete L-1 learning (Levine 1997). Among the features discussed by Levine is the loss of a distinction in the past-tense AUX *zajn* vs. *hobn*; incomplete L-1 speakers in America have only *hobn*. Still, caution must be exercised in discussions of language death. Many features which some might be tempted to view as indicative of language loss are found within vibrant spoken EY (e.g., collapse of case and gender distinctions in much of spoken EY; the loss of AUX *zajn* is characteristic for much of NEY).

The widespread rise of identifiably Jewish ethnolects represents an important peripheral area for Yiddish linguistics. M. Weinreich (1923: 50) recognized the importance of the systematic investigation of Jewish German as a post-Yiddish phenomenon. Van Ginneken (1914) devoted much space within his discussion of Jewish speech (including Yiddish in the Netherlands) to Jewish Dutch.[41] In a similar vein, see Gold (1986) on Jewish English; on Jewish German, see Matras (1991) and Jacobs (1996c); Jacobs and Hinskens (1997) for Jewish Dutch; Brzezina (1986) for Jewish Polish. The appearance of Yeshivish represents a new manifestation of Jewish English (Weiser 1995), involving a complex mixing of "traditional" Jewish English in the context of internal Jewish bilingualism, with an admixture from newly observant Jews who were formerly English monolinguals.

Post-Yiddish Jewish ethnolects exhibit many features typical of language shift – in word order, intonation, pronunciation, etc. Thus, typical of Jewish German (Matras 1991: 277; Jacobs 1996c: 192) is the proximity of AUX and main verb, as is the use of finite verb in initial position to mark a discourse boundary. Ashkenazic Jewish Dutch also exhibits shift features, e.g., in intonation, and syntax (Jacobs and Hinskens 1997). For example, Ashkenazic Jewish Dutch permits Yiddish-style topicalization, as well as the postposing of direct object after the verb complex: *ik heb daar gezien een kalle* 'I have there seen a bride.' A further characteristic of Ashkenazic Jewish Dutch is obligatory preposition *aan* with dative objects: *ik heb het aan hem gegeven* 'I gave it (on) him'; non-Jewish Dutch does not require this (van Praag 1948; Jacobs and Hinskens 1997). Also characteristic of post-Yiddish Jewish ethnolects are calques from Yiddish; thus, Jewish Dutch *een goed uur*, lit. 'a good hour,' used, however, in Jewish Dutch in the sense of wishing good luck; cf. Yiddish *in a mazldikər šo* 'in a lucky hour,' modern Israeli Hebrew *bešaʕa tova* 'in hour good';

[41] While there is much useful material in van Ginneken's study, it is rife with bigoted statements and formulations concerning the Jewish people.

Jewish English *make a blessing* (< Yiddish *maxn a broxə*) vs. non-Jewish *say a blessing*.

The identifiably Jewish ethnolects are typically stigmatized in the general (non-Jewish) speech community. The internalization by some Jews of this stigmatization has also led to a type of hyperlectal speech which seeks to rid itself systematically of the stigmatized features. Herzog (1978: 53–54) notes a type of monotone speech employed by some Jews in their English as a way of avoiding the stigmatized Jewish (= Yiddish) intonation. Acculturating German Jews of the late eighteenth century innovated hypercorrect front-round vowels, e.g., *eigenhöndig* 'with one's own hand,' *anzeugen* 'indicate,' *fünden sich* 'find oneself' (M. Weinreich 1973, III, 293); the hypercorrection is based on the perception that Yiddish has "incorrect" unrounded vowels corresponding to front-rounded vowels (*ü, ö, eu*) in "correct" German; however, cf. StG *eigenhändig, anzeigen, finden sich*. On hyperlectal Jewish German in the twentieth century, see Jacobs (1996c: 199–201).

The large number of words of Yiddish (and/or HA) origin in post-Yiddish ethnolects presents a special challenge to the Thomason and Kaufman model, where characteristic of shift are inherited features in syntax and phonology, much less so in morphology and lexicon. The lexicon of the prior language typically is jettisoned in the shift process. However, typical of the post-Yiddish ethnolects are many words of Yiddish origin; see, e.g., Weinberg (1969) for Jewish German; Voorzanger and Polak (1915), Beem (1967) for Jewish Dutch. Jewish speakers typically possessed competence in both Jewish and non-Jewish varieties of the new vernaculars, and could modify their style according to interlocutor. In the presence of non-Jews, HAisms (as well as other "Jewish" markers) could be avoided (Beem 1974: 34; Beckermann 1989: 118). Conversely, such words could be consciously inserted as markers of intragroup solidarity in other sociolinguistic situations.[42] The point is that many Ashkenazic Jews had competence in multiple varieties of the new vernacular, and these varieties existed within a specialized type of diglossia. Finally, new borrowing directly from HA may occur in a post-Yiddish Jewish ethnolect; this is quite evident in Yeshivish.

A desideratum for the field remains a comprehensive ethnography of Ashkenazic speech. This will encompass both internal Jewish bilingualism in traditional Ashkenaz and the linguistic milieu of modernity, where new linguistic "soups" have emerged. According to Birnbaum (1979a: 14) the social split into traditionalist/orthodox and modernist sectors was creating the

42 Many "Jewish" words crossed over to become part of the language (frequently, slang) of the broader general population. Thus, many Germans use *meschugge* 'crazy,' *mies* 'ugly,' *pleite* 'bankrupt,' etc. Some general varieties (e.g., Viennese German, Dutch) show especially high numbers of such words.

basis for two different styles of Yiddish, and the conditions for an eventual split into two Yiddishes.[43] This is only partly true. Traditional internal Jewish bilingualism, with its regular code-switching, continued to serve as a template for Talmud study among English-dominant modern orthodox Jewry (Heilman 1981). A generalized form of this template carried over as a model for a Jewish discourse style in post-Yiddish Jewish ethnolects. This style involves regular code-switching in, e.g., storytelling narrative (Kirshenblatt-Gimblett 1972: 330–384), macaronic Yiddish folksongs (U. Weinreich 1950; Rothstein 1993), and Jewish cabaret (Jacobs 2003). The term *Ashkenazic verbal code* (Jacobs 2000) may be employed to refer to this code-switching template in the broadest sense. The Ashkenazic verbal code goes beyond grammatical features to include pragmatic and discourse features, conversational style, etc. (Tannen 1981). In ways as variegated, nuanced, and linguistically interesting as it has been from the start, Ashkenazic speech continues.

[43] Harshav (1993: 33–34) writes of a "Jewish polysystem" and "a whole new Jewish secular polysystem."

References

Aronson, Howard. 1985. On aspect in Yiddish. *General Linguistics* 25: 171–188.

Avé-Lallemant, Friedrich Christian Benedict. 1858–1862. *Das deutsche Gaunertum in seiner social-politischen, literarischen und linguistischen Ausbildung zu seinem heutigen Bestande.* 4 vols. Leipzig: Brockhaus.

Baker, Zachary. 1992. History of the Jewish collections at the Vernadsky Library in Kiev. *Shofar* 10(4): 31–48.

Beckermann, Ruth. 1989. *Unzugehörig: Österreicher und Juden nach 1945.* Vienna: Loecker Verlag.

Beem, H. 1967. *Sjeëriet. Resten van een taal. Woordenboekje van het Nederlandse Jiddisch.* Assen: Van Gorcum & Comp. BV.

1974. *Uit mokum en de mediene: Joodse woorden in Nederlandse omgeving.* Assen: Van Gorcum & Comp. BV.

Beranek, Franz Josef. 1965. *Westjiddischer Sprachatlas.* Marburg: Elwert.

Berliner, Note. 1981. [= 1938]. Vegn litvishn dialekt in kongres-poyln. In Joshua Fishman (ed.), *Never say die! A thousand years of Yiddish in Jewish life and letters,* 667–668. The Hague, Paris, and New York: Mouton.

Bernshteyn, Mordkhe. 1959. A bintl verter fun klezmer-loshn. *Yidishe shprakh* 19: 22–25.

Bin-Nun, Jechiel. 1973. *Jiddisch und die deutschen Mundarten.* Tübingen: Max Niemeyer Verlag. (See also: Fischer 1936.)

Birnbaum, Salomo (Solomon, Shloyme). 1915. *Praktische Grammatik der jiddischen Sprache.* Vienna and Leipzig.

1930. *Yidishkayt un loshn.* Warsaw: Yeshurun.

1933. Ungern oder lite? *Yivo-bleter* 5: 329–332.

1934. Di historye fun di alte *u*-klangen in yidish. *Yivo-bleter* 6: 25–60.

1971. *The Hebrew scripts.* Leiden: E. J. Brill.

1979a. *Yiddish: A survey and a grammar.* Toronto and Buffalo: University of Toronto Press.

1979b. Soviet Yiddish. *Soviet Jewish Affairs* 9(1): 29–41.

1981. (= 1938). Zeyer gerekht. [Editor's comment to Berliner 1981 (= 1938).], In Joshua Fishman (ed.), *Never say die! A thousand years of Yiddish in Jewish life and letters,* 668–669. The Hague, Paris, New York: Mouton.

1988. *Grammatik der jiddischen Sprache: Mit einem Wörterbuch und Lesestücken.* Hamburg: H. Buske. (Reprint of Birnbaum 1915.)

Boeschenstein, Johannes. 1514. *Elementale introductorium in hebreas litteras teutonice et hebraice legendas.* Augsburg: Erhard Oeglin.

Booij, Geert. 1995. *The phonology of Dutch*. Oxford: Clarendon Press; New York: Oxford University Press.

Borokhov, Ber. 1966 [1913]. Di oyfgabn fun der yidisher filologye. In Sh. Niger (ed.), *Der pinkes: yorbukh fun der yidisher literatur un shprakh, far folklor, kritik un bibliografye*, 1–12. Vilna: Kletskin. Reprinted in Nakhman Mayzel (ed.), *Shprakh-forshung un literatur-geshikhte*, 53–75. Tel Aviv: Farlag I. L. Perets.

Borsley, Robert. 1999. *Syntactic theory: A unified approach*. London and New York: Arnold.

Bratkowsky, Joan. 1974. Sharpness in Yiddish: A fifth riddle in bilingual dialectology. Indiana University doctoral dissertation. Ann Arbor: University Microfilms International.

1988. *Yiddish linguistics: A multilingual bibliography*. New York and London: Garland.

Brzezina, Maria. 1986. *Polszczyzna Żydów*. Warsaw and Krakow: Państwowe Wydawnictwo Naukowe.

Burnadz, J. M. 1966. *Die Gaunersprache der Wiener Galerie*. Lübeck: Verlag für Polizeiliches Fachschrifttum.

Buxtorf, Johann. 1609. *Lectionis hebræo-germanicæ usus et exercitatio. Thesaurus grammaticus linguæ sanctæ hebrææ*. Basel: Conrad Waldkirch.

Chambers, Jack. 1994. An introduction to dialect topography. *English World Wide* 15: 35–53.

den Besten, Hans, and Corretje Moed-van Walraven. 1986. The syntax of verbs in Yiddish. In Hubert Haider and Martin Prinzhorn (eds.), *Verb second phenomena in Germanic languages*, 111–135. Publications in Language Sciences 21. Dordrecht: Foris Publications.

Diesing, Molly. 1990. Verb movement and the subject position in Yiddish. *Natural Language and Linguistic Theory* 8: 41–79.

1998. Light verbs and the syntax of aspect in Yiddish. *Journal of Comparative Germanic Linguistics* 1(2): 119–156.

2000. Aspect in Yiddish: The semantics of an inflectional head. *Natural Language Semantics* 8(3): 231–253.

2003. On the nature of multiple fronting in Yiddish. In Cedric Boeckx and Kleanthes K. Grohmann (eds.), *Multiple fronting*, 51–76. Amsterdam: John Benjamins.

Dushman, Leon. 1928. Fakh-leshoynes. *Tsaytshrift* 2–3: 875–877.

Dyhr, Mogens, and Ingeborg Zint. 1988. *Lubliner Jiddisch: ein Beitrag zur Sprache und Kultur des Ostjiddischen im 20. Jahrhundert anhand eines Idiolekts*. Phonai 37. Tübingen: Max Niemeyer Verlag.

Eckardt, Guido. 1911. *Wie man in Riga spricht*. (Separat-Abdruck aus der *Baltischen Monatsschrift* 1904, Heft. Nr. 7). Riga: Kommissionsverlag von Jonck und Poliewsky.

Eggers, Eckhard. 1998. *Sprachwandel und Sprachmischung im Jiddischen*. Franfurt am Main, Berlin, Bern, New York, Paris, Vienna: Peter Lang Verlag.

Elzet (= Yehude-Leyb Zlotnik). 1920. Melokhes un bale-melokhes. In his *Der vunder-oytser fun der yidisher shprakh*, part 4, 32–42. Warsaw: Bracia Lewin-Epsztein.

Encyclopedia Judaica. 1971. Jerusalem: Keter Publishing House.

Erlich, Rachel. 1981. Politics and linguistics in the standardization of Soviet Yiddish. In Joshua Fishman (ed.), *Never say die! A thousand years of Yiddish in Jewish life and letters*, 699–708. The Hague, Paris, New York: Mouton.

Estraikh, Gennady. 1994. Soviet Yiddish vernacular of the 1920s: Avrom Abchuk's *Hershl Shamaj* as a socio-linguistic source. *Slovo* 7(1): 1–12.

1999. *Soviet Yiddish: language planning and linguistic development*. Oxford: Clarendon Press.

Faber, Alice. 1987. A tangled web: Whole Hebrew and Ashkenazic origins. In Dovid Katz (ed.), *Origins of the Yiddish language*, 15–22. Oxford: Pergamon Press.

Faber, Alice, and Robert King. 1984. Yiddish and the settlement history of Ashkenazic Jewry. *Mankind Quarterly* 24: 393–425.

Falkovitsh, E. 1966. Evreiskij iazyk (Idish). In V. V. Vinogradov *et al.* (eds.), *Iazyki narodov SSSR*. Vol. I: *Indoevropeiskie iazyki*, 599–629. Moscow: Nauka.

Ferdman, Shoylik. 1958. *Yidishe shprakh. Lernbukh fun gramatik un ortografye far der gruntshul. Driter teyl (sintaks)*. Warsaw: Państwowe Zakłady Wydawnictw Szkolnych.

Fischer, Jechiel. 1936. *Das jiddische und sein Verhältnis zu den deutschen Mundarten, unter besonderer Berücksichtigung der ostgalizischen Mundart. Erster Teil* – Lautlehre (einschliesslich Phonetik der ostgalizischen Mundart). Erste Hälfte: Allgemeiner Teil. Leipzig: Buchdruckerei Oswald Schmidt. (See Bin-Nun 1973.)

Fishman, Joshua. 1965. *Yiddish in America: Socio-linguistic description and analysis*. Bloomington: Indiana University Center for Anthropology, Folklore and Linguistics.

1967. Bilingualism with and without diglossia, diglossia with and without bilingualism. *Journal of Social Issues* 23(2): 29–38.

1981a. The sociology of Yiddish: A foreword. In Joshua Fishman (ed.), *Never say die! A thousand years of Yiddish in Jewish life and letters*, 1–97. The Hague, Paris, New York: Mouton.

1981b. The sociology of Jewish languages from the perspective of the general sociology of language: a preliminary formulation. *International Journal of the Sociology of Language* 30: 5–16.

1981c. Epilogue: Contributions of the sociology of Yiddish to the general sociology of language. In Joshua Fishman (ed.), *Never say die! A thousand years of Yiddish in Jewish life and letters*, 739–756. The Hague, Paris, New York: Mouton.

1985. Why did Yiddish change? *Diachronica* 2(1): 67–82.

Frakes, Jerold. 1989. *The politics of interpretation: Alterity and ideology in Old Yiddish studies*. Albany: State University of New York Press.

1993. Vorwort des Herausgebers. In Max Weinreich, *Geschichte der jiddischen Sprachforschung*, ed. Jerold Frakes. South Florida Studies in the History of Judaism, 27, vii–xxiv. Atlanta: Scholars Press.

Friedrich, Carl Wilhelm. 1784. *Unterricht in der Judensprache und Schrift, zum Gebrauch für Gelehrte und Ungelehrte*. Prenzlau: Chr. Gottf. Ragoczy.

Gartner, Theodor. 1901. Texte im Bukowiner Judendeutsch. *Zeitschrift für hochdeutsche Mundarten* 2: 277–281.

Geller, Ewa. 1994. *Jidysz: język Żydów polskich*. Warsaw: Państwowe Wydawnictwo Naukowe.

2001. *Warschauer Jiddisch*. Tübingen: Max Niemeyer Verlag.

Gerzon, Jacob. 1902. *Die jüdisch-deutsche Sprache: Eine grammatisch-lexikalische Untersuchung ihres deutschen Grundbestandes*. (University of Heidelberg doctoral dissertation, 1902.) Frankfurt am Main: J. Kauffmann.

Gilman, Sander. 1986. *Jewish self-hatred: Anti-Semitism and the "hidden language" of the Jews.* Baltimore and London: Johns Hopkins University Press.

Gininger, Khaim. 1949. A bukh tsu lernen di yidishe kultursprakh. *Yivo-Bleter* 33: 204–211.

Glanz, Rudolf. 1968. *Geschichte des niederen jüdischen Volkes in Deutschland. Eine Studie über historisches Gaunertum, Bettelwesen und Vagantentum.* New York.

Glasser, Paul. 1990. A distributional approach to Yiddish inflection. Columbia University doctoral dissertation. Ann Arbor: University Microfilms International.

1999. Introduction to Schaechter 1999: v–vii.

Gold, David. 1986. An introduction to Jewish English. *Jewish Language Review* 6: 94–120.

Green, Eugene. 1969. On accentual variants in the Slavic component of Yiddish. In Marvin I. Herzog, Wita Ravid, and Uriel Weinreich (eds.), *The field of Yiddish: Studies in language, folklore, and literature. Third collection*, 216–239. London, The Hague, Paris: Mouton.

Guggenheim-Grünberg, Florence. 1954. The horse dealers' language of the Swiss Jews in Endingen and Lengnau. In Uriel Weinreich (ed.), *The field of Yiddish: Studies in language, folklore, and literature*, 48–62. New York: Linguistic Circle of New York.

1966. Review of Beranek 1965. *Zeitschrift für Mundartforschung* 33: 353–357.

1968. Zum Westjiddischen Sprachatlas: II. *Zeitschrift für Mundartforschung* 35: 148–149.

1973. *Jiddisch auf alemannischem Sprachgebiet: 56 Karten zur Sprach- und Sachgeographie. Beiträge zur Geschichte und Volkskunde der Juden in der Schweiz* Zurich: Juris. 10.

Gutman, T. 1926–1928. A pruv fun a fonetik fun lodzher yidish. *Filologishe shriftn* 1: 377–388; 2: 508.

Gutman, Teodor. 1928. Di konsonantn-asimilatsye in zats. *Filologishe shriftn* 2: 107–110.

Gutmans, Teodor. 1958. Di shprakh fun a yidisher radyo-stantsye in nyu-york. *Yidishe shprakh* 18: 65–72.

Haines, James. 1975. *Proto-Yiddish and the history of Yiddish phonology: the front rounded vowel phonemes.* Working Papers in Yiddish and East European Jewish Studies 9. New York: YIVO Institute for Jewish Research.

Hall, Richard. 1967. Yiddish syntax: Phrase structure rules and optional singulary transformations of the modern standard language. Unpublished doctoral dissertation, New York University. Ann Arbor: University Microfilms International.

Harshav, Benjamin. 1993. *Language in the time of revolution.* Berkeley: University of California Press.

Haudricourt, A. G., and A. G. Juilland. 1949. *Essai pour une histoire structurale du phonétisme français.* Paris: Klincksieck.

Heilman, S. C. 1981. Sounds of modern orthodoxy: The language of Talmud study. In Joshua Fishman (ed.), *Never say die! A thousand years of Yiddish in Jewish life and letters*, 226–253. The Hague, Paris, New York: Mouton.

Hergershausen, Aaron ben Shmuel. 1709. *Liblikhe tfile oder kreftige artsnay far guf un neshome.* Fürth.

Herzog, Marvin. 1964. Channels of systematic extinction in Yiddish dialects. In Lucy S. Dawidowicz, Alexander Erlich, Rachel Erlich, Joshua A. Fishman (organizing committee), *For Max Weinreich on his seventieth birthday: Studies in Jewish languages, literature, and society*, 93–107. The Hague: Mouton & Co.

1965a. *The Yiddish language in Northern Poland: Its geography and history*. (*International Journal of American Linguistics*, 31 [2], April. Bloomington: Indiana University.

1965b. Grammatical features of Markuze's *Sejfer refues* (1790). In Uriel Weinreich (ed.), *The field of Yiddish: Studies in Yiddish language, folklore, and literature. Second Collection*, 49–62. The Hague: Mouton.

1969. Yiddish in the Ukraine: Isoglosses and historical inferences. In Marvin I. Herzog, Wita Ravid, and Uriel Weinreich (eds.), *The field of Yiddish: Studies in language, folklore, and literature. Third collection*, 58–81. London, The Hague, Paris: Mouton.

1978. Yiddish. In Herbert Paper (ed.), *Jewish languages: Theme and variations. Proceedings of the Regional Conference of the Association of Jewish Studies held at the University of Michigan and New York University in March–April 1975*, 47–58. Cambridge, Mass. Association for Jewish Studies.

2000. *The language and culture atlas of Ashkenazic Jewry*. Vol. III. *The Eastern Yiddish – Western Yiddish Continuum*. Tübingen: Max Niemeyer Verlag.

Herzog, M., U. Kiefer, R. Neumann, W. Putschke, A. Sunshine, V. Baviskar, and U. Weinreich 1992. *The Language and Culture Atlas of Ashkenazic Jewry*. Vol. I: *Historical and theoretical foundations*. Tübingen: Max Niemeyer Verlag and YIVO Institute for Jewish Research.

Hoge, Kerstin. 1991. From "anti-daytshmerish" to the "hidden standard": The dynamics of the Yiddish standardization process. MA thesis. The Ohio State University.

Hutton, Christopher. 1999. *Linguistics and the Third Reich: Mother-tongue fascism, race and the science of language*. Routledge Studies in the History of Linguistics 1. London and New York: Routledge.

Isaacs, Miriam. 1999. Haredi, *haymish*, and *frim*: Yiddish vitality and language choice in a transitional multilingual community. *International Journal of the Sociology of Language* 138: 9–30.

Jacobs, Neil G. 1975. Yiddish origins and creolization. Unpublished MA paper. University of Texas, Austin.

1979. How hybrid is hybrid phonology? Historical evidence from Yiddish. Paper delivered at Linguistic Society of America Summer Meeting, Salzburg. Abstract of paper in meeting handbook.

1982. Reconstructing Proto-Yiddish vowel 25 through its hidden partner. Paper delivered at Linguistic Society of America Annual Meeting. San Diego. Abstract of paper in meeting handbook.

1989. Hebrew-Aramaic origin verbs in Yiddish: The interplay of inherited form and synchronic phonology. *Mediterranean Language Review* 4–5: 97–108.

1990a. *Economy in Yiddish vocalism: A study in the interplay of Hebrew and non-Hebrew components*. Mediterranean Language and Culture Monograph Series, 7. Wiesbaden: Otto Harrassowitz. (= Ph.D. dissertation, Economy in Yiddish vocalism: The case of Central Yiddish. Columbia University, 1984.)

1990b. The faces of a raising rule in Yiddish. In Paul Wexler (ed.), *Studies in Yiddish Linguistics*, 23–33. Tübingen: Max Niemeyer Verlag.

1990c. Northeastern Yiddish gender-switch: abstracting dialect features regionally. *Diachronica* 7(2): 69–100.

1991. A reanalysis of the Hebrew *status constructus* in Yiddish. *Hebrew Union College Annual* 62: 305–327.

1993a. On pre-Yiddish standardization of quantity. *Diachronica* 10(2): 191–214.

1993b. Central Yiddish breaking and drawl: The implications of fusion on a phonological rule. In David Goldberg, Marvin Herzog, Barbara Kirshenblatt-Gimblett, and Dan Miron (eds.), *The field of Yiddish, fifth collection. Studies in Yiddish language, folklore, and literature*, 99–119. Evanston: Northwestern University Press and YIVO.

1994a. On a structural "Fifth Column" in sociolinguistic change: The diffusion of a Standard Yiddish feature in Yiddish dialects. In Howard I. Aronson (ed.), *NSL.7: Linguistic studies in the non-Slavic languages of the Commonwealth of Independent States and the Baltic Republics*, 133–150. Chicago: Chicago Linguistic Society.

1994b. Structure, standardization, and diglossia: The case of Courland Yiddish. In Dagmar C. G. Lorenz and Gabriele Weinberger (eds.), *Insiders and outsiders. German-Jewish, Yiddish and German literature and culture in contact*, 89–99. Detroit: Wayne State University Press.

1995a. The phonology of spoken Tshernovits Yiddish in 1901. Paper delivered at Ninth International NSL Conference, May 3–6, 1995, University of Chicago.

1995b. Diminutive formation in Yiddish: A syllable-based account. In Irmengard Rauch and Gerald Carr (eds.), *Insights in Germanic Linguistics*, 169–184. Berlin: Mouton de Gruyter.

1996a. Phonemic and phonetic vowel length in Yiddish dialects. Paper delivered at 2nd Germanic Linguistics Annual Conference (GLAC), University of Wisconsin, Madison, April 26–28, 1996.

1996b. Toward a phonological description of *l*-palatalization in Central Yiddish. In Rosina Lippi-Green and Joseph Salmons (eds.), *Recent advances in Germanic linguistics*, 149–168. Amsterdam: John Benjamins.

1996c. On the investigation of 1920s Vienna Jewish speech: Ideology and linguistics. *American Journal of Germanic Linguistics and Literatures* 8(2): 177–217.

1998. Introduction: A field of Jewish geography. In Neil G. Jacobs (ed.), *Studies in Jewish geography. Special issue, Shofar* 17(1): 1–18.

1999. Post-Yiddish Ashkenazic speech: The linguistics and sociolinguistics of Jewish-German and Jewish Dutch. Paper presented at conference "Multilingualism in Western Ashkenazic Jewry: ideology, intertextuality, and transmission," October 24–27, 1999, Middelburg, Netherlands.

2000. The Ashkenazic verbal code and the linguistic negotiation of modern Jewish identity. Paper delivered as a part of Distinguished Lecture Series commemorating the 75th anniversary of the founding of the YIVO Institute for Jewish Research. YIVO: New York. December 11, 2000.

2001a. Yiddish in the Baltic region. In Östen Dahl and Maria-Koptjevskaja-Tamm (eds.), *The circum-Baltic languages*, 285–311. Amsterdam: John Benjamins.

2001b. Review of Eckhard Eggers (1998). *Journal of Germanic Linguistics* 13(1): 68–77.

2003. Soirée bei Kohn: Jewish elements in the repertoire of Hermann Leopoldi. *Zutot 2002*, 200–208.

2004. Syncope and foot structure in pre-Ashkenazic Hebrew. *Diachronica* 21(2).

Jacobs, Neil G., and Frans Hinskens. 1997. Reconstructing Jewish Dutch: Characteristics and conceptual framework. Paper presented at Germanic Linguistics Annual Conference (GLAC), April 25–27, 1997, University of California, Los Angeles.

Jacobs, Neil G., and Joseph C. Loon. 1992. The geography of Ashkenaz: on the development of an ethno-geographic information system (EGIS). *Shofar* 10(4): 6–30.

Jacobs, Neil G., and Dagmar C. G. Lorenz. 1998. If I were King of the Jews: Germanistik and the Judaistikfrage. In Dagmar C. G. Lorenz and Renate Posthofen (eds.), *Transforming the center, eroding the margins: Essays on ethnic and cultural boundaries in German-speaking countries*, 185–198. Columbia, S.C.: Camden House.

Jacobs, Neil G., Ellen Prince, and Johan van der Auwera. 1994. Yiddish. In Ekkehard König and Johan van der Auwera (eds.), *The Germanic languages*, 388–419. Croom Helm Series in Germanic Linguistics. London: Routledge.

Jochnowitz, George. 1981. Bilingualism and dialect mixture among Lubavitcher Hasidic children. In Joshua Fishman (ed.), *Never say die! A thousand years of Yiddish in Jewish life and letters*, 721–737. The Hague, Paris, New York: Mouton.

Jofen, Jean. 1953. The dialectological makeup of East European Yiddish: Phonological and lexical criteria. Columbia University doctoral dissertation. Microfilm dissertation no. 6639. (Privately published as: *A Linguistic Atlas of East European Yiddish*. New York. 1964.)

Kahan-Newman, Zelda. 1983. An annotation of Zaretski's *Praktishe yidishe gramatik*. Unpublished doctoral dissertation, University of Michigan. Ann Arbor: University Microfilms International.

1990. Another look at Yiddish scribal language. In Paul Wexler (ed.), *Studies in Yiddish Linguistics*, 35–46. Tübingen: Max Niemeyer Verlag.

Katz, Dovid. 1977. First steps in the reconstruction of the proto vocalism of the Semitic component in Yiddish. Presentation to course in Yiddish linguistics. Department of Linguistics, Columbia University, New York.

1982. Explorations in the history of the Semitic component in Yiddish. Unpublished doctoral dissertation, University of London.

1983. Zur Dialektologie des Jiddischen. In Werner Besch *et al.* (eds.), *Dialektologie: Ein Handbuch zur deutschen und allgemeinen Dialektforschung*, 1018–1041. Berlin: de Gruyter.

1985. Hebrew, Aramaic and the rise of Yiddish. In Joshua Fishman (ed.), *Readings in the sociology of Jewish languages*, I: 85–103. Leiden: Brill.

1986. On Yiddish, in Yiddish and for Yiddish: 500 years of Yiddish scholarship. In Mark Gelber (ed.), *Identity and ethos: A festschrift for Sol Liptzin on the occasion of his 85th birthday*, 23–36. New York: Peter Lang.

1987a. The proto-dialectology of Ashkenaz. In Dovid Katz (ed.), *Origins of the Yiddish language*, 47–60. Oxford, New York: Pergamon Press.

1987b. *Grammar of the Yiddish language*. London: Duckworth.

1993. The phonology of Ashkenazic. In Lewis Glinert (ed.), *Hebrew in Ashkenaz: A language in exile*, 46–87. New York and Oxford: Oxford University Press.

1994. Naye gilgulim fun alte makhloykesn: di litvishe norme un di sikhsukhim vos arum zikh. *YIVO Bleter, Naye serye* 2: 205–257.

Kerler, Dov-Ber. 1999. *The origins of modern literary Yiddish.* Oxford: Clarendon Press.

Kiefer, Ulrike. 1990. Interlinguale Sprachgeographie: Distributionelle Strukturen im deutsch-jiddischen Kontinuum. Columbia University doctoral dissertation.

1995. *Gesprochenes Jiddisch: Textzeugen einer europäisch-jüdischen Kultur.* Tübingen: Max Niemeyer Verlag.

1997. The significance and principles of transcribing the LCAAJ holdings. Paper delivered at the 12th World Congress of Jewish Studies, Jerusalem 1997.

King, Robert D. 1979. Evidence of the German component. Paper placed before the First International Conference on Research in Yiddish Language and Literature at the Oxford Centre for Postgraduate Hebrew Studies, August 6–9.

1980. Final devoicing in Yiddish. In Marvin I. Herzog, Barbara Kirshenblatt-Gimblett, and Dan Miron (eds.), *The field of Yiddish. Studies in language, folklore, and literature. Fourth collection*, 371–430. Philadelphia: Institute for the Study of Human Issues.

1987. Proto-Yiddish morphology. In Dovid Katz (ed.), *Origins of the Yiddish language*, 73–81. Oxford, New York: Pergamon Press.

1988. Two of Weinreich's four riddles revisited. In Dovid Katz (ed.), *Dialects of the Yiddish language*, 85–98. Oxford: Pergamon Press.

1990a. On the origins of the *s*-plural in Yiddish. In Paul Wexler (ed.), *Studies in Yiddish linguistics*, 47–53. Tübingen: Max Niemeyer Verlag.

1990b. A konspiratsye un a frage-tseykhn, *Oksforder Yidish* 1: 247–251.

Kiparsky, Paul. 1966. Über den deutschen Akzent. *Studia Grammatica* 7: 69–97.

Kirshenblatt-Gimblett, Barbara. 1972. Traditional storytelling in the Toronto Jewish community: A study in performance and creativity in an immigrant culture. Indiana University doctoral dissertation. Ann Arbor: University Microfilms International.

Kloss, Heinz. 1952. *Die Entwicklung neuer germanischer Kultursprachen von 1800 bis 1950.* Munich: Pohl.

König, Werner (ed.). 1978. *Dtv-Atlas zur deutschen Sprache.* Munich: Deutscher Taschenbuch Verlag.

Landau, Alfred. 1895. Das Deminutivum der galizisch-jüdischen Mundart. *Deutsche Mundarten* 1: 46–58.

1901. Die Sprache der Memoiren der Glückel von Hameln. *Mitteilungen zur jüdischen Volkskunde* 7: 20–68.

1913. Zur russisch-jüdischen 'Klesmer' sprache. *Mitteilungen der Anthropologischen Gesellschaft in Wien* 43.

Landau, Alfred, and Bernhard Wachstein. 1911. *Jüdische Privatbriefe aus dem Jahre 1619.* Quellen und Forschungen zur Geschichte der Juden in Deutsch-Österreich 3. Vienna and Leipzig.

Lefin-Satanover, Mendl. 1819. *Seyfer koholes shloyme.* Poland.

Leibel, Daniel. 1965. On Ashkenazic stress. In Uriel Weinreich (ed.), *The field of Yiddish: Studies in Yiddish language, folklore, and literature. Second collection*, 63–72. The Hague: Mouton.

Lemkhen, Khatskl. 1995. Di hashpoe fun litvish oyfn yidishn dialekt in Lite. *Oksforder Yidish* 3: 6–130. See his original paper: Lemchenas, Ch. 1970. Lietuvių kalbos įtaka Lietuvos Žydųtarmei. Lietuviškieji Skoliniai. Vilnius: Mintis.

Levin, Jules. 1987. Computer-modeling language change. Paper presented at Linguistic Society of America Annual Meeting, December 27–30, 1998. San Francisco.

Levine, Glenn. 1997. Incomplete L1 acquisition in the immigrant situation: The case of Yiddish in the United States. University of Texas doctoral dissertation. Ann Arbor: University Microfilms International.

Lévy, Ernest-Henri. 1924. Langue des hommes et langue des femmes en judéo-allemand. In *Mélanges offerts à M. Charles Andler par ses amis et ses élèves*, 197–215. Strasbourg: Librairie Istra.

Lifshits, Y.-M. 1867. Di daytsh-yidishe brik. *Kol mevaser* (Odessa) 36: 239–241.

1869. *Risish-yudisher verter bikh*. Zhitomir.

1876. *Yudesh-rusisher verter bikh*. Zhitomir.

Lior, David. 1959. Bendiner dialekt. In A. Sh. Shteyn (ed.), *Pinkas Bendin*, 156–157. Tel Aviv: Association of former residents of Będzin in Israel.

Liptsin, Sol. 1944. Tsi iz yidish "di shprakhe der ungebildetn yudn?" *Yidishe shprakh* 4: 120–122.

Louden, Mark. 2000. Contact-induced phonological change in Yiddish: Another look at Weinreich's riddles. *Diachronica* 17(1): 85–110.

Lowenstamm, Jean. 1977. Relative clauses in Yiddish: A case for movement. *Linguistic Analysis* 3: 197–216.

1978. Yiddish diphthongs. Paper delivered to the North Eastern Linguistic Society Conference.

1979. Topics in syllabic phonology. University of Massachusetts Ph.D. dissertation. Ann Arbor: University Microfilms International.

Lowenstein, Steven. 1979. The Yiddish written word in nineteenth-century Germany. *Leo Baeck Yearbook* 24: 179–192.

1995. Center and periphery: The shifting boundary between eastern and western Jewry. Read before the 40th Anniversary Conference of the Leo Baeck Institute, March, 1995, Jerusalem. (Published in *Jewish Social Studies* 4(1): 60–78.)

Manaster Ramer, Alexis. 1997. The polygenesis of Western Yiddish – and the monogenesis of Yiddish. In Peter Michalove *et al.* (eds.), *Festschrift for Vitaly Shevoroshkin. Journal of Indo-European Studies. Monograph Series.* Washington: Institute for the Study of Man.

Manaster Ramer, Alexis, and Meyer Wolf. 1997. Yiddish origins: The Austro-Bavarian problem. *Folia Linguistica Historica* 17(1–2): 193–209.

Mansch, Ph. 1888–1890. Der jüdisch-polnische Jargon. *Der Israelit (Lemberg)*, 21–22.

Marchand, James. 1965. The origin of Yiddish. In *Communications et Rapports du Premier Congrès International de Dialectologie générale*, 248–252. Louvain: Centre international de Dialectologie générale.

1987. Proto Yiddish and the glosses. In Dovid Katz (ed.), *Origins of the Yiddish language*, 83–94. Oxford: Pergamon Press.

Mark, Yudl. 1938a. Yidishe anglitsizmen. *Yorbukh fun Amopteyl* (New York: YIVO), 296–321.

1938b. A por gor vikhtike sfeykes fun undzer itstiker klal-shprakh. *Yidish far ale* 9: 233–244; 10: 265–272.

1951. Undzer litvisher yidish. In M. Sudarski, Urye Katsnelnbogn, Y. Kisin, Berl Cahen (eds.), *Lite*, Vol. I: 429–472. New York: YIVO American Branch.

1958. Yidish-hebreishe un hebreish-yidishe nayshafungen. In Shloyme Bikl and Leybush Lehrer (eds.), *Shmuel Niger bukh*, 124–157. New York: YIVO.

1978. *Gramatik fun der yidisher klal-shprakh*. New York: Alveltlekher yidisher kultur-kongres.

Markuze, Moyshe. 1790. *Seyfer refues*. Poryck.

Matisoff, James. 1979. *Blessings, curses, hopes, and fears: Psycho-ostensive expressions in Yiddish.* Philadelphia: ISHI.

Matras, Yaron. 1991. Zur Rekonstruktion des jüdischdeutschen Wortschatzes in den Mundarten ehemaliger "Judendörfer" in Südwestdeutschland. *Zeitschrift für Dialektologie und Linguistik* 58(3): 267–293.

1996. Sondersprachliche Hebraismen: Zum semantischen Wandel in der hebräischen Komponente der südwestdeutschen Viehhändlersprache. In Klaus Siewert (ed.), *Rotwelschdialekte. Sondersprachenforschung,* I: 43–58. Wiesbaden: Otto Harrassowitz Verlag.

Mieses, Matthias. 1924. *Die jiddische Sprache. Eine historische Grammatik des Idioms der integralen Juden Ost- und Mitteleuropas.* Berlin and Vienna: Benjamin Harz.

Miller, David Neal. 1990. Ashkenaz: Paradigm and resistance. Paper delivered at conference: "The role of geography in Jewish civilization – Perceptions of space, place, time, and location in Jewish life and thought," The Ohio State University, October 21–22, 1990, Columbus, Ohio.

Miller, Sh. 1955. Nusekh Amerike: vegn etlekhe prepozitsyes. *Yidishe shprakh* 15: 120–123.

Neumann, Robert. 1995. The computerization of the language and culture Atlas of Ashkenazic Jewry. In Andrew Sunshine, Uriel Weinreich z"l, Beatrice S. Weinreich, and Robert Neumann (eds.), *The Language and Culture Atlas of Ashkenazic Jewry.* Vol. II: *Research tools,* 14–19. Tübingen: Max Niemeyer Verlag and YIVO Institute for Jewish Research.

Niger, Shmuel. 1913. Shtudies tsu der geshikhte fun der yidisher literatur. Di yidishe literatur – un di lezern. In Shmuel Niger (ed.), *Der Pinkes*, 138–185. (= *Yorbukh far der geshikhte fun der yidisher literatur un shprakh, far folklor, kritik un biblyografye.*) Vilna: Kletskin.

Noble, Shlomo. 1939. The survival of Middle High German and Early New High German words in current Judeo-German translations of the Bible. Unpublished doctoral dissertation, The Ohio State University.

1943. *Khumesh-taytsh: An oysforshung vegn der traditsye fun taytshn khumesh in di khadorim.* New York: YIVO.

1958. Yidish in a hebreishn levush. In Shloyme Bikl and Leybush Lehrer (eds.), *Shmuel Niger bukh,* 158–175. New York: YIVO.

Noyman, Yoysef. 1947. A por bamerkungen tsum loshn fun varshever yidn. *Yidishe shprakh* 7: 75–79.

Paper, Herbert. 1954. An early case of standard German in Hebrew orthography. In Uriel Weinreich (ed.), *The field of Yiddish: Studies in Yiddish language, folklore, and literature,* 143–146. New York: Linguistic Circle of New York.

Peltz, Rakhmiel. 1990. Spoken Yiddish in America: variation in dialect and grammar. In Paul Wexler (ed.), *Studies in Yiddish linguistics*, 55–73. Tübingen: Max Niemeyer Verlag.

1998. The politics of research on spoken Yiddish. In Dov-Ber Kerler (ed.), *The politics of Yiddish. Studies in Language Politics and Society*, 63–73. Walnut Creek, London and New Delhi: Altamira Press.

Perlmutter, David. 1988. The split morphology hypothesis: Evidence from Yiddish. In Michael Hammond and Michael Noonan (eds.), *Theoretical morphology. Approaches in modern linguistics*, 79–100. San Diego: Academic Press.

Preston, Dennis. 1999. *Handbook of perceptual dialectology*. Amsterdam, Philadelphia: John Benjamins.

Prilutski, Noyekh. 1917. *Der yidisher konsonantizm* 1 [= *Yidishe dialektologishe forshungen* 1.] Warsaw.

1920. *Tsum yidishn vokalizm: Etyudn. 1.* [= *Yidishe dialektologishe forshungen* 4; *Noyekh Prilutskis ksovim* X.] Warsaw.

1921. *Dialektologishe paraleln un bamerkungen.* [= his *Yidishe dialektologishe forshungen* 3 = *Noyekh Prilutskis zamlbikher far yidishn folklor, filologye un kulturgeshikhte*, Vol. II, part 2.]. Warsaw.

1924. *Mame-loshn. Yidishe dialektologishe forshungen 5.* [= *Yidishe shprakhvisnshaftlekhe forarbetn* 1]. Warsaw.

1927. Di yidishe bine-shprakh. *Yidish teater* 2: 129–144.

1937. *Dialektologishe forarbetn.* [= *Mame-loshn* II = *Yidishe dialektologishe forshungen* VI]. Vilnius: YIVO.

1940. *Yidishe fonetik: Elementarer kurs far lerer un aleynlerner.* Vilne: Aroysgegebn fun di firvokhn-kursn far yidishe lerer (derloybt durkhn bildungs-ministerium).

Prince, Ellen. 1987. Sarah Gorby, Yiddish folksinger: A case of dialect shift. *International Journal of the Sociology of Language* 67: 83–116.

1989. Yiddish wh-clauses, subject-postposing, and topicalization. In Joyce Powers and Ken de Jong (eds.), *ESCOL '88*, 403–415. Columbus: Ohio State University.

1993. On the discourse functions of syntactic form in Yiddish: expletive *es* and subject-postposing. In David Goldberg, Marvin Herzog, Barbara Kirshenblatt-Gimblett, and Dan Miron (eds.), *The field of Yiddish. Studies in Yiddish language, folklore, and literature. fifth collection*, 59–86. Evanston: Northwestern University Press and YIVO Institute for Jewish Research.

Prokosch, Eduard. 1939. *A comparative Germanic grammar*. Philadelphia: Linguistic Society of America and University of Pennsylvania.

Rée, Anton. 1844. *Die Sprachverhältnisse der heutigen Juden im Interesse der Gegenwart und mit besonderer Rücksicht auf Volkserziehung*. Hamburg: Verlag von Hermann Gobert.

Reyzen, Zalmen. 1920. *Gramatik fun der yidisher shprakh. Ershter teyl.* Vilna: Sh. Shreberk.

Rockowitz, Anna C. 1979. *201 Yiddish verbs*. Woodbury, N.Y.: Barron's Educational Series.

Rothstein, Robert. 1990. Review article of Yiddish aspectology (Aktionen im Jiddischen by Mordkhe Schaechter). In Paul Wexler (ed.), *Studies in Yiddish linguistics*, 143–153. Tübingen: Max Niemeyer Verlag.

1993. "*Geyt a yid in shenkl arayn*": Yiddish songs of drunkenness. In David Goldberg, Marvin I. Herzog, Barbara Kirshenblatt-Gimblett, Dan Miron (eds.), *The field of Yiddish. Studies in language, folklore, and literature. Fifth collection*, 243–262. Evanston: Northwestern University Press and YIVO Institute for Jewish Research.

1998. Klezmer loshn. *Judaism* 47(1): 23–29.

Rubin, Ruth. 1979. *Voices of a people: The story of Yiddish folksong*. Philadelphia: Jewish Publication Society of America.

Sadan, Dov. 1963. Der eltster gram in yidish. *Goldene keyt* 47: 158–159.

Sadock, Jerrold. 1998. A vestige of verb final syntax in Yiddish. *Monatshefte* 90(2): 220–236.

Şăineanu, Lazar. 1889. *Studiu dialectologic asupra graiului evreo-german*. Bucharest: E. Wiegand.

Santorini, Beatrice. 1993. Jiddisch als gemischte OV/VO-Sprache. In Werner Abraham and Josef Bayer (eds.), *Dialektsyntax*, 230–245. (= *Linguistische Berichte, Sonderheft* 5.)

1994. Some similarities and differences between Icelandic and Yiddish. In Norbert Hornstein and David Lightfoot (eds.), *Verb movement*, 87–106. Cambridge: Cambridge University Press.

1995. The syntax of verbs in Yiddish. Unpublished manuscript. University of Pennsylvania.

Sapir, Edward. 1949. Notes on Judeo-German phonology (1915). Reprinted in: David Mandelbaum (ed.), *Selected writings of Edward Sapir in language, culture and personality*, 252–272. Berkeley, Los Angeles, London: University of California Press.

Schaechter, Mordkhe. 1951. Aktionen im Jiddischen. Ein sprachwissenschaftlicher Beitrag zur Bedeutungslehre des Verbums. University of Vienna doctoral dissertation. Ann Arbor: University Microfilms International 1986.

1969. The "hidden standard": A study of competing influences in standardization. In Marvin I. Herzog, Wita Ravid, and Uriel Weinreich (eds.), *The field of Yiddish: Studies in language, folklore, and literature. Third collection*, 284–304. London, The Hague, and Paris: Mouton.

1999. *Fun folkshprakh tsu kulturshprakh: An iberblik iber der historye funem eynheytlekhn yidishn oysleyg*. New York: YIVO and Yidish-shprakhiker resursn-tsenter bay der yidish-lige. Includes 6th edition of *Takones fun yidishn oysleyg*.

2001. Lecture on Standard Yiddish. Jewish Theological Seminary, New York, June, 2001.

Schaechter, Mordkhe, and Max Weinreich. 1961. *Yidisher ortografisher vegvayzer*. New York: Komisye durkhtsufirn dem eynheytlekhn yidishn oysleyg.

Schwartz, Rosaline. 1969. The geography of two food terms: A study in Yiddish lexical variation. In Marvin I. Herzog, Wita Ravid, and Uriel Weinreich (eds.), *The field of Yiddish: Studies in language, folklore, and literature. Third collection*, 240–266. London, The Hague, and Paris: Mouton.

Sheskin, Khayim. 1965. A bisl terminologye fun shteperfakh in Grodne. *Yidishe shprakh* 25: 59–60.

Sholem Aleykhem. 1888. (= Rabinovitsh, Sholem). Vegn zhargon oysleygn. *Di yidishe folks-bibliotek* 1: 474–476.

Shtif, Nokhem. 1929. Di sotsyale diferentsiatsye in yidish. *Di yidishe shprakh* 4–5: 1–22.

Siewert, Klaus (ed). 1996. *Rotwelschdialekte. Sondersprachenforschung* 1. Wiesbaden: Otto Harrassowitz Verlag.

Slobin, Dan. 1981. Some aspects of the use of pronouns of address in Yiddish. In Joshua Fishman (ed.), *Never say die! A thousand years of Yiddish in Jewish life and letters*, 709–719. The Hague, Paris, and New York: Mouton.

Spangenberg, Karl. 1996a. Die Musikantensprache von Herdeshagen im Eichsfeld. In Klaus Siewert (ed.), *Rotwelschdialekte. Sondersprachenforschung* 1: 94–101. Wiesbaden: Otto Harrassowitz Verlag.

1996b. Zur Sprache der Wandermusikanten aus dem böhmischen Pressnitz. In Klaus Siewert (ed.), *Rotwelschdialekte. Sondersprachenforschung* 1: 102–103. Wiesbaden: Otto Harrassowitz Verlag.

Stankiewicz, Edward. 1965. Yiddish place names in Poland. In Uriel Weinreich (ed.), *The field of Yiddish: Studies in Yiddish language, folklore, and literature. Second collection*, 158–181. The Hague: Mouton.

1985. The Slavic expressive component of Yiddish. *Slavica hierosolymitana* 7: 177–187.

1991. Comment [on Wexler focus article]. *International Journal of the Sociology of Language* 91: 205–213.

1993. The Yiddish thematic verbs. In David Goldberg, Marvin I. Herzog, Barbara Kirshenblatt-Gimblett, and Dan Miron (eds.), *The field of Yiddish. Studies in language, folklore, and literature. Fifth collection*, 1–10. Evanston: Northwestern University Press and YIVO Institute for Jewish Research.

Strauch, Gabriele. 1990. Methodologies and ideologies: The historical relationship of German studies to Yiddish. In Paul Wexler (ed.), *Studies in Yiddish Linguistics*, 83–100. Tübingen: Max Niemeyer Verlag.

Stutshkov, Nokhem. 1950. *Der oytser fun der yidisher shprakh*. New York: YIVO.

Sunshine, Andrew. 1991. Opening the mail: Interpersonal aspects of discourse and grammar in Middle Yiddish letters. Columbia University doctoral dissertation. Ann Arbor: University Microfilms International.

Sunshine, Andrew, Uriel Weinreich z"l, Beatrice S. Weinreich, and Robert Neumann. 1995. *The Language and Culture Atlas of Ashkenazic Jewry.* Vol. II: *Research tools.* Tübingen: Max Niemeyer Verlag and YIVO Institute for Jewish Research.

Szajkowski, Zosa. 1981. The struggle for Yiddish during World War I: The attitude of German Jewry. In Joshua Fishman (ed.), *Never say die! A thousand years of Yiddish in Jewish life and letters*, 565–589. The Hague, Paris, and New York: Mouton.

Tannen, Deborah. 1981. New York Jewish conversational style. *International Journal of the Sociology of Language*, 30: 133–149.

Taube, Moshe. 1987. The development of aspectual auxiliaries in Yiddish. *Word* 38: 13–25.

Thomason, Sarah G., and Terence Kaufman. 1988. *Language contact, creolization and genetic linguistics.* Berkeley, Los Angeles, and London: University of California Press.

Timm, Erika. 1987. *Graphische und phonische Struktur des Westjiddischen unter besonderer Berücksichtigung der Zeit um 1600.* Tübingen: Max Niemeyer Verlag.

Trivaks, Avrom-Yitskhok. 1923. Di yidishe zhargonen. In M. Vanvild [Moyshe-Yoysef Dikshteyn] (ed.), *Bay undz yidn*, 157–174. Warsaw: Pinkhes Graubard.

van Coetsem, Frans. 1988. *Loan phonology and the two transfer types in language contact.* Dordrecht: Foris Publications.

van Ginneken, J. 1914. *Handboek der nederlandse taal. Deel II. De sociologische structuur.* In cooperation with Willem Kea SJ. Nijmegen: L. C. G. Malmberg.

van Praag, Siegfried. 1948. Hoe ze spraken. *Maandblad voor de Geschiedenis der Joden in Nederland onder Redactie van Dr. J. Meyer* (Amsterdam), Aflevering VIII: 225–230.

Varshavski, Yitskhok. 1944. Dos loshn fun a varshever ganef. *Yidishe Shprakh* 4: 122–123.

Verschik, Anna. 1999. Some aspects of the multilingualism of Estonian Jews. In T. Hennoste (ed.), *Estonian Sociolinguistics. International Journal of the Sociology of Language*, 139, 49–67. Berlin: Mouton de Gruyter.

Veynger, Mordkhe. 1925. *Forsht yidishe dialektn! Program farn materyalnklayber*. Minsk.

1926–1928. Vegn yidishe dialektn. *Tsaytshrift* 1: 181–208; 2–3: 613–652.

1929. *Yidishe dialektologye*. Minsk: Vaysrusisher Melukhe-farlag.

Vilenkin, Leyzer. 1931. *Yidisher shprakhatles fun sovetn-farband, afn grunt fun di dialektologishe materyaln vos zaynen tsunoyfgezamlt gevorn durkh der shprakh-komisye fun yidishn sekter fun der vaysrusisher akademye unter M. Veyngers onfirung*. Minsk: Vajsrusishe visnshaft-akademye, yidisher sekter.

Viler, Yankev. 1924. Fonetik fun mizrekh-galitsishn yidish. *Yidishe filologye* 1: 23–33, 141–151.

von Reizenstein, Wolf E. 1764. *Der vollkommene Pferde-Kenner*. Uffenheim.

Voorzanger, Jonas, and Jonas Polak. 1915. *Het Joodsch in Nederland; Aan het Hebreeuwsch en andere talen ontleende woorden en zegswijzen, verzameld en toegelicht*. Amsterdam: H. van Munster & Zoon.

Wagenseil, Johann Chr. 1699. *Belehrung der jüdisch-teutschen Red- und Schreibart*. Königsberg: Paul Friedrich Rhode.

Waletzky, Joshua. 1980. Topicalization in Yiddish. In Marvin I. Herzog, Barbara Kirshenblatt-Gimblett, and Dan Miron (eds.), *The field of Yiddish. Studies in language, folklore, and literature. Fourth collection*, 237–315. Philadelphia: Institute for the Study of Human Issues.

Weinberg, Werner. 1969. *Die Reste des Jüdischdeutschen*. Stuttgart: Kohlhammer.

Weinreich, Max. 1993 [1923]. Geschichte der jiddischen Sprachforschung. Marburg university dissertation. Published as: Max Weinreich, 1993, *Geschichte der jiddischen Sprachforschung*, ed. Jerold Frakes. South Florida Studies in the History of Judaism. Atlanta: Scholars Press.

1923. *Shtaplen: Fir etyudn tsu der yidisher shprakhvisnshaft un literaturgeshikhte*. Berlin: Wostok.

1928. Di yidishe shprakh-forshung in 17tn yorhundert. *Tsaytshrift* 2–3: 689–732.

1931. Vos volt yidish geven on hebreish? *Di tsukunft* 36: 194–205.

1938. Daytshmerish toyg nisht. *Yidish far ale* 1: 97–106.

1939. Yidish. *Algemeyne yidishe entsiklopedye*. Supplementary volume *Yidn* II: 23–90. Paris.

1950. Editor's Preface. In Stutshkov (1950): iv–xvi.

1954. Prehistory and early history of Yiddish: Facts and conceptual framework. In Uriel Weinreich (ed.), *The field of Yiddish: Studies in Yiddish language, folklore, and literature*, 73–101. New York: Linguistic Circle of New York.

1958a. Roshe-prokim vegn mayrevdikn yidish. In Yudl Mark (ed.), *Yuda A. Yofe-bukh*, 158–194. New York: YIVO.

1958b. Bney hes un bney khes in Ashkenaz: di problem un vos zi lozt undz hern. In Shloyme Bikl and Leybush Lehrer (eds.), *Shmuel Niger bukh*, 101–123. New York: YIVO.

1960. Di sistem yidishe kadmen-vokaln. *Yidishe shprakh*, 20(3): 65–71.

1965. On the dynamics of Yiddish dialect formation. In Uriel Weinreich (ed.), *The field of Yiddish: Studies in Yiddish language, folklore, and literature. Second collection*, 73–86. The Hague: Mouton.

1967. The reality of Jewishness vs. the ghetto myth: the sociolinguistic roots of Yiddish. In *To honor Roman Jakobson. Essays on the occasion of his seventieth birthday, 11 October 1966*, III: 2199–2221. The Hague: Mouton.

1972. Internal bilingualism in Ashkenaz. In Irving Howe and Eliezer Greenberg (eds.), *Voices from the Yiddish*, 279–288. Ann Arbor: University of Michigan Press.

1973. *Geshikhte fun der yidisher shprakh: bagrifn, faktn, metodn*. New York: YIVO.

1980. *History of the Yiddish language*. Translated by Shlomo Noble, with the assistance of Joshua A. Fishman. Chicago and London: University of Chicago Press. (= Partial translation of Max Weinreich 1973.)

Weinreich, Uriel. 1949. *College Yiddish*. New York: YIVO.

1950. Di forshung fun "mishshprakhike" yidishe folkslider. *Yivo-Bleter* 34: 282–288.

1952. *Sabesdiker losn* in Yiddish: A problem of linguistic affinity. *Word*, 8: 360–377.

1954. Stress and word structure in Yiddish. In Uriel Weinreich (ed.), *The field of Yiddish: Studies in Yiddish language, folklore, and literature*, 1–27. New York: Linguistic Circle of New York.

1955. Vegn filtrafikn gram. *Yidishe shprakh* 15: 97–109.

1956. Notes on the rise-fall intonation contour. In Morris Halle *et al.* (eds.), *For Roman Jakobson*, 633–643. The Hague: Mouton.

1958a. A retrograde sound shift in the guise of a survival: An aspect of Yiddish vowel development. In *Miscelánea homenaje a André Martinet, Estructuralismo e historia*, II: 221–267. [La Laguna] Canarias: Biblioteka filológica de la Universidad de La Laguna.

1958b. Di klangike struktur fun a podolyer reydenish. In Yudl Mark (ed.), *Yuda A. Yofe-bukh*, 221–231. New York: YIVO. (Originally appeared in *Yidishe Shprakh* 13(1953): 121–131.

1958c. Yiddish and colonial German in Eastern Europe: The differential impact of Slavic. In *American Contributions to the Fourth International Congress of Slavicists, Moscow 1958*, 369–421. The Hague: Mouton.

1958d. Nusah hasofrim haivri-jidi. *Leshonenu*, 22: 54–66.

1995 [1960]. Vegn a nayem yidishn shprakh- un kultur-atlas. *Goldene keyt* 37: 1–12. (Reprinted in Sunshine *et al.* 1995: *1–*7).

1960. Nozn, nezer, nez: A kapitl gramatishe geografye. *Yidishe shprakh* 20(3): 81–90.

1961. The seven genders of Yiddish. An unpublished paper read at the Annual Meeting of the Linguistic Society of America, Chicago.

1963a. Four riddles in bilingual dialectology. In *American Contributions to the Fifth International Congress of Slavists. Sofia, September 1963*. Preprint, 335–359. The Hague: Mouton.

1963b. Culture geography at a distance: Some problems in the study of East European Jewry. In Viola E. Garfield and Wallace L. Chafe (eds.), *Proceedings of the 1962 Annual Spring Meeting of the American Ethnological Society*. Seattle: American Ethnological Society.

1964. Western traits in Transcarpathian Yiddish. In Lucy S. Dawidowicz, Alexander Erlich, Rachel Erlich, Joshua A. Fishman (organizing committee), *For Max Weinreich on his seventieth birthday: Studies in Jewish languages, literature, and society*, 245–264. The Hague: Mouton.

1968. *Modern English-Yiddish, Yiddish-English dictionary*. New York: McGraw-Hill and YIVO Institute for Jewish Research.

1972. Yiddish language. *Encyclopedia Judaica* (Jerusalem: Keter) 16: 789–798.

1991. Roshe-prokim fun a deskriptiver yidisher dialektologye. *Yivo-bleter, Naye serye*, 1: 9–68.

1992. Outlines of Yiddish dialectology. In M. Herzog, U. Kiefer, R. Neumann, W. Putschke, A. Sunshine, V. Baviskar, and U. Weinreich. 1992. *The Language and Culture Atlas of Ashkenazic Jewry.* Vol. I: *Historical and theoretical foundations.* Tübingen: Max Niemeyer Verlag and YIVO Institute for Jewish Research.

Weiser, Chaim (Jonathan). 1995. *Frumspeak: The first dictionary of Yeshivish.* Northvale, N.J. and London: Jason Aronson, Inc.

Weissberg, Josef. 1988. *Jiddisch: Eine Einführung.* Berne: Peter Lang.

Wexler, Paul. 1981a. Jewish interlinguistics: Facts and conceptual framework. *Language*, 57: 99–149.

1981b. Ashkenazic German. *International Journal of the Sociology of Language*, 30: 119–130.

1987. *Explorations in Judeo-Slavic Linguistics.* Leiden: Brill.

1988. *Three heirs to a Judeo-Latin legacy: Judeo-Ibero-Romance, Yiddish and Rotwelsch.* Mediterranean Language and Culture Monograph Series 3. Wiesbaden: Otto Harrassowitz.

1991. Yiddish – The fifteenth Slavic language. Focus article In *International Journal of the Sociology of Language*, 91.

Wiese, Richard. 1996. *The phonology of German.* Oxford: Clarendon Press; New York: Oxford University Press.

Wiesinger, Peter. 1989. The Central and South Bavarian dialects in Bavaria and Austria. In Charles V. Russ (ed.), *The dialects of Modern German*, 438–519. Stanford: Stanford University Press.

Willer, Jakub [= Y. Viler]. 1915. Żargon żydowski na ziemiach polskich. In *Język polski i jego historia z uwzględnieniem innych języków na ziemiach polskich. Encyklopedia polska*, Part 2, Vol. III. Krakow.

Wodak-Leodolter, Ruth, and Wolfgang U. Dressler. 1978. Phonological variation in Colloquial Viennese. *Michigan Germanic Studies* 4: 30–66.

Wolf, Meyer. 1969. The geography of Yiddish case and gender variation. In Marvin I. Herzog, Wita Ravid, and Uriel Weinreich (eds.), *The field of Yiddish: Studies in language, folklore, and literature. Third collection*, 102–215. London, The Hague and Paris: Mouton.

1974. *Contributions to a transformational grammar of Yiddish.* Yiddish and East European Jewish Studies, 4. New York: YIVO.

1977. Fonologishe protsesn bay mertsol-formatsye. In Shmuel Verses, Natan Rotenshtraikh, and Khone Shmeruk (eds.), *Sefer Dov Sadan: Kovets mehkarim mugashim bemilat lo shiv'im vehamesh shana*, 129–137. Tel-Aviv: Ha-Kibuts ha-me'uhad.

Yuasa, Etsuyo, and Jerrold M. Sadock. 2002. Pseudo-subordination: A mismatch between syntax and semantics. *Journal of Linguistics* 38: 87–111.

Yunin, Volf. 1972. Tseyn-tekhnikeray in byalestoker krayz sof tsvansiker yorn. *Yidishe shprakh* 32: 8–14.

Zamet, Leyb. [= Yudl Mark]. 1967. Fun dem loshn fun di Denebarger yatkes. *Yidishe shprakh* 27: 24–25.

Zaretski, Ayzik. 1926. *Praktishe yidishe gramatik far lerers un studentn.* Moscow: Shul un bukh.

1929. *Yidishe gramatik.* Vilna: Vilner farlag.

1931. *Far a proletarisher shprakh.* Kharkov and Kiev: Tsenterfarlag.

Ziskind, Nosn. 1953. Batrakhtungen vegn der geshikhte fun yidish. *Yidishe shprakh* 13: 97–108.

Zuckerman, Richard. 1969. Alsace: An outpost of Western Yiddish. In Marvin I. Herzog, Wita Ravid, and Uriel Weinreich (eds.), *The field of Yiddish: Studies in language, folklore, and literature. Third collection*, 36–57. London, The Hague and Paris: Mouton.

Zunz, Leopold. 1832. *Die gottesdienstlichen Vorträge der Juden, historisch entwickelt. Ein Beitrag zur Alterthumskunde und biblischen Kritik, zur Literatur- und Religionsgeschichte*. Berlin: A. Ascher.

Zwirner, E. 1959. Phonometrische Isophonen der Quantität der deutschen Mundarten. *Phonetica* 4 (suppl.: Symposion Trubetzkoy): 93–125.

Index

LaVergne, TN USA
30 December 2009
168474LV00003B/39/P

9 780521 105781